A World We Thought We Knew

A WORLD WE THOUGHT WE KNEW

Readings in Utah History

Edited by
John S. McCormick and John R. Sillito

University of Utah Press
Salt Lake City

Printed on acid-free paper

Library of Congress Cataloging-in-Publication Data
A world we thought we knew : readings in Utah history / edited by John S. McCormick and John R. Sillito.
p. cm.
Includes bibliographical references and index.
ISBN 0-87480-483-3 (alk. paper). — ISBN 0-87480-484-1 (pbk. : alk. paper)
1. Utah—History. I. McCormick, John S., 1944– II. Sillito, John R.
F826.5.W67 1995
979.2—dc20 95-23446

To our parents
John E. and Irene O. McCormick
John H. and Alta E. Sillito

". . . the old master narrative, a history that consistently failed to capture the painfully rich and diverse truth of the American experience."

—Vincent G. Harding

Contents

PART I

*

Utah Through the Nineteenth Century

Photograph on preceding page: Ute children, 1873.
Courtesy Utah State Historical Society.

*

Introduction

JOHN S. McCORMICK AND JOHN R. SILLITO

Directing the motion picture *Reuben and Ed* in Utah in the late 1980s, filmmaker Trent Harris described Utah as "a whacked out kind of place": placidity and complacency reigned on the surface, but upon probing deeper he found "many different kinds of people cheerfully laying dynamite in the hidden cracks."

Although Harris with both his words and works can be seen as one of the cheerful subversives, his assessment of Utah seems most perceptive, and provides a challenge to the viewpoint that sees (and then dismisses) the state and its culture as a bland, one-dimensional society inspired by such gentle television sitcom images as "Leave It to Beaver" of the 1950s. There is more to Utah, and there always has been. Textured and rich, Utah's culture is rooted in a complex and compelling past.

For too long historians have often failed, or did not want, to understand how multilayered and multifaceted Utah is and has been. They found it easy to write about Utah's past as simply a collection of facts, a series of isolated, unrelated events, or they presented a narrow and selective reading of Utah history that mainly recounted the activities of Mormons and the Mormon church, as if Utah was a one-dimensional society of interest only as a religious utopia. Recent years, however, have brought a change. The version of Utah history that prevailed for so long has been increasingly contested and called into question, and new versions have been constructed, new facts brought to light, and new meanings attached to them. Historians have begun to reread the historical record to see what voices and experiences have been ignored or silenced. As a result, they are presenting accounts that complicate the picture of Utah's past, not merely enriching it but often changing it dramatically.

The selections in this book help make clear the extent to which Utah history has been and is being rethought and remade. They deal with a wide range of subjects—topics that historians have increasingly addressed in recent years as what is considered to be important about Utah history has broadened and deepened. Among them are matters not commonly included in discussions of Utah history, topics long ignored or underemphasized, others that have often seemed inappropriate, aberrant, or marginal to the main story; but all are topics that historians have come to see as important. They include prostitution during the late nineteenth and early twentieth centuries; Utah's radical political tradition; miners' strikes of 1903–04 and 1912; the post-World War I "Red Scare"; bootlegging during the era of Prohibition; the experiences of women wage workers and child laborers; the experiences of Utah's non-Mormon ethnic groups; environmental values and practices; Native Americans and their encounters with the white settlers; the everyday lives of ordinary Utahns; and race, class, and gender and the ways they have intertwined with and shaped attitudes and behavior.

All but one of the essays included in this collection have been previously published, but they have remained scattered in various books, journals, and magazines. In bringing them together, we hope to make them more accessible, illustrate the expanding boundaries of Utah history, and contribute toward building a more complete understanding of the state's past, one that takes into greater account the variety of its peoples, experiences, traditions, values, and ways of life.

It has not been possible to be inclusive in our selections. Our goal was not to be balanced, nor could the volume be comprehensive. Those are other tasks and would require several volumes. Our intention has been to provide a suggestive account of Utah history, emphasizing topics that reveal the depth and breadth of Utah's past, its richness, variety, and complexity. Of necessity, much is omitted and the work of many important Utah historians is not represented. Our choice of material reflects our own values, interests, and estimation of what is most interesting and important. The articles begin to tell the story we think needs to be told. Others would no doubt make different choices.

The selections are divided into three sections—Utah through the nineteenth century, statehood through the Great Depression, and World War II to the present—arranged roughly in chronological order. A headnote introduces each selection, indicating something about the author or authors, the subject of the article, and important points it makes and issues it raises. We conclude the volume with a bibliographical essay in an effort to identify other works of significance.

Until relatively recently historians tended to approach Utah history in fairly narrow terms. Consequently, much of importance was ignored, neglected, denied, or devalued. The essence of Utah history was assumed, both implicitly and explicitly, to be the Mormon experience. The focus was on the epic tale of a brave people trying to demonstrate what the human spirit liberated from prejudice, ignorance, and oppressive authority could do in a remote area of the United States.

There is much to this. Utah is no ordinary place—it never has been—and much of what makes it different is Mormonism. The most prominent feature of Utah history since 1847 has been the dominance of the Mormon church in Utah's social, economic, and political life. Utah history is in part the story of a utopian experiment: the effort to establish a perfect society; its initial success; the movement away from its original ideals in the face of intense economic, political, and social pressure; and its increasing but never complete assimilation into mainstream America. In another sense, the history of Utah is the chronicle of the "failure of a dream," an expression Perry Miller used to describe the history of New England after the arrival of the Puritans in the early seventeenth century. Thus Dale Morgan described Utah's "Americanization" as "the transformation of the Kingdom of God into another among the kingdoms of the world."[1]

It is natural, then, that the study of Utah history should focus on the Mormons and Mormonism, and more specifically on the nineteenth century, since the Mormon experience during that period was particularly dramatic. However, this is essentially ethnocentric history. Both consciously and unconsciously, it leaves out much as inappropriate, irrelevant, or dangerous. Much of what has been written is comfortable, avoids troubling issues, and often seems determined to put the best possible face on a particular subject. Important question often have gone unasked or, if asked, unanswered.

In the last twenty or thirty years, however, historians have broadened their investigations, expanded the scope of their inquiries, and begun to rethink the Utah story. As a result, old silences have been broken and long-repressed voices heard. Perhaps the most important work in this regard is that of Helen Zeese Papanikolas. She has published widely, in particular on the history of the Greek experience in Utah and the Intermountain West, and the volume she edited on the history of ethnic groups in the state, *The Peoples of Utah*, is a landmark in Utah history. This expansion of the concerns of Utah historians paralleled a similar revolution in the writing of American history in general that began in the 1960s as historians moved beyond their long-standing emphasis on politics, war, diplomacy, and the lives and thoughts of great men to examine a much wider range of the human experience. As Lawrence W. Levine said in his 1993 presidential address to the Organization of American Historians, "The United States has always been a multicultural, multiethnic, multiracial society, but in our own times these truths—and their implications for higher education—have become increasingly difficult to ignore," with the result that the story of the United States as the tale of the progressive rise of a white-dominated, fundamentally righteous, and all-conquering nation has been increasingly called into question as an adequate conception of the American experience.[2] As Thomas R. Frazier points out, "The placid picture of an American paradise, idyllic and relatively peaceful, developing its natural and hu-

[1]Dale L. Morgan, "Salt Lake City, City of the Saints," in Ray B. West, ed., *Rocky Mountain Cities* (New York: Norton and Co., Inc., 1949), 197.

[2]Lawrence W. Levine, "Clio, Canons, and Culture," *Journal of American History* 80 (December 1993), 862.

man resources, was shattered," and new ways of looking at and interpreting the American past developed.[3]

What has emerged from the work of recent historians is a sense of the richness and complexity of Utah history. After all, people have lived in what is now Utah for at least 11,000 years. It has attracted not only members of the Mormon church but also a wide variety of others, including Catholic Italian laborers, Greek miners, and African-American soldiers. The nation's first female state senator, Martha Hughes Cannon, was elected in Utah in 1896 and the nation's second Jewish governor, Simon Bamberger, was elected twenty years later. During the Great Depression of the 1930s, when Utah's unemployment rate was the nation's fourth highest, the Communist party staged local protest marches, rallies, and hunger strikes involving thousands of people. In the late 1940s New York City bandleader Fletcher Henderson opened a jazz club in North Salt Lake, and throughout the 1960s Christian anarchist Ammon Hennacy staged his "one man revolution" here.

Utah history, that is to say, is not simple. It is the story not just of one people but of many, and it is filled with, and often conceals, fierce conflicts. Indeed, Utah has been, and continues to be, formed from a process of conflict: of ideas and values; of economic, political, social, and ecological systems; of people with different cultural backgrounds, needs, and ambitions. These conflicts can involve a complex interplay of racial, class, and gender issues, and Utah is fruitful ground for illuminating larger questions and patterns in American history and in the larger society of which it is a part, whose values and practices have shaped and been increasingly reflected in it.

This does not mean that the long-standing interests of Utah historians are unimportant. On the contrary, the significance of their work can scarcely be overstated. The Mormon presence and experience is central to the Utah story; it remains the predominant concern of historians, and they continue to pursue it in important and fruitful ways, finding as they do, Tom Carter points out, that even "the early Mormon world—the world we thought we knew so well—is much less predictable, much less ordered, and ultimately, much more interesting than we have generally thought."[4] Even so, Utah history is much more than the history of a religious utopia. It is more nuanced, complex, and multi-dimensional. It cannot be dismissed as so self-contained, homogeneous, and one-dimensional, so dominated by the Mormon church and, therefore, so exceptional in its past and present that there is little reason for it to engage anyone's attention except as a new Zion. To view it as an isolated episode of little interest except to the believer and the specialist is a mistake. There is more, and the selections in this volume, and the larger body of work of which they are a part, leave little doubt

[3]Thomas R. Frazier, *The Underside of American History,* vol. 1 (New York: Harcourt Brace Jovanovich, 1987), 1.

[4]Thomas R. Carter, "Northern European Horizontal Log Construction in the Sanpete-Sevier Valleys," *Utah Historical Quarterly* 52 (Winter 1984): 71.

about that. They open, enrich, and vitalize Utah history. It is not just that they expand the boundaries of our knowledge, that through them we accumulate additional information about a range of particular subjects and know more than we once did; more importantly, they make it possible to look at and think about Utah history in new ways. They amount to the beginning of a project in rethinking Utah history. They change the very conception of what Utah history is and the way it might be approached and thought about, altering the boundaries of what constitutes a history of Utah. They change the place of things, destroy our preconceptions, displace the illusion that it has all been said, that anything else will simply be a variation on a theme, and suggest how much more remains to be known. They show how limited, and limiting, were our existing knowledge and assumptions. They more accurately allow us to comprehend the nature of the society to which we belong, the history of the groups and traditions with which we interact, and the meaning of the ideas and experiences we encounter. They cheerfully place dynamite in the hidden cracks of history, or, to vary the image, in Vincent G. Harding's words, they help us "to capture the painfully rich and diverse truth" of the Utah experience.[5]

[5]Vincent G. Harding, "Healing at the Razor's Edge: Reflections on a History of Multicultural America," *Journal of American History* 81 (September 1994), 571.

*

"Dwellers in the Cedar Bark"[1]: The Indian Art of Utah

ANN ELIZABETH NELSON

Historians use a fascinating variety of evidence in their efforts to reconstruct and understand the past. This article demonstrates how much can be learned from artifacts, objects used in daily life, or what is called "material culture," that archaeologists have excavated from the dwelling sites of early Utahns. These artifacts are the basis of virtually our entire knowledge of Native American societies in North America before the arrival of European colonizers. The essay also provides a valuable introduction to Utah's Native American peoples, both before and after contact with white settlers, and challenges a number of stereotypic views: of Native Americans as primitive and backward, as opposed to whites who were dynamic, forward-looking, progressive, and civilized; of Native Americans as "noble savages" living an idyllic life perfectly in tune with nature; and of Utah before white settlement as a vacant wasteland, "a land nobody wanted," waiting to be filled up by civilized people.

Ann Elizabeth Nelson, " 'Dwellers in the Cedar Bark': The Indian Art of Utah," in Hal Cannon, ed., *Utah Folk Art* (Provo, Utah: Brigham Young University Press, 1980): 1–21. Reprinted by permission of the publisher.

At the time she wrote this article, Ann Elizabeth Nelson was Curator of Collections, Utah Museum of Natural History, University of Utah.

MAN-MADE OBJECTS are marvelous things. Each one is essentially the physical embodiment of an idea. This was particularly true in preindustrial societies in which the designer/craftsman was a single person, working available materials into the image he held in his mind.

Single objects are also complex things. Creative expression does not occur in a vacuum; every designer is influenced by the requirements and barri-

---

[1]W. W. Hill, "Navajo Trading and Trading Ritual: A Study in Cultural Dynamics," *Southwestern Journal of Anthropology* 4 (1948): 380.

ers of his environment, his culture, and his skills. It is important to place each thing as precisely as possible within the context of the time, place, and circumstance of its manufacture. When that is done, an artifact not only yields an intimate glimpse into a human mind but also acts as a direct signal from another time and culture.

Every man-made object is designed to fill a need. Our twentieth-century Western society often identifies and isolates "art" from other human production. But the concept of art is time- and culture-specific and it is important not to extend a particular concept of art into a culture where it may be invalid.

The prehistoric and historic Indian objects which appeal so much to our twentieth-century aesthetic, and which we may call art, played a distinct and usually utilitarian role in the lives of their creators. One scholar, Kenneth Ames, has suggested that by stripping things of their context, the alchemy of collection can transform objects previously considered tools into art.[2] Describing an unadorned Ute packsaddle in terms usually reserved for twentieth-century sculpture can indeed seem to transform it into sculpture. Its gaunt purity of form is both elegant and abstract. And yet, if asked to fix it in a gradient between the imaginary extremes of absolute art and utility, its maker would place it nearer utility. Indian craftsmen made useful things beautiful as time allowed, without formally segregating the concepts of art and utility.

Perhaps it is best to suppose, with George Kubler, that "the idea of art can be expanded to embrace the whole range of man-made things"[3] and to remember that the material culture of a people is but one dimension of the intricate fabric of song, dance, myth, kinship, religion, and survival skills which constitute a lifeway.

When looking at a series of artifacts, particularly those which are the only remnants of a lost lifeway or culture, it is also important to remember that chance has dictated which objects survive to be collected. Museum collections may contain, as examples of ritual paraphernalia, many intricately beaded moccasins reserved for festive or ceremonial occasions. More ephemeral or everyday things have often deteriorated or worn out. Such regalia as brilliantly colored body paint for man or horse has almost always been lost.

It is also important to remember that things were made to be used—worn, danced in, ridden. Many Indian-made things today are displayed in the clean and carefully lighted atmosphere of a museum or a gallery; therefore, it is important to provide the ingredient of imagination when looking at the everyday and special things in this exhibit. Yucca sandals did not hang on a wall but trudged squeaking across the flashing purple crystals of

[2]Kenneth Ames, *Beyond Necessity: Art in the Folk Tradition* (New York: W. W. Norton, 1977), p. 20.

[3]George Kubler, *The Shape of Time* (New Haven & London: Yale University Press, 1962), p. 1.

spring corn snow. A duck decoy once floated damply in the dawn while its owner waited tensely among lakeshore grasses for waterfowl to settle beside it. Hot coals and smoky pinyon nuts were tossed in a parching basket on a sunny autumn afternoon, while children laughed and played nearby.

The physical properties of an environment provide the stage for and play critically important roles in shaping the cultures which take form in it. The place we call Utah today has within it, but does not completely contain, three major physiographic regions: the Rocky Mountains, the Great Basin (Basin and Range Province), and the Colorado Plateau. The Great Basin is a semiarid and arid region of internal drainage containing dry basins filled with deep, fine sediments, ephemeral lakes, occasional marshes, and isolated remnants of the great inland waters which once nearly filled it. Its higher slopes are forested with juniper, aspen, pinyon, and other conifers and support large and small game and many birds. The Rocky Mountains are an area of great vertical relief with closely spaced life zones: the treeless alpine, forested subalpine, and montane regions. This is the part of the state which has a surplus of water; and its forests once harbored many elk, deer, bear, and other large mammals. The Colorado Plateau is a high tableland of flat-lying rocks, cut with thousands of deep canyons.

It is, of course, important to remember that "Utah" is an arbitrary entity and that a discussion of Indian cultures can perhaps be divided along linguistic, temporal, or environmental lines but not by modern political boundaries. People living in the deep canyons, deserts, pinyon forests, and high mountains of what is now Utah constructed many different lifeways during the long human history of the region. The things that they made changed form over time, allowing historians and archaeologists to discover or impose patterns. Historians see areal differences and temporal developments—distinctive combinations and clusters of traits—and assign names to them: Anasazi, Fremont, Archaic, Shoshoni, Ute. The complex variety and richness of the cultural history of the area can perhaps best be glimpsed through a discussion of some bits of its material culture, ancient and modern, and our current conception of its context.

A most ancient and enduring lifeway found within Utah was the one that some scholars called "Desert" or "Great Basin Archaic." The dry caves and rock shelters of the Great Basin have yielded artifacts constructed over ten thousand years ago by people living a life probably not unlike that of the nineteenth-century Paiute people. "Desert" traditions were characterized by a broad adaptive adjustment to a chronically dry environment.

A critically important survival skill was the ability to transform grasses, shrubs, and low trees into the tools and utensils needed in day-to-day life. *Salix, Apocynum, Asclepias, Artemisia, Juniperus, Yucca,* and other fibers were twisted, coiled, and twined to make cordage, soft bags, rabbit nets, burden baskets, water jugs, cooking bowls, winnowing and parching trays, mats, and a variety of other necessary objects. One amazing artifact that clearly illustrates the Great Basin dwellers' creative use of available plant resources is a duck decoy recovered in a cave in west-central Nevada, near the western verge of the Great Basin. The people who used Lovelock Cave, probably as a cache site, evidently lived on the margins of nearby Humboldt Lake and depended on its fish and waterfowl for some of their food. The delicate and precise craftsmanship of this piece evidences the observant eye and skilled hands of its maker and reveals its importance as a means of acquiring a meal.

Another Utah lifeway, the Fremont Culture, was first defined and named in the 1930s during an archaeological survey of the Fremont drainage area. Fremont people lived throughout most of Utah. They shared many culture traits that together perhaps represent a blend of Anasazi and Northwestern Plains elements that they adapted to the specific environmental conditions in which they found themselves. We know that they were horticulturalists who raised some corn, beans, and squash and employed check dams and other water-control devices to do so. They evidently significantly enlarged their diet with game, wild plants, and the fish and birds they found in adjacent marshlands; wore leather garments and distinctive moccasins; and wove baskets and other textiles.

We also know that they were fine ceramicists whose fired pottery—that most durable and persistent of materials—survives as shards and, rarely, as whole vessels. Archaeologists currently define three major ceramic traditions and at least ten pottery types in the Fremont area.[4] Snake Valley Corrugated pieces illustrate the futility of formally segregating art from utility when examining Indian artifacts. The sturdy graceful forms and integrated stippled and dimpled surfaces of this "cooking ware" are enormously appealing to our twentieth-century aesthetic.

Both Fremont and Archaic people manufactured enigmatic clay figurines who stare down the years at us through shuttered, elongated eyes. The curious male and female anthropomorphic figures, formed of originally unfired clays with (in Fremont figures) small applied strips and blobs representing ear and neck pendants, aprons, eyes, and breasts, were probably ritual or fertility forms of some sort.[5] The forms are strong and seem curiously modern. We glean from them information about the costume and ornamentation of the people who made them, and they remind us of a possibly intricate religious life of which we know practically nothing. Indeed archaeologists can tell us something about the cyclical round of life—about the hunting and gathering techniques, dwelling places, cooking methods, clothing, and even physical stature of the people who lived in the Great Basin before the white man arrived—but we can only guess about a lost realm of magic and ceremony which may have once existed in the familiar desert.

[4]Rex E. Madsen, comp., and Watson Smith and Kathleen Gratz, eds., *Prehistoric Ceramics of the Fremont,* Museum of Northern Arizona Ceramic Series, no. 6 (Flagstaff: Museum of Northern Arizona, 1977), p. v.

[5]Dee C. Taylor, *Two Fremont Sites and Their Position in Southwestern Prehistory,* University of Utah Anthropological Papers, no. 29 (Salt Lake City: University of Utah Press, 1957).

It is perhaps dangerous to draw analogies about prehistoric life from ethnographic data, but the European explorers and trappers who entered Utah in the seventeenth and eighteenth centuries encountered people probably still practicing variations of the triumphantly successful and ancient Archaic lifestyle.

One of these Shoshonean-speaking groups named themselves the Nuwuvi.[6] Today they are called the Southern Paiutes. In the nineteenth century these people had a hunting and gathering lifeway, moving in small groups through their own territories in a creative annual cycle and visiting informally owned springs, aeries, and pinyon trees at specific times of each year. They gathered wild plants, utilizing a bewildering range of seeds, berries, and roots for medicine and food. Pinyon nuts were a staple of existence, so all objects connected with their harvesting and preparation must have been of great importance to the Nuwuvi. Graceful, fan-shaped twined baskets were once used to clean the nutritious nuts before they were roasted and to hold the rich pinyon flour after it was ground.[7]

Nineteenth-century Paiute people displayed great ingenuity in the construction of fiber objects, including cordage, nets, water jugs, cooking and eating baskets, burden baskets, cradles, hats, seed-beaters, and a range of other utensils. Construction materials were gathered at precise times throughout the year and were perhaps woven together often during the cold winter days when people gathered around their fires.

Most things were made without much decoration. Fringes, beadwork, quillwork, and even vegetal dyes rarely obscured the natural hues and fine stitching of the basketry or the utilitarian lines of the clothing. People moved through the lean, white winter days into spring and from the hot, flickering summer into autumn, weaving a timeless, seasonal pattern that is perhaps very ancient in its rhythms. The appearance of face paint, feathers, and a few beads marked festive ceremonial or social events, but these bright interludes were probably infrequent.

Another Shoshonean-speaking people living in the Great Basin at the time of European entry were the Utes, the horsemen for whom the state is named. In the early nineteenth century they seem to have been a loosely organized people who could claim as their inheritance a successful and adaptive "Archaic" adjustment to their environment but whose culture had acquired an overlay of Plains traits (which grew thinner from east to west). Plains traits include the colorful objects associated with the horse: elaborate equestrian equipment; the use of the parfleche, travois, and tipi; a strong reliance on the use of hides instead of vegetal fibers; and other organizational and ceremonial elements.

Some Ute groups seem to have maintained early vigorous trade contacts with the Hispanic northern borderland settlements (such as Santa Fe) and

[6]*Nuwuvi: A Southern Paiute History* (Reno: Intertribal Council, 1976).

[7]Isabel T. Kelley, *Southern Paiute Ethnology*, University of Utah Anthropological Papers, no. 69 (Salt Lake City: University of Utah Press, 1964), pp. 1–65.

the northern Plains, which argues for a long history of similar commercial enterprises. There is no doubt that by the early eighteenth century some Ute groups consisted of highly mobile, mounted traders who had adapted their material culture and lifeway to the horse.[8]

North American Indian equestrian equipment was probably originally modeled on the designs of late medieval Spanish horse gear, the first any Indians would have seen. Frame saddles such as the Utes constructed were made of forked or curved horn and soft wood covered with sinew-stitched green rawhide, which added great strength to the much-used objects. Other necessary accoutrements of an equestrian people are the girths, quirts, saddle bags, cruppers, and martingales which the Ute people constructed of raw and tanned hides. They learned to mold rawhide into the brightly painted parfleches which were dragged on the long poles of the travois. People packed these indispensable suitcases with their possessions and transported their mobile households from place to place. Ute women became adept leatherworkers; and creamy, brain-tanned Ute hides were in demand.

In the nineteenth century, the Utes enjoyed from neighboring groups the deference due a powerful people. The Kaibab Paiutes eyed the Utes with wary respect, flatly believing that "the Utes know everything. They know how to make buckskin dresses and gloves and how to make beadwork."[9] And Navajos, exchanging blankets for hides, pelts, robes, saddle bags, bandoliers, and other skin articles, found the Ute people to be congenial and sophisticated traders.[10]

Logically, though somewhat reluctantly, the Utes extended their trade relations to include the Anglos who drifted into their territory in the early nineteenth century. Visiting fur trappers' rendezvous and the commercial forts which had been established in the Uintah Basin,[11] the Utes acquired guns, ammunition, blankets, strike-a-lights, and other metal tools and trinkets. Life was enriched and adorned with the benevolent products of an industrialized society: spark-makers, warm woolen blankets, metal tinklers, and rainbows of colored, faceted, iridescent seed beads. The Ute people quickly learned beadwork techniques. An unusual and whimsical pair of dyed gauntlet gloves, made during the early reservation period, illustrates the sophisticated artistry which Ute women once achieved with beads and deerskin.

In addition to their material culture, the Utes were a people possessed of a lively oral tradition. We are lucky to know something about their engaging coyote tales, music, and ceremonial and social dances. One very old Ute

[8]Joseph G. Jorgensen, "The Ethno-history and Acculturation of the Northern Utes" (Ph.D. diss., University of Indiana, 1965), p. 14. It is possible that some Ute groups had the horse by the mid-seventeenth century.

[9]Hill, p. 377.

[10]Kelley, p. 33.

[11]Floyd A. O'Neil, "A History of the Ute Indians of Utah until 1890" (Ph.D. diss., University of Utah, 1973). Fur trappers and traders from the Hispanic colonies of New Mexico were established in the Uintah Basin by the 1830s and were undoubtedly trading with the Utes.

springtime dance, originally probably both a social and a religious event, is the Bear Dance. The Ute people explain that they originally learned the dance from the brown and grizzly bears which lived in great numbers on their lands.

John Duncan described the coming of the Bear Dance to his people:

> Long ago a man dreamed he saw a bear way back in the mountains, dancing in front of his horse. He danced to a pole and back again and kept repeating this, as the people dance forward and backward now. The man then set out to seek the bear. After traveling in the mountains he found him dancing in this manner. The bear taught the dance to the man, who returned home and introduced it to his people.[12]

Dancers arranged in two long lines were accompanied by musicians playing *moraches* (rasps) placed in resonators. A rare and energetic Ute painting illustrates the Bear Dance and the Sun Dance, a ceremony which the Utes acquired from the Plains people.

The people who gathered at Bear Dances in the mid-nineteenth century, dressed in brilliantly beaded clothing and perhaps gambling away some of the profits of another year's successful trade with the white man, did not know that such good times were almost at an end. Many Paiute groups realized early that the arrival of the new strangers was not a fortunate turn of events. White trappers, failing to understand the ingenious and precisely adjusted material culture of the "Archaic" Paiute people they encountered in the Great Basin, contemptuously dismissed them as "diggers." As late as 1874, John W. Powell's expedition photographed the Kaibab Paiutes in deeply fringed Plains buckskin costumes instead of their own clothing.[13] Many white men accepted the vivid, "barbaric" material culture of the Plains Indians as a romantic symbol of the wild, new western land they intended to conquer; but they found the hunting and gathering lifeway of some Great Basin peoples to be primitive and incomprehensible. Unfortunately the Ute people, too, would ultimately suffer from the often disastrous cultural collision which marked the white settlement of this country.

A series of signed and broken treaties in the second half of the nineteenth century slowly forced Indian groups onto reservation lands in Utah. Resistance must have seemed futile to the Indian people. In 1865 Brigham Young summarized the situation for the Utes.

> If you do not sell your land to the government they will take it, whether you are willing to sell it or not—and it won't make one particle of difference whether you say they may have the land or not, because we shall increase and we shall occupy this valley and the next and so on until we occupy the whole of them.[14]

[12]Julian H. Steward, "A Uintah Ute Bear Dance," *American Anthropologist* 34 (1932): 265.

[13]Kelley, p. 59, quoting Frederick S. Dellenbaugh, "Kaibab Paiute," ms.

[14]U.S., Washington, D.C., National Archives, Social and Economic Branch, Indian Record, Unratified Treaty Files, Treaty Negotiations Ute-U.S. Govt., Spanish Fork, Utah, June 1865; quoted in O'Neil.

The Ute people were finally segregated into two large groups designated as the Northern and Southern Utes. The Southern Utes are settled near the Colorado-Utah border and consist of the Capote and Mouache groups, who once lived in northern New Mexico and southern Colorado. The Uintah and other scattered Utah bands moved to the bleak Uinta-Ouray Reservation in northeastern Utah, where they were joined by the White River group, who had lived near the Yampa River in Utah and Colorado, and the Uncompahgres, the high-mountain people of Colorado.[15]

Some generalizations can be made about the Utes' material culture and that of other Indian peoples of Utah just before the reservation era. Like many generations of their ancestors, they tended to be conservative and traditional with little internal specialization. Knowledge was shared and activities were homogeneous. Innovation was probably somewhat proscribed and repetition rewarded. "Unique" or even highly individual objects, possessing a personally distinct assemblage of traits, were rarely produced. Survival needs and cultural norms dictated production.

Indian people had a rich and eclectic material culture which was increasingly impacted by their changed and diminished lifeway. In the late nineteenth century most Ute and Paiute people still remembered how to construct basketry utensils, although they no longer played a significant role in Indian life and at that time had little commercial appeal to anyone else. One pitch-lined coiled water bottle, once a necessary tool for people who lived and traveled in an arid landscape, is an artifact demonstrative of the change that began to take place. The prehistoric form has acquired horsehair lugs and, in eloquent testimony to the new western symbolism, has a bottom patch made from the denim pocket of a pair of Levi Strauss trousers. Although it is over seventy years old, it still fills the air with the sweet smell of sap when it is lifted. Water stored in such baskets must have had a pleasant, clean tang not found in metal canteens.

On the reservation Ute women continued to bead native tanned products, although geometric designs were increasingly replaced with the floral patterns which many Indian groups adopted in the early twentieth century. Some of these were obviously derived from china and chintz patterns. Gradually cotton thread and commercially tanned leather replaced sinew and soft, native-tanned skins. Some of the early twentieth-century articles were sloppily constructed and resemble other poignantly poor tourist trinkets made throughout the West during the unhappy early reservation period. Purses, hatbands, ration-ticket bags, and lapel ornaments replaced the magnificent beaded clothing, equestrian equipment, blanket strips, and paint, strike-a-light, and "medicine" bags of the nineteenth century.

Two rasps, one made in the late nineteenth century and the other in the

[15]Floyd A. O'Neil and Kathryn MacKay, *A History of the Uintah-Ouray Ute Lands,* American West Center Occasional Paper no. 10 (Salt Lake City: American West Center, 1978). Another Ute group, the Ute Mountain Utes, consisted mostly of the Weeminuche Utes at the time of settlement on the Ute Mountain Reservation.

twentieth evidently to be sold as a tourist trinket, reflect the changing character of Ute culture. The simple lines and faint natural ochre coloration of one contrast with the lurid colors and alien shape of the other.

By the early twentieth century, most Indian peoples of Utah had completely abandoned their traditional clothing for everyday wear. The men often dressed in an extreme version of Anglo cowboy garb. Shawls, tall-crowned Stetsons, and cowboy boots were the most popular merchandise in reservation stores.[16] Years of reservation life with sometimes unjust or dishonest agents, the resentment of Anglos who wanted Indian land for farming and mining, and the loss of an independent and traditional lifeway seemed to strip many Indians of their heritage.

By the mid-twentieth century many Utes wished to ignore their history. As one observer noted, "The Utes have what might be termed a short historical memory. There seems to be a great deal of resistance to the re-telling of past events in the life of the Ute. The reasons for this are not altogether clear, but there seems to be evidence that there has been an attempt to forget the past."[17]

Fortunately, Indian people are once again discovering their identity and their past. This phenomenon probably springs from the pan-Indianism of the 1960s and the mythicization and popularization of Indian culture among all Americans, as well as from deep and enduring loyalties and traditions. For many years, caricatures of Indians have appeared in American popular culture and commercial art. However, again in the 1960s, Indian material culture enjoyed an enormous surge in popularity and began to appear in art as well as natural history museums.

People living in a mechanized and plastic society find the objects of daily and ceremonial Indian life beautiful and appealing. Too often they are placed in a context which isolates them from their source. Properly understood, these are evocative and haunting objects which speak to us of our human history.

[16]Gottfried O. Lang, *A Study in Culture Contact and Culture Change: The Whiterocks Utes in Transition,* University of Utah Anthropological Papers, no. 15 (Salt Lake City: University of Utah Press, 1953), p. 53.

[17]Ibid., p. 3. Perhaps this student encountered a natural resistance to telling past Ute events to a white man.

*

Prelude to Dispossession: The Fur Trade's Significance for the Northern Utes and Southern Paiutes

JOHN R. ALLEY, JR.

The fur trade disrupted the lives and cultures of Native Americans throughout North America and prepared the way for permanent white settlement and the ultimate dispossession of Native Americans from their land. This article describes the impact of the fur trade in Utah on the Northern Utes and the Southern Paiutes. An important part of the fur traders' legacy was the image of Indians as savages and, thus, obstacles to progress—a view that however inaccurate and unfair prevailed in Utah as it did elsewhere and was used to justify the harsh treatment Indians received from white immigrants. The elimination of the Native Americans could be and often was rationalized as the extinction or domination of an inferior, cultureless, and barbaric people.

John R. Alley, Jr., "Prelude to Dispossession: The Fur Trade's Significance for the Northern Utes and Southern Paiutes," *Utah Historical Quarterly* 50 (Spring 1982): 104–23. Reprinted by permission of the publisher and the author.

A specialist in Native American history, John R. Alley, Jr., earned a Ph.D. degree in history from the University of California, Santa Barbara, and is an editor at Utah State University Press.

WRITING IN THE 1840s, Rufus B. Sage mentioned a native people who had come increasingly to the American public's attention during the previous two decades:

> The Taos Utahs are a brave and warlike people, located upon the del Norte a short distance to the northwest of Taos. These subsist principally by hunting, but raise large numbers of horses.
>
> . . . The Lake Utahs occupy the territory lying south of the Snakes, and upon the waters of the Colorado of the west, and south of the Great Salt Lake.
>
> These Indians are less warlike in their nature, and more friendly in their disposition, than the Taos Utahs. The persons and property of whites, visiting them for trade or other purposes, are seldom molested; and all having

> dealings with them, so far as my information extends, unite to give them a good character.
>
> . . . The Diggers, or rather a small portion of them, are a division of the Utah nation, inhabiting a considerable extent of the barren country directly southwest of the Great Salt Lake. They are represented as the most deplorably situated, perhaps, of the whole family of man, in all that pertains to the means of subsistence and the ordinary comforts of life.

The people Sage described are known today as the Southern Utes, the Northern Utes, and the Southern Paiutes.[1] When he wrote, the Southern Utes had been trading with Euro-Americans for some one hundred and fifty years. But the Northern Utes' and Southern Paiutes' relationship with Euro-Americans developed at a slower pace: it did not significantly affect their lives until the early nineteenth century. The attitudes and situations of these two peoples, who at first accepted but then resisted Mormon settlement in Utah, emerge only through an understanding of the years during which their lives developed under the influence of expanding trade.

Sometime shortly before 1813 New Mexican traders established direct trade with the Northern or Utah Utes. This was followed in the 1820s by the equally important arrival of American fur trappers who spread across Ute and Paiute territory. As a result, the international position of these tribes changed dramatically. This trade established patterns of intercultural contact which laid the groundwork for the later dispossession of the Utes and Paiutes by white settlers and the United States government. Long before this process was complete, the fur trade introduced new technology and new forms of social and economic organization that significantly changed the life-style of Utah Indians. Thus, although the fur trade in Utah built on earlier, culturally influential contacts with New Mexicans, it had effects similar to those long identified by historians in other parts of North America.[2]

The journal of the Domínguez-Escalante expedition of 1776 provides a glimpse of Northern Ute and Southern Paiute life at the end of the eighteenth century. It is clear from the descriptions therein that neither had yet been directly affected by the introduction of European culture. The most revolutionary Spanish introduction, the horse, had reached only those Utes

[1]Rufus B. Sage, *Scenes in the Rocky Mountains . . .*, in *Rufus B. Sage: His Letters and Papers, 1836–1847,* eds. LeRoy R. Hafen and Ann W. Hafen, 2 vols. (Glendale, CA: Arthur H. Clark, 1956), 2:91–92. As used in this paper Northern Utes refers to those bands who resided most of the time north and west of the Colorado River and generally within the present boundaries of Utah. Notably, this includes the Tumpanawach and Uinta Ats bands. It might also include the Yamparika band of Colorado, although the primary sources of the fur trade era do not mention them by name. The San Pitch and Pahvant bands in Utah did not, as will be seen, play the same role as other Northern Utes. Southern Paiutes refers to members of that tribe living north and west of the Colorado River, with the primary focus on those occupying the Virgin River and Sevier River drainage basins. Unless otherwise specified, references to Utes and Paiutes in this paper are to the above-named groups.

[2]For a recent discussion of this process in relation to the central Rockies fur trade see David J. Wishart, *The Fur Trade of the American West, 1807–1840: A Geographical Synthesis* (Lincoln: University of Nebraska Press, 1979), pp. 214–15.

who lived southeast of the Colorado River. Although Comanches to the north had horses, the journal does not mention horses or metal tools among either the Northern Utes or Southern Paiutes. The Utes were concentrated at Utah Lake and farther south, having been pushed out of much of northeastern Utah, including the Uinta Basin and Strawberry Valley, by the Comanches.[3] Many of the latter may have been Shoshones, whom the Spanish later called "Comanches Sozones," but it is also quite possible that all of the Comanches proper had not yet moved on to the plains from their original homes in Wyoming. Some Northern Utes, whom the padres called Lagunas or Timpanogotzis, were visiting Colorado Utes when the expedition arrived, so they were obviously aware of the flow of Spanish goods that had reached their cousins; but the Comanches appear to have cut them off from this northward flow. Those Southern Paiutes who lived north of the Colorado River had also heard of the Spanish, notably Fray Francisco Garces who had recently contacted Chemehuevi Paiutes on the lower river. The Paiutes who met the explorers demonstrated greater involvement in a trade network then the Utes. The journal mentions Paiute trade with Hopis, Havasupais, Mojaves, and Apaches.

In most regards the Utes and Paiutes lived similar lives in 1776. Their housing, clothing, and hunting-gathering subsistence patterns were basically the same, although the Utes relied on fish from their lake and occasionally hunted bison while some of the Paiutes practiced horticulture. The Utes lived in more concentrated villages on Utah Lake and showed signs of more defined political leadership. This was probably due to the dependable food supply the lake provided and to Comanche pressure, since these social characteristics were not evident among the Bearded Utes farther south. Although the padres recognized the Utes and Paiutes as different nations, the only other distinctions they mentioned were slight linguistic variations and greater Southern Paiute timidity.

After 1776 the Southern Paiutes disappear from the record until the arrival of trappers in the 1820s. During this fifty-year interval only a few documents mention the Northern Utes, but these sources make it clear that their life-style had begun to change. By 1805 the "Yutas Timpanoges" were resisting their Comanche or Shoshone nemeses more successfully and apparently obtaining horses in the bargain. In that year Manuel Mestas journeyed to Utah Lake and recovered horses and mules the Comanches had stolen from New Mexicans and then lost in a war with the Northern Utes.

By 1813 the initial tentative contacts of Domínguez and Escalante and Mestas were transformed into direct trade with the Utes. According to re-

[3]It should be pointed out that on one occasion the padres seem to designate the Uinta Mountains as the boundary between Utes and Comanches, but later they clearly designate the Uinta Valley as Comanche territory. Fray Francisco Atanasio Domínguez and Fray Silvestre Vélez de Escalante, *The Domínguez-Escalante Journal,* trans. Fray Angelico Chavez, ed. Ted J. Warner (Provo, Ut.: Brigham Young University Press, 1976), pp. 40, 43, and 45.

ports in that year, a company of traders led by Mauricio Arze and Lagos García visited the Timpanogos Utes, the Sanpuchi or San Pitch Utes, and the Bearded (probably Pahvant) Utes. The Spanish traded horses for slaves and pelts. The trade was still not completely secure, since the Utes threatened to destroy the traders on several occasions, but a link had been created that only awaited the arrival of more extensive markets to turn the Northern Utes into a major trading nation. This would not happen until the fur traders began to compete with the New Mexicans because, as David Weber has pointed out, "Aside from being illegal, the Spanish trade with Utes . . . was a small-scale, individual, and rather shabby affair."[4]

In 1822 the Southern Utes indicated to Thomas James their desire to increase the trade:

> You are Americans, we are told. . . . We want your trade. Come to our country with your goods. Come and trade with the Utahs. We have horses, mules, and sheep, more than we want. We heard that you wanted beaver skins. . . . Come over among us and you shall have as many beaver skins as you want. . . . These Spaniards . . . wont even give us two loads of powder and lead for a beaver skin, and for a good reason. They have not as much as they want themselves.

American fur traders responded. Within two years they had moved north from New Mexico through the lands of the Southern Utes and into the Utah homelands of the Northern Utes. Of the several parties that entered Utah in 1824, none was more important than that led by Etienne Provost. After Shoshones under Bad Gocha killed eight of Provost's men on the Jordan River, Provost turned to nearby Utes for protection as well as trade. When Peter Skene Ogden met him the next spring in Weber Canyon, Provost was accompanied by a band of twenty Utes, three of whom wore Spanish crosses. He apparently obtained many of his furs that year from the Utes.[5]

Ogden, of the Hudson's Bay Company, was part of the northern frontier of the fur trade which also approached Ute lands in the mid-1820s. However, the British left the Ute country to their American competitors who had recently come west across South Pass. Americans may have encountered Utes in this area as early as 1812 when a returning party of Astorians mentioned the "Black Arms, about 3,000 strong . . . whose territories extend to the neighbourhood of the spainards." Probably Utes, these "Black Arms" were at war with the Arapahoes and in possession of "the best beaver coun-

[4]Joseph J. Hill, "Spanish and Mexican Exploration Northwest from New Mexico into the Great Basin," *Utah Historical Quarterly* 3 (1930): 16–19; David J. Weber, *The Taos Trappers: The Fur Trade in the Far Southwest, 1540–1846* (Norman: University of Oklahoma Press, 1968), p. 27.

[5]Thomas James, *Three Years among the Indians and Mexicans,* ed. Milo Milton Quaife (New York: The Citadel Press, 1966), pp. 160–61. For Provost and other Taos trapping parties of 1824–25 see Weber, *Taos Trappers,* pp. 71–78; "The Diary of William H. Ashley, March 25–June 27, 1825," in Dale Morgan, ed., *The West of William H. Ashley, 1822–1838* (Denver: Old West Publishing, 1964), pp. 113–17; and Peter Skene Ogden, *Peter Skene Ogden's Snake Country Journals, 1824–25 and 1825–26,* ed. E. E. Rich (London: Hudson's Bay Record Society, 1950).

try on this side the mountains."[6] By 1825 Americans in the employ of William H. Ashley were moving south to test this conclusion which their fellow citizens moving north from New Mexico had already confirmed.

The records Ashley and his men kept from 1825 to 1827 provide the first substantial post-1776 description of the Northern Utes. In May 1825 Ashley himself met a band of Utes near the junction of the White and Green rivers. They met him "with great familiarity and Ease of manner" and showed signs of having prospered since 1776. The Utes, who would later be renowned among the trappers for their quality animal skins, "were clothed in mountain sheep skin & Buffalloe robes superior to any band of Indians in my knowledg west of Council Bluffs." They not only had "a great number of good horses" but also had enough English fusils to arm half their number. Since the only source of English guns was to the north and since there is no evidence of Ute trade with the Hudson's Bay Company, these guns were probably acquired from Shoshones. Ashley's account provides other evidence that the Utes were doing better in their relations with the Shoshones although the two tribes remained at war. The Shoshones' territory still extended down the Green River as far as Brown's Hole, but the Utes controlled the Uinta Basin, and some of them lived north of Utah Valley on the Weber River near present Wanship. Provost, accompanying Ashley's party, went even farther down the Weber to trade with another Ute encampment.[7]

The following year Jedediah S. Smith opened trade with Utes at Utah Lake. Despite greater mobility, the largest concentration of Utes still lived near the lake much of the year and depended on it for their principal food supply of fish. Smith, however, found most of them up nearby Spanish Fork Canyon gathering service berries. He confirmed a number of Ashley's comments: the Utes had many horses, were clothed in well-cared-for mountain sheep and antelope skins and buffalo robes, and had even more guns than the Shoshones. He disagreed with Ashley about the source of the latter, concluding that they came from Spanish New Mexico rather than the English; but given the general spread of firearms in North America, Ashley's conclusion seems more reasonable. Smith was greatly impressed by the character of the Utes, describing them in terms most of the trappers who followed him would repeat:

> I found these Indians more honest than any I had ever been with in the country. They appear to have verry little disposition to steal and ask for nothing unless it may be a little meat. . . . The Uta's are cleanly quiet and active and make a nearer approach to civilized life than any Indians I have seen in the Interior.

Anxious to encourage their friendship, Smith "concluded a treaty with these Indians by which the americans are allowed to hunt & trap in and pass

[6]Robert Stuart, *The Discovery of the Oregon Trail: Robert Stuart's Narratives,* ed. Philip A. Rollins (New York: Charles Scribner's Sons, 1935), p. 86.

[7]"Diary of Ashley," pp. 113–17.

through their country unmolested." Before moving on he purchased three horses at an unspecified high price and gave the Utes a "handsome present" of "1 Tin Kettle, 3 yards Red Strouding, 4 Razors, 2 durk knives, 50 balls 1 lb Powder, 3 looking Glasses, 2 dozen Rings, 1 dozen combs 4 hawk Bills, 2 stretching needles, 2 doz. awls, Buttons 1 large green handle knife."[8]

Most important for the future of Ute trade, Smith invited them to meet him at the rendezvous the following year to conclude a treaty with the Shoshones that should make the country safer for Indians and whites alike. The Utes agreed and thus were present to earn the trappers' "great applause for their bravery" in a battle with the Blackfeet. They also concluded the treaty with the Shoshones, sending repercussions as far as Mexico City where the Mexican secretary of state protested to the American minister in 1828 that

> at four days' journey beyond the lake of Timpanagos, there is a fort situated in another lake, with a hundred men under the command of a general of the United States of North America . . . that the said general caused a peace to be made between the barbarous nations of the Yutas Timpanagos and the Comanches Sozones, and made presents of guns, balls, knives, &c., to both nations; . . . that the Yuta Timpanago Indian, called *Quimanuapa,* was appointed general by the North Americans, and that he states the Americans will have returned to the fort by the month of December.

Quimanuapa, one of the few Northern Utes mentioned by name during the trapping era, was apparently the "principal Chief" whom Smith had met the year before. The trappers called him Conmarrowap when in 1834 he reappeared in their journals. Ironically, his reappearance coincided with a renewed outbreak of war between the Shoshones and Utes. This war did not last long, for both Ute and Shoshones were at the rendezvous the following summer.[9] In later years the two tribes still demonstrated a cautious attitude toward each other but remained generally at peace.

The 1827 rendezvous was a turning point for the Northern Utes. They had not only mitigated the Shoshone threat, which had long restricted them, but they had also opened up trade with Americans on their northern frontier through the reciprocal arrangement of annual visits to the rendezvous coupled with trapper excursions into their country. This trade complemented and expanded that with the American trappers and New Mexican

[8]Jedediah S. Smith, *The Southwest Expedition of Jedediah S. Smith: His Personal Account of the Journey to California, 1826–1827,* ed. George R. Brooks (Glendale: Arthur H. Clark, 1977), pp. 41–43, 208.

[9]Daniel T. Potts, letter, July 8, 1827, *Philadelphia Gazette,* October 19, 1827, in Charles L. Camp, "The D.T.P. Letters," *Essays for Henry R. Wagner* (San Francisco: The Grabhorn Press, 1947), pp. 18–19; House Doc. 351 (Ser. 332), 25th Cong., 2d sess., pp. 228–30, quoted in Dale Morgan, *Jedediah Smith and the Opening of the West* (Lincoln: University of Nebraska Press, 1953), p. 229; W. A. Ferris, *Life in the Rocky Mountains,* ed. Paul Phillips (Denver: Old West Publishing, 1940), pp. 266, 275–78; William Marshall Anderson, *The Rocky Mountain Journals of William Marshall Anderson,* ed. Dale Morgan and Eleanor Towles Harris (San Marino: The Huntington Library, 1967), pp. 160–63, 168–69. The editors of Anderson have included a short biography of Conmarrowap on pages 290–91.

traders who continued to visit the Utes from a base in Taos and Santa Fe. The friendship of the Utes was probably even more important to the Americans. The late 1820s and early 1830s were the heyday of Rocky Mountain trapping. During those years Taos became an increasingly important competitor with the rendezvous for mountain man business. Hundreds of trappers moved back and forth between the two, trapping for furs and trading with Indians. It was therefore necessary to maintain the trust and cooperation of the Northern and Southern Utes who occupied the land the whites had to cross.

Kit Carson's travels in 1833 and 1834 provide a good example of this movement. In the fall of 1833 he joined a trapping party that followed the Spanish Trail north to the Uinta Valley. On the Uinta River (the trappers included the present Duchesne below its junction with the Uinta under this name) they found another party under one of the Robidoux brothers trapping and trading with the Utes. The combined parties went into winter camp at the mouth of the Uinta River near a Ute village. During the winter Carson and one of the Utes pursued a California Indian who had stolen some horses from his employer, Robidoux. The pursuit covered some one hundred miles before the horses were recovered. The following spring Carson joined Jim Bridger and Thomas Fitzpatrick in northwestern Colorado, accompanying them to the summer rendezvous on Green River.[10]

The fur trade began a long decline in the late 1830s as both the supply of and demand for furs diminished. Stationary trading posts appeared during this time as traders turned more and more to the alternative of buffalo robes while trying to stabilize trade for other animal skins. The beaver trade remained extensive, though, and some posts, such as those built by Antoine Robidoux in the Ute country, still concentrated on these smaller animals. Although Robidoux's primary business was with independent trappers, the Ute trade was an important supplement. At his post on the Uinta River near present Whiterocks the Utes provided "horses, with beaver, otter, deer, sheep, and elk skins in barter for ammunition, fire-arms, knives, tobacco, beads, awls, &c." In 1844 the Southern Utes went to war with New Mexico after an attack on one of their camps. They attacked Robidoux's Fort Uncompahgre and killed all the Mexican employees. Although they did not kill American citizens and did send word to the Uinta fort that Robidoux and his peltry were safe, this long-time Ute trader decided to abandon the post and retire from the trade, possibly because he felt that his practice of supplying guns to the Utes would ultimately involve him in the war.[11]

Other posts such as Fort Hall, Fort Davy Crockett in Brown's Hole,

[10]"The Kit Carson Memoirs, 1809–1856," in Harvey Lewis Carter, ed., *'Dear Old Kit': The Historical Christopher Carson* (Norman: University of Oklahoma Press, 1968), pp. 58–61.

[11]Sage, *Scenes in the Rocky Mountains,* p. 97; Janet Lecompte, *Pueblo, Hardscrabble, Greenhorn: The Upper Arkansas, 1832–1856* (Norman: University of Oklahoma Press, 1978), pp. 137–38; Weber, *Taos Trappers,* pp. 213–17.

Bent's Fort, and the Platte River posts also traded with the Utes, occasionally dispatching traders to the Ute camps in northern Utah. The companies established different trading rates for Indians and trappers, resulting in a higher percentage profit from the former. As the Ute trader Richens Wootton said, "Trading with the Indians had its attractions, the chief of which was of course, the very handsome profits which we made out of the business." At the Uinta fort one of the Utes' excellently finished and large sheep and deer skins could be purchased for the equivalent of eight or ten charges of ammunition or two or three awls and then resold in New Mexico for one or two dollars. Wootton noted that even if the Utes "knew nothing about money," they could drive a hard bargain when it came to barter. Once an agreed value was set, though, one or two thousand dollars' worth of trade could be conducted in half a day. Although the Utes were considered keen traders, they were also known as honest collectors of "considerable fur" and thus profitable trading partners.[12]

Besides the men who actively sought out Ute trade, all trappers regularly carried such things as knives, tobacco, awls, vermillion, blankets, and beads when traveling through Ute lands. If Utes who had furs were then found, trade would occur. In addition, it was usually necessary to engage in formal gift exchange as a sign of friendship. Associated with this practice are the frequent trapper allusions to Ute demands for tribute. Having opened their territory to outsiders, the Utes commonly insisted that the intruders pay for the privilege. After the "tribute" or "presents" were provided the Utes would formally grant rights to travel and trap in their territory. Although considered honest, hospitable, and friendly, the Utes could be forthright and candid in their demands if the trappers were not willing to share food and other items while in Ute country. Such incidents occasionally led those who did not fully understand to accuse the Utes of begging. Taken as a whole, though, the trapper accounts make it clear that the Ute practice was consistent, and the whites had little excuse for ignoring a well-established tradition.[13]

The only reported battles between trappers and Utes involved trapper unwillingness to pay tribute. In 1839 traders from Bent's Fort in Colorado traveled to the Uinta River in an effort to compete with Robidoux for the Ute trade. The Utes informed them that "on no account could they enter the Eutaw country without paying tribute in some form." The traders refused, and some fighting occurred before the outnumbered whites decided to leave

[12]Osborne Russell, *Journal of a Trapper,* ed. Aubrey L. Haines (Lincoln: University of Nebraska Press, 1955), pp. 120–22; Howard Louis Conrad, *"Uncle Dick" Wootton: The Pioneer Frontiersman of the Rocky Mountain Region* (Chicago: W. E. Dibble, 1890), pp. 101, 110–11; Sage, *Scenes in the Rocky Mountains,* pp. 97–98; William T. Hamilton, *My Sixty Years on the Plains Trapping, Trading, and Indian Fighting,* ed. E. T. Sieber (New York: Forest and Stream Publishing, 1905), pp. 97–98.

[13]Charles L. Camp, ed., *George C. Yount and His Chronicles of the West* (Denver: Old West Publishing, 1966), pp. 70, 86; John Charles Fremont, *Report of the Exploring Expedition to the Rocky Mountains* (Washington, D.C.: Gales and Seaton, 1845), p. 272. These are two examples among many.

the area. In the fall of 1842 a more serious battle was reportedly fought near the Great Salt Lake after a band of trappers refused to pay tribute.[14]

Northern Utes were most commonly met by trappers at Utah Lake which was considered their "headquarters," on the Sevier River, near Brown's Hole, and on the Uinta River, particularly near the junction of it and the White with the Green River. They were also seen occasionally in Shoshone territory along the Bear and upper Green rivers. They became particularly noted for their fine horse herds. One trapper called them "by far, the most expert horsemen in the mountains." The horses provided a link between the Spanish Trail traders from whom the Utes frequently purchased or stole them and the trappers who then bought them from the Utes. Whites also frequently remarked on how well-armed the Utes were. By the late 1830s a diarist could typically note that "These Indians are the best marksmen in the mountains and are armed with good rifles" as well as the earlier fusils.[15]

Between the mid-1820s and mid-1840s the Utes developed an important and mutually respectful relationship with the fur hunters of the Rocky Mountain West. News of the favorable reception the Utes had given the trappers had spread back east as early as 1826, the year the *Missouri Advocate and St. Louis Enquirer* announced that

> *The Indians,* west of the mountains are remarkably well disposed toward the citizens of the United States; the Eutaws and Flat-heads are particularly so, and express a great wish that the Americans should visit them frequently.[16]

When the trappers included respect with their trade goods, the Utes welcomed them into their territory without realizing that once the Anglos came they would never leave.

It is easy to overlook the importance of the fur trade to the Utes. The central Rockies fur trade was different from that in much of the rest of North America, particularly with regard to the organization and makeup of the labor force. White trappers did the trapping in the Rockies and then traded their catch at rendezvous. In other parts of the continent the basic work was done by unsupervised Indians who traded their pelts at posts. However, the assumption cannot be made that Rocky Mountain fur men were solely trappers. Trade with Indians continued to be an important, if

[14]Thomas J. Farnham, *Travels in the Great Western Prairies,* Early Western Travels, 1748–1846, ed. Reuben Gold Thwaites, vol. 28 (Cleveland: Arthur H. Clark, 1906), pp. 166–70, describes the 1839 incident while the conclusions stated here are based on Lecompte, *Pueblo, Hardscrabble, Greenhorn,* p. 162. For the 1842 incident see Hamilton, *Sixty Years on the Plains,* pp. 104–14.

[15]Ferris, *Life in the Rocky Mountains,* p. 312; Hamilton, *Sixty Years on the Plains,* pp. 97–98, 117; "The E. Willard Smith Journal, 1839–1840," in LeRoy R. Hafen and Ann W. Hafen, eds., *To the Rockies and Oregon, 1839–1842* (Glendale: Arthur H. Clark, 1955), p. 180.

[16]*Missouri Advocate and St. Louis Enquirer,* March 11, 1826, quoted in Morgan, *Ashley,* p. 141.

supplementary, source of pelts. Over the years its contribution became more and more important as whites abandoned a depressed industry. Moreover, it was not a fur trade alone. Isolated, annually supplied trappers often depended on the Indians for many items that could not wait for the next rendezvous. Horses and food, among other things, were often supplied by Indians. The Utes, like all the Rockies tribes, were eventually connected to the European market system that followed the trappers.

Although portions, and only portions, of their territory were outside the prime trapping areas, the Utes were in a crucial geographic position between Taos to the south and the Snake country to the north, between Santa Fe to the east and California to the west. The north-south trade route connected Taos-based trappers with the rendezvous while the east-west Spanish Trail linked the northern Mexico provinces of California and New Mexico.

The Spanish Trail's importance to the Northern Utes was a direct continuation of the few pre-1820s contacts they had made with New Mexican traders. Such traders continued to visit the Northern Utes during the trapping era.[17] The 1830 opening of the Spanish Trail between Santa Fe and Los Angeles gave a new boost to this trade. Annual Mexican caravans loaded with woven goods moved over the trail to California where they exchanged their loads for horses and mules to drive back to New Mexico. Along the way they traded with Utes and, occasionally, American trappers. By the 1840s the Utes were meeting the returning caravans annually to trade and levy tribute. Even as early as 1834 W. A. Ferris noted that Conmarrowap had recently acquired ten of the finest horses the trappers had ever seen from the passing traders. Ferris claimed to know of many instances when Conmarrowap had taken such animals by force.[18] Besides furs, the Utes traded Indian captives for these horses, demonstrating that they had gained considerable power over neighboring tribes such as the Southern Paiutes.

The man most closely associated with the Spanish Trail is the Ute leader Wakara. He first emerged to importance in 1840 when, in association with a band of trappers who had left the depressed fur trade for more lucrative pursuits, he raided the ranches of southern California and made off with hundreds of horses and mules. Many of the animals that survived the transit east were later traded to trappers in the mountains. Wakara and other Utes continued to join trappers in these raids throughout the 1840s, carrying on the practice into the 1850s after the American conquest of California ended trapper participation.[19]

Wakara and the Utes who followed him are representative of a portion of the Northern Utes who eventually made trading and raiding their primary means of support. During the 1840s Wakara's activities carried him

[17]For example, Weber mentions an 1827 party which included the same Pedro Leon who is well known in Utah history for his 1851 conflict with Brigham Young over the Indian slave trade; see *Taos Trappers*, p. 162.

[18]Ferris, *Life in the Rocky Mountains*, p. 277.

[19]LeRoy R. Hafen and Ann W. Hafen, *Old Spanish Trail: Santa Fe to Los Angeles* (Glendale: Arthur H. Clark, 1954), pp. 236–57.

over a great amount of territory, trading with New Mexicans and Americans alike. He was seen pursuing his business at places as widely separated as San Luis Obispo in California, southern Wyoming, the San Juan River, and the Sevier River. In 1843 when Theodore Talbot found him in the company of the American fur trader Louis Vasquez, he noted that "He owes his position to his great wealth. He is a good trader, trafficking with the Whites, and reselling goods to such of his nation as are less skillful in striking a bargain."[20]

Many Utes adopted to some degree the trading life-style of men like Wakara, which meant greater mobility, increased dependence on white goods and technology, and considerable adjustment in traditional subsistence patterns. While most of them still depended on the traditional activities of hunting, fishing, and gathering and still resided much of the year in the old villages like those on Utah Lake, they were no longer the same people who had visited with Domínguez and Escalante. There were other Utah Utes, however, who had shared very little in this transformation. Throughout the trapping era the San Pitch Utes, for example, reportedly led lives more consistent with the hunting and gathering, nonequestrian life-style of the Southern Paiutes. Although trappers occasionally met the San Pitch, there is no evidence that they played a role in the trade like that of other Utes.

The Utes always displayed forthright confidence in their meetings with Euro-Americans. This confidence must have reflected an awareness of the power that trade had brought to them. When George Brewerton met them in 1848 at the end of one era in their history and the beginning of another, they were at the pinnacle of their political strength. Brewerton noted that "The Eutaws are perhaps the most powerful and warlike tribe now remaining on this continent. They appear well provided with fire-arms, which they are said to use with the precision of veteran riflemen."[21] Their location on the axis of the north-south and east-west trade routes heightened the Utes' power and importance while also providing them with that tool which best represents the advance of European culture, the firearm. Ironically, a similar strategic location had an opposite effect on the Southern Paiutes during these same years.

The Southern Paiutes' experience during this time can be more easily summarized. They did not acquire horses or firearms in the early years when the Northern Utes were obtaining them. Their isolation in southwestern Utah made these items less accessible, and the Paiutes were not at first under the same pressure that the Northern Utes were encountering from the mounted Shoshones. They probably saw little need for the animals or the guns. By the time they were under such pressure and therefore had such a need, they were cut off by their primary enemies, the Utes. The Utes had

[20]Theodore Talbot, *The Journals of Theodore Talbot*, ed. Charles H. Carey (Portland: Metropolitan Press, 1931), p. 42.

[21]George D. Brewerton, *Overland with Kit Carson*, ed. Stallo Vinton (New York: Coward-McCann, 1930), pp. 99–100.

learned that New Mexicans would exchange horses for Indian slaves, so they began to take captives from neighboring tribes such as the Paiutes. It is difficult to say how extensive this traffic in Southern Paiute slaves was before 1830, though it is clear that the southwestern slave traffic in general was very extensive. After the Yount-Wolfskill party of trappers opened the Spanish Trail in 1830, capture of Paiute slaves became regular and persistent. The trail ran directly through the heart of Southern Paiute territory, allowing New Mexican slave traders direct access to potential victims.[22] Thus threatened, the Southern Paiutes were a harassed people leading disrupted lives when they first met Anglo-Americans.

Fur trappers only rarely visited Southern Paiute territory. With the possible exception of Thomas Smith they did not consider this region where the borders of Utah, Nevada, and Arizona now meet good beaver country. In 1828 Smith during a few weeks reportedly "secured enough skins to make a cargo" from the valleys of the Virgin River basin, but he was the exception.[23] Most trappers lumped the area in with the bulk of the Great Basin which was known as the "land of starvation." Nevertheless, the Americans, while adding little to Paiute culture, left a definite legacy with these people.

Jedediah Smith was the first American trapper to meet the Paiutes, passing through their lands twice, in 1826 and 1827. Moving south in 1826, Smith and his party began encountering shy "Pa utch" and "Sam-pach" on the Sevier River. He drew little distinction between the two groups, but he did note that their appearance "strongly contrasted" with the Utes. Farther south the Paiutes tended to avoid him, but when they approached him near the Santa Clara River, they brought a rabbit "as a token of friendship" and an "ear of corn as an emblem of peace." In return for some small presents, they supplied the hungry trappers with corn and pumpkins. Smith's men were pleased but surprised to find these crops in what they considered an inhospitable region. Here, at the junction of the Santa Clara and Virgin rivers and at the mouth of the Muddy River, the Paiutes grew corn, pumpkins, squash, and gourds. They had dammed the Santa Clara and were irrigating their fields through a tree trunk. While the whites needed to replenish their food supply, the Indians were interested in acquiring pieces of iron that could be used for knives and arrow points. The Paiutes also wore deer, antelope, and mountain sheep skins, and a few of them had beaver moccasins; but the lack of beaver in the area hindered potential trade.[24]

When Smith reached the Santa Clara the following year the situation had changed: "Not an Indian was to be seen, neither was there any appearance of their having been there in the course of the summer their little lodges had burned down." Wherever he went in their country, the Paiutes

[22]For discussions of the slave trade see Hafen and Hafen, *Old Spanish Trail,* and Carling Malouf and A. Arline Malouf, "The Effects of Spanish Slavery on the Indians of the Intermountain West," *Southwestern Journal of Anthropology* 1 (1945): 378–81.

[23]Camp, *Yount's Chronicles,* p. 235.

[24]Smith, *Southwest Expedition,* pp. 49–63.

avoided him. Clearly something or someone had changed their attitude. When Smith reached the Mojave villages, the Mojaves informed him that, as he had suspected and had seen various signs of, another party of whites had recently visited the area. James O. Pattie has left a confused account of this party of Taos trappers. They had traveled up the Colorado in late 1826, had fought with the Mojaves, and had then had two battles with the Paiutes, on the Colorado and later on a tributary, probably the Paria River.[25] By 1827 the Paiutes had a totally different image of the trappers than the one the friendly Smith had left.

In the spring of that year still another party of American trappers met "Pic-Utaws" on the Sevier and Fremont rivers. For three nights the Indians harassed the trappers, stealing two horses and wounding four others with arrows. When they later made another attempt on the animals, the whites attacked, but the Indians escaped across the river. The trappers then returned north. Jedediah Smith had remained fairly objective in his descriptions of the Indians residing in central and southern Utah, but Daniel Potts of this 1827 party introduced an image of them that remained firmly entrenched in the minds of the trappers. Referring to the Sevier, Potts wrote:

> This river is inhabited by a numerous tribe of miserable Indians. Their clothing consists of a breechcloth of goat or deer skin, and a robe of rabbit skins, cut in strips, sewed together after the manner of rag carpets, with the bark of milk weed twisted into twine for the chain. These wretched creatures go out barefoot in the coldest days of winter. Their diet consists of roots, grass seeds, and grass, so you may judge they are not gross in their habit. They call themselves Pic-Utaws, and I suppose are derived from the same stock.[26]

This description, while containing some information on actual cultural traits, is in large part a variation on the Digger image trappers applied to nonequestrian hunters and gatherers throughout the West. Although applied to many tribes, one of the most consistent usages of this ethnocentric terminology was in reference to Southern Paiutes and neighboring bands of Utes such as the San Pitch and Pahvant.

George Yount, who met the Paiutes in 1830, recorded one of the most offensive example of this kind of characterization:

> These people are an anomaly—apparently the lowest species of humanity, approaching the monky—Nothing but their upright form entitles them to the name of man. . . . Their food consists of occasionally a Rabbit, with roots and mice, grasshoppers & insects, such as flies, spiders & worms of every kind—Where nuts exist, they gather them for food—They also luxuriate and grow fat when they find a patch of Clover—On many kinds of grass

[25]Maurice S. Sullivan, ed., *The Travels of Jedediah Smith* (Santa Ana: Fine Arts Press, 1934), pp. 28–29: James Ohio Pattie, *The Personal Narrative of James O. Pattie of Kentucky*, ed. Timothy Flint (Chicago: Lakeside Press, 1930), pp. 132–38.

[26]Potts, letter, July 8, 1827, pp. 18–19. These "Pic-Utaws" may have been Pahvant or Koosharem Utes, bands closely related to the Paiutes. If so, they, like the San Pitch Utes, were included in the Digger characterization of the Paiutes.

> they feed like cattle—They are covered with vermine and whenever they take these from their heads or persons they appropriate them for food—Hence in point of economy they are truly remarkable—These are the lowest grade of species of the Digger Indians, which are found spread over all the eastern & middle portions of California—Probably there is not in all the world a race of human beings more low and degraded than the Diggers.[27]

Yount, at least, could justify his remarks on the basis of first-hand observation. However, although few Americans had actually met the Southern Paiutes and San Pitch Utes, such descriptions of them appear in numerous accounts. The image performed an ideological role far beyond factual observation.

Personal observation also does not adequately explain the extreme value judgments in Yount's remarks. Their accuracy need not be accepted simply because he was there. More careful modern investigations lead to the conclusion that the Southern Paiutes lived quite well within the limits of a varied environment. They developed carefully balanced patterns of exploiting the available resources. As one ethnologist put it, "These . . . patterns show the Southern Paiute Indians not as pawns of a harsh environment, but rather as culturally adapted peoples capable of exploiting a variety of conditions in numerous ways." The image of the Paiutes corresponded with the attitude trappers had toward Paiute territory. Yount felt that a "half starved, nakid" Paiute "well corresponded with the region where he dwelt." Warren Ferris mentioned "the barrenness of their country, and scarcity of game."[28] Paiute territory contained alpine forests as well as arid deserts, but it produced little fur, so it is not surprising that the fur hunters considered it barren. The Paiutes also gave little to the trade, and the trappers' attitude toward Indian tribes was always based on whether a particular tribe contributed to or hindered the business.

The image of Diggers fit nicely into the Anglo-American ideology of savagism. Indians as savages acted as symbols of all that progress left behind. Whites felt that Indians had ultimately to pass away or be destroyed in order to prove the worth of civilizing ideals. In their minds the savage Indian stood in direct opposition to the civilized American. Despite the romance that has surrounded and obscured the actuality of their lives, trapper values were not far from those of most Americans of their time. Even when referring to more respected Indians like the Utes, trappers made it clear that they considered Indians inferior to themselves and other men whom they considered civilized.[29] They used Paiutes and other "Diggers" to confirm American ideas of the Indians' basic nature, a nature that at its heart had to be miserable, impoverished, and degraded to justify the ethno-

[27]Camp, *Yount's Chronicles,* p. 89.

[28]Catherine S. Fowler, "Environmental Setting and Natural Resources," in Robert C. Euler, *Southern Paiute Ethnohistory,* University of Utah Anthropological Papers no. 78 (Salt Lake City: University of Utah Press, 1966), p. 14; Camp, *Yount's Chronicles,* p. 88; Ferris, *Life in the Rocky Mountains,* p. 269, referred specifically to San Pitch Utes.

centrism of the savagism/civilization dichotomy. The danger in these negative images was that they provided justification for overlooking the Paiutes' stake in their world.

Trapper images of the Northern Utes and the Southern Paiutes present a great contrast. In one sense this contrast is valid: it is clear that the two peoples, who appear to have led quite similar lives as late as the last quarter of the eighteenth century, had moved in different directions in the first half of the nineteenth century. The Utes had increasingly moved away from a traditional life-style toward one involving more wide-ranging hunting, trading, and raiding. The Southern Paiutes' traditional life-style had also changed as a result of outside pressure, but for them the change had been in the direction of disintegration of cultural stability as others violently invaded their lands and enslaved their people. Yet, both tribes had a similar reaction when Mormon settlers arrived in the late 1840s. Both seemed to welcome or at least accept settlement and the opportunity for increased trade, but they probably had different reasons for doing so.

The Utes had no reason to fear such an intrusion. They had gained wealth and power through their contact with outsiders. There were some obvious negative results of the fur traders' invasion. Intensive trapping and hunting undoubtedly had reduced game. Buffalo, for example, no longer ranged onto Northern Ute lands. But damage to the local eco-system would not become a serious problem until alternative forms of economic support were no longer available. Although it did not take the Utes long to recognize the danger of permanent white settlement, at first it must have seemed a source of more stable trade, especially since the initial settlement lay between Shoshone and Ute lands. The Southern Paiutes actually asked the Mormons to settle in their area, with good reason.[30] The settlers offered a buffer for the Southern Paiutes, a barrier to their many enemies. Moreover, they offered access to the technology and knowledge neighbors had so long used to the Paiutes' disadvantage.

Thus, the trappers and traders of the early nineteenth century prepared the way for later dispossession of the Utes and Paiutes. These harbingers of more permanent change had helped alter the lives of the Utes. Through their participation in the trade the Utes had augmented their stature among the varied populations of the Intermountain West. Their cooperation had become, if not necessary, at least very important to the fur trade's success. But while increasing their short-term power, trade had connected the Utes to the forces of Euro-American expansion that would eventually end their sway in the Utah region. The Paiutes, on the other hand, while struggling

[29]See Roy Harvey Pearce, *The Savages of America: A Study of the Indian and the Idea of Civilization* (Baltimore: Johns Hopkins Press, 1953), especially pp. 73–75, 154, 168, 223, 232; William H. Goetzmann, "The Mountain Man as Jacksonian Man," *American Quarterly* 15 (1963): 402–15; and Wishart, *The Fur Trade,* pp. 205–7. For example, see Conrad, *"Uncle Dick" Wootten,* pp. 118–19.

[30]John Brown, *Autobiography of Pioneer John Brown, 1820–1896* (Salt Lake City: John Z. Brown, 1941), p. 110; John D. Lee to editor, *Deseret News,* September 4, 1852.

to survive their contact with the Spanish Trail trade, had received little besides hostility from fur trappers. The importance of the Paiute-trapper encounter, then, was not due to its role in the fur trade, which was negligible, but derived rather from the fact that trappers helped open the region to later whites who accepted and reinforced the Digger image and, like their predecessors, allowed themselves maximum leeway in their treatment of the Paiutes.

*

Open Hand and Mailed Fist: Mormon-Indian Relations in Utah, 1847–1852

HOWARD A. CHRISTY

The story of relationships between whites and Indians in Utah after the arrival of Mormon settlers in 1847 is a tragic one and not easy to acknowledge or contemplate. Mormon settlers encroached upon Native American lands; Indians, once they realized the extent and impact of the white presence, resisted. Conflict ensued, and the Indians ultimately were defeated. In recounting part of that story in the following essay, Howard A. Christy challenges the long-standing myth that white-Indian relations in Utah were based on benevolence and conciliation and were thus fundamentally different than they were elsewhere in the United States. Rather, he writes, hostility and bloodshed characterized Mormon-Indian relations in Utah almost from the first, and the impact of white immigration on Native Americans was immediate and disastrous: "The Indians," he points out, "especially the Utes, declined rapidly as a result of extreme poverty brought on by usurpation of their lands, selective extermination, disease, and starvation."

Howard A. Christy, "Open Hand and Mailed Fist: Mormon-Indian Relations in Utah, 1847–52," *Utah Historical Quarterly* 46 (Summer 1978): 216–35. Reprinted by permission of the publisher and the author.

Howard A. Christy is currently Senior Editor of Scholarly Publications at Brigham Young University. The author of several articles on Native Americans in Utah, he was also associate editor of the *Atlas of Utah* and co-editor of *Community Development in the American West: Past and Present Nineteenth and Twentieth Century Frontiers.*

WHEN HISTORIANS DISCUSS Mormon policy toward the Indians they usually mention attitudes of fairness, benevolence, and conciliation exemplified in the phrase coined by Brigham Young: "It is cheaper to feed them than fight them." Virtually all the prominent Utah scholars have pointed out such a policy, emphasizing or at least implying its essentially beneficent nature. A typical treatment is that of Juanita Brooks who wrote:

"When the natives gathered around to watch the new-comers . . . they were treated with kindness and tolerance. Brigham Young early made the pronouncement that became a basic Mormon tenet, 'It is cheaper to feed the Indians than fight them.' "[1]

Though the existence of this policy is not questioned, the interpretation of its essential beneficence flies in the face of evidence that is, at the least, ambiguous. Hostility and bloodshed, as much as benevolence and conciliation, characterized Mormon–Indian relations in Utah before 1852. The policy actually carried out, though couched in terms of beneficence, had as one of its major elements, in addition to assistance, stern punishment when deemed appropriate or necessary. The best evidence indicates that Brigham Young's first mention of his now famous statement was in July 1851 following a number of punitive campaigns carried out between March 1849 and June 1851. By then, experience had demonstrated that it was indeed cheaper to feed the Indians than fight them.

I

Though the Mormons did not arrive in Utah until July 1847, they established their initial policy toward the Indians before the first group left their Winter Quarters in Nebraska and Iowa. It was a practical policy centered on two aspects: separation and fairness. Brigham Young established the basic approach as early as 1846 when he presented his position to the high council at a special meeting. He remarked that it was his impression that the committee should not enter into any specific agreement with the Indians but endeavor to create a friendly feeling and have a meeting at a future time: "We should not invite the Indians to our camp," said the president on August 15, "we can go and see them." Young continued:

> We want the privilege of staying on their land this winter, cutting timber, building houses, perhaps leaving some families and crops; suggest that we might do them good, repairing their guns, and learning them how, and teaching their children and if they want pay for occupancy of their lands, we will pay them.[2]

[1]Juanita Brooks, "Indian Relations on the Mormon Frontier," *Utah Historical Quarterly* 12 (1944): 1–48. Also see Hubert Howe Bancroft, *History of Utah* (Salt Lake City: Bookcraft, 1964), p. 471; Andrew Love Neff, *History of Utah: 1847 to 1869,* ed. Leland Hargrave Creer (Salt Lake City: Deseret News Press, 1946), p. 368; Orson H. Whitney, *History of Utah,* 4 vols. (Salt Lake City, 1892), 1: 425; and S. George Ellsworth, *Utah's Heritage* (Salt Lake City and Santa Barbara, Calif.: Peregrine Smith Inc., 1972), p. 162.

[2]"Journal History of the Church," August 15, 1846, Archives Division, Historical Department, Church of Jesus Christ of Latter-day Saints, Salt Lake City (hereinafter cited as JH). Young later had occasion to deny that he may have actually promised payment to nearby Indians for use of their lands. Responding to a letter from Indian agent Maj. John Miller reporting that an Ottoe chief had demanded money the Mormons had promised for use of his tribe's land, Young stated: "we do not owe them any thing for the land, we never agreed to pay them any thing, the government of the United States stopped us here and if there is any thing due to the Indians it is due from the General Government, not from us." See George W. Wear to Young, May 7, 1848, and Young to Miller, May 8, 1848, Brigham Young Collection, LDS Archives, Microfilm reel 92, box 57, folder 5 (hereafter cited as BYC).

There were many contacts with Indians in the vicinity of Winter Quarters. Though friendship generally prevailed, Indians stole a considerable number of horses and cattle.[3] Each loss was considered serious, as the Mormons were in a desperate condition following their premature expulsion from Illinois. Horses and oxen were essential for the westward trek. Yet, the prophet strongly counseled against killing Indians for theft. Young's clerks reported in his manuscript history that in March 1847 just before heading west he

> told the Council that if any of the brethren shot an Omaha Indian for stealing, they must deliver the murderer to Old Elk to be dealt with, as the Indians shall decide, as that was the only way to save the lives of the women and children.
>
> I felt that it was wrong to indulge in feelings of hostility and blood-shed toward the Indians, the descendents of Israel, who might kill a cow, an ox or even a horse; to them the deer, the buffalo, the cherry and plum tree, or strawberry bed were free. It was their mode of living to kill and eat. If the Omahas would persist in robbing and stealing, after being warned not to do so, whip them. I realize there were men among us who would steal, who knew better, whose traditions and earliest teachings were all against it. Yet such would find fellowship with those who would shoot an Indian for stealing.[4]

Mormon leaders obtained valuable information regarding the Ute Indians at Fort Bridger three weeks before the advance party of settlers reached the Great Basin. James Bridger warned the party that "the Utah tribe of Indians [centered in Utah Valley] are a bad people; if they catch a man alone they are sure to rob and abuse him, if they don't kill him."[5] Young's concern was described in a letter written by Willard Richards and George A. Smith, both Mormon leaders. Young "felt inclined for the present not to crowd the Utes until we have a better chance to get acquainted with them. . . . The Utes may feel a little tenacious about their choice lands on the Utah Lake, and [we] had better keep further north towards Salt Lake. . . . "[6]

Within a few days of the Mormons' arrival in the Great Basin, small groups of Shoshonis and Utes came to trade horses for guns. The situation soon became complicated when the Shoshonis claimed that the Utes were trading on Shoshoni land and interfering with their rights. They also desired to sell land to the Mormons for ammunition.[7] Concerned that trouble might ensue, Heber C. Kimball, speaking for Brigham Young who was ill, responded the next day by establishing a strict policy of separation. He exhorted the Mormons to build their houses together in the form of a stockade and to cease trading their guns and ammunition. Kimball then established a far-reaching policy regarding land ownership. Rather than contracting with the Indians for purchase of land, or paying for the *use* of the land—policy proposed by Brigham Young in 1846 in Iowa—Kimball declared that the Indians did not own the land in the first place.

[3]JH, February 13 and 24, and December 6, 1847.
[4]Brigham Young Manuscript History, 1847:74, LDS Archives (hereafter cited as HBY).
[5]JH, June 28, 1847.
[6]Ibid., July 21, 1847.

> He discouraged the idea of paying the Indians for the lands, for if the Shoshonis should be thus considered, the Utes and other tribes would claim pay also. "The land belongs to our Father in Heaven, and we calculate to plow and plant it; and no man shall have the power to sell his inheritance for he cannot remove it; it belongs to the Lord."[8]

The Indian position, as if in response to the above, was reported three weeks later at a special conference. They claimed "all the land was their own" and that they "were in the habit of taking a share of the grain for their use of the land."[9] There is no indication that such a proposition was ever seriously considered in Utah.

On August 26, 1847, Young and most of the church leadership left the Great Basin to return to Winter Quarters for the purpose of bringing more settlers west the following season. They left to those remaining an epistle that in part reiterated the policy of strict separation and added, "if you wish to trade with them, go to their camp and deal with them honestly."[10]

The remainder of 1847 and most of 1848 was a period of generally peaceful relations with the Indians, though in March 1848 a forty-five-man posse was sent in pursuit of Indians "about Utah Lake" who had stolen seventeen cattle and one horse. Contact was made east of Utah Lake but no fighting broke out. The Indian chief whipped the "two principal thieves" and "all promised to do better." The high council at Great Salt Lake City reported that the marshal of the posse "was sent out with discretionary power and plenty of force," an indication that the Mormon settlers were stiffening in their attitude toward the stealing of stock and that further such "depredations" might be dealt with harshly.[11]

During the remainder of 1848 survival was the Mormons' primary concern, and the new settlers expended most of their energies on bringing in a food crop for the expanding settlement as soon as possible.[12] Exploring parties scouted adjacent areas, but the settlement remained confined to greater Salt Lake Valley. Still, the local Indians, especially the Utes, were confused and angered by this attempt at a permanent white settlement in their domain. Hostile action was restrained, however, possibly due to the location of the settlement in the buffer zone between the Shoshonis and Utes.[13]

By early 1849, however, relations between the Mormons and the Utes had begun to deteriorate. Responding to reports of many horses being stolen and cattle being killed by renegades, Brigham Young dispatched a

[7]Ibid., July 31, 1847.

[8]Ibid., August 1, 1847.

[9]Ibid., August 22, 1847.

[10]Epistle of the Quorum of the Twelve Apostles as recorded in JH, September 9, 1847.

[11]JH, March 1, 5 and 6, 1848.

[12]Brigham Young returned to Utah with another large contingent of settlers in the summer of 1848.

[13]See Edward W. Tullidge, "History of Provo," *Tullidge's Quarterly Magazine* 3 (1884): 241; Paul Bailey, *Walkara, Hawk of the Mountains* (Los Angeles: Westernlore Press, 1954), pp. 49–50; and Paul Bailey, *The Claws of the Hawk* (Los Angeles: Westernlore Press, 1966), pp. 131–39.

company of militia, under Col. John Scott, with orders (according to Hosea Stout's account) "to take such measures as would put a final end to their depredations in future."[14] Scott, with his detachment of thirty-five men, entered Utah Valley on March 3 and was informed of the location of the renegade band by a local Ute Indian named Little Chief. The detachment then proceeded to surround the band and, on March 5, laid siege. The Indians answered a challenge to surrender with a shower of arrows and a two-hour battle ensued. All four warriors were killed, but there were no militia casualties. Scott's detachment returned to Great Salt Lake Valley the next day, followed by the "squaws and children of the slain."[15] The action, carried out with determination and dispatch, was apparently in contravention of Brigham Young's previously proposed policy that Indians would not, or should not, be killed for stealing.

Though the militia killed all the men of the renegade band, they failed to "put a final end to . . . depredations in future." In fact, their actions may have had an opposite effect. Even the Indians who had recommended that the renegades be killed and who had led the militia to the renegade camp bemoaned the ruthlessness with which the action was carried out. Little Chief "howled, cried, . . . screamed and smote his breast in the greatest agony" and "blamed and cursed the whites, and said it would not be good medicine for two or three to come there alone as they had done before."[16]

Just five days later the Mormon leadership voted to send out a small colony to settle in the midst of the Utes in Utah Valley. The settlers, led by John S. Higbee and numbering about 150 persons, set out on March 18.[17] They were stopped en route by the Ute Indians. As no effort had been made to treat with the Indians before the colony was dispatched, the Indians demanded to know the intent of the settlers before allowing them to proceed. Dimick B. Huntington, interpreter for the colony, parleyed with the Indians and promised that though their intent was to establish a permanent settlement, the settlers would not drive the Indians from their lands or take away their rights.[18]

Nevertheless, as early as April 17, President Young had some indication that the Utes were planning an attack on the settlement.[19] Young warned the colony the next day "to look out for the Indians, not to make them any

[14]Hosea Stout Diary, 8 vols., 4:48, typescript, Lee Library, Brigham Young University, Provo, Utah. The stock was taken from herds in Tooele Valley and southern Great Salt Lake Valley by a renegade band of Ute Indians who had declared their hostility toward the white settlers some time before. The band was led by three brothers, "Roman Nose," "Blueshirt," and one other (possibly "Cone"). Reportedly they had been driven out of Utah Valley by their chief because they refused to stop stealing cattle from the Mormons. See Oliver B. Huntington Diary, pp. 52–53, Lee Library.

[15]For accounts of the March 5, 1849 skirmish, see JH, February 27 and 28, and March 10, 1849: Stout Diary, 4:48–56; and Huntington Diary, pp. 53–55.

[16]Huntington Diary, p. 55.

[17]Tullidge, "History of Provo," p. 233.

[18]*Provo: Pioneer Mormon City,* comp. Writers Program, Work Projects Administration (Portland, Ore.: Binfords and Mort, 1942), p. 45. A treaty with the Utah Valley Utes was proposed as early as March 1848 for at least fishing rights, but there is no evidence that it was carried out. See JH, March 6, 1848.

presents, but, if they would be friendly, to teach them to raise grain and to quit stealing."[20] In May he remarked that old Indians will not "enter into the new and everlasting covenant" or gain knowledge, "but they will die and be damned." He admonished the people to "stay at home and mind your own business and the Indians will do the same. And if they come and are not friendly, put them where they can't harm us. . . . "[21]

As a precaution, Young directed that a letter of friendship be sent to the Ute war chief Walkara on May 14, and a few days later he again warned the Utah Valley settlers—this time instructing them to finish their fort quickly—to strictly control the number of Indians to be allowed in the fort at any one time, and to beware of deception. Later, he enlarged upon his previously stated policy of separation by urging the settlers not to be so familiar with the Indians, because, he said, "it makes them bold, impudent, and saucy, and will become a source of trouble and expense to you. Keep them at a respectful distance all the time, and they will respect you the more for it."[22]

On June 13, Brigham Young, his two counselors, and an interpreter met in council with Walkara and twelve of his warriors. During the discussion Young and Walkara expressed friendship. Walkara, having temporarily mellowed, indicated his antagonism toward the Utah Lake Utes and invited the Mormons to settle in his lands to the south of Utah Valley. Young responded affirmatively and went on to propose that the Mormons could help the Indians grow crops, develop herds, and learn to read.[23]

Despite growing concern over Indians, expansion was a primary theme during the summer of 1849 and the following October church general conference. A new settlement in San Pitch (Sanpete) Valley, south of Utah Valley, was announced and an appeal went out to members worldwide: "We want men. Brethren, come from the States, from the nations, come! and help us to build and grow until we can say enough—the valleys of Ephraim are full."[24] The San Pitch company, numbering 224 people led by Isaac Morley, departed Salt Lake City on October 28.[25] Later in the year a party under the leadership of Parley P. Pratt embarked on an extensive exploration of the valleys further south.

[19]JH, April 17, 1849. In Bailey, *Walkara, Hawk of the Mountains,* pp. 66–67, the author tells of Walkara's wrath upon seeing the new Utah Valley settlement. Had it not been for the lack of warriors—and the lack of support from Chief Sowiette—Walkara may have attacked the settlement then and there.

[20]JH, April 19, 1849.

[21]Ibid., May 7, 1849.

[22]Ibid., May 14, 19 and 28, 1849.

[23]Ibid., June 13, 1849. In Bailey, *Walkara, Hawk of the Mountains,* pp. 19–21, the author indicates that residual hostility by Walkara toward the Utah Lake Utes (Timpany Utes) was because Timpany Utes had killed Walkara's father. Walkara and his brother Arapeen avenged their father's murder and fled south, eventually settling in Sanpete Valley.

[24]Second Epistle of the First Presidency of the LDS church as reported in JH, October 12, 1849.

[25]JH, October 28 and November 22, 1849. At a public meeting, President Young was quoted as having called young men to San Pitch Valley " . . . and to take possession of all good valleys."

On October 15, Isaac Higbee, who had replaced John S. Higbee as leader of the Utah Valley colony, wrote that Indians had been troublesome for several weeks. Three men were shot at, two animals were killed, and some corn was stolen. The Indians were reported as "very saucy, annoying and provoking, threatening to kill the men and the women."[26] President Young answered with a letter repeating his previous counsel to build up their fort, attend to their own affairs, and to leave the Indians alone. He went on to scold them for mixing "promiscuously" with the Indians.[27]

II

Events came with a rush in 1850 and forced total reversal of the policy of fairness. Ironically, the reversal was precipitated by three Mormon settlers. In early January the three men accosted "Old Bishop," a member of one of the Indian bands living in Utah Valley, reportedly for stealing a shirt. The men shot him, cut his stomach open, filled it with rocks, and dumped the body into the Provo River. They returned to the settlement and openly boasted of their exploit.[28] Indians soon found Old Bishop's body and furiously called for revenge. Their hostile communications to the settlers, and increased killing and stealing of cattle, led to alarm. One of the Utah Valley settlers, Alexander Williams, wrote to Brigham Young requesting that action be taken to quell the increasingly troublesome Indians. Young responded on January 9 and once again reiterated his policy. He warned that

[26]Ibid., October 15, 1849; and HBY, October 15, 1849.

[27]Ibid., October 18, 1849. Young stated: "Let any man, or company of men be familiar with the Indians, and they will be more familiar: and the more familiar, you will find the less influence you will have with them. If you would have dominion over them, for their good, which is the duty of the Elders, you must not treat them as your equals. You cannot exalt them by this process. If they are your equals, you cannot raise them up to you."

[28]JH, January 31, 1850; HBY, 1850:17–18. The HBY account reads: "Statement made by Elder James Bean (June 12, 1854).

"Early in January, 1850, Jerome Zobriski, Richard A. Ivie, and John Rufus Stoddard were going out from the fort in Utah Valley, professedly to hunt cattle; shortly they met an Indian who was wearing a shirt which R. A. Ivie claimed, alleging that it had been stolen from him and demanded it; the Indian refused to give it up, saying he had bought it; whereupon they tried to take it from him forcibly, he struggling all the time against them, to defend himself drew his bow, when John R. Stoddard shot him through the head killing him instantly; they then dragged his corpse to the Provo River and sunk it near the Box Elder Island.

"The Indians became suspicious, instituted a search and found the body; then they commenced depredations by stealing horses and cattle. The Indian shot by Stoddard was known among the whites as "Old Bishop" on account of his appearance and gestures which somewhat resembled Bishop Whitney's.

"The settlers in Utah Ft. then made a law to keep all Indians out of the fort. Old Elk who was sick with the measles came in for some medicine, went to Sister Hunt's house, where Alexander Williams saw him and took him by the nape of the neck and kicked him out of the fort. That same evening the Indians stole three cows out of Mrs. Hunt's yard and continued stealing, which was the commencement of Indian difficulties."

"James Bean heard Ivie relate the occurrence. Zobriski and Stoddard have boasted of it.

"Elder James Goff subsequently stated that the murder of the Indian was talked of at the time by many of the settlers, and that it was asserted that the men who killed the Indian ripped his bowels open and filled them with stones preparatory to sinking his body. . . . "

Other accounts give the date of the murder as early as August 1849. If true the increase of hostility reported by Isaac Higbee in October 1849 would thereby be explained.

if they killed Indians for stealing they would have to "answer for it."[29]

Leaders of the Utah Valley settlement were not persuaded. Determined to take action, Isaac Higbee traveled to Salt Lake City to petition personally for authority to launch a punitive expedition. On January 31 he attended a meeting with President Young, his counselors, the Quorum of the Twelve, and militia commander Daniel H. Wells. Apostle Parley P. Pratt, who had recently returned from his southern exploration, argued that the only alternatives were abandoning Utah Valley (with the resultant break in communications with settlements further south), defending the Utah Valley settlement, or leaving the Utah Valley settlers to their destruction. He recommended "it best to kill the Indians." Higbee responded that "every man and boy [in Utah Valley] held up their hand to kill them off. . . . " The record does not indicate that Higbee made any mention of the murder of Old Bishop—the incident that had precipitated the dilemma. Willard Richards added to the above by declaring "my voice is for war, and exterminate them." Young, convinced of the need for action, and persuaded by the unanimous recommendation of all those present, ordered a selective extermination campaign to be carried out against the Utah Valley Indians. He ordered that all the men were to be killed—women and children to be saved if they "behave themselves"—and military orders were immediately drafted to that effect by General Wells. Wells's "Special Order No. 2," dated January 31 and addressed to Capt. George D. Grant, commander of the militia company sent from Great Salt Lake City, reads in part:

> You are hereby ordered . . . to cooperate with the inhabitants of said [Utah] Valley in quelling and staying the operations of all hostile Indians and otherwise act, as the circumstances may require, exterminating such as do not separate themselves from their hostile clans, and sue for peace.

The next day Young met with Capt. Howard Stansbury, head of a unit of U.S. Army Topographic Engineers carrying out land surveys in Utah, who encouraged an attack on the Utah Valley Indians and offered his fullest support. On February 2, 1850, Young addressed the general assembly and announced his decision.[30]

[29]Ibid., January 29, 1850. Young proposed: "Why should men have a disposition to kill a destitute, naked Indian, who may steal a shirt or a horse and think it no harm, when they never think of meting out a like retribution to a white man who steals, although he has been taught better from infancy?"

[30]An account of the dialogue of the January 31 meeting can be found in BYC, Microfilm reel 80, box 47, folder 6. Brigham Young is quoted as stating: "I say go [and] kill them. . . . Tell Dimick Huntington to go and kill them—also Barney Ward—let the women and children live if they behave themselves. . . . We have no peace until the men [are] killed off—never treat the Indian as your equal." Wells's Special Order No. 2 can be found in the Utah State Archives, State Capitol, Salt Lake City, Utah Territorial Militia Correspondence, 1849–1863, ST-27, Microfilm reel 1, Document No. 5 (hereafter cited as State Archives). General Wells wrote in his narrative, written some years later, that he left for Utah Valley (ten days later) with orders "not to leave the valley until every Indian was out." See "Daniel H. Wells Narrative," *Utah Historical Quarterly* 6 (1933): 126. On February 14, 1850, Brigham Young instructed: "If the Indians sue for peace, grant it to them, according to your discretion and judgment in the case.—If they continue hostile pursue them until you use them up—*Let it be peace with them or extermination.*" See State Archives, ST-27, Young to Wells, February 14, 1850, Microfilm reel 3, Document No. 1,312.

The campaign was carried out with zeal. On February 8, 1850, a voluntary force made up of militia from Salt Lake City and Utah Valley, supported by cannon, surrounded and laid siege to a group of about seventy Indians under Big Elk (Old Elk) who were dug in at a nearby location on the Provo River. After two days of heavy fighting the Indians withdrew, leaving eight dead, including one woman whose legs were severed by cannon shot. One militiaman was also killed in the battle. The Indian wounded and sick retreated up Rock Canyon and the main body fled in the direction of the Spanish Fork River.[31] General Wells then departed for Utah Valley on February 10 and personally directed a relentless pursuit. Unit commanders were instructed to "take no hostile prisoners" and "let none escape but do the work up clean." One party entered Rock Canyon, finding eight or nine Indians, including Big Elk, dead of wounds, disease, or exposure. Wells and a two-company force of 110 men pursued the main body of Indians who were withdrawing south.[32]

What happened next is recorded in General Wells's field dispatch to Brigham Young written on the night of February 13. Wells reported that a force of "15 or 20" warriors, with their families, surrendered to the militia unit under Captain Grant on the lake shore west of Table Mountain (near Payson). The Indians, stated Wells,

> came rather through fear than otherwise and seemed determined but to give up refusing to smoke the pipe of peace we shall deal with them in a most summary manner as soon as another day favors us with light. . . .

Then, in a postscript appended the next morning, Wells wrote: "Please to make some suggestion in relation to the disposal of some 15 or 20 squaws and children who probably belonged to some 11 warriors who met their fate in a small skirmish this morning." Apparently General Wells had seen to it that his orders were carried out not to take hostile prisoners nor to let any escape.[33]

After the killings, Dr. James Blake, a U.S. Army surgeon, with the assistance of two militiamen, decapitated the bodies, ostensibly for future research.[34] Units dispatched later in the day of February 14 spotted and fired

[31]Accounts of the first two days of battle can be found in *Provo: Pioneer Mormon City*, pp. 52–59; Tullidge, "History of Provo," pp. 237–39; and HBY, 1850, 23–25.

[32]Special Orders No. 10, February 9, 1850, State Archives, ST-27, Microfilm reel 1, Document No. 16; and Lt. George W. Howland to Brigham Young, February 15, 1850, Ibid., reel 3, Document No. 1,311. Also see *Provo: Pioneer Mormon City*, p. 58; and Tullidge, "History of Provo," pp. 239–40.

[33]Wells to Brigham Young, February 13–14, 1850, State Archives, ST-27, Microfilm reel 3, Document No. 1,309. For some interesting secondary accounts, see John W. Gunnison, *The Mormons, or Latter-day Saints, in the Valley of the Great Salt Lake* . . . (Philadelphia, 1852), p. 147; and *Provo: Pioneer Mormon City*, pp. 58–59.

[34]See typescripts of the autobiographies of Epsy Jane Williams Pace and Abner Blackburn, Lee Library, for accounts of the mutilations, although the *Provo: Pioneer Mormon City* quotation of the original documents (pp. 58–59) is probably more accurate. Dr. Blake accompanied the militia from Salt Lake City with the permission of Capt. Howard Stansbury, commanding officer of the U.S. Army Topographic Engineers company then in Utah surveying routes for the transcontinental railroad.

upon five Indians thought to be scouts, killing three. Three more warriors were killed in their camp on Peteetneet Creek on February 15. Another Indian (probably a woman) was killed in Rock Canyon by militiamen on February 17. The following day, General Wells and the main militia force, in response to instructions from Brigham Young, started back to Great Salt Lake City, taking Indian women and children prisoners with them. An eleven-man detachment of the Great Salt Lake City force remained to assist the local (Utah Valley) militia in further pursuit and to escort other prisoners—and wounded militia—northward when they were able to travel. The campaign came to a close a few days later when militia responded to a report of Indian fires being spotted nearby. The force came upon twenty-four Indians, who were reported to be "very hostile." No fighting broke out, however, the forces being equal, and all repaired to the fort where a truce was negotiated.[35]

Brigham Young's decision to launch an extermination campaign was seemingly in total contradiction of his position stated only three weeks before. The reason for this reversal—and his reluctance to do so—is suggested by this statement at a meeting held with his counselors and the Twelve on February 10, 1850:

> I am sent now to confiscate all their property—and then put them in the heat of battle and kill them—if men had taken a different course there—there would not have been any trouble—I have told them the cause of their difficulties—shooting with the Indians—gambling—and running horses with them. . . .

He went on to indicate his fear that the loss of the Utah Valley might lead to ultimate loss of the entire Utah settlement.

> They must either quit the ground or we must—we are to maintain that ground or vacate this—we were cold [told] three years ago—if we don't kill those Lake Utes, they will kill us—every man told us the same—they all bore testimony the Lake Utes lived by plunder and robbing—if we yield in this instance—we have to yield this land.[36]

Captain Stansbury also recorded that "the President was at first extremely averse to the adoption of harsh measures. . . . [37] In 1854, when Young heard of the Old Bishop murder for the first time, he inserted the account in his manuscript history with the following comment: "These facts, which were

[35]State Archives, ST-27; Microfilm reel 1, Document Nos. 36, 39, 44, and 45; Microfilm reel 3, Document No. 1,312. Another woman in Rock Canyon was reported as having fallen to her death from a precipice in an attempt to escape. Ibid. Also see Tullidge, "History of Provo," pp. 235–40; *Provo: Pioneer Mormon City,* pp. 52–59; Conway B. Sonne, *The World Of Wakara* (San Antonio: Naylor Co., 1962), pp. 85–98; and Wells, "Daniel H. Wells Narrative," p. 126.

[36]BYC, Microfilm reel 80, box 47, folder. 6.

[37]Howard Stansbury, *Exploration and Survey of the Valley of the Great Salt Lake of Utah* . . . (Philadelphia, 1852), p. 148.

hid at the time, explained to me why my feelings were opposed to going to war with the Indians; to which I never consented until Brother Higbee reported that all the settlers in Utah were of one mind in relation to it."[38]

III

After the Utah Valley expedition it became customary for reports of depredation to be followed by militia action—and more killings. Whereas policy towards the Indians had been geared initially to benefit both sides, it had, by February 1850, deteriorated to a policy favoring only the new settlers. The best land was to be taken up as fast as possible without payment, the Indians were to be strictly excluded, and stealing by Indians was often to bring swift punishment.

The peace hoped for as a result of the Utah Valley expedition was not to be, contrary to most contemporary and historical treatments of the period. Hatred on the part of at least some of the survivors was intense. On April 29, Alpheus Baker, returning alone from Sanpete Valley, was murdered by two Utes—the first Mormon settler to be murdered by Indians in the Great Basin. A posse rounded up and brought in nineteen suspects. One of them. Patsowett, was summarily tried by a local court at Manti, Utah, convicted, and executed.[39]

In May 1850, Walkara invited Brigham Young to attend the annual Indian trade gathering in Utah Valley. Young went with a Mormon trade delegation and met in council with several chiefs. Hope of a good peace was dashed, however, when a band of Shoshonis raided a Ute camp and stole several horses. Walkara planned a retaliation raid and asked for Mormon militia support. His request was justifiably denied, and Walkara, incensed at both the Shoshonis and the Mormons, rode off with his warriors to do battle with his Indian adversaries. Upon his return after effecting bloody retaliation on the Shoshoni raiders, Walkara and his band made a gruesome demonstration in front of the settlement fort at Manti, then decided to move north and attack the Provo settlement. Rebuffed by another chief, Sowiette, Walkara called off the attack and withdrew.[40]

[38]HBY, 1850: 18. See footnote 28.

[39]JH, April 19 and 20, 1850; and Hosea Stout Diary, 4:93–94. In a letter from Dimick B. Huntington to Brigham Young, on April 19, 1850, Huntington reported that Patsowett's brother had been killed previously. Ibid. A letter from Isaac Higbee and Peter W. Conover to Daniel H. Wells, dated April 28, 1850, reads in part: "I understand that Patsowett is in your city, or was last Monday. He and his brother have been killing cattle since the war with the Indians and threatening to kill every white man he can. We have been searching for him to kill him, but have not found him yet. But we found his brother and killed him. We wish you would search for him, and, if he can be found in your valley, to kill him before he can do any more mischief." Quoted in Juanita Brooks, ed., *On the Mormon Frontier: The Diary of Hosea Stout, 1844–1861*, 2 vols. (Salt Lake City: University of Utah Press, Utah State Historical Society, 1964), 2:368.

[40]See JH, May 14, 18, 20 and 31, and June 27, 1850; Tullidge, "History of Provo," pp. 240–41: Bailey, *The Claws of the Hawk*, pp. 253–60; Sonne, *The World of Wakara*, pp. 108–15; and "Reminiscences of the Early Days of Manti," *Utah Historical Quarterly* 6 (1933): 117–18.

In the late summer of 1850 the killing of an Indian for stealing once more caused trouble. This time it was in Shoshoni country (near Ogden) and retaliation was immediate and vicious. A Mormon farmer, Urban Van Stewart, caught Terikee, a Shoshoni chief, in his corn patch and killed him. The Shoshonis were enraged. They murdered a nearby millwright named Campbell and threatened to massacre all the settlers and burn their property if Stewart was not delivered up to them for punishment by nine o'clock the next morning. Alerted, a large militia force under Gen. Horace S. Eldredge rode out from Great Salt Lake City with orders to quell the disturbance but to do it peacefully if possible. Brigham Young and Daniel Wells were aware of the hitherto friendly relations with the Shoshonis and apparently had been informed that Stewart's act may well have been unwarranted. At the approach of Eldredge's force, the Indians broke and fled and the incident terminated without further bloodshed.[41]

Still, as if convinced that their policy toward the Indians had been unsuccessful, the First Presidency of the Mormon church sought to rid themselves of the problem by having the Indians removed completely beyond the boundaries of the territory. On November 20, 1850, the day after receiving information by mail that Congress had voted to organize the territory of Utah,[42] the LDS First Presidency wrote a letter to John M. Bernhisel, agent for church and state of Deseret interests in Washington, D.C. Brigham Young explained later that the letter's purpose was

> to endeavor to effect the extinguishment of the Indian title and the removal to, and location of the Indians at, some favorable point on the eastern slope of the Sierra Nevada where forests, game and streams are plenty: or to the Wind River chain of mountains, where fish, and game abound; or on the Snake River: at neither of which points white men dwell. The progress of civilization, the safety of the mails and the welfare of the Indians themselves called for the adoption of this policy.[43]

[41]See JH, September 16, 17, 1850; HBY, 1850: 85–86; *Tullidge's Histories* 2 (Salt Lake City, 1889): 15–16; and State Archives, ST-27, Microfilm reel 1, Document Nos. 64–88.

[42]Hosea Stout Diary, p. 126.

[43]HBY, 1850:108. The strongly worded letter reads in part:

"It is our wish that the Indian title should be extinguished, and the Indians removed from our Territory Utah and that for the best of reasons, because they are doing no good here to themselves or anybody else. The buffalo had entirely vacated this portion of the country before our arrival; the elk, deer, antelope and bear, and all eatable game are very scarce, and there is little left here (abating the white population) save the naked rocks and soil, naked Indians and wolves; the first two we can use to good advantage, the last two are annoying and destructive to property and peace, by night and by day, and while we are trying to shoot, trap and poison the wolves on one hand, the Indians come in and drive off, butcher our cattle, and steal our corn on the other, which leaves us little time between the wolves and Indians to fence and cultivate our farms: and if government will buy out and transplant the Indians, we will endeavor to subdue the wolves, which have destroyed our cattle, horses, sheep and poultry by hundreds and thousands. . . .

" . . . Do we wish the Indians any evil? No we would do them good, for they are human beings, though most awfully degraded. We would have taught them to plow and sow, and reap and thresh, but they prefer idleness and theft. Is it desirable that the barren soil of the mountain valleys should be converted into fruitful fields? Let the Indians be removed. Is it desirable that the way should be opened up for a rapid increase of population into our new State or Ter-

On December 2, 1850, just two weeks after the letter to Bernhisel was written, Brigham Young addressed the General Assembly of the state of Deseret to inform them of the creation of Utah Territory. He spoke of the Indians. Without reference to the request for removal that had been dispatched only days before, he commented on the serious cultural gap that existed and implied that the gap might be impossible to bridge.

> All the Indians with whom we have had difficulties, are detached or broken off bands from the main tribes; with them, our peaceful relations have never been interrupted. We have spared no time or expense in endeavoring to conciliate the Indians, and learn them to leave off their habits of pilfering and plundering and work like other people. But habits of civilization seem not to be in accordance with their physical formation; many that have tried it, pine away, and unless returned to their former habits of living, die in a very short time. Could they be induced to live peacefully and keep herds of cattle, then conditions would very materially be ameliorated, and gradually induce a return to the habits of civilization.[44]

The Bernhisel letter was never specifically acted upon; title to Indian lands in Utah was never extinguished completely.[45] As no documented response by Bernhisel can be found, it is assumed that he opted to respond in person upon his return to Great Salt Lake City in the spring of 1851, and that he counseled against any formal action. The significance of the letter is that it reflects the attitude of the Mormon leaders at the time and indicates that they despaired of a solution that might be mutually beneficial. Complete removal seemed the only way out.

IV

Hostilities continued in 1851—again in Utah Valley and later in Tooele Valley, west of Utah Lake. On January 17, 1851, a Mormon settler named Stewart killed an Indian whom he had reportedly mistaken "for a wolf in the grass." Stewart successfully mollified the dead Indian's family by giving them an ox, 300 pounds of flour, and "making a feast for the Indians."[46] Three weeks later, the militia responded to the report of the theft of fifty cattle and horses in Tooele Valley by dispatching a twenty-man party to that vicinity. The party returned without making contact due to deep snow.[47]

ritory, also to California or Oregon? Let the Indians be removed, we can then devote more time to agriculture and raise more grain and feed the starving millions desirous of coming hither.

"For the prosperity of civilization, for the safety of our mail routes, for the good of the Indians, let them be removed." See BYC, Microfilm reel 31, box 12, folder 14.

[44]HBY 1850:121.

[45]Several attempts were made to extinguish the Indian title by treaty purchase as legal ownership of occupied lands could not be accomplished otherwise, nor could much financial assistance otherwise be gained from federal funds to assist the Indians—also a concern. See Leland Hargrave Creer, *Utah and the Nation* (Seattle: University of Washington Press, 1929), pp. 180–91.

[46]JH, January 17, 1851. On the same day, two Indians, a man and a boy, were captured for crippling a yoke of oxen (one of the oxen was killed) in Iron County to the south. "An exchange was made satisfactory, by taking the boy for the ox which was crippled."

[47]Ibid., February 11, 1851.

Indians continued to drive off stock in Tooele Valley, and another party was sent in pursuit in April. This group, under the command of Orrin Porter Rockwell, captured thirty Indians. In an escape attempt, one white, Lorenzo D. Custer, and five Indians were killed. The remainder of the natives made good their escape, except four who were recaptured and probably slain.[48]

In June, the theft of another sixty head of cattle again led to a mobilization of militia. General Wells issued orders on June 13 to Maj. George D. Grant, Capt. Peter W. Conover, and Capt. William McBride to raise forces totaling ninety men for the purpose of trapping the Indian cattle thieves in the mountains between Tooele and Utah valleys. Instructions to Conover indicated the necessity to "chastise them in the most summary manner"; and those to Grant—and subsequently to McBride—were "to down them . . . and if possible let no hostile Indians escape. . . . " The next day, however, the orders to Grant and Conover were rescinded, and only the twenty-man force under Captain McBride went out. Having trailed the Indians to their camp, McBride held up and sent back a request for reinforcements. On June 20, reinforcements under Capt. William F. Kimball headed for Tooele with orders to "endeavor to rout the Indians and recover the stolen property." McBride and Kimball, supported by local militia, moved against the Indian camp, severely wounding two warriors in a fire fight on June 24, then killing nine in an assault on the camp on June 25. The militia returned to Great Salt Lake City on June 27 and claimed eleven Indians killed. There were no militia casualties.[49]

Though the attack was carried out with zeal on the part of Captain McBride, General Wells had begun to reverse himself regarding the extermination strategy. In his June 14 rescinding orders to Major Grant he rhetorically stated:

> If we pursue the same course that people generally do against the Indians we may expect to expend more time and money in running after Indians than all the loss sustained by them. . . .

Wells stated essentially the same to Captain Conover, adding that "all might be saved by proper care and watchfulness and the lives of the Indians spared."[50]

[48]Ibid., April 22, 1851; Stout Diary, 4:155; and Tullidge, *Tullidge's Histories,* 2:83–84. Tullidge reports that the prisoners were later killed by Rockwell's party who: "deemed it unwise to turn the thieves in their power loose to commit more depredations and perhaps shed the blood of some useful citizen and they were sacrificed to the natural instincts of self-defense."

[49]JH, June 10, 13, 20, 25 and 27, 1851; State Archives, ST-27; Microfilm reel 1, Document Nos. 120–22, 126; Microfilm reel 3, Document Nos. 1,326–27; Stout Diary, 4:160; Peter Gottfredson, *Indian Depredations in Utah* (Salt Lake City: Skelton Publishing Co., 1919) pp. 39–40; and Tullidge, *Tullidge's Histories,* 2:84.

[50]State Archives, ST-27, Microfilm reel 1, Document Nos. 123–24. On June 20, Captain McBride pointedly requested arsenic be sent for the purpose of poisoning the water supply at the Indian camp. Ibid., Microfilm reel 3, Document No. 1,328.

A turning point had been reached. The June 1851 Tooele expedition was the last extermination effort against Indians in Utah, though militia actions against thieving Indians continued in 1852, and sporadically in later years. Additionally, the rhetoric inserted into General Wells's orders of June 14 may well have been the basis for the "cheaper to feed them than fight them" statement of policy to come. Brigham Young elaborated on the thoughts expressed by Wells just three weeks later in a letter to Lorin Farr in Ogden. In response to Farr's report of a militia action against Shoshonis for stealing horses, Young stated: "do not the people all know that it is cheaper by far, yes hundreds and thousands of dollars cheaper to pay such losses, than raise an expedition . . . to fight Indians."[51]

Whether or not the territorial leadership had forsworn extermination as strategy in 1851, local militia actions were carried out in 1852, again in the vicinity of Tooele. Some of the militiamen, however, opposed ruthless killing of the Indians that had continued raiding their herds. Jacob Hamblin, a Tooele militia lieutenant, recounted that he brought a number of prisoners into Tooele after assuring them that they would not be injured:

> On my arrival home, my superior officer ignored the promise of safety I had given the Indians, and decided to have them shot.
>
> I told him I did not care to live after I had seen the Indians whose safety I had guaranteed, murdered, and as it made but little difference with me, if there were any shot I should be the first. At the time I placed myself in front of the Indians. This ended the matter and they were set at liberty.[52]

Juanita Brooks, in her biography of Dudley Leavitt, mentions a similar incident where Leavitt brought in a prisoner to Tooele and refused to allow his being shot. Brooks reports that the Indian's fate was decided by Brigham Young, who was contacted by letter (or dispatch). Young "told them to feed the Indian and let him go."[53]

V

Apparently some sort of practical policy had evolved after the Mormon settlers arrived in Utah that was a combination of separation (based on the need for security), fair dealing, and assistance—tempered by a determination to take ruthless action whenever the Indians refused to accept the quantity of largess offered.

Brigham Young strongly indicated the practical nature of such a policy in an address to the Utah Territorial Legislature in December 1854 when he

[51]Farr to Young, July 10, 1851, JH; and Young to Farr, July 11, 1851, BYC, Microfilm reel 31, box 12, folder 15. Farr reported that one Indian was killed in an initial contact. Later, a militia force made a search into Cache Valley, but made no contact.

[52]James A. Little, *Jacob Hamblin: A Narrative of His Personal Experience as a Frontiersman, Missionary to the Indians and Explorer,* 2d ed. (Salt Lake City: Deseret News, 1909), p. 29. (First edition published in 1881.) See also an account of one of the militia actions carried out in March, 1852, in State Archives, ST-27, Microfilm reel 3, Document no. 1,332.

[53]Juanita Brooks, *On the Ragged Edge: The Life and Times of Dudley Leavitt* (Salt Lake City: Utah State Historical Society, 1973), pp. 46–47.

stated: "I have uniformly pursued a friendly course toward them, feeling convinced that independent of the question of exercising humanity towards so degraded and ignorant a race of people, it was manifestly more economical and less expensive, to feed and clothe, than fight them."[54] Earlier that year Young spelled out what appears to have been actual policy in a letter to Colonel Thomas Kane:

> We have ever pursued this policy toward them to feed and clothe them and then if they presumed upon forbearance to become ugly saucy and hostile beyond endurance to chastise them. Yet we have never lost sight of this policy to conciliate them as soon as possible.[55]

Unfortunately, for a period of time the element of "chastisement" received the major emphasis.

Beginning in 1851, stimulated by establishment of the Utah Territorial Indian Agency by Congress in February 1851 and the subsequent proclamation of that superintendency by Governor Young in July 1851, some considerable efforts were inaugurated to aid the Indians. "Indian farmers" were called by Young in the fall and winter of 1851. Two "Indian farms" were also designated in late 1851 to go into operation under those called by spring 1852. Throughout 1853 a policy of conciliation was zealously carried out during the Walker War. Following the war, other farms were established, as well as several Indian missions, from 1854 to 1857. However, commendable as these later efforts were, in most respects they came too late. The Indians, especially the Utes, declined rapidly as a result of extreme poverty brought on by usurpation of their lands, selective extermination, disease, and starvation.

Five observations seem warranted. First, conflict over who would control the limited usable land was inevitable. The Mormons poured into the valleys of the Wasatch oasis and displaced the Indians from their choicest lands. Having no idea how massive the Mormon immigration would be, the Indians put up only slight resistance to early expansion; they even invited settlements in the southern valleys in 1849, believing that there was room for all and that both groups could benefit by the other's presence. Not only were the Indians displaced, but the extensive conversion of the grassland to grain fields ruined their native food supply. Angered at the loss of their lands, rapidly becoming impoverished, having no other place to go, and refusing to take up the white man's farming methods, the natives increasingly relied on theft for survival. Their stealing and expressions of hostility led to bloody reprisal on the part of the Mormons, who felt that the land rightly belonged to those who would develop it.

Second, there was an awesome cultural gap between the two peoples. The Mormons perceived slovenly, naked Indians of small stature living

[54]B. H. Roberts, *A Comprehensive History of the Church of Jesus Christ of Latter-day Saints,* 6 vols. (Salt Lake City: Deseret News Press, 1930), 4:51.

[55]BYC, Microfilm reel 32, box 13, folder. 73.

primitively in rude huts made of brush, eating roots and crickets. They perceived other Indians of a higher cut who brutally exploited their lesser brethren, sold them as slaves, and brazenly carried out the vilest sort of atrocities, seemingly without conscience.[56] The Mormons had some minor success at converting but almost no success at acculturating their new associates. The Indians, on the other hand, looked upon the agrarian life-style of the Mormons with almost total disdain. Most were proud of their gatherer-hunter-warrior way of life and had no desire to settle down on small plots of land and grow grain or tend cattle. The Utes under Walkara were famous and wealthy (by their standards) when the Mormons arrived in 1847. Throughout the 1840s they made massive raids in California and brought away thousands of horses. Walkara was hailed throughout the West as a great Indian chief.[57] Reluctance to being reduced to the status of farmers and herders is understandable.

Third, and closely related to the cultural conflict, the Mormons were convinced of the inferiority of the Indian race. There was little desire to allow assimilation. Though a considerable number of Indian children were brought into Mormon homes and raised to maturity, the general policy was strict separation based on a desire for security and a belief that the Indians would never rise to the level of the white man if treated as equals. This policy of separation was similar to the general American experience. Robert F. Berkhofer closes his book *Salvation and the Savage* on a point that could as well be made with regard to the Mormons: "In many cases the failure of the aborigines to achieve [the] goal of Christian civilization was due to civilized Christians not accepting them on equal terms, for American society traditionally discriminated against non-Caucasian peoples."[58]

Fourth, there was little real compassion on either side. Mormons and Indians alike, inured to suffering and struggle and bent upon survival, had little tolerance for those who stood in the way. Feelings of benevolence—expressed by spokesmen of both groups from time to time—were often eclipsed by less forgiving men.

[56]See Catherine S. Fowler and Don D. Fowler, "Notes on the History of Southern Paiutes and Western Shoshonis," *Utah Historical Quarterly* 39 (1971): 96–113; Julian H. Steward, "Basin-Plateau Aboriginal Sociopolitical Groups," Smithsonian Institution, *Bureau of American Ethnology Bulletin 120* (Washington, D.C.: Government Printing Office, 1938), pp. 1–264; and Brooks, "Indian Relations on the Mormon Frontier," pp. 1–48. Brigham Young, in his report to the commissioner of Indian Affairs dated August 13, 1851, describes the Snake (Shoshoni) Indians: " . . . the Snake diggers . . . who can scarce be said to have any habitation, clothing, arms, or anything else which is generally supposed would contribute to a person's comfort, or even be necessary for one's simple existence. In my first acquaintance with them, they appeared inoffensive, in fact utterly incompetent, and unable to be otherwise, of small stature which appeared to be the result of suffering with cold and hunger, and filthiness, they presented the lowest, most degraded and loathsome specimen of human existence that I ever beheld."

[57]Bailey, *Walkara, Hawk of the Mountains*, pp. 29–45; and Sonne, *The World of Wakara*, pp. 16–43.

[58]Robert F. Berkhofer, Jr., *Salvation and the Savage: An Analysis of Protestant Missions, and American Indian Response, 1787–1862* (Lexington: University of Kentucky Press, 1965), p. 159.

Fifth, the Mormons put no viable programs into effect before 1852 to support a policy of benevolence. The policy was never more than ad hoc, relying mostly upon the good will of individuals. Whatever individual generosity and kindness that existed was overwhelmed by other attitudes—and the regrettable strategy of selective extermination.

The significant tragedy of the Mormon–Indian experience before 1852 is that it was not unique. In spite of the Mormons' much-quoted feelings of benevolence, they performed typically. The Mormon experience, like that stated by Roy Harvey Pearce in his book *The Savages of America*, showed that "practice did not support theory. Indians were not civilized, but destroyed."[59]

[59]Roy Harvey Pearce, *The Savages of America: A Study of the Indian and the Idea of Civilization* (Baltimore: Johns Hopkins Press, 1953), p. 4.

*

One Man's Meat Is Another Man's Poison: A Revisionist View of the Seagull "Miracle"

DAVID B. MADSEN AND BRIGHAM D. MADSEN

One of the best-known and most celebrated episodes in Utah history is the story of the seagulls and the crickets. The following article offers an alternative interpretation to the standard one, suggesting that the seagulls were predators, not saviors, and that they should have been viewed with dismay rather than adoration. It also suggests that a sensible response on the part of Mormon settlers would have been to eat the crickets, as Native Americans of the area had long done, and kill the seagulls. In advancing this interpretation, the authors invite the reader to consider the extent to which, consciously and unconsciously, we construct ourselves, our past, and past events to suit our own purposes; the extent to which myths are limiting and restrictive and need to be challenged; the inadequacies and insensitivities of particular myths; the forces at work in persuading people to accept an ideology as fact; and other realities or facts that might be taken into consideration.

David B. Madsen and Brigham D. Madsen, "One Man's Meat Is Another Man's Poison: A Revisionist View of the Seagull 'Miracle'," *Nevada Historical Society Quarterly* XXX (Fall 1987): 165–81. Reprinted by permission of the publisher and the authors.

David B. Madsen is Utah State Archaeologist and Adjunct Professor of Anthropology and Geography at the University of Utah. He has written extensively on the prehistory of the Great Basin area. Brigham D. Madsen is Professor Emeritus of History at the University of Utah and has written more than a dozen books on Utah and western U.S. history.

INTRODUCTION

CURRENT BIOLOGICAL AND ANTHROPOLOGICAL THEORY suggests that human behavior is based, to a large extent, on economic realities. Essentially these theories boil down to the hypothesis that those who get more for less are more reproductively successful than those who get less for more. They suggest further that it is possible to rank behavior in terms of energetic costs (that is, the amount of calories of energy earned for the amount of time invested) and predict that over the long-term human groups and individuals should tend toward behavior that ranks at the higher end of the list.[1] This is over the long-term, however, and short-term departures from the norm can and do occur. Here we examine what appears to be one of these unusual aberrations: the cricket/seagull/farming encounter of 1848.

The cricket plague of 1848 which racked the farms of early Mormon pioneers and the "rescue" of domestic crops by swarms of seagulls is one of the most prominent events in eastern Great Basin history. It is often elevated to the status of legend, and much that is said about the event falls more within the realm of folklore and myth than in the realm of historical reality. There is a decided ideological component to these folk-tales in that the coming of the seagulls is often viewed as divine intervention, with the birds having been sent in the nick-of-time to save the crops from ravaging hordes of crickets and the Saints from winter starvation. A particularly "miraculous" aspect of these tales is that the birds are reported to have repeatedly gorged themselves on the crickets and disgorged the crickets into the Great Salt Lake in an unnatural (that is to say supernatural) fashion. In short, there is something of a morality play to these stories with the crickets representing disaster, the seagulls representing salvation and the early Euro-American settlers representing the players whose belief system is both tested and reinforced by the sequence of events.

We have neither the desire nor the ability to describe the supernatural aspects of these stories, but we do wish to review the crickets-as-disaster/seagulls-as-saviors contrast since it so directly contradicts a number of other lines of evidence which suggest exactly the opposite. A variety of ethnohistorical, ethnological and archaeological evidence suggests that insects such as crickets and grasshoppers were widely used as a winter storage food resource in the eastern Great Basin by Native American groups. Further, this widespread usage is consistent with recent cost/benefit tests which suggest that the caloric return-rate for time invested is at times as high, and often much higher, than any other wild or domestic food source. Given the events of 1848, it would have been more appropriate, in terms of energetic efficiency, to view the crickets as the saviors and the seagulls as the disaster. Not only were the settlers of 1848 not faced with starvation as a result of the cricket plague, they were faced with a surfeit of food. As a result, the manner in which the pioneers of 1848 reacted to the cricket invasion, as well as the subsequent development of the seagull 'miracle' stories, must clearly be seen in a social rather than an economic context.

[1]James F. O'Connell, Kevin T. Jones, and Steven R. Simms, "Some Thoughts on Prehistoric Archaeology in the Great Basin," eds., David B. Madsen and James F. O'Connell, in *Man and Environment in the Great Basin,* Society for American Archaeology Papers II, 227–40.

THE ETHNOHISTORIC AND ETHNOLOGIC RECORD

Ethnohistorical and ethnological data on the use of insects as a subsistence resource abound for groups in and adjacent to the eastern Great Basin. Not only did every identified group use them, many were dependent on one or more species as their primary resource and principal winter storage food. At the same time, the type of insects used as well as the degree to which they were incorporated into the subsistence system was highly variable.

Groups around Mono and Owens Lakes in the western Basin, for example, collected the larval form of the brine fly for use as a dried winter food and considered it "a favorite food."[2] Around the Great Salt Lake, on the other hand, where they were equally if not more abundant, the use of brine fly larvae was specifically denied by a variety of Gosiute and Shoshoni informants.[3] This variability is also evident for a variety of other insect species. Grasshoppers were widely used in the eastern Basin,[4] but were "eaten only when hungry" in the central Great Basin.[5] Among some western Basin groups, such as the Northern Paiute, they were apparently not eaten at all.[6] Larvae of the pandora (or other similar moths) on the other hand, were extensively used in the western Great Basin,[7] but were apparently rarely if ever used in the eastern Basin.[8]

Despite this variation, the reliance on insects was widespread and common. Early trapper journals and pioneer diaries are replete with reference to insects as a major food resource. Heinrich Lienhard's report in 1846 of a Paiute man along the Humboldt River who when asked for food returned with grasshoppers and roots that tasted like parsnips, is but one of many similar examples.[9] A more extensive description from Peter Skene Ogden's journal of February, 1826, concerning "Snake Indians" north of the Great

[2]Julian H. Steward, "Ethnography of the Owens Valley Paiute," *University of California Publications in American Archaeology and Ethnology,* vol. 33, no. 3 (1933). See also Philip J. Wilke and Harry W. Lawton, eds., *The Expedition of Capt. J.W. Davidson from Fort Tejon to the Owens Valley in 1859* (Socorro: Ballena Press, 1976).

[3]Julian H. Steward, "Culture Element Distributions: XXIII—Northern and Gosiute Shoshoni," *University of California Anthropological Records,* vol. 8, no. 3 (1943).

[4]Omer C. Stewart, "Culture Element Distributions: XVIII—Ute-Southern Paiute," *University of California Anthropological Records,* vol. 6, no. 4 (1942). Steward, "Culture Element Distributions: XXIII . . . "; Don D. Fowler and Catherine S. Fowler, "Anthropology of the Numa: John Wesley Powell's Manuscripts on the Numic Peoples of Western North America, 1868–1880," *Smithsonian Contributions to Anthropology,* #14 (1971 Washington); Isabel Kelly, "Southern Paiute Ethnography," *University of Utah Anthropological Papers,* no. 69 (1964).

[5]Julian H. Steward, "Culture Element Distributions: XIII—Nevada Shoshone," *University of California Anthropological Records,* vol. 4, no. 2 (1941).

[6]Omer C. Stewart, "Culture Element Distributions: XIV—Northern Paiute," *University of California Anthropological Records,* vol. 4, no. 3 (1941).

[7]Catherine S. Fowler and Nancy Peterson Walter, "Harvesting Pandora Moth Larvae with the Owens Valley Paiute," *Journal of California and Great Basin Anthropology* (in press).

[8]Omer C. Stewart, "Culture Element Distributions: XVIII—Ute-Southern Paiute," *University of California Anthropological Records,* vol. 6, no. 4 (1942). Steward, "Culture Element Distributions: XXIII. . . . "

[9]G. Erwin and E.K. Gudde, *From St. Louis to Sutter's Fort 1846* (1961 Norman).

Salt Lake, bears repeating both for its description of insect use as a winter storage resource and for the ethnocentrism common at the time:

> I had often heard these wretches subsisted on ants, locusts and small fish, not larger than minnies, and I wanted to find out if it was not an exaggeration of late travelers, but to my surprise, I found it was the case; for in one of their dishes, not of small size, was filled with ants. They collected them in the morning early before the thaw commences. The locusts they collect in Summer and store up for their Winter; in eating they give the preference to the former, being oily; the latter not, on this food these poor wretches drag out an existence for nearly 4 months of the year they live contented and happy; this is all they require.[10]

This use of grasshoppers, crickets and other insects as a winter storage staple was apparently quite prevalent. Lorenzo Young reports another example from around the Great Salt Lake at the time the first settlements were constructed:

> The ground was covered with black crickets; millions of them. . . . An unusual number of Indians . . . gathered together . . . were harvesting them . . . [they] depended upon this food as one of their principle [*sic*] suppliers for winter use.[11]

Insects were collected and prepared in a variety of ways. The most common method of collecting jumping or crawling insects, such as grasshoppers, was to either simply pick them off bushes in the early morning while they were still cold or to dig ditches, line them with brush or grass, drive the insects into the ditches and fire the brush. John Wesley Powell provides a good general description for the Ute/Southern Paiute:

> Grasshoppers and crickets form a very important part of the food of these people. Soon after they are fledged and before their wings are sufficiently developed for them to fly, or later in the season when they are chilled with cold, great quantities are collected by sweeping them up with brush brooms, or they are driven into pits, by beating the ground with sticks. When thus collected they are roasted in trays like seeds and ground into meal and eaten as mush or cakes. Another method of preparing them is to roast great quantities of them in pits filled with embers and hot ashes. . . . When these insects are abundant, the season is one of many festivities. When prepared in this way these insects are considered very great delicacies.[12]

Howard Egan described a cricket drive northwest of the Deep Creek Mountains in the early 1850s during which a "large group" dug trenches for a number of days, drove crickets into trenches containing dry grass, fired the

[10]T.C. Elliot, ed., "The Peter Skene Ogden Journals," *The Quarterly of the Oregon Historical Society,* vol. 10, no. 4: 325–65.

[11]Anonymous, "Early Experiences of Lorenzo D. Young." Ms. of interview conducted for Hubert H. Bancroft, Bancroft Library, University of California, (1884 Berkeley): 3–4.

[12]Don D. Fowler and Catherine S. Fowler, "Anthropology of the Numa: John Wesley Powell's Manuscripts on the Numic Peoples of Western North America, 1868–1880," *Smithsonian Contributions to Anthropology,* #14 (1971 Washington): 48.

grass and placed more on top. When they had finished, the trenches were "half full of dead crickets," and one woman carried away a large and a small carrying basket containing "over four bushels" to camp some three–four miles away. Bushels of crickets remained to be gathered later in the day.[13] Young reported a slightly different kind of drive in the Salt Lake Valley in which:

> They made a corral twelve or fifteen feet square, fenced about with sage brush and grease wood, and with branches of the same drove them into the enclosure. Then they set fire to the brush fence and going amoungst them, drove them into the fire. Afterward they took out these bodies by the thousand, rubbed off their wings and legs, and after two or three days gathered the meat, which was an ounce or half an ounce of fat to each cricket.[14]

Both trenching/driving insects and picking them from bushes like berries are labor intensive operations, and higher return methods were often used. For example, in the Sevier River drainage in the east central Basin, Peter Gottfredson described an 1864 cricket drive in which crickets were driven into a stream where:

> The squaws (placed) baskets in the ditch for the crickets to float into. The male Indians with long willows strung along about twenty feet apart whipping the ground behind the crickets driving them towards the ditch. . . . [The crickets] tumbled into the ditch and floated down into the baskets. . . . They got more than fifty bushels.[15]

A method common around many of the interior drainage lakes in the Basin was simply to let nature do most of the work. For example, at Owens Lake in 1859:

> . . . the Indians gather them at this season as they are driven ashore by the wind. They then dry them and separate, by threshing and winnowing, the shells, or skeletons, of the Larva from the grub, which they pack away in cakes. I may safely say that I saw hundreds of bushels of this food, in process of preparation and prepared.[16]

Insects appear to have been prepared in a number of ways. Occasionally they were simply eaten:

> During interview with KL, granddaughter brought her a grasshopper. I asked if it was kind they used to eat. She said it was, and because she was hungry she said she would eat that one. Thereupon she swallowed it whole and alive. She had no teeth with which to chew she gagged a little, but said insect kicking caused that.[17]

[13]William M. Egan, ed., *Pioneering the West 1846–1878: Major Howard Egan's Diary* (1917 Richmond, Utah): 230–33.

[14]Anonymous, "Early Experiences . . . ," (1884 Berkeley): 3–4.

[15]Peter Gottfredson, "Journal of Peter Gottsfredson, from the Gottfredson Family History." MSS, Utah State Historical Society (n.d. Salt Lake City): 15.

[16]Philip J. Wilke and Harry W. Lawton, eds., *The Expedition of Capt. J.W. Davidson from Fort Tejon to the Owens Valley in 1859* (Socorro: Ballena Press, 1976): 30.

[17]Omer C. Stewart, "Culture Element Distributions: XVIII—Ute-Southern Paiute." *University of California Anthropological Records,* vol. 6, no. 4 (1942): 337.

More often they were roasted and ground into a flour or made into cakes of what has been called "desert fruitcake," a concoction variably consisting of insects, pine nuts, and various berries mashed together and dried in the sun. Egan describes being fed "a cake of black bread" made of crickets, pine nuts, and possibly other foods,[18] while Gottfredson and Edwin Bryant are more descriptive:

> Three females . . . made their appearance, bringing baskets containing a substance, which, upon examination, we ascertained to be service-berries, crushed to a jam and mixed with pulverized grasshoppers. This composition being dried in the sun until it becomes hard, is what may be called the "fruitcake" of these poor children of the desert. . . . We purchased all they brought with them. . . . The prejudice against the grasshopper "fruitcake" was strong at first, but it soon wore off, and none of the delicacy was thrown away or lost.[19]

And:

> They had a lot of berries that they gathered before which they crushed with the crickets and made into loaves the size of a persons head. They then dug holes in the ground about eighteen inches deep and buried the loaves and left them for about a month. . . . The berries they used were service berries which were plentyful in the hills, and wild currents, both black and red that grew along the creek, and some squaw berries and chokecherries.[20]

While flavor and taste are probably some of the least objective observations that can be made, the gusto with which insects were eaten deserves at least some mention. They are usually described as quite flavorful and were considered, as Powell noted above, "great delicacies." According to Egan's informant, crickets " . . . make the bread good, the same as sugar used by the white woman in her cakes,"[21] while the Honey Lake Paiute used dried crickets and locusts in a soup which had the " . . . flavor of dried deer meat."[22] Even modern non-native informants find them to be more than just palatable. During a recent ethno-archaeological experiment, participants coined the term "desert lobster" to describe the taste of freshly roasted grasshoppers.[23] There is some disagreement, however, since Captain J.H. Simpson considered a seed and root cake version of desert fruitcake he tasted (insects are not specifically mentioned) to be " . . . precisely like cattle-ordure, and having anything but an agreeable taste, I soon disgorged it."[24]

[18]Egan, ed., "Pioneering the West . . . " (1917 Richmond, Utah): 233.

[19]Edwin Bryant, *What I Saw in California* (1967 Palo Alto): 162.

[20]Gottfredson, "Journal of Peter Gottfredson. . . . " (n.d. Salt Lake City): 15.

[21]Egan, ibid.

[22]Francis A. Riddell, "Honey Lake Paiute Ethnography," *Nevada State Museum Occasional Papers* vol. 3 (1978 Carson City): 51.

[23]Steven R. Simms, 1985, personal communication.

[24]Captain J.H. Simpson, *Report of Explorations across the Great Basin of the Territory of Utah for a Direct Wagon-route from Camp Floyd to Genoa, in Carson Valley,* Engineer Department, U.S. Army (1876 Washington): 54.

THE ARCHAEOLOGICAL RECORD

Archaeological data on insect use from in and around the eastern Great Basin is limited when compared to the abundance of ethnographic information from the same area. However, this limitation is probably due more to a bias in the archaeological record resulting from a lack of suitably well preserved sites and the use of rather coarse excavation techniques, than to reduced reliance on insects in the prehistoric period.

To the north and east of the Great Salt Lake area in western Wyoming and northwestern Colorado, insect use has been identified at three sites. Leigh Cave, on the west flank of the Bighorn Mountains, contained a hearth, dating to about 4,200 years ago, with the "cooked remains of several hundred large insects . . . commonly known as the Mormon cricket. . . . "[25] It is interesting to note that these cricket remains were associated with large amounts of wild onion, large quantities of chokecherry pits, some limber pine seeds, buffalo berry, and wild rose, all items which form the basic ingredients of "desert fruitcake." The Eden-Farson site in the upper Green River Basin, Wyoming, is a "proto-historic Shoshonean" site radiometrically dated to 230 years ago.[26] Pigweed seed-cakes containing insect parts were found together with "charred fragments of Mormon crickets . . . and large red ants . . . " in three of the twelve-house floor excavated at the site, and the insects " . . . were almost certainly being used as food."[27] Grasshoppers were recovered from a storage cist along the Yampa River on the Utah-Colorado border. They are poorly dated, but appear to have been deposited about 3,000–1,000 years ago. The hoppers had been "mashed or chopped or ground up into a solid mass" prior to storage.[28]

Within the Great Basin proper, insect consumption has been identified through the analyses of coprolites (dried fecal matter) from sites on both the eastern and western Basin margins. West of the Great Salt Lake, a significant portion of coprolites at Danger and Hogup Caves contain "insect parts," but the species of insects were not identified.[29] The situation is similar in the western Basin, where coprolites at Lovelock Cave also contained "insects."[30] A wooden grasshopper effigy was also recovered from the site,

[25]George C. Frison, "Leigh Cave, Wyoming: Site 48WA304. *The Wyoming Archaeologist,* vol. 11, no. 3 (1968 Cheyenne): 22.

[26]George C. Frison, "Shoshonean Antelope Procurement in the Upper Green River Basin, Wyoming. *Plains Anthropologist,* vol. 16, no. 1 (1971 Lincoln): 258–84.

[27]Ibid., 261.

[28]Robert F. Burgh and Charles R. Scoggin, "The Archaeology of Castle Park Dinosaur National Monument," *University of Colorado Studies Series in Anthropology* no. 2 (1948 Boulder): 98.

[29]Gary F. Fry, "Analysis of Prehistoric Coprolites from Utah." *University of Utah Anthropological Papers* no. 97 (1976 Salt Lake City).

[30]Richard A. Cowan, "Lake-margin ecological exploitation in the Great Basin as demonstrated by an analysis of coprolites from Lovelock Cave, Nevada." *University of California Archaeological Survey Reports* no. 70 (1967 Berkeley): 21–35; Lewis K. Napton and Robert F. Heizer, "Analysis of human coprolites from archaeological contexts with primary reference to Lovelock Cave, Nevada," *Contributions of the University of California Archaeological Research Facility* no. 10 (1970 Berkeley): 87–130.

suggesting the insect was of some importance to the Lovelock Cave occupants.[31]

A cache of grasshoppers was recovered from Crypt Cave along the lower Humboldt River, but its age and archaeological context is poorly described.[32] Apparently the hoppers were stored in a finely woven net bag in one of a series of "cache caves" in the region. A variety of other food resources such a dried fish were also found in the caves.

The most well documented use of insects in the eastern Basin is at Smith Creek Cave in the Snake Range on the Utah-Nevada border and at Lakeside Cave, a site on the north end of the Lakeside Mountains along the western margin of the Great Salt Lake. Grasshopper parts *(Melanoplus sanguinipes)* were identified at both sites in very large numbers. At Smith Creek Cave they occur in a depositional unit dating to about 2,100 years ago,[33] while at Lakeside Cave they are found throughout the deposits but occur in heaviest concentrations in stratigraphic units dating from 4,700 to 4,400 years ago.[34] In a sample of the Lakeside deposits, up to 1.5 million grasshopper parts occur in any one stratigraphic unit. Coprolites are associated with all strata where grasshopper parts occur and contain oolitic sand and hopper parts as their principal components. The hopper parts in the Lakeside coprolites are fragmented and broken, but are large enough to suggest they were eaten whole rather than ground into a flour. The presence of the very large number of grasshoppers, the combination of oolitic sand and hopper parts in the coprolites, and the proximity of the cave to a number of long oolitic sand beaches suggest that the occupants were collecting windrows of grasshoppers washed up on the beaches and were consuming them directly.

A PLAGUE OF CRICKETS

Clearly, both the historic and prehistoric Native occupants of the Great Basin were dependent on harvests of crickets, grasshoppers, and other insects and undoubtedly rejoiced when they appeared in great numbers. The Euro-American settlers had a different view, however, and the Mormon pioneers of 1847 looked on with apprehension as they entered Salt Lake Valley on July 24th and observed the "Mammoth crickets [which] abound in the borders of the Valley."[35] William Clayton summed up the general impression of the first party of settlers, "The ground seems literally alive with

[31]A.C. Jones, J.R. Weaver and F.H. Stross, "Note on Indian Wood Carving in the Form of a Grasshopper Found in Lovelock Cave, Nevada." *University of California Archaeological Survey Reports* no. 70 (1967 Berkeley). 123–28.

[32]Philip C. Orr, "Preliminary Excavation of Pershing County Caves," *The Nevada State Museum Bulletin* no. 1 (1952 Carson City).

[33]Alan L. Bryan, "Smith Creek Cave," in "The Archaeology of Smith Creek Canyon, Eastern Nevada," Donald R. Tuohy and Doris L. Rendall, eds., *Nevada State Museum Anthropological Papers,* no. 17 (Carson City 1979): 162–253.

[34]David B. Madsen and James E. Kirkman, "Hunting Hoppers," *American Antiquity* (in press) (n.d. Washington).

[35]Clair Noall, *Intimate Disciple: A Portrait of Willard Richards* (Salt Lake City, 1957), 538.

very large black crickets crawling around up grass and bushes."[36] But, disregarding their fears and as the spring of 1848 came, the approximately 1,700 Mormons now gathered in the valley prepared the soil and planted about 1,000 acres of grain to provide food for themselves and the large group of new arrivals anticipated for that year.[37]

The new shoots had hardly appeared when disaster came. Mrs. Lorenzo Dow Young recorded in the May 27 entry of her husband's journal:

> Today to our utter astonishment, the crickets came by millions, sweeping everything before them. They first attacked a patch of beans for us and in twenty minutes there was not a vestige of them to be seen. They next swept over peas, then came into our garden; took everything clean.[38]

The next day Isaac Haight wrote, "Frost again this morning. . . . Corn hurt some and some wheat killed and the crickets are injuring the crops."[39] And Mrs. Young also noted that day, "today the crickets have commenced on our corn and small grain. They have eaten off 12 acres for Brother Rosacrants, 7 for Charles and are now taking Edmunds."[40] On June 4, John Steel explained in his diary entry how the frost had injured the crops and "to help make the disaster complete, the crickets came by the thousands of tons."[41] As these and other diary entries of the time emphasize, the pioneers began to face the prospect of starvation, and at least some of them considered sending word to Brigham Young in Iowa to stop the emigration to Utah for that year.[42]

Unlike the Native Americans of the area who welcomed such a food resource as a godsend, the Saints could see only evil in the arrival of the "Mormon crickets." Anson Call, one of the pioneers of 1847, probably spoke for all when he wrote of the cricket pest, "It has an eagle-eyed staring appearance and suggests the idea that it may be the habitation of a vindictive little demon."[43] Even friendly non-Mormon Thomas L. Kane could engage in descriptive horror of the "Black Philistines," "Wingless, dumpy, black, swollen-headed, with bulging eyes in cases like goggles, mounted upon legs of steel wire and clock spring, and with a general appearance that

[36]William Clayton, *William Clayton's Journal: A Daily Record of the Journey of the Original Company of "Mormon" Pioneers . . .* (Salt Lake City, 1921), 311.

[37]Orson F. Whitney, *History of Utah* (Salt Lake City, 1892), I, 375–77; the best account of the cricket plague of 1848 and the part played by seagulls in helping to save some of the crop is William Hartley, "Mormons, Crickets, and Gulls: A New Look at an Old Story," *Utah Historical Quarterly*, vol. 38, no. 3 (Summer 1970): 224–39.

[38]J. Cecil Alter and Robert J. Dwyer, eds., "Journal and Biography of Lorenzo Dow Young," *Utah Historical Quarterly*, vol. 14 (1946): 166.

[39]Isaac C. Haight, "Biographical Sketch and Diary of Isaac Chauncy Haight, 1813–1862" (Provo, Utah: Brigham Young University), 49, as quoted in Hartley, "Mormons, Crickets, and Gulls," 227.

[40]Alter and Dwyer, Lorenzo Dow Young, "Journal . . . of Lorenzo Dow Young," 166.

[41]John Steele, "Extracts from the Journal of John Steele," *Utah Historical Quarterly*, vol. 6 (January 1933): 22

[42]*Journal History*, June 9, 1848 (Salt Lake City, L.D.S. Archives).

[43]Whitney, *History of Utah*, I, 377.

justified the Mormons in comparing him to a cross of the spider on the buffalo.[44] But a few of the more realistic of the Mormon pioneers recognized a kinship with the Natives, as Erastus Snow later explained in an address in the *Salt Lake Tabernacle,* July 25, 1880:

> The savages had learned in their destitution to profit by these visitations [crickets and grasshoppers], for when the insects would devour all the green things, they would turn in and devour the insects. And on this ground, on this city plot, the first company of savages who visited the pioneer camp, after the exchange of salutations, retired to prepare their evening repast, and they emptied out of their sacks bushels of dried grasshoppers, on which they made their supper. Our people had not learned to do this yet, but had it not been for the providential appearance of the gulls, we would have been brought to the same necessity—to gather up the crickets and salt and dry them to subsist upon.[45]

However, despite the recognition by some that the crickets could provide a substantial resource for winter subsistence, to most of the settlers of that summer it seemed the only recourse was to battle the marauding insects with every possible means. Both fire and water were employed: tin pans were beaten to frighten the crickets away from the fields; ropes were drawn across the heads of the grain to dislodge the attackers; and every conceivable weapon was used to beat the insects off the grain stalks. All of this was to little avail as the invading army continued relentlessly across the fields.[46]

Some relief soon came in the form of flocks of seagulls from nearby Great Salt Lake. Many of the early accounts were rather prosaic and matter-of-fact in describing how the gulls devoured the crickets and aided the embattled Mormon farmers in destroying the insects. John Smith wrote on June 9, 1848:

> The first I knew of the gulls, I heard their sharp cry. Upon looking up I beheld what appeared like a vast flock of pigeons coming from the Northwest. It was about three o'clock in the afternoon. . . . There must have been thousands of them. Their coming was like a great cloud; and when they passed between us and the sun, a shadow covered the field, I could see gulls settling for more than a mile around us.[47]

In a letter to Brigham Young in Iowa, John Smith wrote on June 21, 1848, "The crickets are still quite numerous and busy eating, but between the gulls, our efforts and the growth of our crops we shall raise much grain in spite of them."[48] In response to the same letter, John D. Lee, who was

[44]Thomas L. Kane, "The Mormons." A discourse Delivered Before the Historical Society of Pennsylvania, March 26, 1850 (Philadelphia, 1850), 66.

[45]*Improvement Era,* vol. 16 (Salt Lake City), 753. For a similar recognition of insect utility see also Anonymous. "Early Experiences . . . " 4.

[46]For a good description of the battle against the crickets, see Hartley, "Mormons, Crickets, and Gulls . . . " 229, and W.W. Henderson, "Crickets and Grasshoppers in Utah." *Utah Agricultural Experiment Station.* Circular 96, November 1931 (Logan, Utah), 10–11.

[47]*Journal History,* June 9, 1848.

[48]Ibid., June 21, 1848.

usually eager to record any singular heavenly visitation or ministration, merely wrote, "Although crickets had played a heavy hand on the Wheat, yet there would be an abundant raised for all in the valley."[49] These quotations are representative of the general tone of most of the early reports of the seagull intervention, but William Hartley has done the best job of pointing out the "Problems with the traditional account," citing a number of diary entries to illustrate the "non mention" of gulls and that these journals say "nothing about the gulls."[50]

In short, the appearance of the seagulls in the event was evidently somewhat less miraculous than subsequent interpretations often imply. As the authoritative *First Annual Report of the United States Entomological Commission for the Year 1877* points out, all kinds of birds, not just seagulls, have been involved in the eradication of crickets, grasshoppers and locusts. The report provides a long list of such feathered predators: prairie-chickens, plovers, larks, pigeons, grouse, quail, snipes, robins, domestic fowl, and above all and from nearly every observer, blackbirds.[51] As one reads the detailed report, it can be wondered at why the people of Nebraska and other Plains states have not erected monuments to the yellow-billed blackbird.

THE SEAGULL "MIRACLE"

The case of the Saints in Utah was, nevertheless, unique because of their special religious tradition and their tendency to ascribe to the intervention of the Almighty any unusual occurrence in their behalf. At least some of the settlers immediately announced, "it seems the hand of the Lord is in our favor."[52] Another reported, "all looked upon the gulls as a God send, indeed, all acknowledged the hand of the Lord was in it, that He had sent the white gulls by scores of thousands to save their crops."[53] And to the desperate Mormon farmers, it was particularly significant, and again because of help from heaven, that the gulls would eat their fill, drink some water, and then immediately regurgitate before commencing to gorge again and to thus continue the process for many hours. What the Saints of the time did not know was that, as ornithologist F.E. Beale could explain later, "these 'lumps of crickets' were undoubtedly 'pellets' of indigestible parts habitually disgorged by the birds."[54]

To the grateful Mormon settlers, this explanation would not have changed their opinion about divine intervention anyway, as they at once

[49]Robert Glass Cleland and Juanita Brooks, eds., *A Mormon Chronicle: The Diaries of John D. Lee 1848–1876* (Salt Lake City, 1983), I, 64.

[50]Hartley, "Mormons, Crickets, and Gulls . . . " 233–36.

[51]U.S. Department of Interior, United States Geological Survey, *First Annual Report of the United States Entomological Commission for the Year 1877* (Washington, 1878), 334–49.

[52]Quoted in Pauline Udall Smith, *Captain Jefferson Hunt of the Mormon Battalion* (Salt Lake City, 1958), 136–37.

[53]Henry W. Bigler, "Diary of Henry W. Bigler, 1846–1850" (Provo, Utah: Brigham Young University), 11, as quoted in Hartley, "Mormons, Crickets, and Gulls . . . ," 232.

[54]W.L. McAtee and F.E.L. Beale, *Some Common Game, Aquatic and Rapacious Birds in Relation to Man,* U.S. Department of Agriculture Bulletin No. 497 (Washington, 1912), 22.

took legal measures to protect their feathered benefactors. As Thomas L. Kane wrote in 1850, the Saints of Utah were thereafter "careful not to molest them in their friendly office, and to this end declared a heavy fine against all who should kill or annoy them with firearms."[55] Later, in 1897, the State of Utah enacted the prohibition into a state law by declaring, "It shall be unlawful for any person to kill, ensnare, net or entrap at any time in any year any gull, owl, hawks, lark, whippoorwill, thrush, swallow snowbird or other insectivorous or song birds."[56] No one was surprised that gulls led the list. And finally, to cap the devotion of the people of Utah to their favorite bird, the seagull was designated as the State Bird by a Legislative Act of February 9, 1955.[57]

From the early announcements that "the hand of the Lord is in our favor" to an acceptance of the "Miracle of the Gulls" has been an interesting story. Evidently, Apostle Orson Hyde was the first important Mormon authority to proclaim in a General Conference of the L.D.S. Church that the gulls had been messengers sent by divine providence.[58] This conviction of miraculous intervention grew in the minds of the people of Utah until historian B.H. Roberts made it official with the proclamation in his *A Comprehensive History of the Church of Jesus Christ of Latter-day Saints* (finally published in 1930, but written long before) that, "Then the miraculous happened. I say it deliberately, the miraculous happened, as men commonly view the miraculous."[59]

The "Miracle of the Gulls" was, of course, made official with the October 1, 1913, dedication of the now-famous Seagull Monument, sculpted by Utah artist Mahonri Young, and placed on the temple grounds in Salt Lake City. The inscription reads:

SEAGULL MONUMENT
ERECTED IN GRATEFUL REMEMBRANCE
OF THE MERCY OF GOD
TO THE MORMON PIONEERS

In his peroration of the day, the dedicatory speaker intoned, "Though from afar the Seagulls came and destroyed the destroyer, it was Thy voice, O Lord, that called them—they did but do thy bidding—the deliverance was of Thee and by Thee."[60] In remembering the events of 1848, L.D.S. Church President Joseph F. Smith later recalled, "I remember an incident

[55]Kane, "The Mormons," 67.

[56]*Laws of the State of Utah, Passed at the Second Regular Session of the Legislature of the State of Utah* (Salt Lake City, 1897), 96.

[57]*Laws of the State of Utah, 1955, passed at the Regular Session of the Thirty-First Legislature* (Kaysville, Utah, 1955), 286.

[58]Orson Hyde, "Discourse, September 24, 1853," *Journal of Discourses,* 26 vols. (Liverpool, England, 1854–1886), II, 114; see Hartley, "Mormons, Crickets, and Gulls . . . " for a general discussion of the development of the "miracle" story.

[59]B.H. Roberts, *A Comprehensive History of the Church of Jesus Christ of Latter-day Saints* (Salt Lake City, 1930), III, 333.

[60]Benjamin Goodard, "The Sea-Gull Monument," *Young Woman's Journal* (November 1913): 667–73.

when an Indian was arrested for killing a gull. When we told the Indians that our lives had been saved in a miraculous manner by these gulls they, too, learned to respect them."[61] While these Native Americans may have heeded the advice of the Mormon leader, they undoubtedly considered such remonstrations to be just a further example of the often bizarre and unaccountable actions of white settlers and may secretly have wondered about the loss of a valuable food resource eaten by the gulls they were asked to protect.

But to the Mormons, the story of their temporal deliverance during the dark days of June and July of 1848 by seagulls with their "long wings, that arched in flight 'like an angel's,' "[62] a monument to these friendly birds was only a small token of thanks from a grateful people. As Orson F. Whitney wrote, "They were rescued, as they believed, by a miracle—a greater miracle than is said to have saved Rome, when the cackling of geese roused the slumbering city in time to beat back the invading Gauls."[63] As a poet of 1941 expressed Mormon sentiment:

> The shrill calling of the sea gull
> Showed the cloud a living thing
> Like a myriad of bright angels
> Were the sea gulls on the wing.
>
> Soon the ground was grey and gleaming,
> As the sudden fall of snow;
> While God's answer, swift in coming,
> Bade the plague of locusts go.
>
> Soon the sea gulls had devoured
> Every locust in the land
> That the Lord had heard and answered
> No one failed to understand.[64]

MANNA FROM HEAVEN

This view of large numbers of crickets and grasshoppers as an evil plague and seagulls as delivering angels contrasts sharply with the subsistence practices of Native American groups in the same area. The two views are so different that it is worthwhile examining the energetic efficiency of insect use to determine what the most economically appropriate response should be of a group of people (be they native or transplanted) in the Salt Lake Valley, faced with the prospects of starvation, to the appearance of "clouds" of insects.

Direct information on the cost effectiveness of cricket use is only now being collected, but a related study on the efficiency and utility of grasshopper procurement has been conducted along the Great Salt Lake.[65] During

[61]Ibid., 669.

[62]Kane, "The Mormons," 67.

[63]Orson F. Whitney, "The Sea-gull Story," in *Utah: Its People, Resources, Attractions and Institutions* (Salt Lake City, 1913), 36–37.

[64]Margaret Ball Dickson, "A Tale of the Sea Gulls," *Improvement Era*, vol. 30: 491–92.

years when grasshoppers occur in noticeable amounts, they fly or are blown into the Great Salt Lake and are formed by wave-action into lines of salted and sun-dried windrows of grasshoppers stretching for tens of kilometers along the beaches. The occurrence of these windrows around the lake is apparently a common, but unpredictable event.[66] In recent years, "plagues" occurred in '79, '84, and '85; and it appears that similar population explosions have occurred at least once or twice in every decade since 1847. References to vast swarms of hoppers are particularly common during the 1850s. According to Egan:

> There along the shore (of the Great Salt Lake) could be seen great windrows of their bodies that had been washed ashore by the north winds. Near Black Rock there were three such rows, so wide and high that a man could have filled a wagon bed with them as quick as he could have shoveled that much sand, and the whole shore line facing the north was just the same. Millions of bushels of preserved or pickled grasshoppers.[67]

The experimental tests of grasshopper procurement were conducted by collecting them without much processing from the oolitic sand beaches which surround the lake in a fashion similar to that suggested by the prehistoric evidence. In experimental cost/benefit tests, a resource is collected for a given period, processed in the appropriate fashion (such as grinding of seed resources) and subjected to laboratory analysis to determine the number of Calories/kg present. Based on these figures, the number of Calories produced in an hour's effort can be calculated and resources can be ranked according to their relative return-rates.

The sun-dried grasshoppers from around the lake are 60% protein, 10% carbohydrate, and 2% fat by weight and contain roughly 3,010 Calories/kilogram. Based on the results of five samples, the return rates for grasshopper procurement around the Great Salt Lake exceed by extremely high amounts any other known "collected" (as opposed to hunted) resource. Return-rates varied from 41,598 Cals/hr for the smallest windrow to 714,409 Cals/hr for the largest, with an average of 272,649 Cals/hr. Put more descriptively and assuming a daily caloric requirement of 2500 Cals, this means that, on the average, one person, in one hour, could feed four people for nearly a month.

These return-rates are considered tentative, but even at 1/10th of the measured rate, it is much higher than that of any other collected resource. Seeds such as bulrush (1700 Cals/hr), pine nuts (1083 Cals/hr), and sunflower (500 Cals/hr) are substantially lower than even this arbitrarily reduced return rate.[68] Grasshoppers collected in this fashion are also much

[65]Madsen and Kirkman, "Hunting Hoppers: . . . "

[66]Davis Bitton and Linda P. Wilcox, "Pestiferous Ironclads: The Grasshopper Problem in Pioneer Utah," *Utah Historical Quarterly*, vol. 46 no. 4: 336–55.

[67]Egan, ed., *Pioneering the West. . . .* (1917 Richmond, Utah): 150.

[68]Steven R. Simms, *Aboriginal Great Basin Foraging Strategies: An Evolutionary Analysis*. Ph.D. Dissertation, Department of Anthropology, University of Utah (1984 Salt Lake City).

higher than pandora moth larvae (2000/Cals/hr), the only other insect yet tested.[69]

Given these rankings, optimal foraging models used in biology and anthropology predict that grasshoppers should be used as a principal resource whenever they are available.[70] The return-rate is so high, and the abundance so great, that other, lower-ranked, resources will ordinarily be less well represented in the diet. These neo-Darwinian evolutionary models suggest further that individuals and groups who do select these higher-ranked resources will be the most reproductively successful in the long-run. Assuming this has some validity, it would appear that prehistoric groups around the Great Salt Lake were operating in an ecologically sound fashion and were responding to the presence of large amounts of insects in an energetically efficient manner.

Tests on the return-rates of cricket collecting have just begun and, unlike the grasshopper studies, have focused first on determining rates for the most inefficient collecting techniques.[71] Even these low-end procedures produced return-rates which equal or exceed those of other Great Basin "collected" resources. The ethnohistorical accounts of more efficient collecting methods and the 1848 accounts of high abundance levels suggest that crickets probably have an energetic return-rate roughly equivalent to that of grasshoppers. If so, it would seem that during periods when crickets appear in great numbers, the most appropriate response would be to sing hallelujah and start reaping the harvest. Native American groups in the Salt Lake Valley apparently did just that. Euro-American pioneers, facing the possibility of winter starvation, did just the opposite.

The pioneers of 1848 were, of course, part of a large state society with resources which allowed them to be successful with such aberrant behavior in the short-run. Moreover, all cultures contain mechanisms which tend to dampen out rapid change, and many of the actions of the pioneers must be attributed to the conditioning process that structures all learned behavior. However, the degree to which learned behavior and energetic efficient behavior do or do not correspond, the rapidity with which such behaviors become congruent, or the complex interplay of urban and rural forces that allow a local group to act in an ecologically inappropriate fashion, is not at issue here. What is at issue is the nature of the myths which surround the episode of the crickets and the seagulls.

First, and most important, the crickets were far from the disaster that they have been portrayed to be. In a situation in which sufficient food resources must be collected to support an existing population as well as an additional expected influx through the winter, the crickets were manna

[69]Catherine S. Fowler and Nancy Peterson Walter, "Harvesting Pandora Moth Larvae with the Owens Valley Paiute, *Journal of California and Great Basin Anthropology* (in press).

[70]Simms, Aboriginal Foraging Strategies. . . .

[71]David B. Madsen and George Tripp, "Leap and Grab: Energetic Efficiency Tests of Cricket Use." Paper presented at the 20th Great Basin Anthropological Conference—1986. Las Vegas.

from heaven, a gift of the gods. They had only to be collected. Unless the pioneers had no access to seed for the next year's crop, and obviously they had such access, the crickets which invaded their fields would have returned more calories of food than the crops they were trying to protect. Clearly, lack of knowledge is not critical here since the pioneers were fully cognizant of both the utility of the crickets and methods of collecting/processing them. Second, it appears that the seagulls were not quite the saviors that they have subsequently been made out to be and were but one of many predators living off the highly productive cricket resource. Moreover, it follows that if the crickets were indeed a useful and valuable resource for human groups in the valley, then the seagulls which consumed them were actually competitors and perforce should have been viewed with dismay rather than adulation. While it may be that the socio/cultural structure in which early Euro-American settlers operated made it more appropriate to see crickets and grasshoppers as disasters rather than as a windfall, a much more appropriate behavior in terms of energetic efficiency, and one that would most certainly have been followed by native peoples, would have been to eat the crickets and kill the seagulls.

*

"At Their Peril": Utah Law and the Case of Plural Wives, 1850–1900

CAROL CORNWALL MADSEN

Although polygamy has generated much interest among historians, some aspects of it have received relatively little attention. These topics include the legal status of plural wives and the impact of the law on them—the subjects of this article. Following a discussion of early Mormon attitudes toward divorce and laws regarding marriage and divorce, inheritance as related to wives and children, property rights, voting rights, and the testimony of plural wives in courts of law, the author concludes that plural wives experienced the difficulties and penalties of being in violation of the law and living beyond its boundaries to a greater extent than that experienced by either their husbands or children.

Carol Cornwall Madsen, "'At Their Peril': Utah Law and the Case of Plural Wives, 1850–1900," *Western Historical Quarterly* 21 (November 1990): 425–43. Reprinted by permission of the publisher and the author.

Carol Cornwall Madsen is Professor of History in the Joseph Fielding Smith Institute for Church History at Brigham Young University.

VARIOUS STUDIES HAVE EXAMINED the politics, the sociology, the economics, and the evolution of the relationship between the Mormon church and the federal government attendant to the Mormon practice of polygamy during Utah's territorial history. A relevant but lesser known aspect of the subject is the impact of Utah's domestic relations laws on plural wives, as these laws were shaped by polygamy and the federal efforts to abolish it. While all polygamists were at legal risk, plural wives were vulnerable not only to criminal prosecution but also to permanent legal discrimination because of their unorthodox marital choice.

Joseph Smith, Mormon church founder, introduced the practice of plural marriage in 1843 as a restored biblical principle in Mormon theology.[1] It

[1]Joseph Smith also taught that marriages performed by the proper ecclesiastical authority,

was practiced privately until 1852, three years after the church settled in isolated Utah. Then it was publicly announced as a tenet of Mormon doctrine. While personal disputes arising from and within the practice were theoretically governed exclusively by ecclesiastical authority, the Mormon-dominated legislature sought to bring those issues under legal protection as well. Though never inserting the word "polygamy" into any statute, the Utah legislature framed laws that favored the practice without seeming unduly incongruent with the law in other states and territories, thus avoiding special scrutiny by the U.S. Congress.

Initial efforts to legally safeguard the practice were generally successful for several reasons. When Utah obtained territorial status in the Compromise of 1850, it became subject to the control of a federally appointed governor and judiciary. With the appointment of church president Brigham Young as first governor and the election of an all-Mormon legislature, however, Mormon legislative initiative was insured. Secondly, an unusual, though not unique, legislative move attempted to place judicial control in Mormon hands as well. One of the first acts of the legislature in 1851 was to extend the prerogatives of the probate courts, which normally heard only civil cases. Broadly construing the meaning of the territorial Organic Act, which stipulated that the authority of the probate courts "shall be limited by law," the legislature granted original jurisdiction in both civil and criminal cases to the probate courts, whose officers the legislature was also empowered to appoint.[2] Thus, probate courts possessed concurrent jurisdiction with the district courts and offered an alternative to the federally appointed, non-Mormon officers of the district courts.[3]

Another effort by the territorial legislature to enact protective legislation was rejection of the common law in 1854. Since bigamy was prohibited at common law, this legislative act could be construed as permitting legal recognition of plural marriage.[4]

---

namely the current church president or one of his assignees, would be binding in heaven as well as on earth, a principle known as "eternal marriage" and considered an essential saving ordinance in Mormon doctrine. Marriages performed without this authority endured for time only, that is, until death separated the couple.

[2]An Act Providing for a Probate Court, Section 30, 4 February 1852, 1851–52 Laws of Utah 42.

[3]Nebraska, Colorado, Montana, Idaho, and Nevada also awarded their probate courts extended jurisdiction, but none as extensively as Utah. See Earl S. Pomeroy, *The Territories and the United States, 1861–1890* (Philadelphia, 1947). For an overview of Utah's probate courts see James B. Allen, "The Unusual Jurisdiction of County Probate Courts in the Territory of Utah," *Utah Historical Quarterly* 36 (Spring 1968), 132–41. Detailed studies of two probate courts are Jay E. Powell, "Fairness in the Salt Lake County Probate Court," *Utah Historical Quarterly* 38 (Summer 1970), 256–62; and Elizabeth D. Gee, "Justice for All or for the 'Elect'? Utah County Probate Court, 1855–1872," *Utah Historical Quarterly* 48 (Spring 1980), 129–47.

[4]14 January 1854, Section 1, 1853–54 Laws of Utah 16. Utah and New Mexico were the only two Rocky Mountain territories to initially reject the common law, but most western states altered or adapted it to suit their own conditions, when its precedents proved to be inapplicable. See Gordon M. Bakken, "The English Common Law in the Rocky Mountain West,"

Thus, until Congress passed the Morrill Act in 1862, the first federal law specifically prohibiting bigamy, and the 1874 Poland Act restricting the jurisdiction of the Utah probate courts, the legal protection of Mormon institutions was relatively free of federal intervention.[5]

Most Mormons simply avoided the courts, as far as possible, by settling their disputes within an ecclesiastical court system established early in the history of the church. Presided over by bishops of each ward (ecclesiastical unit) at the first level, it provided an appellate system rising from the bishop's court to the high council court (comprising representatives from several wards), and ultimately reaching to the first presidency of the church (the president and two counselors).

On 4 February 1831, a year after the church was organized, Edward Partridge was appointed bishop over the church and empowered to "see to all things as it shall be appointed unto him" regarding the laws given to govern the church.[6] Four days later, Joseph Smith outlined the procedure for removing unrepentant members from the church in a statement embracing "the law and discipline" of the church. For murder, theft, and lying, the offender was subject to the law of the land, but for adultery and other domestic disputes, the case was to be brought before the elders of the church (ordained male members), including the bishop, if the dispute could not be settled privately.[7]

On 1 August 1831 the bishop was instructed that he was "to judge his people by the testimony of the just, and by the assistance of his counselors."[8] While this directive established the framework for what came to be known as bishops' courts, early practice varied as to the number of elders and church members who attended them. Disciplinary action was often interspersed with other church business and generally voted upon by all those assembled.[9]

On 17 February 1834 the first high council for the church was organized in Kirtland, Ohio, then church headquarters, to settle difficulties unresolved by the bishops' courts.[10] In the council minutes, additional procedural due

---

Arizona and the West 11 (Summer 1969), 109–28, and Bakken, *The Development of Law on the Rocky Mountain Frontier,* (Westport, CT, 1983). For a more detailed view of Utah see Shane Swindle, "The Struggle Over the Adoption of the Common Law in Utah," *The Thetean: A Student Journal of History* (May 1984), 76–97; and Michael W. Homer, "The Judiciary and the Common Law in Utah Territory, 1850–61," *Dialogue, a Journal of Mormon Thought* 21 (Spring 1988), 97–108.

[5]Throughout this period, numerous Utah Supreme Court cases resulted in conflicting opinions regarding the applicability of the common law in Utah, until the Poland Act affirmed its validity. See Swindle, 94–97.

[6]*The Doctrine and Covenants of the Church of Jesus Christ of Latter-day Saints* (Salt Lake City, 1957) (hereafter D&C), 41:10. This is a book of revelations, doctrine, and commandments accepted as scripture by Mormons.

[7]*D & C*, 42:79–93.

[8]*D & C*, 58:18.

[9]Donald Q. Cannon and Lyndon W. Cook, eds., *Far West Record: Minutes of the Church of Jesus Christ of Latter-day Saints, 1830–1844* (Salt Lake City, 1983), 35–67.

[10]*D & C*, 102.

process is detailed. Though intended to act as an appellate body to review decisions of the "bishop's council," in practice the high council often assumed original jurisdiction.[11] The first presidency of the church or a member thereof presided over the high council.[12] This pattern was further modified on 28 March 1835 when the first presidency was retained as the presiding quorum of the church; and the Quorum of Twelve Apostles, next to the first presidency in authority, was designated a "traveling Presiding High Council" to serve as a supervisory and appellate body above the "standing" high councils.[13]

Church leaders urged members to use ecclesiastical courts rather than traditional legal courts, even in Mormon-dominated Nauvoo, Illinois, where the church was headquartered from 1839 to 1846. Though the city court judge was a Mormon and the resident justice of the peace was a friend of the Mormons, later converting to Mormonism, church members settled most of their disputes in bishops' or high council courts, a situation which prefigured Utah practice.

With the exodus west, settlements were established along the way, complete with wards, bishops, and high councils (where appropriate), the most notable of which were at Winter Quarters, Nebraska, and Kanesville, Pottawattamie County, Iowa. In these frontier settlements, bishops' courts and high councils became, for the first time, the de facto civil, as well as ecclesiastical, tribunals.

A hearing held by the Pottawattamie high council on 9 July 1847, presided over by Apostle Orson Hyde, illustrates the informality of the procedure. The case involved a dispute between Joseph Meakam and William Carter. Testimony indicated that Carter had married or "covenanted" with Meakam's daughter, Cordelia, as a plural wife, and when she discovered him "to be a scoundrel," she had returned to her father's home, followed by Carter, who threatened that she and all wives who broke their covenants with him would be damned. Her father blamed her subsequent death on the stress she endured because of Carter's threats. Although Carter strenuously denied the charges, Apostle Hyde detected "a spirit manifest here for covering up facts."[14] Others testified to hearing William assert that covenant breakers would be damned, and Hyde reaffirmed "the spirit's prompting" to him in an interview with Carter that Carter was indeed untruthful.

Hyde then admonished Carter to confess, since he "had the witness within him," that Carter had lied in denying that he had preached false doctrine. When threatened with the loss of his church membership, his priesthood, as well as his wives, Carter finally confessed and pled for mercy. The

[11]Stephen J. Sorenson, "Civil and Criminal Jurisdiction of L.D.S. Bishops' and High Council Courts, 1847–1852," *Task Papers in LDS History,* No. 17, Historical Department, Church of Jesus Christ of Latter-day Saints (Salt Lake City, 1977), 21–27.

[12]*D & C,* 102:3, 11.

[13]*D & C,* 107:33.

[14]Minutes, Pottawatamie High Council, 9 July 1847, LDS Church Archives, Salt Lake City, Utah (hereafter LDS CA).

unanimous vote of those assembled was to extend mercy to the defendant.[15]

Even though this court was the only governing judicial entity in Kanesville at the time, the sanctions it threatened to impose were ecclesiastical in nature. Though church courts were not uniformly consistent, the nature of the sanctions, the informality of the proceeding, and the presiding judge's reliance "on the spirit" for a just decision were generally typical of subsequent church court proceedings.[16]

Church courts were especially useful in settling domestic conflicts involving polygamy because of the practice's extralegal character. Nevertheless, Mormon legislatures also attempted to protect the women and children involved in plural marriage by enacting laws based on principles governing church court decisions. Most of these protective laws fell into the category of domestic relations, including marriage, divorce, and succession or inheritance. Their checkered history illustrates the escalating tension between local attempts to preserve a religious practice and federal efforts to destroy it and the legal consequences for plural wives.[17]

For its first four decades, Utah law had no provisions for the civil licensing and registration of marriage. The only marriage law of the period was included in an ordinance incorporating the church, which authorized it to "solemnize marriages compatible with the revelations of Jesus Christ."[18] This ordinance provided for "a registry of marriages," but it was to be kept only in the branches or stakes of the church. No civil record was required until the Edmunds-Tucker Act established regulatory measures in 1887. Thus, polygamous alliances did not need to become a matter of public record. In 1862, the Morrill Act specifically declared bigamous marriages illegal, but not until 1876 did the church-owned *Deseret Evening News* concede that the practice was "not recognized by the law of the land."[19] Polygamy continued to be practiced by church members, however, for an-

[15]Ibid.

[16]For detailed studies of church courts see Sorenson, "Civil and Criminal Jurisdiction"; R. Collin Mangrum, "Furthering the Cause of Zion: An Overview of the Mormon Ecclesiastical Court System in Early Utah," *Journal of Mormon History* 10 (1983), 79–90; and Raymond T. Swenson, "Resolution of Civil Disputes by Mormon Ecclesiastical Courts," *Utah Law Review,* no. 3 (1978), 573–95. A recent book-length study of Mormon courts in Edwin Brown Firmage and Richard Collin Mangrum, *Zion in the Courts, A Legal History of the Church of Jesus Christ of Latter-day Saints, 1830–1900* (Urbana, 1988).

[17]Non-Mormon Utah residents found these laws particularly irksome. As quoted in Orson F. Whitney, *History of Utah,* 4 vols. (Salt Lake City, 1893), 3:61, in an 1878 appeal to Mrs. Rutherford B. Hayes, the newly organized Anti-Polygamy Society protests that the Utah legislature, "composed almost entirely of polygamists and members of the Mormon priesthood," has "thrown around polygamy every possible legislative safeguard in their power."

[18]An Ordinance, Incorporating the Church of Jesus Christ of Latter-day Saints, 6 February 1851, 1851–52 Laws of Deseret 66. The ordinance did not prohibit any other ecclesiastical or legal entity from performing marriages. As a result of the lack of marriage registration, it is difficult to trace marriages performed in Utah between 1847 and 1887, except through ecclesiastical records and the personal papers of ecclesiastical and civil authorities, most of which are incomplete. See Lyman D. Platt, "The History of Marriage in Utah, 1847–1905," *Genealogical Journal* 12 (Spring 1983), 32–33.

[19]Journal History of the Church, (a chronological manuscript collection of journal entries and newspaper articles) 3 May 1876, LDS CA.

other fourteen years, until 1890, when church president Wilford Woodruff suspended the performance of any further plural marriages.

Though polygamy was denounced as a system of female bondage by non-Mormons, the liberality of Utah's divorce laws and the ease with which church divorces were granted belied this perception. As historian Lawrence Foster has noted, in polygamous Utah, contrary to prevailing opinion, women enjoyed more freedom in terms of marriage and divorce than women in other polygamous cultures.[20] Though easy divorce seems incongruous with the Mormon theological focus on the eternity of marriage and propriety of plural marriage, the religious faithfulness and mutual affection of the participants were the primary determinants of a successful union. As early as 1842, according to one account, Joseph Smith taught that marriage was a covenant between two people and if it had not been conducive of blessings and peace, they were free to separate since "it was a sin for people to live together and raise or beget children, in alienation from each other."[21] The sin, according to Mormon thought, was not in divorce but in perpetuating the form of marriage and the begetting of children without the cementing bond of affection. The decision in an 1847 divorce case brought before the high council in Winter Quarters, Nebraska, invoked this tenet: "No man or woman should ever be compelled to live together who cannot live in union. You two now are to separate and not come together again."[22]

In 1861, Brigham Young, successor to Joseph Smith, reiterated this principle. "When a woman becomes alienated in her feelings and affections from her husband, it is then his duty to give her a bill and set her free," he said in a church conference. To continue to live together when a wife had become alienated from her husband was to violate the marriage covenant. Moreover, if a man proved to be an "unworthy" husband and father, he automatically forfeited his marriage covenants, and his wife or wives were "free from him without a bill of divorcement."[23] The sanctity and perpetuation of a marriage, as a holy sacrament, were contingent on the righteousness of the couple and the retention of affection between them. Two cases brought before a Fillmore, Utah, bishop in 1883 illustrate the value placed on affection in marriage. "Although her [the applicant's] grounds are not

[20]Lawrence Foster, "A Little Known Defense of Polygamy," *Dialogue, a Journal of Mormon Thought* 9 (Winter 1974), 29.

[21]Recorded in his journal and later printed in John D. Lee, *Mormonism Unveiled: Or the Life and Confessions of the Late Mormon Bishop, John D. Lee* (St. Louis, 1877), 146; see also Foster, "A Little Known Defense," 29.

[22]Ecclesiastical Court Cases Collection, General Court Trials 1847, Fd. 17, LDS CA, quoted in Sorenson, "Civil and Criminal Jurisdiction," 32.

[23]"Few Words of Doctrine given by President Brigham Young in the Tabernacle in Great Salt Lake City," reported by George Watt, 8 October 1861, LDS CA. Also reported in J. Beck, I Notebook, 1859–65, 8 October 1861 and 11 December 1869, Special Collections, Marriott Library, University of Utah. The case of Emma and Alisha Mallory is illustrative, though Emma desired a certificate of divorce, which was granted her on 1 August 1862 "because her husband . . . has been cut off from the Church of Jesus Christ of Latter-day Saints for apostacy, and therefore *forfeited his privileges and blessings*" (author's emphasis). Brigham Young Papers, Box 64, Reel 99, LDS CA.

just," the bishop reported to church president John Taylor (successor to Brigham Young), "in our opinion it would not be wise to compel her to continue to be the wife of her husband inasmuch as she claims that she does not now nor never did have any affection for him." In another instance, though the bishop again felt the complaining wife did not have sufficient grounds for divorce, she had expressed such hostility to her husband that he was willing to recommend a divorce and "leave the matter to the judgment of President [John] Taylor."[24]

Church leaders continually preached against divorce and urged the reconciliation of estranged couples, but when conciliatory efforts failed, then they advised an expeditious separation and settlement. "Parties should be advised to learn how to live together in peace," Brigham Young counseled in 1851, "but if it is best for them to separate," the husband should give the wife and children "a large proportion of the property."[25] Plural wives were particularly admonished to bear their burdens uncomplainingly and "not to expect heaven on earth but to prepare for it in due time."[26] Nevertheless, they were speedily granted divorces when desired. Extant records show that more than 1,600 applicants, most of them women, received ecclesiastical divorces before polygamy was suspended in 1890.[27]

While both men and women appealed to church courts for divorce, men were almost routinely refused, except in compelling circumstances, while women were seldom denied their requests.[28] In typical earthy imagery, Brigham Young told one male petitioner, "If you have drawn a red hot iron between your legs and scorched yourself, bear it without grunting, and if it smarts, grease it. . . . I want the brethren to stop divorcing their wives, for it

[24]Ecclesiastical Court Cases Collection, 1880, Fd. 6; 1883, Fd. 6, LDS CA, noted in Firmage and Mangrum, *Zion in the Courts,* 327.

[25]Sorenson, "Civil and Criminal Jurisdiction," 31.

[26]Brigham Young Office Journals, 1857–1860, 19 April 1858, 21, LDS CA, quoted in Linda P. Wilcox, "Brigham Young as a Domestic Counselor," 15, unpublished paper in possession of author. See also Firmage and Mangrum, *Zion in the Courts,* 322–36 for examples of the efforts made by bishops and other ecclesiastical officers at reconciling couples and resolving family difficulties.

[27]An analysis of these certificates of divorce is found in Eugene E. Campbell and Bruce L. Campbell, "Divorce Among Mormon Polygamists: Extent and Explanations," *Utah Historical Quarterly* 4 (Winter 1978), 4–23.

[28]The opportunity through polygamy for a dissatisfied husband to take an additional wife mitigated the necessity of divorce for men. Firmage and Mangrum's survey of LDS ecclesiastical court records (since closed to researchers) and Wilcox's survey of Brigham Young's letterbooks (copies of outgoing correspondence, LDS CA) show that divorces were granted primarily to wives, although a male applicant was expected to pay a fee of ten dollars "for his foolishness." *Journal of Discourses* (1875; Salt Lake City, 1966) 17:119. The liberal attitude toward female applicants is demonstrated in such statements of Young's as, "When women tease for a divorce, and are determined to have one, what can be done better than to give them one?" Brigham Young to Benjamin F. Johnson, 20 March 1865, Brigham Young Letterbook 7:517; or " . . . I should feel a little ashamed to require a wife to ask me twice for a bill of divorce, or to refuse signing and paying for it at once"; or "If the brethren were but a small part as anxious, diligent and prompt in this particular, [agreeing to divorce] as they are in having women sealed to them, it would prevent much needless annoyance and perplexity to the sisters," Young to Bishop Philo T. Farnsworth, 22 November 1859, Letterbook 5:132, quoted in Wilcox, "Brigham Young," 16–17.

is not right. I do not want to grant divorces."[29] The preferential treatment given women is consistent with Young's explanation of the sin of begetting children in alienation of affections and reflects the relative ease with which women could remarry in polygamous Utah, as well as the voluntary nature of the practice of polygamy. A church divorce confidentially and expeditiously released women unable to bear the emotional or physical burdens of plural marriage.

The governing policies for church divorces transferred into civil law in 1852, when the territorial legislature attached an incompatibility clause to the traditional grounds for divorce (impotency, adultery, desertion, habitual drunkenness, felony conviction, and abusive treatment). In words similar to those used in church divorce actions, the statute provided that divorce could be granted "when it shall be made to appear to the satisfaction and conviction of the court, that the parties cannot live in peace and union together, and that their welfare requires a separation."[30] The law also provided a minimal residency requirement. Anyone who was or "wished to become" a resident of Utah could invoke the jurisdiction of the court.[31] While various explanations have been tendered for Utah's adoption of such a liberal statute, it is consistent with Mormon legislative efforts to facilitate and protect the practice of polygamy with laws that reflected church court policies and practices.[32]

Although Utah was among the 20 percent of states and territories with the highest divorce rate, it was lower than nearly all of its western neighbors during the first twenty-year period for which national divorce statistics were compiled (1867–1887).[33] More than a third of Utah civil divorces during this time utilized the incompatibility clause, 71 percent of them granted during a single three-year period, 1875 to 1877. In fact, the total number of civil divorces granted in Utah more than tripled between 1875 and 1877, dropping back to its 1874 level in 1878. Four Utah counties registered precipitous increases, but the most dramatic occurred in the small southern Utah county of Beaver, where divorces jumped from two in 1874 to 108 in

[29]Brigham Young to Jonathan Pugmire, Jr., Journal History of the Church, 17 December 1858, LDS CA.

[30]An Act in Relation to Bills of Divorce, Sections 2, 3, 1851–52 Laws of Utah 82.

[31] Ibid., Section 2.

[32]See, for example, Richard I. Aaron, "Mormon Divorce and the Statute of 1852: Questions for Divorce in the 1980s," *Journal of Contemporary Law* 8 (1982), 20–22; and Firmage and Mangrum, *Zion in the Courts,* 324–27. Utah's divorce laws were not so unusual as to provoke undue interest by Congress. Other states that had similar provisions at that time were Indiana, North Carolina, Illinois, Connecticut, Iowa (which had almost the exact wording as the Utah law), and Maine. Arizona, Louisiana, South Dakota, and Washington followed Utah in adopting similar "omnibus" clauses. The others, however, did not include both an incompatibility clause and an open residency requirement as did Utah. For a general discussion of early divorce laws see George Elliott Howard, *A History of Matrimonial Institutions,* 3 vols. (Chicago, 1904), 3:3–106. A brief, comparative analysis of these divorce laws is in Aaron, "Mormon Divorce," 10–12.

[33]Carroll D. Wright, *Marriage and Divorce in the United States, 1867–1886* (1889; New York, 1976).

1875 and 358 the next year. Of a total of 691 divorces in Beaver County during this twenty-year period, 91 percent were granted between 1875 and 1877. This aberration did not reflect an unusual season of marital discontent, but an exploitation of Utah's divorce law by non-Utah divorce lawyers, who found its open residency requirement and completion of the transcontinental railroad (in 1869) an irresistible combination. For example, of the 691 Beaver divorces, only seventy-five involved bonafide Utah residents. All the others were migratory divorces brought by residents of eastern states "wishing," for a day, to become residents of Utah.[34] The probate judges in these counties facilitated the use of their courts by eastern divorce lawyers, creating a short-lived, but active, divorce mill in Utah.

Alarmed at the flagrant abuse of Utah's divorce law, Governor George W. Emery strongly urged the legislature to amend the law in 1876, but not until a grand jury investigation the following year and another urgent appeal by Governor Emery, in 1878, did the Mormon legislature reluctantly eliminate the offending provisions.[35] A *Deseret News* article explained the reluctance: "Polygamy would be considered a system of bondage, if women desiring to sever their relations with a husband having other wives, were refused the liberty they might demand."[36] Though plural wives could not utilize civil courts for divorce, first wives could. Moreover, the liberal divorce law contradicted the popular image of the enslaved wife in Utah. Thus, Mormon legislators agreed to reformulate the law only when convinced its abuse by non-Mormons had overshadowed its value to Mormons.

Rigid jurisdictional distinctions were not always maintained in divorce suits. In 1872, when Emmaline Kesler elected to divorce her husband, Frederick, of thirty-six years, she filed in district court. Three weeks later, at her husband's urging, she withdrew her suit from the gentile-governed district court and refiled it in the Mormon-administered probate court, where the judge awarded her a bill of divorce three weeks later on the grounds that "said parties cannot live together in peace and union."[37]

Thirteen months later, Abigail Kesler, Frederick's plural wife of fourteen years, also left him. Informing Kesler by mail that she would not ask for a divorce for the sake of her children, she requested only a portion of his property to support them. Before receiving a reply, however, Abigail visited Brig-

[34]Divorce Docket, Beaver County Probate Records, 1856–1882, copy in LDS Church Family History Library, Salt Lake City, Utah.

[35]An Act Amending Sections 1151 and 1154 of the Compiled Laws of Utah, Section 1, 2 February 1878, 1878 Laws of Utah 1. See also *Journals of the Legislative Assembly of the Territory of Utah,* (Salt Lake City, 1876), 31 and (1878), 44–45; and report of grand jury, "Divorce," *Salt Lake City Deseret News Weekly,* 3 October 1877. The grand jury report indicated that of 300 divorces under investigation, 80 percent were applied for by non-residents who never appeared in court. Attorneys appeared for only sixty-seven of 150 of the cases. Decrees were granted before defendants had had time to respond and sometimes with complete disregard for contested suits.

[36]"Divorce," *Salt Lake City Deseret News Weekly,* 3 October 1877.

[37]Frederick Kesler Papers, Special Collections, Marriott Library, University of Utah, Salt Lake City, Utah.

ham Young and secured a bill of divorce and his word that she was entitled to a third of her husband's estate, valued then at $12,000. In response to Kesler's inquiry about the matter, Brigham Young wrote: "Your wife Abigail called upon me, stated her feelings and requested a bill, which under the circumstances we thought proper to grant her, as is usual when a woman insists upon one. . . . "[38] While appeals for church divorces generally originated in bishops' courts, from which recommendations were sent to the first presidency for decisions, some applicants skirted this procedure and appealed directly to the church president. Moreover, Brigham Young sometimes suggested a choice of venue. In 1870, he advised Maria Jarman to apply "either to Bro. Elias Smith, Probate Judge of Salt Lake County, or to this office, and procure a bill at any time." It is not clear whether Maria Jarman was a first or plural wife, but it is clear that Young and Smith did not have comparable jurisdiction. Young also occasionally instructed probate judges on the disposition of cases, as he did in the divorce suit of Sarah Hutchenson, advising Judge Elias Smith "that it would be proper" to grant Sarah a divorce from her long-absent husband.[39]

Numerous legal entanglements resulted from this blurring of jurisdictional boundaries. For example, in 1870 Eleanor and Elbridge Tufts decided to terminate their marriage of one year and were granted a church divorce. Both remarried. Upon learning twenty years later that the church divorce was not valid, Eleanor ceased living with John Wickel, her second husband, and sued Tufts for divorce. The divorce was still pending in 1895 when Tufts died. Eleanor then filed claim for a dower interest in his property as his only legal wife. The claim was granted by the trial court and affirmed by the Utah Supreme Court.[40] In a similar case decided three years later, John R. Park, an early Utah educator, married Annie Armitage, a young convert, in 1872 at her bedside, believing her to be on her deathbed but wishing to secure an eternal marriage for them both. When Annie unexpectedly recovered, the two agreed to separate and obtained a church divorce the following year. Park never remarried, but Annie married and bore ten children. At Park's demise in 1902, Annie sued to recover a dower interest in property conveyed by Park before his death, claiming her right as his widow, since her church divorce from him was not valid. Though she lost her case in trial court, the Utah Supreme Court reversed the decision and she recovered her widow's share.[41]

Divorce became less relevant following the 1890 suspension of church-sanctioned plural marriage, and a clear distinction between ecclesiastical and civil marriages and divorces took effect in Utah. The next several decades represented a period of legal adjustment for plural wives and chil-

[38]Ibid.

[39]Brigham Young to Maria Jarman, 15 January 1870, "Brigham Young Letterbook" 11:954; Brigham Young to Elias Smith, 19 January 1870, "Brigham Young Letterbook" 11:959, LDS CA.

[40]*Norton* v. *Tufts,* 19 Utah 470 (1899).

[41]*Hilton* v. *Roylance,* 25 Utah 129 (1902).

dren, many of whom found themselves in a state of legal limbo regarding their inheritance rights.[42]

Like Utah's early marriage and divorce laws, laws of succession also attempted to accommodate the needs of plural wives and children.[43] An 1852 statute rather ambiguously provided that in the absence of a will, and after payment of the liabilities of a man's estate, whatever property remained would "descend in equal shares to his children or their heirs; one share . . . through the mother of such children . . . or if he has had more than one wife, who either died or survived in lawful wedlock, it shall be equally divided between the living and the heirs of those who are dead. . . . "[44]

Written ten years before passage of the Morrill Act outlawing bigamy, the phrase "lawful wedlock" as it referred to additional wives was not necessarily contradictory. The following section, however, went beyond the implied rights of plural wives in the first section to provide that "illegitimate children and their mothers" shall inherit "in like manner."[45]

Mary Ann Maughan, widow of Peter Maughan of northern Utah's Cache Valley, noted the inherent inequity in the "equal distribution to all heirs" of the property in a polygamous marriage. Though she was married thirty years and raised ten children, she was irked to learn that since it was ruled "best for all to share alike," the two-year-old son of her sister wife, Lissy, "was awarded just as much as I was"[46]

A further provision of the 1852 law allowed illegitimate children and their mothers to inherit from the father, whether acknowledged by him or not, if it could be demonstrated that he was the father. Succession cases indicate this was the statute that granted plural wives inheritance rights.

In 1876, at the urging of Governor George W. Emery, the legislature amended the statute to require that the father acknowledge the illegitimate heirs before they inherit to avoid the possibility of fraudulent claims and to prevent injustice to legitimate heirs. It also reluctantly removed the heritable rights of mothers of illegitimate children to conform to the requirements of the Morrill Act, which not only made bigamy a crime, but also nullified all territorial laws that appeared to "establish, support, maintain, shield or countenance polygamy."[47] Since the Mormon-controlled probate courts

[42]Polygamy continues to be disallowed in the church and those Mormons who currently practice it, known as fundamentalists, are excommunicates or out of fellowship. A more detailed discussion of some of these cases is in Lois J. Kelly, "Polygamy and the Law, the Legal Status of Polygamous Wives After the Manifesto of 1890," unpublished paper in possession of author.

[43]These laws were established to protect the property interests of the heirs of a husband or father who died intestate.

[44]An Act in Relation to the Estates of Decedents, Section 24, 1876 Compiled Laws of Utah 268.

[45]Ibid., Section 25. In *Cain Heirs* v. *Young,* 1 Utah 361 (1876) the court construed a widow's interest (in a monogamous marriage) to be "a child's part during her life or widowhood," which in this case amounted to a one-third interest since there were two children.

[46]"Journal of Mary Ann Weston Maughan," in *Our Pioneer Heritage,* ed. Kate B. Carter, 20 vols. (Salt Lake City, 1959) 2:396.

[47]"Acknowledgement" was a common law doctrine and assumed formal requirements in some jurisdictions. These later acts also provided that the mother was the intestate heir for an

were allowed to retain jurisdiction in the settlement of estates after the federal Poland Bill of 1874 transferred all other civil and criminal jurisdiction to the district courts, succession claims could continue to be settled before sympathetic judges. Where succession or inheritance claims were heard, however, depended on the disposition of the first wife, who could press her legal claims in a territorial court or defer to an ecclesiastical court to decide the distribution of the estate. The Gunnell wives of Cache Valley, unlike Mary Ann Maughan, were subject to the later laws providing only for illegitimate children. When Francis Gunnell died in 1889, his second wife Emma "was left nothing, not being recognized by law as a wife. Everything was left to the first living wife, Aunt Esther, and some property divided among the children." The children combined their small inheritance and built a home for their mother.[48] The silence of the law on plural wives' inheritance from their intestate husbands required them to find relief primarily through church courts or through the generosity of their children. Even plural wives who were beneficiaries of a will found themselves in a state of dependency. Emily Dow Partridge Young, widow of Brigham Young, shared in his estate, but found the limitations of her widowhood demeaning. A widow "is left to the mercy of his [*sic*] children," she complained. "They are given preeminence, while the wife and mother is ignored. Even my home, that I hold the deed of," she angrily noted, "is given to my children and I am not allowed the right to own anything but am fed with a spoon like a baby."[49]

When prosecution of polygamists under the Morrill Act failed, Congress passed more stringent anti-polygamy legislation in 1882 (Edmunds Act) and 1887 (Edmunds-Tucker Act). The Edmunds Act affirmed the legality of the inheritance rights of illegitimate children born prior to January 1883, but did not acknowledge any rights of plural wives. In debate on the bill, Senator George F. Edmunds (R-VT) declared that "this bill does not leave any polygamous woman in any worse condition in point of law than she is at the moment, but it leaves her children in an infinitely better condition, because it makes them legitimate."[50] The Edmunds-Tucker Act, while annulling all laws providing for the capacity of illegitimate children to inherit, also included a "saving clause" as to those children legitimated by the Edmunds Act and all others born within twelve months after its own passage in 1887.[51]

---

illegitimate child. See An Act Relating to Estates of Decedents, Sections 30, 32, 28 February 1876, 1876 Compiled Laws of Utah 276; see also An Act Relating to Estates of Decedents, Sections 4, 5, 13 March 1884, 1884 Laws of Utah 75.

[48]Ruth Victor, "Emma Jeffs Gunnell," and Louis Jeffs Gunnell, "Lewellyn (Louis) Jeffs Gunnell," TS in possession of author.

[49]Emily Dow Partridge Young, Autobiography and Diary, TS, 28 February 1880, LDS CA.

[50]U. S. Congress, *Congressional Record,* 47th Cong., 1st Sess. (1881–82), 1213.

[51]Section 11, 24 Statutes at Large 637. The Edmunds Act amended the Morrill Act by changing the crime designated as bigamy to polygamy, making cohabitation a criminal offense, and legitimating children born of polygamous marriages, enabling them to inherit. The 1887 Edmunds-Tucker Act, which amended the Edmunds Act, among other provisions disallowed the right of illegitimate children born after March 1888 to inherit from either mothers or fathers. In 1891, however, the Utah Supreme Court in *Pratt* v. *Pratt* found that "A statute enact-

In *Chapman* v. *Handley,* a suit brought in 1890 by the "illegitimate" offspring of George Handley, who died in 1874, and his plural wife Mary, the Utah Supreme Court held that the 1852 territorial law that gave illegitimate children the right to inherit from their fathers had been superseded by the 1862 Morrill Act, which disallowed any laws that supported polygamy. The Court thus denied the petitioners their claim of inheritance.[52] The United States Supreme Court, however, ruling on a similar case, *Cope* v. *Cope,* reversed the judgment of the Utah court and found that the legislature was free to provide for illegitimate children to inherit from their mother, father, or both, declaring that it was "unjust to visit the sins of the parents on the heads of the children."[53] The United States Supreme Court seemed more willing than Utah's judiciary to interpret the Morrill Act broadly, distinguishing between the rights of illegitimate children to legal protection and the illegal actions of their parents. The irony and ultimate tragedy, however, derive from the obvious disparity between the intent of Congress to protect the moral and social interests of Mormon women by freeing them from polygamy and its subsequent failure to protect their economic or legal status.[54]

Nor were plural wives given legal status by the first legislature of the State of Utah that, in 1896, passed a law legitimating *all* issue of bigamous and polygamous marriages contracted prior to that year and providing that such children could inherit from both parents, but making no provisions for plural wives.[55] The importance of writing wills was never so apparent. One astute daughter, Anne Leischman of Cache Valley, Utah, urged her father to make a will. "My mother would come in all right if he dies for a home and things," she explained, "but Aunt Betsy [his plural wife] would only be treated as a child. . . . She can't write a check, she can't sign a deed, she can't do anything."[56] More than her husband or children, the plural wife experienced the penalties of living beyond the boundaries of the law.

---

ing that illegitimate children and their mothers inherit from the father is not repealed by the Act of Congress which annuls all acts and parts of acts of the Legislative Assembly of Utah Territory, . . . " 7 Utah 278 (1891).

[52]*Chapman v. Handley*, 7 Utah 49 (1890).

[53]*Cope* v. *Cope,* 137 U. S. 832 (1890) *In Re Estate of Thomas Cope,* 7 Utah 63 (1890). See also *In The Matter of the Estate of Orson Pratt,* 7 Utah 278 (1891).

[54]While plural wives had no legal rights, the government did not entirely leave them without recourse. In 1886, at the urging of moral crusader Angelia (Angie) Thurston Newman of the Methodist Woman's Home Missionary Society, Congress appropriated $40,000 for the construction of the Industrial Christian Home for Women in Utah, a refuge for unsupported or discontented plural wives. For varied reasons few women availed themselves of this sanctuary and its offer of industrial training and economic rehabilitation. For more details see Peggy Pascoe, *Relations of Rescue: The Search for Female Moral Authority in the American West, 1874–1939* (New York, 1990).

[55]An Act Relative to the Heritable Rights of Issue of Polygamous Marriages, 9 March 1896, 1896 Compiled Laws of Utah 128. An attempt to allow new trials in those cases decided adversely to the offspring of polygamous marriages was declared unconstitutional by the Utah Supreme Court.

[56]Anne W. G. Leischman Oral History, Interview by John Stewart, 1973, TS, 6, Utah State University Voice Library Interview, LDS CA.

The common law right of dower, granting a widow a one-third interest in her husband's real property, if he died intestate, and a one-third inchoate interest during his life-time, was obviously inoperative in polygamy, and the Utah legislature formally abolished dower in 1872.[57] Since dower had been abolished, never enacted, or modified in other areas in the United States, Utah's legislation could not be construed as a wholly unique accommodation to the imperatives of plural marriage, but was clearly enacted to equalize the claims of plural wives on their husbands' estates.[58] It also left polygamous husbands free to distribute their estates equitably by will. Mormon critics viewed the law as one more legal support of polygamy by breaking down the distinction between lawful and plural wives. One 1882 critic observed that abolition of dower rendered "a polygamous wife slavishly dependent on the husband's favor for any share of his property after his death" and urged repeal of the measure to protect the interests of the legal wife who, in polygamy, he said "is not the favorite as a general rule."[59] Absence of dower effectively diminished a legal wife's claim, by withdrawing her inchoate interest in her husband's property during his lifetime and granting her only an equal share with all of her husband's direct heirs at his death.

In 1887, dower was reinstated by the Edmunds-Tucker Act. Its reinstitution continued to work against the legal interests of plural wives, even as sole surviving wives of their husbands. In one case, for example, the first wife died and the surviving plural wife claimed at the death of her husband that she was entitled to dower as the legal wife under the principles of common law marriage. The court denied her claim, rejecting the evidence of common law marriage and ruling in essence that her original marriage as a plural wife was invalid and did not assume legality upon the death of the first or legal wife.[60] In another instance, Emily P. Raleigh sued for her dower right, as a sole surviving wife, in a piece of property willed by her husband to a mutual investment company. Though she had occupied the property for

[57]An Act Concerning the Property Rights of Married Persons, 16 February 1872, 1876 Compiled Laws of Utah 342. Since dower was implicitly abolished by the 1854 statute abrogating the common law in Utah, the "equitable right of a married woman to a separate estate" was legally recognized early. Subsequent court cases, however, continually raised questions about the validity of the statute. See *Hatch* v. *Hatch,* 46 Utah 116 (1915); and Swindle, "The Struggle," 94–97.

[58]Some of the states that did not recognize the common law right of dower were Texas (dower repealed in 1840), Arizona (1865), Colorado (1868), Kansas (1879), Mississippi (1880), California (community property state), and Louisiana (never had dower). In place of dower, laws of succession were enacted providing for the descent and distribution of property. For an extensive nineteenth-century analysis of dower laws in the United States see Charles Scribner, *A Treatise on the Law of Dower,* 2 vols. (Philadelphia, 1883), 1:22–58. A comparative historical review of married women's legal rights in four western states, including Utah, is Helen S. Carter, "Legal Aspects of Widowhood and Aging," in *On Their Own, Widows and Widowhood in the American Southwest, 1848–1939,* ed. Arlene Scadron (Urbana, 1988), 271–300.

[59]As quoted in Jennie Anderson Froiseth, *The Women of Mormonism or the Story of Polygamy* (Detroit, 1882), 360–61.

[60]*Beck* v. *Utah-Idaho Sugar Company,* 59 Utah 314 (1921).

forty-six years and claimed it as a gift from her husband, the court ruled against her claim declaring that whatever misfortune she felt had befallen her was a result of her own volition. She made the choice to become a plural wife, the court asserted, "at her peril," failing thereby "to acquire the status of a lawful wife." She was, therefore, "without the pale of the law, of inheritance as to any property which her husband had acquired or might thereafter acquire."[61]

Polygamy impinged less directly upon the development of Utah's property law. While dower clearly mitigated the property claims of a plural wife, passage of a Married Person's Property Act at the same time dower was abolished in 1872 protected the property owned by all women at marriage. The act allowed each spouse to retain and control the property each brought to the marriage, as well as that acquired afterwards.[62] While the repeal of dower was opposed by non-Mormons, the Property Act was hailed by Mormon women as progressive and far more in keeping with the times respecting the advancing legal rights of married women.[63]

Utah law was amended by federal statute or judicial decree in two nondomestic ares that also affected the status of plural wives. In 1870, the territorial legislature enfranchised women, only the second legislature in the country to do so. Originally proposed by several members of the U.S. Congress as a means of empowering plural wives to throw off the yoke of polygamy, woman suffrage was seized on by Mormon lawmakers to counteract the perception of the subjugated plural wife. From 1870 until 1887, woman suffrage was inextricably linked to polygamy by non-Mormons, who feared it would strengthen Mormon political hegemony. Every congressional measure proposed to curtail the practice included repeal of woman suffrage in Utah. Though eastern suffragists forcefully lobbied against repeal, the Edmunds Act finally denied polygamists the vote in 1882, and the Edmunds-Tucker Act disenfranchised all Utah women in 1887. While a presidential amnesty in 1893 restored the vote to men who gave up polygamy, women were not reenfranchised until statehood in 1896.

A major tool in the prosecution of polygamists was the testimony of plural wives. But Utah's civil code, adopted in 1870, exempted husbands and wives from testifying against each other, unless the action involved one

[61]*Raleigh* v. *Wells,* 29 Utah 217 (1905).

[62]An Act Concerning the Property Rights of Married Persons, 16 February 1872, 1876 Compiled Laws of Utah 342.

[63]Many Mormon women viewed dower as a form of "vassalage" and "relic of the old common law" and acclaimed the passage of a married person's property act as more reflective of social and economic change. See "Woman's Right of Dower," *Salt Lake City Woman's Exponent,* 1 December 1882; see also "A Woman's Assembly," *Salt Lake City Woman's Exponent,* 1 March 1894. Nineteenth-century feminists generally welcomed the proliferation of married women's property acts as a major step forward in the emancipation of women. By 1850, at least 17 states had some form of legislation that enabled married women to control their property, a number that expanded to 29 by 1865. See Lawrence M. Friedman, *A History of American Law* (New York, 1973), 186; and Norma Basch, *In the Eyes of the Law: Women, Marriage, and Property in Nineteenth Century New York* (Ithaca, 1982), 28.

against the other. It was later amended to allow testimony against one by the other in cases of crimes committed by one on the other.[64] Federal prosecutors sought ways to circumvent this husband/wife privilege. While testimony from wives other than the first was admissible, since they were not legal wives, various approaches were applied to obtain testimony from first wives. In *United States* v. *Bassett,* in which the defendant's first wife agreed to testify, her testimony was ruled admissible by the Territorial Supreme Court, on the basis that polygamy was a crime against *her,* and, thus, under the civil code, she could testify. Moreover, it ruled that polygamy was also a crime of violence to her feelings, personal security, and her liberty, and she was, thus, allowed to testify under the criminal code as well. Since an exception to the husband/wife communication privilege was permitted under the criminal code when a "violent" crime was committed by one against the other, the prosecutors hoped to utilize that exception by declaring polygamy a crime of violence. When the case was appealed to the United States Supreme Court, however, it reversed the lower court's decision. It defined polygamy as a crime against the marital relation, rather than against the lawful wife and refused to acknowledge it as a crime of violence.[65] Thus, the right of immunity excused first wives from testifying, but not being subject to this law, plural wives were required to testify against their husbands. Those who refused were cited for contempt, and several women were imprisoned.[66] In one more instance, plural wives stood outside the boundaries of the law.

While in most respects the development of law in territorial Utah followed principles of the common law, despite legislative efforts to disclaim it, Mormon lawmakers attempted to shape the law, as far as possible, to fit the necessities of a unique family structure. Throughout Utah's territorial period, the law underwent repeated modification, as federal law and judicial decree reshaped it to match the legal contours of the larger society. The Mormon-federal conflict, among other things, demonstrated the fluidity of law in its response to the social factors influencing it. On the local level, Utah laws protecting Mormon interests continually met defeat by the federally appointed judiciary. Yet, on the national level, while congressional lawmakers carved away those protective statutes, the U.S. Supreme Court often exerted a meliorating influence. The weight of congressional legislation, however, ultimately prevailed. Though their children, as innocent victims, were granted legal protection, polygamous husbands faced criminal prose-

[64]An Act Regulating Proceedings in Civil Cases in the Courts of Justice of this Territory and to Repeal Certain Acts and Parts of Acts, Section 379, 17 February 1870, 1876 Compiled Laws of Utah 506; An Act to Amend Title XX, Section 30, 9 March 1882, 1882 Compiled Laws of Utah 79.

[65]*Basset* v. *United States,* 137 U. S. 762 (1890).

[66]See "A Few Facts," *Salt Lake City Woman's Exponent,* 15 July 1885, which lists Annie Gallifant, Belle Harris, Nellie White, Lydia Spencer, Elizabeth Ann Starkey, and Lucy Devereux among those who were charged with contempt of court and who were willing to be imprisoned rather than testify against their husbands. Belle Harris kept a journal, located in the LDS CA, of the three months she served in the Utah prison.

cution and their plural wives, legal discrimination. While many polygamists escaped federal prosecution altogether and others paid the requisite penalties of a fine and a relatively brief imprisonment, all plural wives experienced the legal consequences of living outside the protective limits of the law. Moreover, while polygamous husbands ultimately regained their legal and political rights through a presidential amnesty, plural wives did not. Because far more women than men practiced polygamy, the legal ramifications for women were not only more permanent, they were more pervasive.

While polygamy contributed to the shaping of Utah's territorial law, it is instructive to recognize that the law was so formulated as to accommodate a marital style involving only about 25 or 30 percent of Utah's residents.[67] Rather than reflecting or regulating the practices of the larger population of the territory, the law, in this case, attempted to protect the rights of the minority, sometimes at the expense of the majority. Only when met by coercive measures did Utah/Mormon lawmakers finally "render unto Caesar" the legal prerogatives they had claimed for themselves in pursuit of the establishment of their religious commonwealth, yielding to federal measures to bring the territory into legal harmony with the rest of the nation.

[67]Exact figures were virtually impossible to ascertain, but several recent community studies indicate that the percentages are higher than originally believed. For example, in 1880, a representative year for the practice before federal prosecution, the percentage of the Mormon population involved in polygamy varied from 5 to 66 percent, depending on the locale, with an average around 25 to 30 percent. See Lowell "Ben" Bennion, "The Incidence of Mormon Polygamy in 1880: 'Dixie' versus Davis Stake," *Journal of Mormon History* 11 (1984), 27–42; and Larry Logue in *A Sermon in the Desert: Belief and Behavior in Early St. George, Utah* (Urbana, 1988), especially chp. 3, indicates that more than a third of the husbands in St. George and a majority of the wives were engaged in plural marriage.

*

In Their Own Behalf: The Politicization of Mormon Women and the 1870 Franchise

LOLA VAN WAGENEN

In 1870 the Utah Territorial Legislature granted women the right to vote. Though the decision was an important one, historians have not often thought to ask what part women themselves played in the making of it. In this article Lola Van Wagenen examines the role, specifically of Mormon women, who made up the vast majority of the territory's female population. Her intention, in part, is to help restore women to the historical stage and make clear the range, power, and significance of their contributions. Mormon women, she concludes, "helped gain suffrage by being activists in their own behalf." The 1870 decision was not merely a case of women being given the right to vote but of their winning that right through their own efforts. Those actions were part of a tradition of political activity, thoughtful debate about gender definition, and continued efforts to widen women's traditional roles that began almost with the founding of the Mormon church in 1830.

Lola Van Wagenen, "In Their Own Behalf: The Politicization of Mormon Women and the 1870 Franchise," *Dialogue: A Journal of Mormon Thought* 24 (Winter 1991): 31–43. Reprinted by permission of the publisher and the author.

Lola Van Wagenen has a Ph.D. in history from New York University.

IMMEDIATELY UPON THE PASSAGE of territorial legislation enfranchising Utah's women in 1870, almost fifty years before the Nineteenth Amendment extended the vote to American women, arguments erupted between the Mormon and non-Mormon community over the reasons behind this legislation. Since that time, historians have continued to disagree about the motives of the Mormon-dominated legislature. Some dismiss this early woman suffrage in Utah as a fluke; others believe Mormon women were passive recipients of the vote or pawns of the male leadership. Still others are convinced the act was progressive, the result of a generally egalitarian ideology.[1]

Amidst this array of opinions, it is somewhat surprising to find that what has been overlooked is the possibility that Mormon women themselves had a role in securing their suffrage. This oversight is no doubt due in part to the fact that Mormon women did not publicly draft petitions, nor did they hold public demonstrations to seek enfranchisement. As a result, many historians have concluded that they were not politically active until after suffrage, and then only in response to attempts to disfranchise them.[2] Had these scholars studied the actions of Mormon women within their church, a different view might have emerged.

There is ample evidence that Mormon women were not disinterested recipients of the vote. Their reaction to enfranchisement readily demonstrates their involvement. Moreover, they had *not* been politicized overnight: many were well prepared in 1870 to assume an active political role in their communities (Scott 1986–87). Both their religious and community activities politicized Mormon women and helped lead to the 1870 franchise. Although Mormon women did not openly seek suffrage, I believe they were activists in their own behalf, and their actions contributed to their enfranchisement. The record also shows that Mormon women were not totally isolated in faraway Utah. They engaged many of the same problems and sought similar solutions as did women's advocates in the States.

For Mormon women, 1870 signaled the end of a politicization that had begun in the 1840s and the beginning of a visible and aggressive political activism. This process occurred in three stages. The first began in Nauvoo, where some Mormon women were taught that all the doctrines of the restored gospel, including polygamy, signaled a new era for women. Promised equality and privileges greater than they had ever known, women partici-

[1]Eleanor Flexner notes a difference between Mormon and non-Mormon interpretations of this event. Mormon historians, she states, see the enfranchisement as the "logical extension of an egalitarian attitude toward women basic to the Mormon creed." But to Flexner, a non-Mormon, woman suffrage was an interplay of other forces, the most significant being the need of the hierarchy to "enlist the help of women" against the passage of anti-polygamy legislation (1959, 165). In contrast, non-Mormon historians Mari Jo Buhle and Paul Buhle see woman suffrage in Utah as the act of a "progressive Mormon hierarchy" (1978, introduction); likewise Mormon historian Thomas Alexander states that woman suffrage was a reflection of "progressive sentiment in advance of the rest of the nation" (1970, 38), while another Mormon historian, Richard Van Wagoner, sees the activities of Mormon women as "orchestrated by the Mormon hierarchy" (1986, 109). Beverly Beeton concludes that Mormon women are "pawns" (1986, 37), and Anne F. Scott sees woman suffrage as "to some extent a gift from the male hierarchy" (1986–87, 10). Today, as in other aspects of Mormon history, the old line between Mormon and non-Mormon interpretations is becoming increasingly blurred.

[2]Several sources suggest but do not develop the idea of women's activism. See Arrington in *Brigham Young* (New York: Alfred A. Knopf, 1985, 364–5). Maureen Ursenbach Beecher, Carol Cornwall Madsen, and Jill Mulvay Derr, "The Latter-day Saints and Women's Rights, 1870–1920: A Brief Survey," *Task Papers in LDS History,* No. 29 (Salt Lake City: Historical Department of the Church of Jesus Christ of Latter-day Saints, 1979). Edward Tullidge, *Woman of Mormondom* (1877; Salt Lake City, 1975) states that women worked for passage but does not document the statement.

pated in Church governance through the "religious franchise," the Church's method of voting (Cannon 1869; Gates n.d.; Gates and Widtsoe 1928, 7–9).

Clear evidence of a new era was most expressly manifest by the founding of the Female Relief Society of Nauvoo in 1842. Sarah Kimball is credited with the original idea for the society, although the Prophet Joseph Smith blessed and sanctified the organization (Derr 1987; Crocheron 1884, 27; Derr 1976; Jenson 1901, 4:373). The Relief Society helped the sisters develop many of the same skills other American women were learning in similar benevolent associations (see Berg 1978). But in addition, Mormon women took their first united political action when they drafted—and delivered—a petition to the governor of Illinois seeking protection for the community of Nauvoo.[3] Sarah Kimball later claimed that when the Relief Society was established, "the sure foundations of the suffrage cause were deeply and permanently laid" (1892). In the upheaval following the death of Joseph Smith, the Relief Society was temporarily disbanded by Brigham Young. The Mormon sisters, however, resented giving up their organization and were firm in their conviction that they had specific powers in relationship to it. Angered by these assertions, Brigham Young lashed out saying, "When I want Sisters or the Wives of the members of the church to get up Relief Society I will summon them to my aid but until that time let them stay at home & if you see Females huddling together veto the concern and if they say Joseph started it tell them it is a damned lie for I know he never encouraged it" (in Derr 1987, 163).

The women, however, were steadfast in their belief that the Society was rightfully their own organization. They frequently asserted their convictions by quoting Joseph Smith's promise: "I now turn the key to you in the name of God and this Society shall rejoice and knowledge and intelligence shall flow down from this time" (Minutes, Nauvoo, 28 April 1842). The activism that Mormon women initiated in Nauvoo established a pattern of participation that defined the first critical stage of their process of politicization. By the time the Saints were forced to leave Nauvoo, an inchoate sisterhood had emerged, one that quickened on the Great Plains. Survival on the westward trek dictated cooperation among Mormon women, and many learned through that ordeal and what followed both leadership and independence.

The second stage of politicization dates from the Saints' 1847 arrival in the Great Basin to the end of the Civil War. It was a time of severe stress for Mormon women. Plural marriage, combined with the frequent calling of males on Church missions, left many women alone to provide materially and emotionally for the welfare of their families. In addition, Leonard Arrington has described this era as marked by "harsh hyperbole, offensive rhetoric and militant posturing" on the part of Brigham Young and federal

[3]Several hundred Mormon women signed the petition, which Emma Smith and other women then took to the governor. Joseph Smith attended a Relief Society meeting in August of 1842 and thanked the women for having taken "the most active part" in his defense ("Minutes," Nauvoo, Aug. 1842; Crocheron 1884, 3; Newel and Avery 1984, 127).

officials. The passage of the 1862 Anti-bigamy Act reinforced the national attitudes toward Mormons and polygamy (Arrington, 1985, 300). When that rhetoric was directed toward Mormon women, it appears, at best, insensitive and at worst anti-female (Evans 1980, 13). These were difficult years for Sarah Kimball, who taught school for several years under "very trying circumstances" and, according to an early biography, became "even more than ever convinced" of the need to change working conditions for women who were in competition with men. She saw "no other method that could be so effectual as the elective franchise" (Jenson 1901, 4:190). It is not clear, however, how broadly her sentiments were shared.

In spite of these difficulties and constraints, Mormon women continued their organizational efforts. They established a Female Council of Health in 1851 to discuss personal health matters and were active participants in the Polysophical Society, a western version of the lyceum which sponsored lectures by visiting scholars or dignitaries. Finally, on women's initiative, between 1847 and 1856, various forms of the Relief Society made brief reappearances in a decentralized and ad hoc form (Jensen 1983; Naisbitt 1899; Beecher 1975, 1). Throughout this second stage, 1847–65, women participated in various public efforts to help their own poor as well as Native Americans in the territory and promoted the health and well-being of other women. In these efforts, they learned to move forward carefully enough to avoid problems, but forcefully enough to break new ground.

The third stage of politicization ran from 1865 to the end of the decade. Though benign, the Utah War had been expensive for the Saints, and anti-Mormon sentiment was on the rise. Realizing that he had to find a less combative way to deal with the national government, Brigham Young began reassessing past economic policies and renewed an emphasis on cooperative efforts, including home manufacturing. In this climate, Mormon women worked for the permanent reestablishment of the Relief Society. Eliza R. Snow, President Young's most trusted female counsel, was not officially set apart as president of the "sisterhood" until 1880 but was authorized to reorganize the Relief Society in 1867 (Derr 1987, 172). "The time had come," she stated, "for the sisters to act in a wider sphere" (Minutes 1867).

While each ward Relief Society was officially under the "guidance" of the bishop, programs and priorities reflected the counsel of Eliza R. Snow and the vision of individual ward presidents. In the Salt Lake City Fifteenth Ward, Sarah Kimball was determined to prove that women could contribute economically to the community. She tenaciously promoted home manufacturing, which included a variety of homecrafts such as straw hats and handmade gloves as well as food items, and the construction of a storehouse financed, owned, and operated by women (Minutes 4 Jan., 15 Feb., 18 June, 16 July, 14 Aug. 1868). Her statement when the Salt Lake City Fifteenth Ward chapel's cornerstone was laid indicates her support for women's economic independence: "A woman's allotted sphere of labor is not sufficiently extensive and varied to enable her to exercise all [her] God-given powers . . . nor are her labors made sufficiently remunerative to afford her that independence compatible with true womanly dignity" (Minutes 12 Nov. 1868).

Whether Kimball, Snow, and others saw economic independence as a step toward political activity is unclear. However, Kimball thought it right for women to be independent, but she was careful not to appear *too* autonomous. Programs were always approved by local male authorities. Eliza Snow also promoted programs of self-improvement and instructed the sisters that the time would come "when we will have to be in large places and act in responsible situations" (Minutes 25 April 1868). At the same time, she consistently reminded women of their duty as wives and mothers and of the importance of obedience. Nevertheless, the practical experience in domestic commercial enterprises, the commitment to self-improvement, and the constant affirmation of their spiritual powers had produced a vibrant sense of sisterhood. The Relief Society provided a sanctioned setting in which to discuss women's rights and responsibilities.

By 1869, the success of various Relief Society efforts was gaining public attention in Zion—many men who had been skeptical began praising the women's accomplishments. Among the women, pride and growing self-esteem were palpable. Change was aloft in the community of Mormon women. As an example, in the past when they were portrayed in anti-polygamy attacks as degraded victims, Mormon women had chosen not to respond; now increasingly they came to their own defense.

Ironically, finding a way to end polygamy was the motivation behind the earliest proposal to enfranchise Utah's women. The underlying assumption among non-Mormons was that Mormon women would vote to end polygamy. This tactic was suggested by the *New York Times* in 1867 (reprint, *Deseret News,* 15 Jan. 1867; Beeton 1986, x)[4] and was subsequently introduced as a bill in the United States Congress. To the surprise of the bill's sponsors, both Utah's territorial representative and the press in Utah received the proposal favorably; as a result it was subsequently abandoned. But from this time forward, the issue of woman suffrage was increasingly discussed in the territory—by women as well as men.

January 1870 signaled a turning point in the politicization of Mormon women. They had strengthened the position of their most valuable activist organization, the Relief Society. Widening their sphere of activity, they had thoughtfully debated women's roles. Their gender consciousness appears clear. They had moved into a highly visible public arena that they energetically sustained for the rest of the century.

Two events mark 1870 as a watershed in the history of Mormon women and political activism. First, in early January three thousand women gathered in a "great indignation meeting" to protest anti-polygamy legislation introduced in the national Congress. Then in February, acting Governor

[4]Gary Bunker and Carol Bunker note that the first suggestion that woman suffrage could be an "antidote" to polygamy came from William Ray in 1856 (1991, 33).

S. A. Mann, a non-Mormon, signed the woman suffrage bill passed by the territorial legislature. The circumstances surrounding these events show Mormon women as outspoken public activists in their own behalf.

The arrival in the territory in December 1869 of a new anti-polygamy bill, the Cullom Act, propelled Mormon women into political activism. Among other things, the Cullom Bill stipulated that anyone believing in polygamy would be denied the right to vote or serve on a jury. Though the Saints no doubt knew the bill had been introduced in Congress, seeing it in print must have been a shock—both the substance and language were outrageous and insulting. In fact, a number of non-Mormons found the bill offensive and spoke against its passage (*Deseret News,* 9 March 1870).

Mormon women were especially outraged, which was nothing new, but now their response was boldly public. They called for a meeting 6 January to plan a women's public protest; in probability it was approved by Church leaders.[5] Sarah Kimball opened the discussion stating, "Mormon women would be unworthy of the names we bear or of the blood in our veins, should we longer remain silent." Eliza Snow added that it was "high time" for Mormon women to "rise up in the dignity of our calling and speak for ourselves." The group voted unanimously to hold a protest, and a committee drafted resolutions. After the resolutions were read and approved, the meeting took an even more aggressive turn. Bathsheba Smith stated that she was pleased with the actions thus far, then moved "that we demand of the Gov. the right of franchise." The women voted, and the "vote carried." Then Lucy W. Kimball, stating that "we had borne in silence as long as it was our duty to bear," moved that the women "be represented in Washington." Eliza Snow and Sarah Kimball were "elected as representatives" (Minutes, 19 Feb. 1870).

In response to such bold action, one might have expected newspaper headlines the next day to have read "Women to Seek Franchise from Utah Governor," or "Snow and Kimball Elected to Represent Mormon Women in Washington." Instead *five* days later, the *Deseret News* headline read, "Minutes of Ladies Mass Meeting." The article, which included the comments by Sarah Kimball and Eliza Snow as well as a full copy of the protest resolution, blandly concluded: "Miss E. R. Snow, Mrs. L. W. Kimball and Mrs. B. Smith made a few very appropriate remarks expressing their hearty concurrence in the movement and in the measures adopted by the meeting." The article was signed by Sarah Kimball.[6] It fails to mention both the mo-

[5]The *Deseret News* 9 March 1870. Sixteen years later, in 1886, Mormon women requested permission from President John Taylor to hold a similar meeting (Kimball, Pratt, and Horne 1886).

[6]Two different essays by historians report on this part of the meeting, but neither refers to a vote on the suffrage motion or to Lucy W. Kimball's motion. Beverly Beeton states: "A 'Sister Smith' even demanded of the governor that women be allowed to vote. At the close of the meeting Eliza Snow . . . " (1986, 31). Reported in this way, what happened becomes only one insignificant woman demanding the vote, rather than a motion made and passed by the whole Society. Maureen Ursenbach Beecher, Carol Cornwall Madsen, and Jill Mulvay Derr state: "Later in the meeting one Sister Smith rose to move that 'we demand of the governor the right

tion to seek the franchise and Eliza Snow's and Sarah Kimball's election as representatives to Washington.

This represents a fascinating editorial decision. While the organizing meeting minutes show solid evidence of the quickening political behavior of Mormon women, excluding both motions from the public record obscured their efforts from immediate public (and eventual historical) scrutiny. There are several possible reasons for the omission. The sisters themselves may have worried about appearing too aggressive or about using the Relief Society for their own agenda—accusations that had been leveled at Emma Smith in Nauvoo—thereby endangering the position of the Relief Society; or the women may have wanted to discuss their resolutions with the Brethren before announcing them publicly. The discrepancy may also show one reason why Mormon women's political activities are so difficult to trace: the women were more interested in being effective than visual. A low profile may have been critical to their success, and they knew it. Clearly, however, Mormon women had been talking privately about suffrage, and prior to their enfranchisement they were trying to do something about it.

Another possible reason for not publicizing their 6 January action on woman suffrage was the immediately upcoming mass protest meeting, which needed planning. This "Great Indignation Meeting," held 13 January 1870, brought three thousand women to the Salt Lake Tabernacle to hear the "leading sisters" of the Church speak from its pulpit for the first time. Though the meeting's stated agenda was to protest the Cullom anti-polygamy bill, proceedings indicate that some Mormon women had come to see polygamy as a women's rights issue. Although nine of the fourteen recorded speakers spoke directly to the defense of polygamy without raising the issue of women's rights or suffrage, five did broach the topic. In a surprising opening remark, Sarah Kimball stated, "We are not here to advocate woman's rights but man's rights" (*Deseret News,* 14 Jan. 1870). The 8 February *New York Times* picked right up on her statement: "One of the speakers declared they had not met to agitate for "women's rights" but "men's rights"; as did the *New York Herald:* "In these days when women threaten to become tyrants, it is refreshing to read such earnest pleadings in favor of the rights of men" (in *Deseret News,* 16 Feb. 1870). Those anxious about the danger of "strong-minded" women would undoubtedly be reassured by Kimball's comment. Most likely, that was her intent. She did not, however, overlook women's interests. She ended her speech, noting that not only would the legislation "deprive our fathers, husbands and brothers" of their constitutional privileges, but "would also deprive us, as women, of the privilege of selecting our husbands, and against *this* we most unqualifiedly protest" (*Deseret News,* 14 Jan. 1870, emphasis added).

Ultimately the protest served a number of purposes. Mormon women at last had a chance to show the outside world that they were articulate

---

of franchise.' Whether the motion carried or not, and whether or not the demand reached the legislature is not known" (1979, 10).

and willing to defend their beliefs. The newspaper coverage was perhaps the most positive account ever given of Mormon women, and that reflected well on the whole community. The *Ogden Junction* on 23 March commented, "If the Cragin and Cullom legislative burlesques have no other good effect, they have drawn out the ladies of Utah from silence and obscurity, exhibited them before the world as women of thought, force and ability, who are able to make strong resolutions and defend them with boldness and eloquence."

The anti-polygamy campaign had unintended consequences for Mormon women as well. The protest meeting proved to Mormon men that the women could organize a successful public demonstration and could be, in a "wider sphere" of action, a valuable asset "to the cause of Zion." Mormon men could only applaud the women's public defense of polygamy. The women would not be accused of acting outside their appropriate sphere; defending polygamy became a sanctioned mechanism by which women increased their public participation.

Only four months before the meeting, Brigham Young had commented that he wished more women would assume their rights: "the right to stop all folly in [their] conversation" and "the right to ask their husbands to fix up the front yard" (JD 14:105; Evans 1980, 13). Obviously he was not grappling seriously with woman's rights or suffrage. However, almost immediately following the protest meeting, attitudes changed; male Church leaders moved in support of woman suffrage. Historian Leonard Arrington asserts that in the "aftermath" of the meeting, Brigham and other Mormon leaders—both men and women—decided it would be helpful if the Utah legislature should pass an act granting woman suffrage" (1985, 364). By 12 February the territorial legislature had passed the woman suffrage legislation. Women actively lobbied acting governor S. A. Mann, and, a week later he signed the bill into law (Arrington 1985, 365).

At a subsequent meeting on 19 February at the Salt Lake City Fifteenth Ward, Eliza Snow suggested a committee draft an "expression of gratitude" to the acting governor (Minutes 19 Feb. 1870).[7] That task completed, the meeting became a "feast of woman's anticipations" (Tullidge 1877, 502). If this group shared a single political perception, it was that they had entered a new phase in the "era of women." Several speakers expressed their pleasure in gaining the vote, which they referred to as the "reform." Prescenda Kimball said she was "glad to see our daughters elevated with man," while Bathsheba Smith "believed that woman was coming up in the world." Other women expressed words of caution. Margaret Smoot said that she "never had any desire for more rights," that she had considered "politics aside from the sphere of woman." But Wilmarth East disagreed. "I cannot agree with Sister Smoot in regard to woman's rights," she declared, adding that she had always wanted "a voice in the politics of the nation, as well as to rear a family." Phebe Woodruff said she had "looked for this day for years. . . . [The] yoke on woman is partly removed," she noted, adding "Let us lay it by, and wait till the time comes to use it, and not run headlong and abuse the privilege" (Minutes 19 Feb. 1870).

For Sarah Kimball, however, suffrage was a turning point. She told the women that she had "waited patiently a long time, and now that we were granted the right of suffrage, she would openly declare herself a woman's right's woman." She then "called upon those who would do so to back her up, whereupon many manifested their approval" (Minutes 19 Feb. 1870). These are not the words of a woman who had been recently politicized. Moreover, the rights she was referring to were not religious rights, but the secular rights of women: political, economic, and social. It is hardly surprising that some women at the meeting were unready to "manifest their approval" and "back up" Sarah Kimball on woman's rights. Declaring oneself a "woman's rights woman" was no doubt a bold move for any woman. The implication is that Kimball now allied herself with the more militant American suffragists. The statement was so daring, in fact, that Sarah Kimball waited until after suffrage was granted to declare herself publicly.

Woman suffrage refocused the political activity of Mormon women. No sooner were they enfranchised than the outside world moved to disfranchise them. For the rest of the century, they were defenders of their own suffrage and were joined in that defense by many woman suffrage activists from the States. In turn, Mormon women were activists for the passage of woman suffrage for all women and were outspoken defenders of woman's rights. The degree of help that Mormon women received in return was uneven. Anti-polygamy activists tried to dissuade national suffrage advocates from defending woman suffrage in Utah, claiming that it only reinforced the power of the Mormon church and the strength of polygamy. As a result, support for Mormon women waxed and waned at various times for twenty-five years, and it differed between woman suffrage organizations and among individual suffragists.

Despite the efforts of many national and local advocates of women suffrage, in 1887 all women in Utah were disfranchised by a federal law designed to destroy polygamy and to reduce the political and economic power of the Church. Three years later the Mormons officially discontinued plural marriage and began a vigorous campaign to secularize political life and to secure statehood. In 1895 woman suffrage was vigorously debated during the constitutional convention, and despite fears that its inclusion might damage the bid for statehood, its advocates prevailed.

A month later national suffrage leaders, including a vigorous but aging Susan B. Anthony, were on hand to celebrate the victory with their sister-suffragists in Utah. In a tribute to Anthony, Sarah Kimball discussed the dif-

[7]The 23 February *Deseret News* reported that after the meeting, a committee took the letter of thanks to the governor, who told the women "that the subject has been much agitated . . . [and] will be watched with profound interest." He hoped, he added, that "the women would act so as to prove the wisdom of the legislation." According to George A. Smith, "the ladies said they thought the Governor was about as much embarrassed as they were" (1870).

ficulty of the early years of the woman suffrage movement in Utah. She said that when she first read Anthony's publication the "Revolution" (1869), she would not have "dared to say the bold, grand things that Miss Anthony said. . . . That," she states, would have made her "so unpopular," she would have hardly "dared to shoulder it." She continued, "As time rolled on we were very careful" ("Conference" 1895).

If a single word could describe the operative mode for Mormon women, it would be "careful." They consistently guarded their words and actions to make sure the hierarchy never felt threatened or interpreted the women's goals as inconsistent with the goals of the Church. But the women tenaciously defended their right to participate in the political process. They knew that success was essential, but it was equally critical to succeed in the right way. A year after they were enfranchised, the leading sisters wrote a circular stating that "God through His servants had conferred on us the right of franchise for a wise purpose. This privilege has been granted without our solicitation, and in this as well as in many other respects, we realize that women in Utah possess advantages greatly superior to women elsewhere" (Gates n.d.). The document is a good example of the careful way Mormon women operated. They bypass credit, express their gratitude, and yet secure their continuing activity, in this instance by claiming divine purpose for their enfranchisement. By deflecting credit for their achievements, however, Mormon women themselves contributed to the illusion that they were not agents in their own behalf. Hiding their agency was not uncommon for other nineteenth-century women, and it is not uncommon today. But it is one reason their political activism prior to 1870 has been overlooked.

Mormon women helped gain suffrage by being activists in their own behalf. Suffrage was not granted women in 1870 because of an overwhelming egalitarian impulse on the part of the Brethren; rather the usual pragmatic decision-making process was at work. Four months before women were enfranchised, the male leadership was still undecided about the wisdom of woman suffrage.[8] The women of Utah appear to have been enfranchised only after they had proved their potential for political usefulness. And, in fact, Mormon women did much to buffer growing criticism of the Church and of polygamy by securing the support of many non-Mormon suffragists and by presenting to the American public an alternative vision of Mormon womanhood. Between 1870 and 1890, Mormon women defended plural marriage as a First Amendment right and woman's rights issue, but they also continued to agitate for woman suffrage after polygamy was no longer a central issue. In 1895 when woman suffrage was restored, support for woman's political equality in Utah, while not unanimous, clearly was broadly based. Thus the advocacy of woman suffrage was more than just expedient.

[8]For comments showing a lack of resolve on woman suffrage from both George Q. Cannon and Brigham Young, see *Deseret News,* 6 August 1869, and the *JD* 14:105.

By the time women in Utah were reenfranchised, Mormon suffragists had earned the respect and friendship of many of their sister-suffragists, even though they steadfastly maintained the divinity of their church and continued to sustain and obey its male leaders. But apart from religious issues, when it came to political, economic, and social rights of women, Mormon women were, as Sarah Kimball would have said, "heart and hand" with the female activists of the world.

REFERENCES

Alexander, Thomas. "An Experiment in Progressive Legislation: The Granting of Woman Suffrage in 1870." *Utah Historical Quarterly* 38, no.1 (1970): 20–30.

Arrington, Leonard. *Brigham Young: American Moses*. Alfred A. Knopf, 1985.

Beecher, Maureen Ursenbach. "Three Women and the Life of the Mind." Utah Historical Quarterly 43, no. 1 (1975): 26–40.

Beecher, Maureen Ursenbach, Carol Cornwall Madsen, and Jill Mulvay Derr. "The Latter Day Saints and Women's Rights. 1870–1920: A Brief History." *Task Papers in LDS History,* no. 29. Salt Lake City: Historical Department of the Church of Jesus Christ of Latter-Day Saints, 1975.

Beeton, Beverly. *Women Vote in the West: The Woman Suffrage Movement, 1869–1896*. New York & London: Garland Publishing Outstanding Dissertation Series, 1986.

Berg, Barbara J. *The Remembered Gate: Origins of American Feminism*. New York: Oxford University Press, 1978.

Buhle, Mari Jo, and Paul Buhle. *The Concise History of Woman Suffrage*. Urbana: University of Illinois Press, 1978.

Bunker, Gary L., and Carol B. Bunker. "Woman Suffrage. Popular Art, and Utah." *Utah Historical Quarterly* 59 (Winter 1991): 32–51.

Cannon, George Q. Untitled article. *Deseret News*, 6 August 1869.

"Conference N.A.W.S.A. . . . May 13 and 14, 1895." *Woman's Exponent* 15 August 1895.

Crocheron, Augusta Joyce. *Representative Women of Deseret*. Salt Lake City: J. C. Graham and Co., 1884.

Derr, Jill Mulvay. "'Strength in Our Union': The Making of Mormon Sisterhood." In *Sisters in Spirit*, edited by Maureen Ursenbach Beecher and Lavina Fielding Anderson, 153–207. Chicago: University of Illinois Press, 1987.

———. "The Liberal Shall Be Blessed: Sarah M. Kimball." *Utah Historical Quarterly* 44 (Summer 1976): 205–21.

Evans, Vella. "Woman's Role and Pioneer Mormon Rhetoric." Unpublished paper presented at the University of Utah, 1980. Copy in possession of the author.

Flexner, Eleanor. *A Century of Struggle*. Cambridge, Mass.: Harvard University Press, 1959.

Gates, Susa Young. Susa Young Gates Collection, Box 17, Manuscript Collection, Utah State Historical Society, Salt Lake City, Utah.

Gates, Susa Young, and Leah D. Widtsoe. *Women of the "Mormon" Church*. Independence, Mo.: Press of Zions Printing and Publishing Co., 1928.

JD. *Journal of Discourses*. 26 vols. Liverpool and London: LDS Booksellers, 1855–86.

Jensen, Richard L. "Forgotten Relief Societies, 1844–67." *Dialogue* 16 (Spring 1983): 105–25.

Jenson, Andrew. *Latter-day Saint Biographical Encyclopedia*. 4 vols. Salt Lake City: The Andrew Jenson History Company, 1901.

Kimball, Sarah M., *Woman Suffrage Leaflet*. Salt Lake City: n.p., 1892. LDS Church Archives.

Kimball, Sarah M., R.B. Pratt, and Mrs. Horne. Letter to President John Taylor, 20 February 1886. John Taylor Letterbooks, Special Collections, Marriott Library, University of Utah, Salt Lake City, Utah.

Minutes. Female Relief Society of Nauvoo. Photocopy in my possession, courtesy of Maureen Beecher. Original in LDS Church archives.

Minutes, Salt Lake City Eighth Ward Female Relief Society, 16 December 1867. LDS Church Archives.

Minutes. Salt Lake City Fifteenth Ward Female Relief Society, 4 January, 15 February, 18 June, 16 July, 14 August, 12 November 1868; 19 February 1870. LDS Church Archives.

Minutes. Salt Lake City Thirteenth Ward Female Relief Society, 25 April 1868. LDS Church Archives.

Naisbitt, Henry W. "'Polysophical' and 'Mutual.'" *Improvement Era* 2 (1899): 745.

Newell, Linda King, and ValeenTippets Avery. *Mormon Enigma: Emma Hale Smith*. Chicago: University of Chicago Press, 1984.

Scott, Anne F. "Mormon Women, Other Women." *The Journal of Mormon History* 13 (1986-87): 3–19.

Smith, George A. Letter to Wm. Hooper, 19 February 1870. Copybooks. LDS Church Archives.

Tullidge, Edward. *The Women of Mormondom*. Salt Lake City: Tullidge and Crandall, 1877.

Van Wagoner, Richard. *Mormon Polygamy: A History*. Salt Lake City: Signature Books, 1986.

*

The Buffalo Soldiers: Guardians of the Uintah Frontier, 1886–1901

RONALD G. COLEMAN

African-Americans have been in Utah since before white settlement began in 1847, though their experiences have received relatively little attention from historians. As educator Alberta Henry once remarked, when blacks are discussed, mention of them is often relegated to the back of the book, literally or figuratively, just as they once were confined to the back of the bus. The subject of the following essay is the experience of black soldiers in the last decade and a half of the nineteenth century, at the Uinta Basin's Fort Duchesne, where they were stationed with the primary charge of controlling the Native Americans of the area. Of particular interest are the attitudes the soldiers encountered in Utah and the interracial adjustments that took place between them and the local Anglo and Indian populations.

Ronald G. Coleman, "The Buffalo Soldiers: Guardians of the Uintah Frontier, 1886–1901," *Utah Historical Quarterly* 47 (Fall 1979): 421–39. Reprinted by permission of the publisher and the author.

Ronald G. Coleman is the leading historian of the African-American experience in Utah. He has a Ph.D. degree from the University of Utah, where he is a member of the Department of History. He has also been Director of Ethnic Studies and is currently Associate Vice President for Diversity and Faculty Development at the University of Utah.

THERE HAVE BEEN SEVERAL STUDIES on the history of black soldiers in the post–Civil War years.[1] More than one historian has noted their presence at Fort Duchesne, Utah, but none has examined the soldiers' on-duty as well as off-duty activities during their years on the Uintah frontier.[2] The pop-

[1]For examples see Jack D. Foner, *Blacks and the Military in American History* (New York, 1974); William A. Leckie, *The Buffalo Soldiers: A Narrative of the Negro Cavalry in the West* (Norman: University of Oklahoma Press, 1967).

[2]See Marvin Fletcher, *The Black Soldier and Officer in the United States Army, 1891–1917* (Columbia: University of Missouri Press, 1974), p. 80; Thomas G. Alexander and Leonard J.

ulation of this region of eastern Utah was heterogeneous; Native Americans and whites were in substantial numbers. Various companies of soldiers, white and black, were stationed at Fort Duchesne in the last decade and a half of the nineteenth century. White troops were from the Twenty-first and Sixteenth Infantry and the Seventh and Fifth Cavalry, while the black units were all from the Ninth Cavalry. Except for a six-month period in 1898 when the troops were fighting in the Spanish-American War, the post from September 1892 until March 1901 was garrisoned entirely by the Ninth Cavalry's "buffalo soldiers."[3] Black soldiers at Fort Duchesne gave Uintah County the second largest black population in Utah from 1890 until early in 1901. Thus, the stationing of black troops in the region provides an example of interracial adjustments on the western frontier.[4]

With the exception of racial antipathy from Indians and whites, the experiences of black soldiers there and in other western stations were similar to those of white soldiers. Black troops were used to subdue and control Native Americans. They assisted in quelling disputes among whites, protecting stage and railway lines, building and maintaining military posts, opening and clearing roads, and seeing to the general well-being of frontier settlers. All military units practiced their skills in horsemanship, marching, and marksmanship. Drill exercises, inspections, and annual marches kept the men in a state of preparedness. Black troops, like their white counterparts, performed ceremonial duties, such as participating in parades and serving as honor guards at Memorial Day observances.[5]

OPPOSITION FROM THE UTES

Reports of conflict among the White River, Uncompahgre, and Uintah bands of Ute Indians, the Utes' lack of respect for government employees, and concern for the safety of white settlers had influenced the War Depart-

---

Arrington, "The Utah Military Frontier, 1872–1912, Forts Cameron, Thornburgh, and Duchesne," *Utah Historical Quarterly* 32 (1964): 344–52.

[3]Returns from United States Military Posts, Fort Duchesne, 1886–1902. Microfilm copies of the holograph post returns are available at the Marriott Library, University of Utah.

Some claim the term "buffalo soldiers" originated when Native Americans first came in contact with black soldiers. One story says the term started when black troops serving in the northern plains area started wearing buffalo hides as overcoats on cold winter marches. The black faces peering from the hides resembled the buffalo. Another story says the name was given by Native Americans to black troops because of the similarity between the hair of black soldiers and the mane of the buffalo. Noting that the buffalo was sacred to the Indians, historian William Leckie says: " . . . it is unlikely that he would so name an enemy if respect were lacking." At times the term applied to all black soldiers but was more often associated with the cavalry units. The men of the Tenth Cavalry had a regimental coat of arms with the head of the buffalo for an insignia. John M. Carroll, ed., *The Black Military Experience in the American West* (New York, 1973), pp. 179–80; Leckie, *Buffalo Soldiers,* pp. 25–26.

[4] In 1890 there were 127 blacks in Uintah County; by 1900 the population had increased to 214. See George Ramjoue, "The Negro in Utah: A Geographical Study in Population" (M.A. thesis, University of Utah, 1968), pp. 9–10, 12.

[5]Fletcher, *The Black Soldier and Officer,* pp. 80–82, 85–90; Arlen L. Fowler, *The Black Infantry in the West, 1869–1891* (Westport, Conn.: Greenwood Press, 1971), pp. 10–11.

ment to build a military post on the Uintah frontier in 1886.[6] A site was selected between the Indian agencies of Whiterocks and Ouray on the Uinta River, approximately eight miles above its confluence with the Duchesne River. Troops B and E of the Ninth Cavalry under the command of Maj. Frederick W. Benteen were sent from Fort McKinney, Wyoming, to join four companies of the white Twenty-first Infantry from Fort Steele, Wyoming, and Fort Sidney, Nebraska, for duty at the new post.[7]

The Utes were disgruntled over the decision to build a military post in their midst. A few white men circulated rumors among the Indians that the soldiers were coming to kill several of the Ute chiefs, place others under arrest, and remove the remaining Utes to another area, following which the reservation lands would be given to settlers. The white men urged the Utes to drive all the whites away from Uintah and Ouray, take whatever beef and supplies they wanted, and then attack the soldiers in the canyons. Spurred by the rumors, some Uintah Utes joined the Uncompahgre and White River bands. Women and children were sent to the mountains and the men prepared for war.

Several Uintah chiefs rode to the Uintah Agency in Whiterocks and told special Indian agent Eugene E. White of the impending crisis. White called for a council the following day with all of the White River and Uintah Utes and also asked that an invitation be sent to the Uncompahgres for a council in Ouray the day after that. The Utes agreed to hear White in council.[8]

In the meetings with the Ute bands, White sought to allay their fears concerning the soldiers. They were not, he told them, a threat to the Utes as long as the Indians behaved themselves. An attack on the soldiers by Ute warriors would only bring more soldiers, and eventually the Utes would be subdued and removed from their land. White told the Ute bands that their alleged white friends wanted their land and knew it would become available if the Utes initiated an attack against the United States Army. As an example of what would happen to the Utes if they attacked the soldiers, White pointed out that Geronimo, the Apache chief, had been relentlessly pursued by the army, captured, and sent to Florida where he was away from his people and probably plagued by mosquitoes and alligators.[9]

White asked the Utes for help in keeping peace and suggested that they return their women and children from the mountains. He promised to arrest the whites who had circulated the rumors if they came on the reservation again and admonished the Utes to put away their weapons except

[6]Alexander and Arrington, "The Utah Military Frontier," pp. 343–44; Floyd A. O'Neil, "A History of the Ute Indians of Utah until 1890" (Ph.D. diss., University of Utah, 1973), pp. 171–75.

[7]Alexander and Arrington, "The Utah Military Frontier," pp. 344–46; Special Post Return, Fort Duchesne, August 24, 1886; Post Return, Fort Duchesne, August, 1886; *Provo Sunday Herald,* March 14, 1954.

[8]E. E. White, *Experiences of a Special Indian Agent* (Norman: University of Oklahoma Press, 1965), pp. 122–31, 145–46.

[9]Ibid., pp. 134–39.

when hunting game and to behave "like sensible men." The Utes accepted White's counsel and Chief Sowawick of the White River band said, "If the soldiers want to sit down on the Reservation, all right—just so they do not try to hurt us without cause or take our country away from us."

Apparently, the Utes had assumed that all of the soldiers stationed at Fort Duchesne would be white men. As agent White returned to Uintah from his council with the Uncompahgre he was met by five fast-riding Utes coming from Uintah, among them an old headman named Sour who shouted excitedly:

> Buffalo soldiers! Buffalo soldiers! Coming. Maybe so tomorrow. Indians saw them at Burnt Fort yesterday, coming this way. Don't let them come! We can't stand it! It's bad very bad! . . . You did not tell us that buffalo soldiers were coming, and we did not agree for them to come. We did not think about them at all. Our arrangement applies only to white soldiers. That is all right. We told you they might come, and they may. But all the Indians want you to come back quick and send them back. We cannot stand for them to come on our Reservation. It is too bad. . . .

Leaping from his pony, Sour rushed up to White's buggy, grabbed White's black coat sleeve, and rubbing it over his (Sour's) hand and face, exclaimed, " . . . All over black! All over black, buffalo soldiers! Injun heap no like him!!" With a jerk of his hand, the old man then rubbed his head all over and shouted, "Wooly head! Wooly head! All same as buffalo! What you call him, black white man? NIGGER! NIGGER!"[10]

White was surprised to learn of the Utes' dislike for the black soldiers. He tried to mitigate Sour's fears by telling him that the leaders of the black soldiers were white men. He promised Sour that the black soldiers would conduct themselves honorably. Somewhat relieved, "Sour agreed that they might come and gave . . . his word that he would hurry back and satisfy all the Indians." Upon returning to the agency, White learned "that Sour's excitement had been shared by the entire tribe." He was told:

> The Utes had a strange and irreconcilable antipathy to negroes. Up to that time they had never suffered one to live on their Reservation. Several had dropped in among them from time to time in the past, but only to soon disappear and never be heard of again.

When the four companies of the Twenty-first Infantry arrived to establish the post, the Indians gathered at several high points and with anxiety watched the men organize the camp or "sit down" as the Utes called it. The next day Major Benteen and approximately seventy-five buffalo soldiers arrived, increasing the military personnel to nearly two hundred fifty men.[11]

On August 23, 1886, Fort Duchesne was officially established.[12] The Utes harangued agent White, several of them intimating a violent confronta-

[10]Ibid., pp. 139, 141, 146–47, 147–48.

[11]Ibid., pp. 148, 149.

[12]Post Return, Fort Duchesne, August 1886.

tion if the soldiers were not kept within their cantonment area.[13] On the second night following the arrival of the black troops, a commotion spread through Sowawick's village and several camps near the agency. Rumors that the soldiers were coming toward their encampment and that they might be buffalo soldiers ran throughout the reservation. Women and children fled toward the mountains. White left his home to investigate the rumors; puzzled that soldiers would be out at night, he sent a message to Sowawick, asking him to send several of his chiefs to accompany him (White) to discover the facts. The party left the agency and rode toward Antero's camp, located five miles away in the direction of Fort Duchesne. When they arrived at Antero's they discovered that the camp had been abandoned in haste.

The Utes in the party surmised that the Indians had all been captured by the soldiers. They wanted to return immediately, but the agent suggested they make an inquiry at the garrison. Although apprehensive, the Utes agreed. As they rode toward the post they encountered other Utes who had heard the rumors and were searching for the soldiers. The commanding officer of the post assured White and the Utes that all of the soldiers were present at the fort and that the officers would make sure the men remained orderly.

White returned to the agency and learned that a young herder from Antero's camp had seen a party of Uncompahgres coming from Ouray and in the dark had mistaken them for soldiers. He then ran to the camp and sounded the alarm, thus explaining the hasty abandonment of the camp by Antero and his people.[14] Although clearly a "false alarm," the episode indicates the nervousness in the Indian community caused by the presence of the new troops.

There are two possible explanations, or a combination of the two, that may shed some light on why the Utes showed a greater aversion to black soldiers than to their white counterparts. The buffalo was an important symbol for Plains Indians and figured prominently in their superstitions, taboos, dances, societies, visions, and cures.[15] Perhaps the Northern Utes had a particular fear of black soldiers based upon the similarity of the mane of the buffalo and the "woolylike" hair of many blacks. The second possibility is that the White River Utes remembered that black soldiers had come to the aid of Maj. T. T. Thornburgh in the fall of 1879 during the Battle of Milk River in western Colorado. In that action, Capt. Francis Dodge, who had been commanding a scouting party near Milk River, learned that Thornburgh's command was under siege and led Company D of the Ninth Cavalry to the battle. Thirty-five buffalo soldiers and their officers joined the beleaguered men in trenches at Milk River. The soldiers were able to sustain themselves for three additional days until a large contingent of sol-

[13]White, *Experiences of a Special Indian Agent*, p. 149.

[14]Ibid., pp. 150–57.

[15]Tom McHugh, *The Time of the Buffalo* (New York: Alfred A. Knopf, Inc., 1972), pp. 110–11.

diers from the Fifth Cavalry arrived and forced the Utes to retreat.[16]

The Battle of Milk River, together with the killing of Indian agent Nathan C. Meeker at the White River Agency, influenced the decision to remove the White River Utes as well as the Uncompahgre from their lands in western Colorado to reservations in eastern Utah.[17] There may well have been in the minds of reservation-dwellers an association of blacks with these earlier unhappy events.

Although the Utes did not like having black troops nearby, their initial fears were allayed so that within a few weeks of their arrival the Indians were "harvesting quietly and going about their usual occupations." Commenting on the Utes' attitude toward black soldiers, the post trader said, "the dislike is not sufficient to cause apprehension." Within several years the initial distrust was diminished and the Utes no longer feared coming to the post.[18]

ROUTINE AT THE POST

With the immediate threat of conflict with the Utes abated, the soldiers' attention and efforts were turned to regular garrison duties and the building of the fort. Canvas tents, banked with soil for warmth, were used as temporary housing until more permanent quarters could be built. Each tent also contained a stove.[19]

The daily routine of soldiers throughout the army began with reveille at 5:45 A.M. Following breakfast, the men had a fatigue call at 7:30 A.M., lunch at 12:15 P.M., and a return to fatigue or school for some of the enlisted men and NCOs at 1:00 P.M. At 4:30 fatigue duty ended, and from 4:45 to 5:15 P.M. the men went through drills and had guard mount at 5:30. After dinner the men were free until tattoo at 9:00 P.M. followed by taps. This routine was broken on Sundays and holidays when officers relieved the troops of all but the necessary fatigue and guard duties.[20]

The foods eaten by soldiers were basically the same during the years of the Indian wars: beef or bacon, beans, potatoes, fresh vegetables from the

[16]The Southern Utes did not oppose the presence of blacks. John Taylor, a black man who had served in the Union army, was accepted by the tribe. He married a Ute woman and they had several children. The descendants are recognized and accepted as members of the tribe. This information was given to me by Dr. Floyd O'Neil, an authority on the Ute Indians. For information on the Battle of Milk River, see Carroll, *The Black Military Experience,* pp. 223–43, 381–87.

[17]Alexander and Arrington, "The Utah Military Frontier," pp. 339–40.

[18]*Salt Lake Tribune,* September 12, 1886; *Salt Lake Herald,* June 13, 1897.

[19]Alexander and Arrington, "The Utah Military Frontier," pp. 344–45; Stephen Perry Jocelyn, *Mostly Alkali* (Caldwell, Ida., 1953), pp. 311–12. Capt. Stephen Jocelyn was an officer with the Twenty-first Infantry. He served at Fort Duchesne from 1886 until the spring of 1888. At that time he was transferred to Fort Douglas. His son, Stephen Perry Jocelyn, the author of *Mostly Alkali,* made extensive use of his father's diary in writing the biography.

[20]Fletcher, *The Black Soldier and Officer,* p. 80. Fatigue duty included repairing roads and clearing snowbreaks between the fort and Price as well as between the fort and other points. Details were also sent to work at the sawmill, and there were various jobs within the fort itself. See Post Returns, Fort Duchesne, January 1888, February 1889, March and December 1890.

post garden, fruits, and bread.[21] In the years after the Indian wars some of the food served black regiments was different from that of white regiments and reflected the cultural differences between the races. Mostly the different foods were served on holidays, but at times they were included on the regular menu. A typical menu for a black regiment by 1895 was:

> Breakfast: puffed rice, sugar and cream, stewed beef, baked potatoes, toast, tea or coffee
>
> Lunch: cream of potato soup, oyster crackers, beef pot pie, steamed rice, lima beans, radishes, steamed pudding, vanilla sauce, bread
>
> Dinner: pickled pigs' feet, chile con carne, hot biscuits, butter, syrup, and tea.[22]

The solders' living quarters were typical of most military posts built during that period. In 1890 they were described as being good, except for water leaking in several of the quarters occupied by married men. Bathing facilities at the post were poor. Weather permitting, the soldiers bathed in the nearby "mosquito-infested, rocky-bottomed river." The post surgeon reported that the "lack of bath tubs, lack of conveniences for warming water . . . and lack of privacy makes bathing uncomfortable, so it is frequently neglected."[23]

In anticipation of the coming winter the garrison was a beehive of activity. By the end of October 1886 a sawmill was installed thirty miles north of the post and operated around the clock, cutting lumber obtained from the nearby canyons. A quarry and kiln were also established, and the quarried stone was hauled to the fort. Many soldiers were assigned the duty of improving the road between Fort Duchesne and Price for hauling supplies. Others worked on building a telegraph line between the two points.[24]

New recruits, civilian employees, and a few women increased the garrison's population to approximately three hundred fifty by the end of the autumn. Two or three of the women were black, the wives of soldiers. They supplemented their husbands' income by taking in washing for post residents. Five of the six white women were wives or relatives of military personnel, the sixth was the wife of the post trader.

The winter of 1886–87 was difficult for residents of Fort Duchesne, as well as for settlers throughout the West. The temperature often fell to twenty degrees below zero or lower. The continual winds blew sand into the tents from all directions. Despite the harshness of the weather the garrison was relatively free of sickness, and as spring approached construction of the post resumed. Building plans called for construction of a hospital, commis-

[21]Carroll, *The Black Military Experience,* p. 178.

[22]Fletcher, *The Black Soldier and Officer,* p. 80.

[23]Herbert M. Hart, *Old Forts of the West* (Seattle: Superior Publishing Co., 1965), p. 135; Fletcher, *The Black Soldier and Officer,* p. 80.

[24]Jocelyn, *Mostly Alkali,* p. 314; *Provo Herald,* March 14, 1954. Shortly after the telegraph line was completed, several young Utes cut the line and made firewood from the poles. A group of cavalrymen were sent to apprehend the culprits and bring them to the fort. Their punishment was a brief stay in the guardhouse on a bread and water diet. See *Builders of Uintah: A Centennial History of Uintah County, 1872–1947* (Uintah County: Daughters of Utah Pioneers, 1974), pp. 187–88.

sary, storehouse, and larger quarters for both officers and enlisted men. After visiting the fort in July 1887 Gen. George Crook, commander of the Department of the Platte, expressed satisfaction over the developments.[25]

Military duty at Fort Duchesne was typical of frontier duty throughout the West. The reservations had to be patrolled and disturbances quelled. Potential danger arose every year when some of the Ute bands came back to hunt deer and other game on their old hunting grounds in western Colorado. White Coloradans resented the Utes' annual return, and the cavalrymen were assigned to locate and send the Utes back to the Utah reservations.[26]

Sometimes the Coloradans attempted to drive the Utes out without the help of Fort Duchesne cavalrymen. In August 1887 the Colorado militia pursued a group of Utes, led by Colorow, from the former hunting grounds to the eastern boundary of the reservation. There the militiamen encountered black soldiers who had been sent to prevent the Coloradans from invading the reservation lands. On another occasion a company of buffalo soldiers commanded by Capt. Henry H. Wright was sent to investigate rumors that two white men and five Indians were killed during a fight on the Snake River near Lily Park, Colorado. On their way to Lily Park the soldiers met a party of Utes who had just left there. According to the Utes, the Colorado game warden and twenty-four deputies rode into a camp of seven Indians and started shooting. Two Ute women were wounded and two men were killed. Another account said a dispute arose between the game wardens and the Utes over hunting rights, and the Coloradans used the argument to start a fight. The returning black soldiers "were of the universal opinion that the Indians killed . . . were wantonly massacred by the game warden and his deputies."[27]

Rumors kept the buffalo soldiers busy. Reports that part of the Uncompahgre reservation land was to be opened for non-Indians brought hundreds of "sooners" into the area. Many left the reservation on learning they had been misled. However, two to three hundred decided to remain, and twenty buffalo soldiers under the command of Capt. M. W. Day were sent to eject the intruders. Recognizing that many of the trespassers were there because of a misunderstanding, Captain Day was ordered to avoid, if possible, any conflict that might lead to bloodshed. All but about twelve men heeded the soldiers' orders to leave. Those who refused were arrested and taken to the fort. After removing the "sooners," the troops and agency officials destroyed the locations and monuments posted by the intruders.[28]

Providing escort for Indian agents when large amounts of money, annuities to the Indians, were being transported was an important duty for black

[25]Jocelyn, *Mostly Alkali,* pp. 312, 315–17; *Provo Herald,* March 14, 1954; *Salt Lake Tribune,* July 16, 1887.

[26]*Salt Lake Tribune* August 13, 1887; *Vernal Express,* November 17, 1895; *Salt Lake Herald,* October 27, 1897.

[27]Post Return, Fort Duchesne, August 1887; *Salt Lake Herald,* October 27, 1897; *Vernal Express,* October 28, November 4 and 11, 1897.

[28]*Salt Lake Tribune,* March 10, 12, 1897.

cavalrymen. Extra precautions were taken in March 1898 when hearsay of an impending robbery attempt began circulating between the fort and Price, Utah. The reports were reinforced by the sighting of several members of the Robbers Roost gang in the vicinity of Price and Helper. It was said that the thirty thousand dollars to be paid to the Indians was lucrative enough to justify the robbery attempt.[29]

Captain Wright and Troop F were sent to the railroad depot at Price, and a detachment was sent from Price to Helper when the officer in charge heard that the attempted robbery was to take place at the second depot. When the train arrived at Helper it was guarded by the Ninth Cavalry troops, and no attempt was made to rob the train. The buffalo soldiers returned quickly to Price making sure that a holdup did not occur between stations. When the train arrived in Price approximately forty armed soldiers stood guard on the platform while the money was transferred to an open government wagon. The soldiers then escorted the Indian agent, Capt. G. A. Cornish, and the money from Price to Fort Duchesne. Although rumors persisted that the Robbers Roost gang would attack between Price and the fort, the holdup did not take place.[30]

BLACK-WHITE RELATIONS

Relations between black and white soldiers stationed at the post were generally amicable. A visitor to the fort said, "The white infantrymen and the black cavalrymen at the fort fraternize without any fine discrimination as to color." The men associated with one another, ate together, and according to the same visitor may have slept and fought "the festive bed bug together."[31]

During the summer of 1888 the two companies of black cavalrymen participated along with white companies from Fort Duchesne, Fort Douglas, and Fort Bridger in extensive maneuvers held in Strawberry Valley. The maneuvers took place near the reservations to demonstrate the military force that could be brought against the Utes should they break the peace. Later, with the closing of the post at Fort Bridger, Wyoming, in 1890, the Fort Duchesne troops would become responsible for guarding the entire Indian frontier areas of eastern Utah, western Colorado, and southwestern Wyoming.[32]

[29]Robbers Roost was an outlaw refuge in eastern Wayne County, Utah, on an elevated plateau near the summit of the San Rafael Swell. It was difficult to approach and thus an ideal hideout. Butch Cassidy was the most famous outlaw to use the Roost. For more information see Charles Kelly, *The Outlaw Trail: Butch Cassidy and His Wild Bunch,* rev. ed. (New York: Devin-Adair Co., 1959), pp. 141–47, 302–3; *Salt Lake Tribune,* March 1, 1898.

[30]*Salt Lake Tribune,* March 1, 5, 1898.

[31]The relationship between black and white soldiers at Fort Duchesne was typical. See Carroll, *The Black Military Experience,* p. 185. *Salt Lake Tribune,* October 28, 1886. It is unlikely that black and white soldiers shared the same sleeping quarters, even in tents. By 1888 the fort had permanent quarters and the soldiers, except for married men, would have been quartered according to units. See Hart, *Old Forts of the West,* p. 135.

[32]Jocelyn, *Mostly Alkali,* pp. 323–24; Alexander and Arrington, "The Utah Military Frontier," pp. 345–46.

The cooperation between black and white soldiers stationed at Fort Duchesne does not imply that racial prejudice was nonexistent. Maj. F. W. Benteen, who was commander of Fort Duchesne from August 23 to December 18, 1886, commented in a letter written after his retirement that in 1866 he had turned down a promotion to major in the Tenth Cavalry and had remained a captain in the Seventh Cavalry rather than be associated with black troops. Blaming fate for his later association with the Ninth Cavalry, Benteen felt secure enough financially to retire after thirty years, saying, "it was not proper to remain with a race of troops that I could take no interest in and this on account of their 'low-down,' rascally character."[33]

The ill-disguised contempt that some white officers felt toward blacks was not limited to black enlisted men but to black officers as well. Between 1866 and 1917, a commission in the army could be obtained by three methods: graduating from the United States Military Academy at West Point, which supplied most of the officers; by enlisted men with at least two years of army service passing a qualifying examination; and by civilians successfully completing the same examination. Very few blacks applied for qualification in the last two categories, but blacks did seek appointments to West Point. Of the twenty-three who received appointments between 1870 and 1889, twelve passed the entrance examination. Only three graduated.[34] In 1880 Gen. J. M. Schofield, superintendent of the academy, said:

> To send to West Point for four years' competition a young man who was born in slavery is to assume that half a generation has been sufficient to raise a colored man to the social, moral, and intellectual level which the average white man has reached in several hundred years. As well might the common farm horse be entered in a four-mile race against the best blood inherited from a long line of English racers.[35]

Blacks at the academy were ridiculed and harassed by white cadets. Between 1866 and 1900 West Point graduates filled all available positions for officers in the army. The antipathy shown blacks at the academy would be extended to black officers and enlisted men in the military garrisons of the West.[36]

Two of the three black West Point graduates, John H. Alexander (1887) and Charles Young (1889), served at Fort Duchesne between 1888 and 1901. Both men were from Ohio; Alexander's success inspired Young to emulate him. John Alexander was stationed at Fort Duchesne from June 1888 to October 1891. During that time he performed the regular duties as-

[33]Carroll, *The Black Military Experience,* pp. 191–92.

[34]Fletcher, *The Black Soldier and Officer,* p. 72.

[35]Foner, *Blacks and the Military in American History,* p. 65.

[36]Henry O. Flipper (1877) was the first black graduate from West Point. During his years at the academy, the white cadets ignored his presence. Flipper was court-martialed in 1882 and dismissed from the service. It was alleged that some irregularities occurred in the records of the commissary when Flipper was in charge of the books. He was cleared of the charges in 1978, and his remains were reburied with full military honors. Johnson Parker was assaulted by white cadets in 1880. See Ibid., p. 64; Fletcher, *The Black Soldier and Officer,* pp. 72–73, 74.

signed an officer. He directed fatigue details, led a patrol to remove intruders from the reservations, and took the soldiers on practice marches.[37]

Col. Edward Hatch, commander of the Ninth Cavalry, protested when he learned that Lt. Charles Young was to be assigned to his regiment. Noting that Lieutenant Alexander was already assigned to the Ninth, Hatch said the addition of Young might cause white "officers not to apply for assignment to the regiment." The War Department responded that Young was one of several new West Point graduates who had not been assigned to a regiment. To avoid the possibility that the next available cavalry vacancy might be in a white regiment, the War Department had assigned Young to the black Twenty-fifth Infantry with the agreement that he would be transferred to a black cavalry regiment when a vacancy became available. The next vacancy was in the Ninth, Young's new assignment. Charles Young arrived at Fort Duchesne in October 1890.[38]

Although the two Ohioans were stationed at Fort Duchesne together for nearly a year, they had little time to fraternize. Lieutenant Alexander was in charge of the government sawmill seven of the twelve months. Young was on leave for six weeks, and Alexander spent the month of September 1891 on detached duty in North Carolina. The following month Alexander was transferred to Fort Robinson, Nebraska.[39]

Lieutenant Young was stationed at Fort Duchesne until the fall of 1895. He later was reassigned to Fort Duchesne after the Spanish-American War but did not return to the fort until September 1899. He remained there until January 1901 but was periodically assigned detached service duty away from Utah. As professor of military science he taught at Wilberforce University in Ohio. During the Spanish-American War he took a leave of absence from the regiment in order to become a major with the Ninth Battalion Colored Ohio Volunteers. After the war ended he served as assistant mustering officer in Macon, Georgia, and once again taught at Wilberforce University before returning to Fort Duchesne. While on duty at Fort Duchesne Lieutenant Young, like Alexander, carried responsibilities common to junior officers throughout the army. In addition to leading patrols, he served as commissary officer, post exchange officer, and was in charge of the post school at various times.[40]

[37]Post Returns, Fort Duchesne, 1887–1901; Fletcher, *The Black Soldier and Officer,* pp. 73–74; Post Returns, Fort Duchesne, June and July 1888, April, June and October, 1890.

[38]Fletcher, *The Black Soldier and Officer,* p. 84.

[39]Post Returns, Fort Duchesne, October 1890 to October 1891. Alexander died of natural causes in 1894. See Fletcher, *The Black Soldier and Officer,* p. 73.

[40]Post Returns, Fort Duchesne, January 1894 to February 1901; November 1890; October 1891; April 1892; September 1899 to January 1901.

Young tutored and encouraged Benjamin O. Davis, Sr., who had joined the regular army after serving as an officer in one of the black volunteer regiments during the Spanish-American War. At Fort Duchesne, Davis studied, with Young's help, for the qualifying examination given for commission in the U.S. Army. He scored 91 percent on the final examination, received his commission, and was transferred to the Tenth Cavalry. Davis was the first black general in U.S. military history. His son Benjamin O. Davis, Jr., graduated from West Point in 1936 and later became a general in the U.S. Air Force. See Fletcher, *The Black Soldier and Officer,* p. 74; Foner, *Blacks and the Military,* pp. 93–94.

A deterioration in the relations between black and white residents of Fort Duchesne appeared in 1896 and could have been the result of racial prejudice by white officers. During the spring of that year many of the black troops began to clamor for a change of station. They complained that the post had become "a prison instead of a military reservation." The white population of the garrison organized the Owl Club in August of that year and blacks were excluded. The club was to provide social activities such as card parties, theatrical performances, and other amusements during the coming fall and winter.[41]

Relations between the black soldiers at Fort Duchesne and civilian citizens in the area continued to be amicable, however, and there was a general absence of the blatant contempt for black soldiers expressed in some frontier communities such as San Angelo, Texas, and Johnson County, Wyoming. It has been suggested that "racism may have been mildest and whites most tolerant of black soldiers in communities near Indian reservations." White residents of the Uinta Basin firmly believed there was a need for military protection and vigorously opposed any plans that might lead to a removal of the troops. In addition, the fort and its military personnel contributed handsomely to the local economy. Yet, white civilians referred to the black soldiers as "darkeys" and "coons." During a dispute in a saloon Jack Thomas, a local white rancher, drew a gun and said, "You black son of a bitch, I will kill you." Racist manifestations, while few, leave little doubt of the existence of race prejudice among civilians.[42]

Nevertheless, prejudice did not prevent the black soldiers and white civilians from occasionally engaging in social activities. The troops might entertain the residents of Vernal with an evening of comedy at the local opera house, and before the performances the post band would play and march in a street parade. Capt. F. H. E. Ebstein of the Twenty-first Infantry had organized a band comprised of both black and white soldiers at the fort during the winter of 1887–88, and both officers and enlisted men had contributed money for the instruments. Also, on occasion, a racially mixed group sang for post residents. Sports brought the races together as well. Black and white companies competed against each other in baseball contests, and the Fort Duchesne baseball team competed with the team from Vernal.[43]

[41]New officers were transferred to Fort Duchesne during this period. See Post Returns, Fort Duchesne, March to August 1896; *Vernal Express,* May 28 and August 6, 1896.

[42]Carroll, *The Black Military Experience,* pp. 186–87; Frank N. Schubert, "The Suggs Affray: The Black Cavalry in the Johnson County War," *Western Historical Quarterly* 4 (1973): 57–68; Frank N. Schubert, "Black Soldiers on the White Frontier: Some Factors Influencing Race Relations," *Phylon* 32 (1971): 415 [for a similar opinion see Thomas A. Phillips, "The Black Regulars," in *The West of the American People,* ed. Allen G. Bogue, Thomas D. Phillips, and James Wright (Itasca, Ill., 1970), pp. 138–40]; *Vernal Express,* November 17, 24, December 1, 29, 1892; Alexander and Arrington, "The Utah Military Frontier," p. 346; *Salt Lake Tribune,* July 10, 1887; *Provo Herald,* March 14, 1954; Phillips, "The Black Regulars," p. 140, suggests that merchants in towns near forts manned by blacks allowed economic consideration to overcome race prejudice; *Vernal Express,* May 4, November 25, 1899.

[43]*Salt Lake Herald,* March 22, 1898; *Vernal Express,* March 24, 1898; Jocelyn, *Mostly Alkali,* pp. 320, 322; *Uintah Papoose,* May 29, 1891: *Eastern Utah Telegraph,* April 16, 1891; *Vernal Express,* June 23, July 7, 1898, June 23, 1900.

In May 1897 Troop B was sent on a practice march to Fort Douglas in Salt Lake City. There the cavalrymen played a baseball game with the Twenty-fourth Infantry team. Although previously strong competitors, they could have suffered fatigue from the long trek, for they lost by a score of 23 to 9. Two months later Troop F received orders to travel to Fort Douglas on a practice march. The actual purpose of the trip was for the cavalrymen to participate in Utah's Jubilee Celebration. The men were absent from Fort Duchesne from July 13 to August 2. The brief duty in Salt Lake City probably seemed like heaven to soldiers accustomed to the isolation of the Uinta Basin. On the evening of July 24 Troop F gave a "thrilling exhibition of horsemanship" for the civilians and soldiers in attendance on the lower parade ground at Fort Douglas.[44]

OFF-DUTY HOURS

The off-duty activities of black soldiers at Fort Duchesne were similar to those of soldiers at other frontier posts. Some spent their off-duty hours drinking and gambling. Others sought the temporary companionship of prostitutes who frequented the saloon in an area known as the Strip. The Strip encompassed a triangular-shaped piece of land between the Uncompahgre and Uintah reservations, approximately one and a half miles from Fort Duchesne. Federal, state, and county law enforcement agents were uncertain as to who had jurisdiction over the area, and this proved an advantage to the Indians, whites, and blacks who visited there for liquor, gambling, and other pleasures.[45]

Tempers often flared in the Strip, and soldiers were sometimes involved in the ensuing disputes. The previously mentioned Jack Thomas, a white rancher, was killed there. Thomas often gambled in the Strip with members of the black troops. He was killed and a black soldier wounded in the brothel adjoining the saloon. The incident occurred when Thomas intervened in a dispute involving black soldiers. The white man drew his gun and struck William Carter before shooting him. Thomas was then shot and killed by the wounded Carter. During the melee Abraham McKee, another black soldier, joined in the shooting spree. At the inquest the jurors ruled that the shooting was justifiable and Carter was exonerated. The less-fortunate McKee was taken to Fort Logan, Colorado, where he faced a military court for his participation in the affair.[46]

To prevent black troops from going to the Strip, a guard was placed on

[44]*Salt Lake Herald,* May 24, 1897; Post Returns, Fort Duchesne, July and August 1897; *Salt Lake Herald,* July 24, 1897.

[45]*Salt Lake Herald,* May 2, 1899.

[46]Ibid. The circumstances that led to the shootings are confusing. One report claims that two soldiers were arguing when one drew a gun. Orrin Curry, an employee, was attempting to get the gun when Thomas entered the room (*Vernal Express,* May 4, 1899). Another report (*Salt Lake Herald,* May 6, 1899) says the black soldiers were arguing with prostitutes when Thomas entered the room and confronted the soldiers. On May 2, 1899, the *Herald* had reported that the dispute was over the attentions a white prostitute, Sarah Allred, was paying to the black soldiers. See also, *Vernal Express,* May 4, 1899; *Salt Lake Tribune,* May 26, 1899.

the Duchesne bridge. Soldiers evaded the guard by walking beyond the bridge and swimming across the river. When the soldiers returned to the bridge, they were arrested, taken to the guardhouse, and fined a month's pay. The men were angered at Capt. John Guilfoyle's attempts to keep them from the Strip. There were rumors that a recent fire at the post had been deliberately started in retaliation. Other rumors blamed the fire on Indians or white businessmen on the Strip who were equally incensed with Guilfoyle.[47]

Almost all of the disputes involving black soldiers, however, were with their own army mates. For example, the two cooks of Troop I became embroiled in an argument that led to a fight. One of them died as a result of his injuries. Some of the fights did not involve soldiers. Dennis Ford, a black employee of the post trader, quarreled with the Chinese Ho Sing at the latter's restaurant. Ford stabbed Ho in the breast, was arrested, and placed in the guardhouse. Violence was a regular occurrence on the Strip and was by no means limited to blacks.[48]

Off-duty hours were also spent in activities other than drinking and gambling. A number of soldiers used their free time to further their education at the post school. The troops had a Masonic military lodge on the post. The isolation from a black civilian population forced black soldiers and their families residing on military garrisons to initiate their own social activities. On special occasions, such as holidays or when a favorite member of the company was leaving the post, a dinner party and dance were often given and all of the black residents joined in the festivities.[49]

Black soldiers organized a brass band and others performed in a minstrel group. Baseball, boxing, and track attracted the interest of many troops. Baseball was by far the most popular athletic activity of the black troops at Fort Duchesne as well as of other black regiments. As noted earlier, the company teams played against one another and with white company teams when they were stationed at Fort Duchesne, and sometimes challenged the local team from Vernal. Besides competing in team sports, many soldiers spent their leisure hours swimming or fishing in nearby rivers.[50]

DEPARTURES

Citizens from Price and nearby towns turned out in large numbers to say farewell to the buffalo soldiers in April 1898. The men of Troops B and F were leaving for Tennessee before going to Cuba to fight in the Spanish-

[47]*Salt Lake Herald,* July 10, 17, 1899.

[48]*Vernal Express,* April 21 and 28, 1900; December 29, 1892.

[49]The educational opportunities at posts varied, depending on facilities and personnel. Lt. Charles Young was in charge of the Fort Duchesne school from November 1899 to January 1901. According to the 1900 census schedule all the black soldiers at Fort Duchesne were able to read and write. See also Post Returns, Fort Duchesne, 1899 to 1901; Fletcher, *The Black Soldier and Officer,* pp. 74, 104–5; *Broad Ax,* October 9, 1897; *Vernal Express,* January 11, 1894, May 7, 1896.

[50]*Vernal Express,* March 24, 1898; Fletcher, *The Black Soldier and Officer,* pp. 104–5; *Uintah Papoose,* May 29, July 17, 1891; *Eastern Utah Telegraph,* April 30, 1891; *Vernal Express,* June 8, 1893, June 28, 1894, July 7 and 28, 1900.

American War. The companies, including officers, number about 127 men. In Price the soldiers were feted by the local community with a lunch at the town hall. As the soldiers entered the hall they were serenaded by two lines of children from Wellington and Price singing "Rally 'Round the Flag, Boys" and other patriotic songs. After lunch soldiers and civilians played baseball. That evening both the civilians and soldiers entertained the community. The troops departed the next day by train amidst cheers and best wishes for their success.[51]

The black troops were replaced at Fort Duchesne by two companies of white soldiers from the Seventh Cavalry. Then, in October 1898 Troops C and I of the Ninth Cavalry arrived at Fort Duchesne from Montauk Point, Long Island, New York. Black troops from the regular army units had been sent to Montauk Point for rest and recuperation after a gallant display of bravery and patriotism in Cuba. The new men quickly adjusted to the rigors of a frontier post.[52]

Rumors of an impending departure from Fort Duchesne begin circulating among the troops in June and July 1900. In June 1899 Troop C had been sent to Fort Douglas in Salt Lake City to replace members of the Twenty-fourth Infantry who were being sent to San Francisco and from there on to the Philippines. It was widely believed that the Ninth Cavalry would be going to the newly acquired colonial possession. Many soldiers were excited over moving from Fort Duchesne, but the rumors were premature and the troops remained at the post. The disappointment was short-lived. In March 1901 Troop H of the Fifth Cavalry was sent to Fort Duchesne from Fort Wingate, New Mexico, and Troops I and K of the Ninth Cavalry were dispatched to the Philippines via San Francisco. The 192 buffalo soldiers and their 2 officers left the post on March 4, 1901, bringing to a close nearly fifteen years of black military duty on the Uintah frontier.[53]

[51]*Eastern Utah Advocate,* April 28, 1898.

[52]Post Returns, Fort Duchesne, Special Returns, April, October, and November 1898; Fletcher, *The Black Soldier and Officer,* pp. 44–45.

[53]*Vernal Express,* June 16, July 18, 1900; *Salt Lake Tribune,* June 21, 1899; *Vernal Express,* July 28, 1900; Post Returns, Fort Duchesne, March, April, and July 1901. The main body of black soldiers left the post in March; however, eight men remained at the fort until July 1901.)

PART II

*

Utah from Statehood through The Great Depression

Photograph on preceding page: Utah leaders of the Western Federation of Miners at the Second Annual Miners' Day at Lagoon, June 1904. Courtesy Utah State Historical Society.

*

Respectable Reformers: Utah Socialists in Power, 1900–1925

JOHN S. McCORMICK AND JOHN R. SILLITO

Utah has a long-standing radical political tradition, though it is easily overlooked, and historians generally have paid little attention to it. Many early Mormons were critical of their contemporary American society and viewed immigration to Utah as an opportunity to escape deeply rooted inequities and begin anew. Subsequent generations of Utah radicals included Godbeites of the 1860s, Populists of the 1890s, Socialists, Anarchists, and Wobblies of the early twentieth century, Communists of the 1930s, and New Leftists of the 1960s.

The following essay examines the socialist movement in Utah in the early twentieth century when it was a significant political and social force in the state. Utah socialists hated capitalism and felt that it served only a small, powerful class and could provide neither economic nor spiritual welfare for the general population. The essential question the essay asks is, "What did such people do once they actually held political power?" The assumption upon which the essay proceeds is that radicalism is more than an esoteric footnote to Utah's past, and that Utah was not isolated from the forces that developed elsewhere in the United States. The study of socialism illustrates larger themes and patterns in the state's history, provides a more rounded view of Utah's past, and helps broaden the conception of what Utah is really like, both past and present.

John S. McCormick and John R. Sillito are co-editors of this volume. See note about them at the end of this volume.

THE HISTORIOGRAPHY OF SOCIALISM in the United States is curious in that overviews have preceded case studies.[1] As a result, judgments about the overall pattern of American socialism, and answers to the ques-

[1]See review of Richard W. Judd, *Socialist Cities: Municipal Politics and the Grass Roots of American Socialism* (Albany, New York: SUNY Press, 1989), in *Labor History* 36 (Spring 1990): 231–32.

tion the German economist Werner Sombart asked in the title of his 1906 book, *Why Is There No Socialism in the United States?* were sometimes premature. In recent years important case studies have appeared that challenge earlier conceptions.[2]

In the following pages we focus on the experience of socialists who were elected to public office in Utah during the first two decades of the twentieth century—a time when socialism was a significant presence in Utah and throughout the nation, exciting the hopes of thousands of people and alarming tens of thousands more. Socialists hated capitalism. For them it was an immoral and unjust economic system that could not last, and they sought to fundamentally reconstruct the social order. We are interested here in what people with such views actually attempted to do once they achieved political power.

First, a little background. As John Graham points out in a useful survey of the subject, socialism first found practical expression in the United States in the many utopian communities that arose during the early and middle years of the nineteenth century, of which the Owenite, Fourierist, and Icarian settlements were the most influential.[3] Toward the end of the century new forms of socialist organization developed, including the Socialist Labor Party, Bellamyite Nationalism, Christian Socialism, and the American Fabian Society; but it was not until the first decade of the twentieth century that a true mass movement for socialism could be said to have developed.

A convention in Indianapolis in 1901 that was designed to unify various radical groups resulted in the creation of the Socialist Party of America and brought about a coherence previously unknown to the American left. The creation of the new party ushered in a period when it enjoyed such widespread and growing support that a transition to power seemed more than mere possibility to socialists and non-socialists alike. By 1912 the party had a membership of 118,000 people; its presidential candidate, Eugene V. Debs, received nearly one million votes; 340 cities and towns elected more than 1,200 Socialist party candidates to office, including seventy-nine mayors in twenty-four states; two socialists also served in the U.S. Congress. More than 300 socialist-oriented papers were being published throughout the country; it was claimed that thirty percent of unionized workers sup-

[2]The most recent is Judd. Others include Jerry W. Calvert, *The Gibraltar: Socialism and Labor in Butte, Montana, 1895–1920* (Helena, MT: Montana Historical Society Press, 1988; Donald T. Critchlow, ed., *Socialism in the Heartland: The Midwestern Experience, 1900–1925* (Notre Dame, IN: University of Notre Dame Press, 1986); James R. Green, *Grass Roots Socialism: Radical Movements in the American Southwest, 1895–1943* (Baton Rouge: Louisiana State University Press, 1979); Garin Burbank, *When Farmers Voted Red: The Gospel of Socialism in the Oklahoma Countryside, 1910–1924* (Westport, CT: Greenwood Press, 1976); Bruce M. Stave, ed., *Socialism and the Cities* (Port Washington, New York: Kennikat, 1975); and Henry Bedford, *Socialism and the Workers in Massachusetts, 1886–1912* (Amherst: University of Massachusetts Press, 1966).

[3]John Graham, ed., *"Yours for the Revolution": The Appeal to Reason, 1895–1922* (Lincoln: University of Nebraska Press, 1990), 173.

ported socialist policies; five state federations of labor endorsed the Socialist party; and socialists were an important force in many of the reform movements of the time, including women's suffrage.[4]

Socialist patterns in Utah closely followed national patterns, and for the first twenty years of the twentieth century the Socialist Party of America was a significant presence in the state. Party locals existed in all but the most isolated and thinly populated of Utah's twenty-nine counties and carried on a wide range of activities to spread the gospel of socialism and provide mutual support for party members. Nine Utah newspapers at one time or another claimed the socialist label. The largest of them, the *Intermountain Worker,* had a circulation at its peak of five thousand copies. Socialists wrote a regular socialist column in many local newspapers. Others founded social science clubs in Salt Lake City and Ogden that for ten years sponsored weekly lectures "on all phases of civic affairs and social problems," including such topics as "Marriage As It Has Been and Is and Marriage As It Is To Be." The party held overnight and weekend "encampments," such as one in Duchesne County during the 1915 Fourth of July weekend that featured socialist speakers, music, singing, skits, and theatrical performances, and educational classes and discussions. In 1910 several of its members established the second Modern School in the United States, based on the educational theories of Spanish anarchist Francisco Ferrer.[5]

Between 1911 and 1913 the Utah Federation of Labor officially endorsed the Socialist party, resolving in 1912 "that as a state organization, we aid in the propaganda of Socialism, that we may hasten the day when the emancipation of the working class from the bonds of wage slavery shall be proclaimed in America and throughout the world." A diverse group of predominantly native-born supporters were attracted to the party, including journalists, educators, clergymen, small businessmen, and farmers, along with a solid working-class base. Significantly, more non-Mormons than Mormons belonged to the party, even though in the early twentieth century Utah's population was seventy-five percent Mormon. This was in part because the Mormon church was moving away from its communitarian roots and church leaders were becoming increasingly critical of radicalism; it was also partly because of the Socialist party's own ambivalence about the

[4]Much has been written about American socialism on the national level during its "Golden Age" in the early twentieth century. Major works include David Shannon, *The Socialist Party of America* (New York: Macmillan and Co., 1955); Howard Quint, *The Forging of American Socialism* (Columbia University of South Carolina Press, 1953); Ira Kipnis, *The American Socialist Movement, 1897–1913* (New York: Columbia University Press, 1952); Daniel Bell, *Marxian Socialism in the United States* (Princeton, New Jersey: Princeton University Press, 1967); and James Weinstein, *The Decline of Socialism in America, 1912–1925* (New York: Monthly Review Press, 1967. A convenient summary of the dimensions and impact of the movement is in Graham, "*Yours for the Revolution,*" 173–78.

[5]Documentation follows in subsequent notes. See also John R. Sillito, "Women and the Socialist Party in Utah, 1900–1920," *Utah Historical Quarterly* 49 (Summer 1981): 220–37, and John S. McCormick, "Hornets in the Hive: Socialists in Early Twentieth-Century Utah," *Utah Historical Quarterly* 50 (Summer 1982): 235–50.

church and the likelihood of drawing Mormons to its ranks. Yet, even so, more than forty percent of party members belonged to the Mormon church.

Most socialists believed that the fundamental economic, political, and cultural changes they sought in American capitalism's developing industrial and financial order could be brought about peacefully through the electoral process. For the most part, Utah Socialists shared that view and were active in electoral politics, eagerly entering state and local election campaigns and running for offices of all kinds. Electoral success began in 1901 with the election of a Socialist party justice of the peace in Elsinore, a city marshal in Lehi, and a mayor in Salina. It peaked in 1911 when thirty-seven socialist candidates, including six mayors and twenty-two town council members, were voted into office, and continued until 1923, when Eureka voters elected two Socialist party city council members. In all, the party elected one hundred men and seven women in more than two dozen cities and towns and eleven counties—ranging from towns of several hundred people to Salt Lake City.

Most of those elected were not in a position to accomplish much. They either held minor offices with limited powers, such as constable or justice of the peace, or they were in the minority of a city council or other governing body. For example, Henry W. Lawrence received more votes than any other candidate in the 1911 Salt Lake City Commission election, but he was the only socialist member of the city commission during his four-year term. Likewise, socialist mayors in Salina from 1902 to 1903 and in Cedar City from 1906 to 1907 and again from 1912 to 1913 had to work with entirely non-socialist town councils. On seven occasions, however, five Utah towns elected administrations with Socialist party members in the majority: Bingham (1906–07); Joseph and Murray (1912–15); Stockton (1912–13 and 1916–17); and Eureka (1912–13 and 1922–25). With the exception of the farming community of Joseph, all were mining or smelting towns and ranged in size from Stockton, with a population in 1910 of 340, to Murray, whose population in 1910 was 4,057.

Once elected to office, Socialists in these places did not have to be content with merely raising certain issues, introducing various measures, and trying to influence their colleagues to their way of thinking; they now could actually implement policy. Thus, we are particularly interested in looking at what they did after they achieved political power and why they acted as they did.

We have found that, despite rhetoric that stressed class division, class warfare, and the evils of the profit motive, once in office Utah socialists were moderate reformers who sought to broaden their appeal and be re-elected by cultivating an image of honesty, efficiency, and attachment to conventional values. They generally worked diligently for civic improvements, such as better sewage systems and paved streets, sought to be above the criticism of Mormon bishops or Baptist preachers for their stand on drinking establishments and gambling, and hoped that even people concerned with the "immigrant menace" could vote the Socialist ticket comfortably.

Let us now elaborate. The explicit and overriding goal of Utah's socialist officials, as Eureka's socialist Mayor Andrew Mitchell said prior to taking office in 1908, was to provide "good, clean, capable administration of city affairs."[6] Virtually every socialist who ran for local office in Utah echoed those sentiments and regularly criticized previous Republican or Democratic administrations for their failure to do just that. The 1905 Salt Lake City Socialist party platform was typical in its assertions that Democratic and Republican officials did not view public office as a public trust and that socialist administrations alone "can prevent the corruption and graft which is inevitable under the rule of the capitalistic politicians and can enforce measures which will make for the uplifting of the material and moral standards of life for the masses of the people."[7]

J. Alex Bevan, a socialist representative from Tooele County elected to the state legislature in 1914 and re-elected in 1916, promised "to tell what no other member from the last Legislature dare tell about graft in our Legislature."[8] Though it is not known if he kept this promise, Bevan illustrates that Utah Socialists were primarily reformers preoccupied with immediate demands who worked within the existing framework of government and the economic system, pursuing a program calling for honesty in office, economy and efficiency in government administration, modernization of city services, and sound fiscal management—measures that were not peculiar to Socialists and that appealed to anyone with progressive inclinations and a social conscience. In the view of Major Church, Socialist mayor of Eureka from 1919 to 1922, most voters did not care what party city officials belonged to or what they called themselves as long as they were honest and capable, demonstrated a capacity to deal with actual problems, and provided "good government."[9] It was a question of competence, not of ideology.

Once in office, Utah Socialists spent the bulk of their time dealing with routine matters. They issued business licenses, purchased supplies, paid bills, and devoted entire meetings to discussing such issues as the problem of "young men carrying flippers and air guns."[10] They did not seem to resent or resist dealing with such mundane matters but welcomed them as a way of proving to voters that they were capable administrators in touch with their constituents and able to respond to their concerns, no matter how routine.

Beyond the day-to-day matters of city business, however, Socialist officials were particularly interested in public health and safety. The overriding concern of Bingham's socialist administration during its two years in office, 1906–07, was "the improvement of sanitary conditions"—in particular, the protection of the city's water supply and expansion of its sewer system.[11]

[6]*Eureka Reporter*, 3 November 1907.

[7]*Deseret News*, 2 October 1905, p. 5.

[8]Political flyer, n.d. [1915], reproduced in McCormick, "Hornets," 224.

[9]*Eureka Reporter*, 10 November 1917.

[10]Eureka City Council Minutes, 2 June 1922, Utah State Archives, Salt Lake City, Utah.

[11]Bingham Town Board Minutes, 25 April 1906, Utah State Archives, Salt Lake City, Utah.

The leaders also selected a site for the first city dump and began regular garbage collection, required the removal of "manure piles" within city limits, and prohibited animals "from being at loose or at large on streets or public grounds."

During its first term Stockton's socialist town board completed the town's water system; required the local electric power company to insulate all power lines in the town limits; and, because of anxiety about rabies, specified that all dogs be muzzled or confined to their owner's property for a ninety-day period. During their second term they established a "Special Relief Fund" for "sick, transient persons in immediate need"; notified owners to remove all manure piles deemed a "nuisance"; and upgraded the water system. Sensitive to the charge that Socialists would bankrupt a city and ruin its credit, they also kept a close eye on city finances and constantly practiced the smallest of economies. In May 1912, for example, officials refused to pay the city's electric bill in full because one street light had been out of repair for a month.

In Eureka Socialists built the city's first sewer system, began to pave streets, started a program of regular street cleaning and maintenance, provided for periodic garbage collection, and appointed the first dogcatcher. Murray's socialist officials oversaw a program of street sprinkling, installed public drinking fountains, and supervised construction and operation of a city-owned electric power plant.

Maintenance of a proper "moral climate" was also an important concern for Utah's socialist office holders. Eureka Socialists pledged in their 1907 platform to enforce city ordinances banning the sale of liquor on Sunday and prohibiting gambling; they also criticized previous city officials for past failures to do just that. When asked at the end of his four-year term as mayor what he considered to be his greatest accomplishment, socialist Andrew Mitchell replied, "Closing the gambling houses and bringing about a more strict regulation of the saloons."[12] After Stockton citizens voted for Prohibition in 1917, the socialist town board pledged to "strictly enforce the liquor laws."[13] They also licensed pool and billiard halls and prohibited minors from entering them.[14] After assuming office in 1912, Murray socialist leaders were as interested as were their comrades in other Utah towns in enforcing liquor regulations, which, because of the city's local prohibition ordinance, meant keeping the city "dry." They also sought to enforce Sunday closing laws and ordinances prohibiting cigarette smoking by minors. They regulated boxing matches, and throughout their two terms in office they spent considerable time enforcing the city ordinance that made it

> unlawful for any person in any public dancehall in Murray City to dance any improper, close hugging, indecent, obscene, rowdy, or boisterous dance or dances in any position where the faces or heads of the dancers shall be in

[12]Ibid., 20 December 1911.
[13]Stockton Town Board Minutes, 9 April 1917, Stockton Town Hall.
[14]Ibid., 1 October 1917.

> contact, or where the arm or arms of the dancers encircle or are folded around or about his or her dancing partner, in such a way as to suggest close-embracing or hugging, or where the arm or arms of the dancing couple are folded between them, or where the knee or knees, leg or legs of the dancers are between the knees or legs of his or her partner, providing that nothing herein shall be construed to forbid or prohibit dancing in what is known as the waltz position.[15]

Though this might seem quaint and trivial, it was in fact important because it demonstrated that the Socialist party shared the values and concerns of the larger community, showing that Socialists could identify with "respectable" elements of their society. As Richard Judd points out, Socialist administrations throughout the country typically showed similar concern.[16]

The impact of ethnic divisions was often evident in such efforts at moral reform. Elected officials throughout the United States were judged in part on their ability to keep social disturbances and open vice at a minimum, and in many Utah towns, including those under consideration here, that was seen to require controlling the behavior of a growing "new immigrant" segment of the population.

Throughout the nineteenth century Utah was a territory composed of recent immigrants. In 1880 nearly one-third of Utah's population was foreign-born and another one-third was second-generation immigrants, most of them Mormon converts from the British Isles, Scandinavia, and western Europe. Toward the end of the century that situation began to change. New groups of immigrants, mainly from eastern and southern Europe, part of a stream of twenty million people who reached the shores of the United States between 1880 and 1914, began to arrive in Utah in increasing numbers. For at least the first generation they worked at pick-and-shovel jobs, particularly on the railroads and in the mines and smelters. Their experience in Utah was much the same as that of their fellow immigrants in the rest of the United States, including the alarm their presence occasioned and the prejudice and discrimination they encountered.

In the early twentieth century the beliefs were as widespread in Utah as elsewhere in the country that only the Anglo-Saxon race had the qualities necessary for American society to survive, that the future of the country depended on its having a relatively homogeneous population, and that new immigrants were a threat to community morality, security, and jobs.[17] A headline in the June 27, 1907, *Deseret News,* "Vicious Dago Scoundrel Murders Inoffensive White Railroad Worker," expressed sentiments that were all too common.

[15]Murray City Ordinances, typescript, Chapter XL, Section 809, "Public Dancing," 1909, Murray City Hall Archives.

[16]*Socialist Cities,* 40–43.

[17]On the experience of immigrants in Utah in the late nineteenth and early twentieth centuries see Helen Zeese Papanikolas, ed., *The Peoples of Utah* (Salt Lake City: Utah State Historical Society, 1976), and Papanikolas, *Toil and Rage in a New Land* (Salt Lake City: Utah State Historical Society, 1972).

Many Utah Socialists—predominantly old-stock, native-born members of the working class—shared these beliefs, and in their dealings with the "foreign element" showed little understanding or sympathy. This was evident in Murray, located eight miles south of Salt Lake City and settled in 1849. Initially a rural agricultural village with a largely Mormon, native-born, and old immigrant population, by the early twentieth century Murray had changed considerably. The population increased from under 1,000 in 1870 to more than 4,000 in 1910 and was much more diverse. The town was no longer primarily a farming community, but a major smelting center. By 1910 the lead smelter of the American Smelting and Refining Company (ASARCO) was the largest in the world and employed 43 percent of Murray's workforce. More than half of the population—54 percent—were new immigrants, primarily Greek, along with what were at the time commonly referred to as Austrians but in fact were Slavs, Serbs, and Croats, as well as a smaller number of Italians. As the population grew more diverse, anxiety among native-born and old immigrant residents increased.[18]

Murray was incorporated in 1902 in order to have more control over its own affairs than it did as an unincorporated part of Salt Lake County. In particular, local residents wanted to be able to more tightly regulate the lives and activities of the new immigrants. The initial set of city ordinances was designed to do that, and the first city commission frequently complained about the "foreign element" and repeatedly cited "Dago houses" for their unsanitary conditions. In January 1903, Murray businessmen charged ASARCO with employing too many "Greeks, Italians, and Hungarians," petitioned the company to hire only native-born workers, and asked the city commission for help in seeing that they did.[19] In November 1904, Mayor Joseph Stratton asserted that, in general, Greeks in Murray "live six or more in a 10 foot by 12 foot room that reeks so with filth an ordinary person cannot stay in it for 5 minutes" and called for the removal of all Greek residents from the community.[20]

Emotions periodically erupted in response to particular events. Following an unknown assailant's assault on a Murray woman in November 1904, Mayor Stratton announced that a "foreigner" was no doubt responsible, advocated forcing all new immigrants to leave the community, and called a series of public meetings to consider the matter. As he saw it, Murray's increasingly "heterogeneous elements . . . do not fit into the scheme of American society or community life." The city was "going steadily downhill because of the presence of this low element," he said. "We want to see our town go ahead. It will continue to get worse so long as these foreigners stay here and work for cheap wages. We must get rid of them

[18]David L. Schirer, "The Cultural Dynamics of Urbanization: Murray City, Utah, 1897–1919," (M.A. thesis, University of Utah, 1991).

[19]*Deseret News*, 10 January 1903, 8; Murray City Commission Minutes, 9 January 1908, Murray City Hall Archives.

[20]*Salt Lake Tribune*, 19 November 1904, p. 1.

now."[21] The next day he proposed that pressure "be brought to bear upon the smelter management that will convince them that it is to their interest as well as ours to employ a less dangerous class of labor. The community will simply not put up with it any longer." Several months later, Murray's local newspaper reported that ill-feeling between the city's native-born and new immigrant population continued to run so high that an outbreak of violence was inevitable.[22]

Ethnic division clearly ran deep in Murray. It was perhaps the most striking fact about the city in the early twentieth century. Public officials were expected to address the "immigrant problem," and from the outset of their terms in office Murray Socialists made it a priority, at their first commission meeting instructing city marshal Fred Peters "to make a thorough investigation and inspection of Greek coffeehouses and restaurants for the purpose of observing the manner in which these places are conducted."[23] At the next meeting Peters reported that coffeehouses had no regular time of closing, allowed card playing and gambling seven days a week, and tolerated improper behavior, and he recommended that city ordinances be enforced requiring midnight and Sunday closing and prohibiting gambling, that "all boisterous singing by these foreigners" be stopped, and that "white girls be prohibited from being employed there."[24] Three weeks later, city officials included those recommendations in a new ordinance regulating coffeehouses and in subsequent months rejected all appeals from owners that they be allowed to retain their female workers, in one instance giving an owner "one day in which to get rid of the girl, otherwise his license will be revoked,"[25] and in another refusing to allow a woman who was part owner of a coffeehouse to continue working there.[26] On October 11, 1912, seventy-four of Murray's Greek residents petitioned the city commission to repeal the new ordinance. They were particularly hopeful that coffeehouses would be allowed to remain open on Sunday because "the Greeks have no homes or places to congregate except these coffeehouses." City officials refused.

The Socialist bias against the "foreign element" in Murray was also clearly visible when employees of ASARCO went on strike in April 1912. In similar circumstances it was not unusual for Socialist administrations across the country to support strikers by protecting picketers instead of strikebreakers, offering strike arbitration services, or providing strikers with temporary employment, for example. In contrast, the 1912 Murray strike featured a Socialist party city government siding with employers against the very workers their national platform pledged them to support. Murray's socialists sought "to make provisions for maintaining peace and quiet as

[21]Ibid., 23 November 1904, p. 12.
[22]*American Eagle,* 21 January 1905, p. 8.
[23]Murray City Commission Minutes, 2 January 1912.
[24]Ibid., 3 January 1912.
[25]Ibid., 25 January 1912.
[26]Ibid., 26 April, 1912.

much as possible" by hiring extra deputies and allowing the Salt Lake County sheriff's department "to take hold of the matter and place a sufficient number of special deputies in Murray to control the situation." At a city commission meeting "Representatives of various nationalities were informed that they will be treated fairly, but that the law will be strictly enforced."[27] The next day, the *Salt Lake Tribune* reported that "Fifty sharpshooters and rifles have been sent in to stop the unrest at ASARCO."[28]

During a strike of smelter employees three years earlier, non-socialist city officials had responded in essentially the same way, but in an earlier strike in 1900 local officials had assisted strikers. The difference, David Schirer points out, was that in 1900 smelter workers were mainly native-born citizens and old immigrants from the British Isles and Scandinavia, and the strike was seen as American workers striking for decent wages, whereas in 1909 and 1912, because the workforce was largely composed of new immigrants, the unrest was viewed as "foreigners" striking for no good reason and acting illegally and without the support of American workers.[29]

Despite their moderate actions and efforts to appeal to the nativist sentiments of "respectable" voters, Utah's socialists met with intense and continuing opposition. As Richard W. Judd says, such opposition was a consistent feature of "socialist cities" in the United States in the early twentieth century.[30] Murray again provides a good example. When it became clear during the 1911 campaign that Socialist party candidates might have enough support to be elected, a "Non-Partisan League" was organized to oppose them. Most of its founders and officers were local Mormon church leaders. The main issue during the campaign was prohibition of alcoholic beverages, which voters had narrowly approved in a special election the previous June. The League charged that Socialists did not support prohibition and if elected would not enforce the law mandating it. Following the Socialist victory the Non-Partisan League disbanded, but a Law and Order League was established. In part a quasi-vigilante group, its members again included local Mormon church leaders, among them the Socialist mayor's opponent in the recent election, as well as seven "anonymous detectives charged with identifying law breakers and presenting evidence to the City Commission." Its announced aim was "to bring about better conditions in the city and be an aid in keeping the youth from evil and destructive influences"; in particular it sought "the betterment of the community and cleaning up the illicit liquor trade."[31] Especially active during the next election in 1913, the League charged that Socialist officials had not enforced the liquor laws and would not in the future. When Socialists retained control of city government following the election, the League continued to monitor their actions.

[27]Ibid., 2, 9, 14, and 17 May 1912.
[28]*Salt Lake Tribune,* 18 May 1912, p. 12.
[29]Schirer, "The Cultural Dynamics of Urbanization," 91–100.
[30]*Socialist Cities,* 40–43.
[31]*Deseret News,* 10 January 1912.

In June 1914 an election was held to decide whether or not Murray would remain dry. The League led the fight for continued prohibition. In its view, the election was not only a referendum on liquor but also on socialism, since it asserted that those in favor of ending prohibition were socialists and those who wanted it retained were not. Voters narrowly decided to continue prohibition. League officials and the Mormon church-owned *Deseret News* afterwards charged that "the socialist vote was very strong in favor of the saloon men."[32] Why, the *News* asked, "is there such a close alliance of the liquor people and the city administration? Is it possible, many citizens ask, that the officials have allowed a job to be put up on the people whom they were sworn to protect?"[33] A week after the election the League met to discuss ways to ensure that the administration would enforce the law. "Near clashes were frequent between friends of the city administration and those who inferred that more might be done by the present administration in the matter of enforcing the law," the *Deseret News* reported. "The nearest open rupture came when it was declared by a supporter of Mayor Huscher that the Law and Order League exists for the sole purpose of discrediting the present city administration."[34] At the city commission's next meeting, League officials sent a letter "offering their assistance as an organized body of citizens to work with the city officials in administering the sale of intoxicating liquors in Murray City." In response, the commission resolved that "Our city police department make every effort to enforce laws pertaining to the sale of liquors and tobacco and encourage all help from outside organizations of enforcement of same."[35] A week later, the League asked the commission to pay several of its members to collect evidence leading to the conviction of people illegally selling liquor. The commission instead authorized the city marshal to offer a reward of $25.00 for evidence leading to such convictions.[36] Not satisfied with this, the League renewed its attack, charging that Socialist officials failed to enforce the laws and were "apologists for the illicit liquor dealers." Violations were "open and flagrant," League members asserted several months later, and a generally "lawless climate" existed in the city. As proof, commission opponents pointed to a recent incident at a Greek coffeehouse where a "foreigner" shot and nearly killed a native-born worker.[37] Following the 1915 election, when control of the city commission passed from socialist hands and socialist government influence was no longer an issue, the League disbanded.

This evidence indicates that Socialists elected to office in Utah were what might be called "respectable reformers." In comparison with other Socialists in the United States, they were among the most moderate. Like their counterparts elsewhere, they recognized a limit to what even radicals

[32]Ibid., 1 July 1912.
[33]Ibid., 3 July 1914.
[34]Ibid., 7 July 1914.
[35]Murray City Commission Minutes, 9 July 1914.
[36]Ibid., 17 July 1914.
[37]*Deseret News*, 14 December 1914.

in office could do, and they knew they could not bring socialism to some cities while the rest of the country remained capitalistic. Even considering all this, however, they did less than they might have. A number of socialist cities and towns in the United States sought to go beyond moderate reform, hinting at what socialism might ideally mean, taking small steps forward towards the nationalization of the means of production and distribution, democratic planning, and production for use rather than profit. For example, Milwaukee Socialists looked beyond providing new and improved public services. They advocated the establishment of municipal lodging houses, ice houses, slaughterhouses, and markets; opened a free employment bureau; offered strike arbitration services; and tried to make the police department become working-class in orientation.[38] Flint, Michigan, Socialists made similar reform efforts, seeking to provide a medium through which workers could voice demands not traditionally considered the business of politicians. They called for labor unions, denounced factory conditions, and broadened their criticism to include attacks upon economic as well as political institutions.[39]

What is striking about Utah Socialists is how little of this they did. They did not test the existing limits, question the dominant ideology, try to change the nature of capitalist relations, present a new vision of society, or act as if there were alternatives to existing arrangements. They did not aggressively seek to help people perceive that a new social order was necessary in order to address the problems of capitalism. What they did try to do was provide "good government"; in this way they hoped to attract broad support and widen their appeal. They sometimes even agreed with the views that political parties might not be particularly important in local politics, that what was needed in office were skilled administrators, not broad ideals, and that voting was essentially a matter of making a calculated technical choice. Although they spoke of themselves as the party of the working class, they showed little understanding of, or tolerance for, an increasingly important part of that class, the growing population of new immigrants.

In *The Decline of Socialism in America* James Weinstein identified four groupings within the Socialist party in the early twentieth century. Utah socialists, at least those elected to public office, were part of the conservative, or "constructive," wing, which saw no immediate prospect for a transition to socialism and had only a vague idea of how such a transition might come about. Why did socialists in Utah adopt this approach? There were several reasons. In the first place, they sometimes seemed not to know what else to do. In some ways, theirs was a "romantic socialism,"[40] nurturing a dream but having little strategy for its implementation beyond the faith and hope that the election of good men and women to office would provide the foun-

[38]Sally M. Miller, "Casting a Wide Net: The Milwaukee Socialist Movement to 1920," in Critchlow, *Socialism in the Heartland,* 33.

[39]Richard W. Judd, "Restoring Consensus in Flint, Michigan: The Socialist Party in Municipal Politics, 1910–1912," in Critchlow, *Socialism in The Heartland,* 94–100.

dation or pave the way to such a goal. In 1914, for example, socialist George C. Lindsay became county commissioner in newly created Duchesne County. Several weeks later he wrote to the Socialist party's national office for help:

> The unexpected has happened, and I, a poor socialist, have been elected county commissioner for the four year term. . . . The socialists in this new county will look to me to do all that I possibly can do to advance the interests of our party by passing, or at least introducing, socialist measures . . . and I must have some help as I realize my own weakness. . . . I would be grateful if you could send me whatever you can so that when another election rolls around our campaign can truthfully say that the lone socialist who has been in office has been on the job all the time."[41]

More commonly, however, such an approach was a deliberate strategy, undertaken not because Socialists did not know or could not imagine what else to do but because it made sense to them as a means of moving the masses toward socialism, given the negative images of Socialists that were common in Utah and the kinds of criticism socialists faced. In 1911, as part of its campaign against local Socialist party candidates, the *Eureka Reporter* described the experience in Bingham following the election of a Socialist administration six years earlier: "The promises made by the socialists of Bingham were about the same as the socialists of Eureka are making to the working men of Eureka. They were never kept; they were never meant to be kept. It would be impossible for any party to carry out the wild theories advanced by the socialists and preserve a government of law and order—or even a semblance of it." It was soon apparent, the paper continued, that Bingham's Socialist officials were "thoroughly incompetent." They were consequently "rooted from office and replaced by a business-like administration," and voters interested in "the real progress and welfare of Eureka City" would vote against Socialists, not only because they were revolutionaries but because "they cannot provide a safe, sane, and sensible city government."[42] In a similar vein, Mormon church apostle Anthony W. Ivins recorded his reaction to a socialist street speaker in 1912: "His remarks were bitter, vindictive, just calculated to stir up the hearts of men to anger one against another and create war, rapine, and plunder. . . . One had but to look at him to know that he was a man without character or ability, one who had failed himself and was ready to drag everybody else down to his level."[43]

Utah Socialists always conducted their campaigns and tenure in office under the shadow of such assertions and they were determined to disprove them. Indeed, they felt they must if they were to have any hope of success.

[40]The term is Sheila Rowbotham's. See Rowbotham, "In Search of Edward Carpenter," *Radical America* 14 (July–August 1980), 49–60.

[41]George Lindsay to Carl D. Thompson, 24 November 1914, Socialist Party of America Papers, Duke University.

[42]*Eureka Reporter,* 3 November 1911.

[43]Anthony W. Ivins to W. A. Jameson, 20 April 1912, Anthony W. Ivins Papers, Utah State Historical Society, Salt Lake City, Utah.

Until Socialists were no longer viewed in such negative terms, little progress would be possible. They sought to provide good, efficient government as a way of gradually building popular support for socialism. Until people understood that socialists were neither dangerous nor impractical, but instead were honest, hard-working, capable men and women, as well as genuine idealists who sought a better world, no progress could be made toward the ultimate establishment of the cooperative commonwealth and the triumph of the working class. As they saw it, the issue was not ideology but competence. Before they could discuss socialist ideology or get people to listen to them they first had to be taken as people of substance, not as crackpots, dilettantes, or troublemakers. Having once achieved legitimacy, they could move to reform. But it would take time. In their own view, Utah Socialists had not abandoned socialism; they simply saw its achievement as a slow process built on a foundation of trust.

Their strategy did not work. By 1920 the socialist movement had all but disappeared from Utah, as was the case also throughout the United States. There is no doubt that Utah Socialists were competent and progressive people who helped make their communities better places in which to live and work, but competence in office did not translate into long-term popular support for socialism. Indeed, it seems to have had just the opposite effect. It made socialism irrelevant. The argument that Socialist party members were more honest and efficient than members of other political parties meant, in effect, that the reason to vote for them was because of their personal qualities of mind and character, and not because they espoused socialism and would work toward a fundamental transformation of society.

What can we conclude about Utah's socialist experience? In the first place, it helps illuminate important features of the state in the early twentieth century—in particular the existence of mutually antagonistic cultures and the tensions that existed between them, the pervasiveness of racial divisions, and the challenges elected officials faced in responding to them. It also clarifies the choices that old-stock, American working-class socialist administrators had to make in order to stay in office and the conditions under which they were forced to make those choices. Squeezed between a growing ethnic constituency and a particularly illiberal political culture represented by the middle class, they could expand their constituencies by either turning to immigrant neighborhoods or by reaching out to "respectable" middle-class voters. They chose the latter.

The history of socialism in Utah also suggests an answer to an old but important question, "Why is the United States the only major industrial nation without a viable socialist or other left-wing alternative?" Answers have ranged from government repression, employer opposition, the success of capitalism, internal division within the socialist movement itself, the inadequacy of Marxian analysis when applied to the United States, the existence of the frontier, the absence of a feudal past, and the myth and reality of American mobility. All have explanatory power, but the experience of Utah socialists suggests that an important reason for the ultimate failure of the Socialist party was its actual behavior once in power. Socialists should not be seen as merely misguided reformers, given the conditions under which they made their choices, where conservative social norms permeated local political culture and presented a stark contrast to the new immigrant culture. Yet in failing to differentiate themselves from traditional politicians and their movement from traditional politics and traditional parties, Socialists may have been seen as betraying their principles. By becoming mere politicians, by ignoring the disadvantaged, they may have dampened enthusiasm, leaving their actual and potential supporters dissatisfied and disillusioned.

Socialists sought to create a truly humane world, one that was non-exploitative and classless, and they were motivated by a democratic, utopian vision of collective and individual freedom. However, that was not entirely clear from the actions of Utah Socialists. They did little to distinguish themselves from reformers who assumed the essential validity of the status quo and sought only to make adjustments in a system they saw as basically sound. There were few hints in the actions of Socialists that they questioned the very system itself and viewed particular conditions as symptoms of a larger economic problem. They were not open to the charge, which Daniel Bell leveled at American socialists in general, that they were hopelessly incompetent idealists who lived in the world but were not of it, who had their eyes so focused upon utopian goals that they "could not relate to the specific problems of social action in the here and now, give-and-take political world."[44] Instead, they were open to the charge Melvin Dubofsky leveled at New York City Socialists during the same period: they "lived too fully in this world and were too much political men."[45] They were competent, but only competent; effective reformers, but little more; their political work was too compromised; in turning their backs on their ideals, they drained the phrase "socialism in action" of meaning or reality.

Utah's Socialists thought they were keeping the faith. They did not deliberately undermine the cause, but undermine it they did. Their respectable, modest efforts made it difficult to hold the loyalties of people whose support stemmed from a conviction that the Socialist party was fundamentally different. They acted like the "party of dentists" Trotsky accused American socialists of being, middle-class reformers who would never be more than the left-wing of the Progressive movement. Sensitive to the charge that they were too radical, the Utah experience suggests that Socialists failed because they were not radical enough.

[44]*Marxian Socialism in the United States*, 217.

[45]"Success and Failure of Socialism in New York City, 1900–1918: A Case Study," *Labor History* 9 (Fall 1968), 373.

*

The "Foreign Element" and the 1903–1904 Carbon County Coal Miners' Strike

ALLAN KENT POWELL

Labor history has been a relatively unexplored topic among Utah historians. The worker has often seemed neither as interesting nor as important a subject as has the entrepreneur. Attention has focused more readily on people like Thomas Kearns, who, legend has it, arrived in Park City in the late 1880s with only a pack on his back and a dime in his pocket and a decade later was a multimillionaire and a U.S. Senator, than it has on the men and women whose labor built his fortune. In recent years, however, the situation has begun to change. This article provides an account of Utah's most serious labor dispute to that time—the Carbon County coal miners' strike against the Utah Fuel Company that began in 1903 and lasted for more than a year—and reveals how fruitful the study of Utah's labor history can be. Rich in detail, the essay concludes that the strike failed because the company was able to effectively play on the widespread nativist sentiment of the time and portray the striking miners, who were mainly Finnish, Slavic, Italian, and other "new immigrants" from eastern and southern Europe, as un-American, radical, and dangerous.

Allan Kent Powell, "The 'Foreign Element' and the 1903–4 Carbon County Coal Miners' Strike," *Utah Historical Quarterly* 43 (Spring 1975): 125–54. Reprinted by permission of the publisher and the author.

Allan Kent Powell has a Ph.D. degree in history from the University of Utah and is Director of Field Services at the Utah State Historical Society. His publications include *The Next Time We Strike: Labor in Utah's Coal Fields, 1900–1933* and *Splinters of a Nation: German Prisoners of War in Utah.*

THE FIRST YEARS of the twentieth century were a time of tremendous growth for the labor movement in the United States. In 1900 nationwide union membership was 868,500, and by 1904 it had more than doubled to 2,072,700.[1] Unionism moved forward on two fronts: increased membership

[1]Selig Perlman and Philip Taft, *History of Labor in the United States, 1896–1932,* 4 vols.

in already established unions and increased numbers of new unions. Among the important elements in the burgeoning labor movement were the new immigrants from southern and eastern Europe. In the coal fields of Carbon County, Finnish, Slavic, and Italian miners provided the strength behind the new state's most serious labor confrontation to that time, a confrontation that began in the fall of 1903 and lasted more than a year.

Frustrated in their past efforts to unionize, Utah miners found fresh hope in events taking place outside the state. Following the successful anthracite strike of 1902 in Pennsylvania, the United Mine Workers conducted an extensive campaign to expand their control. Prime areas of concern were the far western coal regions of Colorado, Wyoming, and Utah.[2] Consequently the UMW responded immediately to a call for organizers from the Carbon County strikers in 1903. The Utah strike also coincided with strikes in the northern and southern coal fields of Colorado. The Colorado strike proved both an asset and a liability to the Utah strikers. Because of it the national UMW provided funds and organizers that otherwise might not have been available. Also, the movement of organizers back and forth between Utah and Colorado and the fact that some of the Utah miners, especially the Italians, had worked in the Colorado mines, provided ties between the two groups during the strikes. Psychologically this helped sustain the Utah strikers. On the other hand, the Colorado strike soon developed into virtual civil war, and many Utahns feared that the Carbon County strike would follow the same course. The strikers were therefore denied public sympathy from the beginning.

While several emotionally charged issues clouded the Utah strike, labor and management were irrevocably split on the right of workers to organize and would remain so throughout the strike. Because the coal miners' strike in Colorado had begun three days before the Utah strike, the Utah Fuel Company argued that Utah miners had no real grievances but were only striking in sympathy with the Colorado miners. The strikers denounced this assessment and put forth a number of specific grievances. They charged that they were commonly cheated at the weighing scales (miners were paid by the amount of coal they mined, not the hours they worked), that they were taken advantage of through the scrip and company store system, and that the coal operators frequently violated Utah's eight-hour workday law for miners. In addition to settlement of these grievances, the miners also demanded an increase in pay and recognition of the United Mine Workers

---

(New York, 1935), 4:13. However, it should be noted that during this time less than ten percent of the nation's wage earners were involved in the unions as members. Foster Rhea Dulles, *Labor in America, A History* (New York, 1966), 186.

[2]In January 1901, the miners at Scofield-Winter Quarters and Clear Creek, Utah, had gone out on strike. The striking miners sent an urgent request to United Mine Workers headquarters in Indianapolis for an organizer. The organizer never arrived. For an account of this strike, see Allan Kent Powell "Labor at the Beginning of the 20th Century: The Carbon County, Utah, Coal Fields, 1900–1905" (M.A. thesis, University of Utah, 1972) 80–105.

Union.[3] The Utah Fuel Company had offered the miners a ten percent raise two days before the strike was called. (This was to be accompanied by a twenty-three percent increase in the price of coal to dealers.) The miners would probably have accepted the offer had the company been willing to recognize the UMW. Realizing that concessions won without union recognition were temporary at best and that without the union to protect them they would probably lose their jobs, the strikers remained firm in their determination to achieve union recognition.

The Utah Fuel Company responded to the strike by announcing that the company store was to go on a strictly cash basis and that credit would be given to no one until the trouble was settled. The company then posted notices assuring employees who remained loyal every possible protection from interference or menace by the strikers. The company's chief detective, C.W. Shores, hired guards to ensure the enforcement of these policies. His recruiting methods were simple and straightforward:

> . . . Applicants arrived in large numbers. Immediately on the arrival of an applicant and a statement from him that he desired employment, Shores handed him a Winchester rifle, "Let's see you load and unload that before we can know whether or not you will suit," said Shores.[4]

The Utah Fuel Company's public response to the strike appealed to nativistic sentiments. Company officials argued that support for the strike came from single men without families, those who had recently arrived in the coal fields, and the "worst element of foreigners." The old-time English-speaking miners, officials claimed, did not support the strike. The company continued to brand the walkout as simply a sympathy strike for the miners of Colorado[5] and blamed labor organizers and agitators from that area for stirring up the previously contented miners.

The company accusation that outside agitators had caused the strike lacked any basis in fact. The move for a strike at Sunnyside had been spearheaded by local American leaders of the United Mine Workers who were supported, initially, by all classes of miners but who ultimately received their most dedicated support from the Italian miners. Immediately after the

[3]The strikers' demands were reported in a letter from union representatives Thomas Phelps, Sunnyside; Louis Jones, Winter Quarters: Thomas Potter, Clear Creek: and Thomas Lewis, Castle Gate; to G. W. Kramer, vice-president of the Utah Fuel Company, quoted in the *Salt Lake Tribune,* December 20, 1903, p. 18, and in State of Utah, *Report of the Coal Mine Inspector for the Years 1903 and 1904* (Salt Lake City, 1905), 63–64.

[4]*Salt Lake Tribune,* November 19, 1903, p. 1.

[5]In a letter from John Mitchell, president of the United Mine Workers of America, to Edwin F. Homes, president of the Salt Lake City Commercial Club, November 27, 1903, Mitchell denied that the Utah strike had been called as a sympathetic strike for the Colorado strikers. "Utah miners are not striking in sympathy with miners of Colorado. On the contrary, they demand an increase of 20 percent in wages. Not to exceed three organizers are stationed in Utah. It is unreasonable to suppose that two or three organizers could intimidate Utah miners and prevent their working if they desired. I am anxious for an amicable settlement and am willing to meet representatives of the coal company for the purpose of arranging conditions of settlement." Quoted in the *Salt Lake Tribune,* November 28, 1903, p. 11.

vote to strike was taken on November 12, local leaders requested that organizers be sent to Sunnyside. The first attempt to bring in union organizers failed when a delegation of six strikers on their way from Sunnyside to Price to meet the incoming officials was intercepted by a party of armed men (supposedly employed by the Utah Fuel Company) and forced at gunpoint to return to Sunnyside. But for the union this proved a temporary setback only. By November 17, union leaders with the aid of the Italian organizer Charles DeMolli, who according to local legend secretly entered Sunnyside in a wagonload of hay, had succeeded in organizing a miners' union with an enrollment of 468 members.

Officials reacted quickly to the unionizing effort. On November 17, a regular payday at Sunnyside, all men not working were paid in full and notified to consider themselves discharged. Those occupying company houses were ordered to vacate. The company then launched an active recruiting program among farmers in the local areas to work the mines, in this manner succeeding in keeping the Sunnyside mines in operation, although production was curtailed greatly.

Following the initial success of Sunnyside, the UMW organizers turned their attention to the remaining Carbon County camps: Castle Gate, Clear Creek, and Scofield-Winter Quarters.[6] On November 19, the *Tribune* reported that the "Colorado agitators" had met with poor success at Castle Gate. Yet by November 21 the mines at Castle Gate were closed as a result of the strike—a feat the union was unable to duplicate in any of the other coal camps. On November 28, 627 men paid the $1.25 initiation fee and joined the United Mine Workers at the upper camps of Clear Creek and Scofield.

On November 21 the strike entered a new phase when Carbon County Sheriff Hyrum Wilcox, fearing the eruption of violence, requested help from Gov. Heber M. Wells[7] who responded by sending Gen. John Q. Cannon of the Utah National Guard to investigate conditions in Carbon County. Cannon found the coal camps in a state of emotional excitement. Union organizers were at the pinnacle of their success in recruiting members, approximately twelve hundred miners having joined the union. Parades were held daily by the strikers, and at Castle Gate the parades were led by the Italian brass band.[8] The articulate organizers effectively appealed to the miners'

[6]According to the *Eastern Utah Advocate* (Price), December 3, 1903, the mining population of the Carbon County camps was as follows:

Camp	*Italian*	*English Speaking*	*Austrian*	*Finn*
Castle Gate	356	108	10	
Sunnyside	246	356	222	
Clear Creek	172	95		128
Winter Quarters	74	181		126

[7]See *Report of the Coal Mine Inspector,* 47, for the text of the letter dated November 21, 1903, from Hyrum Wilcox to Gov. Heber M. Wells.

[8]The parades were colorful affairs. On February 18, 1904, the *Eastern Utah Advocate* noted that a parade had been held at Helper in which the strikers masqueraded as capitalists, miners, and slaves.

dignity as men. In one speech William Price, a prominent organizer, reported:

> I met the attorney general of Utah the other day and he said to me: "The men who dig coal in Utah make nearly as much, if not all as much, as the men who handle the pen." Now, in the name of God, are not the men who dig coal entitled to as much as men who whirl the pen? The attorney general told me he went into the homes of the miners in Scofield. "You didn't see any Brussel carpet there did you?" I said to him. Then I said: "Hasn't my wife as much right to wear a silk dress as your wife, Mr. Kramer's wife or Mr. Williams' wife." He said he supposed of course, if I could afford it, but I tell you, my friends, what these men say to us is: "Calico was made for you people and silk for us."[9]

The labor organizers continually urged their members to avoid any threats or acts of violence toward those who continued to work in the mines. They argued that only by peaceful means could they win public support for the strike. Nevertheless, threats were made and acts of intimidation were committed by a few of the strikers. The antiunion forces magnified these incidents until public opinion, for the most part, was swayed against the strikers. Some of the alleged acts included calling miners who were willing to work "scabs." James Polve was threatened with expulsion from the Italian lodge at Castle Gate if he continued to work.[10] Some men were prevented from going to work when their clothes were stolen or soaked with water so that they could not be worn. At Sunnyside strikers were accused of burning a partly loaded boxcar and the "murder" of a company guard's cow.[11] At Castle Gate and the upper camps the Italian strikers were accused of showing disrespect for the American flag when they carried it upside down in their parades. (Charles DeMolli, the Italian organizer, claimed that this was done out of ignorance, not disrespect.) Threatening letters were also sent to certain miners. One of the most colorful notes was written to John Knudsend:

> Mr. John Kundsend [*sic*]: You are hereby notified that if you scab here any more you had better be buying a coffin, and that pretty soon, too. And if you ride that rope tomorrow you will be hung tomorrow night. Now, you ——— ——— ——— ———, you look out, because we mean just what we say. The men that rote this letter belong to the White Cap society, and if you work tomorrow you will see them tomorrow night.[12]

On the other hand, the situation was aggravated by the presence of numerous company guards who had been deputized. They served without pay from the county but were given five dollars a day plus room and board by

[9] *Salt Lake Herald,* December 11, 1903, p. 2.

[10] Reports of various intimidations of miners by the strikers were sent by H. G. Williams to Adjt. Gen. Charles S. Burton. See State of Utah, Industrial Commission, Coal Mine Inspector, "Report—Militia At Scofield During Miners Strike, 1904," Utah State Archives, State Capitol, Salt Lake City.

[11] *Salt Lake Telegram,* December 2, 1903, p. 4.

[12] *Deseret Evening News,* November 24, 1903, p. 2.

the Utah Fuel Company. Some company guards were sympathetic to the strikers; however, the extremely high wages paid the guards—many of them farmers who sought winter jobs to supplement their income—compromised their sympathies.[13] Some guards were guilty of intimidating and bullying strikers, trying to provoke them to lawlessness.[14]

Upon General Cannon's return to Salt Lake City Governor Wells held a conference with state officials and members of the legislature. The group reached a unanimous decision, based on General Cannon's report, that sufficient cause existed for ordering the state troops into the coal fields to preserve order.[15] The following day, November 23, 1903, Governor Wells issued a proclamation calling out the Guard; and by November 24, the entire National Guard was in the coal fields of Carbon County.[16] They took up positions at Castle Gate, Scofield, and Clear Creek. The strength of the National Guard was given as 34 officers and 399 men. Although the entire force had been called out, only three hundred or so actually went to Carbon County. Some guardsmen who were university students, farmers, or ranchers were excused unless conditions worsened.[17]

According to newspaper reports and instructions given by National Guard officers, the troops were to aid county officials in protecting company property from destruction by the strikers and to prevent threats and intimidation against those miners who wanted to work. Some guardsmen held this procompany, antiunion attitude throughout the strike. However, many others, as a result of friendly relations with the strikers and growing disgust with the coal company, found their sympathies swayed.[18] J.L. Ewing, sergeant in the Nephi Company and editor of the *Nephi Record*, noted this shift in one of his editorials:

[13]Lott Powell, one of the guards at Sunnyside, said that although he agreed with the miners' grievances, the unbelievable pay offered men to become company guards could not be turned down. Lott Powell, interview, Salt Lake City, January 3, 1971.

[14]One such guard, C. L. "Gunplay" Maxwell, who continually sought to become a bona fide member of the Robber's Roost gang, was the antithesis of the gallant Butch Cassidy. One story from eastern Utah tells how Gunplay Maxwell rode into a camp of prospectors who were looking for gilsonite in the Hill Creek country east of the Green River. To demonstrate how bad he was, Maxwell tried to pick a fight with one of the smaller men. The prospectors invited Maxwell to take off his guns and fight. He boastfully replied, "I never take my guns off." "The hell you don't!" shouted the prospectors as they stripped Maxwell of his guns and turned the man loose on him. Following the fight, the half-dead badman was loaded on his horse and sent on his way. In 1898 Maxwell had been sentenced to prison for eighteen years for robbing the Springville bank, but on November 21, 1903, his sentence was commuted by influential friends, presumably Utah Fuel Company officials, and he went to Carbon County as a company guard. Charles Kelly, *The Outlaw Trail* (New York, 1959), 185.

[15]For the text of General Cannon's report see *Report of the Coal Mine Inspector*, 55–56.

[16]For an account of the role of the National Guard in the strike, see Richard Campbell Roberts, "History of the Utah National Guard: 1894–1954" (Ph.D. diss., University of Utah, 1973), 58–72.

[17]Matt. T. Howard, interview, Nephi, Utah, February 4, 1971. Mr. Howard was a member of the Nephi Company called out in 1903.

[18]Citizens of Sunnyside, including the strikers, were quite hospitable to the troops. "Whenever a soldier enters the hut of a miner, wine, beer, and whiskey is at once produced and offense is taken if their hospitality is not accepted." *Salt Lake Tribune*, December 20, 1903, p. 8.

When the militia was sent out it was supposed to be to protect the coal trust's property and the lives of its employees from a lot of anarchists and lawless people; but investigation so far has shown that the strikers are quite as law abiding as are the emissaries of the coal trust and that the striking miners are just as much in need of protection from the hired guards of the trust, as the company property and men are in need of protection from the striking miners. . . .

We have but little sympathy with the miners out there, and we have still less sympathy for the coal trust. In the first place if the trust is paying $3 to $8 a day to miners as they claim, or an average of $3.50 to $3.75 a day they have no need to hire Finns or Dagos. They can get the best miners in the country for such pay; and if they have imported under contract or otherwise a lot of anarchists, as they claim they are, from the old countries, they have brought their trouble upon themselves and ought to suffer for it. As time goes on it is becoming plainer and plainer that the companies have been trying to prejudice the public by coloring the reports that have gone from the coal camps to favor the companies and to grossly misrepresent the strikers.

It is a very significant fact that most of the militiamen who have returned are in sympathy with the strikers, and when they left for the coal camps the very reverse was true. . . . [19]

One of the National Guard's first duties was to assist Sheriff Wilcox in arresting the Italian organizer Charles DeMolli whose background and personal magnetism made him a strong adversary. DeMolli was born in 1870 in Brussels, Belgium. His father was a horse trainer from Milan and his mother a native of Como in Italy. He was educated at the Institute of Milan and served three years in the Italian army before going to work in the silk mills of Como. In 1895 he became involved in a strike and revolution at Como and was banished from Italy.[20] Coming to the United States he began writing for Italian newspapers in the East. He drifted to the coal mines in Pennsylvania where he renewed his interest in unionism. Later DeMolli worked in the coal mines of Colorado until he became associated with the newspaper *Il Lavoratore Italiano,* published at Trinidad, Colorado, that served as the organ of the United Mine Workers among the Italians. The *Salt Lake Herald* described DeMolli's charismatic appeal:

DeMolli, the silver-tongued, whose influence with his fellow countrymen is so feared by the Utah Fuel Company officials . . . is in appearance far from being the wild-eyed anarchist he is pictured by his enemies. A tall handsome

[19] *Nephi Record,* December 11, 1903, p. 4.

[20] In an interview printed in *Salt Lake Herald,* December 7, 1903, DeMolli described the Como strike: "It is true that I am an exile and cannot go back to my country for three years more. I took part in what has been called the Como revolution in 1895. At that time 40,000 workers struck. The general command there in the city of Como telegraphed King Humbert—the king is dead now: may his soul rest in peace—and asked what he should do. King Humbert wired back 'You are the general, do as you please.'

"The general then moved on the city with four regiments of soldiers and began arresting men, women and children. Many thousand of us went to the military district and got rifles and resisted. There were several killed and many wounded. They sent a man to treat with us and offered us terms. We were close to the border of Switzerland there, and they demanded that some of us who had been prominent should go over into Switzerland and stay. The leader on our side who was a deputy in the Italian parliament advised us to do this and I went. I was exiled for ten years. . . . "

> man in appearance, dressed in the rough chin-in jacket, flannel shirt, corduroy trousers and laced boots of a miner, he has a handsome face, typically Italian, with a small slooping mustache. His voice is soft and his manners suave. . . .
>
> Besides being big and strong and handsome, and with a magnetic personality, DeMolli is eloquent with tongue and pen in the Italian language. Not only this but he can talk in their native tongues with Finlanders, Slavs, French, or representatives of other nationalities. With his level head, shrewd judgment, college education, suave manner, and great magnetism, he is regarded as one of the strongest men affiliated with the United Mine Workers and he is idolized by his followers.[21]

On November 20 DeMolli and several other organizers went by train to Scofield, intending to organize the miners at Winter Quarters and Clear Creek. A committee of the Citizens Alliance and coal company employees met the organizers at Scofield and refused to let them detrain. DeMolli and his aides were told that it was useless for them to visit the camps because the miners had signed an agreement that they would not strike. DeMolli returned to Helper and enlisted the services of two cowboys who assured him that they would furnish an escort of twenty-five men if necessary and see to it that he arrived in Scofield without injury.[22] The trip was made overland by horseback on November 23, evading company guards covering the railroads and highways. DeMolli's influence was felt immediately; within two days the strike had been organized in the northern fields, and the entire county was then involved in the dispute.

The success at Clear Creek and Winter Quarters was marred by DeMolli's arrest at Scofield by Sheriff Wilcox on the morning of November 25 on a charge of disturbing the peace. A detachment of guardsmen accompanied Wilcox to the Lone Star Saloon where DeMolli was speaking to a group of several hundred. The strikers could have easily overpowered the detachment. Reflecting apprehension and fear, one guardsman nudged the soldier next to him and said, "God! This looks like this is about the end. If they rush us we'll look like rag dolls laying around here."[23] However, when DeMolli saw the sheriff he held up his hands and said in English, "Quiet down boys. Everything's all right."[24] As he left with the sheriff, DeMolli once again cautioned the strikers to preserve the peace and avoid disturbances of any kind. The organizer was immediately taken before the local justice of the peace, found guilty of disturbing the peace, and sentenced to thirty days in the county jail at Price.

On November 30 a special court session at Price heard evidence in habeas corpus proceedings brought against the sheriff and jailer of Carbon County. After hearing the evidence Judge Jacob Johnson quashed the proceedings. An appeal was made to Justice William Burrows at Scofield. The

[21]Ibid., p.1, and December 8, 1903, p. 6.
[22]*Salt Lake Tribune*, November 24, 1903, p. 3.
[23]Howard interview.
[24]Ibid.

appeal and a change of venue to Clear Creek were granted. At Clear Creek the trial lasted all day and late into the evening of December 4. But after ten minutes of deliberation the four jurymen returned a verdict of not guilty. DeMolli was free.

Meanwhile, the last days of November saw the arrival of Dr. Guiseppe Cuneo, the Italian consul, from Denver. Newspaper reports said he had come at the solicitation of the coal company. In any event, he quickly alienated the striking Italians.[25] First, they heard rumors that he had come to persuade them to go back to work. Further, he had not bothered to inform any of his countrymen of the visit, and upon his arrival at Scofield he met with General Cannon and other officials before seeing any of the strikers. When he finally issued a request for several of the leading Italians to meet with him, some refused, and those who did agree to see him were almost prevented from doing so when deputy marshals tried to break up a meeting at union headquarters called to elect representatives to speak with the consul. The deputy marshals retreated upon being shown an order from General Cannon granting permission for the meeting. In avowing a position of neutrality, Dr. Cuneo failed the striking Italians of Carbon County. With his strong support, the strike might have acquired a kind of legitimacy that it did not have. Ultimately the failure of Dr. Cuneo to sustain the Italians was seen by the public as testimony that the strike was unwarranted.

Before his arrest, DeMolli had expressed a desire to meet with Governor Wells to discuss the strike. Following his acquittal he traveled to Salt Lake City where he, John Thal of the Utah Federation of Labor, and two union attorneys, A.B. Edler and J.S. Fowler, met with the governor. DeMolli denied that the walkout had been called in sympathy with the Colorado strike and insisted that all the miners wanted was for the company to allow union men to work alongside nonunion men. The company was still demanding that miners foreswear any union affiliation as a prerequisite for returning to work. Union officials failed to obtain any support from the state. In fact, the union cause was struck a severe blow when Governor Wells was quoted as saying, "Mr. DeMolli, you are not welcome. We don't want you, and the sooner you are out of the state, the better we will be pleased. We will facilitate your going in every way possible."[26] The day after the conference the *Salt Lake Herald* denounced DeMolli:

> We submit that a man whose ideas of government justify that sort of striking [referring to the Como strike of 1895] is not fit representative of either unionism or American citizenship; and we question whether any union

[25]Cuneo had supported the Pinkerton Detective Agency in suppressing the Italians in the Colorado coal fields by aiding in the search for possible fugitives from Italian justice. George Graham Suggs, Jr., "Colorado Conservatives Versus Organized Labor: A Study of the James Hamilton Peabody Administration 1903–1905" (Ph.D. diss., University of Colorado, 1964), 490. Charles DeMolli, one of the Italians harassed by the Pinkerton detectives, described Cuneo as "a tooth puller, pork butcher and sausage maker." *Il Lavoratore Italiano* (Trinidad, Colorado), March 14, 1904, p.2.

[26]*Salt Lake Tribune,* December 8, 1903, p. 1.

> of American citizens would tolerate his leadership a single day. . . . Every friend of the miners will hope that DeMolli will be discarded at once and invited to go elswhere. If he isn't, the union might well prepare to lose its case with the general public.[27]

Within a week DeMolli had left the state, but not permanently. In February of the following year he would return to Carbon County.

In the coal fields several isolated incidents kept the situation in a state of tension, but no serious violence occurred. Sheriff Wilcox, while at Clear Creek, was forced to give up his rifle by two shotgun-wielding Italian women. A Finn was arrested and charged with assault for throwing rocks at another Finn who wanted to work. On the road between Scofield and Winter Quarters, a fight took place when two Finns called John Burgess and Joe Ruff "scabs"; with the arrival of a soldier the Finns tried to run away but were caught and arrested. Reports of threats and intimidations against those who wanted to work were common. The peace of the area was further jeopardized by the arrival of a carload of wine for the Italian strikers on the same day the National Guard entered the northern camps. W. Lloyd Adams, a member of the Nephi Company, gave the following account of his first experience on guard duty:

> . . . My first beat was between two large square houses filled with Italians. They had unloaded a great many fifty gallon barrels of wine during the day. It seemed to be a celebration in these houses as I walked my beat up and down between those houses sometimes women would shake their fists at me and talk in a foreign language and sometimes men. I wasn't more than 16 and of course I kept walking. I didn't rest a minute on that beat.[28]

Meanwhile, the Utah Fuel Company accelerated its efforts to curtail the activities of the union organizers. Exerting great influence upon the civil authorities, the company saw to the arrest of most of the leading union officials. On December 8, William R. Lewis, a secretary, and William Marinelli, president of the Scofield union, were arrested, convicted, and sentenced to twenty days in jail on charges of vagrancy. David Wilson, secretary of the Sunnyside union, was arrested on a charge of disturbing the peace. Most sensational, however, was the arrest of A.B. Edler, attorney for the United Mine Workers. When Edler arrived at Scofield on December 9 to defend the union men who had been arrested, he was served with a warrant for his own arrest on a charge of criminal libel. The charge grew out of comments that Edler had made to the newspapers about the company guards.

During the proceedings that followed, William H. King, attorney for Edler, in one of his encounters with M.C. Braffet, attorney for the Utah Fuel Company, was quoted as saying:

[27] *Salt Lake Herald,* December 8, 1903, p. 4.

[28] W. Lloyd Adams, "Memoirs of W. Lloyd Adams," pp. 6–7. A typescript copy of this portion of his unpublished memoirs was obtained by the author from Adams's niece, Sadie Greenhalgh, Nephi, Utah.

> I have practiced before many courts, but I have never seen a place where the desire to railroad a man through to jail was so manifest. It is outrageous, and there is not another place where an attorney for a corporation is supreme to the court.[29]

At the preliminary hearing Edler was released on bonds of $1,500. According to observers, the court session continually bordered on physical violence between the opposing lawyers. The Edler affair brought a strong warning from Governor Wells to the Utah Fuel Company officials, telling them to be careful and to keep a tight rein on the actions of their guards. The governor also requested General Cannon to make an investigation and submit a report on the Edler arrest and trial. After discussing the episode at some length, Cannon, in his report to the governor, concluded:

> I am of the opinion . . . that the whole incident has been ridiculously magnified by Mr. Edler himself in the interest of his own notoriety, and by the "war correspondents," who in the absence of anything at all exciting in a campaign so entirely uneventful and peaceable as this, seize upon the merest pretext around which to weave a "story." The episode would not have warranted more than an inch of space in the ordinary newspaper column if occurring under normal conditions.[30]

The newspapers were critical of the general's assessment of the Edler affair. A *Salt Lake Herald* editorial attacked him severely:

> . . . Cannon has demonstrated his inability to observe clearly and state facts without prejudice. If his sentiments and attitude have been construed fairly he has no business in a position of judicial or semijudicial responsibility . . . he seems to assume that the state forces have been sent to Carbon county to be placed at the disposal of the Utah Fuel Company till further orders, the taxpayers to settle all the bills.[31]

Tension continued to percolate through the coal camps. At Sunnyside Sunday evening, December 20, a public confrontation resulted in the arrest of thirty-three Italians. While at a dance, Virginio Bonvicini was asked if he would rather go back to work than move into a tent. He replied that he would rather return to work. At this point six or seven men began calling him a "scab" and other offensive names. When Bonvicini reported the matter to Justice George Hill, the Italians were arrested and charged with disturbing the peace. Nineteen of the thirty-three were found guilty: thirteen were fined five dollars plus costs; five were fined ten dollars plus costs; and one was fined twenty-four dollars plus costs. Two men paid their fines, but seventeen served time in the county jail in default of the money. They were described as being a "jolly good-natured set and accepted their sentences of imprisonment laughingly."[32] Each Italian wore in his cap a feather plucked from a stuffed eagle in the Knights of Pythias hall of Sunnyside where they had been confined under guard.

[29] *Salt Lake Tribune*, December 11, 1903, p. 1.
[30] Cannon's report was published in the *Deseret Evening News*, December 14, 1903, p. 5.
[31] *Salt Lake Herald*, December 14, 1903, p. 4.
[32] *Salt Lake Tribune*, December 23, 1903, p. 1.

As the strike continued, expressions of antiforeign sentiments grew more frequent. The coal company continually placed the blame for the strike on the Italians, claiming that it was the foreigners, not the English-speaking miners, that the labor agitators were able to stir up. The *Salt Lake Herald* echoed the refrain: "It is a satisfaction to know that . . . these threats have not come from American citizens, but from an alien class, ignorant in most cases, unlettered, and led by individuals who have little regard for the law and less for the institutions of civil liberty."[33] The editors also noted that while there was no better citizen than the Italian from the north, there could not be any more undesirable citizen than the southern Italian.

As part of the antistrike rhetoric, Italians were sometimes characterized as opportunistic and niggardly. For example, James A. Harrison, Carbon County commissioner, commented:

> The Italians as a class, live on about one-third what it costs the American miner, while at the same time they make the same amount of money for the same work. They have money saved to leave the country or remain in idleness for months. . . . [34]

The *Deseret Evening News,* reflecting a similar point of view, charged that "these Italians have refused to amalgamate with Americans or learn the English language and have lived with the intention of getting out of this country all they could and then returning to their native land of olives and dirt."[35] When Adjt. Gen. Charles S. Burton visited the coal camps local citizens told him that while the Italians were posing as the most peaceful and inoffensive people possible, they stood with a dagger concealed ready to plunge it into someone's back.[36]

Discontent with the situation in Carbon County spread to the National Guard, many of whom found their experience unpleasant for a variety of reasons. For the first twenty days the common soldier was paid a dollar and fifty cents a day from state monies, but beginning with the twenty-first day of active duty the Guard went on the federal pay scale of forty-three cents a day. This caused much discontent, as many of the men had had to leave good paying jobs with no assurance that their positions would be held for them. Additionally, temperatures during November and December were very low, and the inexperienced guardsmen suffered accordingly; at least one private on guard duty was overcome by the cold and found unconscious at his post.[37] Company H at Castle Gate became infested with lice and had to be fumigated.[38] With little to do except carry out the monotonous task of guard duty the soldiers suffered

[33] *Salt Lake Herald,* November 25, 1903, p. 4.

[34] Ibid., November 20, 1903, p. 2.

[35] *Deseret Evening News,* December 7, 1903, p. 4.

[36] Ibid., p. 1.

[37] Ibid., p. 4.

[38] Quoting from a letter written by Gen. John Q. Cannon to Adjt. Gen. Charles S. Burton, December 14, 1903: "The two companies here [Castle Gate] are so widely separated as to their camps that it is found necessary to have them mess seperately. . . .

"Another reason for causing the two companies to mess separately I dislike extremely to mention, but feel that perhaps I should do so. It is in brief that quite a number of the members

also from boredom. One sergeant from Salt Lake City had written home so often describing the inactivity of the troops with the phrase "war is hell" that he began receiving letters addressed to "War is Hell" Tobias.[39]

As weather permitted the guardsmen engaged in sports such as baseball and football. At Clear Creek the Nephi troops borrowed sleighs from the local Finnish children for use on the snow-covered hills of that camp. Occasionally, dances were held by the guardsmen where the only way to tell the "males" from the "females" was that the former wore hats and the latter did not. But idleness remained a problem and created strained relations among the soldiers. At one point two Nephi soldiers, after a disagreement, got their guns and started for the woods. One of them was heard to say, "We're going up into that timber and one of us isn't coming back."[40]

For a time some of the soldiers tried their hand at mining in the employment of the coal company, but this lasted only a few days. Certain guardsmen became jealous of others working for pay; and the company, after some soldiers barely escaped a cave-in, decided that the hiring of soldiers might create an unpleasant situation and no longer sought their employment.[41]

While the National Guard had been enthusiastically welcomed by the local coal company, it was received with mixed feelings by the strikers. At Clear Creek the Finnish community offered the soldiers the use of its social and cultural facility, Finn Hall, for their barracks. But at Winter Quarters the Finnish miners denied the soldiers use of a similar hall. In a practical sense the strikers were glad the National Guard was there, in the words of Charles DeMolli, "to protect them from the company guards and sheriffs." From an ideological standpoint, however, the strikers disliked the presence of soldiers because it implied a state of lawlessness—a condition attributed to the strikers, not the company.

Despite newspaper reports and statements by government officials to the contrary, the public was not convinced of the necessity of the Guard's remaining in the coal fields. From the day the Guard was called out, friends and relatives had tried to persuade the officers that certain soldiers were not needed or that conditions warranted their remaining at home.[42] Many citi-

---

of 'H' company are found to be lousy. We are taking the most heroic measures to eradicate the evil, and upon the receipt of certain supplies tomorrow shall thoroughly fumigate all bedding and tentage; have the men thoroughly bathed and put into new clothing, which at their expense we have been able to get from the store here. The first indication of the most lamentable condition was noted two or three days ago in one man who was immediately isolated from the others; but it has spread with considerable rapidity, though the company itself is made up of men who are on the whole rather superior as to their habits of cleanliness." Cannon to Burton, December 14, 1903, in "Report—Militia At Scofield During Miners Strike, 1904."

[39]*Salt Lake Tribune,* December 18, 1903, p. 4.

[40]Howard interview.

[41]Ibid.

[42]*Salt Lake Tribune,* December 3, 1903, p. 12. One of the most clever appeals was sent by a man from Provo in behalf of his son who had recently been married. Enclosed in the letter to General Cannon was the following scripture found in Deuteronomy 24:5. "When a man hath taken a new wife, he shall not go out to war, neither shall he be charged with any business; but he shall be free at home one year, and shall cheer up his wife which he has taken."

zens resented the large expenditure necessary to maintain the Guard in the coal fields. Others were skeptical of the Guard's purpose in Carbon County, especially after the Utah Fuel Company had said it would continue to discriminate against union men.[43]

With the cold weather, inactivity, and approach of Christmas, many guardsmen became anxious to return home. Discontent was expressed in the following letter from a soldier in the field and quoted in the *Salt Lake Herald:*

> We have seen no trouble and there has been evidence of none. I understand public sentiment is against the whole thing and it ought to be. We wouldn't any of us kick if there were need of us, but as it is this stunt will finish the national guard. I will ask for a discharge as soon as I reach Salt Lake, and almost all the company will do the same. . . . [44]

Only two problems prevented the return of the militia before Christmas: the reopening of the mine at Castle Gate and the eviction of strikers from company houses, scheduled for the first of January.

The reopening of the Castle Gate mine was significant for a number of reasons. First, it was the only mine that had been shut down by the strike. In addition, the mine was a hard place to work, and there was some concern that sufficient miners could not be found to reopen it. On December 11, representatives of the strikers met at Helper and voted unanimously to return to work, providing the company did not discriminate against union men. The following day David Crow, mine superintendent at Castle Gate, posted a notice that the mine would reopen on December 21 and that applications from strikers and other miners would be accepted until noon on December 15. Newspapers were jubilant with the expectation that the coal company would agree to this concession. However, company officials demanded that prospective employees foreswear the union. They argued that those miners who had remained loyal to the company would refuse to work if the union men were hired. The strikers, on the other hand, charged that the company wanted to break the union completely. As a result the call to apply for work was ignored to a man by the union miners.

At another meeting held at Helper on December 18, union representatives drafted a formal address to company vice-president C.W. Kramer that contained a list of their grievances and at the same time expressed the desire to return to work provided no discrimination was made against members of the union. They waited in vain for a reply. The union had played its last hand, and now its strategy was to wait and see if the newly recruited men would be capable of taking over the strikers' jobs.

[43]Ibid., December 14, 1903, p. 4. Commenting on this the *Salt Lake Tribune* said: " . . . the public has no interest whatever in supporting a blacklist against union men; and the time has come when the public must be considered, above any claim or contention of either party to the dispute."

[44]*Salt Lake Herald,* December 20, 1903, p. 4.

At 5 A.M. December 21 the whistle at Castle Gate called the miners from their sleep to work. Deadlines had been drawn at the east and west ends of the camp, and groups of six company guards patrolled them. On a hill overlooking the camp, guardsmen with their Gatling guns in place were ready for any trouble. Estimates of the labor force recruited throughout the state ranged from the union calculation of 25 men to the company figure of 103 men. Regardless, the company succeeded in reopening the mine.

The eviction of strikers from company houses and their removal from company property was accomplished, with one exception, without violence. That exception occurred at Winter Quarters on December 27 when about twenty guards were in the process of evicting the unmarried Finnish strikers. The guards had also ordered three married men to move and attempted to force them out of their homes, even though the married strikers had been given until the first of January to leave. The guards were attacked by the Finns and several were severely beaten. The fate of the guards might have been worse had not one of their number escaped and run to the National Guard for assistance. Company F of Manti hurried to the scene. The company guards ordered the soldiers to open fire on the mob, but the order was ignored. Through a simple request, the soldiers were able to persuade the Finns to cease hostilities. Company F had been the Christmas guests of the Finnish strikers the night before and were recognized as friends.

After their eviction, strikers from various company towns gathered in such labor union camps as Mitchellville (apparently named for John Mitchell, president of the United Mine Workers) near Sunnyside or the Half-Way House between Helper and Castle Gate. Here, and at other places, the strikers lived in tents provided by the union. Some men felt that the newly recruited labor force would soon prove inadequate, and the company would be forced to take them back. Others, less optimistic, left after a short stay. They were encouraged in this by the coal company which made arrangements with the Denver and Rio Grande Railroad to give the strikers a reduced rate, one cent a mile, on one-way tickets from Carbon County.

The company faced a particularly ticklish problem with the houses, some 225 of them, built by strikers on company land. Legally the houses belonged to the coal company, but public sympathy would not rest with the company in evicting strikers from houses built by miners. A compromise was negotiated between G.W. Kramer of the Utah Fuel Company and William H. King, attorney for the strikers. A committee of three appraisers was appointed: one by the company, one by the union, and one by the two appointed appraisers. The committee would appraise the value of each house and improvements made by the strikers. They would also fix a reasonable rental value on the property. The strikers would then leave the homes but be paid the rental value fixed by the appraisers, in advance, for a period of six months. The strikers would also have the right to sell the property at any time before October 31, 1904, subject to the approval of the company. All of the strikers, with the exception of a group of Italians at Castle Gate, agreed to the compromise.[45]

Following the peaceful reopening of the mine at Castle Gate and the relatively peaceful eviction of the striking miners, it was apparent to almost everyone that the National Guard was no longer needed.[46] In retrospect, many citizens commented that the calling out of the entire National Guard had been unnecessary from the beginning and that the same duty could have been performed by a corporal's guard in each of the coal camps. By the first week of January more than half of the soldiers in Carbon County had been relieved, and by January 24 all of the troops had returned home.

The Utah Fuel Company continued its recruiting attempts throughout the state, and as a result an issue that had been brewing finally surfaced. Since most of the strikebreakers were Mormon, the church attitude towards labor and unionism suddenly demanded definition. When Angus M. Cannon, president of the Salt Lake Stake, announced in the tabernacle that employment in the coal fields of Carbon County was available to anyone who wanted it, the issue burst into the open. Con Kelliner, organizer for the United Mine Workers, reacted to Cannon's announcement by charging that "the Mormon church had commenced a fight to annihilate union labor in Utah" and warning that "union men must be aroused to the true situation and defend themselves and appeal to national labor organizations throughout America to assist in unseating Reed Smoot, who is a member and who would be a dangerous foe to labor in Congress."[47] Kelliner also sent letters to Samuel Gompers, president of the American Federation of Labor, and John Mitchell, president of the United Mine Workers, calling upon them to use their power to prevent the seating of Reed Smoot in the U.S. Senate. Kelliner reasoned that Smoot in the Senate would be a dangerous and powerful foe to labor and that his unseating would serve as rebuke to the Mormon church for its intervention in the Carbon County labor dispute.

Kelliner's charges prompted a telegram from the LDS First Presidency to Gompers and Mitchell in which the official church position was defined:

[45]No records have been found as to how many houses were sold or how successful the compromise actually was. In 1923 attorneys for the striking miners of that year made the following comments regarding this 1904 agreement: "Houses and improvements, valued by a disinterested arbitration committee at approximately $60,000.00 were confiscated, and in only three or four instances was restitution ever made." Samuel A. King, "Statement and Brief Concerning the Campaign of the Coal Operators in Utah against Organized Labor and the Unionizing of the Utah Coal Fields," photocopy. Utah State Historical Society Library, Salt Lake City.

[46]Some Carbon County citizens felt that the evacuation of the National Guard was premature. Strikers were among those who requested that the militia remain. " . . . the strikers themselves, in the form of a petition in one instance, and in repeated personal requests to and converstations with me urged that the troops remain. It was peculiarly gratifying to feel that in a situation of such delicacy, our soldiers had gained the confidence of all elements of the community." Cannon to Burton, December 31, 1903, in "Report—Militia at Scofield During Miners Strike, 1904."

[47]*Salt Lake Tribune,* December 29, 1903, p. 4.

> Reports have been circulated that the Mormon Church had used its influence against organized labor, and had endeavored to fill the places of union strikers with non-union men, we hereby emphatically deny that the Church over which we preside has taken any such steps or issued any instructions on this matter. The whole story originated in a false newspaper report. Joseph F. Smith, John R. Winder and Anthon H. Lund.[48]

Thus the issue was played down. The church did not want labor unions as enemies in its attempt to seat Reed Smoot, and the labor union did not wish to fight both the coal company and the Mormon church in Utah.

Because Mormon miners did not remain in sufficient numbers, the company was forced, despite public promises to the contrary, to fall back on "foreign labor." Initially, a few Blacks and Japanese were hired. Later a group of twenty-five Greeks arrived to work in the mines, thus beginning the great influx of that important ethnic group into Carbon County.[49]

Meanwhile, during the first part of February 1904, Charles DeMolli, who had left the state at the governor's request in December 1903, returned to Carbon County. While at Sunnyside he and Joseph Barboglio, treasurer for the United Mine Workers, were arrested by company guards when they tried to cross a deadline on their way from Sunnyside to Helper. They were taken to the city jail and held without charges being preferred against them. That evening when company guards arrived to take their prisoners to the company boarding house for supper they found that the men had escaped by taking off the bolts on the inside of the door. DeMolli and Barboglio were caught late that night below the coal camp, taken before Justice Hill, and found guilty of breaking jail. They were sentenced to thirty days in jail and fined thirty dollars. After an appeal both were released on a $250 bond.

A week later John Trewarther, president, and Thomas Casley, secretary, of the Scofield miners' union were arrested, tried, and found guilty of conspiracy. Bonds were placed at $1,000 which Trewarther and Casley were unable to obtain. Three weeks later their attorney succeeded in having the bonds reduced to $500, and the men were released from jail.

Strategically the arrest of union leaders continued to be an effective tool used by procompany individuals to crush the strike. Although legal justification for the arrests and convictions was highly questionable, the policy as stated by one company guard seemed to be "damn the legality, so long as we make it stick."[50] The arrest of union officials was insignificant, however, when compared to the arrest of 120 Italian strikers following the arrival of Mother Jones in Carbon County.

Mother Mary Jones was one of the most forceful and colorful individuals in the history of American labor. Born in 1830 in Cork, Ireland, she emigrated to America as a child. In 1861 she married, but six years later while

[48] *Deseret Evening News,* January 4, 1904, p. 4.

[49] Helen Zeese Papanikolas, *Toil and Rage in A New Land: The Greek Immigrants in Utah,* published as *Utah Historical Quarterly* 36 (Spring 1970).

[50] *Deseret Evening News,* December 8, 1903, p. 10.

living in Memphis, Tennessee, she lost her husband and four small children in a yellow fever epidemic. Following this tragedy, she went to Chicago where she engaged in dressmaking. To working men, Mother Jones represented the best qualities of Joan of Arc and Mother Mary. But to her enemies she was a "vulgar, heartless, vicious creature, with a fiery temper and a coldblooded heart brutally rare even in the slums."[51] She was accused of being a well-known character in the red light districts of Omaha, Kansas City, Chicago, and San Francisco. In Denver she allegedly had her own brothel and the *Deseret Evening News* reported that she was a good friend of the notorious Kate Flint, one of the pioneer scarlet women of Salt Lake City.[52]

Mother Jones was active in Colorado until April 1904 when she came to Utah. Her arrival at Helper, as described by the *News*, was typical of her flamboyant style:

> She walked to the best hotel and announced who she was. Later she entered the dining room and sat down to dinner. At the close of her meal the waitress placed a finger bowl before her. "Take it away my girl," she said in a voice that could be heard all over the dining room, as was doubtlessly intended, "such things are not for me, they only give some poor overworked girl extra work at washing dishes."
>
> The sentiment was applauded as being as noble a one as ever uttered by the white haired old woman dressed in black. The words were passed from mouth to mouth and the railroad hands who boarded at the hotel were filled with admiration for her sterling qualities.[53]

On the first Sunday after the arrival of Mother Jones, April 17, a meeting of all the strikers was held at Helper. Following the meeting she and several Italians visited William Price, an organizer for the United Mine Workers who had been active since the first days of the strike in Utah. Because of her exposure—Price was in quarantine with smallpox—officials attempted to put Mother Jones in quarantine for the customary fifteen days. A shed had been constructed at Helper for those exposed to the disease, and Mother Jones was to spend the fifteen days there. Just before her consignment, however, the shed mysteriously caught fire and burned to the ground.[54] Mother Jones refused to remain in voluntary quarantine, and on

[51]Ibid., April 30, 1904, p. 6.

[52]Ibid.

[53]Ibid.

[54]Dr. J.J. Dalpiaz in an interview with Philip Notarianni at Helper, Utah, February 5, 1972, gave the following statement about his father, Salias Dalpiaz and another Italian, Angelo Pilatti, regarding the burning of the shed: " . . . later when Mother Jones, the old union organizer, came through the country down here they were all going to lock her up. They built a house right over here right toward the east side of Helper over here. On the big flat and they were going to lock her up in this house. My dad and a fellow by the name of Angelo Pilatti walked over the hill way back there. They came over that hill way back and came down. They both had a gallon of kerosene. They both came down and went over that place. The shingles were not dry. They were still kind of green and it was wet and they couldn't. . . . They spread this thing all over and they set the thing on fire and then they went over the hill down in and they went around Helper and went back. But my dad says by the time we got to the hill it was burning pretty good, but he said by the time we got on top it was smoldering out. They ruined it so that it couldn't be used."

the morning of April 21 Deputy Sheriff Harry World moved to arrest her and two Italians, Sylvester Tedesco and Caesar Antonia, for violating quarantine regulations. World later testified that upon his arrival at the Half-Way House, headquarters for the Italian strikers located between Helper and Castle Gate, he was prevented from making the arrests by at least one hundred armed Italians who occupied positions at the house and at all the rocks and prominent points surrounding the camp. Deputy World and county officials then requested that Governor Wells send the National Guard back to Carbon County to prevent possible violence and to see that the arrests were made.

Governor Wells again asked Gen. John Q. Cannon to inspect conditions in Carbon County to see if the situation warranted recalling the Guard. Once more emotions ran high. Rumors circulated that Mother Jones planned to lead the strikers in a march to Castle Gate in an attempt to regain possession of the houses built or occupied by the strikers before their eviction by the coal company. Company guards at Castle Gate reported that they had been fired upon by Italian strikers and that some thirty shots had been exchanged. When the strikers persuaded Italian coal heavers working for the Rio Grande Railroad to leave their jobs, the strike seemed suddenly to be gaining momentum.

Despite the anxiety of the county officials, Governor Wells decided against sending the National Guard back into Carbon County after hearing Cannon's verbal report. The governor could not forget that the $25,000 he had been forced to borrow from a New York bank to finance the Guard's earlier activities in Carbon County had become a serious blemish on his administration's record. Furthermore, Wells had received enough criticism of the first mobilization of the Guard to become hesitant about a repeat performance.

Following the refusal of Governor Wells to send the National Guard, Sheriff Wilcox began organizing a posse to go to the Half-Way House to arrest those guilty of violating quarantine regulations. The sheriff recruited between twenty-five and forty-five men, and at two o'clock on the morning of Sunday, April 24, the posse left Castle Gate for the Half-Way House. Concealing themselves in the rocks above the camp, the posse waited for daylight. At dawn they charged down the hill and within a short time had taken 120 Italians into custody. In her autobiography Mother Jones gives the following account of the raid:

> On Saturday night I got tipped off by the postoffice master that the militia was going to raid the little tent colony in the early morning. I called the miners to me and asked them if they had guns. Sure, they had guns. They were western men, men of the mountains. I told them to go bury them between the boulders; deputies were coming to take them away from them. I did not tell them that there was to be a raid for I did not want any bloodshed. Better to submit to arrest.
>
> Between 4:30 and 5 o'clock in the morning I heard the tramp of feet on the road. I looked out of my smallpox window and saw about forty-five

> deputies. They descended upon the sleeping tent colony, dragged the miners out of their beds. They did not allow them to put on their clothing. The miners begged to be allowed to put on their clothes, for at that early hour the mountain range is the coldest. Shaking with cold, followed by the shrieks and wails of their wives, and children, beaten along the road by guns, they were driven like cattle to Helper. In the evening they were packed in a box car and run down to Price, the county seat and put in jail.
>
> Not one law had these miners broken. The pitiful screams of the women and children would have penetrated Heaven. Their tears melted the heart of the Mother of Sorrows. Their crime was that they had struck against the power of gold.[55]

The *Deseret Evening News,* in much more restrained words, also found sympathy for the Italians.

> . . . When light enough the sheriff gave the order to charge the camp, compel every man to come out of his tent and put him under arrest. The orders were carried out. Many were hustled out of bed in their night clothes but were allowed to return and dress. The women also were forced out while the tents were searched for firearms. Some guns and ammunition were found. . . .
>
> When the officers were taking the strikers away the women were very abusive in their language and some threats were made. The men were very peaceable and made no resistance. As the strikers were being marched to the train, their wives and children who had followed them down to Helper, were weeping as they said good-bye. The scene will not be forgotten soon by those who witnessed it.[56]

Since the country jail at Price was far too small to house 120 prisoners, the Italians were sent to a bullpen owned by E.M. Olson where they were housed in a shed that had been used to store carriages. The entire area was surrounded by a high fence, and guards were hired to patrol.[57] Local residents and hotels were asked to help by cooking meat for the prisoners. The Mormon bishop, Ernest S. Horsley, gathered food for the Italians, and water was obtained from private cisterns and hauled from the Price River. Sheriff Wilcox claimed that the Italians were better off in the bullpen than they had been at home, but others argued that the prisoners were suffering from lack of adequate shelter.[58] Although the situation seemed quiet, there were some portents of violence. One prisoner was transferred to the jail after he threatened to burn down the shed inside the bullpen. Rumors were circulated that an attempt would be made to set all of the prisoners free. Attorney M.F. Braffett of the coal company called the prisoners "desperate marauders." The *Salt Lake Herald* accused the Italian women of abusing the officers and guards in broken English which "put to shame a drunken pirate."[59]

[55]Jones, *Autobiography of Mother Jones,* ed. Mary Field Barton (Chicago, 1925), 105–6.
[56]*Deseret Evening News,* April 25, 1904, p. 10.
[57]Powell interview.
[58]*Salt Lake Herald,* April 27, 1904, p. 1: *Deseret Evening News,* April 26, 1904, p. 5.
[59]*Salt Lake Herald,* April 26, 1904, p. 1.

On the morning of April 27, the 120 Italian prisoners were loaded in three boxcars of a special train and taken to the schoolhouse at Helper to appear before Justice M.A. Ward. The charge covered a multitude of alleged lawless acts, including resisting an officer, rioting, intimidating men and driving them from work, and disturbing the peace. Attorneys for the Italians pleaded not guilty in each case. The next morning the court began trying each of the strikers individually. The outlook in Helper was for a judicial marathon. The *Salt Lake Herald*'s tongue-in-cheek assessment was that the trials would take at least two months, not counting Sundays.

By May 13 eleven Italians had been found guilty of the charges, and an equal number had been discharged. At this time the eighty-nine Italians remaining at the Price bullpen were also discharged. Several factors led to the dismissals: the wish to avoid lengthy court proceedings, insufficient evidence, the high cost to the county of feeding the prisoners, and a good deal of public sentiment against the arrest and imprisonment of seemingly peaceful and innocent Italians.[60]

From the time the governor was asked to send the National Guard back to Carbon County until the end of the court proceedings against the Italians, a very vocal segment of the public had protested the actions against the strikers. The unofficial leader of this group was the ambitious and imaginative Sam Gilson. Prior to his arrival in Price, Gilson had led an exciting life. At the age of fifteen he had left Illinois and traveled to Nevada where he entered the livestock industry and supplied horses to the Pony Express. As U.S. marshal he supervised the execution of John D. Lee at Mountain Meadows. Later he discovered and promoted many mining properties and invented several successful machines, including a hydraulic ore concentrator or separator. The mineral gilsonite took its name from him.[61]

In reply to Deputy World's request for National Guard troops to help serve warrants for the arrest of strikers violating quarantine regulations, Gilson, in a letter to the *Salt Lake Herald,* described the situation as he saw it:

> The facts are that neither the sheriff nor his deputies have ever tried to serve papers upon anyone as an officer gifted with any sense of judgement would have done. It is a notorious fact that all they have done has been in the interest of the Utah Fuel Company and not for the peace and quiet of the county.[62]

In another letter to the *Herald,* Gilson denounced the treatment of the Italians who had been arrested:

[60]However, this was not the end of the episode. A few days after his release, Joseph Barboglio, treasurer of the United Mine Workers and later founder of the Helper State Bank and the Carbon Emery Bank, brought a $5,000 suit against Wilcox. The charge was false imprisonment. Apparently the suit was either dismissed or dropped because no further mention was made of the case in newspapers or court records.

[61]Newell Christy Remington, "A History of the Gilsonite Industry" (M.A. thesis, University of Utah, 1959), 36–40.

[62]*Salt Lake Herald,* April 25, 1904.

> What the charges against these men are I could not find out from the guards or deputies. The citizens, seeing that they were given but little to eat and that of the worst kind of food, started a subscription and raised $100. When they went to take provisions to the starving men they were told by Harry World, chief deputy sheriff, they would not be allowed to give them a thing. They are herding them inside the court house and will not allow anyone to speak to them. They don't give them a trial to which they are entitled, but say they will try them when they get ready. They have preferred no charges, and no one seems to know what the men were arrested for.[63]

On the day following the arrest of the 120 strikers Gilson himself had been arrested on a charge of abusive language when he allegedly swore at Sheriff Wilcox and Deputy World. He was released on a twenty-five-dollar bond. In the next few weeks several indignation meetings were called by Gilson to protest the actions of the coal company and county officials.

While the strike dragged on, union support was gradually eroding. During the first week of the Italian imprisonment at Price, the executive board of the United Mine Workers adopted a motion instructing union officials to close up affairs in District 13, which included Colorado and Utah.[64] On May 26 Harry Bousfield addressed a letter to H.G. Williams asking that they meet to discuss the strike. Clearly, Bousfield was attempting to carry out the executive council motion and obtain permission for the miners still on strike to return to work. The company, realizing that the union was anxious to call off the strike, became determined to make it as humiliating as possible.

By late July the union had ceased direct financial support of the strikers, leaving them with only two dollars a week assistance, the money coming from voluntary contributions from the miners of Butte, Montana, and elsewhere. This meagre income was not sufficient to support the strikers, and several of them turned to rustling local cattle for food.[65]

During the last week of November $7,000 was sent to the First National Bank of Price by the United Mine Workers. The money was to be used for railroad fares and other necessities in aiding the remaining two hundred and fifty strikers to leave Carbon County. James D. Ritchey and R.M. Smith, officers of the union, visited the strikers and encouraged them to accept the offer and seek employment elsewhere. Some of the strikers did ac-

[63]Ibid., April 27, 1904, p. 1.

[64]In a letter to Harry Bousfield, President John Mitchell admitted union defeat: "Close inquiry upon the part of our representatives satisfied us that the mines are being operated with reasonable success and there is no possibility of winning the strike. For this reason we have decided to bring the strike to a close at the earliest possible date. . . . The strike in district 15 has been more expensive to the national organization than any other strike in history. . . . It is our sincere hope that all those who have participated in the struggle may be able to secure speedy employment, that they may retain their interest in the organization and prepare themselves for a more successful movement at the first opportunity. It is not our intention to abandon the work of organization in Colorado and Utah." Quoted in U.S., Congress, Senate, Commissioner of Labor. *A Report of Labor Disturbances in the State of Colorado, from 1880 to 1904, Inclusive, with Correspondence Relating Thereto,* Doc. No. 122, 58th Cong., 3d sess., 1904–5 (Washington, D.C., 1905), 331.

[65]*Eastern Utah Advocate,* August 11, 1904, p. 1.

cept and were sent to the mines of Colorado. However many of the men voted to decline the offer and were left to their own resources, the union refusing to provide further aid.

The remaining strikers, most of whom were Italians, never did return to the mines. Many became farmers along the Price River, raising produce for the miners who had replaced them. Others went into business in Helper. Although the Rio Grande Railroad was the parent company of Utah Fuel, a number of Italians were able to find work on the railroad gangs.

The union members had suffered defeat, but they were not alone. Ironically, the working miners were presented with a reduction of wages in January 1905. In this and other ways the coal company continued to abuse the miners, and the Carbon County coal fields simmered with labor unrest, culminating in another strike in 1922. This one was led by the Greeks, the unknowing "scabs" who had begun to replace the Italian miners in 1904.

From today's perspective, the demands made by the union in 1903 were clearly justified. The Utah Fuel Company showed a willingness to negotiate on all demands except union recognition. To the miners, however, this was the most important item. As a result the struggle became a fight for union recognition with the question of working conditions deemphasized. This gave an advantage to the coal company, because many Americans regarded the union as a foreign import that, with its radical tendency toward socialism, had no place in democratic America. Given the prevailing fear of communism, the strike failed even though the public had no particular sympathy for the coal company.

Company forces made the most of the public's nativistic sentiments, charging that the strike was led and supported by foreigners who could not and would not allow themselves to be assimilated into American society. Thus one's patriotism was challenged if he supported the union. The dispute was seen by many as a struggle between a ruthless company, which was at least American, and a foreign-dominated labor union.

In the beginning the company was able to convince the public that a state of lawlessness existed in the coal fields and that the strikers were to blame. Later it was apparent that the company guards were as guilty, if not more so, of violence and intimidation as the strikers.

A remarkable characteristic in light of the confrontation between strikers and guards was the relatively little violence during the strike. This was due in large measure to the belief of union officials that the blame for any violence would be charged to them. Therefore they continually urged the strikers to conduct themselves peacefully. The presence of the National Guard in the coal fields served as another deterrent. Although the top officers of the Guard were procompany, the men maintained a fairly neutral position throughout the strike. In time many guardsmen became good friends with the strikers, and although they did not sympathize with the union, some did react strongly against the company.

Governor Wells tried to appear neutral, but he exerted a good deal more pressure on the union than on the coal company. He backed off from his attempt to settle the strike when the Utah Fuel Company refused to arbitrate. He also failed to act against the use of the courts by the company to restrict the activities of the union officials. Company guards who were causing serious problems received better treatment than union members whose offenses were minor. No company employees or supporters were arrested for their activities. The rights to free assembly and free speech were also denied union officials. Much of the situation was out of the governor's control and in the hands of local officials who were naturally cautious about attacking the company that was largely responsible for the economy of the area and that paid seventy-eight percent of the local taxes. During a period of prosperity it was not as easy to find fault with the company as it would be during a time like the depressed thirties.

For its part, the union was strengthened by the nationwide efforts at unionization of the coal fields and by the ability of the organizers: Charles DeMolli, Con Kelliner, and William Price. At the same time, Utah coal miners were hurt by the violence of the Colorado strike. While the union was successful in signing about two-thirds of the miners, it failed to maintain the loyalty of many of those who joined, and they soon left the area. The continuing support of the foreign strikers proved a liability in obtaining public sympathy for the union.

In the end, the strike failed because the union simply did not have enough support, either internally or externally, to win against a powerful and influential company that effectively played on radical, antiforeign sentiments in defending its position.

*

Padrones and Protest: "Old" Radicals and "New" Immigrants in Bingham, Utah, 1905–1912

GUNTHER PECK

In the late nineteenth and early twentieth centuries Utah's population grew increasingly diverse as a new wave of immigrants arrived in the state. Many of them worked at "pick and shovel" jobs in the mines and on the railroads. In this article. Gunther Peck examines the relations between new immigrants and native-born American workers in Bingham, Utah, before, during, and after the dramatic 1912 strike when more than 1,000 miners working for the Utah Copper Company walked off their jobs, and armed themselves with rifles and dynamite in their struggle for better working conditions. Peck shows how intertwined and mutable were racial, ethnic, and class formations and how strong nativism was in Bingham, whose population by the early twentieth century included people from several dozen national groups. He finds that just as nativism is a key to understanding the coal miner's strike a decade earlier in Carbon County, so too is it a key to understanding the Bingham strike. As in Carbon County, the strike was broken and the company's successful exploitation of ethnic divisions was a main reason why.

Gunther Peck, "Padrones and Protest: 'Old' Radicals and 'New' Immigrants in Bingham, Utah, 1905–1912," *Western Historical Quarterly* 24 (May 1993): 157–78. Reprinted by permission of the publisher and the author.

Gunther Peck received a Ph.D. degree in history from Yale University and is a member of the history department at the University of Texas at Austin. The article was awarded the Bryant-Spann Memorial Prize by the Eugene V. Debs Foundation.

IN THE FALL OF 1912, over one thousand employees of the Utah Copper Company in Bingham, Utah, walked off their jobs and armed themselves with rifles and dynamite in one of the most dramatic strikes in the Western Federation of Miners' (WFM) violent history. Twenty-four national groups cooperated in the walkout, digging trenches, breastworks, foxholes, even constructing a makeshift cannon. Their militancy and organization greatly impressed one socialist reporter from the *New York Call*, who wrote:

> Out of the practically unorganized mass of workers has sprung up a remarkably strong organization. Bingham now boasts the second largest miners' local in the United States. . . . In the face of a common crisis nationalities have been lost and national prejudices have disappeared.[1]

To the *New York Call* reporter, an American working class, united across all skill and ethnic lines, was finally emerging in Bingham and industrial sites like it across the United States. Ethnicity and racial difference—those traditional stumbling blocks to class consciousness—were being miraculously set aside, it seemed, as immigrants of all backgrounds finally embraced the WFM's assertion that "the working class knows but one foreigner and that is the capitalist class."[2]

The overzealous reporter did not see, however, the formation of vital connections between ethnicity, race, and class in the origins and fashioning of the Bingham strike movement. The hundreds of Southeast European and Asian immigrants defending the union barricades had not spontaneously arisen from an "unorganized mass" of workers, but from groups of immigrants already familiar with the strike as a tool of collective action. Like many radicals of the American left, though, the *New York Call* reporter expressed a commitment to a rigid and idealized notion of class consciousness that precluded its potential compatibility with ethnic and racial identities. Consequently, he neglected one of the most remarkable features of the Bingham strike. The American born leadership of the WFM, headed by union president Charles Moyer, maintained only marginal control of the strike movement. Immigrant strikers possessed their own agenda for striking. They advocated abolishing the padrone hiring system that had brought so many unskilled immigrants to Bingham in the first place.[3] Although the Utah Copper Company never recognized their union, immigrant strikers succeeded in forcing the company to fire its most powerful and notorious labor agent, Greek entrepreneur Leonidas Skliris.

Until recently, western labor history accepted many of the same idealized notions about class that shaped the *New York Call* reporter's reading of the dramatic events in Bingham. A generation of western labor historians have debated whether western miners were radical or conservative.[4] Al-

[1]*New York Call,* 3 October 1912, p. 3.

[2]*Miner's Magazine* (Denver), 24 October 1912, p. 9.

[3]Gunther W. Peck, "Crisis in the Family: Padrones and Radicals in Utah, 1908–1912," in *New Directions in Greek American Studies,* ed. Dan Georgakas and Charles C. Moskos (New York, 1991).

[4]Marxists such as Melvyn Dubofsky argue that the West was the site of an exceptionally pure form of class conflict, one that produced the most radical class consciousness in the nation. See Melvyn Dubofsky, "The Origins of Western Working Class Radicalism, 1890–1905," *Labor History* 7 (Spring 1966): 131–54; Melvyn Dubofsky, *We Shall Be All: A History of the Industrial Workers of the World* (Chicago, 1966), 25. Revisionists such as Richard H. Peterson have argued that "labor exploitation and instability" have been overemphasized in the West, a position subsequently expanded and modified by Mark Wyman and Ronald Brown. See Richard H. Peterson, "Conflict and Consensus: Labor Relations in Western Mining," *Journal of the West* 12 (January 1973): 17; Mark Wyman, *Hard Rock Epic: Western Miners and the Industrial Revolution, 1860–1910* (Berkeley, 1979): Ronald C. Brown, *Hard-Rock Miners: The Intermountain West, 1860–1920* (College Station, TX, 1979).

though an important question, both sides of the debate have accepted the assumption that class consciousness and socialism were virtually synonymous terms. Western class relations have been conceptualized as a history of western radicalism and its celebrated "heritage of conflict."[5] Two separate teleologies have supported this conceptual approach to western class relations, one Marxist, the other Turnerian. The former assigns ethnicity and race the status of false consciousness, much as the *New York Call* reporter did, while the latter denies the existence of class in the West altogether, or roots its rapid emergence in the frontier's disappearance. Both paradigms lend themselves to exceptionalist interpretations of western labor history in which historians of all political stripes have assessed western workers by the ahistoric yardsticks of civilization or a pristine socialism with a capital *S*.[6]

Recent path-breaking work by David M. Emmons and Elizabeth Jameson has freed western labor history from many of its exceptionalist moorings, in part because they grapple with the critical connections between western labor, immigration, and women's history.[7] This article follows their lead by exploring the complex relationships between Bingham's "new" immigrants—principally Japanese, Italian, Slavic, and Greek—and the American-dominated union local before, during, and after the 1912 strike. How does an understanding of the ethnic and racial tensions between "new" immigrants and "old" American-born radicals change our story of western radicalism—its origins, its growth, and its decline? Put another way, what are the connections between the traditionally separate histories of ethnicity, race, and labor radicalism in the West? Bingham's labor history provides an unusually rich case study for examining their interconnections and underscores some of the conceptual challenges facing the new western labor history.

Before examining the relationship between Bingham's new immigrants and the local union, it is important to establish what I mean by "radical" and to assess briefly the content and context of the Western Federation of Miners' radicalism in 1912. For the purposes of this essay, I use "radical" in the literal sense to refer to any individual or group ideologically committed to changing society at its roots.[8] Although the WFM had recently affiliated

[5]Vernon H. Jensen, *Heritage of Conflict: Labor Relations in the Nonferrous Metals Industry Up to 1930* (Ithaca, NY, 1950).

[6]An important exception to this pattern is Carlos A. Schwantes, "The Concept of the Wageworkers' Frontier: A Framework for Future Research," *Western Historical Quarterly* 18 (January 1987): 39–55.

[7]See David M. Emmons, *The Butte Irish: Class and Ethnicity in an American Mining Town, 1875–1925* (Urbana, 1989) and Elizabeth Jameson's forthcoming study of gender and class in Cripple Creek, Colorado. Any reformulation of western labor history, as Jameson shows, must also grapple with the importance of gender. My inattention to gender in this article reflects my judgement that the Bingham episode best exemplifies the relationships between ethnicity, race, and class.

[8]My broad definition includes the Industrial Workers of the World, the Western Federation of Miners, and the Socialist Party of America in 1912. I am less interested in designating one sectarian group the true American radicals, than in assessing how one particular group responded to immigration.

with the allegedly conservative and craft-oriented American Federation of Labor in 1911, the WFM's constitution of 1912 still proclaimed that "a class struggle in society" would continue "until the producer is recognized as the sole master of its product."[9] In Bingham, the WFM local remained strongly committed to organizing a working class of skilled and unskilled male workers and supporting the Socialist party, which represented a powerful minority party throughout the first decade of the twentieth century. The Socialists attained a powerful position in Bingham's City Council, electing members every two years between 1905 and 1911. They nearly won control of the council in 1909 when they took 47 percent of the vote and were defeated only by a last-minute coalition between Republican and Democratic candidates.[10]

In spite of the WFM local's commitment to the Socialist party, very few of Bingham's new immigrants were enlisted into the local class struggle. Japanese workers, for example, were never recruited or initiated into the miners' union, despite their prominent role in the 1912 strike. At the national level, the WFM's socialist politics had long been racialized. In 1902, the same year the WFM endorsed the Socialist party's platform, the WFM also excluded all Asian workers from its ranks, institutionalizing one of the most enduring boundaries in the western labor movement.[11] Although the union accepted Greek, Italian, and South Slavic workers into its membership and promoted Slavic immigrant Yanco Terzich to its executive board, its relationship to these new immigrants remained ambivalent. In Bingham, only a handful of Italians and Greeks joined the union before the 1912 strike, even though they attained numerical prominence in the work force by 1907. Local union leaders E. G. Locke and Thomas Burlison discussed "the Greek problem," including their grievances against the padrone hiring system, as early as 1908 when they proposed using the union library to teach Greek workers the English language. But little appears to have come from their inclusionist proposal; the number of Greeks joining the local remained very low—one or two a month—before and after the union's discussion about whether to encourage Greeks to join. Efforts to publish local union news and announcements in foreign languages were sporadic at best, despite a smattering of Greek and Italian members and a more sizeable number of Slavic and Finnish members. In 1905, the only occasion for

[9]Preamble, Constitution of the Western Federation of Miners, in *Official Proceedings of the 20th Annual Convention of the Western Federation of Miners* (Denver, 1912).

[10]*Appeal to Reason* (Kansas City, MO), 20 November 1909, p. 5; City Council Minutes of Bingham Canyon, UT, 14 November 1904, 11 November 1907, 9 November 1911, and 10 November 1913, Utah State Archives, Salt Lake City, UT.

[11]*Official Proceedings of the 10th Annual Convention of the Western Federation of Miners* (Denver, 1902). Herbert Hill and Gwendolyn Mink have studied the racially exclusionist nature of American labor unions, of which the WFM was clearly no exception. See Gwendolyn Mink, *Old Labor and New Immigrants in American Political Development: Union, Party, and State, 1875–1920* (Ithaca, NY, 1986) and Herbert Hill, "Race, Ethnicity, and Organized Labor: The Opposition to Affirmative Action," in Herbert Hill, *Race and Ethnicity in Organized Labor* (Madison, forthcoming).

translation came when union officials posted signs in three languages demanding the immediate payment of back dues. Declarations of class solidarity, by contrast, such as the local's support for the Industrial Workers of the World, were read, delivered, and published only in English.[12]

The strength of nativisim in Bingham reflected the intensity of economic and social change that the community had experienced between 1900 and 1910. In 1900, the population of Bingham, already something of an anomaly in the state of Utah, consisted mostly of non-Mormon men, nearly half of them foreign born.[13] Most of Bingham's labor force worked underground in silver mines and had emigrated to the United States from Sweden, Ireland, England, and more recently, Finland. By 1910, however, not a single silver mine remained in Bingham and newly arrived Greek, Italian, and Japanese immigrants comprised nearly half the local work force. The overall skill level of the work force dropped significantly as the number of unskilled laborers in Bingham increased elevenfold.[14]

The spectacular growth of the Utah Copper Company, which pioneered the largest and most successful open-pit copper mine in the world, fueled a dramatic demographic and social transformation.[15] Incorporated in 1903 and backed by Guggenheim family capital, the company, by 1907, had begun mining and smelting an entire mountain of low-grade copper ore above Bingham Canyon, using steam shovels that operated on train tracks to dig and load the ore directly onto boxcars for smelting. A booming market for copper ensured the company's rapid growth and hastened the displacement and deskilling of Bingham's underground silver miners. Deskilling proved a complex and uneven process in Bingham. Certain immigrant groups such as the Swedes seemed to have benefited from the reorganization of work by becoming skilled machine tenders.[16] Former skilled miners did not usually fill most of the new unskilled positions at the Utah Copper Company. In-

[12]Minutes of the Bingham Miners' Union, No. 67, Western Federation of Miners, 20 May 1905, 1 August 1909, and 28 September 1908, Labor and Management Historical Documentation Center, School of Industrial Relations, Cornell University, Ithaca, NY.

[13]Although Bingham Canyon was originally settled by a Mormon family in the 1860s, Mormons played only a peripheral role in the mining community's subsequent development. In 1900, there were only about fifty or sixty Mormon men, women, and children in the town, out of a population of 1,881. By 1912, Mormon church services still attracted only between twenty-five and fifty members each week. Membership records of the Mormon Church, West Jordan Stake, 1897–1918, Historical Research Library, Church of Jesus Christ of Latter-day Saints, Salt Lake City, UT.

[14]In 1900, 88 percent of Bingham's occupation holders had been born in either Britain, Sweden, Finland, or the United States. By 1910, that percentage dropped to just 53 percent of all occupation holders. The number of unskilled workers in the one-in-ten sampling of the 1900 and 1910 censuses increased from 11 to 128. U. S. Bureau of the Census from the Twelfth and Thirteenth Census (1900 and 1910), Bingham Canyon, Salt Lake County, UT, enumeration districts 58 and 59 for 1900 and 90 and 91 for 1910, microfilm, State Historical Society of Wisconsin, Madison, WI.

[15]Leonard J. Arrington and Gary B. Hansen, *"The Richest Hole on Earth": A History of the Bingham Copper Mine* (Logan, UT, 1963).

[16]Between 1900 and 1910 the percentage of Swedes engaged in unskilled and semiskilled occupations dropped from 70 to 30 percent. U. S. Bureau of the Census from the Twelfth and Thirteenth Census (1900 and 1910), Bingham Canyon, Salt Lake County, UT.

stead Greek, Italian, and Japanese immigrants, who performed the arduous tasks of laying and relaying railroad track for the cumbersome steam shovels, moved into those positions. Though deskilling affected different national groups in strikingly different ways, citizens of Bingham across the occupational and political spectrums blamed the community's wrenching dislocations on these new unskilled workers, a pattern evidenced in the rapid growth of the anti-immigrant and anti-Mormon American party.

Although the dramatic success of Simon Guggenheim's investment prompted industrial rival John D. Rockefeller to call Bingham "the greatest industrial sight on earth" in 1911, the Utah Copper Company's modern expansion produced two paradoxical developments.[17] Not only did mechanization with steam shovels greatly increase the amount of pick and shovel work performed in Bingham, it also necessitated the expansion of a seemingly archaic method of obtaining these strong arms and backs—the ethnic padrone system.[18] A labor contractor who imported his countrymen and provided them with jobs in America, the padrone also exploited his intermediary position by charging fees to all immigrant workers for getting and keeping their industrial livelihoods. In Bingham, three men imported unskilled immigrants for the burgeoning number of railroad and mining jobs: Leonidas Skliris, also known as the "Czar of the Greeks," imported all Greek and Slavic workers; Edward Daigoro Hashimoto, importer of Japanese laborers into Utah; and Moses Paggi, labor agent for Bingham's Italians.[19]

While nativism and cultural differences kept many new immigrants from joining the WFM local, class solidarities nonetheless quickly developed within Bingham's immigrant communities. Paid the least, Greek, Italian, Slavic, and Japanese workers formed the bottom tier of the Utah Copper Company's ethnic and skill hierarchy and assumed some of the greatest occupational risks in the open pit. Most Greek and all Japanese workers earned $1.75 a day as muckers, laying track for the steam shovels in the open pit, or unloading ore with pick and shovel at the smelter. Most muckers, in work gangs of five or six people, labored next to and were supervised by one of their own countrymen.[20] Although the localistic organization of mucking prevented much interaction between different ethnic groups of workers, job-

[17]Frank O'Connor, *The Guggenheims: The Making of an American Dynasty* (1937; reprint, New York, 1976), 269.

[18]See discussion of mechanization in David Montgomery, *The Fall of the House of Labor: The Workplace, the State, and American Labor Activism, 1865–1925* (Cambridge, ENG, 1987), 60. For a description of the Utah Copper Company's padrone system see Helen Zeese Papanikolas, "Life and Labor among the Immigrants of Bingham Canyon," *Utah Historical Quarterly* 33 (Fall 1965): 289–315, and her subsequent short monograph, "Toil and Rage in a New Land: The Greek Immigrants in Utah," *Utah Historical Quarterly* 38 (Spring 1970): 100–203.

[19]Much of my evidence of padrone business activity has been gleaned from court cases involving Skliris, Paggi, and Hashimoto. See, for example, Stavros Skliris v. Leonidas Skliris, Case #8637, 8 November 1906; E. D. Hashimoto v. Showell Brothers, Case #8641, 19 November 1906; and Moses Paggi v. G. Milana, Case #19657, 23 March 1915, Third District Civil Court, Salt Lake County, Utah State Archives.

[20]Papanikolas, "Toil and Rage," 123; *O Ergatis* (Salt Lake City), 22 August 1908, p. 1.

related disputes and dangers could provoke moments of intense class feeling among muckers. In 1908, when an American foreman attempted to fire a Greek worker without notifying his fellow workers, six Greek workers "beat their American supervisor with sticks, fists, and stones." After a small avalanche of copper ore buried two Greek cousins alive that same year, an anonymous Greek worker articulated similar rage in an eloquent statement published in the local Greek newspaper O *Ergatis* (The Worker): "May thunder and fire fall upon the smelter, which has poured poison into the glasses of many parents."[21]

If class solidarities among immigrant workers developed within ethnic boundaries at the smelter and open pit, Bingham's many saloons encouraged bonds both within and between groups of immigrant workers. By 1911, nearly every major ethnic group in Bingham possessed its own drinking establishment. But such facilities did not serve merely as safe havens where immigrants spoke their own languages. One of the most popular sporting events in Upper Bingham's Greek coffee houses, the weekly wrestling contests between Japanese and Greek workers encouraged immigrants of many nationalities to bet on the likely winner. Although intensely competitive affairs, contestants and spectators of all nationalities observed common codes of "fair" conduct and male honor.

Between 1908 and 1912, groups of foreign-born men celebrating both particular ethnic holidays as well as American national holidays frequently monopolized the streets of Bingham. Even the most ethnic of holidays, Greek Orthodox Christmas, provided an occasion for interethnic sociability. On the night of 8 January 1911, Greek and Serbian workers welcomed Orthodox Christmas with revolvers and giant explosions of powder that "struck terror into the hearts of the peaceful citizens of Bingham." Far more than a parochial ethnic celebration, these immigrant workers also had a larger American audience in mind; the only property damaged during the celebration, despite the many gunshots and powder blasts, was the home of an American supervisor at the Utah Copper Company. Such public events and saloons that provided drinks to thirsty celebrants forged both ethnic and working-class identities among Bingham's new immigrants.[22]

Though few Greek immigrants had much contact with the union prior to the 1912 strike, they nonetheless demonstrated a remarkable capacity for collective action. In August 1908, over three hundred Greek laborers walked off their jobs at the Utah Copper Company's smelter and demanded a restoration of a pay cut made during the recent recession. The walkout occasioned considerable comment in the Greek community of Utah, particu-

[21]O *Ergatis,* 1 August 1908, p. 1; 10 October 1908, p. 2. O *Ergatis* was published in Katharevousa Greek in Salt Lake City between September 1907 and October 1908, when Leonidas Skliris acquired formal control of the newspaper and shut it down. All citations from O *Ergatis* were translated by the author with the help of Lena Nikolaou.

[22]Papanikolas, "Toil and Rage," 122; for an account of Bingham's Christmas celebrations, see the *Salt Lake Tribune,* 10 January 1911, p. 3 and the *Deseret Evening News* (Salt Lake City), 6 January 1911, p. 1.

larly from Panayiotis Siouris, newspaper editor of *O Ergatis*. He wrote with astonishment that "three hundred Greeks, without supervision, without being united in an association, agreed upon everything." Just one week later, the Utah Copper Company granted Greek workers their demand and restored the former wage rate of $1.75 a day. Although Greek workers struck without any union affiliation or cooperation from other immigrants, their success derived from the existence of the WFM local in Bingham, which company officials loathed; better, after all, to grant the demands of Greek workers without union recognition than to drive them into the arms of the Western Federation. The walkout did not produce a single comment in the local union's minutes, however, suggesting just how much cultural and political distance continued to exist between Greek and American workers.[23]

Class loyalties in Bingham did not emerge only in union hall meetings, nor did they develop roots purely within the work place or Bingham's many ethnic saloons. Perhaps the most crucial factor in Greek workers' growing awareness of their exploited condition was their volatile relationship with the padrone, Leonidas Skliris. Born in the village of Vresthena, high in the mountains above Sparta, Skliris's career in the United States began in 1898 when he arrived in New York and began selling flowers to businessmen on Wall Street.[24] Skliris quickly mastered English and, by 1901, moved to railroad work as a section foreman on the Baltimore & Ohio Railroad. A year later, Skliris had moved to Utah, at the exhortation of childhood friend and labor agent, William Caravelis of Pocatello, Idaho. By 1908, however, Skliris remained only one of several prominent Greek labor agents in the intermountain West.

When *O Ergatis* editor Siouris called for Greek workers to send in any information regarding alleged abuses within the labor contracting system, most of the forthcoming letters condemned the excesses of Caravelis, who imported Greek immigrants for work on the Oregon Short Line in Utah, Idaho, and Oregon. Several correspondents accused Caravelis of charging his compatriots too much for the "right" to work, often from $20 to $50 for a single temporary job. Such prices were "unfair" and, more importantly, unpatriotic. One Greek worker, for example, compared Caravelis to the hated Turk, describing him as the "Ali-Pasha of Pocatello." Other letters, by contrast, praised Skliris for being a good protector; one letter, signed by thirteen Greeks, wrote that Skliris was "never tired, ever energetic, and always successful in defending the laborer in his every care and need." These letters cohered in making distinctions between good and bad padrones. Even the most militant protests against Caravelis condemned only his particular abuses, rather than labor contracting itself.[25]

[23]*O Ergatis,* 22 August 1908, pp. 1, 5; Minutes, Bingham Miners' Union, August and September 1908.

[24]These details of Skliris's early career were gleaned from the court case Walker Brothers v. William Caravelis, Nicholas P. Stathakos, and L. G. Skliris, Partners, 18 April 1908, Case #1938, Third District Civil Court, Salt Lake County, Utah State Archives.

[25]*O Ergatis,* 29 February 1908, p. 1; 1 August 1908, p. 3.

By 1911, however, Skliris had greatly expanded his operations as a labor contractor. Unlike the Greeks who immigrated to Bingham in 1908, most of those arriving in 1911 came from the island of Crete rather than from villages near Skliris's own hometown in the southern Pelopponese.[26] Skliris had also expanded his power in America by purchasing the Panhellenic Grocery store in Bingham from a Cretan businessman. Like many company town superintendents, Skliris required that Greek workers shop there or risk losing their jobs. Such extensions of the tribute system galvanized the militancy of Greek workers, few of whom would have proclaimed Skliris a defender of the laborer.

To the contrary, Greek immigrants, led by the Cretans, began organizing themselves to remove Skliris as the Utah Copper Company's labor agent and to abolish the padrone system altogether. In the spring of 1911, fifty Greek laborers sent a letter to the governor of Utah, William Spry, demanding the abolition of Skliris's tribute system:

> Do you think this is right for Skliris to sell livelihoods to the poor workman . . . and to thus suck the blood of the poor laborer? Where are we? In the free country of Amerika [*sic*] or in a country dominated by a despotic form of government? Hoping you liberate us from this padrone, who is ravaging the blood of the poor laborer, and that too, of his fellow countrymen.[27]

These Greek workers did not describe Skliris as a bad protector, or a Turk, but in stark class terms, as an oppressor of the "poor laborer," a man whose authority violated their rights as workers in America. When Governor Spry failed to reply, over five hundred Greek immigrants, all of them employees of Utah Copper, wrote him another letter. The workers typed this one, refined the English usage, and demanded that "Skliris and his agents be restrained," that all immigrants be hired directly by the company, and that all Greek employees be "at liberty to do their purchasing wherever they wish." Spry replied this time, but suggested they take their complaint directly to the Utah Copper Company management for "an impartial hearing." Most Greeks recognized that the company had facilitated Skliris's rise to power and began searching for more direct means of abolishing padronism.[28]

Although Greek workers were increasingly well organized during the summer of 1911, tensions continued to divide American and immigrant workers. The appeal to a more powerful and supposedly neutral authority in Governor Spry was itself a revealing commentary on Greek workers' distrust of the American-led union local. By 1912, however, local union lead-

[26]Passenger lists of ships arriving in the port of New York reveal the broadening geographic scope of Skliris's power. In March 1907, eighteen Greek immigrants listed Bingham Canyon as their final destination; all of them came from villages near Sparta in the Pelopponese. By March 1912, fully seventy-five Greek immigrants checked through to Bingham, 64 percent of them from Crete. Passenger Lists, Port of New York, National Archives, Washington, DC.

[27]Fifty Greek laborers to Governor William S. Spry, 2 February 1911, William S. Spry Papers, Personal Correspondence, Box 10, File "G," Utah State Archives.

[28]Mike Lakis et al. to Governor Spry, 10 August, 11 August 1911, Spry Papers.

ers, such as E. G. Locke, recognized the organizing potential of the padrone system and wrote a letter to the ambassador of Turkey, with copies to Governor Spry, demanding that he investigate the existence of peonage among "his subjects from Crete." By publicizing Skliris's villainy, Locke hoped to win allies among Bingham's militant Cretan miners. Locke, however, overlooked the fact that these same miners loathed their official Turkish protectors as much as their new-world protector Skliris. Not surprisingly, Locke's letter earned the union little support from Bingham's patriotic Cretans, although it did provoke an angry response from Greek banker Nicholas P. Stathakos, who wrote to Spry, excoriating the radical Locke for his unauthorized intervention into the affairs of Greek workers. A naturalized American citizen, Stathakos portrayed himself as both a good American—law abiding and patriotic—as well as an honorable Greek immigrant. For Stathakos, both national identities were predicated on middle-class notions of respectability and loyalty to authority, and were thus compatible, even reinforcing identities. Although Stathakos may have persuaded the governor of his political virtue, Greek workers probably remained unconvinced. They knew that Stathakos provided the economic support for Skliris's expanding business operations by providing him the capital to finance the passage of increasing numbers of Cretan immigrants to Bingham Canyon.[29]

Until the summer of 1912, working-class Greeks in Bingham remained unclear about what kind of Americans they planned to become. As Greek workers' anger against Skliris and the padrone system mounted, their sense of cultural distance from the Bingham local narrowed. Having witnessed the indifference and complicity of one group of Americans, they soon turned to the only group of American willing to listen to their complaints, E. G. Locke and the Bingham local. The union's membership grew spectacularly that summer, from 250 members in June, to 700 in July, to nearly 1200 by September. Precisely who encouraged the Greeks' participation remains unclear. Certainly the handful of Greeks in the Bingham local had some influence in recruiting their countrymen as did John Leventis, a Cretan immigrant who owned Bingham's most popular coffee house and who proved an outspoken champion of labor during the strike. Although the union hired no official Greek organizer, it did translate its entire constitution and organizing literature into Greek that spring and probably relied on E. G. Locke and Greek union members to disseminate the WFM literature. The federation also hired an Italian organizer, Steve Oberto, who worked in Bingham throughout the summer of 1912.[30]

[29]E. G. Locke to His Excellency the Ambassador of Turkey in Washington, 12 May 1912, and Nicholas Stathakos to Governor William Spry, 14 August 1912, Spry Papers, Personal Correspondence, Boxes 18 and 19, Utah State Archives. For evidence of Stathakos's business connections to Skliris, see Walker Brothers v. Caravelis, Stathakos, and Skliris, Case #1938, Third District Civil Court, Utah State Archives.

[30]State of Utah, *First Report of the State Bureau of Immigration, Labor, and Statistics for the Years 1911–1912* (Salt Lake City, 1913), 30; *Official Proceedings of the 20th Annual Convention of the Western Federation of Miners* (Denver, 1912), 110, 117.

The Greek immigrants demonstrated their already established internal mobilization in the way they took over the union's business. In early September, recently initiated Greek immigrants decided to exercise their newfound rights by pressing American union leaders for a strike vote. When Charles Moyer, president of the WFM, heard of their plans, he rushed to Bingham by train to dissuade the strike-hungry immigrants. Moyer's reluctance to strike highlighted some of the growing tensions in the WFM between its radical constitution and its organizing strategy. With a strike fund nearly bankrupt and the union's legal resources stretched thin, Moyer hoped to avoid a protracted and expensive strike, as had recently occurred at the Homestake Mining Company in Lead, South Dakota.[31] Perhaps more important, Moyer remained reluctant to relinquish control over the expanding Bingham local to recently initiated Greek and Italian immigrants, whose militancy and solidarity with Japanese workers challenged the authority of American-born radicals such as himself and the organization they had built.

After an impassioned speech by Moyer against striking, the membership, led by Greek miner John Stanopolis, voted to walk and began celebrating with gunshots and victory toasts. The next morning, over one thousand immigrants laid down their tools and set up pickets around the Utah Copper mine and smelter works. Hundreds of non-union immigrants soon followed them, including all two hundred Japanese laborers in Bingham, many of whom joined the picketing effort. By contrast, a number of skilled American workers, many of them union members, refused to join the strikers and attempted to go to work. When American steam shovel operators began revving up their engines, "a number of strikers, principally Greeks, appeared on the mountainside above the workman [*sic*] and pelted them with stones and rolled boulders down the mountainside, driving the workers from their places." By noon of the first day, over five thousand workers were idle and "the greatest industrial sight on earth" had been completely shut down.[32]

The drama of the Bingham strike inspired reporters of all political stripes to discern and define the event's meaning and significance. If the *New York Call* reporter saw the emergence of an American working class, local Utah newspapers focused on the manifold racial tensions between American and immigrant workers. The Salt Lake City *Deseret Evening News,* for example, reported that:

> The "white" element has been forced against its will [to strike]. . . . The Bingham camp is today a divided camp. . . . One one side is a mob of . . . 3500 aliens. . . . On the other . . . are perhaps 1500 men who refused to strike . . . and in addition to these the merchants and citizens of Bingham itself.[33]

[31]Joseph H. Cash, *Working the Homestake* (Ames, IA, 1973).

[32]*Deseret Evening News,* 16 September 1912, p. 7; *Salt Lake Evening Telegram* 18 September 1912, p. 1.

[33]*Desert Evening News,* 20 September 1912, p. 2.

By defining Greeks, Italians, and South Slavs as nonwhite, this reporter reduced to race what the *New York Call* reporter had reduced to class.

Given the popularity of these competing reportorial narratives—the emergence of race war or a raceless working class—how did union leaders in Bingham negotiate such reductive alternatives? Moyer's strategy, consistent throughout the strike, focused on winning public support for the union's cause by attempting to "Americanize" the efforts of its militant immigrant membership. For Moyer, this meant not only obeying American laws regarding firearms, but respecting the authority of the union's American leadership. Initially, this seemed an impossible task because immigrant strikers controlled the mine with guns and dynamite and fired at all who came near, including Moyer himself. Subsequently, Moyer distanced himself publicly from Greek laborers. To the *Deseret Evening News,* Moyer disavowed violence and stated that he could not be held "responsible for the individual conduct of 4000 members."[34] Moyer feared that a nativist backlash would ruin his chance to win political support for an arbitrated settlement of the strike. Moyer's concession to Utah's nativist political climate seemed double-edged, however, for by distancing himself from Greek strikers, he also undercut his authority and reputation as a union leader to an American public. Wrote the Ogden *Evening Standard,* "Moyer . . . seems to be but a nominal leader of the strike, . . . and it seems that more radical leaders have the ears of the men."[35]

Moyer sought to regain control over the rebellious membership by orchestrating an open-air meeting between strikers, himself, the governor of Utah, and middle-class immigrant leaders. Nicholas Stathakos spoke first to the crowd of angry strikers: "For the glory of our nation, you should be law-abiding here." Not surprisingly, Stathakos's appeal to Greek patriotism "deeply agitated" a great number of Greek strikers. Greek Orthodox priest Vasilios Lambrides followed Stathakos, but the priest's appeal to patriotism likewise failed to calm the angry strikers. Greek workers' angry reaction to Stathakos and Lambrides underscored the sharply different meanings that honor and patriotism possessed for working-class and middle-class Greeks. After Lambrides left the podium, a number of Greek strikers denounced Skliris as a capitalistic traitor and demanded that company officials abolish the padrone system. One laborer from Crete emphasized the importance of this demand by asserting that Greek strikers would return to work if Skliris were fired. The meeting ended with a stern speech by Governor Spry, who warned immigrants not to take the law into their own hands; afterwards Spry took a walking tour of the strikers' fortifications with Moyer as his guide.[36]

Moyer's effort to regain control of the Bingham strike by attempting to Americanize the immigrant workers' struggle had produced quite a different

[34]Ibid., 19 September 1912, p. 1.

[35]*Evening Standard* (Ogden, UT), 19 September 1912, p. 1.

[36]*Salt Lake Tribune,* 20 September 1912, pp. 1–2; *Deseret Evening News,* 20 September 1912, p. 3.

result. If Moyer regained a measure of control over the strikers, immigrants succeeded in redefining the strike's agenda and purpose. This mutual accommodation marked the beginning of a more cooperative and coordinated relationship between immigrant strikers and the WFM. Greeks became the core of a disciplined but now unarmed strike force that patrolled company grounds, inspected all incoming trains for strike-breakers, and manned the picket lines. The fusion of immigrant and union demands was dramatically evident just one week after the open-air meeting when Leonidas Skliris announced his resignation from the Utah Copper Company. Greek workers promptly held a meeting to consider the possibility of returning to work, and although they engaged in an animated discussion, they voted unanimously to continue striking for both union recognition and abolition of padronism.[37]

Skliris responded to the worst crisis of his career by wrapping himself in the paternalistic ideology that had once undergirded his power as a padrone. In a two-page letter printed in the *Deseret Evening News* on the day of his resignation, Skliris asserted that his Greek countrymen loved him because he alone served as their true defender. His letter conveyed a clear sense of betrayal and exemplified the ties of reciprocity that had once existed between himself and his compatriots in Bingham. Yet it likewise illustrated the profound ideological distance that had developed between Skliris and Greek workers. Skliris refused to believe that Greek strikers remained committed to unionism and the abolition of the padrone system. In his own mind, he had always been a good padrone, providing his countrymen with jobs and job security at a fair and reasonable price. Rather than criticize his countrymen for being radical, and therefore both un-Greek and un-American, Skliris embraced the notion that a Greek rival had conspired to take his rightful place as the protector of Greek workers. Skliris concluded his letter by denouncing certain unnamed "vicious characters" who were plotting "machinations against my countrymen."[38]

Skliris's resignation produced a crisis within Utah's small middle-class Greek community, which tried to distance itself from Skliris while simultaneously defusing the public perception that Greek strikers were in fact committed to industrial unionism. On the day after Greek workers voted to continue striking, George Photopoulos, editor of the Greek newspaper *To Fos* (The Light), stated in the *Salt Lake Evening Telegram* that "the Greeks in Bingham do not understand the significance of a union" and "are ignorant of such American customs." On the same day, Stathakos announced the formation of a local chapter of the Panhellenic Union, whose purpose in Utah was to "establish schools where Greeks can become familiar with the American language and customs . . . and learn to respect the laws of America and in that way become more desirable citizens." Clearly, industrial

[37]*Deseret Evening News,* 23 September 1912, pp. 1–2; 24 September 1912, p. 1; 27 September 1912, p. 1.

[38]Ibid., 23 September 1912, p. 2.

unionism was not one of the "American customs" the Panhellenic Union would teach. Founders of the union in Utah committed themselves to an upwardly mobile, middle-class type of Americanization, one that stood in direct opposition to the working-class form of Americanization that Greek workers had embraced in the WFM.[39]

Greek strikers responded to these statements and actions with their own letter to the *Salt Lake Evening Telegram* that highlighted the class conflicts dividing the Greek community of Utah. Signed by Greek striker George Gatzouros, the letter stated:

> We denounce all those self-posed leaders of the Greeks once and for all. . . . It is to their best interests to desist from making themselves prominent and misleading the public regarding the strike situation, or we will be compelled to show them up.[40]

Gatzouros's sentiment captured the combative and boastful quality of Greek strikers' militancy and underscored their abiding commitment to the struggle for union recognition. Despite the efforts of Photopoulos and Stathakos to the contrary, Greeks continued to work at the forefront of the ethnically heterogenous strike movement, guarding the breastworks and searching incoming trains for strikebreakers. Their efforts, no less militant than at the strike's outset, now earned the praise of working-class Americans to the WFM. Reflecting the sentiments of E. G. Locke and others, William O'Neill, editor of the *Miner's Magazine,* stated, "the Greeks must be given the greatest credit for showing the greatest spirit of solidarity and discipline."[41]

If the accommodation of working-class Greeks in the WFM left Skliris and Stathakos bewildered, its implications for other members of Bingham's working class were all too obvious. The Japanese workers who had walked out with other immigrants remained excluded from the union. The boundaries of working-class organization continued to be racialized in Bingham, boundaries that in fact eased the Americanization of working-class Greeks and Italians. Although the boundaries of race appeared highly mutable in Bingham, the term "Americanization" connoted whiteness for all classes during the conflict. Joining the WFM thus culminated a process of both working-class acculturation and racial assimilation for Greek and Italian immigrants.[42] Unlike Mexican sugar beet workers in Oxnard, California, who refused to join the AFL in 1903 unless the offer included their Japanese cohorts, Bingham's formerly nonwhite Greeks sundered ties with their Japanese co-workers as WFM leadership brought the strike under more

[39]*Salt Lake Evening Telegram,* 30 September 1912, p. 12.

[40]Ibid., 2 October 1912, p. 9.

[41]*Miner's Magazine,* 3 October 1912, p. 8.

[42]For an analysis of the larger impact of racial ideology on the formation of an American working class, see David R. Roediger, *The Wages of Whiteness: Race and the Making of the American Working Class* (London, ENG, 1991) and Alexander Saxton, *The Rise and Fall of the White Republic: Class Politics and Mass Culture in Nineteenth-Century America* (London, ENG, 1990).

direct control.[43] The Utah Copper Company attempted to take advantage of these enduring racial divisions by offering special wages to the Japanese during the strike. Most Japanese laborers responded to this tragic dilemma with their feet, however, and left Bingham altogether.[44]

The continued exclusion of the Japanese from the union weakened the WFM's ability to maintain pressure on the Utah Copper Company. Nevertheless, Moyer succeeded in building a tension-fraught alliance between unskilled immigrants and skilled American workers in Bingham during the strike. By the second week, even skilled craft unions such as the American Brotherhood of Railway Workers had joined the shutdown. The union was also successful in increasing the economic pressure upon the Guggenheim copper interests by pulling out an additional four thousand copper workers from Ely and McGill, Nevada. But such collective economic leverage proved too little to gain a union contract; the Guggenheims still controlled two more open-pit copper mines in New Mexico and Arizona. One illustration of the Utah Copper Company's formidable financial power is that the value of its stock increased throughout the strike's initial stages.[45]

The Utah Copper Company broke the strike not merely with superior financial resources, but by dividing working-class ethnicity from within each immigrant group, thus pitting Italian worker against Italian worker and Greek laborer against Greek laborer. In this endeavor, the company benefited from events far from Bingham. On 1 October 1912, the Greek government issued an executive draft order recalling to active duty all male subjects between the ages of eighteen and thirty. For Bingham's Greek strikers, the outbreak of the Balkan Wars posed a profound dilemma: Should they return to Greece to vanquish their traditional enemy or finish the fight against labor padronism and the Utah Copper Company? Initially, most Greeks stayed in Bingham in solidarity with other strikers; they also stayed because Skliris assumed control of Utah's repatriation effort to the Balkan War.[46]

With the help of Stathakos and former business partner Will Caravelis, Skliris transformed the newly created Panhellenic Union from an organ of middle-class Americanization to one of Greek nationalism, and took on the task in Utah of exporting "patriotic" Greeks back to their homeland. Skliris made the most of his self-appointed role as the nationalistic spokesman of Utah's Greek community in the *Salt Lake Tribune:*

> To be sure, the empire of the Ottoman is great and its soldiers are fierce and fanatic fighters, but history has yet to show where the Caucasian Race . . . ever went down to defeat in a war so important as this will be. The Turk is doomed.[47]

[43]Montgomery, *Fall of the House of Labor,* 87.

[44]*Deseret Evening News,* 30 September 1912, p. 7.

[45]The value of Utah Copper Company stock rose from $64 to $68 between 12 September and 28 September 1912. *Wall Street Journal,* 12 September 1912, p. 3; 28 September 1912, p. 3.

[46]*Salt Lake Tribune,* 1 October 1912, p. 1; 8 October 1912, pp. 3, 5; *Evening Standard,* 4 October 1912, pp. 7, 9.

[47]*Salt Lake Tribune,* 22 October 1912, p. 3.

More than a touch of irony shadowed Skliris's bravado, given his own recent experience with "fierce and fanatic fighters." Perhaps more remarkable, however, was Skliris's identification of Greeks as "Caucasian." Like Moyer, Skliris also sought to redeem Greek workers to a nativist public by emphasizing their Americanness and whiteness. Skliris thus used the Balkan War not only to rehabilitate the padrone system, but to whiten himself and his rebellious constituency in the eyes of Utah's middle class.[48]

The Utah Copper Company capitalized on these events by acquiring much-needed strikebreakers. Although Leonidas Skliris had resigned as the company's labor agent, his subordinate, Gus Paulos, sent one hundred Greek strikebreakers to Bingham on 10 October. Hundreds of angry Greek strikers confronted their countrymen at the mine gates, but enough of these newly imported workers remained on the job to start up three steam shovels that day.[49] Most of these Greeks hailed from Rhoumeli, a province in the central Greek mainland. During the ensuing weeks, hundreds more Italian, Greek, and Mexican workers poured into Bingham, enabling the Utah Copper Company to resume full production by 15 November. The devastating impact of this strategy was graphically demonstrated on 25 October 1912, when thirty strikers from Crete ambushed and killed Greek strikebreaker Harry Spendon on his way to work; Spendon was the first immigrant worker to die in Bingham's labor unrest.[50]

With the strike appearing completely lost, *Miner's Magazine* editor O'Neill sharply criticized those Greeks who abandoned the class struggle in Bingham to fight in the Balkan wars:

> The Greeks who have gone back belong to the working class, and these men of labor . . . forget the conditions that drove them to the new world. . . . But the Greek, like the American, is moved by that sentiment of prejudice, which is commonly known as patriotism.[51]

O'Neill condemned patriotic Greeks for fighting the wrong war, but he overlooked the fact that without a "sentiment of prejudice" Greek workers might not have rebelled against Skliris and the Utah Copper Company in the first place. Yet O'Neill's recognition of the Balkan War's divisiveness underscored just how fragmented the solidarity of working-class Greeks had become. For the Greek strikers and strikebreakers who remained in Bingham, the 1912 episode left enduring ideological divisions that would take more than a generation to heal. Not coincidentally, copper miners in Bingham remained without a union until 1946, when the International Union of Mine,

[48]Ibid., p. 4.

[49]Ibid., 11 October 1912, p. 1; Paul Borovilos, 1 April 1970; Jack Tallas, 18 January 1971; James Korobas, 3 October 1974; Mrs. Isidore Kastanis, 2 March 1973; Peter Argentos, 4 December 1974, Greek Oral History Collections, Marriott Library, University of Utah, Salt Lake City, UT. These interviews, conducted under the supervision of Helen Papanikolas, confirmed the same basic facts about breaking the strike with Greek laborers supplied by Gus Paulos.

[50]*Evening Standard,* 25 October 1912, p. 4; 26 October 1912, p. 3.

[51]*Miner's Magazine,* 7 November 1912, p. 4.

Mill, and Smelter Workers, an offspring of the WFM, finally won a union contract. Many of the 1912 strike's most militant Greek participants scattered throughout the West; some, such as Louis Theos, became organizers for the IWW, while others joined fellow union members in the coal fields of Ludlow, Colorado, the site of the infamous Ludlow Massacre of 1914.[52]

If immigrant workers emerged from 1912 a class divided, padrones emerged more unified than ever before. The reorganization of padronism that occurred during the strike became dramatically evident in the cross-ethnic alliances that resulted. In December 1912, as the strike wound down, Skliris formed a seven-year business partnership with Italian padrone Moses Paggi to provide immigrant laborers to the Utah Power & Light Company.[53] Skliris and Paggi charged immigrant workers five cents a day rather than a dollar a month, and deducted the tribute directly from workers' wages, bypassing any troublesome problems of collection or enforcement. Equally if not more significant, padrones also imported men from beyond their home country's borders. The Mexican strikebreakers who arrived in Bingham in 1912 were not brought there by a Mexican padrone, but by Japanese contractor E. D. Hashimoto, whose connections among nonwhite workers in Mexico served him well after 1912.[54] In the process, Mexicans became the newest of Bingham's many new immigrants—like the Japanese, a nonwhite group whose admission into American labor unions would be vigorously resisted for years to come.[55]

For Bingham's American-born residents, the strike thoroughly discredited any formal working-class organizations. The Bingham local survived for a few years, but only as a shell of its former self. Although the Socialists still commanded 20 percent of Bingham's electorate during the strike, they polled barely 3 percent in congressional elections two years later. At the city council level, the Republicans acquired a virtual monopoly on power, polling 74 percent of the vote and winning all five seats in the fall of 1913. Formerly one of Utah's most politically radical communities, the town of Bingham Canyon had quickly become one of its most conservative. For the American-born radicals who stayed in Bingham such as E. G. Locke, the Bingham defeat meant not only the loss of his job as the union's financial secretary, but a subsequent lifetime of blacklists and temporary work.[56]

[52]Helen Papanikolas, "Toil and Rage," 122; Zeese Papanikolas, *Buried Unsung: Louis Tikas and the Ludlow Massacre* (Salt Lake City, 1982).

[53]Case #3216, 12 March 1919, Utah State Supreme Court, Utah State Archives. My thanks to Phil Notarianni of the Utah State Historical Society who brought this case to my attention.

[54]Conversations with Helen Papanikolas, who interviewed Hashimoto's son, Edward I. Hashimoto, in Salt Lake City, 14 and 16 April 1975, just before he died.

[55]For a study of the role of Mexican copper miners in the western labor movement, see A. Yvette Huginnie's forthcoming book, *Strikitos: Race, Class, and Work in the Arizona Copper Industry, 1870–1920*.

[56]Bingham Canyon City Council Minutes, 10 November 1913, Utah State Archives; conversation with Vernon Jensen, who interviewed Locke in his home in Salt Lake City just before he died in 1948.

For western social historians, the significance of the impressive, but short-lived militancy of Greek, Italian, and Japanese workers does not lie in the event's typicality or its far-reaching impact on the western labor movement. The WFM's loss of the Bingham local did not cripple the union, nor did other groups of unskilled immigrants subsequently begin "taking over" WFM locals. Rather, it is precisely the atypical features of the Bingham strike—the unusual prominence of rank and file immigrants and their demands against both immigrant elites and would-be union leaders—that suggest its importance to western social historians. The tensions and loyalties within and between immigrant groups underscore just how intertwined and mutable racial, ethnic, and class formations could be in the West. Organizers mobilized Greek strikers as both workers and immigrants, and, at different moments of the strike, as both white and nonwhite workers. The relationships between race, ethnicity, and class could cut in different and sometimes unpredictable directions, inducing the same Greek workers to fight both Leonidas Skliris and Charles Moyer at distinct moments. The choices Greek workers and Skliris made about their ethnicity occurred within an intensely nativist and polarized political context, one that at least partially defined the very meaning of being Greek in racial and political terms. Ethnicity for these immigrants existed as an invention of American society, as suggested by Werner Sollors, but it emerged as an identity whose meaning was forged out of conflicts between different classes and different races of immigrants.[57] The struggle to construct ethnicity in Bingham also demonstrated the conflict over the elastic but always racialized definitions of both Americanization and radicalism, a struggle in which an immigrant working class, an immigrant middle class, and American radicals all participated.

The Bingham strike also suggests ways of rethinking some of the conceptual challenges—both new and traditional—confronting western labor history. It is only by examining the intersections between race, ethnicity, and class, so richly intertwined during the Bingham strike, that their historical meaning and significance begin to emerge. Recognizing how the category of Caucasian worker changed and expanded during the Bingham strike, for example, helps us make distinctions between different ethnicities and different forms of racism; and it encourages us to avoid flattening the meaning of race and ethnicity across the nineteenth and twentieth centuries.[58] To conclude that the WFM declined in Bingham merely because it accepted racist practices and therefore could no longer be considered truly radical, would obscure the complexity of the union's social history by failing to historicize the meaning of *either* racism or radicalism. From its inception, the WFM's socialist politics coexisted with a commitment to ex-

[57]Werner Sollors, ed., *The Invention of Ethnicity* (New York, 1989).

[58]On historicizing western race relations, see Richard White's "Race Relations in the American West," *American Quarterly* 38 (Bibliography 1986): 396–416, and his *The Middle Ground: Indians, Empires, and Republics in the Great Lakes Region, 1650–1815* (Cambridge, MA, 1991).

cluding nonwhite workers, a connection that problematizes idealized definitions of western labor radicalism and narratives of its growth and decline. If race and ethnicity constituted highly mutable social constructs in Bingham, so too did radicalism and Americanization remain contested concepts whose meanings developed out of the conflicts between working-class and middle-class immigrants, "old" radicals and "new" immigrants. Recognizing the tensions between Charles Moyer and Greek strikers does not mean the WFM was conservative, but suggests that more and more diverse kinds of radicals worked and organized in Bingham than previously thought. It was the militancy and, by 1912 standards, the radical cross-ethnic and cross-racial solidarity of Greek, Italian, and Japanese immigrants that redefined the union's strike agenda and challenged, at least temporarily, the WFM's increasingly nativist politics. The challenge to western labor historians should not be to examine how ethnicity and race necessarily weakened the growth of an indigenous and ideologically pure western radicalism, but how the ethnicity and race of western radicals—"old" native-born and "new" immigrant alike—shaped *both* the growth and decline of western labor radicalism.

*

Red Lights in Zion: Salt Lake City's Stockade, 1908–1911

JOHN S. McCORMICK

The history of prostitution is not merely a sensational or colorful subject. Nor is it trivial. Prostitution is deeply woven into the fabric of a community, and its study can provide insight into social structures and cultural values and practices. It can function as a lens through which to focus on a range of issues, including politics, women's economic and social status, and aspects of race, class, and gender. This article discusses prostitution in Salt Lake City in the late nineteenth and early twentieth centuries, with an emphasis on the operation between 1908 and 1911 of the city's westside "stockade" operated by one of Utah's best-known madams, "Belle London," of Ogden's "Electric Avenue."

"Red Lights in Zion: Salt Lake City's Stockade, 1908–1911," *Utah Historical Quarterly* 50 (Spring 1982): 168–81. Reprinted by permission of the publisher and the author.

John S. McCormick is co-editor of this volume.

THE HISTORY OF PROSTITUTION in the United States is not a frivolous subject, though it is often treated that way, and in recent years a number of historians have given it the serious treatment it deserves. They have focused particularly on the midwestern and western United States, writing, for example, about prostitution in late nineteenth- and early twentieth-century Saint Louis, Kansas, Helena, Nevada's Comstock, San Diego, and San Francisco.[1]

---

[1]John C. Burnham, "The Social Evil Ordinance: A Social Experiment in Nineteenth Century St. Louis," *Missouri Historical Society Bulletin* 27 (April 1971): 203–17; Carol Leonard and Isidor Wallimann, "Prostitution and Changing Morality in the Frontier Cattle Towns of Kansas," *Kansas History* 2 (Spring 1979): 34–53; Elliott West, "Scarlet West: The Oldest Profession in the Trans-Mississippi West," *Montana, the Magazine of Western History* 31 (April 1981): 16–27; Paula Petrik, "Capitalists with Rooms: Prostitution in Helena, Montana,

Thus far, historians have had little to say about prostitution in Utah. Yet, the situation here was little different from the rest of the country. In Salt Lake City, as in other cities in the United States, laws prohibiting prostitution were on the books. In general, local officials saw them as politically expedient concessions to middle-class morality. Prostitution, it was felt, could not be eliminated. It could only be controlled, The best way to do that was to confine it to particular parts of town, known as "red-light districts," where it could be watched and regulated. As Arthur Pratt, Salt Lake City police chief in 1895, said,

> I think the best plan is to put them [prostitutes] in one locality as much as possible and keep them under surveillance. The evil cannot be suppressed, but it must be restrained and kept under strict police control. It is a more difficult problem to handle when the women are scattered out than when they are kept together.[2]

Red-light districts existed in most late nineteenth-century American cities and towns. They varied from place to place, ranging from a discreet house or two in or near small towns to the block after bawdy block of New York City's "Tenderloin," Chicago's "Levee," Baltimore's "Block," San Francisco's "Barbary Coast," New Orleans's "Storyville," and San Diego's "Stingaree." In Salt Lake City a red-light district was well established near the central business district within a generation of settlement; and in the early twentieth century, Salt Lake, following the example of other cities, adopted a "compound," or "stockade," policy. Under the direction of the mayor and city council, the interior of a block on the city's westside near the railroad tracks was walled off, "cribs" and "parlor houses" were built within the enclosure, and prostitutes were allowed to work essentially unhindered within the stockade and were arrested only when they plied their trade elsewhere. Though little known,[3] the history of the stockade is not

---

Goldman, "Sexual Commerce on the Comstock Lode," *Nevada Historical Society Quarterly* 21 (Summer 1978): 98–129; Elizabeth C. MacPhail, "When the Red Lights Went Out in San Diego," *Journal of San Diego History* 20 (Spring 1974): 1–28; Neil Larry Shumsky, "Vice Responds to Reform; San Francisco, 1910–1914," *Journal of Urban History* 7 (November 1980): 31–47. Other valuable studies include David J. Pivar, "Cleansing the Nation: The War on Prostitution, 1917–1921," *Prologue* 12 (Spring 1980): 29–40; Pivar, *Purity Crusade* (Westport, Conn.: Greenwood Press, 1976); Mark Connelly, *The Response to Prostitution in the Progressive Era* (Chapel Hill: University of North Carolina Press, 1980); Robert E. Riegel, "Changing American Attitudes Toward Prostitution, 1800–1920," *Journal of the History of Ideas* 29 (July–September 1968): 437–52; and John C. Burnham, "The Progressive Era Revolution in American Attitudes Towards Sex," *Journal of American History* 59 (March 1973): 885–908.

[2]*Salt Lake Tribune,* January 4, 1895, p. 8. For similar statements see the comment of Frank B. Stephens, a member of the Salt Lake Police and Fire Commission, in *Salt Lake Tribune,* February 8, 1896, p. 5; an editorial in *Salt Lake Tribune,* February 9, 1896; and a note in *Truth* 1 (September 6, 1902): 6.

[3]Reuben J. Snow's master's thesis, "The American Party in Utah: A Study of Political Struggles during the Early Years of Statehood" (University of Utah, 1964), deals with the stockade at various points in its discussion of the American party. There is no other study concerned, except in passing, with the stockade nor with any other aspect of the history of prostitution in Utah.

only fascinating in itself but is a rich source of information about the larger history of Salt Lake City and, in combination with other studies, contributes to the history of prostitution in the United States.

The origin of Salt Lake's first red-light district is unknown. It is not clear whether it evolved gradually or whether city officials at some point unofficially established it. What is clear is that by the early 1870s, what is now Regent Street in downtown Salt Lake was the center of a red-light district. Then, it was appropriately named Commercial Street. In 1903 the *Salt Lake Tribune* referred to the area as a "resort of gamblers and fast women."[4]

According to the *Deseret News*, half a dozen years later, the occupants of Commercial Street were "the demi-monde, the male parasite, the dope fiend, the gambler, and the begger."[5]

John Held's description is one of the most interesting. A native of Salt Lake who became a nationally known illustrator in the 1920s, Held said his account came from considerable first-hand experience.

> Within the street were saloons, cafes and parlor houses, with cribs that were rented nightly to the itinerate 'Ladies of the Calling.' Soliciting was taboo, so these ladies sat at the top of the stairs and called their invitation to 'come on up, kid.' The parlor houses allowed no such publicity. There was no outward display to gain entrants to a parlor house. One pushed an electric bell and was admitted by a uniformed maid or an attendant. The luxury of these houses always included a 'Professor' at the piano. There was none of the brashness of the mechanical piano; those were heard in the saloons and shooting galleries of the street. The names of two of the madams are engraved on my memory, just as they were cut on the copper plates that Dad had made for printing the ladies' personal cards. In Dad's engraving shop an order for cards from the madams was always welcome. They demanded the finest and most expensive engraving, and the cards were of the finest stock, pure rag vellum. . . . One of the madams called herself Miss Ada Wilson. Hers was a lavish house on Commercial Street. Another gave her name as Miss Helen Blazes. Her establishment catered to the big money, and in it only wine was served. In other houses, beer was the popular refreshment, at one dollar a bottle, served to the guests in small whiskey glasses.[6]

Of the several dozen buildings on Commercial Street that were once houses of prostitution, three remain standing at 165, 167, and 169 Regent Street. A restaurant occupies two of the buildings and an electrical supply company the third. Throughout the United States, leading citizens commonly owned land and buildings in red-light districts,[7] and that was also the case in Salt Lake. In 1893, for example, Gustave S. Holmes constructed the buildings at 165 and 167 Regent Street. A well-known businessman, he owned the fashionable Knutsford Hotel (which stood on Third South and State streets), served as a director of the National Bank of the Republic, had extensive mining interests, and in 1909 was reportedly the fifth or sixth

[4]March 31, 1903, p. 11.
[5]June 24, 1909, p. 2.
[6]*The Most of John Held, Jr.* (Brattleboro, Vt.: Stephen Greene Press, 1972), pp. 99–100.
[7]See, for example, Goldman, "Sexual Commerce on the Comstock Lode," pp. 106—8.

largest taxpayer in Salt Lake County.[8] "Female boarders," a common euphemism for prostitutes, occupied the upper floors of each building. In 1909, according to the *Deseret News,* the prostitutes at 167 Regent Street were "French women."[9] Legitimate businesses were located on the first floor of both buildings. A cigar factory, one of about a dozen in the city at the time, was originally in one building, and a printing establishment was in the other. The liquor business was always closely associated with prostitution, and in 1900 a saloon replaced the printers.[10]

The third building has a similar history. It was built in 1899 for Stephen Hays, a Salt Lake merchant, real estate speculator, and, like Holmes, a director of the National Bank of the Republic.[11] A prominent Utah architect, Walter E. Ware, designed the building. Other buildings Ware designed in Salt Lake include the First Presbyterian Church, the First Church of Christ, Scientist, Saint Mark's Hospital, and the Westminster College gymnasium.[12] For several years, Martin E. Mulvey, a member of the Salt Lake City Council from 1906 until 1912, operated a saloon on the first floor of the building.[13] Upstairs was a parlor house, so named because prostitutes received their customers in a common parlor or sitting room. Though long vacant, its original design and layout remained unchanged in the 1980s: a large center room surrounded by 8-by-10-foot rooms, or "cribs," just large enough for a bed, washstand, and one or two chairs.

As in other American cities at the time, an unofficial licensing system for prostitutes existed in Salt Lake. Typically in cities throughout the country, police periodically arrested prostitutes and escorted them to the police court where they routinely paid a fine for being an "inmate" or a "keeper" of a "disorderly house." In many places the money derived in this way became an important part of the city's revenue, so that, in fact, the aim of antiprostitution ordinances and periodic arrests and fines was not so much to suppress prostitution as to produce revenue for the city. In Wichita, Kansas, for example, the city treasurer reported at the end of August 1873 that the city income from fining prostitutes was so large that general business taxes were unnecessary.[14]

[8]For biographical information on Holmes, see his obituary in the *Deseret News,* July 3, 1935, p. 3, and *Sketches of the Inter-Mountain States* (Salt Lake City: Salt Lake Tribune Publishing Co., 1909), pp. 226–27.

[9]June 24, 1909, p. 22.

[10]*Insurance Maps, Salt Lake City, Utah* (New York: Sanborn-Perris Map Co., 1898), 2:103; *Salt Lake City Directory, 1894–95* (Salt Lake City: R. L. Polk and Co., Publishers 1894–95), p. 824; *Salt Lake City Directory, 1898,* pp. 844, 846, 893, 643; *Salt Lake City Directory, 1899,* p. 505; *Salt Lake City Directory, 1900,* pp. 440, 512; *Salt Lake City Directory, 1901,* p. 926.

[11]For biographical information on Hays, see his obituary in the *Deseret News,* January 29, 1927, p. 1, section 2, and the *Salt Lake Tribune,* January 30, 1927, p. 22, section 3.

[12]For information on Ware see the Architects File, Preservation Office, Utah State Historical Society, Salt Lake City.

[13]*Salt Lake City Directory, 1900,* p. 517; *Salt Lake City Directory, 1901,* p. 926. For biographical information on Mulvey, see his obituary in the *Salt Lake Tribune,* April 22, 1951.

[14]Leonard and Wallimann, "Prostitution and Changing Morality in the Frontier Cattle Towns of Kansas," pp. 44–45.

The way the system operated in Salt Lake City varied from time to time. In 1886 police regularly arrested several dozen prostitutes, fined them a maximum of fifty dollars each, gave them physical examinations, and released them. Between arrests, according to the *Salt Lake Herald,* the women were "allowed to go along without fear of molestation, as long as they did not ply their trade so openly and brazenly as to offend the public eye."[15] By 1908 a registration system existed. Police kept track of names and addresses of madams and their houses. The madams in turn gave up-to-date lists of their "girls" to police. Every month each woman was expected to pay a "fine" of ten dollars. The *Deseret News* examined the book in which the list of prostitutes was recorded and found that during the summer of 1908 an average of 148 women paid fines each month. The nearly $1,500 collected monthly went into the city's general fund.[16] In the mid-1910s city policy was to license brothels as "rooming houses" and require prostitutes to work only in them.

Around the turn of the century various individuals and groups began to advocate that city officials end prostitution on Commercial Street and relocate the red-light district farther from the business area. In 1903 the *Deseret News* reported that "It is now proposed to purge Commercial Street and move it to a less public district where their presence will not be a constant blot, defacing the business center and forcing itself upon public attention." In the view of the *News,* "The project is commendable. . . . Whether it is practicable remains to be seen."[17] In another story, the *News* quoted Nephi W. Clayton, a prominent businessman and Mormon church leader, as favoring the continuation of a restricted red-light district but relocating it on the far west side of the city.[18] The *Salt Lake Tribune,* on the other hand, preferred to "open up a new street into the interior of some of the downtown blocks."[19] The general feeling was that prostitution could not be entirely eliminated and to try to do so was wasted effort; but when located near the downtown area, a red-light district had a harmful effect on business. It offended and drove away potential customers and led to higher rents, since space for legitimate business was scarce. In addition, it was pointed out, prostitution had begun to spread beyond the bounds of Commercial Street. Several brothels were operating on Main Street itself, another was located on Brigham Street, and the notorious Helen Blazes was reported to have opened a parlor house near the corner of Seventh South and Main streets.

Formal involvement of Salt Lake City officials in the relocation of the city's red-light district came in 1907 when Police Chief Thomas D. Pitt recommended in his annual report that a change be made in the city's method of dealing with prostitution. In his view, the red-light district needed to be

[15]June 2, 1886, p. 4.
[16]*Deseret News,* September 23, 1908, p. 1.
[17]April 3, 1903, p. 4.
[18]Ibid., p. 1.
[19]March 31, 1903, p. 11.

moved from Commercial Street to another location, and a "stockade" needed to be established. As Pitt saw it,

> This question [of prostitution] is certainly a question hard to dispose of, and, being a necessary evil, there is only one way in which it can be successfully handled, which is as follows: Let the city set aside a piece of ground of sufficient size to accommodate several hundred of these prostitutes. Enclose same carefully with high fences; build cottages or houses to accommodate these inmates; charge them rent; license them and place them under control of the Police Department as to their safety and confinement, and to the Board of Health as to their cleanliness and sanitary conditions.[20]

Mayor John Bransford and the Salt Lake City Council accepted Pitt's recommendation and in the spring of 1908 began to plan the stockade.

A prominent businessman, deeply involved in real estate and mining activities, Bransford was a member of the American party, as were nine of the fifteen members of the council.[21] This explicitly anti-Mormon political party was founded in 1904 and made up of people opposed to what they saw as the Mormon church's continued domination of political affairs in Utah. In many ways a reincarnation of the Liberal party, which existed in Utah from 1870 to 1893, it was never successful in the state as a whole; but it grew rapidly in Salt Lake City and between 1906 and 1912 dominated city government.[22] However, the stockade policy was not merely a policy of the American party but received support from council members of all parties. The clearest indication of that came when Chief Pitt changed his mind and refused to help implement the stockade policy. Mayor Bransford fired him, and the city council supported the mayor by a vote of twelve to two.[23]

The city council made no public announcement of their intention to establish the stockade until December 1908 when it was nearly completed and about to open. Bransford then held a press conference and frankly explained his own attitude toward prostitution and outlined the way the stockade had come about. "With reference to the new district," he said, "the houses of which are in the process of construction, I wish to say that I am thoroughly in favor of it and that it was at my suggestion that the work was begun." Prostitution would always exist, Bransford asserted. It could not be eliminated but only minimized and controlled. The best way to do that was to establish an isolated area where it would operate under official sanction and supervision. Accordingly, he said, "I propose to take these women from the business section of the city and put them in a district which will be one of the best, if not the very best, regulated districts in the country."[24]

[20]*Message of the Mayor, with the Annual Report of the Officers of Salt Lake City, Utah, for the year 1907* (Salt Lake City, 1907), pp. 374–75.

[21]For a short biography of Bransford, see *Sketches of the Inter-Mountain States*, p. 97.

[22]The only study of the American party is Snow, "The American Party in Utah."

[23]Salt Lake City, "Minutes of the Meeting of the City Council," December 7, 1908, p. 831; December 14, 1908, pp. 856–58.

[24]*Salt Lake Herald*, December 8, 1908, p. 1.

Having explained his approach to the problem of dealing with prostitution, Bransford went on to outline the stockade's history. In the spring of 1908, he said, he and Councilman Martin E. Mulvey, with the approval of the rest of the council, met with Mrs. Dora B. Topham. Perhaps Utah's most notorious madam, she was better known as "Belle London" and operated much of the business of prostitution on Ogden's "Electric Avenue."[25] Bransford and Mulvey asked her to form a corporation, purchase land on Salt Lake's westside in the center of Block 64, Plat A, which was between 500 and 600 West and 100 and 200 South streets, and set up and operate a stockade. According to Bransford, "I told her that if she did as I wished, and followed out the directions, . . . I would see to it that the women of the downtown district were removed to the new location."[26] London agreed. Later she explained:

> I know, and you know, that prostitution has existed since the earliest ages, and if you are honest with yourselves, you will admit that it will continue to exist, no matter what may be said or done from the pulpit or through the exertions of women's clubs. I believed that I could segregate the evil, that I could control it, and that I could decrease disease by an intelligent management, and while profiting financially myself, do some good. . . . [27]

In the summer of 1908, Belle London formed the Citizen's Investment Company. During the next two months it purchased land in the interior of Block 64 and commissioned architect Lewis D. Martin, a member of the city council, to draw up plans for a stockade. In September 1908 construction of the stockade began. Work was completed three months later.

On the evening of December 18, ten days after Mayor Bransford's press conference, city police told all prostitutes on Commercial Street and nearby Victoria Alley that they had until 4:00 A.M. the next morning to vacate the area. According to Councilman Mulvey,

> The women of the town will not be told that they must reside within the shelter, but they will be given to understand that if they do not, things will be made unpleasant for them, while they will be given to understand that they will be allowed to live undisturbed within the stockade.[28]

In other words, the women had three choices: they could leave town, they could go to jail, or they could go to the stockade. Evidently, most of the women, perhaps one hundred in all, went to the stockade.

Salt Lake City newspapers, in particular the *Deseret News* and the *Intermountain Republican,* provided lengthy descriptions and photographs of the stockade. The 1911 Sanborn Fire Insurance Maps of Salt Lake City are also an important source of information. The stockade occupied the interior

[25]Little biographical information is available on London. For some fragments see Lyle J. Barnes, "Ogden's Notorious 'Two-Bit Street,' 1870–1954" (Master's thesis, Utah State University, 1969), pp. 19–20.

[26]*Salt Lake Herald,* December 8, 1908, p. 1.

[27]*Salt Lake Tribune,* September 28, 1911, p. 2.

[28]*Salt Lake Herald,* December 10, 1908, p. 12.

of the block and consisted of about one hundred small brick and frame dwellings called "cribs," built in rows, or on "line." Hence, the phrase, "Going down the line." Belle London rented these cribs to prostitutes for from one to four dollars a day. Each crib was about ten feet square, with a door and a window in the front. Soliciting was usually carried on from the windows. According to the *Deseret News,* "At the windows, only two feet above the sidewalk, sits the painted denizen of the underworld calling to the passers between puffs on her cigaret."[29] A curtain or wooden partition divided the inside of the crib. In the front half were a chair or two and a combination bureau and washstand. In the rear half was a white enameled iron bed. Also in the stockade were half a dozen larger buildings known as "parlor houses." A "landlady" operated each parlor house, renting it from Belle London for $175 a month. The half a dozen or so women in each house split their earnings with their landlady. A large structure at the end of one row of cribs served as a storehouse for beer and liquor, always an important part of the stockade operation. A brick wall partially enclosed the compound. Outside the stockade, on First South, Belle London built a two-story brick building as her office and residence. Its architect was Councilman Martin. There were three entrances to the stockade, one on Second South and two on First South, with a guard at each one. Their job was to keep children out of the block and to warn stockade occupants of the periodic police raids that were conducted largely as a matter of form. To give warning, an elaborate alarm system was installed. The effectiveness of the system, and the extent of cooperation between police and prostitutes, is shown by the fact that in March 1910, 453 warrants were issued for the arrest of women in the stockade. Not one was served. The reason, the police officers in charge explained, was that each night when they went to the stockade to serve the warrants, they found it dark and deserted.[30]

Why was the stockade located at that particular place on the westside? No one wanted to be near it, Mayor Bransford explained, but it had to be somewhere. Those in charge of the project looked for an area where it would have as little negative effect as possible. According to Councilman Mulvey:

> The location of the new district is the best which could possibly have been secured. There are railroad tracks on two sides of the district, and when the Western Pacific tracks are completed, the tracks will surround the district on three sides. The block is the dividing line between two school districts, and no children will be compelled to pass the place on their way to and from school. From the outside, nothing can be seen of the movements within, and the offensive sights which have greeted passers-by in the neighborhood of Commercial Street will be absent.[31]

There was a second reason why city officials chose this location for the stockade, Mulvey said: "We found that most of the better class of residents

[29]May 18, 1909, p. 1.
[30]*Salt Lake Times,* July 23, 1910, p. 1.
[31]*Salt Lake Herald,* December 18, 1908, p. 2.

were leaving the area anyway, because of the influx of Italians and Greeks who live in that neighborhood."[32] The particular conclusion Salt Lake City officials drew was that the "foreign element" had so destroyed the area that establishing prostitution there would not harm it any further and could even be rationalized as catering to the "immoral foreigners."

Mayor Bransford and Councilman Mulvey failed to mention one other fact that played a role in the selection of the site of the stockade: Bransford owned property across the street. On it he built a large two-story building. Its upper floors served as a rooming house for prostitutes, while the ground floor housed a variety of small Greek businesses, including, originally, a saloon, a barbershop, and a coffeehouse.[33]

The stockade operated for nearly three years. During that time reaction to it was mixed. On December 13, 1908, a few days before it opened, a group of fifty westside residents submitted a petition to the Salt Lake City Council endorsing the stockade policy. It would keep prostitution from spreading, they said, would not interfere with business nor "contaminate" residents of the area, and it would "add to the safety and respectability of that portion of the City known as W. Second South."[34] At the same time, other residents formed a West Side Citizens League, submitted petitions to the city council, and held mass meetings at which they protested the establishment of the stockade on the westside and demanded the prosecution of those responsible.[35] The league remained in existence for the life of the stockade. Of Salt Lake's five daily newspapers, the *Salt Lake Tribune* and the *Salt Lake Telegram* supported the stockade, while the *Deseret News*, the *Salt Lake Herald*, and the *Intermountain Republican* opposed it. In December 1908 and again in May 1910, the *Deseret News* ran a series of sensational articles purporting to expose conditions in the stockade. Mayor Bransford and a majority of the city council continued to support the stockade; but Bransford's own American party, on the other hand, opposed it, as did both the Republican party and the Democratic party. Salt Lake City Police Chief Samuel Barlow supported the idea. Salt Lake County Sheriff John C. Sharpe did not and conducted raids, on dubious authority, on the stockade. Women in the stockade, including Belle London herself, were periodically arrested. Charges were usually dismissed, however, and only a handful of women were ever convicted. When convicted, they were usually given the choice of paying a fine, going to jail, or leaving town. The Salt Lake Ministerial Association periodically spoke out against the stockade, on one occasion characterizing it as "a system of brutality, debauchery . . . that Rome never out did."[36] Mormon church leaders, in contrast, made no public statements about it.

[32]Ibid.

[33]*Salt Lake City Directory, 1911*, pp. 108, 153, 774, 987.

[34]*Salt Lake Herald*, December 13, 1908, p. 7.

[35]See, for example, Salt Lake City, "Minutes of the Meeting of the City Council," June 21, 1909, p. 448.

[36]*Intermountain Republican*, December 15, 1908, p. 7

On September 28, 1911, Belle London made an unexpected announcement: "The stockade will be closed on Thursday and the same will not be opened again. So soon as I can arrange my business I shall advertize the property for sale."[37] Reaction to the announcement was mixed. The *Salt Lake Telegram* published an editorial expressing regret at the stockade's closing. Prostitution was inevitable, the paper said; a "segregated district" was the best way to control it, and closing the stockade would make regulation more difficult.[38] Police Chief Barlow agreed, saying that with the closing of the stockade, control of prostitution in Salt Lake would be "infinitely more difficult."[39] The *Deseret News* and the *Salt Lake Herald* were skeptical that London really intended to close the stockade permanently. As the *Herald* saw it, her intent was "merely to embarrass the good citizens of the community by turning a flood of scarlet women into the streets, thus creating a condition more horrible, if possible, than the stockade itself."[40] That accomplished, the paper predicted, the stockade would soon reopen. The *Deseret News* agreed, pointing out that "This turning loose of 300 prostitutes in Salt Lake where they will infiltrate the business district, flaunt themselves on the streets, and offend the public morals," would occur during the weekend of the Mormon church's general conference when the city would be filled with out-of-town visitors.[41]

According to the *Salt Lake Telegram,* the decision to close the stockade was made at a meeting of Belle London, Mayor Bransford, and Councilman Mulvey. London denied that, saying that the decision had been entirely her own. She had reached it, she said, because "there is a strong public sentiment in favor of such a course."[42] Bransford agreed, without being specific, that "opposition from various sources" led to the stockade's closing.[43]

The precise circumstances surrounding the closing of the stockade remain unclear. The important point, however, is that its demise brought no substantial changes. It did not mean the end of prostitution in Salt Lake City nor the end of segregated vice districts. Prostitution continued to exist, and everyone knew it; though, as before, the subject was excluded from polite conversation. According to newspaper reports, no more than a dozen women accepted the offer of the Women's League to "leave their lives of sin" and come to the Women's Rescue Station where jobs as maids and domestic servants would be found for them. The rest of the former occupants of the stockade either returned to Commercial Street or remained near West Second South. Laws prohibiting prostitution remained on the books but were only selectively enforced. The continued goal of public officials was not the elimination of prostitution but its regulation by de facto licensing

[37]*Salt Lake Tribune,* September 28, 1911, p. 1.
[38]September 29, 1911, p. 4.
[39]*Salt Lake Telegram,* September 28, 1911, p. 10.
[40]September 29, 1911, p. 1.
[41]September 28, 1911, p. 1.
[42]*Salt Lake Tribune,* September 28, 1911, p. 1.
[43]Ibid.

and attempted confinement to certain areas of the city. Commercial Street remained a red-light district until the late 1930s, and West Second South until the late 1970s. Prostitution continued to be an integral part of the life of Salt Lake City.

*

Women in the Utah Work Force From Statehood to World War II

MIRIAM B. MURPHY

Though the history of women in Utah has increasingly engaged the attention of historians, it remains a relatively neglected area of study. This article explores women's work in Utah between statehood in 1896 and World War II. On the basis of both statistical data and extensive interviews with women about their experiences, the author finds that Utahns, with only slight variations, generally fit into the statistical pattern for working women in the United States: the number of women wage workers gradually increased during the period; most were unmarried; though women were found in a wide range of occupations, they tended to be concentrated in a few, traditionally female, areas of employment; race and ethnicity affected the nature and conditions of a woman's work; and the wages working women received were significantly less than those of similarly employed men.

Miriam B. Murphy, "Women in the Utah Work Force From Statehood to World War II," *Utah Historical Quarterly* 50 (Spring 1982): 139–59. Reprinted by permission of the publisher and the author.

Miriam B. Murphy is associate editor of the *Utah Historical Quarterly* and has published on a range of historical subjects, including several articles on women in Utah.

IN THE EARLY 1900s Charles O. Harris of the Utah Independent Telephone Company visited the Maxfield homestead in Big Cottonwood Canyon. He asked two daughters of the house if they would be interested in working for the new venture. The girls' father was outraged: "No daughter of mine will ever be a telephone operator. Most of them are nothing but little hussies." As the chagrined Harris quickly explained to his host, such a notion was incorrect. The Independent was looking for "good girls." Lois and Josie Ellen Maxfield were surely that, and, more to the point, they were experienced workers eager to learn new skills. Like so many young women of their time, they had labored not only at home but as poorly paid domestics in the homes of others. With their father's worst fears allayed, the two sisters—one just in her middle teens—went to work in Salt Lake City for the promising, but short-lived, competition to the Bell System.

Utah's capital was a growing, bustling city of about a hundred thousand in the first decade of the twentieth century. Probably many a parent shared R. D. Maxfield's anxiety about letting daughters, especially, work there. However sheltered their lives may have been, the two sisters soon became street wise. The UITC offices were on State Street near the old police headquarters and no more than a silver dollar's throw from the heart of Salt Lake City's red-light district. The young women saw policemen drag prostitutes by the hair of the head into the station for booking. They knew something of the patrons of Regent Street, too—pillars of the community, many of them. These men would telephone from one of the notorious hangouts to ask the young operators to call home for them: "Tell my wife I've been detained at the Alta Club." Such experience neither tempted the Maxfield girls nor made them cynical. Rather, they learned to cope in a complex, changing world where good and evil continually contend.

In 1909 the younger girl accepted a job offer from John E. Clark, manager of the Lyric Theatre, to work as a cashier. Clark cautioned twenty-year-old Josie Maxfield not to engage in any conversation with male patrons of the silent movie palace. She never doubted the wisdom of this warning. A year later, in pursuit of better wages and working conditions, she started to clerk at a dental and surgical supply house. After two years and the disappointment of seeing another, less experienced girl promoted ahead of her, she decided to move on.

About that time, the Independent folded, and both Lois and Josie Maxfield began new careers as saleswomen for the city's leading department stores. Employment there was not necessarily safer—one store owner had a reputation as a womanizer, and a buyer for another firm was deeply involved in a complex thievery plot. Despite these perils, the two women succeeded at their new line of work and rose in the retailing hierarchy. They married in 1919, and having no children continued their careers. Fortunately for their many relatives, the two women and their husbands remained employed steadily throughout the depression years. They continued busily at work in their own restaurant-resort enterprise as World War II ushered in a period of prosperity and different opportunities for working women.[1]

[1]Interview with Lois Maxfield Recore and Josie Ellen Maxfield Reenders, May 10, 1979, Salt Lake City.

The offices of the UITC were at 115 South State Street, and the old police station was around the corner at 120 East First South. Regent Street runs intermittently north-south between Main and State streets; the particular block referred to as a red-light district was between First and Second souths. The old Lyric Theatre at 321 South Main was a silent movie house at the time Josie Maxfield worked there. The restaurant-resort business was the original Maxfield Lodge in Big Cottonwood Canyon east of Salt Lake City.

There is something very typical about the experiences of the Maxfield sisters and something less typical as well. These young women went to work originally out of necessity. Their parents were not wealthy, nor even middle class, and children from such families were expected to shoulder some of the economic burden. Not until 1919 was compulsory school attendance through high school in effect in Utah.[2] Working children were hardly exceptional. Compiled employment statistics through at least the 1930 census include persons ten years of age and older.[3]

Paid housework brought the girls their first pay. That seems typical of the times. Domestic help was the most frequently advertised need in the female help wanted columns of the newspapers. But when other, more lucrative opportunities came along, the Maxfield sisters and their peers were quick to seize the bright ring of bigger paychecks and better hours and working conditions. The positions they filled were typical—telephone operator, clerk, saleswoman, and occasionally department head or assistant buyer. Only their eventual leap into the employer class near the beginning of World War II was atypical.

They encountered, or at least were made very aware of, sexual harassment on the job. That, too, was a fairly common experience, one of the hazards of employment for women.

Their paychecks helped to support ailing parents and relatives laid off work during the depression. Other women in Utah were also breadwinners. Coming from a large family, the sisters were unusual in having no children themselves. That would undoubtedly have changed their employment pattern as it did for most women of that time.

It is a temptation for researchers in Utah history to look for the unique, the unusual, indeed, for the "peculiar." One can resist that temptation in studying working women. Utahns generally fit into the statistical pattern for working women in the United States and varied only slightly from the norm, as did the Intermountain region, to the extent that the area was less heavily industrialized than other sections of the country and therefore provided fewer job opportunities.[4]

[2]John Clifton Moffitt, *A Century of Service, 1860–1960: A History of the Utah Eduction Association* (Salt Lake City: Utah Education Association, 1960), pp. 464–65. To cope with the need for more personnel, since funds were insufficient to support the extended compulsory education law, local school boards hired teachers at lower salary levels, to which the UEA, not surprisingly, objected.

[3]In 1910 there were 90 females and 1,040 males between ages ten and thirteen employed in Utah, mostly in agriculture, although 24 girls and 19 boys are listed as servants. By 1930 employment in this age group had dropped sharply to 281 males and only 24 females. See U.S., Department of Commerce, Bureau of the Census, *Thirteenth Census of the United States . . . 1910*. Vol. 4, *Population 1910: Occupation Statistics* (Washington, D.C.: Government Printing Office, 1914), p. 73; U.S., Department of Commerce, Bureau of the Census, *Fifteenth Census of the United States: 1930; Occupation Statistics, Utah* (Washington, D.C.: Government Printing Office, 1931), p. 13. The 1940 census lists employed persons over age fourteen, an indication of declining child employment.

[4]Another regional variation in 1910 was the higher proportion of employed females in the professions and in domestic and personal service in the Mountain Division (Montana, Idaho,

There is a popular song—written in 1909—titled "Heaven Will Protect the Working Girl."[5] Heaven certainly seems to have favored the Maxfield sisters during their working years. But other forces also attempted to protect working women or advance their cause. During the 1895 constitutional convention in Salt Lake City several rather fascinating events occurred. To begin with, on March 12 the question arose of who would win the coveted position of convention clerk. Miss B. T. MacMasters and Miss Henrietta Clark were among the women nominated along with several men. George M. Cannon, who was to prove the champion spokesman for women at this all-male convention, came out strongly for MacMasters: " . . . She is perfectly capable of doing the work required, and . . . we will by this means give representation to the fair sex." Forwarding the skills of Clark was delegate David Evans who, with truth but no gentlemanly class, said: "She is thoroughly competent, I understand, and that will recognize the sex, as she is willing to work cheap. She is an honest lady devoted to her work and does not seem to be very much devoted to the gentlemen around her." The backhanded compliments notwithstanding, according to the *Deseret News*, MacMasters and Clark won the day and were "employed after a . . . rather unparliamentary set-to lasting fully an hour." The two women were exuberant about their employment as convention clerks and saw it as a "good omen."[6]

Two delegates, George B. Squires and Samuel R. Thurman, contested for the title of "uncompromising champion of the fair sex," with Squires claiming to be "in favor of woman having whatever she wants in this world."[7] Despite the good Squires's claim, however, to George M. Cannon goes the credit for espousing several revolutionary ideas.[8] On March 15,

---

Wyoming, Colorado, New Mexico, Arizona, Utah, and Nevada) than in any other geographic region. See *Thirteenth Census . . . Occupational Statistics*, p. 51.

Nationally in 1910 23.4 percent of the females age ten and older were employed; the figure for Utah was 14.4 percent. (In Utah's two largest cities, however, female employment was appreciably higher: 17.7 percent in Ogden and 19.7 percent in Salt Lake City.) Males were also underemployed in Utah, 76.9 percent as opposed to 81.3 percent nationally.

[5]The song was "a satire on the sentimental ballads of the 1890s, introduced by Marie Dressler in the Broadway production *Tillie's Nightmare.*" The lyrics were by Edgar Smith and the music by A. Baldwin Sloan. The song was revived in musicals in 1926 and 1944. See David Owen, *American Popular Songs from the Revolutionary War to the Present* (New York: Random House, 1966), p. 139.

[6]*Official Report of the Proceedings and Debates of the Convention . . . 1895 . . . to Adopt a Constitution for the State of Utah,* 2 vols. (Salt Lake City, 1898), 1:120–25; *Deseret News,* March 13, 1895. MacMasters told the *News* that she intended to remember "the names of all the delegates who voted against her employment in order . . . to show her lady friends at the first election of equal suffrage in the Territory, that the men who did so—if candidates—should not receive their votes. 'And,' with manifest assurance she concluded, 'I'll see that they don't get them, either.' "

[7]*Deseret News,* March 14, 1895.

[8]A son of Angus M. and Sarah Mousely Cannon, George M. Cannon was reportedly the first white boy born at St. George. He graduated from the University of Deseret (Utah) in 1881 and shortly thereafter was elected Salt Lake County recorder. He organized his own real estate company and also served as cashier of the Salt Lake Security & Trust Co. A Republican, Cannon was elected to the first state senate and was named senate president. See Press Club of Salt Lake, *Men of Affairs in the State of Utah* (Salt Lake City, 1914), p. 168.

1895, he introduced to the convention a proposition that would prohibit any organization from discriminating against a person on the basis of sex in "acquiring knowledge of any trade or profession" or in limiting the number of persons of each sex that could be employed in a given field. What a blow that might have been to some unions and professional organizations had it been approved.[9]

The defeat of this measure did not stop Cannon from introducing another, more controversial concept—equal pay for equal work. In a most eloquent, but nonetheless futile, plea, he proclaimed:

> There has been in almost all ages a discrimination on account of sex, not because of the difference in work, not of the . . . amount performed, but simply because of sex. There are instances in this Territory where parties at the present time contract for certain kinds of work. I would instance the case of tailors . . . where there has been a discrimination on account of the sexes that were employed. The articles made are sold to the public without a difference in price. The work is performed just the same by the lady tailors as by the men. . . . There has been, too . . . a difference in the amount paid to those who were engaged as typesetters . . . and this provision is intended to prevent anything of this kind.[10]

Needless to say, Cannon's fellow delegates did not concur. One claimed the measure would interfere with the rights of citizens to make contracts, another that it brought women down to the level of men, a third that it was an impossible task, wages being subject to supply and demand.

Women did achieve some gains in the new state constitution, however. Chiefly, they regained the right to vote that had been taken away from them in 1887 by the Edmunds-Tucker Act. And subsequent sessions of the state legislature also dealt with the problems of working women. Frequently, the legislation enacted in the early twentieth century limited the scope of female employment and often lumped adult women and children under a certain age together, as if they had similar needs. For example, women, along with children under the age of fourteen, were prohibited by the constitution from working in underground mines. Other statutes and local ordinances enacted in the period between statehood and World War I forbade the employment of women in saloons at any time or their hire as musicians in dance halls, public gardens, railroad cars, steamboats, and other such spots. Nor were women to be hired as dancers except for legitimate theatre performances. Women under twenty-one could not work where alcoholic beverages were made or dispensed, and girls under sixteen were forbidden to sell newspapers or other merchandise on the streets or in public places. Finally, employment agencies were warned not to send females to find work at any place of bad repute.[11]

[9]*Official Report of the . . . Convention . . . 1895*, 1:164.

[10]Ibid., 2:1169–70.

[11]See, for example, George L. Nye, comp., *Revised Ordinances of Salt Lake City,* Utah . . . 1903 (Salt Lake City, 1903), sec. 323; P. J. Daly, comp., *Revised Ordinances of Salt Lake City, Utah . . . 1913* (Salt Lake City, 1913), secs. 4243, 4244, 1339–6, 1339–8, 1339–9, 722.

Of greater potential consequence to women, other state laws of that time provided for uniform compensation for female and male public schoolteachers, limited the hours women could work on a daily and weekly basis, established minimum wages for female employees, and instructed businessmen employing women as clerks to provide chairs or other seats for them.[12]

But, as Elise Boulding has pointed out, "A description of the life of women in any society today, from tribal to industrial, based exclusively on a reading of law codes, would be most misleading."[13] Certainly one would be misled by the 1896 law providing equal pay for female and male public schoolteachers. The Utah Education Association has detailed the failure of local school boards to comply.

> An examination of school reports indicates that for many years men were paid more than were women for the same kind of work and with the same training. In 1907, the average salary for men in Millard County was 85 percent more than that of lady teachers. The average salary of men in Box Elder County in 1909–10 was more than 40 percent above that of lady teachers. The range of difference was even larger in the high schools than in the elementary.[14]

One result of these rather shocking disparities was high teacher turnover. As the UEA was to ask: Why should a woman prepare herself to teach at a salary of $60 to $85 a month for ten months when a short course at a business college would give her access to jobs paying from $75 to $125 a month the year around, including a two-week paid vacation? Despite continuing efforts by the UEA to boost teacher salaries, little was accomplished. During the 1930–31 school year the average male high school teacher received a salary more than 50 percent higher than the average woman teacher in an elementary school. The following year salaries for both women and men were reduced and teaching loads increased because of the depression.[15]

Besides their generally lower pay, women teachers were saddled with another handicap that cut short their careers and effectively kept them from working toward higher-paying supervisory positions. Most school districts

[12]See Moffitt, *A Century of Service,* p. 455; James T. Hammond and Grant H. Smith, comps., *The Compiled Laws of the State of Utah, 1907* (Salt Lake City, 1908), Title 66, chap. 9, sec. 1853 and Title 43, chap. 3, sec. 1339; Allen T. Sanford and Richard B. Thurman, comps., *The Compiled Laws of the State of Utah, 1917* (Salt Lake City, 1919), Title 58, chap. 4, secs. 3671, 3673, 1677; *The Utah Code Annotated, 1943* (Salt Lake City, 1943), Title 49, chap. 4, secs. 3, 5, 8.

Minimum wages for women in the 1917 compilation were 75 cents a day for minors under age eighteen, 90 cents a day for adult apprentices (with apprenticeships not to exceed one year), and $1.25 a day for experienced adults. In 1933 the Industrial Commission was empowered to determine if women's and minors' wages were adequate to secure "a proper living" (see 1943 reference above). In the 1917 compilation legal hours for women workers were nine per day or fifty-four per week with exceptions made if life or property were in danger. In the *Utah Code Annotated, 1943* legal hours were eight per day or forty-eight per week with domestic service and packing and canning industries excepted.

[13]Elise Boulding, *The Underside of History: A View of Women through Time* (Boulder, Colo.: Westview Press, 1976), p. 220.

[14]Moffitt, *A Century of Service,* p. 455.

[15]Ibid., pp. 462, 470–71.

fired women teachers who married. Some women deeply resented this, and some women kept their marriage a secret as long as they could in order to continue working.[16]

Comprehensive data on working women are found in census reports for the years 1900 to 1940. The statistics reveal what kinds of jobs women had and where, as well as age, marital status, and race or national origin. Charts also compare the number of women and men employed in the same occupation. Several generalizations may be made from this data.

First, women have been employed nationally in almost every occupation defined by the census. However, too much should not be made of this, for in the main most women have worked at jobs where they predominated and men were in the minority; and, likewise, men have predominated in jobs where women were in the minority. In the 1900 census, for example, one can find 14 women miners (presumably not underground miners) in Utah but 6,629 men and in nursing 14 men but 452 women. Although such anomalies teach us the dangers of stereotyping the sexes, they are of little consequence statistically. Nevertheless, as one analyst in the 1920s put it, "It is by no means certain that women have as yet filled the place they will ultimately occupy in the industrial world."[17]

Second, in some job classifications women and men continued to be employed in fairly large—but not necessarily equal—numbers. Teaching was one such occupation. In 1900 there were 1,040 female teachers and 648 male teachers in Utah. By 1930 their numbers had increased to 3,649 females and 1,556 males. The job of waitress or waiter was another that consistently attracted both women and men.[18]

Third, some employment categories in which one sex was well established in 1900 became overwhelmingly dominated by the opposite sex. For instance, at the turn of the century in Utah 40 percent of the stenographers were men. By 1930 men could claim less than 9 percent of such positions. Less dramatic perhaps, in the professional field women accounted for 11 percent of Utah's physicians and surgeons in 1900 and only 3 percent in 1930.[19]

Fourth, new job opportunities created dramatic shifts in employment patterns for women. On the national level the 1920 census recorded very large net losses against the 1910 figures in such occupational classifications as ser-

[16]Helen P. Sheffield, Kaysville, questionnaire, 1979, and interview with Aurelia Bennion Cahoon, May 16, 1979, Salt Lake City. Some fifty women who worked in Utah during the period under consideration responded to a two-page questionnaire on the conditions of their employment. These questionnaires are in the author's possession. Women who requested anonymity will be cited by their initials and city of residence.

[17]Joseph A. Hill, *Women in Gainful Occupations, 1870 to 1920: A Study of the Trend of Recent Changes in the Numbers, Occupational Distribution, and Family Relationship of Women Reported in the Census as Following a Gainful Occupation* (1929; reprint ed., Westport, Conn.: Greenwood Press, 1978), p. 32, see also pp. 46–47; U.S., Census Office, *Twelfth Census of the United States . . . 1900*. Vol. 2, *Population, Part 2* (Washington, D.C.: Census Office, 1902), table 93.

[18]*Twelfth Census . . . Population, Part 2*, table 93; *Fifteenth Census . . . Occupation Statistics, Utah,* table 4.

[19]Ibid.

vants (–20.5 percent), dressmaker (–47.3 percent), home laundress, milliner, and boarding and lodging house keeper, among others. Showing large net increases in 1920 over 1910 were clerk, other than in a store (+288.3 percent), college professor or president (+240.6 percent), semiskilled manufacturing operative (+33.4 percent), stenographer, bookkeeper, saleswoman, and teacher, among others. A similar shift may be seen in Utah employment figures. For example, the job category of female servant suffered a net loss of 31.4 percent during the decade from 1910 to 1920, while female stenographers and typists increased by 106 percent in the same period.[20]

Expounding on these changes for the Bureau of the Census, Joseph A. Hill suggested that

> The inducements may be better pay in many cases, regular and shorter hours, more congenial companionship, and pleasanter surroundings, also probably a better social standing, since the occupation of domestic servant and that of laundress or washerwoman, in particular, are very commonly looked upon as being menial pursuits.[21]

Additionally, there was a lessening demand for some jobs: More women were buying ready-made clothing instead of employing a dressmaker and using the services of a steam laundry rather than a washerwoman. The small boarding houses of the turn of the century were also disappearing from the urban scene.

For many women the changes visible in the twenties seemed to usher in a new era. "A greater proportion of women were receiving Ph.D.s at American universities at that time than at any time since."[22] Commenting on these phenomena, Elise Boulding noted:

> It is no wonder that young women born after 1940 cannot easily imagine how promising the world looked to women beginning their careers in the twenties. The women of the twenties were world shapers. The women of the forties, while they entered the labor force in large numbers as war workers, were already beginning the psychological retreat into the home so graphically described by Betty Friedan.[23]

[20]Hill, *Women in Gainful Occupations,* p. 33; *Thirteenth Census . . . Occupation Statistics,* table 7; U.S., Department of Commerce, Bureau of the Census, *Fourteenth Census of the United States, State Compendium: Utah* (Washington, D.C.: Government Printing Office, 1924), table 25.

[21]Hill, *Women in Gainful Occupations,* p. 35.

[22]Boulding, *The Underside of History,* p. 753.

[23]Ibid., p. 755. The large increase in women as college professors noted earlier was one kind of breakthrough for women in the first decades of the twentieth century. Ralph V. Chamberlain, *The University of Utah: A History of Its First Hundred Years, 1850 to 1950* (Salt Lake City: University of Utah Press, 1960), appendix P, lists teaching staff during 1850–1915. Over ninety women are listed. Of these, only sixteen began their employment prior to 1900. Outstanding among her peers was Maud May Babcock (for whom the Babcock Theatre at the university is named) who rose from instructor to professor of speech and physical education during 1892–1938 and eventually served as chairman of the Department of Speech. She originated one of the first university theatres in the United States. See pp. 175–77. Although more women were teaching at the college level, the stereotype of the male professor persisted. On p. 339 the author lists the "new men" who signed teaching contracts for the university's 1915–16 school year following an academic crisis that had decimated the faculty. Almost 20 percent of the "new men" were women!

Fifth, a higher percentage of women were employed in urban than in rural areas. Looking at Ogden as a case in point, in 1910 17.7 percent of the women of that city who were over age ten were employed. In the state as a whole the percentage was 14.4 percent. This nationwide trend continued. In 1940, among females fourteen years of age or older in Utah, more than one in five living in urban areas was employed. In rural nonfarm areas of the state the number dropped to one in eight, and for rural farm areas to one in ten.[24]

Sixth, race and national origin were significant factors in defining female employment. In Salt Lake City in 1930 more than one-third of the black women over age ten were employed. For native-born whites the figure was slightly less than one-fourth, and for foreign-born whites about one-fifth. For other races the figure dropped to about one-seventh of the females over ten years of age.[25]

The relatively low economic status of blacks, both nationally and in Utah, would seem to account for the higher percentage of employed black women. Quite simply, black women experienced a greater need to find work, and find it they did, although usually at the lower end of the pay scale.[26]

In the case of some foreign-born white women, entirely different factors operated to preclude their employment. Economic necessity notwithstanding, cultural values effectively kept most first-generation Greek, Serbian, and Italian women from entering the job market. A few eastern and southern European women worked unobtrusively in stores operated by their husbands or other male relatives or ran small boarding houses that catered to newly arrived immigrants (usually relatives or others from their old-country villages). Jobs that took women away from home or out from under the eye of a male relative were considered improper. So strong was the proscription that even a poor widowed Greek woman would have been unlikely to seek employment but rather would rely on support from the extended family or the godfathers of her children.[27]

Seventh, age and marital status affected employment among women. The census data for 1930, if laid out in graph form, would show a significant peak for the ages of 18 through 24. Almost half of the women in that age group in Salt Lake City were employed. From age 25 on the percentages decline fairly steadily. Going down the scale one finds one in five women between the ages of 50 and 54 employed. And with no Social Security to look

[24]*Thirteenth Census . . . Occupation Statistics*, pp. 256, 138; U.S., Department of Commerce, Bureau of the Census, *Population, Second Series: Characteristics of the Population, Utah* (Washington, D.C.: Government Printing Office, 1941), table 16.

[25]*Fifteenth Census . . . Occupation Statistics, Utah*, table 6.

[26]Fully 90 percent of employed black women in Utah in 1930 worked in domestic and personal service occupations, primarily as servants.

[27]Interviews with Helen Z. Papanikolas and Philip F. Notarianni, May 1979, Salt Lake City. One Greek woman drove supplies to a sheep camp where her husband worked, and an Italian woman drove the school bus to Notre Dame School; but these were unusual activities for southern and eastern European women and may not, in fact, have been "gainful employment" as defined by the census.

to, one in ten women between 65 and 69 was working in Salt Lake City in 1930. As for marital status, nationally in 1920 one married woman out of eleven was employed. Or, another way of looking at that statistic is to note that two out of nine employed women were married. Utah did not lag too far behind with 17.5 percent of the female work force married in 1920.[28]

Although the census data provide a large body of information on working women, they tell nothing of the conditions of employment such as wages and hours, not to mention those more subtle but very significant evaluations of the employer or boss.

Some of the problems faced by women teachers have already been discussed. Office workers in Utah had no association to champion their cause, but women who worked as secretaries, stenographers, typists, and bookkeepers have expressed opinions—some positive, some negative—about their experiences. Taken as a whole, their employment seems to have been ordinary enough and fits into the national picture.

In her excellent study of the American working woman, Barbara Wertheimer wrote that white-collar positions were, for a time, anyway, almost the exclusive prerogative of young, single, native-born white women. This was the case in Utah in 1910 when native-born white women, in proportion to their numbers in the population, were five times more likely to find employment in office positions than the foreign-born and almost six times more likely than black women. Only three black women had office jobs in Utah in 1910, and it seems highly probable that these were with black organizations.[29]

According to Wertheimer:

> The appeal of office work was real: it was cleaner and less strenuous than factory work, and socially much more acceptable. Workers were paid a weekly salary rather than hourly wages, and work tended to be regular, layoffs less frequent. Most important for young women of that time, it meant working for men on an individual basis, which provided at least the possibility of finding a husband.
>
> That was the credit side of the ledger. On the debit side were the long hours, the often low salaries, the need to dress well (an added cost), and working conditions that ranged from poorly lit desks to rooms filled with cigar smoke from the men who shared office space with the women. Then there were the advances of men who felt the young women were fair game and would not dare to protest.[30]

Utah women office workers generally found conditions similar to Wertheimer's description. These stenographers, bookkeepers, and typists usually received much of their training in high school, taking such courses as short-

[28]*Fifteenth Census . . . Occupation Statistics, Utah,* table 8; Hill, *Women in Gainful Occupations,* p. 75; *Fourteenth Census . . . State Compendium: Utah,* table 26.

[29]Barbara Mayer Wertheimer, *We Were There: The Story of Working Women in America* (New York: Pantheon Books, 1977), p. 233; *Thirteenth Census . . . Occupation Statistics,* table 7. Two of the three black women were clerks (not in a store), and one was a stenographer or typist. There were a few black businesses that may have employed these women.

[30]Wertheimer, *We Were There,* pp. 234–35.

hand, accounting, and typing. A few attended business college. Once on the job they found it fairly enjoyable, and often they were thankful just to have a paycheck of any kind during the depression.[31] As one secretary who worked in the 1930s expressed it:

> We were grateful to have these jobs. We never thought of taking breaks or needing them. I don't recall any of the girls complaining about the amount of work given them and we did work hard. We didn't know about discrimination or breaks then. We didn't know or never considered the possibility of advancing to jobs the men held. Of course, the two jobs I held were exceptionally good for this area. Some girls were clerking at $30.00 a month so I can't speak for them.[32]

The hours worked were generally longer than today—forty-eight in many instances, although some women claim to have worked longer—with time on the job beginning to approach the standard forty-hour work week later in the period under consideration. Their starting wages in the mid-1930s ranged anywhere from 22.5 cents an hour for a secretary at a mill in Logan—with part of that amount in credit at the company store—to about $60 a month. Some women changed jobs when they could to improve their income. (Starting salaries seem to have been higher in the 1920s before the depression, with one woman reporting an $85 monthly stipend in 1924.) Most office workers received a paid vacation after a year's employment, but they enjoyed few other fringe benefits common today such as health and life insurance, retirement programs, or sick and overtime pay. Perhaps for these young women, most of them single, retirement funds and hospital insurance seemed unrelated to their needs, for many of them left their jobs upon marriage or with the birth of their first child. Some who wanted to continue working after marriage were not allowed to do so. One worker who married was jolted to hear upon returning from her honeymoon that "We don't have married women working for us."[33] Another office worker was required to give up her job as a WPA stenographer following her marriage in 1937 "so that an unmarried girl could take over."[34]

The office supervisor was most often, but not always, a man. And that leads into the debit side of office employment. Although a majority of those interviewed found their work experiences pleasant enough, about one-fifth did not. Here are a few of their complaints:

> The pressure . . . was terrible—no time even to go to the rest room. Boss also expected personal attention. Wanted to hire me an apartment and be my "friend."

Conditions improved at this woman's next job, but she objected to "the dirty stories told by the salesmen to each other" in her hearing.[35]

[31] General statements made about Utah office workers are based on compilations from the questionnaires mentioned in n. 16. Only specific statements will be individually identified.

[32] K.W., Provo, questionnaire.

[33] Gwen W. Jensen, Salt Lake City, questionnaire.

[34] Maurine B. Campbell, Delta, questionnaire.

[35] Gwen Jensen questionnaire.

A secretary-typist for two Salt Lake City firms reported excessive overtime on Saturdays, Sundays, and holidays without extra pay. She also resented having a meter attached to her typewriter to keep track of the number of strokes typed. Each typist had to hand in a daily meter reading.[36]

One head bookkeeper found herself in a dilemma. She felt a responsibility to complete the tasks she was hired to do, but that was not easy given an unfortunate precedent.

> When I refused to sit on the assistant manager's lap or kiss him as the former bookkeeper had done, he harassed me and made life miserable at work, so after I got the books all balanced, and had given him adequate notice, I quit my job.[37]

A stenographer in northern Utah disliked

> having to cover for the infidelities of my boss. Having to take part in his petty vendettas. I sometimes left my initials off of his letters. I left with a great sense of relief when I got married. Later he offered me double my pay to work part time. I couldn't do it.[38]

The physical environment was fairly pleasant for office workers, although some women complained about smoking in enclosed spaces, cramped work areas, and excessive heat or cold depending on the season. As one woman described it, she "worked in [a] small cubicle next to the V.P.'s office—no windows—[and it] became very stuffy at times espec[ially] when cigar-smoking men waited for their app[ointment]ts."[39]

Canning or food processing was one of the new industries that beckoned many women workers during the early twentieth century. This was arduous labor in many instances, and as Barbara Wertheimer has suggested,

> Because the industry was seasonal, manufacturers were able to get exemptions from hours limitations for their workers. From the start, women made up over half the work force in canning. . . . Farmers' wives and daughters, sometimes whole families were employed. Some manufacturers preferred to hire newly arrived immigrant women. As one owner told an investigator, "They are the best workers I have; they keep at it just like horses."[40]

Most women cannery workers were between the ages of sixteen and twenty. Blanche Jensen remembers working for three summers at the Del Monte plant in Spanish Fork during the late 1920s. She was sixteen years old when she began. Supervised by a "stern" matron, the women and girls "sat on benches beside a moving belt and took out leaves, damaged peas, or anything not suitable for canning. . . . " The women had to remain alert and work quickly for hours at a time with rest breaks only "if the pea load

[36]L. S. W., Salt Lake City, questionnaire.
[37]V. H., Logan, questionnaire.
[38]Z. W. T., Logan, questionnaire.
[39]K. W. questionnaire.
[40]Wertheimer, *We Were There*, p. 217.

slacked up." The length of lunch and dinner breaks was also determined by the volume of peas to be processed. Depending upon the harvest and the weather, the hours might vary from five one day to ten or twelve the next. The starting wage was 15 cents an hour with seasoned workers making 17.5 cents an hour or about $6 or $7 a week. By 1940, Mrs. Jensen said, one woman worker reported earning 35 cents an hour—more than her farm-worker husband who made only $1.50 a day. The women were required to wear "heavy blue, cotton dresses with matching caps. . . . The uniforms were supplied by the company and a small fee was taken out of each check for the rental of the uniform which was handed back to the company at the termination of work."

String beans followed peas in the canning season. At this task the women worked regular hours from 8 A.M. to 5 P.M. with an hour for lunch. They snipped off the ends of the beans, cut them in even lengths, and placed them in boxes. A supervisor inspected each box and punched the worker's tally card. The pay was about 7.5 cents a box, with two boxes per hour being produced by most of the women. "We grumbled about the job but wouldn't think of quitting," Mrs. Jensen said. The plant had "a waiting list of people who wanted work."[41]

At the Morgan canning factory in northern Utah women also canned peas and beans for wages ranging from 12 cents an hour to 22 cents for floor ladies. Shifts lasting up to nineteen hours during peak times were reported. When some of the women became dissatisfied with the pay and threatened to strike, the plant management vowed to bring in Mexican workers if the women left their jobs.[42]

Women worked in other kinds of factories, too. A Grantsville woman was employed at a nearby plant where she filled, by machine, cans and bags with salt and then pasted on labels or sewed up sacks that weighed as much as twenty-five pounds. The wages at this factory were 30 cents an hour in 1927 and 40 cents an hour by the early 1940s. The workers had few benefits until later when the plant was unionized and better working conditions and higher pay were achieved. Like so many women, this factory worker was grateful to have a paycheck during the depression, for her family depended upon her support. She rode a bus to and from work. As a sidelight on those grim depression days, she remembers being paid in cash during the time the banks were closed. "Payday could be any one of 5 days so we wouldn't be held up on the way home. . . . "[43]

A Salt Lake City factory worker was employed throughout the 1930s as a stacker and packer for wages beginning at 25 cents an hour and eventually climbing to $20 a week. As she described the duties, "The stacker picked cookies off warm pans and placed them in a trough for the packer to

[41]Blanche J. Jensen, Spanish Fork, questionnaire.

[42]Ruth Gregory West, "'Those Good Peas': The Morgan Canning Company in Smithfield, Utah," *Utah Historical Quarterly* 36 (1968): 176.

[43]Ellen B. England, Grantsville, questionnaire.

put . . . in cartons, boxes or caddies." She worked in a large area at a table staffed by sixteen young women. Two conveyors brought the cookies down from the ovens to be stacked and packed. Full boxes were conveyed to the scales for weighing. According to this informant, "the boss screamed and swore at the girls" and often called them back early from their lunch hour. The employees struck for better working conditions in 1937. Although conditions did improve somewhat, the strikers lost and the plant was not unionized.[44]

These factory workers certainly toiled long and hard for their meagre but much-needed wages. Whether some of them "worked like horses," as suggested earlier, is conjectural. However, for Salt Lake City the 1930 census does show that a foreign-born white woman (but not necessarily a newly arrived immigrant) was almost twice as likely to be found working in various manufacturing and mechanical pursuits as a native-born white woman. Black women, on the other hand, were very unlikely to find such employment, at least in 1930.[45] Like their sisters in the East, some women factory workers in Utah struck or threatened to strike, and in these efforts they, too, were unsuccessful at significantly improving employment conditions or gaining union recognition. In fact, during the 1930s Utah women were much more successful at helping their husbands, sons, and brothers achieve union status than in achieving it for their own sex. One remembers, for example, Helen Papanikolas's description of the fearless Milka Dragos and other immigrant women in Carbon County during the 1933 coal miners' strike that led to recognition of the United Mine Workers of America.[46]

If strikers have their folk heroines in women like Milka Dragos and Mother Jones, so, too, do nurses. During the Civil War the tireless Mother Bickerdyke worked at emergency hospitals on the front lines, recruited volunteers, and raised money. When asked by a doctor on whose "authority she presumed to act in his hospital," she supposedly replied. "On the authority of Lord God Almighty; have you anything that outranks that?"[47] More recently, in central Utah, Marva Christensen Hanchett became a heroine of sorts.

Born in the little town of Annabella in Sevier County in 1908, Marva was fascinated by medicine at an early age. In 1927, soon after her eighteenth birthday, she entered the Salt Lake General Hospital School of Nursing.

> The first six months of the nurses training consisted of a full day of classes and demonstrations with long study assignments to be done at night. The nurses who successfully completed this period of schooling were given

[44]A. M., Salt Lake City, questionnaire.

[45]*Fifteenth Census . . . Occupation Statistics, Utah,* table 11. Only 8.3 percent of employed native-born white women in Salt Lake City worked in manufacturing or mechanical pursuits, whereas 15.4 percent of the foreign-born women workers were so employed.

[46]Helen Z. Papanikolas, "Unionism, Communism, and the Great Depression: The Carbon County Coal Strike of 1933," *Utah Historical Quarterly* 41 (1973): 284–85.

[47]Wertheimer, *We Were There,* pp. 135–36.

their caps and, besides continuing the classes and study, were assigned to work an eight-hour shift on one of the wards.[48]

At that time and on into the early 1930s the old Salt Lake County General Hospital had so heavy a patient load that beds were sometimes set up in halls. "Nurses worked six and a half days a week, took regular classes, and studied in their off hours." After three years of this grueling schedule, Marva graduated and returned to Sevier County as the area's only available registered nurse. With no real hospital to work in, she and the local doctors delivered babies and performed surgery in patients' homes. "Many times she was paid with a bucket of honey or a loaf of bread instead of money. Sometimes she received no pay." After her marriage in 1933 Mrs. Hanchett's career took a new turn as she set up Sevier County's first regular public health program, and later she became nursing supervisor for the new Sevier Valley Hospital in Richfield. Few nurses have been responsible for so large a geographic area—almost one-fifth of the state—as was Mrs. Hanchett.[49]

Nursing was another occupation that experienced a dramatic change in the decade between 1910 and 1920. The earlier census showed 225 trained nurses in Utah and 643 midwives and untrained nurses. By 1920 the number of trained nurses had jumped 241.7 percent while the number of untrained nurses (midwives are not mentioned in this census breakdown) showed a slight loss.[50]

Before the turn of the century few nurses had formal training, and working conditions, including wages and hours, were poor. Standards were gradually imposed, and nursing became a true profession. In 1917 a registration law was enacted, and three years later graduating nurses were required to pass a qualifying examination. The first nursing schools in Utah were operated by hospitals, a situation that may have affected the professional status of nurses. As one educator has pointed out, in hospital nursing schools "the doctor became the teacher and supervisor of the nurse, a role which tended to keep the nurse in a subservient position." Not until World War II did nursing programs begin to move from hospitals to universities, with the University of Utah offering the state's first baccalaureate nursing program in 1942. Undoubtedly, university-based education has enhanced the professional status of nurses.[51]

To cover in some detail several occupations typically associated with women has, in a sense, reinforced a stereotype of the working woman as either a teacher or a nurse, a secretary or a saleslady. And, indeed, these occupations have been important to women and important to society as well.

[48]Patricia H. Sorenson, "The Nurse: Marva Christensen Hanchett of Sevier County," *Utah Historical Quarterly* 45 (1977): 166.

[49]Ibid., pp. 168–71.

[50]*Thirteenth Census . . . Occupation Statistics,* table 7; *Fourteenth Census . . . State Compendium: Utah,* table 25.

[51]Sandra Hawkes Noall, "A History of Nursing Education in Utah" (Ed. D. diss., University of Utah, 1969), pp. v–vi, 28.

Nevertheless, it is necessary to shatter the stereotype. A look at St. George in 1900 will do that.

A town of about seventeen hundred in the first years of the twentieth century, St. George offered women a variety of occupations. In addition to jobs as dressmaker and servant, teacher and saleslady, women were employed or self-employed as farmer, gardener, printing compositor, merchant, telegraph operator, postal clerk, photographer, and physician—unexpected diversity for a small rural town in the West. Obviously, the variety of jobs in a city such as Salt Lake or Ogden would be too great to list conveniently. So, St. George can make the point for all of Utah.[52]

In summary, then, what can be said about Utah working women? During the forty-five-year span from statehood to World War II women filled a wide variety of jobs. Many of their occupations were of signal importance to education, health care, manufacturing, communications, retailing, business—the lifeblood of most communities, in fact. Despite unfavorable working conditions in some occupations, the percentage of women employed in Utah increased steadily over the years from 11.2 percent in 1900 to 17.5 percent by 1940. Working out of economic necessity as well as for personal fulfillment, women were harassed or handicapped in some instances because of their sex. Nevertheless, they remained dedicated and persistent. As social and economic conditions changed they abandoned old occupations and took up new ones. Their horizons changed constantly. Young and old, single and married, black, white, and foreign-born, Utah women went off to work as did their sisters in other parts of the country. Yet, they remained essentially invisible in history. In 1929 Joseph Hill noted:

> Whatever opinions may be held as to the proper sphere of woman, the fact is that, to a considerable extent, women's place is no longer in the home. In addition to her social contributions to the preservation and welfare of mankind, the contributions of her sex to economic production in its commercial aspects are of such substantial proportions that not only is it impossible to ignore them as a factor in industrial progress, but they are worthy of serious study as an important element in this progress.[53]

Fifty years later such studies are beginning to be made. The invisible woman is becoming fleshed out, her contributions recognized, her significance to all aspects of human society acknowledged.

[52]Twelfth Census of Population, 1900, Utah, manuscript, National Archives, Washington, D.C., microfilm at Utah State Historical Society, Salt Lake City. See St. George, Washington County. Many of these women were heads of household with several dependents. All are identified by name, marital status, age, and place of birth.

[53]Hill, *Women in Gainful Occupations,* p. xv.

*

Protect the Children: Child Labor in Utah, 1880–1920

MARTHA S. BRADLEY

Child labor was common and widespread in the United States in the late nineteenth and early twentieth centuries. In 1880 one-fifth of the nation's children between the ages of ten and fourteen held jobs, as did a smaller, but significant, percentage of children younger than ten. In this article Martha Bradley examines child labor in Utah during that period, a time when many families sent their children off to work as soon as they could persuade someone to hire them. Bradley provides a wealth of information about the extent of the participation of children in the labor force, the kind of work they did, their working conditions, the reasons they worked, and the importance of their work in helping provide a living for their families. She concludes by discussing the passage by 1920 of legislation regulating the wages, hours, and working conditions of children in the workplace. Those acts, however, did not prohibit child labor altogether, and few Utahns were willing to condemn all types of child labor. The issue was not so much whether children should work as it was what kind of work was appropriate for them.

Martha S. Bradley, "Protect the Children: Child Labor in Utah, 1880–1920," *Utah Historical Quarterly* 59 (Winter 1991): 52–71. Reprinted by permission of the publisher and the author.

Martha S. Bradley has a Ph.D. in history from the University of Utah and taught for several years at Brigham Young University. She is co-editor of *Dialogue, A Journal of Mormon Thought* and has written extensively in Utah history, including *Kidnapped From That Land: The Government Raids on the Polygamists of Short Creek.*

ON FEBRUARY 19, 1903, A SMALL twelve-year-old boy climbed to the top of a ladder and stretched to dust the boxes that lined the top shelf of ZCMI's millinery department. He accidentally fell backward, struck his head, and soon sank into unconsciousness. After the company doctor briefly examined the boy the store manager took him by carriage home to his mother. The family's poverty was immediately obvious to Thomas Webber. They were short of provisions, fuel, and adequate bedding and clothing. During the next two days the boy continued to fail and finally died.

Mrs. Rosina Marti had depended upon her son's wages since her husband's death. She petitioned ZCMI for satisfaction for her loss to the sum of $2,000. She met with the Board of Directors in the institution's third-floor office with an interpreter and her attorney, Daniel B. Richards. Mrs. Marti expressed her gratitude for what the company had done to help but pointed out that because of her pitiful circumstances it was not enough. Her dead son had been the sole means of support for her and her other children. If ZCMI was not willing to pay $2,000, she said, she would accept $1,000.

As a result, "On motion of George Romney the $1000 was awarded to Mrs. Marti to help her obtain a home and support until such time as she could, with the aid of her children, make a living; on condition of full release."[1]

This unnamed boy was part of an anonymous mass of young people who worked alongside adults in the most tedious, thankless jobs in the workplace. He in many ways typified the experience of the child worker—his labor was essential to his family's survival, he prematurely assumed the responsibilities of an adult, and his options were few. He most decidedly was not unique. During the last two decades of the nineteenth century and the first two decades of the next, a dramatic increase in the number of child laborers accompanied the nation's industrialization. At the same time, an increasing number of reform-minded Utahns looked toward the exploitation of the energies of the state's youngest citizens with dismay and saw child labor as a blemish on society.

Child labor was not a problem unique to Utah, but rather a problem with national dimensions. When Theodore Roosevelt called for the conservation of children in 1906 he voiced the progressive goal of putting an end to child labor:

> Remember, that the human being is the most important of all products to turn out. I am eagerly anxious to do everything I can to wake up our people to the need of protecting the soil, protecting the forests, protecting the water; but first and foremost, protect the people. If you do not have the right kind of citizens in the future, you cannot make any use of the natural resources. Protect the children—protect the boys; still more, protect the girls; because the greatest duty of this generation is to see to it that the next generation is of the proper kind to continue the work of this nation.[2]

Roosevelt recognized that legislation was not enough. He knew that the minds of the nation's employers had to be changed to eliminate this "blot" on American civilization.

[1]Minute Book F, March 19, 1903, Zion's Cooperative Mercantile Institution, Salt Lake City, Utah.

[2]Theodore Roosevelt, *The Conservation of Childhood,* National Child Labor Committee, Pamphlet No. 163 (New York, 1911), pp. 2, 4–5, 8, cited in Robert Bremner, *Children and Youth in America* (Cambridge, Mass.: Harvard University Press, 1971).

Before the Civil War all legislative efforts to regulate child labor had failed. Existing labor laws were the work of educational reformers who saw the lack of education among working children as a contributing factor to the nation's crime and poverty rate. This class of legislation sought to enforce compulsory education laws rather than offering protection against the hazards and exploitation of child labor.

Between 1870 and 1900 some 8.5 percent to 18.25 percent of all the nation's children were employed. The percentage rates for boys were substantially higher. In 1870, 19 percent of all boys worked and in 1900, 26 percent of the nation's young men were employed. The number of child laborers was lower in the Rocky Mountain section of the United States than in any other part except the Pacific states. Again, in 1920, of the total 393,563 children in the Rocky Mountain region, 15,612 were employed—4 percent of all children in the states of Montana, Idaho, Wyoming, Colorado, New Mexico, Arizona, Utah, and Nevada. None of the states in the Mountain region was heavily industrialized. More than half of those children at work were employed in agriculture on a full-time basis.[3]

Nationally, over a million children (1,060,858) ages ten to fifteen were reported in 1920 as employed in a wage-earning occupation. Of those, only one-fifth were employed in occupations affected by federal child labor laws and only one-third in occupations affected by state legislation. Child farm laborers at 61 percent were the largest group and were, therefore, subject to almost no direct legal regulation.

Child labor was never a major problem in the state of Utah; nevertheless, it was still a concern. Less than 4 percent of Utah's children were reported as being employed in factories or on farms, although agricultural employment was always under-reported. Compared to the industrial eastern states that often had as many as 17 percent of their young citizens at work, the need for protective legislation was slight. Utah was, however, in the forefront of states creating legislation that regulated employment in mines and smelters. The first legislature of the new state of Utah passed a bill that limited the hours of work in mines and prohibited the employment of boys under fourteen and girls and women of any age. After one Bingham businessman failed to obey the law, the United States Supreme Court upheld the Utah statute and described it as a valid exercise of the state's police power over dangerous work. The case, *Holden* v. *Hardy*, was considered a landmark of progressive jurisprudence.[4]

It is not surprising that employment in mining was outlawed for women and children at the turn of the century. Mining had been traditionally a male profession. Women and children were usually not found in mines. Even

[3]"Prevalence of Child Labor by Region, 1920," testimony of Grace Abbott at U.S. Senate hearings before a subcommittee of the Committee on Labor Reform, Child Labor Amendment, 67th Cong., 1st sess. (1923), pp. 31–32, cited in Bremner, *Children and Youth in America*, 2:607.

[4]*Holden* v. *Hardy*, 159 US 366.

women from the very lowest classes—including immigrants—were not used for such work. Not only were the miners predominately male, they were for the most part non-Mormons. The Mormon prejudice against the mining industry was initiated by Brigham Young who, before his death in 1877, had waged a personal war against the mining industry in Utah. He quite vocally exhibited his disgust for the lifestyle and type of individual that mining attracted. The church sought to impose its values on all the community and found it virtually impossible to do so in the wide-open atmosphere of the mining camp. In addition to this societal prejudice that prevailed in the Mormon-dominated territory of Utah, more practical considerations of health and safety dictated prohibitive legislation as well. Working conditions in the mines were abominable. Health and safety standards were almost nonexistent. Wages paid to miners were low and uncertain at best. The 1896 prohibition on women and children in Utah's mines met these important issues and resolved them for future generations. Despite this important piece of restrictive legislation, by 1910, 3,231 children under age sixteen were recorded by the U.S. Census as employed in some way in Utah.

As previously mentioned, Utah was never prominent as a manufacturing state. In fact, during the territorial period the Latter-day Saints were discouraged by their ecclesiastical leaders from trading with the outside world—self-sufficiency was the primary goal of all church economic planning. Therefore, most factories and industries that were developed served to satisfy local demands. The number of manufacturing establishments located in Utah rose dramatically between 1880 and 1900. In 1880 only 640 businesses with a total value of $2,656,657 employed 2,395 workers. The number of businesses decreased during the next ten years to 531 but the total value rose to $6,583,022. Almost twice as many workers (4,349) were employed by manufacturing firms in the 1890s. By 1900 these figures had doubled again. More than 1,400 businesses were recorded in the census report with a total value of $14,650,948. The 6,615 men, women, and children employed in industry profited by that growth.

Many industries in Utah involved the production of foodstuffs. Businesses like the American Can Company in Ogden or the Ogden Packing and Provision Company produced thousands of cans of green beans, pork and beans, fruit, and peas. Almost every town had a small manufacturing business that employed local citizens and satisfied local needs.

In addition to agriculture, the economy of Utah at the turn of the century was based on certain extractive industries that were related to the availability of natural resources in the area such as the mining of gold, silver, copper, lead, and coal; the beet-sugar industry; raising cattle and sheep; and the manufacture of salt. In addition to these basic industries, factories for the manufacture of metal products, canneries, breweries, creameries, and flour and grist mills were located in Utah's towns and cities. Although there were upwards of fourteen woolen and knitting mills in the state at the end of the century, the garment trades were not an important factor in

Utah's economy. This accounts in large part for the low percentage of children who were employed in Utah. Again, few of the major industries of Utah in this early period lent themselves to child labor.

Statistics describing the number of children employed in agriculture present a false enumeration. A large proportion of children working on family farms worked without wages. After 1910 a more careful effort was made to assess more accurately the number of child farm workers. In that year alone a national increase of 35 percent was recorded.[5]

Most children in Utah worked on farms, most likely alongside their fathers and brothers. As mentioned, agricultural work was often heralded as a great boon to the development of responsible citizenship. Sen. Albert Beveridge of Indiana said in one speech to the Senate on the issue of child-labor, particularly labor in agriculture,

> I do not for a moment pretend that working children on the farm is bad for them. I think it is the universal experience that where children are employed within their strength and in the open air there can be no better training. . . . And I am in favor of and look forward to the time, when as a part of the educational system of the country, children will be taught to work. For, I repeat, there is no training like labor.[6]

Apparently Beveridge and others like him believed in the redemptive value of good, hard work under the influence of kind and loving parents rather than work in the impersonal, unmonitored environment of the factory. It was commonly thought that "By performing certain light tasks, the country child inculcates a habit of industry which is invaluable to him in later life."[7] Like the industrial school philosophy of work, or even the tradition of the Protestant work ethic, work, particularly farm labor, was often the reformer's cure-all for the problems of society. Even to critics of child labor, work on the farm seemed a valuable factor in the development of strong, morally healthy children.[8] Perhaps most important to this concept was that children stayed under the influence of their parents on the farm rather than the disinterested supervision of strangers.

Many children began working on the family farm as early as six years of age, working in the fields, picking potatoes, bagging or sorting—simple, yet essential chores. One young cowboy herded cows and horses each spring from his sixth year until he was twelve. One child's attitude toward play typified the attitude of the importance of a serious and judicious use of one's time.

> I grew up with the idea firmly impressed into my very being that it was my duty to be useful; that play or pleasure—seeking even to a limited extent, while permissable, was not essential; that work, if sufficiently varied, might

[5]U.S. Bureau of the Census, *Statistical Abstract of the United States, 1910* (Washington, D.C.: GPO, 1910).

[6]Hazel Youngberg, "Our Child Labor Problems" (Master's thesis, Brigham Young University, 1907), p. 7.

[7]George Mangold, *Problems of Child Welfare* (New York: Macmillan Co., 1918), p. 271.

[8]*Relief Society Magazine,* 8:185.

> furnish all the necessary exercise and recreation for physical development without having to resort to games or calisthenics.[9]

The fathers of Mormon polygamous families were often gone for long periods of time while attending to other family groups or serving on missions for the church. In one family the fifteen-year old son ran the jewelry store during his father's three-year stay in the state penitentiary on charges of cohabitation.

Girls were kept busy at home knitting, spinning, weaving, and doing other domestic chores. Mary Ann Bosworth was ten years old when she was first employed, earning fifty cents a week for housework. Another young girl, Eliza Horsepool, was twelve when she established independence from her polygamous family.

> I was about twelve years old then and Mrs. Hill was leaving for a trip to England . . . so he took me home with him. I was then old enough to keep house for him . . . as soon as he left for work I put on the boiler and did that washing by myself. I had wanted to do it and he was afraid it was too much for me but from then on I always did our washing. Without father knowing it I went out and washed for other people. I would get 50 cents a day for doing a big wash by hand.[10]

Child labor was a city problem in Utah. The diverse industries and mercantile establishments that hired young workers were usually located in trade centers. Stores, shoe manufacturers, printing and binding works, bottling and brewing companies, knitting works, the paper trades such as cigar and cigar box manufacturers, pickle, candy, and macaroni factories all employed children for substantially lower wages than were paid to adults. In addition, many children, particularly young boys, worked in the street trades as newsboys, messenger boys, office boys, and in service trades. These jobs were common to children in cities across the nation.

The report issued each year by the Bureau of Statistics painted an interesting picture of how extensive the child labor problem was in Utah's cities and what types of businesses employed children. During 1903, for example, of 7,365 employees of the state's mercantile institutions, 302 were under the age of sixteen years. This same proportion, one of every twenty-four, remained constant until 1905.

In response to business growth the number of child workers steadily increased. Out of a total 19,757 boys between the ages of ten and fifteen in 1912, 2,095 or 11 percent were gainfully employed; 6.2 percent, 1,225, worked on farms and 870 in industry. Of 20,046 girls of the same age group 430 or 2 percent were employed. Only 0.1 percent of these girls worked in agriculture.

[9]George Lambert, "Journal of George Cannon Lambert," quoted in Kate B. Carter, ed., *Heart Throbs of the West*, 12 vols. (Salt Lake City: Daughters of the Utah Pioneers, 1939–50), 9:269–384.

[10]Eliza Burdette Horsepool, Historical Records Survey, Biographical Sketches, Utah Collection, Bancroft Library, University of California, Berkeley.

A surprising number of the boys provided the primary support for their families. Of 8,334 native-born white boys between ten and fifteen years of age 808 or 10 percent were the breadwinners, 541 in agriculture and 267 in other businesses. The figure was higher for boys with one or both parents born outside of the United States. Out of a total 10,403 such boys 11 percent or 1,108 were breadwinners of their families. Agriculture was the most common source of work for 6 percent of the total number of boys in Utah.

Fewer girls provided the primary support for their families. Of native-born white girls 1.5 percent (127) were responsible for the finances of their homes. Foreign parentage increased that figure to 2 percent (208).[11] These children collected $1,136 in weekly wages out of the $97,617 total. A child brought home on the average $3.70 a week, whereas a male adult worker would earn almost five times as much. As wages increased over the years the proportion remained the same.

In 1895 ZCMI's cash boys earned a total $2,307. Besides cash boys there were errand boys, delivery boys, and extra hands hired for bargain sales as well as messenger boys. In 1896 that figure rose to $4,500 when girls were hired for similar jobs and as wrappers.[12]

The attitude toward the number of hours a child should work each day was very liberal in Salt Lake City. Although an adult male might work as many as eighteen hours in a single day, and a woman seven, children usually worked only four and one-half hours. In Weber and Utah counties the difference was not as extreme, but adult males still worked more than four times the hours that children worked. These statistics indicate that the typical child laborer in Utah was helping his family to get by but was rarely the most important element in the family income. Children had only a small influence on total output and that may have made their services more expendable.

In 1906 out of 200 children employed in Salt Lake County in the mercantile industries, 184 worked in Salt Lake City. The largest number of children, 47, were involved in general merchandise. Another 34 worked at institutions that sold books, stationery, boots, shoes, clothing, furnishings, jewelry, millinery, and notions. Another large group of children were employed by businesses that furnished farm implements, hardware, lumber, and other building materials.[13]

Many children worked for the same company when they were young that they would as adults. James Maurice Saville first worked at ZCMI in 1883 as a cash boy. In 1903 he was department manager of chinaware.[14] Harold E. Young periodically worked as a cash boy after school and on Saturdays in the shoe or grocery department.[15] George Reed worked in the drug department in the late 1880s when as a boy "it fell to his lot to make

[11]U.S. Bureau of the Census, *Statistical Abstract of the United States, 1912* (Washington, D.C.: GPO, 1912).

[12]Minute Book F, April 7, 1895, ZCMI.

[13]U.S., Bureau of Labor Statistics.

[14]*ZCMI Advocate,* 8:56.

[15]*ZCMI Advocate,* 8:75.

himself generally useful. After graduating from the menial duties that fall to the lot of the average boy, Reed became a salesman 'back of the counter.' " In the 1880s a boy slept on the premises to take emergency calls. Reed remembered that several times during his years as night attendant "distracted fathers would awaken him from his slumber at all hours of the night that they might obtain paragoric for their baby with colic, or some other cause about as serious." Reed eventually became a registered pharmacist.[16]

This sleepy night watchman was no exception. Although men and women were the primary members of the workforce, most industries and businesses employed a few children for low wages and the most menial jobs. For instance, six aerated-water manufacturing establishments reported that five children under sixteen were employed for fifty cents a day for nine hours of work. Adult males averaged five times as much money. The twenty-nine different businesses in the report included a biscuit factory, two broom factories, five candy manufacturers, a carriage works, a clothing factory, a glovemaker and tannery, and salt, sugar, ice, and macaroni factories. The report did not specify which businesses used children.

Printing firms in Salt Lake City accepted as apprentices only those young boys who had finished the work of the eighth grade. The apprentice could advance from one grade of work to the next according to his effort. In one study of the printing trades done in 1906 several boys under age fifteen were found to be working. A few boys had permits from the Board of Education that allowed them to work while continuing their studies at school.

Boys were also hired for errands on a temporary basis. They had no hope of a future in the business but were simply earning money. Those shops that exploited this class of boys by perpetuating their ignorance and delaying their chance for training in another field were labeled by the local labor union "unfair" shops. The "fair" shops, on the other hand, had predictable and consistent programs of advancement for the apprentice as he progressed and learned skills.

In her 1906 study of working conditions in Salt Lake City, Hazel Youngberg described a practice of one paper box company. Boxes were sent home with employees during the Christmas rush, and one family's sweatshop included a child of four who worked through the evenings with her older brothers and sisters during the holiday season.

Young girls were employed by the Salt Lake Umbrella Works and a producer of fluff rugs. One boy at the rug factory who earned $2.50 a week claimed to have a work permit but actually did not. His days were spent ripping up soiled and discarded carpets that were used in the rag rugs. The work was unsanitary, dusty, and tedious. Eventually the probation officer of the Salt Lake Juvenile Court caught up with this boy, who was only ten years of age, and sent him back to school The factory hired a boy of sixteen to fill his place.

[16]*ZCMI Advocate,* 8:106.

Many children worked in the canneries and fruit processing plants. On a national basis, children accounted for 7 percent of all workers in canneries.[17] Cannery work was seasonal and depended on the availability of fresh fruits and vegetables. Pickles, relishes, jams, jellies, ketchups, soups, and baked beans were also made. Processing this type of product helped to extend the work year. Extra workers, particularly children, hired for this type of work prevented regular employees from collecting overtime.

Most of the work of canning could be considered unskilled. Peeling and slicing vegetables and fruits, labeling and wrapping bottles, washing bottles, or boxing finished products could be done by just about anyone. Speed and a certain amount of dexterity were desirable, but little more. This type of factory work was not particularly dangerous, although standing all day was very tiring. Most of the cooking of the food, what one worker called the "responsible" part of the work, was done by men. Women and children did the preparatory work and such final processes as bottling, labeling, and wrapping. In general, sanitary conditions at the canneries were good; certainly the constant handling of food products made cleanliness good business.

Most of the jobs that children did in canneries were very simple. Children under sixteen packed bottles, folded circulars, swept the floors, scrubbed walls, and cleaned the bathrooms.[18]

The candy factories of Salt Lake City typically employed the largest number of children in the state:

> Young girls were engaged at a very small wage, and when old enough and skillful enough to demand more than the pittance they received for their long hours of work, were discharged to make room for younger children, who were exploited in their turn. The Juvenile Court, making effective for the first time the compulsory education law for children under sixteen, greatly interfered with the selfish course of the candy manufacturers.[19]

In 1900, 62 percent of the nation's female candy workers were under twenty-five years old. Work in candy manufacturing could be done by women and girls with no trade experience or education. Candy making was primarily hand work and involved a great deal of machinery for cooking and molding the candy. There were two distinctly busy seasons—the two months before Christmas and another shorter season before Easter. As was true of the canneries, many children were employed to help during the busy seasons.

Although the factories were typically clean, they were often hot and humid when the candy was cooking. When the candy, such as chocolates, cooled, the temperature was kept at around 60 to 68 degrees, or even lower. Girls worked as dippers, packers, wrappers, or labelers. In addition to those jobs that required a certain amount of manual dexterity girls were em-

[17]U.S. Bureau of the Census, *Special Reports of the Census Office, Manufactures, 1905,* part 3 (Washington, D.C.: GPO, 1905), p. 400.

[18]U.S. Bureau of the Census, *Report on Condition of Women and Child Wage-Earners in the United States,* 71st Cong., 2d sess., Doc. 645 (Washington, D.C.: GPO, 1913).

[19]Youngberg, "Our Child Labor Problems," p. 8.

ployed as general helpers to carry trays, clean or tend machines, and pack candy in boxes.

Factories that manufactured paper boxes, cigars, or cigar boxes also employed children in Salt Lake City. The production of paper boxes was a relatively new endeavor that was in direct response to the growing diversity of manufactured products that needed packaging to be sold. Shoes, hats, clothing of every type, foods, cigarettes, and a variety of other goods were boxed in packages that were just about as important as the products.

The work at box factories was messy because of the glue and paste used, but was not unsanitary; however, most of the work was done in proximity to dangerous machinery. Few of the jobs required special skills, and most work was easily done by women and children.

The sanitary and moral environments were not the only factors that affected the child at work. An environment conducive to healthy, happy conditions of work was more difficult to regulate. The character of the work itself, the people working in the factory, and the importance of the job all in turn affected the day-to-day world of the growing child and helped to form the adult he or she would become. One factory that made overalls in Salt Lake City, for instance, had an internal regulation system that failed to provide the necessary safeguards for the child employee. One small girl was given the job of snipping the end threads from a pile of overalls. Her load was placed in a dark, narrow passageway where she bent over her work struggling to see while, quite efficiently, wielding her scissors to put the finishing touches on the product of the factory. One observer felt the enormity of the child's plight, saying:

> Those visitors who brushed past her in the passageway thought nothing of one little girl so employed, but had she been one of a hundred workers the public would have been aroused to decry in indignation an intolerable condition. But alone, or with ninety-nine comrades in misery, her injury is the same.[20]

Contradicting that image, according to Annie H. Bywater, manager of ZCMI's clothing factory, girls working at ZCMI were content, productive, and efficient: "Here, happy Utah girls—with the aid of some of the most modern machinery and methods—are turning out close to 10,000 garments a month, girls and machinery [are] constantly being added to keep pace with the increasing demand for the product."[21] In describing ZCMI's female workforce as "girls," Bywater may have meant both women and girls. But it is obvious in one photograph of ZCMI's shoe factory employees that out of 53 workers—13 were men, 15 were boys, and 25 were girls between the ages of thirteen and sixteen.[22] At least in the clothing and shoe factories of one of Utah's largest companies a significant amount of the work was done by children.

[20]Ibid., p. 9.
[21]*ZCMI Advocate,* 5:164.
[22]Photograph in ZCMI files.

In 1906 there were approximately fifty messenger boys in Salt Lake City, about half under sixteen years of age. The boys received compensation for a percentage of the profit which made deception seem advantageous. Reformers considered the messenger service a

> school in petty thievery, obscenity, and general moral degradation. A boy goes the "pace" down hill, very rapidly after entering the service. Here it is not at all the severity of labor the young boy undertakes, but the bad associations for him, that makes the messenger boy a most serious problem.[23]

No attempt was made to determine the number of girls that were employed as domestics. During the last decades of the nineteenth century and the first of the twentieth it was still common practice for parents to "put out" their young daughters into the service of wealthy families. One such girl was interviewed in 1920 by the Relief Society Welfare Department of the LDS church. She had worked as a domestic since she was twelve years of age and by age sixteen was restless and wanted a change. In addition to her dissatisfaction, she had a goiter and needed immediate medical care she could not afford. She also thought that she was developing a mental disorder. Upon examination, she was diagnosed as suffering from what was then called "melancholia" and needed a change in environment. When more careful investigation into her work conditions was conducted, it was found that she had been employed as a nursemaid and had not been allowed to associate with the family at all. She had no friends, no social contacts, and in fact seemed to have lost the incentive or the ability to make friends. Because of her limited education, her scanty knowledge of the world and how to interact with other young people, she was deprived of her right to a good and rich life. This was seen to be the result not only of the poverty of her parents (which forced her to work) but also of the assumption that a child could be put to work at such an early age.[24]

Poverty was the largest single reason children went to work. In addition, many parents assumed that a child should always contribute to the family pot and that their children were "economic assets on which they hope to declare dividends at the first opportunity."[25] Children worked to increase the family income for a variety of different reasons. One study done by the U.S. Bureau of Labor established that only 30 percent of all children employed actually went to work out of necessity. Another 28 percent went to work because help was desired though not necessarily crucial to the family's wellbeing.[26]

Although 26.6 percent of the children worked because they were dissatisfied with school, only 10 percent of the children questioned actually preferred work over school or play. This was the only time that the attitude of

[23]Youngberg, "Our Child Labor Problems," p. 11.
[24]*Relief Society Magazine,* 12:301.
[25]Mangold, *Problems of Child Welfare,* p. 11.
[26]*Statistical Abstract of the United States, 1912.*

the child himself appears to have been measured in an early governmental study.[27]

In one local instance. C. W. Snelgrove, who later became a prominent Utah businessman, grew tired of school in the third grade and quit for what he deemed a job too good to pass up—setting up pins in the local bowling alley. Before his eighteenth birthday Snelgrove had held a series of odd jobs, including cleaning out ditches and delivering groceries.[28]

For her 1906 master's thesis for the University of Utah, Hazel Youngberg interviewed several children who had been forced to work by their parents. The first boy, a thirteen-year-old named Edward, worked in a printing office for four months before he was apprehended by a truant officer. The visit to his home revealed that Edward, his mother, her husband, and the other children were living on the boy's weekly salary of four dollars. The mother maintained that they would be "utterly destitute" if her son could not work. The four dollars that the boy earned in a week was used to support both adults and three children.

One ten-year-old newsboy stole bottles and junk to support his father's alcohol habit. His parents knew about his theft and did nothing to prevent it. Another boy, this one age thirteen, who also had a "worthless" father, earned three dollars working in a barn. His family had been recently evicted from their home and was living in a nearby field.[29]

In one case of blatant neglect a stepfather refused to support his wife's twelve-year-old dependent son. The boy got a work permit from the school board so that he could work at theaters selling fruit, candy, and popcorn.

Poverty was not the only factor in each situation. Unusual home arrangements caused by divorce, death, or desertion were also important elements that determined whether or not a child worked.

In the early years of the twentieth century three basic pieces of legislation were passed that sought to resolve these and other problems associated with child labor. As a group, these laws indicate the status of Utah on the child labor question. Each was protective and environmental in intent. The first restricted the employment of children in mines, the second established the juvenile court system, and the third was the compulsory education law of 1905.

The compulsory education law included a variety of devices that restricted employment, such as simple literacy tests or compulsory education during certain periods of the school year. Later legislation required completion of specified school grades.

Eventually, a similar grading system was used to assess developmental stages in health and physical growth prior to employment. The earliest such regulation was generally ineffective because it left enforcement to the dis-

[27]U.S. Bureau of the Census, *Report on Condition of Women and Child Wage-Earners in the United States*, p. 46.

[28]Judy Richins, "C. W. Snelgrove," 1987, manuscript in possession of the author.

[29]Youngberg, "Our Child Labor Problems," p. 9.

cretion of the employer. Often factory inspectors or physicians employed by the factory examined children to ensure their physical fitness. The most effective approach specified that each child who desired to enter a new position be examined by a public medical officer who would sign a certificate verifying his sound health and normal development.

The compulsory education law required that every child be sent by his legal guardian to school at least twenty weeks in each school year, ten weeks of which would be consecutive. In cities of the first and second class children were required to attend school at least thirty weeks of the year. The only exceptions to this rule were based on the ability of the parent to provide viable alternatives to public or private education.[30]

Compulsory education kept many children from working during the school year but did nothing to prevent seasonal or summer employment. Another serious drawback to the dependence on education laws for regulating the employment of children was the difficulty of enforcement. The Board of Education in Salt Lake City in a single year issued between 500 and 600 work permits. Most of them were temporary for periods averaging from four to six weeks. Thousands of children continued to work without permits.

By the end of the nineteenth century most of the basic elements of protective legislation were contained in state statutes. During the first decades of the twentieth century these provisions were defined more specifically and strengthened to translate principles into appropriate action. These included laws that more closely protected the rights of the individual child in determining his own future. They included provisions setting out: (1) minimum age at which children could go to work or could choose a particular trade, (2) hour limits that reflected realistic assessments of the child's ability to endure without threatening his health or welfare, (3) educational guarantees that ensured that every child would have a chance at a good education, and (4) exclusions of children from certain occupations that would be either dangerous physically or that would subject them to immoral influences. Another important development was the growing systemization of official supervision over children who did work, especially industrial inspection, the employment certificate system, and compulsory school attendance.

The principles underlying this type of legislation reflected support in the community for the idea that every child had the right to a reasonable opportunity for both physical and mental development and, as one reformer described it, that "it is in harmony with the welfare of society that these rights should be protected."[31] Because of the peculiar social and economic conditions in the Rocky Mountain region, it was acknowledged that child labor was a less complicated problem here than in the East. However, when children were out of school for long periods of time, were allowed to roam the streets and other public places, and had no structure in their young lives the social consequences were similar.

[30]State of Utah, *Code of Laws* (1907), 643.
[31]*Relief Society Magazine*, 8:185.

The 1911 General Child Employment Act was the single most important piece of legislation that affected children after the Juvenile Court Act of 1907. Among other provisions regulating the work conditions and hours of children it prohibited the hiring of children under fourteen in occupations that might be considered dangerous to their health or morals. Children were excluded as well from night work. On March 9, 1911, two separate bills were passed. One written by Carl A. Badger, a member of the committee on labor, provided for the investigation of the conditions of child labor in the state. The second, Senate bill 147, written by Rudolph Kuchler of Ogden, dealt with the broad scope of child labor issues. Surprisingly, for a bill that included such a wide variety of issues, it passed the Senate with a unanimous vote. Apparently the time was right, for support was mustered from every part of the community to limit the labor of children in Utah.

In 1911 laws were passed to protect children from the incidental influences of certain occupations. These included the production of alcoholic beverages and tobacco products or employment where these products were sold. Children could not work around dangerous processes, such as the preparation of paint, colors, or white lead or the manufacture of dynamite, nitroglycerin compounds, or fuses.[32] It was a misdemeanor offense to neglect to provide chairs, stools, or other furniture for the rest periods of female employees.[33]

Boys younger than twelve and girls younger than sixteen could not, after 1911, sell newspapers, magazines, periodicals, or other merchandise in cities of the first and second class, nor could young boys shine shoes on the streets.[34] After 1912 children under fourteen could not work in mills, factories, quarries, or workshops with more than ten employees. Work on the farm, with the exception of domestic service and fruit or vegetable packing, was limited to no more than fifty-four hours in any one week.[35]

The effort was also made to limit the work week to fifty-four hours for women and children. One labor act passed in 1912 prohibited the employment of children under sixteen years during school hours. Children who did work, did so by presenting a certificate issued by the school board. The certificate allowed a child to work no more than nine hours a day and did not permit night work.

The labor bureau of the state government monitored violations of these laws. The commissioner was responsible for investigating and reporting all violations of the law as well as making recommendations about how the best interests of employees could be safeguarded. One method that proved to be very helpful was the permit system mentioned above. In order to be hired by a factory or any type of institution a child had first to obtain a work permit from his school superintendent. This permit verified the age of

[32]State of Utah, *Code of Laws* (1911), 144.
[33]State of Utah, *Code of Laws* (1907), s1339.
[34]State of Utah, *Code of Laws* (1911), s1339.
[35]State of Utah, *Code of Laws* (1907), s1339.

the child, stating that he was developmentally normal and in good physical condition.

By 1920 Utah had a much more definitive and specialized body of legislation to regulate the working conditions, hours, and wages of children than it did at the end of the nineteenth century. It reflected general community support for the ideals of child protection and the effort to improve the lives of the children of the poor. It met many of the standards set by the National Child Labor Committee in 1907.

Child labor was not simply a problem that could be solved by taking children out of the factory. It began in broken families, in families plagued by poverty, and where ethnicity sometimes created barriers. It fostered delinquency and the abuse of children and prevented children from forming a solid basis in intellectual and moral principles essential to the formation of character and good citizenship.

W. D. P. Bliss wrote in 1898 in the *Encyclopedia of Social Reform* that "there is scarcely one subject in the whole range of social reform more important than that of child labor."[36] If that was in fact true, social reform met with marked success in Utah. Although Utah never had a problem of sizeable proportions with child labor, hundreds of children did work on a regular basis to help support their families. The legislation passed between 1896 and 1920 exhibited a conscious effort to define the work children might do and set certain standards for the environment in which the children worked. These acts did not prohibit child labor altogether—and in this Utah was at the same point as the rest of the nation—but they did attempt to prevent the exploitation of this class of citizens unable to speak for themselves.

[36]W. D. P. Bliss, *Encyclopedia of Social Reform* (New York, 1898), quoted in Bremner, *Children and Youth in America,* 2:601.

*

Utah's Ellis Island: The Difficult "Americanization" of Carbon County

PHILIP F. NOTARIANNI

Utahns have always been highly ambivalent about how much they value people from other cultures, about whether diversity is a strength or a weakness, something to be embraced or feared. This article discusses the immigrant experience in Carbon County, Utah's most ethnically diverse area, focusing on the post-World War I period, a time when suspicion of foreign-born residents was particularly high. There was a push at the time for "100% Americanization" and politicians were quick to exploit the sentiment. Several points emerge from the study. In the first place, immigration is not just a movement of people from one place to another but also a movement from one culture to another, and a matter of what happens in the cultures once new people arrive. Secondly, Utahns have been as susceptible as those in other areas of the United States to periodic feelings that the barbarians are at the gates, that we are being overrun with immigrants who take jobs from American citizens, are a drain on society's resources, refuse to assimilate or (more seriously) are incapable of assimilating, and threaten our cultural and political unity. The search for scapegoats for our dissatisfactions is as common in Utah as it is elsewhere.

Philip F. Notarianni, "Utah's Ellis Island: The Difficult 'Americanization' of Carbon County," *Utah Historical Quarterly* 47 (Spring 1979): 178–93. Reprinted by permission of the publisher and the author.

Philip F. Notarianni received a Ph.D. degree in history from the University of Utah and is Director of Museum Services at the Utah State Historical Society. The author of a number of studies relating to Utah's ethnic history, he is also the author of *Faith, Hope, and Prosperity: The Tintic Mining District* and co-author of *The Avenues of Salt Lake City*.

ETHNIC DIVERSITY CHARACTERIZES Carbon County. This variety forms a unique cultural resource around which county residents may identify, either as descendants of an immigrant group or as individuals coming into daily contact with the ethnic mix. In addition to immigration, railroads, coal mining, and labor—reasons for the immigrant influx—form an integral part of Carbon County's history and in turn comprise a key aspect of the industrialization and economic growth of Utah and the nation.

Ethnic diversity raises questions of ethnicity and the adjustment of immigrants to life in America, Utah, and Carbon County. Such questions center around concepts of "Americanization" and "accommodation."[1] The Carbon County experience affords an excellent opportunity to view ideas of adjustment, for in the main, the county functioned as Utah's Ellis Island, a principal entrance point for numerous immigrant groups, primarily southern and eastern Europeans, but including some thirty-two different nationalities.

The present investigation examines the reasons for Carbon County's attractiveness, its ethnic diversity, cultural maintenance in a new environment, and the virtual accommodation of ethnic groups to the existing society—all these factors helping to form a unique social milieu. That this character forms a significant part of Carbon County's past and remains a cultural resource is visually exemplified by the Lynn Fausett murals in the Price Municipal Building.[2] Elements of county history are skillfully and colorfully painted by a native son with ethnic diversity very much a basic theme running throughout the work.

Railroads and the developing coal industry beckoned laborers to the area now known as Carbon County in the late nineteenth and early twentieth centuries.[3] In 1882 the Denver & Rio Grande Western Railroad opened up the vast coal deposits of Carbon County, and the railroad's coal subsidiary, the Utah Fuel Company, by 1900 had become Utah's chief coal supplier.[4] Four main coal mining camps developed: Winter Quarters, acquired by the D&RG in 1882; Castle Gate, 1883; Clear Creek, about 1898; and Sunnyside, 1900.[5] The demand for labor proved the major impetus for immigration.

Responding to the demand for workers were numerous immigrant groups, part of the general influx occurring throughout the United States. In

[1]Other concepts relevant are those of the "melting pot," assimilation, acculturation, and cultural pluralism. A concise bibliographical essay dealing with ethnicity and "the making of Americans" is Rudolph J. Vecali, "European Americans: From Immigrants to Ethnics," in William H. Cartwright and Richard L. Watson, Jr., eds., *The Reinterpretation of American History and Culture* (Washington, D.C.: National Council for the Social Studies, 1973), pp. 81–112.

[2]The Fausett murals and the Price Municipal Building are listed on the National Register of Historic Places owing to their historic and cultural significance.

[3]On March 8, 1894, Carbon County was officially formed, having previously been a part of Emery County.

[4]Thomas G. Alexander, "From Dearth to Deluge, Utah's Coal Industry," *Utah Historical Quarterly* 31 (1963): 237. Also consult Robert J. Athearn, "Utah and the Coming of the Denver and Rio Grande Railroad," *Utah Historical Quarterly* 27 (1959): 128–42.

[5]Alexander, "Utah's Coal Industry," p. 237; and James B. Allen, *The Company Town in the American West* (Norman: University of Oklahoma Press, 1966), pp. 169–72. Some discrepancy over founding dates does exist.

Carbon County the 1900 census figures indicate the presence of Canadians, Chinese, Danes, English, Finns, Germans, Irish, Italians, Japanese, Norwegians, Scots, Swedes, Swiss, and Welsh. Soon after 1900 South Slavs (Serbs, Croats, and Slovenes) and Greeks entered the scene, followed later by Spanish-speaking peoples.

How were these immigrants attracted to Carbon County? Coal company agents and railroad representatives often operated both abroad and at Ellis Island, New York, recruiting foreign laborers with the promise of work and wealth, often promoting a mythical America. Padrones, or bosses, of a particular nationality also provided workers. These labor agents would supply laborers, extracting a fee from both the workers and company to which they were contracted. In Utah and Carbon County the prime example of the padrone system occurred among the Greeks where Leonidas G. Skliris became known as the "Czar of the Greeks." The Japanese labor agent, also providing workers for Carbon County, was Daigoro Hashimoto.[6]

The grapevine also served to increase immigrant awareness of Carbon County. Once settled, laborers would write back to their homelands and send for relatives—mothers, fathers, sisters, brothers, uncles, cousins. Thus, Carbon County and its mining camps became places of destination for tickets purchased in the old country. One incident illustrating a summoned immigrant's arrival into Castle Gate was recounted as follows:

> Then the train coming, we took the train. We got into Castle Gate. It was just getting dark, when the conductor started to holler "Castle Gate next" . . . It was a little place, a mining town. I got off there in Castle Gate. My brother and sister thought I was coming the next morning. I don't find nobody there. . . . There was snow on the ground and you coming out of that air on the train you know, I shiver. The litle depot was a box car. The best thing I thought for me is I got a piece of paper and write my sister's name and my brother's name.[7]

Another significant aspect to the influx of immigrant laborers was their apparent fluidity of movement. That is, the workers often moved from Colorado to Utah and to other work sites throughout the Intermountain region. The flow of men between the coal areas of Colorado and Carbon County appears to have been especially strong.[8] Such a phenomenon transcended nationality and occurred among metal miners as well as coal miners.

Carbon County's ethnic diversity was characteristic almost from the outset or at least from the formation of the area into a distinct county in

[6]Helen Z. Papanikolas, *Toil and Rage in a New Land: The Greek Immigrants in Utah,* 2d ed. rev., 120–33, reprinted from *Utah Historical Quarterly* 37 (1970); Helen Z. Papanikolas and Alice Kasai, "Japanese Life in Utah," Helen Z. Papanikolas, ed. *The Peoples of Utah* (Salt Lake City: Utah State Historical Society, 1976), pp. 336–42.

[7]Interview with Tony Priano, Helper, Utah, July 29, 1975.

[8]This observation was particularly evident in the pension application files located at the United Mine Workers of America Office in Price, Utah. Similar trends were also discovered in the personnel files of the Utah Copper Co. (Kennecott), once located at the R. C. Gemmell Club, Bingham Canyon, Utah.

1894. The county's foreign-born population in 1900 and 1920 was:

	1900	*1920*
Australia	—	6
Austria	—	315
Canada	28	33
China	3	16
Denmark	96	84
England	294	477
Finland	163	83
France	—	110
Germany	29	53
Greece	—	869
Ireland	17	13
Italy	374	1,215
Japan	125	516
Mexico	—	113
Netherlands	—	4
Norway	11	19
Poland	—	19
Russia	—	40
Scotland	113	115
Sweden	36	61
Switzerland	18	11
Wales	202	80
Yugoslavia	—	162
Others	325	136

Census statistics reflect only the settled population. The movement of workers from place to place is not injected; nevertheless, the figures do illustrate the diverse elements, and the fluidity factor would in all probability inflate the figures.[9]

The various mining camps were themselves multiethnic, reflecting the county's quality. In 1903 in Castle Gate there were 356 Italians, 108 English-speaking, and 10 Austrians. Sunnyside contained 358 English, 246 Italians, and 222 Austrians. Clear Creek had 128 Finns, 172 Italians, and 95 English; while 181 English, 126 Finns, and 74 Italians lived at Winter Quarters. By 1914 the population in these four camps was divided as follows: 1,421 Americans, 663 Italians, 138 Japanese, 1,245 Greeks, 434 Austrians, 97 Finns, 21 Negroes, 21 French, 12 Germans, 7 Scandinavians, and 1 Swede. The towns of Price and Helper contained a conglomerate of all groups.[10]

[9]U.S., Department of Interior, *Twelfth Census of the United States, 1900: Population,* vol. 1 (Washington, D.C.: Government Printing Office, 1903), p. 789; U.S., Department of Commerce, *Fourteenth Census of the United States, 1920: Population,* vol. 3 (Washington, D.C.: Government Printing office, 1922), p. 1040.

[10]*Eastern Utah Advocate,* December 3, 1903: State of Utah. *Second Report of the State Bureau of Immigration, Labor, and Statistics, 1913–14* (Salt Lake City, 1915), p. 95. It must

How did immigrants respond to the new environment encountered in Carbon County's camps and towns? In most cases their first impulse was to congregate where others of the same nationality resided. This was either voluntary or forced, as when "Jap" sections of towns developed. Castle Gate had its Italian section, while Helper by 1914 had become an important area of settlement for South Slavs attracted by business opportunities there. Earlier, Finns had settled in the Scofield and Clear Creek area where they suffered greatly in the mine disaster of 1900. Greeks were labeled as "clannish," but the basic need to be among the familiar was only a natural response.

In one instance, a Utah Fuel Company officer offered an interesting explanation of the situation in a 1917 letter regarding ventilation in the amusement halls at Sunnyside and Castle Gate:

> Our primary object in building the amusement halls is to make it a kind of a center for people in the camps, instead of as at present—the tendency for each nationality to keep to themselves. Nothing will tend to help this situation more than a rapid change of atmosphere in the halls eliminating the present practice of Americans moving to other seats in case Greeks or Italians take seats immediately adjoining them. The primary reason for moving usually being that bodily odor from the foreigners is offensive.

Any apparent leniency directed toward the Greeks or Italians was not afforded the Japanese as the same official in various telegrams sought a separate Japanese Hall and "Jap" pool hall for Sunnyside.[11]

Immigrants sought security among those who spoke the same language and who could offer assistance with such exigent needs as finding a job. These people brought with them language, religion, beliefs, and customs, products of their cultural heritage. Congregation in camps and distinct sections of towns only accentuated the elements of cultural difference. The establishment of fraternal groups, coffeehouses, boarding houses, churches, and, later, businesses, all aimed at security and cultural maintenance. Assimilation into American society was not a primary goal because Japanese and most Mediterranean immigrants initially viewed themselves as only temporary workers in America.

Finnish saunas dotted the Scofield and Clear Creek countrysides; individual as well as public saunas enabled the Finns to enjoy their traditional baths created by running water over hot rocks. Greek miners suffering from homesickness, especially because women were not initially present to honor them with feasts on their name days, gathered in coffeehouses for social life. In the Helper and Price coffeehouses, basil plants lined the window sills, and calen-

---

be noted that "Austrians" were in reality Serbs, Croats, and Slovenes. An idea of the ethnic mix in Price and Helper can be found in the *Utah State Gazetteer and Business Directory, 1903–1904*, vol. 2, 2d. ed. (Salt Lake City: R. L. Polk & Co., 1903), pp. 148, 262–65: and vol. 5, 1914, pp. 85, 171–77.

[11]C. H. Gibbs to A. H. Cowie, vice-president and general manager of Utah Fuel Co.; telegrams from A. H. Cowie, April 3 and April 12, 1917, MS 154, box 12, Utah Fuel Co. Manuscripts, Special Collections, Lee Library, Brigham Young University, Provo, Utah.

dars and pictures of Greek patriots hung on the walls. Men drank Turkish coffee and smoked the nargile, played cards, read Greek newspapers, and spent hours talking. Sunday dress for Greeks, and most immigrants, meant a sign of respectability. In Helper, Greeks utilized the YMCA showers to wash prior to donning suits for Sunday visits to the coffeehouse.[12]

Fraternal organizations flourished in Carbon County. Italians organized Stella D'America ("Star of America"), Castle Gate (1898); Principe Di Napoli ("Prince of Naples"), Castle Gate (1902); Fratellanza Minatori ("Miners Brotherhood"), Sunnyside (1902); and Società Cristoforo Colombo ("Christopher Columbus Society"), Castle Gate (ca. early 1910s). The Slovenska Narodna Podporna Jednata ("Slovene National Benefit Society"), affectionately called the "Snappy J," served Slovenes in Carbon County. (The Slovenian National Home in Helper still functions and serves as a testimony to the importance of such groups.) Croatian lodges were also founded in the county, as well as lodges of the Jugoslav Socialist Federation. These organizations were formed to help mitigate the problems of employment in an industrial society. Some functioned as types of labor unions, while others, such as the Jugoslav Socialist Federation and branches of the Italian Socialist Federation in Scofield and Clear Creek, were political. Economic and artistic needs were served by various groups. Greeks also had organizations—Pan Hellenic Unions—fostered by Greece to nourish the idea of repatriation.[13]

The immigrants sought to maintain various customs and traditions while making a living in Carbon County. Italians were either accompanied by or had sent for wives earlier; but by 1910–17 Greeks, South Slavs, and Japanese were taking picture and "mail order" brides from their respective nationalities, with some returning to the homeland to marry. Weddings, funeral processions, open-casket viewings, and the memorial wheat of the Greeks were important customs celebrated in traditional ways. Ethnic foods simmered in all parts of Carbon County. "American" children wondered in horror why pork entrails were being cleaned on public water spouts. Yet, outdoor ovens in Helper summoned many a child, of immigrant parentage or otherwise, to indulge in a piece of homemade bread after school.[14]

[12]For a geographical study of the Finns, with emphasis on the Great Lakes but some map references to Utah, see Matti E. Kaups, "The Finns in the Copper and Irons Mines of the Western Great Lakes Region, 1864–1905: Some Preliminary Observations," in Michael G. Karni, Matti E. Kaups, Douglas J. Ollila, Jr., eds. *The Finnish Experience in the Western Great Lakes Region: New Perspectives* (Vammala, Finland: Institute for Migration, 1975) pp. 55–88. Research on the Finns in Carbon County is in progress by Craig Fuller, Local History Project, Utah State Historical Society. On the Greek coffeehouses consult Papanikolas, *Toil and Rage,* pp. 118–19.

[13]Philip F. Notarianni, "Italian Fraternal Organizations in Utah, 1897–1934," *Utah Historical Quarterly* 43 (1975): 172–87; Joseph Stipanovich, "Falcons in Flight: The Yugoslavs," *Peoples of Utah,* pp. 370–71. Evidence of the existence of the Italian Socialist Federation is found in issues of *Il Proletario* (New York), June 26, 1904, and October 30, 1904, on microfilm. Immigration History Research Center, University of Minnesota, Minneapolis. State locals were listed, Utah having two branches where one R. Anderlini apparently served as president. Information on the Slovenian National Home, listed on the Utah State Register of Historic Sites, is located at the preservation office, Utah State Historical Society. Also see Helen Z. Papanikolas, "The Exiled Greeks," *Peoples of Utah,* pp. 417–18.

Folk beliefs continued in many households. Belief in the occult and in folk cures was especially significant and most often transmitted by the women. The *mal occhio* or "evil eye"—the idea that human envy could cause harm and could be transmitted by a mere glance—was held by many southern European peoples. Among Carbon County Greeks the authority for folk beliefs prescribed cures, explained dreams, predicted the sex of unborn children, and read the shoulder blade of the Easter lamb, feeling its bumps to foretell what the year would bring.[15]

The desire for cultural maintenance was natural, but the realities of the new environment often produced irony in the attempt. In trying to maintain and foster cultural ties, immigrants altered or adapted to new conditions, customs, traditions, and beliefs; thus their practices were assuming new meaning and form. Gradual change occurred as immigrants came into contact with American institutions and ideas, but those who favored 100 percent "Americanization" of the new immigrants sought to expedite the process by the abrupt stripping away of cultural differences. It must be said, however, that many viewed this Americanization as a panacea for the country's ills in the post–World War I period.

As mentioned earlier, some immigrant men began taking brides in the post-1910 years. Greek women were summoned from Greek villages by anxious miners. In some cases prospective brides arrived alone with tags on their clothing that identified future husbands. Such was the case of one Cretan woman who traveled to Carbon County and was left waiting near the railroad tracks in a sagebrush flat thirty miles from Helper. Greek women traveling alone were burdened with the concern that their morals would be suspect, since in the homeland daughters were chaperoned with "paranoid obsession." At the Latuda Japanese camp second cousins were wed, a marriage unthinkable in Japan. Likewise, South Slavs chose brides through correspondence, not only contrary to custom but beset with many difficulties.[16] Italian, Greek, and South Slavic men also eventually intermarried with women of other immigrant groups or resident American women. The Japanese, however, stayed to themselves and did not attempt to enter American social life. Thus, while clinging to old ideas, the immigrants developed new approaches and responses.

The role of unionization in creating a gradual change in immigrant life was especially significant in Carbon County. In the late nineteenth and early twentieth centuries unions struggled for life in Carbon County, and in that fight the immigrants were of signal importance. During the strikes of 1903,

[14]Papanikolas and Kasai, "Japanese Life in Utah," *Peoples of Utah,* p. 342; Papanikolas, *Toil and Rage,* pp. 139–42, 151; Joseph Stipanovich, *The South Slavs in Utah: A Social History* (San Francisco: R&E Associates, 1975), p. 75; Lucile Richens, "Social History of Sunnyside," MS A211, WPA Collection, Utah State Historical Society; interview with Al Veltri, December 18, 1971, Helper, Utah, by Philip F. Notarianni and A. Kent Powell, American West Center, University of Utah.

[15]Philip F. Notarianni, "Italianita in Utah: The Immigrant Experience," *Peoples of Utah,* p. 327; Papanikolas, *Toil and Rage,* pp. 149–50.

[16]Papanikolas, *Toil and Rage,* pp. 141–42; Papanikolas and Kasai, "Japanese Life in Utah," p. 342; Stipanovich, *South Slavs,* p. 75.

1922, and 1933, Italian, Finnish, South Slavic, and Greek miners figured prominently, as they did in keeping the fire of unionism burning throughout the period.[17] The activities of various union organizers, such as Frank Bonacci, make this especially evident.

Many immigrants viewed unionism as a legitimate remedy for solving problems associated with work in mines. The concept was new to some, but others, such as northern Italians who were familiar with unions in the old country, attempted to articulate grievances to fellow workers in an effort to improve the work place. Thus, various immigrant groups came together for a common cause—a cause that transcended ethnic lines. The contact was not always harmonious, as some groups, such as the Greeks in 1903, were used as strikebreakers. Mexicans were brought in primarily after the 1920s. As in other areas the Japanese appeared to have steered clear of unionization efforts.

Once an economic base had been achieved, many immigrants left the labor ranks and entered business and the professions; again, this effected a gradual change in behavior. After the 1903 strike Italians, mostly northerners, were blacklisted from Castle Gate and settled in Helper where they founded a bank and opened stores, saloons, markets, and other small businesses. Many of their children later entered the professions. Also in Helper the South Slavs found an environment conducive to their seeking improved status; they initiated business ventures, some, such as the Mutual Mercantile Company, in joint interest with other nationalities. Greeks likewise broke the labor ranks in the 1920s. On one occasion Mexican laborers entered Carbon County to work under a Greek contractor who was bringing in a water line through Price Canyon. Upon completion of the contract many of the Mexicans remained to work in the mines where they experienced many of the same conditions as other immigrant groups.[18]

Some Italians turned to farming, while other Italians, Greeks, and Basques herded goats and sheep. The first Basque sheepman in Clark's Valley was chronicled as follows:

> Sheepmen began to come into the valley to find grazing land for their flocks. Gratien Etcheborne [*sic*] was the first to arrive. He came in 1910 and filed the first claim on the land in 1916.[19]

Basques, however, never gained a strong foothold in Utah's sheep industry because of the willingness of Mormon sheepmen and their sons to continue herding.[20] Carbon County contained both French Basques and Vizcayan populations, with Price housing a Basque hotel and boarding house.[21]

[17]On labor and unionism the main work is Allan Kent Powell, "A History of Labor Activity in the Eastern Utah Coal Fields, 1900–1934" (Ph.D. diss., University of Utah, 1976).

[18]Notarianni, "Italianita in Utah," pp. 313–20; Stipanovich, *South Slavs,* p. 65; Vicente V. Mayer, "After Escalante: The Spanish-speaking People of Utah," *Peoples of Utah,* p. 442.

[19]William A. Douglass and Jon Bilbao, *Amerikanauk: Basques in the New World* (Reno: University of Nevada Press, 1975), p. 244. Also consult Thursey J. Reynolds, comp. *Centennial Echoes from Carbon County* (Price, 1948).

[20]Douglass and Bilbao, *Amerikanauk,* p. 245. The authors state on p. 320, "Only in some Mormon outfits of Utah does the Anglo sheepherder appear with any regularity."

[21]Ibid., pp. 431, 433.

Post–World War I suspicion of foreign and alien groups provided impetus for formal "Americanization" efforts. In Carbon County immigrants' participation in strikes branded them as "un-American," and their seeming ambivalence toward serving in the military, even though many purchased war bonds, infuriated native Americans. This sentiment prompted an editorial in the *News Advocate* commenting, "Feeling against such dirty low-down grafters is running high in many towns in Utah."[22]

Even prior to the war, stereotyped images of "Wops," "Bohunks," "Japs," and "clannish Greeks" intensified nativistic sentiment. Adding fuel to the fire was the practice by many immigrants of sending money to their families abroad in support of relatives and to provide dowries for sisters. A poignant example of nativistic sentiment appeared in a fifth grade Huntington, Utah, student's essay on "What Utah Day Means to Me."

> . . . In our mining camps, we can, if we will, stop the Greeks and Japs from their work, and give our own men and boys a chance for work, giving them the money instead of others. If Utah paid her money to her own people instead of other places, we might be rich now. . . . [23]

Such fears were deeply rooted; and interestingly, the same fear of foreign labor currently exists in the United States.

In any event, in 1918 a state committee on Americanization was established, with Arch M. Thurman one of the most active members. Thurman stated his fear that "The presence in our state of large alien groups presents the possibility of a real menace to the welfare of the state." He continued by urging the necessity of giving immigrants the opportunity to know American ideals and institutions. If not, those who were preaching discontent would instill them with un-American ideas, thus endangering America's free institutions.[24]

On March 20, 1919, an Americanization bill became law, having been introduced in January by Sen. George H. Dern. It originally maintained that any alien between the ages of sixteen and forty-five residing in Utah—except those physically and mentally disqualified—unable to speak, read, or write English required by fifth grade standards must attend public evening school classes. Willful violation of the act was considered a misdemeanor and was punishable, upon conviction, by a fine of not less than $5.00 nor more than $25.00. The State Board of Education and a state director of Americanization were to oversee the program. Under the 1919 law sixty-three Americanization classes were maintained within the supervision of school authorities. Classes were held in Granite, Salt Lake City, Carbon, Jordan, Tooele, Logan, and Ogden districts. Attendance in 1919 of all classes was 60,253.[25]

[22]*News Advocate,* January 3, 1918.

[23]*Emery County Progress,* May 4, 1912.

[24]State of Utah, *Thirteenth Report of the Superintendent of Public Instruction* (Salt Lake City, 1920), pp. 63–65.

[25]Americanization Act is in *Laws of Utah, 1919,* chap. 93. In 1921 the law was amended and provided for: registration of aliens, an instruction fee of $10.00 from each alien, a lowered age limit, 16–35, an increased penalty of not less than $15.00 nor more than $25.00, and the

In anticipation of the Americanization Act, the University of Utah in the summer of 1919 offered a course of training for teachers in Americanization work. During the summer of 1920 the course was repeated, and similar courses were conducted at Brigham Young University and the Agricultural College in Logan.[26] Dr. R. D. Harriman, a member of the State Committee on Americanization, stated in a report to teachers: "The purpose of this work is not only to acquaint the foreigner with American institutions and ideals, but also to make it possible for him to enter actively into his American life."[27]

Public response to the Americanization law was favorable. The consensus of the citizenry was that aliens should be required to become Americanized. In February 1923 the Salt Lake City Chamber of Commerce established an Americanization committee. A national congress of the Sons of the American Revolution met in Salt Lake City in 1923 to discuss the Americanization effort. The national chairman of Americanization for the organization, Harry F. Brewer, stated:

> You will hear further from this year's committee as soon as possible, but don't let procrastination be the thief of time and opportunity; the anti-American is on the job ALL the time, in season and out; should we let him out do us in Industry?[28]

Americanization of the immigrant was the national vogue. When it appeared that Americanization was not succeeding, residents of Utah, keeping in step with national forces, advocated immigration restriction.

A. C. Matheson, director of registration, thought to propose a law making it incumbent on employers not to hire aliens who had not conformed to the Americanization law, but considering labor shortages and the absence of such laws in neighboring states, he relented.[29] Enforcement was extremely difficult, and the law was destined to fail for reasons set forth in a 1924 report:

> The Americanization law . . . has been found unsatisfactory. The compulsory feature is obnoxious to the foreign people. It creates an attitude of mind not conducive to learning. Its enforcement to the letter is expensive and uninviting to the communities with large numbers of the foreign population.[30]

---

elimination of the director of Americanization. See especially, Leroy Eugene Cowles, "The Utah Educational Program of 1919 and Factors Conditioning Its Operation" (Ph.D. diss., University of California, 1926), p. 56.

[26]State of Utah, *Thirteenth Report of . . . Public Instruction,* p. 64.

[27]R. D. Harriman, "Suggestions for Americanization Teachers," *Bulletin of the University of Utah,* vol. 10, no. 16 (1920), p. 19.

[28]*Chamber of Commerce News* (Salt Lake City), vol. 5, no. 7 (1923), p. 4; *Minute Man,* vol. 19, no. 2 (1924), p. 76. Both these serials are available in Special Collections, Marriott Library, University of Utah, Salt Lake City.

[29]State of Utah, *Fourteenth Report of the Superintendent of Public Instruction* (Salt Lake City, 1922), p. 80.

[30]State of Utah, *Fifteenth Report of the Superintendent of Public Instruction* (Salt Lake City, 1924), p. 109.

Americanization was considered most important in Carbon County schools, and its "desired" results were admirable. But compulsory adherence led to problems. First, what was "Americanization" or the true prototype of an "American"? Immigrants had believed that America was a land of many peoples. Intolerance and prejudice, rampant in the 1920s, forged a negative example of Americanism. Carbon County Italians responded to the movement by organizing the Italian Americanization Club in 1920; but this was ephemeral, and, in the main, response by immigrants was negligible.[31]

Immigrants viewed the law with ambivalence. Forced compliance represented to many a stripping of cultural distinctiveness. A study of South Slavs has shown that the law was unnecessary in some instances, as those who needed language training obtained it voluntarily. Italians, Greeks, and other groups paid relatively little attention to the law. The Japanese, however, were the most compliant. The reasons for this and for prior observations concerning the Japanese have been attributed to their cultural training in patient acceptance and the belief that their position as workers in America was temporary. In addition, the Japanese culture emphasized a law-abiding attitude, and the training of children under the Bushido code stressed good behavior and diligent study.[32] In an ironical sense, by attempting to comply with "Americanization," the Japanese were in essence adhering to their own cultural traits.

The process of accommodation, or adjustment, of Carbon County immigrants to life in Utah proceeded gradually. Tragically, children were torn between the cultural environment at home and the values encountered at public schools. For Greek children, there were Greek schools and American schools. Some found Mormon racial attitudes difficult to understand, and some felt a bitterness at the intense antiforeign sentiment typified by Ku Klux Klan activity in Price and Helper in 1925. A Serb miner summed up his feelings by stating: "They call me everything but white man. . . . Yeah, sure I leave Carbon County. You could die down there and nobody care."[33]

Yet, children were educated in American public schools, and parents committed to life in America encouraged their offspring to betterment through education. Immigrant businessmen were successful, and the turbulence of earlier years waned somewhat after 1933, except for the Mexican-Americans who were recruited to work in Carbon County mines during the labor shortage of World War II. Among these peoples the stigma of prejudice continued longer than for others.[34] Perhaps a reason for this, and an explanation for the dispersion of other groups into American life, can be found in the fact that after the restrictive immigration legislation of the

[31]*News Advocate,* April 8, 1920. See also Philip F. Notarianni, "The Italian Immigrants in Utah: Nativisim (1900–1925)" (M.A. thesis, University of Utah, 1972), pp. 71–74.

[32]Stipanovich, *South Slavs,* p. 91; Papanikolas and Kasai, "Japanese Life in Utah," pp. 342–43.

[33]Interview with Mike Dragos by Joseph Stipanovich, excerpted in Stipanovich, *South Slavs,* p. 64.

[34]Mayer, "The Spanish-speaking People," pp. 461–62, 464, 468.

1920s, Japanese and southern and eastern European populations were no longer being fed by newcomers as in prior years, whereas the Mexican influx continued. So, with regard to the former groups, language maintenance and many traditions and customs were further modified, since many times their significance was tied to Old World conditions. Even though cultural traits were modified in the accommodation process, cultural maintenance in the broad sense was not lost. Ethnic identification continues.

Thus, the legacy left to Carbon County is ethnic diversity. Whether it be the Greek Orthodox Church, Saint Anthony's in Helper or Notre Dame in Price (the former reportedly built in response to Italians, the latter to the French), or the remaining business blocks built by immigrant businessmen—their existence is testimony to the county's past. The character of Carbon County's past is also its future character, because as coal begins its new reign as "king" the diversity of population continues.

In conclusion, a final irony remains: through efforts to force conformity, the result was, in most cases, a stripping away of a certain identity, the same identity that is now sought by people trying to find "roots" or to reidentify with their ethnic heritage. Fortunately for Carbon County residents, the diversity of character that marked its beginning is still evident. Such a cultural resource should indeed be preserved and remain a source of public pride.

*

Monticello, The Hispanic Cultural Gateway to Utah

WILLIAM H. GONZÁLEZ AND GENARO M. PADILLA

What happens to inherited traditions when people from other countries leave behind their kin, friends, language, and culture to settle in the United States? Is an effort made to strengthen those customs and traditions that define social and cultural identity? How much of the old is retained and transmitted to children? What parts are sloughed off? What accommodation is made between the old and new? The following article addresses those questions. Its purpose is to acquaint Utahns with a part of the Hispanic heritage of the state and the ways that culture has changed during the last century. The authors also intend it as a tribute to the strength and devotion of the early Hispanic pioneers who came to Utah buscando tradajo, *"looking for work." After briefly outlining the history of Hispanics in the Monticello area beginning in the late nineteenth century, the authors introduce the reader to the traditional practices of Monticello's turn-of-the-century Hispanic community, discussing such subjects as baptism; marriage customs; funeral rites; and liturgical observances, including Christmas, New Year's Day, and Cinco de Mayo. They then explore the reasons why some of those practices have gradually changed while others have not.*

William H. González and Genaro M. Padilla, "Monticello, The Hispanic Gateway to Utah," *Utah Historical Quarterly* 52 (Winter 1984): 9–28. Reprinted by permission of the publisher and the authors.

William H. González is Professor of Languages and Literature at the University of Utah. Genaro M. Padilla is Professor of English at the University of California, Berkeley. He is co-editor of *Recovering the Hispanic Literary Heritage* and *The Short Stories of Fray Angelico Chavez.*

THE FIRST HISPANICS TO ARRIVE in San Juan County were the men who came from northern New Mexico during the last decades of the nineteenth century to tend sheep owned by the Mormon settlers of the Bluff area. Since the latter had a somewhat limited knowledge of the sheep industry, men who were familiar with this type of livestock were needed; and the Hispanic New Mexican, who carried unbroken the sheep-raising tradition brought from Spain and introduced into New Mexico as early as 1598,[1] was the one to fill that need. These men came on horseback from various New Mexico villages, a trip that took them about a week to make. They would usually work for eight or ten months at a time and then return home to spend a few months with their families. As some men returned to their villages to spend the winter, others would take their place, thus establishing a continuous flow of men over the two-hundred mile or so stretch of land. In time, a few of those who had traveled back and forth decided that they would stay to make their home and their future in a new territory.[2]

In this way, as an example, one such man, Ramón González, brought his wife, Guadalupe, a daughter, Romana, eighteen, and his sixteen-year-old son, Prudencio, to Monticello in March of 1900 to settle permanently. The González family set out from Dixon, New Mexico, by way of Colorado's San Luis Valley in 1899 in an old wagon, bringing their belongings and the few head of livestock they owned. As they made their way through Durango, Ramón discovered that there was a serious drought in Monticello that season, and so he decided to remain through the winter in Durango where he could work for the railroad. The family finally arrived in Monticello the following March and, shortly thereafter, homesteaded a piece of land in the Indian Creek vicinity. González was one of the first Hispanos to homestead in Utah. As though to signal his resolve to remain, his name appeared not only in the county records but also scratched onto Newspaper Rock, which was located on the homestead itself.

Unfortunately, Ramón died in 1902 before he really had much of a chance to work the land he had traveled so far to claim. Because he was a Catholic in a predominantly Mormon community, the town's LDS bishop told the family that Ramón could be buried in a section of the cemetery set aside for non-Mormons. Ramón remains in the original Monticello cemetery alongside other Hispanics who were separated from the Anglo community in death as they often were in life.[3]

Shortly after the arrival of the first Hispanic families into Monticello, the migration of people from various New Mexico villages—Abiquiu,

[1]In 1598 Juan de Oñate led an expedition of some two hundred Spaniards to settle an area of the New World located somewhere near where Santa Fe, New Mexico, stands. Along with wagonloads of the equipment required to establish a permanent settlement, Oñate also brought some six thousand head of livestock, of which nearly four thousand were sheep and rams. For a more detailed catalogue of the supplies Oñate took to New Mexico, see Julian Nava, *The Mexican American in American History* (New York: American Book Co., 1973), p. 30.

[2]Vicente V. Mayer, Jr., ed., *Utah: A Hispanic History* (Salt Lake City: American West Center, University of Utah, 1975), pp. 37, 39.

[3]Ramón González was the co-author's grandfather. The story of his trek to Utah, his homesteading, and the episode with the Mormon bishop upon his death is a matter of family history.

Gallina, Coyote, Canjilón—increased considerably. Many of these families settled the different areas around Monticello—Spring Creek, Carlisle, and La Vega. Yet, even though many Hispanics came to Utah to stay, their cultural roots remained fixed in New Mexico. Largely because of their traditionally close family ties, the new settlers maintained constant contact with their home towns and their relatives. In this manner, there was a continual renewal of cultural traditions in all of their aspects. And, in like manner, this constant interflow led new settlers—brothers, uncles, and friends—into Utah where there was promise of jobs and land. By 1920 the Hispanic population was substantial enough to have created several distinct neighborhoods in and around Monticello. These newcomers occupied themselves by working their homesteads while also hiring themselves out as cowboys and sheepherders on surrounding ranches in San Juan County.[4]

Because of this early presence of Hispanics in Monticello, the town became a gateway for the entrance of hundreds more Hispanos into Utah. As people crossed the border into the state they found that their predecessors in Monticello welcomed them not only with warm greetings but with warm greetings in their native tongue. Surprisingly, what many Hispanos discovered was that they could leave villages where they never had to use English, move to Monticello, and live there without having to learn the new language. In fact, many of the early settlers never bothered to learn English at all, and they were perfectly at home living well into the second half of this century remaining essentially monolingual.

By the late twenties the migration of Hispanics into the area had dwindled, due both to lack of jobs and the scarcity of land open to homesteading. There was little change in the town until the early 1940s with the outbreak of World War II. With the exodus of young Hispanics into the armed forces and the attraction of well-paying war-related jobs, people began leaving their homes for the coal mines in Carbon County, the copper mines in Bingham, the military-industrial plants in the Salt Lake Valley, and the railroad shops of Ogden.[5]

For a time during the early forties, a vanadium processing plant located in Monticello attracted both Hispanic construction workers and plant employees. After the war ended, however, the plant complex was shut down, and people again followed the trail further north in search of work. Since WW II the Hispanic population in Monticello has remained fairly small, only a fraction of what it once was, but there are still Gallegos, Manzanares, Vigil, González, Jaramillo, and Garcia families who are the descen-

[4]Focusing as it does upon the Monticello area, this paper suggests that most people inhabiting the towns in the southeastern part of the state have their roots in Hispanic New Mexico and southern Colorado. It is not our intention, however, to suggest that there was no migration into Utah by people directly from Mexico. As Mayer points out: "By 1920, there were some 2,300 people who were born in Mexico and lived in Utah. The majority of these families found work and made their home in Salt Lake City . . . " (p. 39). This Mexican population entered the state via a southwesterly route and settled mainly along the Wasatch Front.

[5]Mayer, *Utah: A Hispanic History*, p. 61.

dents of the original settlers.[6] With Hispanos such as these the cultural traditions of generations have continued.

As always, it seems, when people find themselves a long way from familiar surroundings and from folks they know intimately, there is a tendency for them to strengthen those customs and traditions that define their social and cultural identity. Since the family was literally the center of life in Hispano culture, the birth of a child, the child's baptism, the relating of *cuentos* (folktales), the singing of sacred ballads, marriage customs, the observance of seasonal religious holy days, and, finally, funeral rites were maintained by families in a communal manner. The same cultural patterns held true for those early Hispano settlers in Monticello. They may have been isolated hundreds of miles from the social and cultural sources of their native villages, but they clung to those customs and traditions, largely rooted in Mexican-Spanish Catholicism, they knew as children. And they clung to those life-cycle rituals as tenaciously as they clung to the new soil.

Although it is not the purpose of this article to present an exhaustive explanation of all traditional practices, we would like, by way of introduction, to touch upon some of the basic life-cycle customs and observances of the liturgical year that have been practiced by Monticello Hispanics. Some of these customs, marriage celebrations for example, have remained vital, if slightly altered by social circumstances, while others like the baptismal presentation of a child to its parents have declined dramatically. A survey of Hispano customs, either still in common use or largely remembered, will, we hope, acquaint Utahns with a part of the Hispanic heritage of the state.

BAPTISM

Soon after the arrival of a child, parents began making preparations for the baptism and the festivities that surrounded that momentous event. As it still is, the sacrament of baptism was the ritual that initiated the child into the spiritual community of the Catholic church, but it also signaled the child's initiation into the social community as well.

For early Monticello Hispanics a baptism could take place anywhere from a few days to several months after the birth of a child, depending upon the health of the child and the availability of a priest, who because of Monticello's isolation and mission parish status only periodically made pastoral visits to the area. Regardless of the date chosen for baptism, the parents were careful to select the *padrinos* (godparents) with utmost care and consideration for the future bond established between the child, the parents, and the *padrinos*. The choice of godparents was open to anyone, but it usually was and continues to be from within the immediate family that the *padrinos* are chosen. More often than not, grandparents were asked to sponsor the first child in a family; thereafter, brothers and sisters of the par-

[6]The 1980 U.S. Census statistics show a total of 307 Spanish-speaking people in the Monticello area and 433 Spanish-speaking people in San Juan County as a whole. *1980 Census: Statistics for Utah,* State Census Data Center, June, 1981, p. 12.

ents, or uncles and aunts, were honored with this responsibility. And that responsibility was a serious one. The godparents were expected to be Christian models for the child; and if the parents died, the godparents were charged with raising the child in an upright Catholic home.

On the day of the baptism the *padrinos* took the child to church or to a home where the priest was baptizing. Nowadays the parents usually accompany the *padrinos,* but years back the godparents were solely entrusted with the child on that day to symbolize their spiritual bond. During the baptism the godparents formally gave the child the name the parents had chosen. One of these was often the name of a patron saint on whose feast day the child was born; sometimes the name was that of a grandmother or grandfather and occasionally that of a special relative or friend.

One of the lyrical customs that used to be followed was the verse greeting with which the *padrinos* returned the child to its parents. Standing with the baby at the threshold of the parents' home, the *padrinos* would present the child to its parents, saying,

> Aquí está esta fresca rosa que de la iglesia salió,
> Con los santísimos sacramentos y la agua que recibió.
> (Here is a rose so fresh which has just come from church,
> With the Blessed Sacraments and the holy water it received.)

Upon accepting the child, the parents would reply,

> Recíbote fresca rosa que de la iglesia salió
> Con los santísimos sacramentos y la agua que recibiste.
> (We receive thee, rose so fresh, newly come from church,
> With the Blessed Sacraments and the holy water received.)

Once this formality was observed, the family and guests would sit down to a special meal and spend the rest of the afternoon admiring the baby, bestowing simple gifts, wishing him or her a long and joyous life, toasting each other, and enjoying each other's company. Today, although some of the specific elements of the baptismal ritual, such as the verse greeting and the naming formalities, have been abandoned, the significance of the sacramental event itself and the festive recognition of the baptism remain vital.

MARRIAGE

In a world that has changed too radically for many strict Hispanic customs to survive, many of the courtship and wedding rituals of yesterday have largely gone by the way. In Monticello, as in other Hispanic enclaves, young lovers now see each other without chaperones and usually decide on their own when and where they will be married. Still, their weddings are marked by many customs that are now hundreds of hears old.

In the old days in Monticello, when a young man was interested in a girl, he first sought permission from her parents to court her in an appropriate manner. If, eventually, he wanted to marry the young woman, he would consult with his father, asking him to visit the girl's parents to ask for her hand in marriage. If the father agreed to ask his *vecino* (neighbor) for his daughter's hand, he was required by long tradition, a tradition that went back to sixteenth-century Spain, to compose a formal letter stating his son's honorable intentions, while also extolling the girl's virtue and beauty.[7] In more recent times, however, the future groom's mother and father simply arranged a formal visit with the girl's parents to discuss the possibility of a marriage between their children. During this visit it was customary to engage in a form of repartee in which the parents praised the physical and spiritual qualities of the respective offspring as a measure of the conditions they expected for their son or daughter. Usually more friendly than confrontive, these meetings gave the parents a chance to reminisce about their *hijo's* and *hija's* childhood, with its moments of joy, near tragedy, comic happenings. Still, if there were serious concerns about the impending marriage, this was a time for all concerned to discuss and reconcile them or to state reasons for opposing the union.

If at the end of such discussion the marriage was agreed upon, a date was set and the parents decided who should be asked to sponsor the young couple at the wedding. Usually an older couple, perhaps an uncle and an aunt who had been married for years, were asked, since it was believed that with their long marital experience they could best advise the couple in times of uncertainty or crisis. Here again, as with baptism, a strong relationship, a lifelong bond, was established between the parents of the couple and the sponsors as well as between the newlyweds and their *padrino* and *madrina* —as the sponsors were called to signify their spiritual tie.

Marriages in Monticello are performed in St. Joseph's Church, but before the church was built in 1935 marriages were celebrated in private homes. If there happened not to be a priest in Monticello, the wedding party traveled to one of the neighboring Colorado towns—Cortez or Durango—to be married. As was usually the case, however, when the wedding was performed in Monticello, after the ceremony there was a formal wedding procession to the home of the bride's parents where, in the company of relatives and guests, the fiesta was held. This procession was accompanied by both a violinist and a guitarist playing a simple wedding tune. It was the first communal gesture of goodwill toward and support for the young newlyweds.

Once at the home of the bride's parents, the guests were served a special dinner. Even as poor as people in Monticello might have been, they set a

[7]In a master's thesis written in 1949 Salvador Pérez describes the tradition of the formal letter pleading for the hand in a girl in marriage:

> If a boy likes a girl and desires to make her his wife, he tells his troubles to his father, who thereupon writes a very businesslike letter to the father of the young lady, asking the hand of his daughter in marriage for his son. When the parents of the boy go to the house of the parents of the girl, they carry the letter proposing the marriage of the girl with their son. The answer is given in another letter by the parents of the girl accepting or rejecting the proposal. It is also understood that if 10 days elapse and there is no letter it means the answer is yes. Salvador Pérez, "Folk Cycle in a New Mexico Village: Customs and Ceremonies of Birth, Marriage and Death" (Master's thesis, University of New Mexico, 1949), pp. 14–15.

well-laid table of various Mexican dishes—chile, *frijoles, pollo* (chicken), and, when possible, lamb. For dessert, there were *bizcochitos* (anise-flavored cookies), cakes, and fruit and mincemeat pies. People sat with their families and friends, enjoying the food and drink while admiring the newlyweds.

That evening there was a wedding dance with musicians brought in from one or another of the large Colorado towns or by musicians from the surrounding Monticello area. Usually, the dances were simple *valses* (waltzes) and polkas played on guitar, violin, and accordion. Nowadays the young couple, in step with the times, want an electric band that can play the latest rock tunes as well as *rancheras,* polkas, and waltzes. Nevertheless, even today there is usually a wedding march, an adaptation of the original march from church to the wedding hall in small villages. This march consists of a series of intricate formations, including a hand-trellis under which the bride and groom pass to signify the community's goodwill toward the couple. There is also a special dance during which people pin dollar bills to the bride's gown and the groom's suit. Often the young couple receives enough money during this dance to pay for their honeymoon.

About halfway through the evening the dance is interrupted so that one of the musicians can sing the *entrega de novios*—the wedding song. A long sustained tradition, this *entrega* ceremony continues to mark the high point of the evening and actually climaxes all the other wedding observances. Now, as in the past, it is here that the newlyweds receive their family's and the community's blessing and testimony. At this moment the couple is reminded by the entire community that the vows they have just taken are sacred, blessed by God himself, old as the bond between Adam and Eve, and, therefore, not to be taken lightly. Always sung in Spanish, this benediction consists of *coplas* or stanzas of rhyming quatrains in which the entire wedding ceremony is described in religious and lyrical terms.

Writing in 1940, Professor Juan B. Rael, one of the great pioneers of Hispanic folkore, characterized the *entrega* content in this manner.

> In the first two or three stanzas of this song, the singer generally requests the attention of the audience and sometimes apologizes for not being a more gifted singer. Then he summarizes the Bible's story of the creation of man, reminding those present of how God created man out of clay in his image and likeness and how the first woman was formed out of one of Adam's ribs. He also passes in review the marriage ceremonies before the altar. The wedding pair is then admonished regarding the sacredness of marriage and its indissolubility, and they are told of their responsibilities and their duties to each other. Even the *padrinos,* or best man and bride's maid, are reminded of their obligation, which, according to the singer consists in bestowing their blessing upon the newly wedded couple and placing the latter in the hands of the parents. The parents are then advised of the need of guiding their children in their new life.[8]

[8]Juan B. Rael, "New Mexico Wedding Songs," *Southern Folklore Quarterly* 4 (June 1940): 55. As Rael points out, the *entrega de novios* is a form unique to the Hispanos of New Mexico. Nowhere else in the Spanish-speaking world is there anything quite similar. It appears that the traditional New Mexican wedding song was adapted from sixteenth-century wedding *coplas,*

The number of stanzas in each *entrega* varies,[9] but depending upon the singer's ability to improvise and the generosity of the guests the singer-poet may continue composing stanzas celebrating the qualities of the bride and groom, the *padrinos,* the parents, and the guests themselves. At the end of each *copla* the audience tosses coins onto a blanket spread before the musicians and requests still another stanza.

One Utah version of the *entrega,* for instance contains the following verses:

A Dios le pido permiso, memoria y entendimiento, para poderme expresar en este fiel casamiento.	I ask God for permission, memory and understanding to be able to express myself at this wedding full of faith.
A Dios le pido permiso, y a este público honrado, para celebrar la boda de los recientes casados.	From God I ask permission and from this honorable gathering to help me celebrate the wedding of this newly married couple.
...	...
Oígame usted esposado que le voy amonestar, esa cruz que Dios le ha dado no vaya a olvidar.	Listen to what I say young man I am giving you some advice, "The Cross which God has given you, you must never forget."
Si deja su cruz por otra ella pegará un suspiro y se llegará responsable ante un tribuno diviono.	"If you leave your Cross for another your spouse will suffer a shock for which you will be held responsible before a Divine Tribunal."
Oígame usted esposada y eschuche lo que le digo, ya no hay padre, ya no hay madre ya lo que hay es marido.	Listen to me young lady and hear what I have to say, "There is no longer father or mother now there is only your husband."[10]

With the termination of the singing, the newlyweds kneel on the floor before their parents, grandparents, and even their godparents to receive a formal blessing which symbolizes their acceptance as *una nueva familia,* a new family, by their parents and the entire community. The *entrega* and the final parental blessing signal the end of the wedding ceremony; both rites serve as lingering reminders for the newlyweds that they are only beginning a long and sacred life together. In parts of Utah the *entrega* remains an inte-

---

but, as Rael notes, the stanza content is distinct in the New Mexico versions. The survival of the *entrega* in Utah, then, is a precise measure of the New Mexican origin of many Hispanics who are now a second or third generation removed from that state.

[9]See, once more, Rael's notes on the stanzaic structure of the *entrega,* ibid., p. 56.

[10]This version of the *entrega* is transcribed from a recording of José Pacheco and his wife, Sophie, performing the wedding song in 1981 in Salt Lake City.

Mr. Pacheco was born in Vallecitos, New Mexico, but moved to Antonito, Colorado, at an early age. He came to Bingham, Utah, in 1923 to work in the mines and eventually settled in Salt Lake City with his wife, who was born and raised in Conejos, Colorado. Mr. Pacheco says

gral part of the wedding celebration, emphasizing not only the present joy of the marriage but also the difficulties and sacrifices of the years ahead.

FUNERAL RITES

In Monticello religious devotions before and after the death of a family member were always observed with great solemnity. When someone was gravely ill, it was customary for relatives and neighbors to visit the home of that person to comfort the family and to pray the rosary. Again, when a priest was available, the person was administered the sacraments of the Catholic church—Confession, Holy Communion, and Extreme Unction, the anointing of the sick.

When someone died, one of the younger members of the family was formally dispatched to visit the homes of all relatives and neighbors to announce the death, even though the church bells rang the death knell. The entire Hispanic community would gather in the home of the deceased to pray over the body, to comfort the family by offering *pésames* or condolences, and to spend the night reciting the rosary and singing *alabados* or hymns. The rosary was usually led by one of the older men of the town who would pray in lilting Spanish while the people responded in chorus. After the rosary, a group of men took seats near the coffin and began chanting *alabados,* a ritual that often lasted through the entire night.

The chanting of *alabados* was the most solemn and traditional part of the *velorio de difunto* or wake. The *alabado* itself is a holdover of the medieval ballad form that originated in Spain hundreds of years ago and was brought over to what is now the Southwest by Spanish settlers in the early seventeenth century. In fact, recent studies have concluded that many of these ballad forms, which long ago disappeared in Spain and Mexico, exist only in Hispanic communities in New Mexico, Colorado, and Utah.[11]

There are many types of *alabados* for different occasions. The *alabados* for funerals typically praise the soul of the departed before God, Jesus Christ, the Blessed Mother, and a host of saints. The deep profession of faith on the part of the deceased's friends, it was believed, would help build a spiritual bridge over which the departing soul could make its way to its Beloved. One such *alabado,* of which we here include a fragment from Prudencio González's hand-copied prayer booklet,[12] is a chant commending the soul of a friend to God:

---

that they visited northern New Mexico and southern Colorado frequently, bringing back with them the musical customs of that region. There were many Hispanos from the region who worked in the mines as well, and it was for them, the Pachecos relate, that they began to play their music and sing the traditional songs at weddings. Mr. Pacheco informs us that he and his wife have been singing the *entrega* at weddings for almost fifty years. They still play a variety of instruments, including the guitar, mandolin, accordion, and harmonica, as accompaniment for the songs they have long committed to memory.

[11]For a summary description of the *alabado* see "El Alabado de Nuevo Mexico," *Kentucky Quarterly Romance* 29, no. 1 (1982) by co-author William H. González.

[12]The co-author's father, Prudencio González, like many other individuals, kept a personal hymn and prayer booklet which contained numerous *alabados*. The co-author is currently at

La encomendación del alma no la dejes de pedir, encomiéndale a Dios y Dios la ha de recibir.	The commendation of the soul Never forget to plead, Recommend it to God And He will surely receive it.
¡Oh divino Redentor, Hijo del eterno Padre, a Tí te encomiendo esta alma que la cuides y la salves!	Oh Divine Redeemer Son of the Eternal Father I recommend this soul to you That you may guard and grant it salvation.
¡Oh Madre mía amorosa yo te ruego Madre amada que vaya esta alma al Cielo de ángeles acompañada!	Oh my beloved Blessed Mary I pray dearest Mother That this soul ascend to Heaven In the company of angels.

Such an *alabado* personalizes the relationship between man and God, the earthly community and the heavenly host, and it also has the effect of removing the sting of death. After all, the soul is winging its way toward Paradise.

On the day of the funeral the casket was carried on the shoulders of the men from the house to the church. After the Requiem Mass the coffin was taken to the *campo santo* or cemetery either by horse-drawn wagon or, in more recent times, by car. Once the rites were completed and the casket had been lowered into the ground, each member of the family, beginning with the eldest, would drop a handful of dirt on the coffin. This ritual symbolized the acceptance of God's will in death, but it was also a reminder to every member of the community that they shared a common fate with the deceased, that they also would sooner or later return to dust.

After the burial it was customary for the family of the deceased to go into a period of mourning for at least a year. This meant that there would be no music in the house, no one would attend dances, and, of course, women dressed in black. Moreover, the family and friends would offer masses, novenas, and daily prayer for the soul of the departed.

In more recent years the solemnity and religious aura that surrounded the death of a loved one has declined, even if the pain of loss has not. Since the *velorio* (wake) has left the house, where the body of the deceased was prayed over and accompanied through the night by neighbors chanting *alabados,* the funeral rites have become much more brief, even businesslike. That is to say that with the removal of the wake to mortuaries, the *alabados* that were once chanted into the first light of the day are seldom sung and have fallen into almost complete disuse. Since the *alabado* and other religious rites that served as constant reminders of the continuing spiritual tie between the living and the dead have sharply declined, so too has the period of mourning. The rites immediate to death have maintained their traditional intensity, with family closely gathered and friends providing material and spiritual comfort, but people now return to their normal activities sooner.

---

work on a project transcribing *alabados* from recorded collections and collating these and copied variants for a collection of Hispanic *alabados* of Utah.

LITURGICAL OBSERVANCES

Christmas, New Year's, Holy Week, Easter, and special patron saint feast days also played a central part in the life of the Hispano in Monticello. Among these, perhaps the most intense and solemn time of the year was *la cuaresma* or Lent—the annual season of spiritual self-examination and penance which begins on Ash Wednesday and continues for forty days to Easter.

In Monticello the Lenten period was characterized by commitment to severe personal sacrifice on the part of each family member. Dancing, for example, was absolutely forbidden. Radios were disconnected. The movie house was shunned. Moreover, to show their devotion to Christ, who had fasted for forty days and forty nights in the wilderness, many Hispanos in Monticello also observed strict fasting during Lent. Nothing but coffee was taken in the morning, perhaps only a piece of tortilla was eaten at noon, and dinner was very meager.

After the evening meal families would retire to a candle-lit room where, kneeling before the crucifix, the father would lead them in the recitation of the rosary. Family devotions would often continue in this manner for hours, with the mother offering special prayers and the father singing *alabados*. In fact, it was during the Lenten season that parents took it upon themselves to give catechismal instruction to their children. And it was in this manner that some of the *alabados* were orally passed on to another generation as they had been since the early fourteenth century. Most of the *alabados* were chanted by memory, giving rise to different versions and variants; others were fixed in carefully penned *cuadernos* or personal prayer books.

The singing of *alabados* and the observance of other devotions, such as daily attendance at church and the praying of the Stations of the Cross, reached a high point during the Holy Week that immediately preceded Easter. During Holy Week many people maintained strict silence, cooked very little or not at all, stopped chopping wood, and simply stayed indoors as much as possible. The only respite from this solemnity was Palm Sunday. Children could not help but feel relief when the palm branches were distributed before mass, for it meant that Lent was almost over. Imagine, palm branches in Monticello in early spring!

Easter Sunday Mass was celebrated in St. Joseph's Church, where the community would listen joyfully to the Gospel telling them the good news that the stone had been rolled away from the sepulchre and that Christ had risen. After church the older people would usually spend a quiet day visiting each other, and, when it was warm enough, the younger people would picnic at South Creek or Soldier Spring and sing and laugh after the long period of penance.

Contrary to the celebration of Christmas as the central Christian holiday in the United States, Christ's Resurrection from the dead and his Ascension into heaven constitute the doctrinal core of Catholic faith. Hence, it is not surprising that although more solemn and self-effacing, the Easter season superseded Christmas in the minds and hearts of Monticello Hispanics, as it did for Hispanics in the Southwest generally.

Nevertheless, Christmas was a time of joy and festivity in Monticello. On Christmas Eve some people would arrange three small stacks of piñon wood in front of their homes and light them when it turned dark. As the older Hispanos explained it to the young people who gathered around these fires or *luminarias,* the Three Kings had already begun their long journey to visit the newborn child, and the *luminarias* would help them to find their way. Another explanation had it that the *luminarias* were actually to light the way for the baby Jesus, so that his small feet would find their way to earth and to his people. The fire from the *luminarias,* in either event, lit up yards, houses, and the faces of youngsters with a warm glow that signaled the coming birth of Christ. How strange this must have seemed to Mormon neighbors in Monticello who were unfamiliar with a custom that had been preserved for so many centuries.

If a priest happened to be in town, *La Misa del Gallo* or Midnight Mass was celebrated with the choir singing the joyous "Mass of the Angels" in Latin and perhaps a Spanish Christmas carol or two. But whether people celebrated Midnight Mass or simply attended church on Christmas morning, after religious observances there was always the customary special food, the most characteristic of which was the *empanada,* a turnover pie filled with meat, raisins, and nuts, or fruit *empanadas* filled with apple slices or *calabaza* (pumpkin). There were also plenty of delicious *bizcochitos* as well. And even though women made these in large batches, the children were quick to make them disappear.

On Christmas morning children rose early to open their gifts, which were few and simple since most families were poor. Then they would dress and visit neighbors to *pedir los crismas,* that is, ask for sweets. Monticello Hispanics brought this residual custom with them from their villages in Colorado and New Mexico, where as children they would knock at the doors of neighbors on Christmas and chant:

Oremos, oremos	Let's pray, let's pray
angelitos semos	Little angels are we
d'el cielo venimos	Who have come from Heaven
a pedir algo venimos.	To ask for charity.
si no nos dan,	If you do not allow us to partake
puertas y ventanas quebraremos.	Your doors and windows we shall break.

Of course, the last line was meant in jest, but both the rhyme and the *pedir los crismas* signified the importance of being hospitable to strangers who might indeed be angels from heaven asking for lodging or food as a sign of charity, no matter how poor a family might be.

New Year's Eve was celebrated by Hispanos in a manner quite distinct from Anglos in Monticello. Usually there was a dance which most of the Hispanos attended; but it was really after the dance that the celebration began, for many of the people who attended the dance would form a group to begin a house-to-house serenade. The serenaders were composed of Hispanos of all ages, and anyone who could play the guitar was not only invited to join but was almost forcibly incorporated into the group. As the group walked from one house to another, people who had either not attended the dance, or those who had gone immediately home, waited expectantly with the lights darkened. As the group approached a house, family members would peek through the curtains and listen as the serenaders sang the traditional Spanish verses of "Los días" or "Good Morning."

Then one of the lead singers would, in the time-honored tradition of the roving troubadour, make up additional verses exalting the qualities of the would-be hosts. The family would then turn on the lights and invite the serenaders into their home where they were offered wine and *bizcochitos*. The group would remain in one family's home for some time where they would sing and dance; then they would graciously take leave and proceed to another house, singing as they went. Occasionally, when they were ignored or refused entry to a house, the serenaders would sing a *copla* or stanza of biting satire aimed at the owner of the house. This serenading continued through the night until all of the Hispanic residences had been visited and serenaded. Any families unintentionally overlooked were serenaded on January 6, the Feast of the Epiphany, or "little Christmas" as it was called by the Hispano.

Two other special religious days observed by Hispanics in Monticello were *El día de San Juan* or the Feast of St. John on June 24 and *El día de San Lorenzo* or the Feast of St. Lawrence on August 10. It was traditionally believed that on June 24 the waters of the rivers and lakes surrounding Monticello were blessed and purified, since in Christian tradition that was the day on which Christ was baptized by John. In addition to signifying that water for the crops would be sweeter, June 24 signaled the day youngsters could go swimming in the reservoirs around Monticello. After this day parents usually allowed their children to go swimming without undue fear, but they also warned them not to forget to wet their foreheads before stepping into the water, "*para que no te pique el agua*" ("so that the water will not sting you"). This is a variation of the Mexican custom of blessing oneself with water before swimming as a symbolic form of self-baptism.

The feast day of San Lorenzo on August 10 signaled the beginning of the harvest. It was upon his intercession that Hispano farmers depended for good weather and gentle winds. In the days when most of the threshing was done by hand and the wheat was separated from the chaff by tossing it into the air, people would chant a little prayer as they worked: "*Viento, viento, San Lorenzo, barbas de oro*" ("Send us a breeze, send us a breeze, St. Lawrence of the golden beard"). Of course, here too there were variations of the rhyme, some of which were playful. It was said, for example, that a man invoking the intercession of St. Lawrence for a favorable breeze was frustrated when his prayers went unheard. Finally, when the farmer could take it no longer, he yelled out, "*Viento, viento, San Lorenzo, barbas de chivato*"

("A breeze, a breeze, Saint Lawrence, beard of a he-goat"). Taking exception to the man's impatience, San Lorenzo, it was said, sent a terrible windstorm that blew his wheat entirely away.

These, then, are some of the life-cycle customs and liturgical observances that Hispanos from Monticello and elsewhere in Utah brought with them on their trek from New Mexico. Some traditions go back centuries and are steadfastly maintained, while time and American social pressures have increasingly eroded other of these customs. Since there is little subsistence farming done by Hispanos anymore, planting and harvest observances such as *El día de San Lorenzo* have declined. Baptisms, weddings, and funerals maintain vital secular elements of traditional practice, while many of the more religious elements have been lost. At weddings, for instance, the *marcha* and the *entrega* remain an integral part of the festivities, but at funerals the chanting of *alabados* has all but been abandoned. But in both cases there are reasons for maintenance or loss; a dance hall allows old wedding traditions to be repeated and perpetuated, while a mortuary that must close its doors to the community by, say, 10:00 p.m. puts an abrupt stop to night-long *velorios* and the singing of *alabados*. Strict Lenten observances of self-denial and penance have relaxed considerably, not because Hispanos in Monticello are necessarily less devout but because we live in a more secular world, a world in which even the Catholic church has relaxed its harsh Lenten observances. Still, when a child is baptized nowadays, he or she undergoes as serious an initiation into both the church and the Hispanic community as ever.

While there are still Hispanos living in Monticello, many of the elders have passed on, their traditions buried with them. Many of the children of the early Monticello settlers have left to settle in Price or the Salt Lake Valley area, and others have gone even further away to Denver or California, returning only occasionally to baptize their children in the now old St. Joseph's Church, or to attend a wedding, or more often a funeral. Yet, despite the gradual decline and change in Hispanic life-cycle rituals, many of the people who grew up in Monticello maintain some part of the best of their cultural traditions which they carry with them wherever they go. That they do so reflects upon the strength and devotion of the early Hispanic pioneers who came to Utah *buscando trabajo,* "looking for work."

*

Utah's Ethnic Legacy

HELEN ZEESE PAPANIKOLAS

This moving and evocative essay was originally delivered as a commencement address at the University of Utah in 1984. In it Helen Papanikolas addresses a number of issues, including the importance of a commitment to diversity; the necessity of people understanding their heritage and feeling connected to it; and the realities, hardships, and causes of prejudice and discrimination. "Only recently have we Utahns acknowledged the importance and richness of culture," she says. "Much has been accomplished since World War II, but we cannot linger in complacency. We have promises to keep for coming generations of children and for our own self-respect." Her vision is of a society where people live in dignity and freedom and children are raised in equality and hope, and she eloquently denounces the complacency of the "well fed and comfortable."

Helen Papanikolas, "Utah's Ethnic Legacy," *Dialogue, A Journal of Mormon Thought* 19 (Spring 1986): 41–48. Reprinted by permission of the publisher and the author.

Helen Zeese Papanikolas is one of Utah's most important historians. She is editor of *The Peoples of Utah* and author of *Toil and Rage in a New Land: The Greek Immigrants in Utah;* a biography of her parents, *Emily-George;* and *Small Bird Tell Me: Stories of Greek Immigrants in Utah.*

AS I LOOK AT YOU graduates, I recognize in your faces, full-blown in some, slight in others, the ethnic people of your past. Among you sit men and women whose sorrowing ancestors were summarily sent to federal reservations when settlers arrived. Those settlers ploughed the land on which for centuries your people had picked berries, gathered nuts, and hunted small animals. Perhaps seated here is a descendant of the Paiute leader who told Major John Wesley Powell:

> We live among the rocks, and they yield little food and many thorns. When the cold moons come, our children are hungry. . . . We love our coun-

> try; we know not other lands. [When] the pines sing, we are glad. Our children play in the warm sand; we hear them sing and we are glad. We do not want [others'] good land; we want our rocks, and the great mountains where our fathers lived.[1]

A great number of you, though, are progeny of those celebrated American Mormons and the later-arriving English converts. The English thought themselves superior to the Scandinavians, particularly the Danish, who followed. Their feuds have left a folklore that is the delight of scholars; their cultural clashes were resolved through intermarriages encouraged by leaders of the fledgling Church. Many of you may be descendants of persevering converts from other parts of Europe who were drawn to this new Zion. Some of you may descend from those few blacks, freeborn servants or slaves brought west by unbelievers and by southern converts in the first migrations. Others may come from those blacks recruited years later by the railroads to work as porters and waiters.

Surely several of you can trace your roots to those early Jews who drove precariously loaded wagons to army posts and mining camps. From lowly beginnings, these peddlers became merchants, then industrialists. Their illustrious names have long been associated with Utah's economy.

Perhaps among you are great-great-grandchildren of those Chinese railroad workers who rushed to reach Promontory, Utah, before the Irish laborers arrived from the East. In one day they laid ten miles of track. Maybe you come from the Chinese in the Carbon County coal fields who used no blasting powder but with picks carved mine entrances that were "as beautiful a piece of work as one would want to see."[2] A few Chinese remained as launderers and restaurant workers and owners. One became a trading post proprietor on the Ute reservation; another, an herbal doctor in Mercur.

Many more of your forefathers were young men from the Balkans, Mediterranean, Middle East, and Japan who began coming to Utah at the turn of the century. They came to supply brawn for rapidly opening mines, mills, and smelters and for railroads, because Mormon leaders counseled their members to stay on the land. During labor wars large numbers of these immigrants were brought in as strikebreakers. They traded the clear air and the sound of sheep and goat bells for the darkness of mines, for the searing heat of smelting furnaces, for the loneliness of isolated railroad gangs.

These newer immigrants, unlike Mormon converts who came to stay, expected to remain in Utah only long enough to help their destitute parents. For mutual aid and protection they settled in neighborhoods known as "towns": the Greeks in Greek Town, the Italians, Lebanese, South Slavs, and Japanese in their towns. Yet they stayed because in America they were

[1] Powell, John Wesley. *Report of J. W. Powell, Exploration of the Colorado River of the West and Its Tributaries,* (Washington, D.C., 1875), 128–29, 130.

[2] Reynolds, Thursey Jessen et al., eds. *Centennial Echoes from Carbon County,* (Price[?], 1948), 37.

assured of bread to eat. From their native countries they brought brides they had seen only in photographs. Crucifixes, icons, and Buddhist shrines enriched modest homes in which Mormons had once lived. The young wives became matriarchs, raising large families within their towns, fearful of the world beyond and its alien language.

Then the Mexicans came to follow this pattern of immigrant experience. Several of you come from those first Hispanics, who drove covered wagons from southern Colorado and northern New Mexico to teach the Monticello Mormons the nurture of sheep and in time homesteaded there themselves. A professor in the University of Utah Department of Languages, William Gonzales, is the son of those first pioneers; his father will be one hundred years old soon. More of your forebears came later, fleeing the Mexican Revolution to become strikebreakers in the Bingham Canyon Strike of 1912, riding freight cars to find any kind of work, anywhere.

All these ethnic groups—Indians, blacks, immigrants—were separated by their distinctive cultures and languages, but they shared the belief that religion, family, and work constituted the highest good in life. Communal celebrations for marriages, baptisms, or confirmations offered them welcome respite from long hours of toil. Even laborers in Utah could afford to provide the hospitality their ancient traditions demanded.

Still, each incoming immigrant group suffered discrimination. When the Irish fled the potato famine in the 1840s, NINA signs appeared throughout eastern cities: No Irish Need Apply. In Utah, Chinese were chased from the mines by subsequent English-speaking workers. Managers and straw bosses ruled the lives of immigrants and blacks, forcing them to trade at company stores, arbitrarily hiring and firing in alliance with labor agents, and at first providing no housing. As elsewhere in the United States, Utahns demanded instant Americanization of these laborers, disdaining their ancient languages and cultures.

Perplexed and wary, immigrants pined for their homelands. Yet, when in old age a few returned to their fatherlands to live more easily on their Social Security, they congregated in places like the Astor Hotel Bar in Athens or in ancestral village squares in Italy and spoke with longing of their lost land, America.

These forebears are receding from memory; they are entering the realm of myth. We must not forget them completely, for because of them we are here.

My parents were immigrants from Greece; I lived among ethnic people during my growing-up days in Helper in Carbon County, where whistles of coal mines and the Denver and Rio Grande Western steam engines drowned out the pandemonium of school recess. The first question a new child was asked was not "What's your name?" but "What nationality are you?" On a hillside just beyond town, a large, whitewashed number 57 advertised the Heinz Pickle Company's varieties, but residents maintained it meant the races and nationalities in town. (The Work Progress Administration [WPA] in the Depression days counted only twenty-six.)

The nostalgia, though, is not all pleasant. Memory reminds me that as a child of immigrants I was uncertain, even though I was born in Utah, that I was an American. When schoolmates taunted us immigrant children to "go back where you came from," we answered with anger and impotence, so unsure were we of our birthrights. How distantly strange it seems to me now that children were teased about eating spaghetti or for going to Greek or Japanese school after regular school. Yet that generation of immigrant children, most of whom began school without speaking English, has succeeded far beyond anyone's expectations.

The success of these Balkan, Mediterranean, and Asian immigrants has been unfairly compared with the experience of native Americans, blacks, and Hispanics. Those who wonder why they have not pulled themselves up by those suspect bootstraps are unaware of the historical forces and the circumstances that make such judgments unjustified and incorrect. Balkan and Mediterranean people survived continuous invasions without complete destruction of their cultures because their conquerors were unlettered tribesmen; the Japanese were proud that their country had never known "the shame of foreign rule." In contrast, Indians, blacks, and the indigenous inhabitants of Mexico were crushed by technologically superior invaders, and their ascent from near annihilation continues, unfinished.

Unlike the immigrants with whom they are compared, Indians, blacks, and Hispanics had no doctors, attorneys, editors, or druggists to champion and lead them. Nor did they have long-established ethnic newspapers and institutions like coffee houses and fraternal organizations to disseminate government news, help them with citizenship papers and legal problems, and provide support while they took the rudimentary steps toward Americanization. Decades would pass before Indians, blacks, and Hispanics would found organizations to aid their people.

Nor in the first twenty-five years of this country, during America's great era of industrialization, did Indians, blacks, or Hispanics have labor agents with the power to represent and ease them into steady work. The Greeks, Italians, Lebanese, South Slavs, and Japanese all had such spokesmen.

In all, the indignities and prejudices inflicted on these racial minorities were far more intense than those suffered by the Balkan and Mediterranean people. Historians researching old newspapers regularly find items recounting that Indians, blacks, and Mexicans were replaced on labor gangs by southern European and Middle Eastern immigrants—solely because of race. The roots of discrimination were in color and physiognomy: the darker the skin or the more distinctive the features, the greater the prejudice.

Mexican immigration differed from that of other groups in significant ways. Most immigrants traveled thousands of miles to Utah, to terrain and weather often far different from that of their native countries. Once in Utah, they were not only physically but psychically cut off from their homelands; they had little choice but to adapt. Mexicans, though, made their way north through arid land of sparse vegetation, a geographical continuation of their own country. Until the treaty of 1848, it had been Mexican territory. The need to modify the old culture with the new was less urgent.

More important, Mexican immigration has never eased. Immigrants from southern Europe, the Middle East, and Japan came mainly during one major era: the first two decades of this century. These people and their progeny passed once and for all through the three-generation immigration experience: the first generation's accommodation to America for survival, the second generation's ambivalence toward its parents' and American cultures, and the third generation's complete assimilation. For Mexicans, however, the immigration experience has never finished. Although Hispanics continually enter the middle class to become educators, small businessmen, building subcontractors, and civil servants, the constant arrival of poor Mexicans with little education gives the erroneous notion that Hispanics are unprogressive and contribute little to the state. Facts contradict this impression; as Utah's largest minority, Hispanics did and do most of the industrial work begun by earlier immigrants. The newest immigrants will always perform the menial labor for the nation. In Utah the newly arrived Mexicans and the refugees of the Viet Nam War join native Americans and blacks in this work. Of the Southeast Asians, the Vietnamese have a decided advantage because of the influence their former rulers' Western culture had upon their own.

Yet the immense amount of industrial labor that gave millions of immigrants a foothold in America is gone. In Utah the railroads, mills, and smelters have already been built. In mines, mammoth cutting machines demolish within minutes veins of coal and ore that would have taken hundreds of men with picks and shovels days to dig out. In this age of the machine, education is the key to survival, and it is the right of every child. That children, many of them immigrants, are lost in our education system to wander, barely literate, their potential for a balanced life blighted, is a tragedy.

Those well-fed and comfortable in their identities find it difficult to understand the souls of Indian, black, Mexican, and Southeast Asian children. These children are forever immigrants, even those whose ancestors were born in this land. How easy to speak of bootstraps and of education available to all and to condemn dropouts and the young unemployed. Future educators will be teaching minority children; all of us will have contact with them. How will we approach them? Others standing here have spoken of Plato and Aristotle's view that education is more than a useful function; it is a liberating force. An educated person is liberated from his limitations and irrationality. Can we expect children to be liberated by education when we are not?

Paternalism—thinking we know what is best for others—is disguised prejudice, as is accepting preconceived ideas about people. The paternalism foisted on immigrants in mining and smelting camps is in the past; a mine manager today would not dare shut off electricity in company houses because the immigrants, in his opinion, did not need or deserve it. Paternalism today is more subtle. Some teachers think of minority children as intellectually or culturally inferior and treat them with condescension. Minority groups are often not invited to help make decisions that affect them. Paternalism did not work in industry; it does not work in education; it is unworthy.

We must keep searching for the best techniques to educate our children. Future educators must be given more than a smattering of instruction in how to teach children from many cultures. Computers and every other teaching aid must be brought into this crusade. Money spent for these programs will surely help stave future dependency on government.

This monumental task is extremely complex. Many parents' most anxious, daily concern is providing food and shelter for their children, not overseeing their school attendance. Other parents come from a cultural background that is highly permissive toward children. They must be taught the worth of education.

Education is difficult for children not knowing English. Native language is usually lost in the Americanization of immigrants by the third generation. But because Mexicans continually arrive, because Indians live mainly on reservations, and because Southeast Asians have been here such a short time, language will remain of paramount concern in the education of these minority students.

Bilingual education is experimental in Utah. The program began ten years ago, but a generation must pass before the results can be seen. Test scores among sixth graders in the Salt Lake City schools are encouraging, and Indian students in Roosevelt, Uintah County, appear to be responding to a bilingual program. The federal government has been lax in fulfilling treaties with Indian nations to provide education for their children. The Indians themselves are forcing the government to face this responsibility. Still, generations of Indian children are poorly educated, becoming aimless, unemployed young people, and little has been done to alleviate their despair. This must stop.

Although we all have an obligation to the children of our country, you ethnic graduates have a double duty. On your way to reaching your highest potential, may you not forget your people. They need you. Colleges founded with the sweat and blood of black educators are struggling to survive today because their graduates are not supporting them financially. Ethnic students who actively work for their rights during college days often lose interest in scholarship programs for those climbing up behind them. Often in their quest for material goods and what they perceive as social acceptance, they turn from their culture. They are wrong. Samuel Ramos, the Mexican philosopher, said culture is not like the brand of a hat. America has room for all cultures. Those cultures made America. Each immigrant and native people has given new vitality to this country. Culture is our soul.

Only recently have we Utahns acknowledged the importance and richness of culture. Until World War II people who thought of themselves as true Americans viewed those unlike themselves as strange and inferior. After the war, soldiers brought home foreign brides, often from enemy countries. The federal government sent vast amounts of economic aid and an army of workers to oversee its disbursement to devastated nations. The government lifted quotas to allow hundreds of thousands of destitute and displaced immigrants to enter the country. With the increase in defense industries and government services, employees moved far and often. Mormon missionaries proselyted in lands where Americans were strange and exotic. The word *isolationism* was almost eliminated from print. We began to appreciate people from many cultures, looking beyond the superficialities of appearance and habit.

Perceptions about ethnic people began to alter in small and significant ways. Racial slang that humiliated was heard less often. American sojourners in other lands returned with a penchant for foreign foods. Second-generation Italians who had been ashamed as children to admit they ate spaghetti opened pasta restaurants. Almost every ethnic food became readily available, and each group's modest communal celebrations, centered in churches, temples, or synagogues, evolved into highly successful festivals for the general population.

Now grandchildren of those first immigrants, whose names were either shortened arbitrarily by officials in Ellis Island, by judges awarding them citizenship, or by themselves in frustration at the reactions of "true" Americans, are at home in America and at the same time proud of their roots. Newer immigrants have left their patronymic names intact; grandchildren of the earlier arrivals often give their children names derived from the ancient histories, literature, and mythology, a startling departure from the custom of their parents.

Signs of goodwill are dramatically reflected in adoptions. Not long ago, adoptive parents would accept only white children of British or North European ancestry; today children of all races are sought. Important, also, is the awareness of the cultural enrichment of speaking languages besides English and perceiving education to be deficient without a second language. The language program for Mormon missionaries has greatly influenced this new attitude.

In education a slower yet steady trend toward hiring minority teachers is belatedly taking place. Utah's universities have opened their doors to ethnic professors. When Louis Zucker, a Jew, arrived in 1928 to join the English department at the University of Utah, he was looked upon as an oddity. When the university established a four-year medical school, other Jews arrived. Several of them, Max Wintrobe, Leo Samuels, and Louis Goodman, were renowned in their fields. After World War II, the number of ethnic educators in higher education increased phenomenally. A few minority educators hold administrative positions in the public school system, and recently the first black principal was hired.

In judicial affairs, a memorable act in Utah history occurred recently when Governor Scott F. Matheson appointed Tyrone E. Medley, a graduate of the University of Utah law school, to the Fifth Circuit Court Bench, making Medley the state's first black judge.

Much has been accomplished since World War II, but we cannot linger in complacency. We have promises to keep for coming generations of children and for our own self-respect.

*

The Strawberry Valley Reclamation Project and the Opening of the Uintah Indian Reservation

KATHRYN L. MACKAY

The story of the construction of Utah's first federal reclamation project, the Strawberry Valley Project (1906–22), on what had originally been part of the Uintah Indian Reservation and its impact on Native Americans is a tragic story, but one important to understand. The following article, powerful in its impact, does not back away from, or try to soften, the tale. On the one hand, the project permitted the development of additional farming land in Utah County, furnished electric power to local towns, stimulated population and industrial growth, and provided recreational facilities for thousands of people. On the other hand, it was built on expropriated Indian lands without Indian consent and in spite of their persistent protests. It exploited Indian resources, both human and material, and revealed an ethnocentrism that evaluated Indian ways and systems as inferior. For all its success in Anglo terms, it is part of the legacy of ignoble dealings with Native Americans. It is also an example of power politics, conflicts of interest within the federal bureaucracy, and disregard for the legal rights of Native Americans.

Kathryn L. MacKay, "The Strawberry Valley Reclamation Project and the Opening of the Uintah Indian Reservation," *Utah Historical Quarterly* 50 (Winter 1982): 68–69. Reprinted by permission of the publisher and the author.

Kathryn L. MacKay has a Ph.D. degree in history from the University of Utah and teaches at Weber State University. A member of the history department, she has also been Coordinator of the Women's Studies Program there and is currently director of its Teaching and Learning Forum.

THE STRAWBERRY VALLEY PROJECT (1906–22), Utah's first federal reclamation project, was part of the opening of the Uintah Valley Indian Reservation in the Uinta Basin to mining, agricultural, speculative, and conservation interests over the vain protests of the inhabitants, the Northern Ute Indians. The project is an example of power politics, of conflicts of interest within the federal bureaucracy, and of the disregard for the legal rights of Native Americans.

The Uinta Basin was the traditional homeland of the small Ute band, the Uinta-ats,[1] and the hunting grounds for several Indian groups. Until the 1840s when they became extinct in the Basin, buffalo were hunted there by the Uinta-ats, other Ute bands, particularly the Yamparika (later called the White River Utes) and the Tumpanawach (also called the Lagunas, the Utah Lake Utes, the Timpanoagos), and by other Indians such as the Northwestern Shoshone.

In the 1820–40s the buffalo and beaver in the Basin attracted non-Indian trappers and traders from the United States and Mexico. These intruders established posts in the area—Fort Kit Carson, 1833–34; Fort Robidoux or Uintah, 1837–44; Ford Davy Crockett, 1837–44. The Utes became involved in an expanded trade economy by which some Ute groups, such as the Tumpanowach led by Wakara, prospered.

In the 1840s the Mormons established their agrarian kingdom in what became Utah Territory, but they were not attracted to the Basin except as it might be protected from settlement by non-Mormons. In 1861 after an expedition sent by Brigham Young had determined the area unsuitable for Mormon agrarian settlement,[2] the Uintah Valley Reservation, of which the Strawberry Valley at the western end composed one-fifth of the area, was established by executive order of Abraham Lincoln.[3] This order was confirmed by act of Congress in 1864, which act also provided for the sale of four other smaller reservations established in 1856 for the Utes and the Gosiutes and provided for the removal of all Utah Indians to the Uintah Valley Reservation.[4]

Most Indian groups found the Uinta Basin as unsuitable for year-round occupation as had the Mormons, and many continued the struggle to use their traditional lands, increasingly occupied by non-Indians. In 1865 Congress empowered the president to treat with the Indians of Utah Territory in order to extinguish Indian title to all agricultural and mineral lands in the territory except lands to be reserved for them at distances far removed from non-Indian settlements.[5] This act was one of several that formed the federal reservation or enclavement policy to deal with the "Indian Problem."

With this legislation the energetic, pragmatic Indian superintendent for Utah, O. H. Irish, negotiated on behalf of the federal government several treaties with various Utah Indians—Gosiutes, Paiutes, Shoshones, and Utes—in order to establish peace between them and the non-Indian intrud-

[1]Julian H. Steward, *Basin-Plateau Aboriginal Sociopolitical Groups, Bureau of American Ethnology Bulletin no. 120* (Washington, D.C., 1938), pp. 223–25.

[2]*Deseret News,* September 25, 1861.

[3]Executive Order 10-3-1861 in *Executive Orders Relating to Indian Reservations, May 14, 1855 to July 1, 1912* (Washington, D.C., 1912), p. 169.

[4]Act 5-5-1864, 13 *Stat.* 63; amended 6-18-1878, 20 *Stat.* 165; and 5-24-1888, 25 *Stat.* 157.

[5]Act 2-23-1865, 13 *Stat.* 432.

ers and to provide for the concentration of these Indians onto lands reserved for their sole occupation and use. The Ute treaty was negotiated on the old Spanish Fork Reservation in June 1865. It provided that the Utes give up all lands in Utah Territory except the Uintah Valley Reservation. They were to move there within one year, receive $900,000 over the next sixty years, and be provided with supplies, homes, schools, etc.[6] Soweett, a Uinta-ats leader, explained that the Utes " . . . did not want to sell their land and go away; they wanted to live around the graves of their fathers." However, all the leaders of the various Ute groups were persuaded to sign the treaty.[7]

Congress, ill-disposed to support Mormon interests, failed to ratify the treaty. However, some of the Utes, acting in good faith, moved to the reservation. When the promised supplies, cattle, and other goods did not arrive, many Utes joined Black Hawk in the series of raids on central Utah settlements that came to be called the Black Hawk War (1865–69).[8] Not until 1867 did a large group of Utes led by Tabby-To-Kwana, a Uinta-ats leader, move from central Utah to the Uintah Reservation, settling in the Strawberry Valley where they had access to cattle being grazed in Heber Valley.[9]

The first agency on the reservation had been built in 1865 at the head of Daniels Canyon.[10] The area was isolated by heavy snowfall in the winter, and agent Albert Kinney did not stock adequate supplies, thereby frustrating and discouraging Ute support. Thomas Carter was made agent the next year and moved the agency into the Basin near present-day Hanna on the upper Duchesne. Two years later the agency was moved to the junction of Rock Creek and the Duchesne River. In the fall of 1868 agent Pardon Dodds moved the agency from this western end of the reservation to the center of the Basin at White Rocks, a location recommended to him by Antero, a Uinta-at leader.[11] White Rocks had been the location of Fort Robidoux and was the crossroads of several trails.

With the placement of the agency in the center of the Basin, most of the Ute groups who used it located their camps around it, although annuities, rations, and crops were not sufficient to maintain the Utes year-round. Agent J. J. Critchlow in his first report in 1871 complained about the lack of attention his predecessors had paid the Utes: "There seems never to have been anything more done for them than to keep them quiet and peaceable

[6]O. H. Irish to Commissioner of Indian Affairs, June 7, 1865, Letters Received, Record Group 75, National Archives.

[7]Ibid.; also Secretary of Interior, *Annual Report 1865* (Washington, D.C., 1866), pp. 318–20.

[8]Carlton Culmsee, *Utah's Black Hawk War, Love and Reminiscences of Participants* (Logan, Ut., 1973).

[9]Commissioner of Indian Affairs, *Annual Report 1867* (Washington, D.C. 1868), p. 175.

[10]Ibid., p. 181. All but one of the buildings were erected by soldiers of the California Volunteers camped there in 1865–66.

[11]James Warren Covington, "Relations Between the Ute Indians and the United States Government, 1848–1900" (Ph.D. diss., University of Oklahoma, 1949), pp. 138–39, 142–43. See also Mildred Miles Dillman, comp., *Early History of Duchesne County* (Springville, Ut., 1948), pp. 79–81.

by partially feeding and clothing them and amusing them with trinkets."[12]

The western end of the reservation, located some fifty miles from the agency and accessible by wagon only on exceedingly rough roads, became less frequented by the Utes, although in 1881 several hundred Uintah Utes moved into the area in response to the influx of White River Utes removed to the reservation from Colorado following the Meeker incident.[13] The Strawberry Valley region, distant from federal supervision, was, therefore, vulnerable to trespass.

The cattlemen out of Heber City, who became powerful influences on the economy and politics of northeastern Utah, were among the first (beginning about 1878) to trespass the western end of the reservation, grazing their cattle in that area. Despite Ute protests,[14] the Indian agent was powerless, both politically and militarily, to either end or tax the practice. By 1887 agent T. A. Byrnes was exasperated:

> These cattlemen have given me more trouble than all my Indians or business of both Agencies [Uintah and Ouray]. *For years* they have controlled this reservation and most of its affairs. They have pastured their cattle for years on this reservation and swindled these Indians at every opportunity.[15]

In 1892 the Indian Office agreed with agent R. Waugh that the Strawberry Valley should be leased, since the Utes had not acquired "stock enough to consume the pasture and since . . . trouble, expense, and annoyance would continue in trying to keep the trespassers off."[16] The southwestern portion of the Uintah Reservation was, therefore, leased by the Utes in 1895 to Charles F. Homer of New York. (Correspondence suggests that neither the agent nor the Utes were desirous of the lease being granted to local ranchers.[17]) Without Ute consent, the agent also began leasing land in the western end of the reservation for sheep grazing.[18]

In addition to ranchers illegally grazing their stock in the Strawberry area, farmers in Heber Valley illegally diverted water from tributaries on upper Strawberry River. Canals were built that carried water across the Basin divide to be turned into Daniels Creek, whence it flowed into irrigation systems built in Wasatch County. White settlers built these canals on Indian land without the consent of the Utes or authorization from the Indian agent or the Indian Office.[19]

[12]Commissioner of Indian Affairs, *Annual Report 1871* (Washington D.C., 1872), p. 547.

[13]The Uncompahgre Utes were also removed from Colorado and settled in Utah. In 1882 the Uncompahgre Reservation was established for them by executive order. This reservation was opened in 1898. See Floyd A. O'Neil and Kathryn L. MacKay, *A History of the Uintah-Ouray Ute Lands, Occasional Papers no. 10* (Salt Lake City: American West Center, University of Utah, 1979).

[14]William Parsons to Commissioner of Indian Affairs, May 29, 1886, LR RG75 NA.

[15]Byrnes to Commissioner of Indian Affairs, November 8, 1887, LR RG75 NA.

[16]Commissioner of Indian Affairs to Waugh, October 6, 1890, LR RG75 NA.

[17]Robert Waugh to T. J. Morgan, October 27, 1892, LR RG75 NA; Waugh to Morgan, December 14, 1892, LR RG75 NA.

[18]Elihu Root to Secretary of Interior, December 6, 1899, LR RG75 NA.

[19]U.S., Congress, House, *Surveys and Examinations of Uinta Indian Reservation, House Document no. 671*, 57th Cong., 1st sess. (June 19, 1902), p. 24

The three-mile-long Strawberry Canal was begun in 1879 by Hyrum Oakes and completed in 1882 by him and others whom he had interested in the project. In 1883 the Strawberry Canal Company was incorporated with fifty stockholders, most of whom were farmers benefited by the diverted water. The Strawberry Canal Company later built the two-mile-long Hobble Creek ditch.[20]

In 1888 Joseph C. and James McDonald dug a one-and-one-half-mile ditch to divert water from Hobble Creek. The seven-mile-long Willow Creek Canal, which included a 1,000-foot tunnel, was begun in 1890 by the Strawberry Canal Company which later abandoned the work. It was subsequently completed by the laborer-farmers who organized in 1893 the Willow Creek Canal Company with forty-five stockholders.[21] By 1904 approximately 991 acres were being irrigated wholly or in part by the illegally diverted water.[22]

In 1892 the Willow Creek and Strawberry Canal companies employed attorney William Buys of Heber to make a survey of the canals. Buys did so and filed the plats and maps describing the area with the Wasatch County recorder and applied for rights to the land and water from the secretary of the interior. The petition was carried in 1894 by Utah Delegate Joseph L. Rawlins who attempted to secure a special act of Congress necessary to divert waters from an Indian reservation. The bill (HR 6636) was stalled in committee.[23]

Later in the session, Congress, bowing to pressures from mining, ranching, and farming interests, authorized a commission to:

> . . . negotiate and treat with the Indians properly residing upon the Uintah Reservation . . . for the relinquishment to the United States of the interest of said Indians in all lands within said reservation not needed for allotment in severalty to said Indians. . . . [24]

The canal owners threw their support to those efforts, relying upon the opening of the reservation to "confirm their rights to the use of said water and the right of way for their said canals."[25]

However, the commission spent its time trying to induce the Uncompahgres to take allotments and give up their reservation within which gilsonite had been discovered in 1888. The Uncompahgres were not induced. The commissioners did not even meet with the Uintahs and White Rivers on the Uintah Reservation.

[20]H. P. Myton to Reed Smoot, December 5, 1904, LR RG75 NA. In his report on the canals, Myton lists the company officers, dates of incorporation, and length of water use. He concludes: " . . . while these people have no legal right to this water, I would recommend if it is all possible that you permit them to continue to use the water." Myton noted there was only one Indian family living in the area. Myton to Commissioner of Indian Affairs, July 1, 1902, enclosed in Tonner to Myton, June 11, 1902, LR RG75 NA.

[21]Ibid.

[22]Ibid.

[23]*Congressional Record,* 26 (April 10, 1894), p. 3657.

[24]Act 8-15-1894, 28 *Stat.* 337.

[25]Myton to Smoot, December 5, 1904.

Joseph Rawlins, who became a United States senator in 1897, therefore, again attempted to pass legislation to secure rights of way for the canal companies. In 1899 he succeeded in attaching an amendment to an Indian appropriations act that would authorize the secretary of the interior

> to grant rights of way for the construction and maintenance of dams, ditches, and canals, on or through the Uintah Indian Reservation in Utah, for the purpose of diverting, and appropriating the waters of the streams in said reservation for useful purposes: Provided that all such grants shall be subject at all times to the paramount rights of the Indians on said reservation to so much of said waters as may have been appropriated, or may hereafter be appropriated or needed by them for agricultural and domestic purposes. . . .[26]

Responding to this proviso, the secretary of the interior directed the U.S. Geological Survey to investigate the Uintah Reservation to determine whether bringing all arable lands on the reservation under cultivation would result in a shortage of water supply for the present and future needs of the Indians. Hydrographer Cyrus C. Babb directed the investigation September 1899 to June 1901. In his 1902 report Babb described the canals illegally diverting water from the Strawberry area. His supervisor F. H. Newell commented that:

> Such diversion is probably without any authority, but at the present time is not injurious to any rights of the Indians. The enlargement or further construction of such ditches might in the future result injuriously to agricultural development along the Duchesne River, but this is too problematical to be now seriously considered.[27]

However, Newell did conclude, based on Babb's survey, that:

> At present, and for many years in the future, the supply of water on the reservation is enormously in excess of the uses by the Indians, but in view of the future needs of the lands which may be allotted to the Indians, there is not much water which can be appropriated without injury to these prospective wants.[28]

Nevertheless, the water was appropriated, the lands were taken, and injury to the wants and rights of the Indians was done.

About 1900 there developed another interest in the lands at the western end of the reservation. While visiting the Strawberry Valley on a summer outing, State Sen. Henry Gardner of Spanish Fork and his friend John S. Lewis conceived the idea of building a reservoir on the east side of the Wasatch Mountains to store water that could be transferred through a tunnel to supplement the streams of the Spanish Fork Valley.[29]

[26]Act 3-1-1899, 30 *Stat.* 941.

[27]*House Document no. 671*, p. 8. Frederick Haynes Newell became chief engineer for the Reclamation Service when it was organized as part of the U.S. Geological Survey.

[28]Ibid.

[29]Thomas G. Alexander, "An Investment in Progress: Utah's First Federal Reclamation Project, the Strawberry Valley Project," *Utah Historical Quarterly* 39 (1971): 289. Also U.S. Department of the Interior, Bureau of Reclamation, *Ninth Annual Report of the Reclamation Service, 1909–1910* (Washington, D.C., 1911), p. 268.

In 1902 the Spanish Fork East Bench Irrigation and Manufacturing Company, later called the Strawberry Reservoir Irrigation and Canal Company, employed an engineer to investigate the project. He confirmed its feasibility but reported that expense beyond the capability of the company would be involved. The state engineer subsequently examined the site and made a favorable report but estimated a cost too expensive even for the state to accomplish.[30]

Early in 1903 the canal company petitioned the Interior Department to obtain permission to enter the reservation, to file water locations, and to make the surveys and obtain the data necessary to apply to the newly established (June 17, 1902) U.S. Bureau of Reclamation in order to involve the federal government in the cost and supervision of the project. The director of the U.S. Geological Survey, Charles D. Wolcott, supported the petition, stating that "the amount of water to be used for this enterprise will not interfere materially with the irrigation of lands within the reservation."[31] Wolcott thus rationalized away the concerns expressed by Babb and Newell in 1902 about injury to the future water needs of the Utes. Concerns for the welfare and rights of the Indians were set aside in the enthusiasm for the possibility of an irrigation project that would transfer water from the Uintah Basin to the Great Basin.

The secretary of the interior had been empowered to "reclaim in a large and comprehensive way the public lands which are susceptible of irrigation."[32] The Newlands Act (1902), which enabled such reclamation, was the culmination of a popular crusade for government support of irrigation projects, particularly the building of dams, in the arid West. The crusade, launched at the first National Irrigation Congress at Salt Lake City in 1891, opened up a twentieth-century homestead frontier on marginal western lands.[33]

The Reclamation Service, with the support of the Utah Arid Land Reclamation Fund Commission, created in 1903 to "take such measures as may be necessary to secure the construction by the United States of such reservoirs and irrigation works as are contemplated by the reclamation law."[34] and with the support of Spanish Fork area farmers, authorized surveys of the proposed Strawberry reservoir site in 1903 and 1904, even though the land was not public but an Indian reservation. However, the Reclamation Service anticipated the opening of the reservation and began maneuvering to have the site reserved for reclamation, thereby making it

[30]"Third Annual Report of the State Engineer to the Governor of the State of Utah," *Public Documents, State of Utah, 1901–2* (Salt Lake City, 1902).

[31]Charles D. Wolcott to Secretary of Interior, February 6, 1903, Strawberry Water Collection, MS B-200, Utah State Historical Society, Salt Lake City.

[32]Wolcott to Secretary of Interior, May 15, 1903, LR RG75 NA.

[33]Lawrence B. Lee, "William Ellsworth Smythe and the Irrigation Movement: A Reconsideration," *Pacific Historical Review* 41 (1972): 290.

[34]U.S., Department of the Interior, Bureau of Reclamation, *Second Annual Report, 1902–3* (Washington, D.C., 1903), p. 45.

unavailable to grazing and homesteading interests which also anxiously awaited the opening.[35]

The service's district engineer in Salt Lake City, George L. Swendsen, was particularly enthusiastic about the project for which he was one of the surveyors. He worked closely with the Strawberry Canal Company and later with the Strawberry Valley Water Users Association and lobbied the service for its approval. His enthusiasm was noted by his immediate supervisor:

> . . . while it is our duty and should be our earnest effort to furnish information when requested to do so by the officers and members . . . of such water users associations, we should be particularly careful not to act as promoters.[36]

The Reclamation Service was, however, not the only federal agency competing for the western end of the reservation. The Forestry Division (organized in 1905 as the U.S. Forest Service) had been directed since 1898 by the indefatigable Gifford Pinchot whose guiding principle was what he called conservation, the managing of the whole environment efficiently for the long-term good of all the people.

The Uinta National Forest, created by presidential proclamation in 1897,[37] included lands of the Uinta Mountains bordering on the south of the Uintah Indian Reservation. In the summer of 1902 chief grazing officer Albert F. Potter was sent by Pinchot to survey Utah's forested areas with the purpose of creating additional forest reserves.[38] As a result of this survey, the Forest Service became interested in appropriating part of the Uintah Reservation as a national forest reserve.

During 1904 and 1905 there was considerable maneuvering between the Reclamation Service (particularly Swendsen) and the Forest Service to coordinate efforts to reserve sections of the Strawberry area upon its opening that each service might be "entirely free" in their plans for that vicinity.[39] The Forest Service eventually had withdrawn lands north of the reservoir project to "protect the watershed supplying the reservoir."[40]

These conservation interests were opposed by farmers and ranchers who had their own schemes for the area. The *Vernal Express* carried several edi-

[35][Swendsen] to Gifford Pinchot, December 9, 1904, SWC.

[36]H. N. Savage to G. L. Swendsen, May 12, 1905, SWC.

[37]Proclamation 2-22-1897, 29 *Stat.* 895.

[38]Charles S. Peterson, "Albert F. Potter's Wasatch Survey, 1902: A Beginning for Public Management of Natural Resources in Utah," *Utah Historical Quarterly* 29 (1971): 238–53.

[39]Swendsen to Chief Engineer, Reclamation Service, December 22, 1904, SWC; C. F. Larrabee to Secretary of Interior, April 10, 1905, LR RG75 NA; Swendsen to Pinchot, May 12, 1905, SWC. At one point Swendsen suggested that the Strawberry Reservoir be made part of the forest reserve, thereby removing it from the reservation but reserving it from public domain. That scheme failed, for a legitimate evaluation of that brush area of few trees could not be deemed forest land. However, the Forest Service did finally support the schemes of the Reclamation Service. Grace Overton to George L. Swendsen, May 20, 1905, SWC.

[40]U.S., Congress, House, *Uinta National Forest, Utah, House Report no. 1633,* 67th Cong., 4th sess. (February 17, 1923), p. 2.

torials during the next years expressing the opposition of Basin farmers who anticipated the opening of the reservation as affording homestead sites:

> . . . there is a scheme on foot by which the people of Utah County propose to use the Strawberry Valley as a huge reservoir, to store the waters of the Strawberry River with which to irrigate the lands of Utah County.
>
> In view of the fact that there are thousands of acres of available land along the Strawberry and Duchesne Rivers which can be irrigated by this same water, and where it naturally belongs, we cannot help but admire the supreme affrontary with which our friends over the range set about apropriating something to which they have no moral right in the world. . . . [41]

On March 28, 1905, a mass meeting was held in Vernal to protest the Strawberry project. Participants declared:

> . . . that all of the water of said streams is necessary for the reclamation and development of the arable land of the reservation, including land allotted to the Indians as well as land soon to be opened for the occupation of actual settlers.[42]

Ranchers were also concerned about the future uses of the Strawberry area. Thousands of cattle and sheep seasonally grazed, legally and illegally there. Babb had commented in his 1902 report that the altitude of the land "is rather high for general agricultural purposes, but the land is splendidly adapted to grazing."[43] An act of Congress in June 1897 had given the federal government the legal authority to administer grazing on public lands. But many ranchers protested the increasing regulation of the land to prevent overgrazing and to protect its other uses, and confrontations between ranchers and forestry personnel occurred.[44] The ranchers received assurances that grazing permits for the forest lands and other ranges would be available after the opening of the reservation. In fact, 60,160 acres of grazing land in the Strawberry Valley were leased to ranchers from the project's beginning in 1905 until 1916 when the land became part of the project, by which time 8,000 of those acres were covered by the waters of the Strawberry Reservoir.[45]

The Strawberry project was supported by "about 1,200 citizens owning more than 26,000 acres of land in the vicinity of Spanish Fork," the influential Sen. Reed Smoot, and the maneuverings of George L. Swendsen. Within two years of the preliminary surveys the project was recommended by the Reclamation Board of Engineers and was authorized by the secretary of the interior on December 15, 1905.[46]

[41]*Vernal Express,* September 5, 1903.

[42]Charles Wolcott to Secretary of Interior, May 6, 1905, LR RG75 NA.

[43]*House Document no. 671* (1902), p. 15

[44]Charles DeMoisy, Jr., "Some Early History of the Uinta National Forest," (n.d.), MS A-625, Utah State Historical Society.

[45]U.S., Department of the Interior, Bureau of Reclamation, *Fifteenth Annual Report, 1915–1916* (Washington, D.C., 1916), p. 419.

[46]Bureau of Reclamation, *Ninth Annual Report, 1909–1910,* p. 268.

The rights of the Utes to the land and water of the Strawberry area and their opposition to the opening of the reservation to non-Indians were ignored. The Indian Service, guided by the long-standing policy of assimilating the Indians into the dominant Anglo society, acted—frequently without protest—to accommodate the interests and influences of non-Indians. The service, usually powerless to do otherwise, rarely acted to protect the interests and rights of the Indians other than with rhetoric or delaying tactics. Even the "friends of the Indians" during this era of reform agitation supported the allotment mechanism for opening reservations as the only means by which Indians could protect themselves from the rapaciousness of whites and the best means by which Indians could be "Americanized"—by breaking up the tribally owned reservations into individually owned plots of land.

Private and federal interests anxious for the opening of the Uintah Reservation secured a series of laws and proclamations that allotted plots of land to individual Indians; reserved certain lands to the tribe, to various federal agencies, and to other concerns; and opened the rest to homestead and claim. The chronology, the changes in rhetoric, the accompanying debates, correspondence, and negotiations of this legislation clearly demonstrate the jockeying of various non-Indian interests and the ignoring of Ute interests.

The sequence by which lands for the Strawberry Valley Project were secured included: (1) reserving the land in March 1905 "to conserve the water supply for the Indians or for general agricultural development," (2) withdrawing the lands in August 1905 "for irrigation works" under the Reclamation Act of 1902, and (3) extinguishing in 1910 the "right, title, and interest" of the Utes to the lands. The Utes, like other noncitizen Indians, lacked influential advocates. Inexperienced in power politics, they were unable to affect this legislation and their concomitant economic security and sociopolitical independence. Despite years of protest, which included a desperate journey to join the Sioux in South Dakota,"[47] the Uintah Reservation was opened and the Strawberry Valley was taken to serve the needs and wishes of non-Indians.

Acting agent James F. Randlett had reported in 1894 that

> . . . the Uintahs could be led to see it would be to their best advantage to relinquish for fair compensation all of their lands west of the Duchesne River above the point of its conflux with the Strawberry River, together with a good portion of the lands south of the Strawberry.

Randlett added prophetically:

> I am of the opinion it will be unjust and it will be positively contrary to my sense of good faith on the part of the Government to ask these Indians . . . at the present time or in the near future to relinquish interest in their lands to any further extent than I have suggested. The minerals that have been or may be discovered on the remaining land are the property of

[47]Floyd A. O'Neil, "An Anguished Odyssey, the Flight of the Utes, 1905–1908," *Utah Historical Quarterly* 36 (1968): 315.

these Indians. The timber lands will eventually become very valuable and are their legal possessions; those possessions should not be taken from these Indians to their pecuniary disadvantage.[48]

In 1896 Commissioner of Indian Affairs D. M. Browning replied to a House inquiry as to why the terms of the 1894 law to treat with the Uintah Reservation Indians to relinquish all lands except allotments, had not been fulfilled:

> The Uintah Reservation is admirably adapted to Indian usage, and it seems to me that it should be kept intact for their use and occupation until it is ascertained beyond question that there is a surplus over and above the present and prospective wants of the Indians thereon and in that region of the country, when such portions as are really not needed might be disposed of for white settlement. I do not think we should be in a hurry to encroach upon it simply because it happens to be attractive to white home seekers.[49]

Councils with the Utes were held the next year by agent Beck who reported their opposition to allotment.[50]

In June 1898 an act was passed that authorized the appointment of a commission to allot lands in severalty to the Uintah Reservation Indians and to obtain "by the consent of a majority of the adult male Indians . . . all the lands within said reservation not allotted or needed for allotment as aforesaid."[51] In August 1899 the newly appointed agent, H. P. Myton, reported:

> If the consent of the Indians is necessary to be obtained in order to open the Uintah Reservation, it will be useless for Congress to pass any more laws or spend any more money for that purpose for I do not believe there is an Indian on the reservation who is willing or favors selling any part of their land. They look with favor on leasing when they can be assured that it will not bring too many white men among them and that they will not be cheated.[52]

In 1899 a bill was introduced in Congress by Senator Rawlins to set aside part of the Uintah Reservation, north of the Duchesne and east of the Lake Fork rivers, for the Utes and open the "residue," which included the Strawberry Valley, to entry and settlement. The bill was an attempt to open the reservation without negotiation and consent of the Utes. It did not pass.[53]

In May 1901 special agent Frank C. Armstrong investigated the Uintah Reservation and reported it to be "one of the finest valleys in Utah and one of the best reservations owned by any Indians." This unrealistic report echoed the attitude toward the Utes of many people—bureaucrats, settlers, and reformers alike:

[48]James F. Randlett to Secretary of Interior, December 12, 1894, LR RG75 NA.

[49]U.S., Congress, House, *Appropriations for Conducting Negotiations with Certain Indians, House Document no. 248,* 54th Cong. 1st sess. (February 18, 1896), p. 5.

[50]William Beck to Commissioner of Indian Affairs, September 1, 1897, LR RG75 NA.

[51]Act 6-4-1898, 30 *Stat.* 429.

[52]Commissioner of Indian Affairs, *Annual Report, 1899* (Washington, D.C., 1899), p. 351.

[53]U.S., Congress, Senate, Senate Bill 93, 56th Cong., 1st sess. (December 6, 1899).

> These people can readily make their own living if the Government will compel them to do it. They are bitterly opposed to selling the land but are willing to lease. Some steps should be taken to utilize the surplus which is now used only for a range for worthless ponies.[54]

This patronizing attitude served to rationalize the opening of the reservation without regard to the desires or rights of the Utes.

In December 1901 Rawlins again introduced his bill to open the reservation. This latest bill, the many applications for leasing the lands, and the number of letters and petitions from citizens urging the opening (the governor and legislature of Utah sent such a memorial to Congress in January 1902) convinced the Senate to hold hearings on the issue. Utah Rep. George Sutherland (later a senator and still later a U.S. Supreme Court justice) was particularly adamant that since no treaty with the Utes had ever been ratified, the latter were not rightful owners of the reservation, which, therefore, could be taken without negotiations and consent. Indian Commissioner Jones reported:

> . . . there is a sort of feeling among the ignorant Indians that they do not want to lose any of their land. That is all there is to it, and I think before you can get them to agree to open the reservation, you have got to use some arbitrary means to open the land.[55]

In May 1902 Congress authorized the secretary of the interior to allot land to the Uintah Reservation Indians and open the rest of the lands to entry and settlement only with the consent of the majority of the adult male Utes.[56] The consent was not forthcoming.

The 1902 act also gave special privilege to the Raven Mining Company. This and other mining companies were the most influential interests in securing this first piece of legislation to open the Uintah Reservation. President Roosevelt apparently refused initially to sign the 1902 act, because of its preference toward these mining interests and for its failure to give to the Utes grazing lands in connection with their allotments.[57]

In June 1902 a joint resolution was passed authorizing the secretary of the interior to set apart for the common use of the Indians such grazing lands as would serve their reasonable requirements. During the Congressional debates on the measure some expressed concern that reserving grazing lands to the Indians merely removed the land from homestead and permitted the secretary of the interior to lease the lands to ranchers, thereby giving them special privilege. The language of the resolution did not clarify the grazing lands as being nonirrigable.[58]

[54]This report contrasted sharply with previous reports on the aridity and rockiness of the reservation lands. Armstrong to Commissioner of Indian Affairs, May 3, 1901, LR RG75 NA.

[55]U.S., Congress, Senate, *Leasing of Indian Lands,* Senate Document 212, 57th Cong., 1st sess. (February 22, 1902), 3.

[56]Act 5-5-1902, 32 *Stat.* 263.

[57]Commissioner to H. P. Myton, June 25, 1902, LR RG75 NA.

[58]*Congressional Record,* 35 (June 16, 1902), p. 6870.

In January 1903 the arbitrary means to open the reservation without Ute consent was found in the U.S. Supreme Court decision *Lone Wolf* v. *Hitchcock* which declared that Congress had plenary authority over Indian relations and had the power to pass laws abrogating treaty stipulations.[59] On March 3, 1903, Congress appropriated funds to carry out the provisions of the act of May 1902. It also provided that if Ute consent could not be obtained by June 1, 1903, the secretary of the interior could proceed to allot lands and open the reservation without it.[60]

The 1903 act also remedied President Roosevelt's objections to the 1902 act by providing grazing lands for the Utes' livestock of not more than 250,000 acres to be located south of the Strawberry River.[61]

James McLaughlin, U.S. Indian inspector, was sent to council with the Utes and to obtain their consent to the 1903 act. He explained the opening of the reservation as a fait accompli:

> . . . until quite recently, the policy of our Government has been that Indians had unquestioned right to all lands of these respective reservations, but a recent decision of the Supreme Court of the United States is that Indians have no right to any part of their reservations except what they may require for allotments in severalty or can make proper use of.[62]

The Utes protested. Happy Jack explained:

> When the white man talks, the Indians are afraid. The Indians understand the white man pretty well. That is the reason they are talking so. When the Indians take their land in allotments, they will lose everything they have. That will not be good. After they lose everything they will be poor. . . . [T]hese white men do not like the Indians anyway.[63]

Charley Mack commented:

> Before they passed such a law, someone ought to have come here and spoken to the Indians first. That is the reason the Indians are so scared—it has come so sudden. They were not expecting anything like this. . . . We are done for. We are afraid of the Mormon people. They do not like the Indians.[64]

McLaughlin was unable to secure a majority in consent of the legislation.

Without Ute consent then, the government proceeded to open the reservation. In October 1904 acting agent C. H. Hall requested of the Indian Service that Congress be persuaded to change the location of the grazing lands to the Deep Creek area. Hall explained "that the indians [*sic*] should

[60]Act 3-3-1903, 32 *Stat.* 997.

[61]Ibid.

[62]Minutes of Council held at Uinta Agency, Whiterocks, Utah, May 18–29, 1903, LR RG75 NA.

[63]Ibid., p. 59.

[64]Ibid., p. 68.

have the best grazing land. That portion of the Reservation south of the Strawberry is not the best, and is only suitable for a winter range."[65]

Hall was, by this time, well aware of reclamation plans to "divert water from the upper Duchesne River, Red Creek, Currant Creek, and Strawberry Creeks across the divide to the district of Provo and other hydrographic works."[66] Whether this knowledge prompted his suggestion to switch the location of the grazing lands is not documented. Hall does seem to have been genuinely concerned about the water rights of the Utes and convinced that one way to protect those rights was by having the "grazing and timber land taken in the headwaters and a goodly portion of the streams upon which they [the allotted Utes] will depend for water."[67]

By the end of 1904 the procedures for making allotments on the Uintah Reservation had still not been implemented. Congress had included in the 1904 Indian Appropriations Act a provision extending the time for opening the unallotted lands to public entry to March 10, 1905.[68]

George L. Swendsen began a barrage of letters to the Reclamation Service, the Forest Service, and the Indian Service, soliciting their support for the reservation of the Strawberry Valley as a reservoir site. He pleaded that:

> This is a very nice piece of grazing country, and will be taken up very quickly by settlers as soon as the Reservation is opened unless we can secure it in some way.[69]

In March 1905 the opening of the reservation was postponed until September 1, 1905, and the president was authorized to set lands "apart and reserve as an addition to the Uintah Forest Reserve," and to

> . . . set apart and reserve any reservoir site or other lands necessary to conserve and protect the water supply for the Indians or for general agricultural development, and may confirm such rights to water thereon as have already accrued. . . . [70]

This act repealed that part of the 1903 act that had provided for a grazing reserve for the Utes in the Strawberry Valley and reserved instead a 250,000-acre grazing area in Deep Creek.[71]

Senator Smoot was instrumental in framing the above legislation. His support of the Strawberry Valley Project is evident in hearings held on the legislation in February 1905.

> SENATOR SMOOT: I want the right of mineral locations on these [lands] preserved, and I want also the water we wish taken down into Wahsatch [*sic*] County preserved.

[65]C. H. Hall to Commissioner of Indian Affairs, October 17, 1904, LR RG75 NA.
[66]C. H. Hall to Tonner, August 3, 1904, SWC.
[67]C. H. Hall to Commissioner, October 17, 1904.
[68]Act 4-21-1904, 33 *Stat.* 207.
[69][Swendsen] to U.S. Reclamation Service, December 22, 1904, SWC.
[70]Act 3-3-1905, 33 *Stat.* 1069.
[71]Ibid.

MR. PINCHOT: The trouble is that this is treated as Indian land.

THE CHAIRMAN: About this joint resolution [SR 100]. . . .

SENATOR SMOOT: It is for the withdrawal of certain sections of land there for the purpose of a reservoir in the Strawberry Valley, as recommended by Mr. Newell. . . . It is on an Indian reservation and we want a resolution to provide for it.

THE CHAIRMAN: You want a reservoir up in the timber land?

SENATOR SMOOT: No; it will be down low in the Strawberry Valley. . . .

SENATOR KEARNS: I would prefer not to load up the bill. I would like to cut out all the House amendments. If Mr. Newell recommends the withdrawal of the reservoir site I would consent to that, but I would like to see the reservation opened at the date set in the last act—in March. . . . [72]

Pursuant to the 1905 act, President Roosevelt issued a proclamation on July 14, 1905, setting the opening of the Uintah Reservation for August 28, 1905.[73] On August 3, 1905, the president withdrew 200,633 acres from disposal, some for agricultural purposes, some for a "reservoir site necessary to conserve the water supply for the Indians, or for general agricultural development." The reservoir site so designated was that of the Strawberry Valley Project.[74]

However, the listing of the reserved lands under "agricultural" and "reservoir" caused some confusion. The acting secretary of the interior, Thomas Ryan, explained:

> At the time this matter was considered by the Department it was understood that both lists were intended only for the conservation of the water supply for the two purposes named, and did not embrace the lands under those headed 'agricultural' that were only susceptible of reclamation.[75]

Ryan further explained that 54,886 acres had previously been reserved as an addition to the Uinta Forest and that the 50,440 acres reserved under the heading "agricultural" were not needed to conserve the water supply, and, therefore, their reservation was not authorized under the act of March 3, 1905.[76]

The matter was resolved in a presidential proclamation dated August 14, 1905, that specifically reserved as a reservoir site the land proposed for the Strawberry Valley Project.[77] On December 15, 1905, the project was approved by the secretary of the interior on the condition that:

> . . . all of the complications involved be adjusted, including all conflicts that may exist in regard to water rights; that a sufficient acreage be pledged

[72]U.S., Congress, Senate, *Indian Appropriation Bill Hearings* before the Subcommittee of the Committee on Indian Affairs of the Senate, 58th Cong., 3d sess. (January 28 to February 13, 1905), p. 26.

[73]Proclamation 7-14-1905, 34 *Stat.* 3119.

[74]Proclamation 8-3-1905, 34 *Stat.* 3142.

[75]Thomas Ryan to Director of Geological Survey, August 10, 1905, Ute Files, American West Center, University of Utah, Salt Lake City.

[76]Ibid.

[77]Proclamation 8-14-1906, 34 *Stat.* 3144.

to secure the return to the reclamation fund of the cost of construction and that a clean-cut feasible reclamation project, free from all complications or difficulties of any kind or character, be secured before a dollar is spent in construction.[78]

On March 6, 1906, construction work was authorized to be commenced by force account. There was one complication. The lands embraced by the project had been reserved "to conserve the water supply for the Indians or for general agricultural development." The land so reserved was "situated in the Uintah Indian Reservation,"[79] and the Utes were entitled to the benefits from the land. However, the Strawberry project was not in the irrigation scheme of the Indian Office[80] which had taken few steps to administer the lands. Therefore, the Reclamation Service was left free to proceed with the project. The Utes seem not to have been consulted in any regard.

In 1907 a question arose as to the liability of the Reclamation Service to pay the Utes rent for the use of the Strawberry lands. Approximately 51,840 acres of land in the project were being leased for grazing. The proceeds were claimed by the Indian Office for the Utes. The Strawberry Water Users Association protested this claim as denying them revenue by which they could repay the cost of the project.[81]

In 1910 Senator Sutherland introduced a bill "making available certain lands [the Strawberry Valley] on the former Uintah Indian Reservation under the reclamation act." The bill would have extinguished the right of the Utes to the lands upon payment of $1.25 per acre. This bill did not pass.[82]

However, when the Indian appropriations bill for the fiscal year 1911 reached the Senate in April 1910, an amendment was attached to it that embodied the Sutherland bill:

All right, title, and interest of the Indians in the said lands are hereby extinguished, and the title, management, and control thereof shall pass to the owners of the lands irrigated from said project whenever the management and operation of the irrigation works shall so pass under the terms of the reclamation act.[83]

The Utes were paid $1.25 per acre for 56,858.51 acres in five annual installment payments totaling $71,085.65. The payments were made to the Indian Office which then used the money as it saw fit for the "benefit" of the Utes.[84]

The 1910 act generated some controversy among the users of the Strawberry Valley. By 1914 the sheep and cattle owners had organized an effort

[78]Bureau of Reclamation, *Ninth Annual Report, 1909–1910*, pp. 268–69.

[79]U.S., Department of the Interior, Commissioner of Indian Affairs, *Annual Report, 1905* (Washington, D.C., 1905), p. 175.

[80]U.S., Congress, House, *House Report no. 1633* (1923), p. 2.

[81]Larabee to Secretary of Interior, May 6, 1905, LR RG75 NA.

[82]U.S., Congress, Senate, *Making Available Certain Lands on Former Uinta Indian Reservations, Senate Report no. 219*, 61st Cong., 2d sess. (February 14, 1910).

[83]Act 4-4-1910, 36 *Stat.* 285; *Congressional Record*, 45 (February 14, 1910), p. 283.

[84]John T. Lant to Franklin K. Lane, December 7, 1914, SWC.

to repeal or amend the act, protesting that section which transferred title to the owners of the lands irrigated by the project. The controversy continued through the early 1920s. In 1923, in an effort to clearly define title of the project to the United States, a bill was introduced to add the lands to the Uinta National Forest. The bill did not pass.[85] The water users assumed control of the project in 1926.[86]

There is no indication that the Utes were involved in any of the actions taken to extinguish their title to the Strawberry Valley. It appears that they were not informed about most of the dealings involving the Uintah Reservation lands. Despite continuing protest of the Utes, both individually and through their leaders, they were powerless to prevent the transfer of title of their lands from themselves to non-Utes.

In 1912 James McLaughlin, who had attempted unsuccessfully in 1903 to secure the consent of the Utes to the opening of their reservation, made an inspection of conditions there. His unpublished observations are a poignant description of the effects on the Utes of the loss of their lands:

> They feel that against their wishes one million acres of land was taken from them and opened to settlement, and that another million was placed in a forest reserve with the understanding they were to receive the revenue until 1920. They have witnessed the settler on the ceded lands improve his claim with timber cut from the forest reserve under a free use permit. They have been helpless to prevent the cattle and sheep of the white men from crossing their exclusive range of 250,000 acres to reach the forest ranges for which the white man pays but no part of which goes to reimburse the Indians, and they realize that greater returns are being derived from the reserved lands than they can ultimately receive from the vestige of the reservation that was allotted them. They know that every dollar received from the sale of the ceded lands has been expended to conserve the water of the former reservation, which will in all probability be appropriated by their white neighbors. Jurisdiction of their rights has been transferred from Federal to State control and they live in a community where they must witness the inexorable march of progress and pay for it the inevitable price of the weaker people.
>
> It is difficult to believe that the rights of these Indians have been sacrificed to meet the demands of local interests, but it is more difficult, after following step by step the administration of their affairs, to reach any other conclusion.[87]

The Strawberry Valley Project, which permitted the development of additional farm lands in Utah county, furnished electric power to local towns, stimulated population and industrial growth, and provided recreational facilities used by thousands of people, has been deemed "successful."[88] But

[85]*House Report no. 1633*, p. 3.

[86]Alexander, "Strawberry Valley Project," p. 295.

[87]"Conditions on Uinta Indian Reservation, Utah," Report of E. P. Holcombe and James McLaughlin, September 24, 1912, LR RG75 NA. See also the published report in U.S. Congress, House, *Conditions on Uinta Indian Reservation, Utah, House Document no. 892*, 62d Cong., 2d sess. (July 27, 1912).

[88]Alexander, "Strawberry Valley Project," p. 304.

this success was built on the expropriation of Indian lands without Indian consent, on the exploitation of Indian resources, both human and material, and on the ethnocentrism that evaluated Indian ways and systems as inferior. The Strawberry Valley Project for all its success in Anglo terms is part of the legacy of ignoble dealings with the American Indians.

*

Beyond the Spotlight: The Red Scare in Utah

ANDREW HUNT

The immediate period following World War I was a time of widespread, hysterical fear throughout the United States that the country was in extreme danger from radical elements—usually presumed to be foreign-dominated. The hysteria culminated in the arrest of several thousand suspected radicals throughout the country in the spring of 1920 and the widespread violation of civil liberties. This article examines what happened in Utah at the time. The story is a distressing one. Utah's Red Scare set a disturbing precedent and left an ugly legacy, including wholesale violations of constitutional rights, while it added fuel for the fires of nativism and intolerance. The Utah State Legislature passed laws that blatantly violated individual civil liberties, but their actions evoked little public outcry. With little public resistance, the Salt Lake City police department openly spied on dissenters. Groups of businessmen systematically stripped labor unions of their power, and ideas and beliefs considered threatening to the status quo were regarded as un-American. Ironically, this followed a war perceived to be a crusade to defeat totalitarianism and to encourage the growth of democracy. A war the American people were asked to fight to make the world "safe for democracy" led to the suppression of their own democratic rights.

Andrew Hunt, "Beyond the Spotlight: The Red Scare in Utah," *Utah Historical Quarterly* 61 (Fall 1993): 357–80. Reprinted by permission of the publisher and the author.

Andrew Hunt is a graduate student in United States history at the University of Utah.

AS THE UNITED STATES BEGAN TO HEAL from the excesses of the McCarthy era during the mid-1950s, a handful of historians turned their attention to the Red Scare of 1919. In studying this turbulent period, they sought to identify parallels between the post–World War I Red Scare and the anticommunism of the Cold War era. Their works chronicled the significant events, the flash points, that occurred. They focused on the thirty bombs sent to leaders and prominent citizens during the spring of 1919, general strikes in Seattle and Winnipeg, May Day riots in New York and Cleveland, the formation of domestic Communist parties, and the rise of nativist beliefs that swept much of the nation. Finally, researchers traced these events to the climax of the Red Scare: the Justice Department raids directed against thousands of suspected radicals in cities across the country in January 1920.[1]

Despite the dearth of secondary sources on the subject prior to the 1950s, two historians produced notable works about the Red Scare within a few years of each other. The first was Robert K. Murray's *The Red Scare: A Study of National Hysteria, 1919–1920* (1955), which historians have traditionally regarded as the premier general history on the subject. The second book, Stanley Coben's biography, *A. Mitchell Palmer: Politician* (1963), appeared eight years later.

While the two books represented significant, exhaustively researched contributions, the extent of the Red Scare has not yet been fully explored. Both Murray and Coben present the Red Scare as being broad in scope and creating an atmosphere of "intense public suspicion and fear."[2] For Murray this was a period when "the national mind ultimately succumbed to hysteria," characterized by "restrictive legislation, . . . [and] mob violence."[3] Although Coben is less dramatic than Murray, he raises the theme of nationwide hysteria throughout his work. He writes that during the Red Scare, there existed a "deeply rooted fear . . . that America stood on the brink of catastrophe."[4] According to Coben, "the xenophobia common in America before the war was greatly exacerbated," resulting in "widespread popular hostility toward radicals" and "a nativistic hostility that swept the land."[5]

Historians such as Murray and Coben are, to some extent, guilty of analyzing and describing abstract wholes based on selectively chosen accounts of significant events, individuals, and pieces of legislation. They assume a unity of society based on a cluster of specific instances. In doing so they run the risk of exaggerating the magnitude of the 1919 Red Scare.

What was the scope of the Red Scare outside of Murray's or Coben's spotlight? To what degree did authorities persecute radicals in areas where

[1]For example, earlier works include Louis F. Post, *The Deportations Delirium of 1920* (Chicago: Charles H. Kerr and Company, 1923); Frederick Lewis Allen, *Only Yesterday: An Informal History of the 1920s* (New York: Harper and Brothers, 1931); Robert Dunn, ed. *The Palmer Raids* (New York: International Publishers, 1948); and Max Lowenthal, *The Federal Bureau of Investigation* (New York: William Sloane Associates, 1950). The most notable later works are Robert K. Murray, *The Red Scare: A Study of National Hysteria, 1919–1920* (New York: McGraw-Hill, 1955); and Stanley Coben, *A. Mitchell Palmer: Politician* (New York: Columbia University Press, 1963).

[2]Murray, *The Red Scare,* p. 18.

[3]Ibid., p. 280.

[4]Coben, *A. Mitchell Palmer,* p. 212.

[5]Ibid., pp. 198, 203, 245.

fears of revolution were less dramatic? As both authors point out, nativism played a big role in the virulent anticommunism of the era. How widespread was nativism in regions with more homogeneous populations? To answer these questions, this article will focus upon Utah, particularly Salt Lake City. Does Utah fit within the standard framework? Were the men and women of Salt Lake City caught up in the hysteria? What light do local moods, perceptions, and behaviors shed upon the Red Scare of 1919?

By 1919 nearly half of Utah's 450,000 residents lived in the state's burgeoning cities. Nestled in fertile valleys west of the Wasatch Mountain range in northern Utah, the two largest cities in the state, Salt Lake City and Ogden, had populations of 118,110 and 32,804 respectively.[6] With its rising skyline, growing population, and expanding neighborhoods, Salt Lake City was beginning to resemble a bustling urban center rather than a Mormon frontier settlement. The largest church in Utah was the Church of Jesus Christ of Latter-day Saints, with approximately 60 percent of the state's inhabitants as members. Nevertheless, the non-Mormon population in the state had grown dramatically since the 1870s.[7] In 1916 Utahns elected the state's first non-Mormon governor, Simon Bamberger, a Jew and a staunch progressive. During World War I there were intense displays of patriotic fervor throughout Utah, with Liberty Gardens springing up across the state, and Liberty Bond drives raising large contributions from Utahns. When the war was over Utah's veterans returned to crowded celebrations in Salt Lake City.[8]

Yet, within months after the armistice of November 1918, the postwar economic recession that ravaged the United States began to take a heavy toll on Utah. The recession hit the state's farms the hardest, with prices of wheat declining after the war from $3.50 a bushel to 98 cents in 1921. The state's large mineral industry did not fare much better. In 1919 Utah's total production of lead, zinc, silver, copper, and gold plummeted 54 percent below the previous year's level. The Utah Copper Company closed its mills, the Bingham Mine laid off thousands of workers, and populations decreased dramatically in the neighboring towns of Magna and Garfield.[9] Throughout 1919 economic hardships led to strikes and labor demonstrations across the state. At the end of the year the State Industrial Commission estimated that the fourteen labor disputes that occurred in Utah had cost the state an estimated $900,000 in lost production.[10]

According to historian Robert K. Murray, the economic hardships of 1919 coupled with postwar demobilization led to widespread "psychologi-

[6]U.S., Bureau of Census, *Fourteenth Census of the United States: 1920, Population: Utah* (Bulletin), p. 1.

[7]Dean L. May, *Utah: A People's History* (Salt Lake City, University of Utah Press, 1987), pp. 170–71.

[8]Ibid.

[9]Ibid., p. 173

[10]Karl Alwin Elling, "The History of Organized Labor in Utah" (Master's thesis, University of Utah, 1962), p. 103.

cal torment and confusion." He argues that, faced with the example of the Bolshevik revolution in Russia of 1917 and widespread postwar political unrest throughout Europe, most Americans rallied behind the "prevailing drive for normalcy" that fostered a "confusing, intolerant, and irresponsible atmosphere."[11] For Murray, the quest for an illusory "normalcy" created tension in the minds of Americans. He contends that much of the confusion plaguing Americans was channeled into attacks against nonconformists, pacifists, and Communists.[12]

To a visitor to Salt Lake City in the early months of 1919 it would have appeared that Murray's thesis was manifesting itself in the corridors of the state's legislature. In February state representatives introduced two bills intended to curb radical activities in Utah. The first, House Bill 28, known as the Red Flag Bill, was a broadly worded piece of legislation that prohibited the "disloyal display of the red flag or any other emblem of anarchy" in Utah. J. E. Cardon, a businessman who introduced the bill the day after a massive general strike began in Seattle, Washington, referred to the law as "a warning to agitators that there is no place for them in this state." The Red Flag Bill passed by a healthy majority of two-to-one, with only ten representatives voting against it.[13]

The following day saw the introduction of a second piece of restrictive legislation, the Sabotage Bill, on the floor of the house. The purpose of the bill was to establish a "strong anti-syndicalism and sabotage law prohibiting the advocacy, teaching, or suggestion of same" and "prohibiting assemblages for such teachings or suggestions, and prohibiting the use of any building for such assemblages."[14] As was the case with the Red Flag Bill, prolabor representatives like Fred Morris and Robert Currie, both union members and representatives from the Salt Lake Federation of Labor, offered rousing condemnations of the Sabotage Bill. Morris, a member of the Typographical Union, Local 115, charged that such bills "emanate from a class who fear that the despotism which they are about to impose upon laboring people will cause a revolt." Currie, a leader in the Salt Lake Carpenter's Union, took a more moderate approach, arguing against the bill from a civil libertarian perspective. In spite of their pleas, representatives overwhelmingly supported the Sabotage Bill, with 24 voting for the measure and 5 opposing it.[15]

Making it a felony to advocate sabotage or syndicalism was clearly aimed at the militant Industrial Workers of the World. Founded in 1905, the IWW, a radical labor union led by native Utahn William D. Haywood, maintained offices in Salt Lake City. The organization enjoyed some success in

[11]Murray, *The Red Scare*, pp. 3–17

[12]Ibid., p. 14.

[13]*Deseret News*, February 8, 1919.

[14]This description of the Sabotage Bill is contained in *Deseret News*, April 23, 1919.

[15]For the Red Flag Bill see *Deseret News*, February 8, 1919. On Sabotage Bill see *Salt Lake Tribune*, February 9, 1919. For Currie and Morris, see Elling, "The History of Organized Labor," pp. 12, 89, 112.

Utah's mining industry, especially after 1910, attracting members from the state's numerous squalid mining camps. Arguing that the "working class and the employing class have nothing in common," the IWW leadership advocated syndicalism—the theory that through the use of general strikes and force, workers would be able to overthrow capitalism and introduce an economic system in which trade unions would control the means of production.

Moreover, following the teachings of French syndicalist Emile Pouget, the IWW advocated the use of sabotage. The organization never offered a precise definition of the term, yet IWW newspapers trumpeted sabotage and frequently published cartoons of its symbols—the wooden shoe and the black cat. For the IWW the word carried broad connotations. Some members of the organization defined sabotage as acts of passive resistance, including "the conscious withdrawal of efficiency," jamming machines, or sending railroad freight in the wrong direction. Others viewed sabotage as "striking on the job," while a handful of members included a violent resistance in their definition. Yet, for opponents of the IWW, sabotage carried one simple definition: the violent destruction of private property.[16]

While legislators intended the Sabotage Bill to undermine the IWW, they aimed the Red Flag Bill at a newly formed organization called the Workers', Soldiers', and Sailors' Council which met for the first time in Salt Lake City in February of 1919. The purpose of the council was to act as an umbrella organization embracing representatives from various local unions and political clubs. In addition to endorsing the infant Soviet republic, the organization called for "mass action to build up a real democratic government, a government of the workers, for the workers and by the workers, to take the control of politics and industry out of the hands of big business." The council sent letters to labor unions throughout the state inviting them to join.[17]

With the passage of the Red Flag and Sabotage bills, conservative legislators sought to suppress organizations like the IWW and the Workers', Soldiers', and Sailors' Council. Yet once the laws were passed, they were never stringently enforced. Under the sabotage law, there were but two known arrests. Police jailed two immigrants in Carbon County on October 31, charging them with "distributing IWW literature and making anarchistic threats." Officials from the Justice Department interrogated the two men, then turned them over to the Department of Immigration for deportation.[18] Salt Lake City Mayor W. Mont Ferry used the sabotage law to prohibit the IWW from holding its annual national convention in the city on June 25.

[16]For a good discussion of the IWW's definition of sabotage see *Roughneck: The Life and Times of Big Bill Haywood* by Peter Carlson (New York: W. W. Norton & Co., 1983), pp. 196–97.

[17]The "Preamble, Resolutions, and Plan of Action" of the Workers', Soldiers', and Sailors' Council is contained in the records of the Utah State Federation of Labor and Utah State Industrial Union Council at Western Americana, Marriott Library, University of Utah, Salt Lake City.

[18]*Deseret News*, November 1, 1919.

Ferry consulted with city, county, state, and federal officials and then announced: "I am determined to enforce this law to the utmost limit and protect our community from anarchistic and revolutionary teachings."[19] Ferry and his advisors ultimately persuaded IWW leaders to select another site for their convention. Curiously, authorities made no attempt to use the sabotage law to repress or shut down the state IWW offices in downtown Salt Lake City.[20] When Ralph Chaplin, editor of the IWW newspaper *Solidarity*, came to Salt Lake City in November, he spoke to an audience of 200 people with no interference from the police.[21]

The police enforced the red flag law even less rigorously than its anti-sabotage counterpart. No known arrests were made under the law in spite of the efforts of law enforcement officials to scrutinize local radical organizations. Beginning in February, plainclothes officers from the Salt Lake City Police Department began attending the weekly meetings of the Workers', Soldiers', and Sailors' Council to monitor the group's activities. Salt Lake City Police Chief J. Parley White called the council a "strictly bolshevist organization," and advised officers investigating the organization "to guard against an emergency in the present state of social unrest." Police officers maintained a close watch over the council until November 1919, but a frustrated Chief White eventually conceded that all meetings were "held in an orderly manner."[22]

That did not deter law enforcement officials from looking for other reasons to arrest council members under the red flag law. In April a flyer appeared in the streets of Salt Lake City announcing a council-sponsored May Day celebration. The flyer, printed in red ink, announced, "Grand International May Day Mass Meeting under the auspices of the Workers', Soldiers', and Sailors' Council. Subject of Speakers to be 'The Class Struggle.'" An alarmed Chief White charged that because they were printed in red ink, the circulars violated the state's red flag law. He urged authorities to treat the distribution of the flyers as a criminal act. But state officials were reluctant to accept Chief White's broad interpretation of the red flag law, and police made no arrests.[23]

Thus, the months leading up to April 1919 saw little hysteria in the state. Utahns from Logan to St. George seemed absorbed in affairs of immediate local interest rather than the "specter of international bolshevism." Events like the Soviet revolution or the general strike in Seattle were too distant and seemed to have no impact on their lives. Yet the shattering events of May 1 would temporarily interrupt the stillness.

[19]*Deseret News,* April 23, 1919.

[20]*Deseret News,* November 19, 1919.

[21]Elling, "The History of Organized Labor," p. 55.

[22]*Deseret News,* November 1, 1919. Although police records pertaining to this matter no longer exist, throughout 1919 there are newspaper accounts of plainclothes police officers attending meetings of the Workers', Soldiers', and Sailors' Council. Other accounts will be noted later.

[23]*Deseret News,* April 29, 1919.

On the morning of May 1 postal carrier Fred Libby delivered a small package to the Judge Building in downtown Salt Lake City. He handled the package in the same manner he dealt with the rest of his mail, calmly delivering it to the sixth-floor offices of attorney Frank K. Nebeker. It was an eight-inch-long narrow box weighing eleven ounces, wrapped in manila paper, with a label pasted to it bearing the address of Gimbel Brothers, a department store in New York City. Stamped on one side of the package were the words "Sample—Novelty," directly above the figure of an old man carrying a pack and holding a staff in his left hand. The unsuspecting postal carrier had no idea that the contents of the box consisted of a wooden tube filled with an acid detonator and a high explosive.[24] Two days earlier Nebeker had left for Chicago on a business trip. When his stenographer, Norma Best, signed for the package she was "on her guard" as a result of reading front-page newspaper accounts of prominent officials in New York City and Washington, D.C., receiving similar packages. In fact, Best later expressed surprise that Nebeker had not received any bomb threats earlier. This particular package piqued her attention because the illustration of the man on the box reminded her of an IWW poem titled "Wail of the Bindle Stiff."[25]

A year earlier, as assistant attorney general of the United States, Frank Nebeker had gained fame as the zealous prosecutor in the case of *U.S.* v. *William D. Haywood, et al.* In that case he had successfully prosecuted a hundred members of the IWW who were accused of violating a number of laws, including the Espionage Act of 1917. Nebeker argued the case before federal Judge Kenesaw Mountain Landis and ultimately convinced the jury that IWW leaders had participated in a conspiracy to sabotage the war effort. The jury deliberated for less than an hour before handing down a blanket guilty verdict giving prison sentences to all of the defendants. One year later, when Nebeker was notified in Chicago that a bomb had been sent to his Salt Lake City office, his only reply was a brief telegram: "If I was selected to receive one of the bombs, then the IWW organization is behind it."[26]

Frank Nebeker was not the only prominent Utahn to receive a bomb in the mail on May 1. Later in the day postal authorities in Ogden, acting on orders from the U.S. postmaster, intercepted a bomb en route to the Salt Lake City offices of U.S. Sen. William H. King. A Democrat, King was one of the most virulently antilabor and anti-Communist politicians in Congress. He advocated the passage of local restrictive laws as a means of stifling dissent, and his speeches often emphasized the threat of radicalism emanating from the remnants of the Seattle general strike. King also received attention in the national press as a member of a Senate committee investi-

[24]For descriptions of the so-called infernal machines see *Salt Lake Tribune,* May 2, 1919, and Murray, *The Red Scare,* pp. 70–71.

[25]*Salt Lake Tribune,* May 2, 1919.

[26]For the best account of Frank Nebeker's role in *The U.S.* v. *William D. Haywood, et al.,* see Carlson, *Roughneck,* pp. 265–82. For Nebeker's comments on the bomb see *Salt Lake Tribune,* May 2, 1919.

gating methods of curbing radical propaganda. Like the bomb sent to Nebeker, the device intended for King was wrapped in Gimbel's paper. Within days after postal clerks announced the discovery of the bomb, King prepared a bill making it illegal to transport bombs in interstate commerce and a capital offense to belong to an organization advocating violent overthrow of the United States government.[27]

Authorities discovered a third bomb mailed to U. S. Sen. Reed Smoot. A conservative Republican and apostle in the Church of Jesus Christ of Latter-day Saints, Smoot was a puzzling choice to receive a bomb. He had never been as outspoken as King or Nebeker, and he showed very little concern about the Soviet revolution or the Seattle general strike. Nevertheless, postal inspectors notified Ogden postmaster W. W. Browning to watch for suspicious packages addressed to Smoot. The following day authorities discovered that the bomb intended for Smoot had never reached Salt Lake City. It was returned to Gimbel's Department Store in New York City for additional postage where it was confiscated by Justice Department agents. Authorities never apprehended the culprit or culprits responsible for the mail bombs.[28]

Nebeker, King, and Smoot were among thirty-six recipients of May Day bombs across the country. Other prominent bomb recipients included Oliver Wendell Holmes, Jr., associate justice of the Supreme Court, Postmaster General Albert S. Burleson, Judge Landis, Attorney General A. Mitchell Palmer, John D. Rockefeller, J. P. Morgan, and Secretary of Labor William B. Wilson. Bomb blasts injured only two people, the wife and maid of former Georgia senator Thomas Hardwick. Yet the bomb scare created blazing headlines in newspapers across the country.[29]

The local press echoed the anti-Bolshevik sentiments of the rest of the mainstream media in the United States. "Death to the Terrorists" screamed bold, block letters above an editorial in the May 1 *Deseret News.* "The country's history records no similar instance of widespread diabolism," the editorial began. "It is almost unbelievable that the human mind can descend to the depravity that this wretched plot bespeaks." The *Salt Lake Tribune* used the incident to call for more legislation to curb bolshevism, referring to the bombs as the product of the "unrestrained menace" of free speech. Perhaps the most succinct response came from the editor of the *Ogden Examiner,* who stated that "red-blooded Americans have no use for the 'Red,' whether it is a red flag, a red badge, a red poem, or any other insignia which is anti-American." Ironically, the *Salt Lake Herald,* an otherwise conservative publication, was the only daily newspaper to suggest that the packages were likely the creation of a lone maniac.[30]

[27]Murray, *The Red Scare,* pp. 65, 71, 80, 83, 95, 232; *Salt Lake Tribune,* May 2, 1919.

[28]*Deseret News,* May 1, 1919.

[29]Murray, *The Red Scare,* pp. 70–71.

[30]See *Deseret News,* May 1, 1919; *Salt Lake Tribune,* May 3, 1919; *Ogden Examiner,* May 3, 1919; *Salt Lake Herald,* May 2, 1919.

The May Day bomb scare also stirred conservative groups in Utah. A month after the incident the Elks Club held its annual state convention in Ogden, with its theme "The Elks vs. Anarchy." Elks president A. R. Diblee began the meeting by praising the record attendance of members from every chapter in Utah, then announced that the organization "is determined to fight against anarchy and bolshevism, while counter-battling for true-blue Americanism." The Utah Kiwanis Club followed the Elks' example by featuring bomb recipient Frank Nebeker as the keynote speaker at its July 3 gathering. Nebeker told the Kiwanis Club that "radicalism is not confined to the long-haired soap-box orator" and warned that "the spread of the doctrine demanding industrial revolution is far more serious than has been admitted." Salt Lake Rotary Club president James W. Collins, speaking before a club luncheon in the Hotel Utah in November, expressed concern about what he perceived to be a growing IWW threat in the mining districts of eastern Utah. He called on state and federal authorities to rid Utah of the "cancerous infection" of the IWW. Eventually, the state American Legion joined the crusade. State Commander Hamilton Gardiner, writing in the Legion's December 1919 bulletin, called on the 101 posts in Utah to campaign for "Americanism." Gardiner urged officials to pass legislation banning radical meetings and encouraged Legion posts to appoint officers from each chapter to monitor local radicals.[31]

Yet, the overall calm that prevailed in Salt Lake City on May 1, 1919, contrasts with Robert K. Murray's assertion that it was a day when "American radicals put on a colossal show," and "numerous riots arising from radical May Day celebrations" erupted. No sizable riots or demonstrations occurred in Salt Lake City, Ogden, or Provo on May 1. Because most accounts of the local bomb scare (with the exception of the *Deseret News*) appeared on May 2, residents of cities such as Provo, Ogden, and Salt Lake City had not yet reacted to the delivery of the "infernal machines" to Nebeker, King, and Smoot.[32]

This is not to suggest that Salt Lake City was completely insulated from momentous events in Cleveland, Boston, New York City, Seattle, and other cities where May Day riots did occur. On May 1, Police Chief J. Parley White assured the public that the local police would "take precaution to suppress all bolshevist and anarchistic sentiment in Salt Lake City." White also indicated that federal authorities were monitoring the activities of local radical organizations.[33]

When the Workers', Soldiers', and Sailors' Council held its May Day celebration at the downtown Musicians' Hall, Chief White personally attended the festivities, accompanied by six plainclothes police officers. Before a crowd of 400 people, council member Bertha Bennett encouraged

[31]*Ogden Examiner*, June 7, 1919; *Deseret News*, July 4, November 19, and December 6, 1919.

[32]Murray, *The Red Scare*, pp. 73–74.

[33]*Deseret News*, May 1, 1919.

members of "the Soviet of Salt Lake" to donate money to the Bolshevik cause. She was followed by speaker R. E. Richardson, a self-proclaimed "poor tramp wobbly," who called the nationwide bomb scares "the bunk." Neither Chief White nor his colleagues attempted to halt the festivities, and no arrests were made.[34]

In other parts of the state clusters of radicals met without interference from police. At a Socialist party forum in Ogden a "few dozen people" listened as local party secretary O. A. Kennedy declared, "The working class of the world is awakening." Kennedy read a statement prepared by the Ogden chapter expressing solidarity with socialists around the world. Unlike the council celebration in Salt Lake City, there is no evidence that police agents even attended the Ogden gathering. Although the meeting was by no means a "colossal show," it serves as evidence of reluctance on the part of police to obstruct the activities of left-wing groups in Utah in 1919.[35]

Almost a month after the May Day bomb scares, a series of mysterious explosions occurred in eight cities in other states, destroying a handful of buildings and killing two individuals. Yet the June 2 bombings failed to arouse the same enthusiasm in Utah's newspapers as the May Day scare. A headline in the *Deseret News* announced "Anarchists in Nationwide Bomb Plot," while the *Ogden Examiner* carried an editorial arguing that foreign-born radicals should be "show[n] the way to their homeland" to test their ideas. Other newspapers, such as the *Salt Lake Tribune,* devoted little attention to the explosions.[36]

The traditional interpretation of the Red Scare maintains that labor unions, like the highly publicized May 1 mail bombs, played a crucial role in provoking hysteria. Coben wrote that 1919 was a "vintage year for strikes," and labor conflicts aggravated "public fear of revolution or economic disaster." Murray regarded organized labor as a "trigger mechanism" that produced "the ultimate manifestation . . . of national psychoneurosis."[37]

The activities of organized labor in Utah are inconsistent with Coben's and Murray's statements. There were strikes, demonstrations, and displays of union militancy in Utah in 1919; nevertheless, the number of strikes in Utah ranked low when compared with national figures during the period. Fourteen major labor disputes occurred in the state throughout the year, some of which, such as the Park City mining strike, lasted no longer than one or two months. Nationally, there were more than 3,600 strikes involving 4,000,000 workers. Utah's contribution to the number of strikes in 1919 was therefore relatively minor. Toward the end of the year the Utah State Industrial Commission released a report praising the state's labor leaders for their conservatism. The report concluded that "employers and em-

[34]*Salt Lake Herald,* May 2, 1919.

[35]*Ogden Examiner,* May 2, 1919.

[36]*Deseret News,* June 3, 1919; *Ogden Examiner,* June 5, 1919.

[37]Coben, *A. Mitchell Palmer,* pp. 173–74; Murray, *The Red Scare,* p. 105.

ployees generally in this state are making an honest effort to adjudicate their differences without resorting to the lockout or strike."[38]

Nevertheless, there were examples of red-baiting directed against some labor unions. A mining strike that erupted in Park City on May 6 and involved nearly 1,000 miners made headlines in local newspapers because of IWW participation. The strikers demanded a six-hour workday, a daily salary of $5.50, and an end to discrimination based on union membership. Two federal investigators and a commissioner from the Department of Labor traveled to Park City to investigate "agitation on the part of active IWW members." The Department of Justice also conducted an investigation of IWW business agent Albert W. Wells for his alleged role in instigating the strike. However, the ill-fated strike lasted only a month and a half. With their modified demands for an eight-hour workday and a daily wage of $5.15 rejected by mine owners, the Park City miners went back to work on June 21.[39]

The Park City strike proved to be the only major IWW-led strike in Utah in 1919. For the most part labor unions in Utah moved to distance themselves from Syndicalist or Communist ideas. The one exception occurred in September at the annual convention of the Utah Federation of Labor, the central body of the majority of Utah's labor unions. At the convention, UFL members voted by a three-to-one majority to endorse the newly formed Soviet government in Russia. The federation released an official resolution declaring the Soviet government to be "controlled by workers . . . in the interest of the working class," and they demanded the withdrawal of U.S. troops occupying the Soviet Union. Federation leaders stated their hostility toward the resolution, yet it passed by a vote of 49 to 13.[40]

Conservative labor spokesmen such as state representative Robert Currie feared the federation's Soviet resolution would cause a backlash in the Utah legislature against labor unions. Their concerns appeared to be justified. At the beginning of the month the Utah Associated Industries, the state's largest businessmen's association, requested that Governor Bamberger repeal a 1917 law introduced by Currie that gave unions the right to organize and picket peacefully. Bamberger immediately called for a special session of the legislature, and a group of Utah senators drafted a bill to overturn the 1917 law. When the special session convened on October 4, labor unions organized effective protests against the bill. Before the bill was even introduced 2,500 workers marched to the State Capitol to rally against its passage. One thousand shopmen from the Denver & Rio Grande and the Oregon Short Line railroads jammed the galleries of the Capitol to capacity. Both unions had declared October 4 a holiday in order to be present for the

[38]Elling, "The History of Organized Labor," p. 103; Coben, *A. Mitchell Palmer,* p. 173; *Deseret News,* December 11, 1919.

[39]Elling, "The History of Organized Labor," pp. 33–35; *Deseret News,* May 9 and June 6, 1919.

[40]*Deseret News,* September 11, 1919.

debate. Eventually, the bill was killed in the Senate by a 10 to 9 vote. Labor was victorious.[41]

The defeat of the antipicketing law undermines the thesis that by the end of 1919 antiunion groups had successfully challenged organized labor and its public support. Few labor unions in Utah lost members in 1919. A number of labor organizations, such as the Amalgamated Carpenters, the United Mine Workers, the Street and Electric Railway Employees, and the Brotherhood of Railway Carmen, flourished in 1919.[42]

According to the traditional interpretation of the Red Scare, nationwide hysteria reached a climax between November 1919 and January 1920 with the infamous Palmer Raids. Attorney General A. Mitchell Palmer organized the Justice Department sweep of foreign-born radicals. An estimated 3,000 Anarchists and Communists were arrested in cities such as New York, Chicago, Detroit, Boston, Kansas City, Portland, and Denver. In his biography of Palmer, Stanley Coben wrote that once the Palmer Raids ended "the American public was ready for a reconsideration of the Red Menace" and "the popular anxiety of 1919 and early 1920 evaporated." Similarly, Murray argued that following the Palmer Raids "anti-Red hysteria subsided almost as quickly as it had developed and . . . the nation rather rapidly regained its composure." To his credit, Murray conceded: "In the west and far-west, while raids were conducted, they were not especially significant."[43]

When the sweeps and arrests began on January 2, 1920, the Justice Department ignored Utah entirely. With the exception of a few headlines and newspaper editorials, the Palmer Raids had no impact on the state. Outside of Coben's and Murray's spotlights, Salt Lake City and its neighbors followed a dramatically different pattern from New York City, Boston, Seattle, and even Denver. It is possible to liken the Red Scare in Utah to a defective stick of dynamite. With Fourth of July speeches warning about the spread of IWW-ism, the passage of laws designed to suppress radicals, police surveillance of the Workers', Soldiers', and Sailors' Council, and a variety of other actions, conservatives attempted to light the fuse of the dynamite. It never exploded.

Clearly, federal, state, and local authorities did not see a need to crack down on Utah dissenters in 1919 and 1920.

William J. Flynn, head of the U.S. Bureau of Investigation (later the FBI), visited Salt Lake City on February 27, 1920, and explained that radicals had a much weaker presence in western states than in the east. "This is due," he explained, "to the fact that the 'reds' and 'the communists' have not found their way, to any great extent, west of the Mississippi river." Yet the feebleness of radicals in Utah during the Red Scare had little to do with their inability to find their way to Utah. Rather, it had a great deal to do

41 Elling, "The History of Organized Labor," pp. 114–15; *Deseret News,* October 4, 1919.

42 Dee Scorup, "The History of Organized Labor in Utah" (Master's thesis, University of Utah, 1935), pp. 70–158.

43 Murray, *The Red Scare,* pp. 217, 239; Coben, *A. Mitchell Palmer,* p. 236.

with a series of events that began nearly a decade before 1919.[44]

After World War I, Justice Department agents, state legislators, and law-enforcement officials saw no reason to devote their time and resources to the repression of dissenters in Utah. This was not because leaders in the state were more tolerant than their counterparts in New York City or Seattle. Sen. William King, Salt Lake City Mayor Mont Ferry, Police Chief J. Parley White, and several members of the legislature were rabidly anti-Communist. The Church of Jesus Christ of Latter-day Saints remained neutral on the issue of the Red Scare, but the church-owned newspaper *Deseret News* frequently expressed antipathy toward Communists, Socialists, and Anarchists.

Nevertheless, authorities were not threatened sufficiently to take drastic action. By 1919 radicals and militant labor organizers in Utah were too few to be regarded as a menace by authorities. However, this had not always been the case. Leftists had obtained a foothold in Utah before World War I, and although their numbers were always relatively small they had some influence on local politics. But the gradual repression of dissenters that began in 1910 and lasted until the war slowly eroded the leadership within the Utah left.

Before World War I the two major radical organizations in Utah were the Socialist party and the Industrial Workers of the World. The Socialist party first appeared in Utah in 1901 and reached its peak between 1905 and 1912. Historian John McCormick, who has exhaustively researched the Socialist party in early twentieth-century Utah, pointed out that at its height in 1911, thirty-three party members were elected in ten communities, including city councilmen, mayors, and city treasurers in such towns as Bingham, Fillmore, Salt Lake City, Cedar City, Eureka, and Mammoth. According to McCormick, many party members were so-called gas and water Socialists—progressive reformists who emphasized electoral politics and sought to work within the system. The party was especially powerful in mining areas.[45]

The IWW first made its presence in Utah known at a miners' convention in Eureka in April 1910. The Western Federation of Miners, which allied itself with the IWW, organized the event. The IWW, like the Socialist party, found much of its support in Utah's mining towns. Two months after the Eureka convention, the WFM attracted 2,000 miners to its annual outing at Lagoon. The union boasted 2,500 members in Utah during the summer of 1912, largely as a result of a huge miners strike in Bingham Canyon. The Bingham strike of 1912 ultimately ended in failure for the miners, but the IWW played a key role in instigating smaller labor disputes, such as a smelter workers' strike in Murray in 1912 and a construction workers' strike in the central Utah town of Tucker in 1912.[46]

[44]*Deseret News*, February 28, 1920.

[45]John S. McCormick, "Hornets in the Hive: Socialists in Early Twentieth-century Utah," *Utah Historical Quarterly* 50 (1982): 226–27.

[46]Gibbs M. Smith, *Joe Hill* (Salt Lake City: University of Utah Press, 1969), pp. 115–19; Elling, "The History of Organized Labor," pp. 29–32.

Despite the organizations' shared radicalism, the IWW and Socialist party in Utah were not always on good terms. The two organizations made their ambivalence toward one another known as early as 1910. Both groups frequently conducted outdoor street meetings in Salt Lake City and Ogden, a popular method of drawing sizable crowds. The large meetings prompted the Salt Lake City Police Department to ban Socialist party meetings during the summer of 1910. The Wobblies (or IWW members) responded to the ban by organizing "free speech" fights in which radical street-corner orators denounced efforts to curb free speech. One of the soap-box speeches, delivered in Liberty Park by W. J. Kerns, was broken up by soldiers under the orders of the police. The Socialist party hastily announced that Kerns was not affiliated with their organization, and party officials emphatically stated that they had nothing to do with authorizing the meeting. The party went to great lengths on a number of other occasions to dissociate itself from the IWW. Prominent Socialist party member William Knerr, who later became chairman of the State Industrial Commission, often emphasized that he had nothing to do with the union. When Knerr gave a speech during the Park City strike of 1919, he criticized miners who held IWW cards and the audience replied with boos and catcalls.[47]

Local No. 69 of the IWW in Salt Lake City retaliated against the Socialist party's criticisms by attacking the efforts of Socialists. Wobblies often referred to those party reformists who believed that gradual change could be achieved in the ballot box as "slow-cialists." For Wobblies, the solution to the ills of society was simple: direct action through strikes, demonstrations, and sabotage. They believed political action was ineffectual. "Let the workers as a class fight the bosses as a class," demanded Lee Pratt, a Salt Lake City Wobbly.[48]

After 1912 the Socialist party began to wane in Utah. McCormick partially attributed its decline to the suppression of the party by law-enforcement officials during free-speech fights in 1910 and 1912. The party also lost much of its labor support at that time. Before 1911 the Salt Lake Federation of Labor and the Utah Federation of Labor had endorsed the Socialist party on many occasions. In September 1911 the latter organization enthusiastically embraced the Socialist party and encouraged all workers to join, referring to it as "the party of the working class." However, after 1911 an increasingly conservative leadership steered the two groups away from the party. As a result, most Socialist party political candidates suffered.[49]

The IWW faced harsher repression in Utah than did the Socialists. Arrests of IWW members in Utah before World War I were common. On June 14, 1912, police arrested and jailed five Wobblies involved in organizing the Tucker strike. A few months later, on August 12, a strikebreaker named

[47]Elling, "The History of Organized Labor, pp. 36–37, 42; *Deseret News,* May 8, 1919.

[48]Smith, *Joe Hill,* p. 117.

[49]McCormick, "Hornets in the Hive," pp. 226–27; Elling, "The History of Organized Labor," pp. 109–11.

Axel Steele and a group of hired "deputies" interrupted Wobbly leader James Morgan in the middle of a speech in downtown Salt Lake City. Steele and his strikebreakers severely beat Morgan and several audience members. When the skirmish ended, police arrested Wobbly Thomas Murphy, who had shot and injured four of his assailants, charging him with intent to commit murder. Police also arrested Morgan and fined him $1,000. Charges were never filed against Steele or his hired deputies. Law-enforcement officials stepped up their efforts to repress IWW activities in Utah when they arrested twenty-one Wobblies, charging them with trespassing on an Oregon Short Line railroad car on their way to an IWW meeting in Salt Lake City. Two years later, on October 30, 1915, Maj. H. P. Myton, a city police officer, shot and killed IWW member R. J. Horton, during an argument. Judge L. R. Martineau charged Myton with voluntary manslaughter and released him on $3,500 bail.[50]

The now-legendary trial of Joe Hill, the famed Wobbly songwriter and poet, accelerated the IWW's decline in Utah. Police arrested Hill on January 13, 1914, charging him with the murder of grocer J. G. Morrison and his son. The so-called "Wobbly bard" was executed on November 19, 1915.

Hill's trial is significant inasmuch as it further undermined the IWW's presence in Utah. Most city, rural, and mining town newspapers viciously attacked Hill and applauded his execution. The Utah Federation of Labor angrily denounced the American Federation of Labor when its leader, Samuel Gompers, appealed to President Woodrow Wilson to intercede on Hill's behalf. Following Hill's execution, the State Bar Association disbarred Hill's attorney, O. N. Hilton, for critical comments he made during a funeral oration. The *Park Record* in Park City vilified Hilton: "His looks alone should debar him from the practice in the courts of Utah—to say nothing of . . . the vile epithets hurled at the state officials in his funeral oration of the murderer, Hillstrom, in Chicago recently." In retaliation, Hilton devoted most of his Hill eulogy to attacking Gov. William Spry, the Utah Supreme Court, and the "humanity of Salt Lake City in this enlightened age."[51]

The trial and execution of Joe Hill disillusioned many IWW activists. Virginia Snow Stephen, an instructor of art at the University of Utah and daughter of former Mormon church president Lorenzo Snow, devoted much of her energy to the Joe Hill Defense Committee. After Hill's execution the university fired Stephen, disclosing that the cause for her dismissal was her involvement in the Hill case. Stephen left Salt Lake City, married a former member of the IWW, and settled in California. Nationally, the IWW denounced Utah; and its songs, poems, and articles about Hill emphasized their belief that the state was a lost cause. Hill's last words to IWW leader Bill Haywood, "I don't want to be found dead in Utah," were made legendary in the Wobbly press. Ralph Chaplin, another IWW poet, declared that

[50]Smith, *Joe Hill*, pp. 115–28; Elling, "The History of Organized Labor," pp. 35–43; *Salt Lake Tribune*, October 24, 1913.

[51]Smith, *Joe Hill*, pp. 179–80, 185–86.

Hill was "murdered by authorities of the state of Utah." IWW leaders placed Hill's ashes in envelopes and sent them to locals in every state but Utah.[52]

Ultimately, the Joe Hill trial weakened the IWW in Utah. When Governor Spry threatened to "bring to bear a force" that would stop inflammatory street speaking after Hill was executed, prominent Salt Lake attorney Harper J. Dininny advised that there was no need for such drastic measures. Dininny estimated that only thirty Wobblies remained in the city, and the sheriff could "handle them with ease."[53]

The final blow to the IWW occurred during World War I. When the federal government rounded up antiwar activists for violating the Espionage Act, the IWW in Salt Lake City was a prime target. On September 6, 1917, federal authorities raided the IWW's Radical Bookshop downtown and its state headquarters in the Boyd Park Building. The government confiscated all IWW property in Salt Lake City, including the organization's records. Between 1917 and the end of the war authorities arrested nine IWW leaders in Utah, most for their involvement in antiwar activities. On September 28, 1918, police arrested Jose Roger, secretary of the local IWW and manager of the Radical Bookstore, for circulating a pamphlet calling for a general strike. They also jailed Alex Zennikos for translating Roger's pamphlet into Greek. Carl Larson, a Swedish member, was arrested in May 1918 and charged with "making seditious utterances" against the war. Finally, federal agents subpoenaed local IWW leader G. H. Perry to stand trial in Chicago with a hundred other Wobblies.[54]

So devastated was the Utah IWW in 1919 that the organization's only show of strength was the poorly organized Park City strike in May which lasted but a month and a half. The IWW also suffered at the hands of Utah's conservative labor unions, which often attacked the Wobblies. On August 24, 1918, during the height of wartime repression, unions organized an anti-IWW gathering in Bingham. Representatives from the Salt Lake Federation of Labor, the State War Labor Bureau, and the International Union of Mine, Mill, and Smelter Workers delivered impassioned speeches against the IWW.[55]

In 1919 the most visible left-wing organization in Utah, the Workers', Soldiers', and Sailors' Council, could not attract significant numbers. The council's letter-writing campaign urging Utah's labor unions to affiliate with it was, at best, unproductive. The "Soviet of Salt Lake" merely stirred paranoia in Salt Lake City's police force and the press. The council faded into obscurity after 1920.

The state's labor unions were another factor decreasing the potency of Utah's Red Scare. Internal conflicts plagued unions and depleted them of re-

[52]Ibid., pp. 90, 172, 179.

[53]Ibid., p. 179.

[54]*Deseret News,* February 11, 1919; Elling, "The History of Organized Labor," pp. 53–55.

[55]Elling, "The History of Organized Labor," pp. 32–33.

sources in 1919. Conservatives clearly had the upper hand in most unions, but they still faced contentious radical elements within. When the Utah Federation of Labor endorsed the Soviet Union at its September convention, it also rejected, by a vote of 32–18, a resolution calling for radical unionism along IWW lines. Similar splits between radicals and conservatives occurred in the Salt Lake Federation of Labor. In the middle of May 1919 a powerful faction of radicals in the SLFL drafted a resolution supporting the Park City strike and calling for affiliation with the Workers', Soldiers', and Sailors' Council. Conservatives steadfastly opposed the Park City strike, and they wanted nothing to do with the council. Ultimately, conservatives triumphed on both issues. SLFL president Otto Ashbridge had the last word when he announced that "no union as a union had become affiliated with the Council in any manner." The cost for that victory was internal division in Utah's unions.[56]

The lack of militancy on the part of unions enabled the Utah Associated Industries, an organization whose goal was "to put an end to industrial disturbances," to implement its American Plan (or the open-shop movement) with virtually no resistance. The American Plan was the product of industrialists and businessmen following World War I. Its purpose was to "combat union tyranny" by "putting an end to industrial disturbances." The open-shop movement proved to be an effective strategy in restructuring work relations by opening up unionized businesses and industries to non-union members, thereby weakening labor's grip on the workplace. In 1919 labor's only resistance to the open-shop movement occurred when Salt Lake City's cooks and waiters joined a Culinary Alliance strike in May. After a year-long walkout the strikers ultimately succeeded in maintaining a closed shop. But in the years that followed, the open-shop movement had a crippling effect on Utah's railroad shopmen, building trades unions, and the typographical union.[57]

One final aspect of the Red Scare that must be explored is nativism. The foreign connections of so many radicals in the United States strengthened widespread suspicion that sedition was chiefly foreign-made. Murray summed up the nativist tone of the Red Scare: "The belief was perpetuated that most aliens were susceptible to radical philosophies and therefore represented an element which particularly endangered the nation." According to Coben, a "fanatical 100-percent Americanism . . . pervaded a large part of our society between early 1919 and mid-1920," and resulted in a "popular clamor for deportation of allegedly subversive aliens." Anti-immigrant animosity was, in most cases, directed against the large influx of immigrants sweeping into the country between 1910 and 1919. Many of those immigrants were from southern and eastern European nations—Greece, Italy, Russia, and so forth. Nativism was often rabidly anti-Semitic, anti-

[56]*Deseret News,* April 29, May 24, 1919; Elling, "The History of Organized Labor," pp. 93–94.

[57]Scorup, "The History of Organized Labor," pp. 28–42.

Catholic, and chauvinistic toward people with different customs, beliefs, and ethnic origins.[58]

How widespread was nativism in Utah? One possible clue to this question is found in U.S. Census records. In 1919 the proportion of foreign-born people living in Utah was comparatively small. Between 1910 and 1919 Utah's population jumped from 373,351 to 449,369. However, in this ten-year span the number of foreign-born residents in the state actually dropped from roughly 63,000 or 16.9 percent in 1910, to 56,455, or about 12.6 percent in 1919. Thus, Utah had a relatively small foreign-born population during the Red Scare.[59]

The Palmer Raids and the deportations of alleged radicals in January 1920 were directed primarily against large pockets of southern and eastern European immigrants living in cities. At that time Utah had a much more homogeneous population than Massachusetts, New York, or Pennsylvania. More than 25 percent of Utah's foreign-born population came from Great Britain. Nearly 25 percent more were born in Sweden and Denmark. In contrast, the number of Russian-born residents was about 684, or 0.15 percent, while only 240 Polish-born residents lived in the state. The number of people who immigrated to Utah from southern European countries was higher. Of the state's foreign-born residents, 3,225 were from Italy, followed closely by Greece with 3,029. In total, immigrants from southern and eastern European countries comprised about 14.5 percent of foreign-born people in Utah.[60]

These figures mean nothing unless placed in a demographic perspective. More than twice the number of Italians lived in the mining areas of Carbon County (1,215) than in Salt Lake City (496). Only 548 Greeks lived in Salt Lake City, as opposed to nearly 900 in Carbon County. More Yugoslavians lived in Tooele, Summit, and Carbon counties than in Salt Lake County. In total, according to the U.S. Census, fewer than 25 percent of foreign-born residents in Utah from southern and eastern Europe lived in Salt Lake City.[61]

The figures for 1920 indicate that the immigrants—who were usually the victims of nativist, anti-alien hostility in other states—were small in number in Utah and most lived away from the lawmakers, police officers, and newspaper editors in Salt Lake City and Ogden. It is not surprising that A. Mitchell Palmer, William J. Flynn, J. Edgar Hoover, and the Justice Department ignored Utah entirely during the Palmer Raids.

The state's homogeneous population was reflected within the membership of the Socialist party between 1900 and 1923. According to John McCormick's findings, 90 percent of its 1,423 members were men, 90 per-

[58]Murray, *The Red Scare,* p. 265; Coben, *A. Mitchell Palmer,* pp. 196–97.

[59]Comparing 1910 population figures see May's *A People's History of Utah,* p. 136. For all figures from 1920 see *The Fourteenth Census* (1920), p. 1040.

[60]*The Fourteenth Census* (1920), p. 1040.

[61]Ibid.

cent were married, two-thirds were born in the United States, and 70 percent of them were native Utahns. Half of the foreign-born members were from the British Isles and the majority of the rest had been born in northern and western European countries. Nearly 42 percent were Mormons. It was not the sort of organization that inspired nativist animosity or even fear in the hearts of Utahns.[62]

The Red Scare manifested itself in different ways in Salt Lake City than it did in New York City, Chicago, or Cleveland. Outside of the historian's spotlight Utah followed a separate pattern and responded to events differently. The region felt the ripples of the Red Scare, but it was distant enough from the nation's centers of conflict that the ripples had little impact. Newspapers devoted more columns to local news and social events than to strikes in Seattle or revolutions in faraway lands.

Nevertheless, a disturbing precedent was set in 1919. Legislators passed laws that blatantly violated civil liberties and, though seldom enforced, evoked little public outcry. With no resistance, the Salt Lake City Police Department openly spied on dissenters. Groups of businessmen systematically stripped labor unions of their power. And even though reports of anti-immigrant hostility were rare, ideas and beliefs considered threatening to the status quo were regarded as un-American. During the Palmer Raids a frustrated *Deseret News* editorial lamented:

> Surely if we have laws by which we can rid ourselves of foreign hyenas and jackals, we must have laws to enable us to sterilize domestic snakes and vipers. . . . Their deeds are of that black type that is properly known as treason, against which, by every consideration of sense and self-protection, the government must move promptly, firmly and mercilessly.[63]

Was Utah representative of other areas outside of the lens of historians? How did events in Utah differ from Red Scares in other areas out of the historical focus, especially states with relatively homogeneous populations? Was the national "hysteria" that Robert K. Murray and Stanley Coben wrote about confined to a handful of cities? Were these scholars guilty of overstating or exaggerating their cases? How much wind was removed from the sails of the Red Scare by the repression of radicals in the United States between 1910 and 1918? Such questions beg for further research.

[62]McCormick, "Hornets in the Hive," pp. 231–32.
[63]*Deseret News*, January 5, 1920.

*

Bootlegging in Zion: Making and Selling the "Good Stuff"

HELEN ZEESE PAPANIKOLAS

Bootlegging flourished in Utah during the era of Prohibition (1917–35), as it did in the rest of the nation. As Helen Papanikolas says, it was the era of "the speakeasy, the silver hip flask, and the padded suitcase," and she discusses the people who were involved, the process of production and distribution, and the areas where illegal production of alcohol flourished. The prohibition experiment probably reduced the total consumption of alcohol in the state, as well as in the country, but most people who wanted to drink during the "noble experiment" did. Efforts of law-enforcement officials to enforce the law were inconsistent, often reflected the anti-immigrant prejudices of the period, sometimes involved corruption, and even promoted contempt for the law. In the end, Papanikolas concludes, "the foisting of Prohibition on the nation was catastrophic."

Helen Z. Papanikolas, "Bootlegging in Zion: Making and Selling the 'Good Stuff,'" *Utah Historical Quarterly* 53 (Summer 1985): 268–91. Reprinted by permission of the publisher and the author.

Helen Zeese Papanikolas is a Fellow of the Utah State Historical Society and author of *The Greek Immigrants in Utah; Emily George,* the biography of her parents; and *Small Bird Tell Me: Stories of Greek Immigrants in Utah.*

"THE GREATEST BLESSING SINCE CHRIST," the *Deseret News* called Prohibition on the evening before Utah went dry. "A splendid measure," Gov. Simon Bamberger said of the Utah dry law that would take effect on August 1, 1917, and the *Salt Lake Tribune* assured its readers that "No Prohibition bill ever became law with a better chance of being enforced." Instead, Prohibition introduced the speakeasy, the silver hip flask, and the padded suitcase. The era of the bootlegger was about to begin in Utah as it had in other dry states.[1]

[1]*Deseret News,* July 31, 1917; *Salt Lake Tribune,* February 3, 1917. Studies of Prohibition

While the legislature was still debating the fine points of implementing statewide Prohibition, opportunists were busily hoarding liquor in anticipation of its advent. An enterprising Marysvale druggist had accumulated 600 gallons, supposedly to be dispensed by physicians in Piute County, which was already dry under a local option law. In Salt Lake City, legally wet until August 1, the *Tribune* reported that residents were "keeping ear and eye open to the call of the 'tangle foot' vendor and many a quart, gallon and barrel has been snugly stowed away for future reference."[2]

Until midnight of July 31 liquor dealers sold their inventories at any cost. People flocked to buy whatever liquor was available, ignoring provisions in the law for stringent fines, jail, or both for possession of it. Throughout the state, throngs celebrated the end of an era by toasting with liquor. The *Deseret News* called the revelry a night of debauchery. The *Kaysville Weekly Reflex* complained that if people were as careful in saving food for the war effort as they had been in the past few days "in conserving the supply of booze there would be a very large surplus this fall." In Richfield "they celebrated the death of John Barleycorn with lots of wetting and washing down. . . . " The *Tooele Transcript* decried "a night of disorder that was much to be regretted by all the sober citizens of Utah." The *Salt Lake Tribune* said, "Old Man Booze . . . died game . . . like the spirit of the west . . . with his boots on . . . [and with] wine, women and song." At midnight in Park City

> a wild scene was enacted on Main Street, and empty barrels and empty ice cream freezers and everything else that would roll down the paved street were set to motion . . . [with] drunken yells and loud hurrahs by the midnight revelers.[3]

By January 16, 1920, the Eighteenth Amendment imposing nationwide Prohibition had been ratified by the states; to enforce it Congress passed the Volstead Act. The evangelist Billy Sunday said:

> the reign of tears is over. The slums will soon be a memory. We will turn our prisons into factories and our jails into storehouses and corncribs. . . . Hell will be forever for rent.[4]

The naive belief that Prohibition would solve the country's social problems was unaffected by the weariness of the population over wartime short-

---

in Utah include Brent Grant Thompson, "Utah's Struggle for Prohibition, 1908–1917" (M.A. thesis, University of Utah, 1979), and Larry Earl Nelson, "Problems of Prohibition Enforcement in Utah, 1917–1933" (M.S. thesis, University of Utah, 1970).

[2]*Salt Lake Tribune,* July 1, 20, 1917.

[3]*Deseret News,* August 1, 1917; *Kaysville Weekly Reflex,* August 2, 1917; *Richfield Reaper,* August 4, 1917; *Tooele Transcript,* August 3, 1917; *Salt Lake Tribune,* August 1, 1917; *Park Record,* August 3, 1917. For a personal account see John Farnsworth Lund, "The Night before Doomsday," *Utah Historical Quarterly* 51 (1983).

[4]Larry Engelmann, *Intemperance: The Lost War against Liquor* (New York: Free Press, 1979), p. xi.

ages and sacrifices, the trauma of the worldwide influenza epidemic that killed more than a half-million Americans, and, most important, the cynicism accompanying the carnage of "the war to end all wars." In the revolt against old virtues, forbidden liquor became the symbol of a new sybaritism. For many, also, Prohibition was an assault on Constitutional liberties.

While ministers, politicians, editors, and the Women's Christian Temperance Union enjoyed a putative victory, speakeasies immediately proliferated in basements and walkups on shabby streets. A knock on a door was answered by the opening of a peephole through which suspicious eyes looked out waiting for the password. "Joe sent me" and the words *flivver, rumble seat, booze, flapper, jazz,* and *bootleg* (an old word for liquor smuggled in a tall boot) became indelible accretions to the American vocabulary.

Joining Americans in these illegal liquor activities were recent immigrants from the Balkans, Mediterranean, and Asia who were free from the American-Puritan attitude toward alcohol. In moderation it was traditionally part of the ceremonial and communal festivities of their cultures. Especially among the Mediterranean people, drunkenness was censured. The immigrants derided Prohibition as peculiar; their wine and *saké* were staples that accompanied meals. A popular Greek phonograph record of the era asked in perplexity, "Why is America dry?"[5]

The foreign-language newspapers subsidized by the LDS church—such as the German *Beobachter* and Danish *Bikuben*—could only mirror its stance in favor of Prohibition, but the Japanese *Utah Nippo* predicted the impossibility of monitoring the law and deplored the evils that followed, in particular blindness that afflicted people who had turned to drinking wood alcohol. The Greek-language *To Fos* ("The Light") said:

> By a large majority doctors consider alcoholic beverages useful for therapy, most priests as well as [other] knowledgable people, want the abolition of this law that rather than saving a few drunkards from degeneracy and catastrophe, has sent a multitude to Hades by means of liquor sold for evil and unscrupulous gain.

To Fos asserted that morphine and cocaine addiction had increased tenfold since Prohibition. "Statistics show the Volstead Act is harmful not beneficial," it said. In ethnic communities bootleggers were not outcasts unless they combined liquor pursuits with prostitution.[6]

In contrast, the predominately Mormon communities of Sanpete County gave Prohibition

> whole-hearted approval, but the law would be violated in Sanpete just as it was in areas with no tradition of abstention. Although possibly exaggerat-

[5]Mentioned in "Tales of Skill and Loss in Greek-American Recorded Humor," paper by Steve Frangos, Department of Anthropology, Indiana University.

[6]*Utah Nippo* (Salt Lake City), February 8, 1919, January 10, 1923; *To Fos* (Salt Lake City), July 5, 1923. The author is indebted to Rev. K. Okuno, Nicherin Buddhist Temple, for researching back issues of *Utah Nippo.*

ing, one former resident recalled that, "Bootleggers almost had to wear badges so they wouldn't sell to each other."[7]

Yet in Utah, immigrants and the American-born never embroiled themselves in bootlegging to the extent of those in large cities beyond the state where young thugs were taking their first steps toward becoming leading gangsters. Utah was only slightly touched with gangsterism, but residents, including mothers and children, became lawbreakers; bootlegging flourished; and shootings were regular events. Drinkers had not resigned themselves to becoming abstinent, even if it meant drinking flavoring extracts that contained a high percentage of alcohol (as much as 85 percent for lemon) and which, in spontaneous accommodation to their need, were being bottled in pints, quarts, and gallons.

Former governor J. Bracken Lee recalled Prohibition's debut: "Whiskey immediately began coming in from Rock Springs, Wyoming." Rolla West, a mayor of Price, Utah, during the Prohibition era, wrote:

> One of the biggest and most astute politicians of the early 1920's discovered that White Mule, Panther wettings, moonshine, embalming fluid, Bootleg or even Bourbon whiskey, by throwing in a little burnt sugar and tobacco juice [for flavor and color], was available in Private distilleries in Wyoming.[8]

The making and selling of liquor had suddenly passed from commercial distilleries to the underground. Immigrants who had used the grape residue from wine-making for their households' liqueurs, Americans who had sporadically made a small amount of whiskey for their own consumption, and an eager number of novices learning the easy rudiments of production set up stills in towns, cities, and isolated areas of the state. The Utah State Legislature was as busily engaged for the next sixteen years in formulating a complex system of rules to govern patent medicines and flavoring extracts (a favorite of young people and housewives), denatured (wood) alcohol, cider, vinegar, mincemeat, and communion wine ("to follow the commands of the Divine Master") as well as fines, imprisonment, and confiscation of liquor apparatus and other property involved in the preparation and selling of liquor, including automobiles used for transportation.[9]

Although the phenomenal new liquor business was surreptitious, bootleggers became instantly known. Usually they carried on a legitimate business as camouflage. Others worked part-time at it, especially after the stock market crash of 1929 and the economic depression that followed. Bootleggers came from the professions, from business, and from labor: unsuccessful doctors and attorneys, successful druggists, sheepmen (who left their

[7] John S. H. Smith, "Localized Aspects of the Urban-Rural Conflict in the United States: Sanpete County, Utah, 1919–1929" (M.A. thesis, University of Utah, 1972), p. 69.

[8] Interview with J. Bracken Lee, June 16, 1983; Rolla West MS., p. 23, American West Center, University of Utah.

[9] Nelson, "Problems of Prohibition Enforcement," pp. 49, 104–16.

wives to run stills while they were in sheep camps for lambing and shearing), railroad workers, miners, and shop owners, particularly those of shoeshine stands.

Many American-born druggists were actively engaged in bootlegging, a natural development since medicinal liquor had always been dispensed by them. In their back rooms, as well as in poolhalls, candy stores, and hotels where "traveling men," the old-time drummers, congregated, liquor was readily available.

Shoeshine shop owners became middlemen through another long-established American custom. Until World War II, doctors, attorneys, and businessmen were in the habit of having their shoes shined during their work day in the business district. According to one shop owner, while the polish was being applied his customers "asked us all the time where to get some whiskey."[10] In Utah, as in the nation, Greek immigrants had almost exclusively taken over shoeshine parlors, once the province of blacks and the Irish, and often owned chains of them. As boys of nine and older they had been brought to the United States by *somatoempori* ("flesh merchants") and indentured in return for their highly inflated ship's passage.[11] In Salt Lake City and elsewhere in Utah they served as conduits between their countrymen's bubbling stills and respected, insatiable citizens. As the shoeshine parlors became increasingly popular fronts the once modestly dressed, obsequious shoeshiners began wearing monogrammed silk shirts and being chauffeured in Cadillacs. Several extended their activities into Canada. As the best man at a wedding in the middle twenties, one of them brought cases of Canadian whiskey as a gift for the large reception, because marriage celebrations in Greek immigrant days were communal.[12]

If illegal whiskey flavored the wedding festivities of immigrants, it also spiced the dancing parties of the American-born. Reports in the *Provo Herald* complained of "immoral dancing" and intoxication in Utah County resorts throughout the early 1920s. L. R. Hebertson, who managed the Geneva resort, "admitted that drinking had been rampant at the resort the entire season. 'There hasn't been a dance at Geneva this summer,' he said, 'when Salt Lake bootleggers didn't come down, loaded with liquor, which was sold to the dancers and others.'" In Vivian Park, another resort in the Provo area, manager J. F. Carter told the *Herald* that "there had been 'drunkenness and improper dancing at the resort all summer.'"[13]

Middlemen did well; bootleggers who sold their liquor directly did even better. In cellars, basements, and empty buildings they set up stills with exhaust pipes leading to chimneys to disperse the potentially betraying fumes. Beyond, on farms and in half-hidden gulleys and washes where scrub oak

[10]A Greek bootlegger of the era who asked, as did many respondents, not to be identified.

[11]Theodore Saloutos, *The Greeks in the United States* (Cambridge, Mass.: Harvard University Press, 1964), pp. 48–56, gives a graphic picture of this dark period.

[12]The author's husband remembers this scene at the wedding of his uncle in the mid-1920s.

[13]Gary C. Kunz, "Provo in the Jazz Age," *Sunstone* 9 (January–February 1984): 34.

and tall sagebrush screened chimneys on shacks, lucrative distillation progressed. Small canyons and mountain draws were ideal: Burch Creek in Weber County, the Mount Olympus area of Salt Lake County, Barney's Canyon north of West Jordan, the junction of Red Creek and the Strawberry River, Johnson's Pass in Tooele County, Twelve Mile Canyon in Sanpete County, the mouth of Provo Canyon, Crandall Canyon north of Castle Gate in Carbon County, and Nine Mile Canyon between Price and Duchesne.

To allay suspicion, bootleggers in Nine Mile Canyon kept a few old ewes grazing outside the shacks because authentic sheepmen left old and injured animals behind when they trailed their flocks into high country for summer grazing.

Fermenting grapes for wine and barley and hops for beer required no special equipment, but setting up a still depended on a coppersmith's craftsmanship to solder sheets of copper into round or box-shaped containers of sizes ranging from a few feet in circumference for individual needs to those of massive dimensions for wholesale business. The "feds," federal liquor agents, sought out coppersmiths as diligently as bootleggers did and at times used ruses to entrap them.[14] Fortunately, stills were made of copper. When a still that used lead coils rather than copper was discovered in Sanpete County, the information "presumably did more to discourage tippling . . . than any number of sermons."[15]

Making whiskey was simple once the still was ready; recipes for mash became common property. Bootleggers drove to farms and grain elevators to buy great amounts of rye, wheat, and corn "for fodder"; to stores for hundred-pound sacks of sugar "for putting up fruit"; and to wholesalers for pounds of yeast "to bake bread." To distill 100 gallons of whiskey a day, a plant in an empty four-story warehouse on First South and Fourth West in Salt Lake City used a ton of sugar, sixty-five pounds of yeast, and a sack of rye every four days.[16] The industry utilized great quantities of raisins, molasses, and a lesser amount of fresh fruit. Tobacco juice or iodine gave the required amber color and "bite" to the whiskey.

Sugar whiskey made without fusil oil that had to be filtered over charcoal was of the highest quality. Grapes were often added to the grain and sugar for taste. The mash was then left to ferment in a crock for seventy-two hours, strained through cloth, and distilled. The first distillation was whiskey. The bootlegger periodically lighted matches to the distillation: the higher the alcohol content, the bluer the flame. When the flame turned yellow, more water than alcohol was being distilled.

"Raw" whiskey, also called "white lightning," was unaged and sold straight from the still.[17] Much cheaper than aged whiskey that was handled

[14]*Salt Lake Tribune,* March 8, 1929.

[15]Smith, "Localized Aspects of the Urban-Rural Conflict," p. 69.

[16]*Salt Lake Tribune,* November 15, 1930.

[17]Raymond Sokolov, "White Lightning," *Natural History* 89 (1980): 86–90.

by trusted bootleggers who supplied men in business and the professions, it satisfied transients, cowboys, sheepherders, and the poor.

Capturing bootleggers was a monumental problem.[18] Following usual political practice, the state legislature had passed a Prohibition bill that entailed an enormous expenditure of time by a vast force of personnel but had not provided commensurate funds to pay officers. Governor Bamberger asked health officials and other state officers to take on Prohibition duties with their regular work, and he deputized others. Gov. Charles R. Mabey continued the policy of giving commissions to people who traveled about the state and were interested in uncovering liquor violations.[19] Not enough honest agents were employed, however, to cope with stills sprouting up everywhere and the ceaseless demand of the public: "People went crazy over whiskey. Looking for it, getting it, hiding it."[20]

After the Utah bill became law, the liquor agents' first duty was to stop whiskey from coming into the state, especially from Wyoming, which was still legally wet. According to Rolla West:

> Any unattached man who had enough money to make a down payment on a fast car and enough money to pay for his 'load' to the Wyoming supplier could get directions [from him] where he could sell his 'load' at a handsome profit. Full time or part time. Part time being preferr[ed] since a regular job was a good front.

When agents found the two-lane dirt roads that bootleggers used between Utah and Wyoming, some shipments were thwarted and local whiskey making increased. In Carbon County

> "Kentucky" moonshine whiskey makers who had never been as far east as Grand Junction, Colo., arrived on the scene on very short notice. Back rooms and basements strategically situated became quietly active and hush-hush. . . . [You could get it] anywhere in town.[21]

To transport liquor, bootleggers used cars, stages, trains, horses, and, in one instance, an airplane. One man recalled:

> I drove the old Bingham Stage Line starting in 1919. We'd regularly pick up two unmarked suitcases in Salt Lake—no name or tag on them—and deposit them outside Johnny Jimson's place in Bingham. This way no one could accuse us of knowing the suitcases were filled with Wyoming whiskey.[22]

An ingenious bootlegger in Wales, Sanpete County, loaded whiskey in the pack saddle of his trained horse and then turned the animal loose to

[18]Frederick Lewis Allen, *Only Yesterday: An Informal History of the Twenties* (New York: Bantam Books, 1952), p. 224, states that appropriations in 1920 provided a force of only 1,520 federal agents.

[19]Nelson, "Problems of Prohibition Enforcement," pp. 108–9.

[20]Statement of Emily Zeese, the author's mother.

[21]West MS., p. 24.

[22]Interview with Joseph Hasalone, August 18, 1983.

make its way home over twenty miles of mountain road. The bootlegger returned home by car on the highway. Although the officers "knew he was bootlegging," when they stopped his car and searched it, they never found any liquor in it.[23]

Agents checked boxcars regularly. Because few officers were available to examine every freight train, they relied on rumors and informers. In Ogden agents discovered two boxcars filled with $100,000 of "fine liquor" and stood guard while curious onlookers came to the railyards and milled about.[24]

Railroaders themselves made deliveries. Engineers, conductors, and brakemen traveled throughout Utah and into surrounding states and were able to buy their own whiskey, but railroad officials and men working in roundhouses and depots in division points had stationary jobs and depended on others for liquor. Two gallons in pint bottles could be fitted into a padded suitcase. Railroaders had few qualms about carrying their heavy luggage into YMCAs, which had been built mainly to house them on their overnight runs.

A long-retired Union Pacific brakeman recalled that as an eighteen-year-old he was introduced to the Milford mayor by a conductor. In reurn for a room above the mayor's drugstore, freedom to read any magazine on the rack, and all the malted milks he wanted, he was recruited to bring Delmuse Whiskey, at twenty dollars a gallon, from Caliente, Nevada.

> It was a good deal. I had the experience. The year before I spent two months in Monterey, California, in an army program for young men to get a taste of army life. The sergeant was confined to the base. He was an alcoholic and he'd whipped all the Monterey police force. His nerves were a jangle and he had to rely on vanilla and lemon extract. Twice a week I went into Monterey for supplies and the sergeant gave me some money and a note to take to this guy in a certain poolhall. I'd go to the toilet and the guy would follow me. I'd give him the note and money and he'd give me the booze.[25]

Using the rails to transport liquor was easiest and least subject to detection, but automobiles were the common means of bootleg travel. When horses carried liquor through impassable draws and canyons, several trips had to be made to highways where cars awaited their arrival. In a dugout a half-mile off the Lincoln Highway in Tooele County, agents found a 200-gallon still, 40 gallons of whiskey, and 1,500 gallons of mash. The bootleggers brought the liquor on horseback to the highway with a cedar tree tied to the horse dragging behind to erase its tracks.[26]

Bootleggers spent a large portion of their time eluding and trying to outwit agents. In Salt Lake City a wholesaler rode streetcars to empty houses

[23]Smith, "Localized Aspect of the Urban-Rural Conflict," pp. 69–70.
[24]*Salt Lake Tribune,* December 29, 1923.
[25]The respondent asked not to be identified because "The U.P. was good to me."
[26]*Salt Lake Tribune,* December 29, 1923.

throughout the city to tend his stills. To cover his trail he stopped off at various corners and transferred to later streetcars. For alleviating the sag at the back of automobiles that gave officials the clue liquor was being transported, bootleggers placed blocks under the rear springs. With loads of liquor in their cars, they drove slowly toward semaphore lights to prevent sloshing in the bottles that would arouse suspicion. Recalling this precaution, the owner of the Grand Central grocery chain, Maurice Warshaw, told a television audience about creeping toward an intersection light while looking apprehensively into the rearview mirror at a sheriff's car following him.[27]

Bootleggers quickly learned it was useless to hide bottles in toilet tanks or pour liquor down the sink, for agents became adept at removing the gooseneck pipe underneath and finding the incriminating residue. However, bootleggers were equally adept at devising new subterfuges to avoid detection.

An imaginative bootlegger in Sanpete County "kept his stocks in bed—with his wife ready to jump in and feign sickness should the law appear with a search warrant." Another Sanpete merchant transported his booze "in a specially designed rumble seat." In Summit County, when the newly elected Coalville sheriff set up road-blocks to stop Wyoming whiskey from coming in, Park City connoisseurs had to drink less desirable brew until the town mortician J. E. "Jimmy" Flynn drove a hearse to Kemmerer, Wyoming, with other town notables following, ostensibly to the site of a mine disaster. After filling the coffin with whiskey, the funeral cortege drove through the roadblock, reverently waved on, and into Park City.[28]

Heine Hernon, who since 1901 had owned a Park City saloon that was converted to a soda fountain the day after Prohibition went into effect ("There were seventeen saloons in Park City before that day and seventeen soda fountains the day after," residents said), installed a partition, suspended by weights, under a second-story window of his saloon. When raided, he rolled barrels of Wyoming whiskey against the partition, which lifted from the pressure, and the kegs came to rest in the attic of the adjacent one-story building. The owners of the Metropol Hotel in Price constructed removable baseboards behind which whiskey bottles could be safely hidden. In the Granger-Hunter area of Salt Lake City County, farmers successfully hid bottles and small kegs in designated sections of irrigation ditches for nighttime retrieval by middlemen.

Copper tubing leading to storage containers was conclusive proof of illegal activities. After a diligent hunt in a combination restaurant and soft-drink parlor near 100 West Second South in Salt Lake City, agents found a copper tube between the woodwork running from the first floor to the basement and back to a supply tank on the second floor.[29]

[27]For Warshaw's other bootlegging experiences in California see his autobiography, *Life More Sweet than Bitter* (Salt Lake City, 1975), pp. 157–59.

[28]Smith, "Localized Aspects of the Urban-Rural Conflict," p. 69; interview with Robert Hernon.

[29]*Salt Lake Tribune,* May 17, 1929.

No one, of course, could explain away the presence of working stills; bootleggers frantically tried to dismantle them when agents swept through neighborhoods on raids. During the 1922 Carbon County coal strike National Guard troops, while systematically searching mine company houses, saw a young South Slav girl running down the road, her long blond hair streaming; sensing she was holding contraband, they ran after her. The girl threw a coil of copper tubing into a clump of bushes, climbed a tree outside Menotti's grocery store, and remained there until a wagon passed below. She jumped into it, hid, and escaped to her house. She then had her hair cut like a boy's and dyed black, and until the National Guard left the county she dressed in overalls.[30]

The potential profit to be made from illegal liquor was so tempting that individuals often took foolish risks. Frank Lyons built a 40-gallon still in his Provo; home, less than two blocks from the courthouse; it was raided in 1921. A number of larger stills were discovered by agents in downtown Provo; the largest, destroyed by officials in 1928, "was capable of producing over 200 gallons of whiskey every 24 hours," with most of the product sold to Provoans in anticipation of the Christmas holiday season.[31]

The elements often helped federal agents. Counting on surprising the immigrant neighborhoods in Magna, agents began a raid after snowfall. Hearing the commotion and the cries, "They're coming!" a millworker emptied several barrels of wine into the gutter in front of his house. The agents followed the red rivulets to his doorstep and arrested him.[32] To absorb fumes a bootlegger in Price dug a trench and buried two parallel pipes that led from his basement still to an underground septic tank. While agents prowled the neighborhood after snow had fallen, they noticed two lines where the snow had melted, dug, and uncovered the pipes.[33]

Stills exploded frequently and neighborhood fires were a constant menace. Firemen repeatedly detected stored whiskey and stills while extinguishing flames. A disastrous 1932 fire in Highland Boy destroyed the school, houses, and businesses a third of a mile on either side of Carr Fork, leaving three hundred people homeless. Above the roar of the fire stills blew up, one after the other.[34]

Agents were also aided by hunters and boys. During every pheasant, duck, and deer season, hunters came upon hidden stills and informed police. Playing football on Fourth South between Tenth and Eleventh East in Salt Lake City, boys discovered a ten-gallon keg of whiskey buried in a hillside to age. They carried the prize a distance and then called police. One of the largest distilleries in the West was found by boys playing near an old westside warehouse, supposedly used to store furs and hides. The

[30]Interview with Zelpha Vuksinick, April 2, 1980.

[31]Kunz, "Provo in the Jazz Age," p. 35.

[32]The godfather of the author's husband.

[33]Interview with Ted A. Poulos, October 26, 1980.

[34]*Bingham Bulletin,* September 22, 1932; *Salt Lake Tribune,* September 9, 1932.

boys saw two men enter the building and notified the police. Nine 500-gallon vats and twelve 55-gallon barrels filled with mash were found. Inadvertently, a small boy betrayed his bootlegging grandfather when several agents appeared at a farmhouse in American Fork and asked him if his grandfather made whiskey. The boy answered that he did and led them to the barn, then watched in horror as they demolished the still and barrels with axes.[35]

Liquor agents were almost always Protestants or Mormons and reflected the anti-immigrant prejudice of the era that culminated in the 1924–25 Ku Klux Klan campaigns.[36] As immigrants from the Mediterranean and the Balkans began marrying American women, hostility against them grew. In retribution, liquor agents often tried to fake bootlegging charges. A young Greek in Magna who eloped with a Mormon woman to Farmington and returned to find crosses burning in front of his cafe and her parents' house was continually on the alert for approaching agents. By banging on the wall, the other side of which was a Greek coffeehouse, he gave the signal to his countrymen to rush over to prevent agents from planting a bottle of whiskey and then arresting him.[37]

Ignorant of or indifferent to immigrant cultures, agents were often harsher than necessary. They trivialized the need of wine for communion, for the common cup from which a bride and groom must drink, and for toasting the health of a newly baptized infant. In Helper the sheriff entered a below-the-sidewalk restaurant to arrest the owner for a liquor violation. The proprietor was eating and lifted his palm in a staying motion. He had come from the island of Crete, from a pocket of land where a large population of Turks lived, and had acquired their Moslem tenet of not rising from the table until a meal was completed. Fuming, the sheriff waited, taking this religious custom as a sign of contempt.[38]

The Price newspaper resented the attention focused on illegal liquor operations in Carbon County by federal Prohibition director Mathonihah Thomas. It accused him of not having "the nerve to tackle the booze problem in Salt Lake City" where "all a man has to do to get booze most anywhere . . . is pay the price. . . . The trouble is that if the Democratic office holder undertook to clean up Salt Lake he would run into too many of his friends. . . . " Accusations that law enforcement officials protected some liquor violators were common during Prohibition. The city marshal of Milford in 1928 was reported by federal official George A. Goates to be protecting his sister, "the chief offender" against Prohibition in his jurisdiction. State legislator Lorenzo Argyle complained to Governor Bamberger that law

[35]*Salt Lake Tribune,* March 30, 1932, February 24, 1923; story related to author by Myra Varanakis.

[36]See Larry R. Gerlach, *Blazing Crosses in Zion: The Ku Klux Klan in Utah* (Logan: Utah State University, 1982).

[37]Interview with Mr. and Mrs. Andrew Dallas, June 26, 1972.

[38]Reminiscence of George Zeese, the author's father.

officers in Spanish Fork were turning a blind eye toward "Bootlegging, Drinking and Carousing."[39]

Caught with liquor in one's possession was not the only hazard in Prohibition days. Lacking reputably made liquor, drinkers consumed canned heat and wood alcohol that could cause blindness. Some learned how to neutralize the methane in this denatured alcohol bought at service stations. Lead salts from car radiators—used by unscrupulous still operators as cheapjack condensers instead of copper tubing—could poison drinkers. Another danger was posed by caves and other poorly ventilated hideouts that nearly asphyxiated bootleggers and agents alike.[40] Proper storage presented problems that sometimes required sophisticated knowledge. J. Bracken Lee recalled:

> Someone gave me a gallon of moonshine and I went to the druggist and asked him if he had any empty wooden casks. He gave me a small, empty formaldehyde barrel and told me to wash it out several times with boiling water. Later that day two friends came by and I offered them a drink. I saw them the next day down town. Their mouths were blistered. I found out you can't ever get formaldehyde out of wood.[41]

Because the liquor business had become clandestine, standards of sanitation belonged to the past, and bootleggers could be as clean and as honest or as unclean and as dishonest as they wanted. Agents raiding a grocery store in Salt Lake City seized forty-four gallons of wine made in a dirty fifty-gallon barrel: "The mash was a conglomeration that respectable pigs would have scorned—being composed of decomposed grapes, apples and other refuse from the store."[42]

Drinkers, therefore, deemed it important to know their bootleggers, and they searched until they found "decent liquor that wouldn't make a person sick." Two men most frequently mentioned as "men you could trust" and who "made good stuff" were John Diamanti of Helper and Jimmy McG— of Salt Lake City who made whiskey in his First Avenue house and sold most of it in the Moxum Hotel; the guests were mainly permanent residents, stockmen, and traveling salesmen.

People needed bootleggers to supply them with liquor, and bootleggers needed attorneys to extricate them from the law. Prohibition brought a period of halcyon days to many lawyers who otherwise would have made a modest or substandard living. Word-of-mouth elevated several attorneys to enviable positions, among them Samuel A. King and R. Verne McCullough, well known also as a businessman. More so than American bootleggers, immigrants required effective attorneys because judges used their discretion in

[39]*News Advocate,* April 29, 1920; Nelson, "Problems of Prohibition Enforcement," p. 117.

[40]*Salt Lake Tribune,* June 11, 1930.

[41]Lee interview.

[42]*Salt Lake Tribune,* January 21, 1928.

handing down sentences and were especially severe toward the foreign-born who had flouted the nation's laws. Meanwhile, local juries refused to convict their fellow citizens of liquor possession often enough that the Utah attorney general's office complained.[43]

Women, too, often faced trial for bootlegging. Among nine Carbon County bootleggers caught in a raid was a Helper women of "old" American stock who owned a "brewery of magnificent proportions." Her operation included a complete bottling plant. Women owners of boardinghouses were under continual scrutiny. The French owner of the Allies Hotel in Price was arrested twice in one week. In Bingham a woman was charged with making whiskey in the old Boston Con Hotel, and in Salt Lake City the mother of nine children pleaded guilty to possession of liquor. Another Salt Lake City mother kept a still going in the basement of her house while her husband was serving an eighteen-month term at McNeil Island for bootlegging.[44]

Many mothers turned to bootlegging during the depression years when federal aid was unavailable to help their indigent families. For others bootlegging was a wondrous opportunity to make money. Some women followed the cultural patterns of their native countries. To have on hand the obligatory liqueur for guests, Greek women in Magna (and elsewhere) made *ouzo* from *chipoura,* the crushed grape skins left after the juice was extricated for wine. To make *mastiha,* the licorice-tasting liqueur, they combined *ouzo* with anise.[45] Italians used the crushed grape skins to make a second-grade, and therefore inferior, wine called *grappa.*

Bootlegging was commonly a family business. Children often left play and chores to deliver liquor.

> I was fourteen years old and drove my dad's fancy Hupmobile to N—'s goat ranch in Butterfield Canyon. I'd load up and drive back to Magna. I'll never forget the time the feds raided our house and one of them pushed my mother out of the way. She bit his hand so hard, he had to go around with it bandaged up.

In Spring Glen, Carbon County

> The appearance of an 8 year old boy on the Highway in the heat of the day garbed in a coat of manly proportions . . . aroused the curiosity of agents, who, upon investigation, discovered two pints of whisky in the pockets of the coat.[46]

Agents frequently overlooked the search and seizure conditions of the Prohibition law and were zealous in their pursuit of liquor violators. In Salt Lake City Sheriff Benjamin R. Harries wounded a fleeing confectioner who

[43]Ibid.; Nelson, "Problems of Prohibition Enforcement," p. 129.

[44]*New Advocate*, July 24, May 13, 1926; *Bingham Bulletin*, March 10, 1932; *Salt Lake Tribune*, February 17, 1933.

[45]Interview with Mrs. John Klekas, May 10, 1979.

[46]Interviews with Theodore Heleotes, September 3, 10, 1983; *News Advocate,* July 29, 1926.

was fearful that invading officers were going to assault him. *To Fos* denounced the shooting of this "American citizen, of very short stature, quiet, a philanthropist, and well known in his business neighborhood." In his fear of agents a seventy-eight-year-old man fell headfirst down an elevator shaft. A widow and her children, who had moved into an alley house behind the Holy Trinity Greek Orthodox Church in Salt Lake City, were terrorized by agents when, failing to find liquor in a neighbor's house, they burst into her kitchen looking for contraband.[47]

Unconcerned about formalities, agents were given a legal precedent when the Utah Supreme Court upheld the conviction for possession of liquor of a Uintah County man who had contested his arrest without a signed warrant. In a unanimous decision the court held that the Fourth and Fifth Amendments of the U.S. Constitution on unreasonable search and seizure did not apply to state governments and state courts. The court, however, ruled in favor of Bertha Jackson, who brought suit against the Salt Lake County sheriff's office for "vigorously" searching her house (with a warrant) and causing her "severe nervous and emotional stress."[48]

Legal maneuvers, speakeasies, rum-running, fashionable cocktail parties, gang wars, and hypocrisy fused into the milieu of the dry years. From its inception Prohibition enforcement was a delusion. Although the liquor traffic was intense in almost every part of the state, the *Salt Lake Tribune* carried the caption "Utah Bone Dry, According to the Official Records." The reality was that during 1923–32 agents uncovered 448 distilleries and 702 stills in Utah along with thousands of pieces of distilling apparatus; over 47,000 gallons of spirits, malt liquor, wine, and cider; and 332,000 gallons of mash. Much more went undetected.[49]

While agents struggled to control the amount of alcohol made in-state by Utah residents, other law enforcement officials tried to stem the tide of liquor entering the United States from foreign countries. Representatives of the federal government and Canada attempted the impossible task of shutting off the supply of liquor and drugs over the border into the United States. Trucks from throughout the country met Canadian ships and left with their disguised loads. A Magna family regularly drove a truck with a half load of lumber to the Pacific Coast, set cases of whiskey and rum under the planks, and returned to Utah. Liquor brought by British ships to the twelve-mile national waters was transported to lighter, faster craft to elude the United States Coast Guard, a small patrol that could not conduct adequate surveillance. Arrests were relatively few; the capture of a British rum schooner with the purported king of smugglers aboard made front-page news.[50]

[47]*To Fos,* September 6, 1923; *Salt Lake Tribune,* November 29, 1923, February 20, 1933; interview with Steve Sargetakis, October 26, 1981.

[48]*Salt Lake Tribune,* November 16, 1923; Nelson, "Problems of Prohibition Enforcement," p. 46.

[49]*Salt Lake Tribune,* November 19, 1923; Nelson, "Problems of Prohibition Enforcement," appendix 1.

[50]*Salt Lake Tribune,* November 26, 1923; *To Fos,* July 5, 1923.

While gang wars escalated in the East and Midwest—the 1929 Valentine's Day Massacre of seven O'Bannions by Al Capone's men a grisly, ingenious performance—violence also erupted periodically in Utah. In Eureka near the Mammoth Mine a bootlegger shot and killed a member of the pioneer McIntyre family. Halfway between West Jordan and Bingham Canyon in a barn where a still worked, a shooting left one of the bootleggers dead. Rival bootleggers shot at each other on a goat ranch near Lark, and in Lakepoint two still operators were killed over liquor and slot-machine competition. Seventeen miles south of Price, near Mounds in Emery County, an agent shot a bootlegger who was protecting his still with a shotgun and paralyzed him. He died soon after. Two Salt Lake City revenue officers were wounded in Silver City when they discovered that the town's water line had been tapped and followed the pipe to an "effectively concealed" dugout. The three young bootleggers refused to come out of the dugout, thinking the officers were hijackers. In the midst of the confrontation, the boiler exploded and one of the bootleggers came out shooting.[51]

The illegality of liquor and the determination of drinkers to get it by any means led to unprecedented corruption. Raids into neighborhoods were often shams: bribed officials telephoned still operators to give them time to dispose of their liquor. An area of West Jordan was under the protection of the sheriff, and deputies were ordered not to enter it. In Summit County a deputy sheriff was indicted for allegedly furnishing a still to a bootlegger and conspiring with him to manufacture liquor. Sheriff Amasa M. Hammon was charged with taking one hundred dollars from "Fats" Davis, owner of an Ogden speakeasy. This occurred in the same week that beer was again being legally sold in Wyoming and long lines of automobiles crossed over the border from Utah as regular Sunday excursions.[52]

A federal grand jury in 1928 indicted deputy sheriffs, federal officers, "and reputed higher ups in [Salt Lake City] bootleg circles." In Clear Creek, Carbon County, the constable was arrested for serving "white mule" in his boardinghouse; and in Helper the mayor and all the councilmen except one asked for bribes from hotels, poolhalls, and candy stores in return for insurance against arrest. The owners notified Henry Ruggeri, the county attorney, who stripped the officials of their positions. In Ogden the mayor, a commissioner, the chief of police, a police captain, a patrolman, the sheriff, and two deputy sheriffs were arraigned in court, indicted for collaboration with a bootlegger. The local Lions' Club passed a resolution in support of the officials.[53]

[51]*Salt Lake Tribune,* January 19, 1931; *Price News Advocate,* January 29, 1931; *Salt Lake Tribune,* January 11, 1931. Until mortuaries began sending obituaries to newspapers, families often neglected to insert death announcements. When relatives were involved in shootings, they were even more reluctant to inform newspapers of deaths. That, along with incomplete files for some newspapers, makes gathering details of shootings difficult. Accounts are often imprecise but vivid. Everett L. Cooley recalled a Boy Scout trek from West Jordan to Bingham and the awe of seeing the barn in which the shootings over the still took place.

[52]*Salt Lake Tribune,* July 30, 1928; *Deseret News,* May 25, 19, 1933.

[53]*Salt Lake Tribune,* April 24, 28, 1928; *Sun,* August 30, 1928; Zeese reminiscence; *Salt Lake Tribune,* January 25, 1923, April 6 and May 23, 1933; *Ogden Standard-Examiner,* April

Citizens had a collective contempt for elected officials and, especially, for agents. Besides their solicitation of bribes or accepting them when offered, agents were often guilty of drunkenness and disorderly conduct. In Carbon County an agent was charged with being "too drunk to call the 'Black Maria' " after making an arrest.[54] The Salt Lake City police chief suspended a policeman caught in a speakeasy raid and three others of intoxication.[55] A Salt Lake City federal agent with "a high-handed manner" was arrested in Helper for criminal assault on a woman he had kept captive for a period of five hours:

> [He] held her nose and tried to force liquor down her throat after which he attacked her. [In his car were] two revolvers, a rifle, several pint flasks filled with moonshine, and an empty small keg.[56]

Agents carried on vendettas against bootleggers who tried to avoid paying bribes; some kept confiscated liquor and openly defied the law:

> The fed telephoned my dad to give him time to hide his whiskey, then walked in with his men, gave a quick look around, and after his men went out, motioned my father to get him a stiff drink.[57]

Bootleggers became bolder in their retaliation against liquor agents. A percentage of each fine was commonly paid to officers on convictions, a policy that was particularly offensive to bootleggers and a reason Helper dry agents became "unpopular with the foreign element." Bootleggers in Bingham Canyon warned "Sheriff Corless . . . not to destroy booze . . . or [he] may come in contact with T.N.T." On Salt Lake City's westside bootleggers fought with two undercover agents, leaving one with a battered face.[58]

On November 15, 1927, the *Salt Lake Tribune* reported: "War between police and bootleggers after nightfall, at the present time, has developed into more or less of a one-sided conflict, in which the rum dealers have the odds." Two years later the newspaper reported federal agents had been threatened with bodily harm, and precautionary measures were taken. Rumors of a similar nature surfaced throughout the era:

> Members of a bootleg ring are believed to be planning a swift revenge, according to officers. Reports intimate that a group of racketeers had been brought to Salt Lake from a distant city to assist with the work.[59]

Agents especially feared going into Carbon County and at times refused to return there. Scoffing at Prohibition was an amusement: a Helper baseball

---

5, 1933. Of the Helper officials, only Charles Bertolino was found innocent, and he became acting mayor.

[54]*News Advocate,* April 15, 1927.

[55]*Salt Lake Tribune,* February 12, 1931.

[56]*News Advocate,* October 31, December 1, 1927.

[57]Heleotes interviews.

[58]*News Advocate,* April 27, 1922; *Bingham Press Bulletin,* August 9, 1918; *Salt Lake Tribune,* January 17, 1925.

[59]*Salt Lake Tribune,* October 25, 1929, January 21, 1932.

team was called the Bootleggers. Carbon County had been described as "wide open" since early settlement days when cattle were rustled from southern Utah and northern Arizona through Nine Mile Canyon to Myton and Vernal for summer range and on to Union Pacific railheads in Wyoming.

> This brought into the county a bunch of hard riding fast shooting men who generally had money. . . . In addition these rustlers required liquor and entertainment and from somewhere these "wide open" items always seemed available.[60]

Carbon County's wide-openness was accepted by almost everyone, but W. F. Olsen, mayor of Price, angrily replied to a derogatory *Deseret News* editorial on the subject with a letter to the editor: "Our two marshalls [*sic*] are good Latter-day Saints even in keeping strictly the word of wisdom."[61]

Complaints about laxness in Carbon County did not abate. Letters to federal government officials, the United States attorney general, and Gov. George H. Dern resulted in a vast raid. Agents met in Scofield at 3:30 on an August afternoon in 1928 and spread out to Colton, Helper, Price, the surrounding coal camps, and Eureka in the Tintic Mining District. They succeeded in making numerous arrests.[62]

When public protests reached a proportion that could not be ignored, raids followed and agents smiled in the foreground of a pile of stills for newspaper photographers. Editors and readers were scornful of thee raids:

> Frequent accounts appear of the destruction of confiscated liquor, in which a great ceremony is made of the event. It is quite the fad to delegate the actual destruction to some dry organization, under the direction of the proper officers of the law. A public place in the streets is selected, due publicity given in advance and then the "Roman holiday." The assembled crowd looks on with varied audible expressions.[63]

The scorn was fueled constantly by contempt for the law that came from the very makers of laws. George Zeese, who accompanied Carl R. Marcusen of Price, state Republican chairman and a candidate for governor, to the August 16, 1928, state GOP convention in Ogden, said: "Whiskey was everywhere in the convention hall. What went on! It was almost impossible to believe. A big drinking party."[64] On another occasion, when a well-known lobbyist dropped one of two quart bottles of pre-Prohibition Scotch whisky on the marble floor of the Utah State Capitol building, he explained, before hurrying off, that it was medicine for the sick wife of a legislator.[65]

The "Era of the Big Lie," a writer characterized the period:

[60]West MS., p. 17.
[61]*Sun,* April 28, 1928.
[62]*Sun,* August 30, 1928.
[63]*Salt Lake Tribune,* December 4, 1926.
[64]Zeese reminiscence.
[65]*Salt Lake Tribune,* February 25, 1931.

> The drys lied to make prohibition look good. . . . the wets lied to make it look bad; the government officials lied to make themselves look good and to frighten Congress into giving them more money to spend, and the politicians lied through force of habit.[66]

The foisting of Prohibition on the nation was catastrophic. The failure of the Volstead Act and the misery of the depression brought a clamor for repeal of the Eighteenth Amendment. Organizations sent resolutions to Governor Blood asking for a special session of the legislature to consider repeal. Yet Prohibitionists fought with valiant, impotent fervor to keep the amendment. At a mass meeting in the Salt Lake Tabernacle to rally against repeal, speakers pleaded for more money and men to enforce Prohibition. "Death is preferable to the iron collar of liquor," a Methodist minister proclaimed.[67]

Prohibition was repealed by the Twenty-first Amendment that required ratification by thirty-six states. Utah won over Maine's bid to become the thirty-sixth state by Governor Blood's quick action in convening the legislature to vote on it.[68] Utah, however, remained a dry state until 3.2 beer became legal in January 1934, and liquor continued to be bootlegged until the present state monopoly was established in 1935. In the interim, Wyoming whiskey from Kemmerer selling for $1.25 was a drinker's "good stuff."

[66]Herbert Asbury, quoted in Engelmann, *Intemperance,* p. 161.
[67]*Salt Lake Tribune,* May 4, 16, April 6, 1933.
[68]*Salt Lake Tribune,* February 21, 1933.

*

Struggle Against Great Odds: Challenges in Utah's Marginal Agricultural Areas, 1925–1939

BRIAN Q. CANNON

The period between World War I and World War II, and the 1930s specifically, were hard times for Utahns, as they were for Americans in general. In this article Brian Cannon discusses the difficulties rural Utahns in particular faced in the 1920s and continuing through the Great Depression years of the 1930s. He examines the nature and impact of the crisis, the suffering it caused, and the government's response to it. What becomes clear is that Utahns, like other Americans, faced with a disaster of unprecedented proportions, turned to the federal government for help. The problems were too great for individuals, private charities, or state and local governments to handle. As a result, a principle was established that federal and state governments not only have a responsibility to provide relief from disaster but also have a duty to work to maintain the economic health of the nation. The Great Depression, in other words, changed the conception of people in Utah and throughout the United States as to what was the nature and proper role of government.

Brian Q. Cannon, "Struggle Against Great Odds: Challenges in Utah's Marginal Agricultural Areas, 1925–39," *Utah Historical Quarterly* 54 (Fall 1986): 308–27. Reprinted by permission of the publisher and the author.

Brian Q. Cannon received a Ph.D. degree in history from the University of Wisconsin and is a member of the history department at Brigham Young University.

DISASTER STALKED MUCH OF UTAH'S AGRICULTURE in the 1920s and '30s. Indeed, the years 1925–39 can be viewed as a round of rural distress. Environmental, sociocultural, and economic factors handicapped farmers and ranchers throughout the state but most acutely in marginal agricultural areas: southern, eastern, and western Utah. Haphazardly extended beyond its environmental and economic limits, agriculture there began to flounder on its wobbly framework. This paper identifies specific flaws within that framework. Taken together, these flaws explain why social planners advocated major agricultural reforms for the state, including rural resettlement.

A host of environmental problems beset farmers and ranchers in marginal areas in the 1920s and '30s. Among them was soil deficiency. Although soils in Utah included rich alluvial loam, soil studies conducted during the '20s and '30s in Uintah, Duchesne, Carbon, Emery, and Millard counties revealed that in many cases farming there had been undertaken on inferior soils. In Uintah County, only 15 percent of all privately owned land offered good soil. Further west in Duchesne County alkaline soils strewn with gravel mocked farming efforts. South of the Uinta Basin, Carbon and Emery county soils were generally "not of farming quality." Impregnated with alkali, much of the soil consisted of mancos shale—an uninviting substance that became sticky when wet and rock-hard when dry.[1]

Yet it was in the western part of the state that soils least adapted to farming had been cultivated. Eighty-five percent of the soil in Millard County's Delta area was difficult to cultivate or maintain a favorable tilth on because of its heavy clay texture. Furthermore, alkali had rendered large tracts entirely unproductive. As land had been brought under irrigation following the completion of Sevier Bridge Reservoir in 1914, seepage from canals and excess irrigation water had caused the water table to rise, saturating the soil. Hot sun and dry air quickly evaporated the moisture, leaving behind a saline residue. Depending upon their concentration, these salts had either reduced the quality of crops produced or sterilized the soil.[2]

Faced with declining productivity, many farmers in Millard County abandoned their lands. In the Delta area 21 percent of the area's homes had been deserted by 1931. Nearly all farms in some towns such as Abraham and Woodrow lay vacant.[3] Once farms had been abandoned plant regression ensued, with inferior plants rather than climax vegetation taking over. Overgrazing and drought combined in other areas to produce similar results. Irrigation water, too, spread weeds throughout the state.

Regardless of its causes, plant regression reduced the land's value for agriculture. Most of the new plants were less nutritious for stock than their predecessors. Some, such as the whorled milkweed, proved lethal to livestock, while others with thorns and spines injured cattle and sheep. Furthermore, the new plants were often annuals with root systems shallow and less drought-resistant than those of perennial plants. As such they offered little protection to the soil.[4]

[1]R. H. Walker, *Pioneering in Western Agriculture,* Utah Agricultural Experiment Station (UAES) bulletin no. 282 (Logan, 1938), pp. 28–299; Russell R. Keetch, "Annual Report of Extension Work in Uintah County, 1936," p. 7, Utah State University Archives (USUA), Logan; and J. Howard Maughan, "Continuation of Study of the Extent of Desirable Major Land-Use Adjustments and Areas Suitable for Settlement" (n.p., 1936), p. 56. Box 01, Independent Commissions: Planning Board-Agriculture, 1934–41, Utah State Archives (SA), Salt Lake City.

[2]D. S. Jennings and J. Darrel Peterson, *Drainage and Irrigation, Soil, Economic and Social Conditions, Delta Area, Utah: Division 2, Soil Conditions,* UAES bulletin no. 256 (Logan, 1935), pp. 8, 34.

[3]Walker, *Pioneering,* p. 120.

[4]A. F. Bracken, "State Report on Land-Use Study for Utah" (n.p., 1935), pp. 71–72, 76, copy in files of Charles S. Peterson. Utah State University (USU), Logan.

In addition to battling new varieties of troublesome weeds, farmers combated an increasingly diverse host of insect pests and plant diseases. These included the beet leafhopper which induced curly top disease in sugar beets, beans, and tomatoes; the lygus bug which decimated alfalfa seed, an important cash crop for Millard County and the Uinta Basin; pale western cutworms; strawberry root rot; grasshoppers; Mormon crickets; and says bugs. Mere percentages and dollar amounts cannot convey the consequences of these pests. Those consequences can be glimpsed, however, through the experience of Cedar Valley dry farmers. For three years, over 25 percent of their planted wheat fell prey to the pale western cutworm. Destitute and unable to combat the worms, many of the growers abandoned their farms.[5]

Not only did agriculture suffer from poor soil, plant regression, and insects, it also experienced recurrent drought. During the thirties, drought hit throughout the state, albeit unevenly. However, the entire state suffered from low precipitation in 1931 and 1934, to that date "the driest (year) of record in the history of Utah on all watershed(s) in the state." Writing to Harry L. Hopkins, in June 1934, Utah emergency relief director Robert H. Hinckley reported, "Large areas of planted wheat have been abandoned, garden crops have been plowed and then left to die so water could be diverted elsewhere. Much of the grain is shrunken. Pests, lacking their natural food, are eating the remaining crops in destitute regions."[6]

Such regions could be found throughout southern, eastern, and western Utah. Beaver County lost 75 percent of its alfalfa to drought. In Millard County, many farmers lost their entire wheat crop. Ranchers near Delta dug water holes and troughs to catch and store water lest their livestock die of thirst. In the state as a whole, farmers planted only 30 percent of the normal acreage in 1934 and harvested only 40 percent of that in some areas. As much as 65 percent of the range withered away.[7]

Plant cover, withered by drought or consumed by livestock, invited erosion, thereby threatening to rob the land of necessary topsoil. State land use planning consultant A. F. Bracken wrote, "The problem of range erosion covers a wide area and affects more people than any other maladjustment from which the population of the state is suffering." In 1934 the Forest Service classified 60 percent of Utah's rangeland and the entire land area of Carbon, Emery, Grand, and Kane counties as "severely eroded." Following heavy rainfall on September 3, 1936, agricultural experiment station per-

[5]Blanche C. Pittman, comp., *How Science Aids Utah Agriculture,* UAES bulletin no. 276 (Logan, 1936), pp. 20–26.

[6]George D. Clyde, "Preliminary Report on Snow Cover of the Principal Watersheds of Utah, February 1, 1935," and Robert H. Hinckley to Harry L. Hopkins, June 29, 1934, FERA Correspondence, both in Henry H. Blood Papers, SA.

[7]Lew Mar Price, "Annual Report of Extension Work, Beaver County," (n.p., 1934), p. 16, USUA; George Whornham, "Annual Report of Extension Work, Millard County," (n.p., 1934), p. 5, USUA; N. Lester Mangum to Robert H. Hinckley, May 5, 1934, FERA Correspondence, Blood Papers, SA; and Leonard J. Arrington, *Utah, the New Deal and the Depression,* Weber State College, Dayton Lecture (Ogden, 1983), pp. 12–13.

sonnel discovered how serious erosion could be. Measuring silt and organic matter within the Duchesne River, they found that 17,500 tons of solid material—enough to bury an acre of land ten feet deep—passed by a single point within one hour. Rapid erosion produced gaping chasms. Three or more gullies per acre cut across nearly 70 percent of Uinta Basin Indian land. Bisecting roads, these chasms made road travel in some areas impossible.[8]

Barren soil invited wind as well as water erosion. On heavily grazed sections of the west desert, between two and six inches of soil had blown away by 1935. Blowing sand blasted plants, cutting them down to mere stumps. Perhaps Utah's severest blow area was near Grantsville where several dust storms in 1934 and 1935 enveloped 40,000 acres in a pall of dust. Billowing soil penetrated homes and barns in the area and halted highway traffic. Clouds of dust limited vision so much that the postman could not deliver mail. To filter out the dust some residents wrapped wet towels around their faces. Lacking such filters, sheep and cattle in the area died from breathing the dust or eating dirt-clogged feed. One man abandoned his ranch, and others seriously contemplated moving away as a result of the storms' destruction.[9]

All of these environmental problems curtailed agricultural production in the 1920s and '30s. In summary, these problems included soil deficiency, plant regression, insect pests, drought, and erosion. They stemmed only partially from human land use: in a dialectical relationship society and nature had forged them. But regardless of their origins, the problems mandated sociocultural adjustments, including changes in agricultural practices and characteristics.

Among those practices requiring adjustment was dry farming. By 1929 Utah dry farms comprised 200,000 acres. At the height of the dry-farm boom earlier in the century, much more land had been involved: over 5,000 homesteaders had patented dry farms as a result of the Enlarged Homestead Act of 1909. Under proper conditions, dry farming could yield impressive harvests. However, it was a tricky business whose success varied with precipitation, temperature, slope of the land, wind, and cultural practices. Untrained farmers simplistically sunk savings in unproductive tracts. Near Fillmore, for example, where precipitation averaged 15 inches annually, farmers planted dry wheat. Harvests were minimal, whereas a few miles north in Levan, farmers harvested a good crop. Precipitation in the two areas was comparable but other conditions were not. In some areas rainfall came too late in the summer to be of much benefit to dryland wheat. Most who had settled such tracts had abandoned them by 1930. However, in 1935 Utah's land planning consultant, J. Howard Maughan, observed that

[8]Bracken, "State Report on Land-Use," p. 51; and L. A. Stoddart et al., *Range Conditions in the Uinta Basin, Utah,* UAES bulletin no. 283 (Logan, 1938), pp. 22–23.

[9]Bracken, "State Report on Land-Use," p. 50; and Harley J. Helm and Graham S. Quate, "Report on the Wind Erosion and Dust Menace, Grantsville, Tooele County, Utah," in Grantsville and Shambys Soils Conservation Districts, *Conservation History of Tooele County* (n.p. 197[?]), in USUA.

"a surprising number still hold on to their land, . . . beaten and broken victims of a false hope that could not be realized." Some form of land use adjustment seemed necessary for these people.[10]

A characteristic typical of but not limited to dry farming was unprofitable small farms. This too required adjustment. In 1925, 47 percent of Utah's farms had fewer than fifty acres, and 22 percent contained 20 acres or less. Soil and climate ruled out intensive cultivation of some of these small farms. Moreover, many of them in marginal areas lacked sufficient irrigation water.[11]

Not only were Utah's farms small, but they were often composed of scattered, oddly shaped parcels of land. Tracts such as these proved difficult to cultivate and irrigate. Furthermore, they facilitated division of farms. This occurred frequently between 1920 and 1930; although the number of acres under cultivation remained virtually the same over the decade, the number of farms under 20 acres in size rose from 4,610 to 6,617. Already too small to sustain a family comfortably, many farms were divided into still smaller units.[12]

In some areas better suited for ranching than farming, residents lacked range rights. Along the Nevada-Utah border in Millard, Juab, and Tooele counties early homestead laws had sharply limited land claims, facilitating absentee ownership of the range. By the 1930s outside livestock interests controlled much of the range. Nonresident ownership impoverished once-prosperous local residents.[13]

Areas of more recent settlement also lacked range rights. Settlers in the Uinta Basin as well as dry-farm owners in Johns Valley, Garfield County; western Box Elder County; and the La Sal area had arrived too late to acquire title to the range. Conditions in these areas proved to be ill-suited to farming, but nonresidents already held key alpine grazing rights there. In the Uinta Basin, 23 percent of all animal-unit months of grazing allotted on federal lands in 1937 went to outside stockmen. Furthermore, the average outside owner of sheep received permits to graze twice as many sheep on the public domain as the average resident.[14]

Taken together, nonresident and resident livestock grazing used 85 percent of Utah's land. The range industry's incorrect seasonal use of that land, improper distribution of livestock on it, and overall surplus of livestock decimated the range in southern, eastern, and western Utah. Although grazing had been restricted within national forest reserves beginning in the first decade of the century, Utah's sheep industry reached an all-time high in 1930.

[10]Marion Clawson et al., *Types of Farming in Utah,* UAES bulletin no. 275 (Logan, 1936), pp. 32, 62, 66.

[11]Byron Alder, "The Poultry Industry in Utah," p. 5, Agricultural College file, 1930, George H. Dern Papers, SA.

[12]Bracken, "State Report on Land-Use," p. 29.

[13]Maughan, "Continuation of Report," pp. 72–73.

[14]Ibid., pp. 59, 65, 69–70; and George T. Blanch, *A Study of Farm Organization by Types of Farms in Uinta Basin, Utah,* UAES bulletin no. 285 (Logan, 1939), pp. 17–18, 65–66.

Grazing restrictions had upgraded some lands, but overgrazing remained a serious problem. Sixty percent of Utah's range and nearly all of Kane and Garfield counties was severely eroded and "badly overgrazed" by 1934. For communities almost entirely reliant upon livestock these statistics spelled disaster. Two such Garfield County towns, Cannonville and Henryville, had an aggregate population of six hundred. With approximately four hundred acres of irrigated land between them and a badly depleted range, these communities faced defeat. Much of the population was on relief. To the east of these town, Escalante, primarily a stock-raising area that had once boasted a per capita income of $1,000, had to import $20,000 worth of feed for livestock from 1933 to 1935. In 1935, 70 percent of the town's 1,000 residents were on relief due to depleted range and crop failure.[15]

Improper management of water paralleled poor range management. Three problems contributed to this: improper drainage, ineffective irrigation networks, and overextended and improperly allocated water resources. One consequence of improper drainage has already been discussed: alkali accumulation in the soil. Another consequence, irrigation-induced erosion and flooding, occurred most frequently in Carbon and Emery counties where soil was highly susceptible to erosion. Gullies formed rapidly on farms where excess irrigation water repeatedly followed the same drainage course. They grew quickly as water undercut their banks, causing adjacent land to cave in. Gorges 100–200 feet deep and 10–70 feet wide became common.[16]

Ineffective irrigation systems, the second water management problem mentioned above, resulted in the loss of vital water. These systems often lacked sound engineering. Some, such as a canal designed to bring water from Lake Fork River to North Myton Bench in Duchesne County, never did work. After residents had invested "thousands of dollars worth of work," the canal's banks "washed out like salt," one resident recalled. Similarly, a dam built by land promoters in southern Utah's Grass Valley "would not hold water" because it was surrounded by a lava flow. Many other systems suffered heavy conveyance losses. The Central Utah Canal near Delta which carried water thirty-seven miles lost 70 percent of its water through evaporation and seepage. Other systems had fallen into disrepair. Long canals serving a handful of people often became dilapidated, for those using the canals could not muster the manpower to maintain them.[17]

The third problem involved overextended and improperly allocated water resources. In the state's twenty principal irrigated counties, 41 percent of all irrigated acreage had a first class water right in 1930. Twenty-five percent had a secondary right, 22 percent a third class right, and 12 percent a fourth

[15]Bracken, "State Report on Land-Use," p. 25; and Maughan, "Continuation of Report," p. 69.

[16]I. D. Zobell, *Soil Management and Crop-Production Studies: Carbon County Area,* UAES bulletin no. 270 (Logan, 1936), p. 7.

[17]LeAnn Wabel, "History of Anna R. Lemon Johnson," (n.p. 1983), Peterson files, USU; Maughan, "Continuation of Report," pp. 35, 49; and Loreen P. Wahlquist, "Memories of a Uintah Basin Farm," *Utah Historical Quarterly* 42 (1974): 169.

class right. Thus, by midsummer many farms had little if any water. In 1934 the state's land planning consultant reported that 160 farms comprising 12,000 acres in the state-developed Piute Project had not been irrigated for years, possessing only a second or third class water right. Not surprisingly, only four of 160 families remained. One resident who abandoned his farm on the project was Rasmus Michelsen. Michelsen had purchased eighty acres of project land to which the state had promised to deliver three acre-feet of water per acre of land. Yet the project had generally delivered only four to six inches of water per acre.[18]

A similar problem with overextension of water emerged along the lower Beaver River on a strip of land known as Beaver Bottoms. Twenty-two farms in the region dried up when developers built Minersville Dam several miles north of the region. Because the dam rarely filled, only a trickle of water ever reached these farms. Unable to pay the cost of lawsuits against the reservoir company, these residents sold their water rights to the company and completely abandoned their homes, farms, and school.[19]

Besides being inadequate, water resources were poorly distributed. Millard County extension agent George Whornham indicated, "In many cases irrigation water is applied to land which never did nor never can economically produce crops in sufficient quantity to produce a living. On the other hand, many good farms are being ruined and made unproductive because not enough water is being applied." The state agricultural experiment station observed similar problems besetting "most irrigation enterprises" in the state.[20]

In summary, agricultural characteristics and practices that bore bitter consequences in southern, eastern, and western Utah included ill-advised dry farming, small farm size, and lack of range rights. Others were poor range management, improper drainage, ineffective irrigation networks, and overextended water resources. All of these practices pointed to the need for land use adjustment.

In addition to environmental and agricultural problems, social challenges plagued the state's marginal agricultural areas in the 1920s and '30s. Foremost among those challenges was population pressure on the land. Utah's rural population increased 16 percent from 1900 to 1910, 16 percent from 1910 to 1920, and 3.3 percent from 1920 to 1930. Already hemmed in by insufficient water and submarginal soil, the state's agriculture could ill accommodate this surge in population. Several phenomena manifest this inability to adjust to the rise in population. Among them was the

[18]Clawson et al., *Types of Farming,* p. 30; Bracken, "Utah Report," 15; and Rasmus Michelsen to Henry H. Blood, November 30, 1940, Land Board Correspondence, Blood Papers, SA. Class I water rights were those with no water shortage during ordinary years. Class II rights experienced some shortages but had enough water to mature crops. Class III rights furnished water during flood season only. Class IV rights were those which during a normal year provided water for no more than thirty days.

[19]Bracken, "Report on Land-Use," pp. 99, 109; and Maughan, "Continuation of Report," pp. 36, 44–45.

[20]Maughan, "Continuation of Report," p. 36; and Clawson et al., *Types of Farming,* pp. 28–29.

large number of unestablished young people. In 1939 Sanpete County's extension agent counted 364 unestablished, young married couples; 383 single, unestablished men ages 18–30; and 276 single, unestablished women ages 18–30 in the county. Millard County's agent predicted that this region's 2,000 men and women ages 16–30 had little chance of starting a home or farm on their own. Another sign of the population-land imbalance surfaced in an overabundance of farm labor. In the reservation area of the Uinta Basin, the average farmer had almost 200 surplus man days of labor each year. A third sign of overpopulation involved division of farms, a trend previously discussed.[21]

In addition to population pressure, rural sociologists noted a second imbalance in rural life: the paucity of social institutions and public services in some areas. At the same time New Deal planners in Washington were extolling the community conveniences and spirit of Utah's Mormon villages, sociologists within the state were detecting deficiencies in rural Utah. Not all rural residents lived in villages, they observed; farms in areas of more recent settlement were often dispersed. Moreover, villages often lacked a variety of high quality community services because of tax delinquency, poverty, and isolation.[22]

A detailed study of the Delta area revealed many such deficiencies. Only 20 percent of state and local taxes levied there in 1931 were collected. This limited revenue could support few community services. Only one town in the area had a public library, only five of the eight communities had mail service, and none had a municipal water system. Several had no playground, baseball diamond, rodeo grounds, or park, and hospital facilities were distant. Oasis, perhaps the most dismal of the eight communities, "was a village in ruins in 1936," according to one rural sociologist. Its small church lacked indoor plumbing, its roads had received "little attention," and its cemetery "was poorly maintained." No village recreational facilities existed. The depression had closed many businesses including a drugstore, dry goods store, meat market, bank, two lumber yards, grocery store, barber shop, service station, and alfalfa seed plant. Not all communities offered as few services as Oasis, but many towns throughout the state in the 1930s were not inviting places to live, according to studies of the state's rural communities.[23]

[21]Walker, *Pioneering,* p. 24; Blanch, *Farm Organization in Uinta Basin,* p. 85; Elmer H. Gibson. "Annual Report of Extension Work, Sanpete County, 1939," p. 69, USUA; and Bracken, "Report on Land-Use," pp. 5–6.

[22]A. F. Bracken, "Utah Report on the Extent and Character of Desirable Adjustment in Rural Land-Use and Settlement Areas" (n.p., 1934), *passim;* Agriculture Planning Board Reports, SA; and Paul K. Conkin, *Tomorrow a New World: The New Deal Community Program* (Ithaca, NY: Cornell University Press, 1959), pp. 13–14, 81. Responsible for much of the idealization of Mormon villages was M. L. Wilson, director of the Subsistence Homesteads Division.

[23]Joseph A. Geddes, Carmen D. Fredrickson, and Eldred C. Bergeson, *Drainage and Irrigation, Soil, Economic and Social Conditions, Delta Area, Utah: Division 4, Social Conditions,* UAES bulletin no. 288 (Logan, 1939), *passim.*

Poor living conditions also plagued marginal agricultural areas. In some conveniences, rural Utah compared favorably with rural areas in the nation at large. For example, Utah ranked third in the percentage of farmhomes with electricity (58 percent), and thirteenth in the percentage of farms having running water (39 percent). Nevertheless, these statistics belied pockets of primitive living conditions. In the Delta area only 28 percent of all homes had running water. Duchesne and Uintah counties (respectively 4 and 21 percent) did not come close to approximating the state's 58 percent of homes with electricity. Similarly, while 27 percent of the state's homes had phone service, only 3 percent in Duchesne County and 14 percent in Uintah County had phones.[24]

Generally, as the isolation of an area increased, so did primitive living conditions. In the isolated Uinta Basin, many homes were shabby. Small and cheaply built, they had unplaned, mud-chinked walls and dirt floors. Because running water was rare (4 percent in Duchesne and 9 percent in Uintah) many households hauled culinary water from irrigation ditches or rivers. Others dipped irrigation water from cisterns near their homes for household use. Typical was the lifestyle of Anna R. Lemon Johnson. During the winter of 1936–37 she and her family lived in a tarpaper shack made of one-inch boards. Eventually most of the tarpaper blew off, allowing snow to whip through the cracks in the wall. Temperatures outside often plunged to 44 below. Anna's husband Frank would arise at 4 A.M., stoke a fire in the kitchen stove to warm the place a bit, and huddle on the oven door for the balance of the night. Anna was pregnant that winter "which made it harder for me," she recalled. She hauled snow for water, which she stored in a fifty-gallon barrel. The following summer she and her family moved to an eighty-by-twenty-four-foot camp cabin. It was a "really strange set up," she recalled, for it had truck doors built into the side with roll-up-and-down windows. Bedbugs, mites, and flies shared the place with the family. New Deal social planners found such conditions to be widespread and deplorable.[25]

By the 1930s many people favored and even demanded government-engineered assistance and improvements. "The people here . . . are crying for help," wrote Uintah County's extension agent. From Millard County came a similar report of people "waiting for the Rehabilitation Division to do something." Personal pleas fill Governor Henry H. Blood's files. Typical is this one: "My farm is being sold at sheriff's sale for interest. I have not the money to pay. I would like help. Wire if you can help me."[26]

Relief came too late or amounted to too little to succor some. Many deserted their farms. Only 2.2 in 1,000 families migrated from the state, according to a WPA study of interstate migration. Of those families, only 7

[24]Blanch, *Farm Organization in Uinta Basin,* pp. 12–23; and Geddes, *Social Conditions, Delta Area,* pp. 51–52.

[25]Blanch, *Farm Organization in Uinta Basin,* p. 13; and Wabel, "Anna R. Lemon Johnson."

[26]Keetch, "Annual Report, 1937," p. 7; George Wornham, "Annual Report of Extension Work, Millard County 1935," p. 15, in USUA; and Glen Gates to Honorable Governor Blood, November 21, 1934, FERA Correspondence, Blood Papers, SA.Z

percent listed farm failure as the principal cause of their move. Though few farmers actually left the state, many did abandon their farms. Twenty-one percent of the Delta area's homes lay vacant in 1930. In the state at large the 1930 farm population was only 81 percent of what it had been in 1920. By 1934 Aaron F. Bracken, Utah's land planning consultant, noted almost total abandonment of sections across the state. In 1940 only 94,352 people were living on farms, down from 106,667 in 1930.[27]

That more did not move from their farms is surprising, given the depth and pervasiveness of disaster. The fact that many of the earlier settlements traced their roots to colonization calls from Mormon church leaders may have contributed to this resilience. This heritage firmly bound farmers to their homes in Utah's Dixie. Even in areas of more recent, economically motivated settlement, religious zeal could reinforce ties to the community. For example, decades following his removal from the town of Widtsoe, one farmer recalled a promise made by Mormon apostle Melvin J. Ballard to the community's residents. The valley would be a Garden of Eden if its inhabitants kept God's commandments and stayed out of debt, Ballard had prophesied. If they did not do so, it would be taken from them. Ballard's words had infused the land with sacred meaning, rendering the valley a symbolic link between the area's residents and God. Remembering that promise, the people clung to their land as long as they physically could. To move away was to admit spiritual as well as temporal failure. Although all but two families eventually moved away, some former residents of the area still remember that promise, speak of their valley reverently, make annual pilgrimages to it, and speculate that it may one day blossom.[28]

In summary, social problems of southern, eastern, and western Utah during the '20s and '30s included a population-land imbalance, insufficient or inadequate social institutions, poor housing conditions, and migration. In their efforts to eradicate these problems, New Deal reformers faced two common attitudes: expectation of government aid and religiously motivated tenacity to even submarginal land.

It has been shown that environmental, agricultural, and social deficiencies and imbalances handicapped farmers in southern, eastern, and western Utah in the 1920s and '30s. Much had also gone awry economically. When the bottom fell out of the stock market in 1929, Utah agriculture had been contributing little to national commerce. Nevertheless, some agricultural sectors marketed most of their products. Commercial surges in Utah in the

[27]John N. Webb and Malcolm Brown, *Migrant Families,* W.P.A. Research Monograph XVIII (Washington, D.C.: GPO, 1938), pp. 137, 151; Geddes, *Social Conditions, Delta Area,* pp. 58, 120; Joseph A. Geddes, *Migration: A Problem of Youth in Utah,* UAES bulletin no. 323 (Logan, 1946), p. 6; and Bracken, "Utah Report," *passim.*

[28]J. Howard Maughan, "A Resume of Community Settlement in Washington County, Utah" (Logan, 1935), p. 6, Land Use folder, Agriculture Planning Board Reports, Independent Commissions, SA: Mabel W. Nielsen and Audrie C. Ford, *Johns Valley—The Way We Saw It* (Springville: Art City Publishing Co., 1971), p. 70; and interview by author with Reed Reynolds and Ileen Reynolds, January 12, 1985.

first three decades of the century had involved sheep, cattle, poultry, fruit, dryland wheat, alfalfa seed, and sugar beets. Producers of these goods had a stake in the national economy by 1929.[29]

A good example of southern Utah's blend of subsistence and commercial farming was Washington County agriculture. In 1914 a new, good road connecting the county with Salt Lake City and Los Angeles made fruit shipments to major urban markets possible. County agricultural agents encouraged increased production and marketing. Wholesale houses in Salt Lake and Los Angeles also sent agents to the county to purchase fruit and vegetables. Yet commercialization remained limited: by 1928 farm size, production, and profits continued to be small, with only 1,900 of the county's 16,000 cultivated acres producing truck crops, fruits, or nuts.[30]

Those farmers who did market their products in the '20s and '30s suffered blistering defeat. Already low farm prices plummeted even more during the first five years of the depression, contributing to that defeat. National agricultural prices fell 40 percent between 1929 and 1934 as supply far outstripped demand. Meanwhile, industrial prices fell only 15 percent. Illustrative of this fact, a bushel of wheat which had sold for $1.03 in 1929 sold for 38 cents in 1932. At that price, ten bushels of wheat would buy only a pair of cheap shoes. Prices paid Utah farmers for agricultural commodities hit rock bottom in February 1933. Prices in 1933 were only 73 percent of parity (average farm prices for 1910–14). Prices then began to rise, until by 1937 they were 123 percent of the prewar level. The Roosevelt recession in 1938 again pushed prices down, to 104 percent. At no time during the decade did prices approach the 139 percent level of the '20s, let along the 170 percent level of World War I.[31]

Falling livestock and land values accompanied declining prices. Having invested when high prices prevailed, farmers could not recover their investments. Utah stockmen were particularly hard hit. While Utah's sheep population declined only 15 percent from 1929 to 1933, the population's value plummeted 78 percent. Utah cattlemen owned 20,000 more cattle in 1933 than they had in 1929, yet the aggregate value of the stock was $17 million lower than it had been in 1927. Farmers also felt the crunch. In Washington County, land values that had escalated 189 percent between 1920 and 1929 fell 31 percent from 1930 to 1935. Farmers could neither pay taxes on their property nor repay their loans. Typical was the struggle of one young couple in the Uinta Basin, Fred and Loreen Wahlquist. In 1928 they "bought a

[29]Bracken, "Report on Land-Use," pp. 21–23, 28. Utah's total yearly cash income from agriculture averaged $54,604,000 for 1926–30.

[30]Clark Knowlton, "Washington County and the Depression," pp. 7–13, copy in the files of Charles S. Peterson, USU.

[31]Richard N. Current, T. Harry Williams, and Frank Friedel, *American History: A Survey,* 2d ed. (New York: Alfred A. Knopf, Inc., 1967), p. 762; W. Preston Thomas and George T. Blanch, *Drainage and Irrigation, Social, Economic, and Soil Conditions, Delta Area, Utah: Division 3, Economic Conditions,* UAES bulletin no. 273 (Logan, 1936), pp. 7–8; and W. Preston Thomas, George T. Blanch, and Edith Hayball, *A Study of Farm Organization by Type of Farm in Sanpete and Sevier Counties,* UAES bulletin no. 300 (Logan, 1941), p. 26.

bunch of cows for a high price." By 1931 prices were dropping, and the Wahlquists were offered $70.00 a head for their five best cows. Unwisely, they chose not to sell. Three years later, lacking feed for the cows, the Wahlquists sold them to the government for $16.00 a head.[32]

Low and decreasing farm production further complicated southern and eastern Utah's agricultural economy. Utah harvested its largest acreage of crops ever in 1922 and its greatest yield per acre in 1925. Following these peak years, production oscillated but diminished overall. The seven-year period from 1931 to 1937 drew yields lower than any period of like length since Brigham Young's time. Particularly hard hit was the state's alfalfa seed production. In 1925, Utah had produced 22 million pounds of alfalfa. Acre yields in the Delta area had averaged 6.4 bushels. Four years later, Utah produced only 3 million pounds with annual acre yields in Delta reaching only 1.5 bushels for 1929–31. Drought more than any other factor constricted Utah's production during the thirties. Other contributing factors included soil problems, lack of crop rotation, and insect pests. Simultaneously, range problems caused livestock production to plummet 30–50 percent.[33]

As farm production and prices fell, farm operation costs became exorbitant. Operating expenses, including hired labor, feed, seed, interest payments, taxes, land and water rent, vehicle costs, repairs, and livestock purchases, drained farm income. Farm prices plunged far more than costs for these items. A bushel of dry land wheat, for example, cost 76 cents to produce in 1926–27 and 68 cents to produce in 1933–34. Meanwhile, the national price per bushel of wheat fell from $1.03 in 1929 to 38 cents in 1932.[34]

Costs of transporting goods to distant markets were among the most onerous operating expenses. In March 1933, 850–950 carloads of peas, cabbage, onions, and potatoes harvested the previous year still had not been shipped due to high transportation costs and low prices. Utah's 1938 apricot and cherry crops largely rotted because of prohibitive shipping costs. Utah peach growers anticipated a harvest of 600–800 carloads of peaches that year. To be competitive, those peaches had to be priced under $1.50 per bushel. The average costs of freighting and refrigeration alone amounted to 70 cents per bushel, far too high to make any profit on the crop. Producers in isolated areas where few highways or railroads existed—most notably Daggett, Rich, San Juan, Duchesne, and Uintah counties—suffered most acutely. They could ill support costs of transporting wheat, oats, barley, or corn to the nearest shipping facilities.[35]

[32]Merrill Stucki, "An Economic Study of Farmers' Cooperative Business Associations in Utah" (M.A. thesis, University of Utah, 1935), pp. 90, 101; Knowlton, "Washington County," p. 22; and Wahlquist, "Memories," p. 169.

[33]Walter U. Fuhriman, *Some Trends in Utah's Agriculture,* UAES bulletin no. 286 (Logan, 1939) pp. 9, 18, 20; and Thomas and Blanch, *Economic Conditions, Delta Area,* p. 6.

[34]Current, Williams, and Friedel, *American History,* p. 784; Walker, *Pioneering,* p. 20; and Stucki, "Economic Study," pp. 87–88.

[35]Stucki, "Economic Study," p. 74; Governor Henry H. Blood to A. J. Seitz, August 26, 1938; and Ward C. Holbrook, Otto A. Wiesley, and Walter K. Granger to A. J. Seitz and O. J. Grimes, August 22, 1938, both in Department of Agriculture Correspondence, 1938–1940,

Farmers in some areas still made enough money to offset operating costs. In Summit County, a livestock producing region, the average farm in 1930 grossed $2,520 in cash. Farm expenditures at $1,391 left $1,129 for family expenditures, a sufficient amount for necessities. Farmers in other areas, though, had less luck. Annual cash farm receipts in the Delta area for 1929–31 averaged $1,461, while average cash expenditures for a farm operation averaged $1,470. Farmers in the Uinta Basin and Carbon and Emery counties faced similar difficulties.[36]

A major component of operating expenses in these areas was drainage and irrigation taxation. It soared to exorbitant heights in the Delta area, largely as a result of drainage bond indebtedness. During the teens and early twenties three of the area's drainage districts had floated two bonds, and the remaining district had floated three bonds to construct drainage systems. Costs eventually totalled far more than originally estimated: farmers in the area thus faced an unpayable yearly assessment of $11 per cultivated acre for forty years. From 1929 to 1931 the drainage districts succeeded in collecting less than 10 percent of these net annual assessments, forcing them to default on bond payments. Drainage and irrigation taxation in the other areas was less than in the Delta area, but still excessive. By 1932 all three of the major water projects with State Land Board loans—Piute, central Utah, and Carbon—were battling "serious financial difficulties" because farmers could not meet their irrigation assessments.[37]

Partly because drainage and irrigation districts were over-capitalized, tax delinquency ran 40 percent in rural Utah by 1932. Delinquency in Kane, Duchesne, Garfield, and Wayne counties all topped 50 percent in that year. By 1933, 70 percent of Duchesne County's taxes were delinquent. The Thatcher-Magleby bill passed on March 1, 1933, extended the payment deadline for taxes accrued between 1928 and 1931 to January 1, 1935. A similar law passed in 1934 extended the deadline to May 1936. Notwithstanding this grace period, the county had taken control of nearly 65 percent of farms in the Delta area by 1936. Similarly, in another hard-hit area, Uintah County, 430 tax sales occurred in May 1936.[38]

Mortgage as well as tax indebtedness plagued farmers in many regions. High interest rates on loans assumed in more prosperous times mocked efforts at payment. Daggett County's state land appraiser, writing to the State Land

---

Blood Papers, SA; and James H. Eager and A. F. Bracken, *San Juan County Experimental Farm: Progress Report 1925–30, Inclusive,* UAES bulletin no. 230 (Logan, 1931), pp. 5, 9.

[36]Walker, *Pioneering,* p. 19; and Thomas and Blanch, *Economic Conditions, Delta Area,* p. 26.

[37]O. W. Israelsen, *Drainage and Irrigation, Soil, Economic, and Social Conditions, Delta Area, Utah: Division 1, Drainage and Irrigation conditions,* UAES bulletin no. 255 (Logan, 1935), pp. 9–11, 19, 46–47; and JFM, Executive Secretary to Governor George H. Dern, to Hon. Reed Smoot, February 11, 1932, Land Board Correspondence, January–February 1932, Dern Papers. SA.

[38]Knowlton, "Washington County," pp. 29, 31; Maughan, "Continuation of Report," p. 36; Russell R. Keetch, "Annual Report of Extension Work, Uintah County, 1936," p. 7, USUA; and Bracken, "Utah Report," p. 16.

Board, recounted the situation of a Mr. Twitchell who owed the state money on a small flock of sheep, a home, and a seventy-acre farm. Twitchell, who had lost his crops to drought in 1931 and could not sell his lambs, was not able to make payments on his loan. Many residents of Daggett County and of the state at large were in similar circumstances, the appraiser believed.[39]

State Land Board and Federal Land Bank records corroborated the appraiser's belief. The Federal Land Bank reported in 1932 that 43 percent of its Utah loans were delinquent. Of 945 mortgages held by the State Land Board on February 1, 1935, 78 percent had fallen delinquent. Although the State Land Board insisted that "in no case have foreclosures been instituted for the reason of interest or principal delinquencies alone," it had foreclosed on 508 farms by February 1935. By that year, the Federal Land Bank in Utah had also foreclosed on $2,140,615 out of a total of $4,690,504 in loans. Other banks had likewise foreclosed on farms. Banks and real estate firms owned nearly one-third of all property in Millard County in 1934, largely as a result of foreclosures.[40]

Mortgage payments, taxes, irrigation and drainage assessments, and operating expenses bled farm income dry. Average farm labor income—the cash income from farming after farm expenses, taxes, and mortgage payments were deducted—amounted to minus $709 for the Delta area, $172 for Sanpete County, and $303 for Sevier County. Farm labor income totaled $36 on Ashley Valley general farms, and minus $108 on Uintah Reservation general farms. Thirty-three percent of all Utah farms in 1929 had a *gross* income of under $1,000. Two extension service studies estimated that in 1929–31 the average farm family needed at least $1,000 to cover family expenses. To survive, farm families turned to off-farm labor where possible. Some made enough money to support themselves. Others did not.[41]

Unable to earn enough money, much of the population applied for relief. Nationwide, over one-fourth of all rural families *sought* relief between 1930 and 1936. The figure in Utah was probably much higher, for at the highest single point, in May 1934, 21 percent of the entire population was receiving relief. Figures escalated beyond this for some rural areas: 30 percent in Uintah County in July 1935, 71 percent in Duchesne County in June 1934, 53 percent in Millard County at one time, and 70 percent in Escalante in 1935.[42]

[39]John S. Bennett to Mr. Mendenhall, State Land Office, February 9, 1932, Land Board Correspondence, January–February 1932, Dern Papers, SA.

[40]Knowlton, "Washington County," pp. 19, 24; "Data Pertaining to the Activities of the State Land Board, State of Utah," February 5, 1935, Land Board Correspondence, 1935, Blood Papers, SA; untitled State Land Board document, Land Board Correspondence, January–February 1932, Dern Papers, SA; and Bracken, "Report on Land-Use," p. 102.

[41]Thomas and Blanch, *Economic Conditions, Delta Area,* pp. 25, 31–32, 35; Thomas, Blanch and Hayball, *Farm Organization in Sanpete and Sevier,* p. 37; Blanch, *Farm Organization in Uinta Basin, Utah,* pp. 37, 47; Clawson et al., *Types of Farming,* p. 37; and Edith Hayball and W. Preston Thomas, *Family Living Expenditures: Summit County, Utah, 1930,* UAES bulletin no. 232 (Logan, 1931), p. 29.

[42]Carle C. Zimmerman and Nathan L. Wetten, *Rural Families on Relief,* W.P.A. Research Monograph no. XVII (Washington, D.C.: GPO, 1938), p. xi: Richard D. Poll et al., eds., *Utah's History* (Provo: Brigham Young University Press, 1978), pp. 483, 487–88; S.R. DeBoer,

To summarize, serious economic problems hampered agriculture in southern, eastern, and western Utah during the 1920s and '30s. Among those problems were low farm prices, falling livestock and land values, and low production levels. Relatively high farm operating costs, mortgage payments, taxes, and irrigation and drainage expenses combined to further reduce farmers' and ranchers' earnings, forcing many onto relief.

For the nation at large, the 1920s exuded prosperity compared to the stark thirties. Real annual earnings in the twenties rose 11 percent, consumers enjoyed an increased selection of conveniences including appliances and automobiles at reduced prices, and the American dream of success attracted new disciples. Signs of prosperity even veiled the nation's agricultural sector, albeit thinly: farm expansion, including the plow-up of 5,260,000 virgin acres on the southern plains between 1925 and 1930, obfuscated the plight of the small farmer, caught in a vortex of high interest rates, dwindling markets, and declining farm prices. No such veil of expansion camouflaged rural distress in Utah: the number of acres under cultivation changed little between 1920 and 1930, and the rural farm population plummeted 19 percent. As the preceding discussion demonstrates, Utah's marginal agricultural regions were buckling long before the calamitous thirties. The twenties provided neither a vivid contrast nor a subtle prelude to the tragedy of the Great Depression. Rather, the stock market crash in October 1929, the subsequent depression, and the drought of 1934 only accentuated an agrarian tragedy well under way before then.[43]

The difference between the twenties and the thirties lay not so much in agricultural conditions as in governmental responsiveness to those conditions, and particularly to the plight of small farmers. Recognizing the plight of farmers in Utah's marginal agricultural regions and in the nation at large, the Resettlement Administration and other New Deal agencies sought to ameliorate rural problems. For those living on arable land but lacking necessary machinery or water they proposed rural rehabilitation loans and small reclamation projects. For those living on submarginal land, they proposed governmental purchase and revegetation of their land, and government-engineered resettlement in economically viable, rural, suburban, and urban environments. Thereby they hoped to promote small family farms and simultaneously to stem land abuse. Though such massive reforms proved untenable, in southern, eastern, and western Utah at least, conditions seemed to warrant them.[44]

"Uinta Basin" (n.p., 1936), in State Engineer 1935, Blood Papers. SA: Whornham, "Annual Report, 1935," p. 15; and Bracken,"Report on Land-Use," pp. 118–19.

[43]Bracken, "State Report on Land-Use," p. 29; Donald Worster, *Dust Bowl: The Southern Plains in the 1930s* (New York: Oxford University Press, 1979), p. 94; William E. Leuchtenberg, *The Perils of Prosperity, 1914–1932* (Chicago: University of Chicago Press, 1958), pp. 178–203; and Irving Bernstein, *The Lean Years: Workers in an Unbalanced Society* (Boston: Houghton Mifflin, 1960), pp. 81–82.

[44]Donald Holley, *Uncle Sam's Farmers: The New Deal Communities in the Lower Mississippi Valley* (Urbana: University of Illinois Press, 1975), pp. 196–97, 272–73; and Resettlement Administration, *First Annual Report* (Washington, D.C.: GPO, 1936).

PART III

*

World War II and After: The Emergence of Contemporary Utah

Photograph on preceding page: Utah women doing, in the words of the Salt Lake *Tribune*, "Man's Work," during World War II. Courtesy Utah State Historical Society.

*

Utah's Rosies: Women in the Utah War Industries During World War II

ANTONETTE CHAMBERS NOBLE

During World War II millions of women in the United States entered the work force for the first time. This article focuses on the experiences of women who worked in military industries in Utah during that war. In particular, it considers the war's influence on women's values, attitudes, and behaviors as well as women's responses to appeals to return to the home at war's end and efforts to see that they remained there. The article concludes that the experiences of Utah women were similar to those of women elsewhere in the United States and illustrates the difficulties women faced in challenging the traditional view of their proper place.

Women entered Utah's work force in unprecedented numbers, many of them finding jobs in areas previously closed to them. Although they proved to be effective workers, no permanent shift in the structure of Utah's labor force followed. Women's work during World War II was not a breakthrough that signaled the end of discrimination against women in the labor market. The war barely shook the notion that a woman's place was in the home, and in the end the rapid demobilization of both military and civilian economic sectors resulted in a basic restoration of former labor patterns.

Antonette Chambers Noble, "Utah's Rosies: Women in the Utah War Industries During World War II," *Utah Historical Quarterly* 59 (Spring 1991): 123–45. Reprinted by permission of the publisher and the author.

Antonette Chambers Noble earned a master's degree in history from the University of Utah and currently lives in Wyoming, where she is a member of the Wyoming Humanities Council.

"WHEN THE BIG PLANES (B-24s) came in, they were started through the hangers by first being washed down. People wore hats and long rain coats and used long hoses to reach," recalled Retha Nielson. "I, with other women, went to see them come in. I got a lump in my throat as I read the names of the men who had piloted them. Some of them had given the planes a name. One was called the Kitty Hawk. I would walk up to the big plane and touch it and wonder if all of the men had come out alive, what had happened, and why they had named it what they had. One plane had a pretty girl painted on it. She was dressed in Air Force clothes."[1] Retha was recalling her employment at the Ogden Air Service Command at Hill Field during World War II. She was one of several thousand women who took employment in a Utah war industry during the war. In addition to earning a good salary. Retha was patriotically serving her country.

When World War II abruptly came to America with the bombing of Pearl Harbor, leaders of economically devastated areas sought war contracts as the country frantically strengthened its military. Unemployment rates had peaked nationally in the 1930s at 25 percent, but in Utah 36 percent of the labor force was out of work. Utah's governor, Herbert B. Maw, and its congressional delegation, not surprisingly, were among the state and national politicians who tried to obtain war contracts for their communities. They advertised local advantages to military planners with fruitful results: war contracts were awarded to the state. The federal war work was implemented in Utah at military facilities and in private industries and with increased production of raw materials.

Women were employed at all Utah military facilities, including the Ogden Arsenal, the Utah General Depot, the Ogden Air Materiel Area at Hill Field, the Naval Supply Depot at Clearfield, and the Tooele Ordnance Depot. Women also worked at the Remington Arms Company, the Eitel McCullough Radio Tube Plant, and the Standard Parachute Company—private industries with military contracts. Furthermore, women substantially contributed to agricultural production in the state. Mining was the only area where women failed to make a large contribution. Utah's prewar laws restricting the employment of women in the mining industry remained unbending despite the wartime crisis.

Personnel directors at military installations and industries with war contracts wanted white males to fill labor positions. Uncle Sam, however, needed the same men for combat which of necessity took priority. The Utah war industries, like those around the country, turned to other groups when the pool of white males diminished. Although women would experience the greatest employment opportunities, nonwhites, the handicapped, and even interned German and Italian prisoners of war were assigned work in the military installations. This article will focus on the experiences of hundreds of women who took advantage of the wartime employment opportunities in Utah. A woman who took a war job became affectionately known as Rosie the Riveter after Norman Rockwell's 1943 *Saturday Evening Post* cover featuring a woman war worker.[2]

[1]Questionnaire completed by Retha Nielson, October 17, 1984, in author's possession.

[2]Scholarly works on American women in the war industries include Karen Anderson, "Last Hired, First Fired: Black Women Workers during World War II," *Journal of American History* (June 1982): 82; *Wartime Women: Sex Roles, Family Relations, and the Status of*

The call for women to enter the work force escalated as more men marched off to war. For example, spanning the *Deseret News* want ads in a banner headline during World War II was, "One Solution For Your Personnel Problem—Hire Women."[3] The *Ogden Standard Examiner* declared in 1942: "It is in the nature of patriotic duty of the highest order to apply at once at the personnel office of the Arsenal, . . . and Ogden women of all ages are urged to lay aside all considerations of need for earning money and come to the Arsenal to make a direct and vital contribution to the United Nations victory in the war."[4]

The calls for women workers were successful. Utah women responded to patriotic appeals and to promises of good salaries, pleasant conditions, and steady work obtainable without experience. Women constituted 17.6 percent of the Utah labor force in 1940 and 36.8 percent by 1944.[5] Government war plants employed a larger percentage of women than any other industrial concern. Still more were needed. On November 1, 1944, the local Minute Women Organizations telephoned house to house in search of women to work outside the home. Both times they were unable to bring more women into the work force, indicating that all the women who could or wanted to had taken jobs.[6]

It was common to encourage women to the workplace and then to keep them there by promoting the idea that war work did not threaten their femininity. War work was sometimes likened to traditional feminine work, as depicted in the *Hill Fielder*'s article on Mary Owens. In discussing her sign-up, training, family arrangements, and job washing ball bearings, the newspaper quoted Mary as saying that her work "is a great deal like doing dishes and the technique is much the same."[7] Women belonging to the Martha Society and "other fancy clubs" and also the wives of "prominent men" who took war jobs were featured in the *Ogden Standard Examiner.* They

---

Women during World War II (Westport, Conn.: Greenwood Press, 1981); D'Ann Campbell, *Women at War with America: Private Lives in a Patriotic Era* (Cambridge, MA.: Harvard University Press, 1984); William H. Chafe, *The American Woman: Her Changing Social, Economic, and Political Roles, 1920–1970* (London: Oxford University Press, 1972); Susan M. Hartmann, *The Home Front and Beyond: American Women in the 1940s* (Boston: Twayne Publishers, 1982); Maureen Honey, *Creating Rosie the Riveter: Class, Gender, and Propaganda, 1939–1945* (Amherst: University of Massachusetts Press, 1984); Valerie Kincade Oppenheimer, *The Female Labor Force in the United States: Demographic and Economic Factors Governing Its Growth and Changing Composition* (Westport, Conn.: Greenwood Press, 1970); "Demographic Influence on Female Employment and the Status of Women," *American Journal of Sociology* (1973); Karen Beck Skold, "The Job He Left Behind: American Women in the Shipyards during World War II," in *Women, War, and Revolution*, ed. Carol R. Berkin and Clara M. Lovett (New York: Holmes and Meier Publishers, 1980).

[3]*Deseret News,* February 6, 1943.

[4]*Ogden Standard Examiner,* September 13, 1942.

[5]*Salt Lake Tribune,* April 20, 1944; U.S., Department of Labor, War Manpower Commission, United States Employment Service, "Monthly Field Operating Report for Utah," April 1944.

[6]U.S., Department of Labor, War Manpower Commission, United States Employment Service, "Field Operating Report, Ogden," November 1944; "Labor Market Survey Report, Ogden," 1942, p. 6.

were waiting until after the war to be active in their clubs again. In the meantime, after a day of work they were "no more tired than [after] an afternoon of playing bridge." Furthermore, "The foreman stated that these women, all housewives and with no previous experience, had readily adapted themselves to the work."[8] Although articles stressing women's ability to maintain their feminine roles in the work place were most common, a few features about working women praised their professional attributes along with feminine qualities. One featured inspector, a "Blond Bomber," was listed as a mechanically inclined woman "who intelligently applied her aptitudes, very successfully." She was also a wife, mother of two, ages seven and eleven, and "a farmerette." Men initially resented her as the first mechanic trainer but by the end of the war accepted and liked her.[9]

The local newspapers frequently reported about the new members of the labor force. Articles were usually favorable to the Utah Rosies, although they carried a tone of surprise when reporting the success of the women. Referring to women as the fair sex was common, as in this frequent headline: "The Fair Sex Invades Another Domain Once Only for Males."[10] Further examples speak for themselves: "A flood of applicants pouring into Hill Field seems conclusive proof that many a woman secretly yearns to drive a jeep and show the menfolk she can handle cars as good as anyone"[11] and "the ego of many a man who has made slighting remarks about women drivers is going to be deflated terrifically."[12] "Femmes Okay on Curves," the title of a *Salt Lake Tribune* article on women drivers at a military installation, represents the all too common presentation of women workers.[13] Another article about women drivers, this feature concerning a training class, noted that women showed a "degree of skill far beyond expectations, and even the men with whom they work are forced to admit that the girls do all right."[14] From Hill Field it was announced that "women always have been accused of ruling the highways, but now they are really going to have opportunity to do so—so hail to women drivers"[15] Furthermore, women drivers were praised as "oblivious to the 'women's place is in the home' adage by driving taxis, jeeps, five ton trucks and buses. Their service and load average are almost parallel to that of men drivers."[16] Women guards were especially intriguing to newspapermen. "Pistol Packin' Mammas in the Flesh," one wrote of the Hill Field auxiliary military police and was so amazed that women had guns "and could shoot!"[17] When the women were

[7]*Hill Fielder,* February 1943.
[8]*Ogden Standard Examiner,* August 26, 1942.
[9]*Salt Lake Tribune,* March 16, 1943.
[10]*Hill Fielder,* April 26, 1944.
[11]*Ogden Standard Examiner,* September 13, 1942.
[12]*Ogden Standard Examiner,* September 11, 1942.
[13]*Salt Lake Tribune,* August 13, 1945.
[14]*Hill Top Times,* January 1943.
[15]*Salt Lake Tribune,* September 12, 1942.
[16]*Ogden Standard Examiner,* August 11, 1945.
[17]*Salt Lake Tribune,* December 6, 1943.

first hired as civilian guards at Tooele and the Ogden Arsenal they were not issued guns or even uniforms because officials could not decide whether to give the women uniform skirts or pants; they gave them a hat and a badge to wear on their civilian dresses.[18] One feature about a woman guard with dogs bragged of her sending a challenging man to a car top.[19] An excerpt from the *Salt Lake Tribune* in 1944 exemplifies the newspapers' presentation of the women:

> These women, driven by the truly feminine urge to stand by their men, are doing practically every job a man can do with the exception of heavy lifting, and as more men are called to the battlefronts we are confident that their places will be taken by courageous, capable, and patriotic women.[20]

Perhaps the most interesting public comment on women is the following excerpt:

> Because Ogden Arsenal employs a large number of women a realistic survey of female employment has been made available to Col. Nickerson by Army ordnance personnel.
>
> Here is what battle-tough experts discovered. Women have greater finger dexterity than men; greater patience; greater enthusiasm.
>
> Women will accept 99 percent responsibility, but they always like to receive a final O.K. on their work from a man.
>
> Women want their job glamorized for them.
>
> Women do not mind getting their hands and faces dirty, but the lack of beauty shops in the community will cause a serious personnel problem.
>
> Women take instruction and direction in a far more personal manner than men.
>
> Women are patriotic without cynicism.[21]

The *Hill Fielder* noted that women did monotonous work better than men.[22] Taken together these comments on women imply that they were willing to work, even in difficult, boring, tedious jobs that men were not always willing to take. Also suggested is women's desire to maintain their feminine identity, including their consistent submission to men, despite their job position. Ironically, while women were hailed for competently handling vital war jobs, they were still viewed as concerned most with their femininity and always submissive to men.

A job in a war industry did not replace a woman's full-time work at home. National and local propaganda throughout the war, even when luring women into the work place, reminded women that their household and family responsibilities could not be neglected. For example, the *Davis County Clipper* printed, "America's Housewife's Part in the War Is an Important One," and "Keeping Her Family Well in Wartime Is Her Special

[18]Helen Worsley to author, Tooele, Utah, October 13, 1984.

[19]*Salt Lake Tribune,* February 6, 1944.

[20]*Salt Lake Tribune,* March 2, 1944.

[21]*Ogden Standard Examiner,* July 22, 1943.

[22]*Hill Fielder,* March 1, 1945.

Task."[23] The Women's Bureau 1941 bulletin *Women Workers in Their Family Environment* analyzed women in two cities, Cleveland and Salt Lake City. Of the 337 Utah families studied, the report concluded that women, regardless of whether they were in households headed by men or not, were principally responsible for housework. Furthermore, two-fifths of the women in these families had no outside help and more than half did all the housework. Working mothers with young children were also primarily responsible for their care."When all the facts are weighed regarding women workers' contributions in time, effort, and money, there is no doubt about the indispensable role they play in their families."[24]

The adequate care of children in Utah, as nationwide, was a perpetual concern for parents, educators, and religious and community leaders. The labor-starved war industries desperately needed all workers, including young women with children. Yet there was a strong sentiment throughout the community that mothers should be the only caretakers of their children and therefore should not work regardless of the wartime emergency. Throughout the war the debate raged, unresolved, on the creation, funding, and use of public child care.

With the dropping of the atomic bombs on Japan, World War II was brought to a sudden halt. America returned to a peacetime economy as quickly as she had converted her industries to the production of war materials. Utah, however, did not experience a radical industrial change at war's end as did other areas of the country. Some adjustments had already been made when the federal government had cancelled three Utah contracts because of overproduction prior to 1945. Other Utah military work was crucially needed at war's end. In addition, the ceasing of hostilities meant the beginning of work for the Utah installations responsible for reclamation and storage of army and navy materials. Some Utah war industries, such as Geneva Steel and the Utah Oil Refinery, successfully continued in operation throughout the post war years. Federal spending would in fact continue to have a significant impact on the Utah economy for decades to come.

Change, nonetheless, did occur in 1945, Significantly fewer employees were needed for postwar military work. Some employees voluntarily left their war jobs. Others quit in hope of obtaining work before the feared postwar depression struck. Many were simply laid off; most of these workers were either women or minorities.

Employee reductions came as no surprise. Inherent in war jobs is the fact that they terminate with peace. Similarly, most people expected that minorities and women would be the first and largest groups released from the labor force. Women had received many signals that their work force participation was only temporary. A predicted postwar depression, as had occurred after the First World War, was expected to limit significantly the jobs

[23] *Davis County Clipper*, September 18, 1942.

[24] U.S., Department of Labor, Women's Bureau, *Women Workers in Their Family Environment* (Washington, D.C.: Government Printing Office, 1941), p. 51.

available. Furthermore, available jobs, it was widely believed, should be given to the returning veterans.

These brief generalizations mask the impact of the war's end on Utah's Rosies. Society issued the Rosies new orders and requested adjustments in roles and expectations. How did Utah's working women respond to appeals to return to hearth and home? How lasting was the war's influence upon their values, attitudes, and behaviors? Did Utah's working women react to their changes in circumstances differently from their sisters in other parts of the nation?

Local newspaper editorials, the Mormon church (expressed in the *Relief Society Magazine*), and Utah politicians encouraged women to return to their homes after the war. Even during the hostilities and at the height of the labor shortage these opinion makers had counseled a similar course. For example, in 1943 the *Deseret News* featured a motor pool driver who "would rather keep house but for the duration she prefers operating a truck." Besides, she commented, "The work keeps me busy while my husband is away—I don't think I worry so much."[25] The *Ogden Standard Examiner* featured female employees in war jobs in 1943. Their work was "fine for the duration, but Weber [College] enrollees are girls at heart. . . . It is nice to know we are as capable as men in their 'own' trades, but the future would take on rather a bleak aspect if we thought that was all there was to look forward to in the years to come." Furthermore, the female workers were socially frustrated because their male coworkers "can't picture us demure little souls in smart dresses and therefore never consider us as ideal 'after hours' companions. This plays havoc with our social life." War jobs, concluded the article, are threatening to femininity and a woman's potential dating career, powerful incentives, one may suppose, to leave a war job as soon as possible.[26]

In 1944 the *Salt Lake Tribune* editorialized that women had proven themselves in industry but that the majority welcomed victory, most especially because it would allow them to return to their homes and families. In March 1945 the Salt Lake Council of Women surveyed war workers to discern their postwar plans. The study found that seven of eight women preferred the hearth and were in war jobs doing men's work only for the duration.[27] The *Relief Society Magazine,* throughout the war, opposed Mormon women working outside their homes. As the war's end neared, the message became stronger. For example, an October 1944 editorial, "Home, After the War," asked, "Have the eyes of some in this day been so full of greediness that mothers have put in jeopardy the very souls of their children?" The article continued, "the great majority, it is hoped, of the men will be coming back; war industries will cease, and the returning members of the armed forces must be given the opportunity to once more earn livelihoods

[25]*Deseret News,* June 28, 1943.
[26]*Ogden Standard Examiner,* February 19, 1943.
[27]*Salt Lake Tribune,* February 11, 1945.

for themselves and their families. When this situation arises, the mother who has left her home should be prepared to face the situation and accept it."[28] Public officials further encouraged women to return to their homes when hostilities ceased. Governor Maw claimed there was no pressure on the working women to leave the work force, though he did encourage them to "give way to their husbands."[29]

To facilitate this study of Utah's Rosies an extensive effort was made to supplement public sources of information with personal histories of war workers. One hundred and thirty-three women working in the Utah war industries were contacted concerning their jobs and families during the war years. While such a sample is not random, the data compiled enhance our understanding of how the war work affected their lives.

War jobs ended for a variety of reasons for the research sample. Not surprisingly, the largest number (28 percent) were caught in the postwar "reduction of force." Fourteen percent terminated their war work for miscellaneous reasons such as sexual harassment, transportation or child care difficulties, or health problems. Another 8 percent quit because the war had ended. "My husband didn't want me to work anymore," said Dora Webb.[30] "It was the policy to be replaced by men who served," answered another. Eight percent discontinued their work to go to school, 19 percent to marry or to follow a husband, and 12 percent for family reasons. Many of the latter women were pregnant, and one, Maudie L. Williams, quit work to adopt two children.

Despite public encouragement to return home after the war many women remained in the labor force. In most cases, though, the jobs available to women during the war, notably those classified as traditional "male work," were not offered to women in postwar years. The reality of a limited job market for women became evident in Salt Lake City even prior to war's end when the Remington Small Arms Plant closed in 1943. The War Manpower Commission reported:

> Of the 3000 estimated as unemployed in the Salt Lake area, approximately 1000 of these workers are thought to be former women employees of Remington Arms who have somewhat inflated ideas of their skills and ability. These women are semi-independent economically and can shop around for the job they think they are qualified for. It is believed a majority of them originally accepted employment without previous training or experience. However, they received good training and orientation at Remington and performed creditably and with a high degree of efficiency during their employment. Many of them were advanced to instructoresses and leaders, and received, as a result, exceptionally liberal salaries compared to wages paid women in other industries in the area.
>
> It is now becoming apparent that these women have a tendency to overestimate their ability and the value of their experience. This is particularly true viewed in the light of current demand for women workers. Unless this

[28]*Relief Society Magazine,* October 1944.
[29]Interview with Herbert B. Maw, Salt Lake City, Utah, December 10, 1984.
[30]Telephone interview with Dora Webb, Salt Lake City, September 5, 1984.

group lowers its estimate of the value of its services, a major portion will probably remain unemployed.[31]

When hostilities ceased, the reality of a tight job market for women became even more evident. Employers advertised in newspapers specifically for male workers, especially veterans.

Requests for women workers did continue after August 1945, but they were distinctly different from the jobs offered during the war years. A month after victory, labor leaders Clarence L. Palmer, state Congress of Industrial Organizations (CIO) president, and J. R. Wilson, state American Federation of Labor (AFL) secretary, said that Utah industry was "too tough for women." They "opposed married women holding jobs in a tight labor market" except for financial need.[32] The Labor Department published the pamphlet *Retool Your Thinking for Your Job Tomorrow.* "Girls who wake up after the war without a job can't say they weren't warned," threatened the booklet. The Labor Department's advice was to obtain training, especially secretarial skills.[33] Dorothy Lemmon lost her wartime job in the tool room at Tooele Ordnance Depot to a returning G.I. She was placed in the secretarial pool where she remained until her retirement. Lemmon and the G.I. accepted the situation. "He felt bad, too," recalled Dorothy.[34]

The War Manpower Commission reported in December 1945 that fewer jobs were available for women, and fewer women were seeking employment. Furthermore, there was a shortage of women filling traditional female jobs. The commission suggested that "Local married women with employed husbands who are holding [traditionally male] jobs would be performing a patriotic service if they resigned such positions and thus created jobs for men who are in much worse need of jobs."[35] Women who wanted to work in the postwar years were advised to select traditionally female, or "pink collar," jobs. This was the case for one member of the research sample who said she could not get a job like the one she had had during the war, when she later "needed it to support self and son, because of discrimination."[36]

When Clearfield Naval Supply Depot published a history as part of its ten-year anniversary in 1953 the pictures of personnel taken during the war included women in all kinds of work. Later photographs showed women only in traditional or secretarial roles. For example, a section titled "Labor or Equipment Branch" sought to demonstrate the evolution of work from the two-wheeled hand truck used to push boxes in 1943 to the 1953 fork-

[31]U.S., Department of Labor, War Manpower Commission, United States Employment Service, "Monthly Field Operating Report, Salt Lake City," January 1944, p. 7.

[32]*Salt Lake Tribune,* September 9, 1945.

[33]*Salt Lake Tribune,* April 3, 1945.

[34]Interview with Dorothy Lemmon, Salt Lake City, July 23, 1984.

[35]U.S., Department of Labor, War Manpower Commission, United States Employment Service, "Labor Market Development Report, Ogden," December 1945, p. 3.

[36]War worker's questionnaire.

lift. The earlier photograph pictured three women working, while in the later picture a man operated the forklift.[37] A Tooele Army Depot informational brochure published in 1967 pictured several workers, all of them men. A feature in the Tooele newspaper in 1984, however, corrected the male-only image and insisted that women had always worked there: "Today [1984] they do all kinds of work from office work to equal terms with men, heaving a hammer, grinding a crank shaft, and producing a mechanical drawing."[38]

Some women, however, were able to find work similar to their war jobs. For a few of the research sample the war working experience was an important steppingstone in their careers. Twelve percent of the sample remained in the same line of work they had entered during the war. For example, Grace M. McLean began her career as an ammunition inspector during the war. When she retired in April 1978 she was the only woman explosives safety specialist in the U.S. Air Force. Still another war worker, Maudie L. Williams, remarked, "I had the experience to get better and more paying work for the government after the war." Nelda Chadwick was promoted to a supervisor's position during the war. When the men returned she was asked to step down and assume a clerk or typist job. She refused and with perseverance remained in supervisory positions until her retirement. Noteworthy as these examples are, the majority of women who continued to work outside the home had to accept pink collar jobs.

Individual income rose sharply in the state during World War II, a fact that was particularly appreciated after the harsh depression. "Before 1940," one historian wrote, "Utah's total personal income was under $300 million. In 1943 it surged beyond the $700 million mark, then dropped back slightly for three years and continued upward thereafter."[39] The war job paycheck significantly affected research sample members and their families. Veda Swain and her husband were out of work during the 1930s. Just prior to the bombing of Pearl Harbor she had obtained a job as an elevator operator at ZCMI department store for twenty-five cents an hour, two hours a day, while the regular attendant took his lunch. When Remington Small Arms Plant opened she gained work there at sixty-nine cents an hours, forty-eight hours a week. Gloria McNally reported that the war "set us up financially. We never were behind economically after that." Renee Christensen's family purchased its first record player, installed a telephone, and bought a natural gas stove, water heater, and typewriter "while mom worked at Remington." The Standard Parachute Company had a crucial economic impact on the Manti community. Parachute seamstresses bought

[37]U.S., Department of Defense, *Tenth Anniversary, Naval Supply Depot, Clearfield, Utah, 1943–1953* (Clearfield, Ut.: Defense Printing Service, Ogden, 1953).

[38]U.S., Department of Defense, *Tooele Army Depot, Utah* (Tooele, Ut.: Information and Education Office of Tooele Army Depot, 1967); *Tooele Bulletin*, February 7, 1984.

[39]John E. Christensen, "The Impact of World War II," in *Utah's History*, ed. Richard D. Poll, Thomas G. Alexander, Eugene E. Campbell, and David Miller (Provo, Ut.: Brigham Young University Press, 1978), p. 505.

family necessities with the paychecks. Workers' purchases included shoes for the children, living room furniture, and installation of indoor plumbing.

War jobs offered higher salaries than other work. Local employers complained that high wage scales made it difficult for them to compete for workers. In 1940 most women in restaurant work in Salt Lake City earned about $13 a week and in Ogden about $12. In Utah department and variety stores women's salaries averaged $10.50 per week, and in laundries women received an average of $12 per week.[40] Pay differentials are obvious when these wages are compared to war job paychecks. Remington Small Arms Plant workers usually earned $22.56 a week. Classified laborers in the military installations earned a minimum of $36.48 a week and as much as $42.24 a week. Clearfield women workers, as supply handlers and lift operators, earned $30.72 a week.[41]

Even though war industries paid women more than other community jobs and more than they had earned prior to the war, women were often paid less than men. Female typists, stenographers, and card punch operators generally were paid between $1,260 and $1,440 per year at the military installations. Men at the same plant working as crane operators, electricians, blacksmiths, and steamers were paid $1,860. Men were also paid higher wages than women in similar work because the men's work was often judged more difficult. For instance, the Tooele Ordnance Depot Salvage Department paid women 67.5 cents an hour, but teenage boys in the same department earned 85 cents an hour because they did heavy lifting. The Rocky Mountain Packing Company paid women five cents less than men, claiming the women handled easier jobs. Military installation employees were often paid on an ascending scale according to experience. For example, in 1942 Hill Field inspectors were paid as follows: juniors, $1,860; regulars, $2,200; seniors, $2,600; and principals, $2,800. Women, with their lack of experience, were assigned to the lower levels and hence received less pay.

Some pay discrepancies were more blatant. "The base pay for unskilled men will be $4.00 per day and the women will receive $3.75 per day as a starting pay," announced the War Manpower Commission in 1941 in Ogden.[42] A year later it reported that in Salt Lake City "The Cudahy Packing Co. is employing women to replace men in many departments, but these women are not paid at the same wage scale as male employees."[43] The

[40]Industrial Commission of Utah, Women's Division, "Utah State Planning Board," March 28, 1940. The Women's Bureau Bulletin, "State Minimum Wage Laws and Orders: 1942," reported that women in retail, restaurant, and laundry work received $14 a week in Salt Lake City and Ogden, and in Utah communities with populations of less than 2,500 received $10 or less a week depending on experience. U.S., Department of Labor, Women's Bureau, *State Minimum-Wage Laws and Orders, 1942: An Analysis* (Washington, D.C.: Government Printing Office, 1942).

[41]Area newspapers regularly carried information on wages offered for war jobs.

[42]U.S., Department of Labor, War Manpower Commission, United States Employment Service, "Labor Market Survey Report, Ogden," November 13, 1941.

[43]Ibid., "Labor Market Survey Report, Salt Lake City," December 15, 1942.

Ogden Standard Examiner noted in 1942 that ammunition loaders at the Ogden Arsenal were paid $4.40 a day if they were women but $5.50 if they were men. Research sample workers Dorothy Lemmon and Helen Worsley, as well as others, were frustrated by this male-female pay differential. Salary inequality in some cases worsened in the postwar years. In late 1945 the *Salt Lake Tribune* reported that jobs were not being filled because they offered wages reduced by from 34 to 49 percent for women. Furthermore, "most available jobs are for men while most of the jobs seekers are women."[44]

Several historians of women war workers argue that the World War II working experience was a watershed for women. For the first time large numbers of married and older women entered the labor force. More significant, these women remained in the work place, permanently changing the female labor force from its prewar young and unmarried character to a postwar older (over thirty-five) married composition. Society accepted older and married women working during the wartime emergency and affirmed its approval in the immediate postwar years. The war also opened new doors for women by stimulating personal, social, and economic involvement beyond the home. These experiences inaugurated some of the fundamental changes in women's status that have occurred since 1945.

This study of Utah women war workers provides support for the interpretation that the war induced lasting changes in women's roles. The most obvious transition is in female labor force participation during and after the war. In 1950 female participation rates decreased from the wartime high in 1944 of 36.8 percent to 24.3 percent, or 57,145 women, which is still higher than the 1940 percentage rate of 17.6 or 33,888 women. The female labor force expanded to 94,103 in 1960, or 32.4 percent, to 41.5 percent, or 145,799, in 1970; and by 1980, 49.6 percent, or 246,963 Utah women, worked outside the home. Furthermore, the majority of Utah women who worked after 1940 were older than those in the prewar period (table 1). The majority of the Utah postwar female workers were also married, as illustrated in table 2. After World War II women who were married and/or over thirty-five years of age joined the work force as never before. The war had induced them to leave the home, and their continued presence in the labor force overshadowed that of young and unmarried women. The national data presented in table 3 delineate this and make state-national comparison possible. Considerably fewer Utah women than nationally worked outside the home in 1940 and 1950 for all marital statuses. The gap grew smaller, however, in 1960 and 1970. With each decade following the war Utah women increasingly followed the national trend of more women entering the labor force in all marital statuses. The group experiencing the largest growth for Utah and the nation was those women married with husbands present.

[44] *Salt Lake Tribune,* November 14, 1945; *Ogden Standard Examiner,* September 13, 1942.

TABLE 1
FEMALE LABOR FORCE PARTICIPATION RATES
FOR UTAH BY AGE, 1940–70

	1940	1950	1960	1970
14 to 19 years	13.7%	21.0%	27.6%	27.6%
20 to 34 years	24.5	26.6	32.1	44.1
35 to 49 years	16.7	29.3	40.4	50.4
50 + years	10.8	19.6	31.4	37.5

Source: U.S. Census. The percentages are for those working within that age group for the given year and not as part of an aggregate for the female working population by age for the given year.

The expanded participation of married and older women in the labor force after the war suggests a social tolerance or even acceptance of this new trend. Furthermore, the prewar depression practice by the state government and private businesses of firing women upon marriage was not reinstated in Utah or elsewhere in the nation.[45] The increased availability of employment also eased the entrance of women into the work force. Perhaps, too, more married women had to work after the 1940s because one breadwinner could no longer meet the escalating financial demands of middle-class life. Two incomes were needed to match inflation and to keep up with society's materialistic values. Rather than working outside the home for pin money, women have most often entered the labor force because of financial necessity. Marie W. Galloway, a Remington Small Arms Plant worker, said at the closing of the plant that she planned to continue working because "I have to."[46]

TABLE 2
FEMALE LABOR FORCE PARTICIPATION RATES
FOR UTAH BY MARITAL STATUS, 1940–70

	1940	1950	1960	1970
Single	35.5%	36.8%	49.9%	47.8%
Married, living with husband	7.8	19.0	29.3	40.0
Divorced, separated, and widowed	26.5	33.7	37.3	39.6

Source: U. S. Census. The percentages are for those working within that age group for the given year and not as part of an aggregate for the female working population by age for the given year.

[45]Lois Scharf, *To Work and to Wed: Female Employment, Feminism, and the Great Depression* (Westport, Conn.: Greenwood Press, 1980).
[46]*Deseret News,* November 17, 1943.

TABLE 3
FEMALE LABOR FORCE PARTICIPATION RATES FOR THE UNITED STATES BY MARITAL STATUS, 1940–70

	1940	1950	1960	1970
Single	48.1%	50.5%	44.1%	53.0%
Married, living with husband	14.7	23.8	30.5	40.8
Divorced, separated, and widowed	34.0	37.0	38.3	36.8

Source: *Historical Statistics of the United States.* The percentages are for those working within that age group for the given year and not as part of an aggregate for the female working population by age for the given year.

Working women point to the war experience as a critical junction in their lives. Those interviewed stressed that they had experienced personal growth from war work. When asked if the war had an influence on them, 81 percent of the sample responded positively. "I developed more confidence in my ability to face new challenges," and "I felt very good about myself, because I was contributing to my country" were typical responses. "I knew I could do housework but not sure I could do work like this—but I did," said Odessa Young Mower.[47] For several women war work brought them in contact with people different from themselves for the first time. Associating with people of various ethnic, cultural, and religious backgrounds was an educational experience made possible in the war industries. Several respondents commented on the feelings of autonomy and independence brought about by having their own paychecks. This meant not having to be dependent upon their husbands for an income. For a few, a paycheck paid for an education, probably not affordable otherwise. Personal gains were therefore numerous: confidence, career possibilities, pride, tolerance for other people, autonomy, and for some, an education.

When analyzing the results of the working experience, the ugly realities of war must be considered also. The war often affected the women workers, for it was a rare war worker who did not have a family member or friend in military service. Day-to-day workers felt the anxiety of wondering if he, or in some instances she, were alive. War worker Marie Adams discussed the darker side of the war work experience.

> War is terrible. For me it was awful as the first man I considered marrying was at Corregidor and all the terrible things they were going through was [*sic*] in my mind constantly even though I was working 10 hours, 7 days a week at Ogden Arsenal and sometimes at a cafe in Ogden in between. . . . I never heard from him again. Eventually he was listed as missing in ac-

[47]Interview with Odessa Young Mower, Fairview, August 4, 1984.

> tion. . . . I don't mention this much, because I just try to forget. . . . It was hard work and a lot of tears.[48]

The war became a daily reality on the job. Workers at the Ogden Arsenal who handled equipment salvaged from the battlefields remember blood stains on much of it. War worker Ellen Jenkins found notes from American G.I.s between gun parts. She turned the notes over to authorities, never knowing what happened to them. Workers on planes at Hill Field cleaned blood, skin, and hair out of the insides of cockpits. Pilots often left messages and drawings inside their planes. "This brought home the reality of what was happening," reported one worker. Retha Nielson, a worker on B-24s, wrote, "I got a lump in my throat as I read the names of the men who had piloted them. Some of them had given the planes a name. . . . I would walk up to the big plane and touch it and wonder if all the men had come out alive, what had happened and why they had named it what they had."[49] Employees at the Tooele Ordnance Depot had similar experiences when refurbishing tanks from the battlefields. Another worker wrote, "My last job was on a bomb shoot [*sic*]—I often wondered if my bomb shoot was used on Japan."[50] Macel Anderson received two letters from the federal government stating that two boys' lives had been saved by the parachutes she had worked on. Each parachute had the maker's name on it. "That made the whole sacrifice of working worthwhile," commented Macel.[51] Perhaps, added to the impact of the women's working experience, was a deeper understanding of how wretched war was. These women experienced it quite closely, despite the battlefields being thousands of miles away.

The trauma of the war did not end when hostilities ceased. The nation counted on the women at home to help the returning soldiers readjust to civilian life. Despite an overwhelming "welcome home" from their country, American G.I.s suffered, in varying degrees, from "combat fatigue." Fortunately, most soldiers did adjust, but it took time. June Anderson wrote, "The time separated from my husband changed our lives so much and we had to make a new start and get acquainted all over again, as he was gone twenty-seven months."[52] Another said of her returning husband, "I have to admit that [it] was almost as bad as when he left." He went to war the day after they had married and was then gone for the duration of the war.

The positive effects of World War II on working women should not obscure the fact that there were areas where women failed to secure changes. Despite the unprecedented opportunities for women to work during the war, they largely remained in lower level, lower paying jobs. Women were also paid less than their male co-workers in many instances while performing the same or similar war work. Most women returned to traditional fe-

[48]Personal letter from Marie Adams, Layton, October 12, 1984.
[49]Questionnaire completed by Retha Nielson, October 17, 1984.
[50]War Workers' questionnaire.
[51]Questionnaire completed by Macel Anderson, November 6, 1984.
[52]Questionnaire completed by June Anderson, November 19, 1984.

male jobs after the war despite their success in handling nontraditional work. Furthermore, the gap between wages paid to men and women often increased in the postwar years.

The enduring effects of women's working experience during the war, though, may have taken place in the socialization of the children who came of age in the 1960s. Work accomplishments during World War II may have created women who saw themselves differently from their more traditional female contemporaries. A new sense of self-worth and self-reliance arose in the minds and hearts of the Rosies. Perhaps children raised by these "different and new" mothers of the 1940s and 1950s responded to the feminist message of the 1960s, finding it conducive to their sense of a woman's place in the home, family, work place, and society. More studies are needed to examine this possibility.

One would suspect that the Utah case study would be unique, rather than similar to the national experience of women during the war because of the dominance of the Mormon church. The patriarchal church discouraged women from participating in the work place and strongly encouraged them to remain at home. Yet, Mormon women both during and after World War II entered the Utah labor market in large numbers. When Latter-day Saint members of the research sample were asked about conflict between their church and the decision to work, no one indicated any problems. Their desire to contribute patriotically to their country and their need for a paycheck outweighed the Mormon church's message not to work outside the home. Perhaps, then, what is most noteworthy about the Utah experience is how similar it was to the national experience.

The historical debate over the war's impact on women has created sharp divisions. For some, the war generated lasting social and economic changes for women. Others acknowledged that the war brought unprecedented opportunities for women but characterized these changes as temporary and with few lasting results. The Utah case, mirroring the national experience, suggests that elements of both interpretations are valid. The war did spur a changed female labor force composition, the effect of which is still being felt. Also, women war workers experienced personal growth. Yet, permanent on-the-job changes did not occur. The war did not eliminate pay inequality and job segregation, problems that continue to plague American women workers. An invisible revolution, however, may have occurred in the thoughts and expectations of Rosies' children who began to come of age in the 1960s. Modeled by this generation of war-working mothers and trained to demand more of themselves and their society, they will perhaps be the creators of a new place for women in the American socioeconomic community.

*

Interned at Topaz: Age, Gender, and Family in the Relocation Experience

SANDRA C. TAYLOR

During World War II, propaganda campaigns sought not only to stimulate patriotism but also to promote hatred for the enemy. Some of this engendered hatred carried over to certain residents of the United States of foreign descent. Some prejudice was shown against both German-Americans and Italian-Americans, but Japanese-Americans—both resident aliens and American citizens of Japanese ancestry—were the object of the greatest concern. Early in the war the U.S. government confined more than 100,000 of these people in concentration camps. It was one of the greatest mass abridgments of civil liberties in American history. One of the ten "relocation centers" the government established was Topaz, near Delta, in Millard County, which at its peak held more than 8,000 people and was the fifth largest population center in Utah.

The subject of this article is how age, gender, family situation, and generation influenced a person's reaction to his or her incarceration; in particular, it looks at the impact on younger inmates. The loss of parents, the breakdown of the family system, and other aspects of life behind barbed wire traumatized young children. Teenagers were swept into gangs. Young girls approaching maturity suffered from the lack of privacy. The author concludes that "coming of age in a concentration camp was a painful thing."

Sandra C. Taylor, "Interned at Topaz: Age, Gender, and Family in the Relocation Experience," *Utah Historical Quarterly* 59 (Fall 1991): 380–94. Reprinted by permission of the publisher and the author.

Sandra C. Taylor is Professor of History at the University of Utah, author of *Jewel in the Desert: Japanese-American Internment at Topaz,* and co-editor of *Japanese-Americans, From Relocation to Redress.*

WHAT WAS LIFE LIKE for the Japanese Americans incarcerated by the American government in relocation camps during World War II? Dillon

Myer, the "keeper of concentration camps,"[1] swore that of the 70,000 people (over half the original number) still in camp in 1944, "probably at least half had never had it so good."[2] Richard Drinnon recently wrote, "incarceration had unintended consequences and by-products, not all of which were negative," a sentiment that evacuee-author Harry Kitano had earlier voiced.[3] What has not been discussed is the extent to which reaction to life in the camps was a function of one's age, gender, family situation, and generation. The experience for the citizen Nisei, the second generation, differed markedly from their alien Issei parents, while the small number of third-generation Sansei were too young to be greatly affected psychologically. This paper will study the impact of the Topaz experience on the Nisei through the use of oral histories.

Topaz, in central Utah, was one of ten so-called relocation centers or concentration camps[4] built by the American government during World War II. These ten bleak sites housed Japanese Americans evacuated from the West Coast by Executive Order 9066, issued by President Franklin D. Roosevelt in February 1942.[5] "Military necessity" was the reason the administration advanced for relocating some 120,000 people from California, Oregon, Washington, and Hawaii. In reality the motives stemmed from economic greed, politics, and above all, racism. The population of Topaz peaked at 8,255 people in the fall of 1942 and diminished by about 15 percent a year until the rapid expulsion of the remainder prior to the closure of the camp on October 31, 1945. During those years Topaz was the fifth largest city in Utah with the Nisei numbering 65 percent of the total interned there.[6]

[1]Richard Drinnon, *Keeper of Concentration Camps: Dillon S. Myer and American Racism* (Berkeley and Los Angeles: University of California Press, 1988).

[2]Dillon S. Myer, *Uprooted Americans: The Japanese Americans and the War Relocation Authority during World War II* (Tucson: University of Arizona Press, 1971), p. 292, cited in Drinnon, *Keeper,* p. 44.

[3]Harry Kitano, *Japanese Americans: The Evolution of a Subculture* (Englewood Cliffs, N.J.: Prentice-Hall, 1969), p. 74.

[4]The terminology used in referring to the internment camps is itself very politically charged. The U.S. government called them relocation centers and described them as "temporary war stations" for the evacuated Japanese Americans from the West Coast. However, they were surrounded by barbed-wire fences and had armed guards in guardhouses. Inmates were warned to stay away from the fences, and one man in Topaz was shot when he did not. They were, in the true sense of the term, concentration camps that forcibly held people who were virtual political prisoners. The term "concentration camp" was used at the time but discarded when it was later applied, incorrectly, to the Nazi death camps.

[5]Basic histories of the internment are to be found in Roger Daniels, *Concentration Camps USA* (New York: Holt, Rinehart, and Winston, 1971); Roger Daniels and Harry Kitano, *American Racism: Exploration of the Nature of Prejudice* (Englewood Cliffs, N.J.: Prentice Hall, 1970); Dorothy S. Thomas, *The Salvage* (Berkeley and Los Angeles: University of California Press, 1952); Morton Grodzins, *Americans Betrayed: Politics and the Japanese Evacuation* (Chicago: University of Chicago Press, 1949); Leonard Bloom and Ruth Reimer, *A Removal and Return: The Socio-Economic Effects of the War on Japanese Americans* (Berkeley and Los Angeles: University of California Press, 1949); Audrie Girdner and Anne Loftis, *The Great Betrayal* (New York: MacMillan, 1971), and Michi Weglyn, *Years of Infamy: The Untold Story of America's Concentration Camps* (New York: William Morrow, 1976). The only work solely on Topaz is Leonard Arrington, *The Price of Prejudice: The Japanese American Relocation Center in Utah* (Logan: Utah State University Press, 1962).

[6]Arrington, *Prejudice,* p. 15.

Topaz was neither the best nor the worst of camps. Its population was quite homogeneous, coming almost entirely from the San Francisco Bay Area. It experienced a minimal amount of mob violence—unlike Manzanar or Tule Lake, which became the resegregation center for those desiring repatriation to Japan—but it did experience the brutality that the white overseers could inflict. One inmate, James Hatsuaki Wakasa, an elderly Issei, was shot by a guard when he strayed too near the fence and allegedly ignored four orders to halt. This certainly had a traumatic effect on the population, especially on the lives of those who resided nearby and knew him, like Karl Akiya, a fellow Issei who had even eaten dinner with him that fateful night, and Nisei teenager Michiko Okamoto, who remembers it to this day.[7] There was no specific draft resistance at Topaz such as occurred in Heart Mountain, Wyoming. The climate in the central Utah desert was extremely hot in the summer, but it was probably worse in the two camps in Arizona and in the swamps of Arkansas.[8] The winters could be bitterly cold but probably no worse than at Heart Mountain. Housing everywhere consisted of uninsulated tarpaper-covered barracks, heated by pot-bellied, coal-burning stoves. The distinguishing feature at Topaz was dust storms that plagued all the residents, especially those suffering from asthma and allergies, which made it impossible to keep oneself or one's quarters clean. Kazu Iijima vividly described a dust storm, telling how they covered their noses and mouths in vain and yet the sand got in everything. "I can still remember how torturous those storms were," she said.[9] Beyond that, it was just an ordinary concentration camp, appalling for that very fact if for no other. As Morgan Yamanaka, a Kibei, termed it, Topaz was a "peaceful, quiet place where people were pretty much left alone."[10]

Oral histories obtained from survivors more than forty years later provide one way of understanding Topaz beyond the voluminous documentary record the War Relocation Authority administration compiled. Yet they suffer from a number of handicaps. First, they are obviously limited to the living, approximately half of the original number. Access and availability played a large part in my selection of interviewees, for there is no single listing of the survivors. Memories also tend to be selective and are influenced by the succeeding events in one's life. Those whom the years treated well

[7]For details on the Wakasa killing see Roger Daniels, *Asian Americans: Chinese and Japanese in the United States since 1850* (Seattle: University of Washington Press, 1988), pp. 228–31. His source was the Russell Bankson Papers, "U.S., War Relocation Authority," at the University of Washington library.

[8]Arrington, *Prejudice,* p. 14

[9]Interview by Sandra Taylor, New York City, October 4, 1987; tapes are on file with the American West Center, University of Utah, and transcripts are shelved in the Western Americana Division, Marriott Library, University of Utah, as part of its Asian American series. Funding for the oral history project was provided by the College of Humanities and the Research Committee, University of Utah, and the Helen Papanikolas Fund, Marriott Library. Hereafter the interviews are cited by name, place, date, and AWC Collection.

[10]Interview with Morgan Yamanaka, San Francisco, September 1988, AWC Collection. Kibeis were Nisei educated in Japan.

may be more positive or at least neutral in their assessment of camp life, while those who suffered traumatic experiences or who have led stressful lives since the war may recall more vividly the negative impact of the internment experience. This sample is not random: the interviewees were recruited by Japanese Americans whom I had met or was referred to and by the Japanese American Citizens' League headquartered in San Francisco. Not all I met wanted to talk, and some who were interviewed later declined to have their interviews used. Those who were unwilling may have been the most traumatized of all.[11]

Prior to the beginning of the Redress movement[12] in which many Japanese Americans, some organized through the JACL, sought apologies and compensation for the wrongs done them, many of the former internees had attempted to put relocation out of their minds. They had reestablished their homes, reunited their families, and found new livelihoods. Sixty percent returned to the West Coast, usually to the communities they had left. Many did not even share memories with their children, for they were ashamed of the experience: a response born both of a kind of "survivors' guilt" and their Japanese heritage. Their desire was to be loyal Americans, to prove by their lives how wrong incarceration had been. By the 1960s they had become the so-called "model minority,"[13] for the most part having achieved economic success at just the time their children, the Sansei, were awakened by the Civil Rights movement to challenge their parents' acquiescence and demand compensation. Nisei silence did not mean that the incarceration had not been traumatic, nor can one say that the scattering effects of relocation, which brought some people more economic opportunity in new locations than they had possessed on the West Coast before the war, justified its

[11]Extensive primary source material on the camps is found in the National Archives, Washington, D.C., Record Group 210. This material is primarily concerned with administrative matters, but individual files are also kept there. The Bancroft Library at the University of California, Berkeley, has a smaller collection of materials, and records on individual camps are sometimes, but not always, located in university archives nearby. One must note that the role of the Japanese American Citizens' League in relocation is still extremely controversial; it counseled an enthusiastic acceptance of the government's plan, and many today are still bitter about its acquiescence. Although no realistic alternative to submission was possible, the JACL virtually collaborated with the jailers.

[12]Redress became an organized movement when it was adopted as a cause by the Japanese American Citizens' League in 1978 after a decade of debate. President Gerald Ford revoked the original order for relocation, Executive Order 9066, in 1976. After much lobbying and work by the Japanese American community, the Redress legislation passed by Congress in 1980 was signed by President Jimmy Carter in 1980. This created the Commission on Wartime Relocation and Internment of Civilians, which held a series of hearings around the country and finally published its report, *Personal Justice Denied* (Washington, D.C., 1982). It set a figure of $20,000 for compensation to survivors. President Ronald Reagan signed the implementing legislation in 1988. See John Tateishi, "The Japanese American Citizens League and the Struggle for Redress," in Roger Daniels, Sandra C. Taylor, and Harry H. L. Kitano, *Japanese Americans: From Relocation to Redress* (Salt Lake City, University of Utah Press, 1986), pp. 191–95. The first payments were made in 1991.

[13]Harry Kitano and Roger Daniels, *Asian Americans: Emerging Minorities* (Englewood Cliffs, N.J., Prentice-Hall, 1988), p. 48. The term was coined by sociologist William Petersen in 1966.

pain. The price of success, as the Commission on Wartime Relocation and Internment of Civilians reported in 1982, was psychologically very high.[14]

The Redress movement required Japanese Americans to dredge up the past and to reflect on the injustice that had been done them. Testimonies at the commission hearings in 1981 were painful. Memories were no doubt affected by the desire for justice—at least official acknowledgement of their innocence and the federal government's colossal blunder in establishing the camps, something termed even at the time by Eugene Rostow as its "worst wartime mistake."[15] Not all Japanese Americans agreed with Redress, at least in the way the JACL had formulated it, and their feelings influenced their responses to my interviews.[16]

Response to the concentration camp experience was the result of many variables. Age had much to do with people's reactions. Most of the Nisei were children in camp, and the experience affected their lives in ways different from its impact on their parents. Children were freed from parental discipline to play, while many adolescents, particularly females going through puberty and the stress of the teenage years, found the lack of privacy and the uncertainty of their futures troubling.

Normally hardworking students, Japanese American youth reacted to their fractured educational experiences in different ways, some working twice as hard as before, while others adopted a style they called "waste time."[17] Anything constructive was "waste time," and anything destructive was all right. Mari Eijima recalled that in 1946–47 "the three r's which were reading, 'riting, and 'rithmetic 'on the outside' now became ruder, rougher, and rowdier. To represent the new three r's best became each individual's goal." Everything was "corroded," as they termed it, the administration, the hospital, the mess halls, the schools, and under such circumstances there was "no shame" in anything."[18]

With teenagers responding to their circumstances in such a way it is clear that the camps had a profound effect on family life through their weakening of parental authority. Meals are a traditional time for reinforcing family values, but lining up for communal mess served cafeteria style

[14]*Personal Justice Denied,* Report of the Commission on Wartime Relocation and Internment of Civilians (Washington, D.C.: U.S. Government Printing Office, December 1982), pp. 295–96.

[15]Roger Daniels disputes this point in *Concentration Camps, USA:* "The legal atrocity which was committed against the Japanese Americans was the logical outgrowth of over three centuries of American experience." xiv. Drinnon, *Keeper of Concentration Camps,* also disputes this label, first applied by Eugene Rostow in 1946 in an article bearing that title in *Harper's* magazine. Drinnon, like Daniels, traces internment to centuries of American racism.

[16]The impact of the Redress movement has strongly affected the way that survivors of America's concentration camps remember their experiences. Only one of those interviewed did not agree that some form of compensation was warranted.

[17]See interview with Fumi Hayashi, Berkeley, California, for a discussion of this. The best study of education in the camps is Thomas James, *Exile Within: The Schooling of Japanese Americans 1942–1945* (Cambridge, Mass.: Harvard University Press, 1987).

[18]Mari Eijima, "How I Saw the Birth of Slang," paper written when Eijima was in college after the war. Copy in author's possession.

made it difficult to eat together. Crowding into one or two small rooms meant a lack of privacy to establish rules and enforce them. Children and parents alike were usually in their uncomfortable barracks room only for sleeping.[19] And above all, the father's authority was undercut by the administrative structure of the camp. He did not set the rules, the Caucasians did.

For some children camp life was fun—but not for all. Separation from one's father could have a profound effect. Some children experienced the temporary loss of their fathers who were community leaders jailed in the Midwest by the Federal Bureau of Investigation because they were influential in the prewar settlements and presumably could have sparked resistance. For other young children camp was a time to be carefree, to have fun and ignore the diminished authority of parents and teachers. Young teenager Abu Keiokan recalled that "I was too busy playing to get involved," running around with friends from Sacramento who were also in the camp.[20]

Young mothers' lives revolved around their small children, much as before, and once the hospital was functioning health was for most a lessened problem. But the distance from barracks to latrine and laundry made sanitary tasks more burdensome on women. The primitive conditions in camp and the extremes of heat and cold made young motherhood doubly difficult.

Young children and the older Issei were perhaps the least marked by the internment experience. Since the Issei were not citizens, incarceration came as less of a shock; they had expected hostilities to bring some form of discriminatory treatment or incarceration, for that was customary in wartime. Those most affected included the older Nisei, whose lives were disrupted just as they were beginning their most productive years, and the younger Issei who were removed from the work force at the prime of their lives and often found reestablishing themselves afterwards difficult or impossible.[21]

The Nisei were also affected in varying ways by the camp institutions: the educational system, the food, their work experiences, and health care. Experiences with Caucasian teachers, administrators, and townspeople in the nearby tiny central Utah town of Delta, as well as in Provo, where some seasonal workers encountered violence, also affected them. For many Issei (and some Nisei) relocation was so traumatic that they feared reentering the Caucasian world that had expelled them and sought to return to Japan or to stay permanently in the relative safety of the camps.

The following assessment of the effects of relocation on the Nisei of Topaz is based on interviews with forty-nine Japanese Americans residing in the California Bay Area and the East Coast, of whom thirty-six were Nisei.

[19]For a discussion of the positive and negative effects of camp life on families see James K. Morishima, "The Evacuation: Impact on the Family," pp. 13–19, in Stanley Sue and Nathaniel N. Wagner, *Asian-Americans; Psychological Perspectives* (Palo Alto: Stanford University Press, 1973).

[20]Interview with Abu Keiokan Guilday, Sacramento, May 14, 1988, AWC Collection.

[21]My interviews document this process. See especially those with Glenn Kumekawa, Wakefield, R.I., June 20, 1988, and Tomoye Takahashi, San Francisco, November 2, 1987, AWC Collection.

It is possible to categorize the respondents by the nature of their reaction to incarceration after forty years of reflection. Although this is a subjective judgment on the part of the interviewer, based on the internal evidence of the words they used in describing camp. I believe the interviews can support a judgment that approximately as many accepted camp life and were relatively undamaged by it as were severely traumatized. Granting this, one then may arrive at some conclusions as to why the internment experience affected this group as it did. This by no means exonerates the actions or the motives of those who imposed it, but it can help us understand the incarcerated better.

The Nisei who were incarcerated in the concentration camps ranged in age from infants to young adults. They outnumbered the Issei by 1920, as immigration ceased in 1924, and they were just beginning to come of age.[22] In 1940 the median age of the Nisei was about sixteen.[23] For most of them then, the years of confinement were those of adolescence, of slipping the parental controls that had previously constrained them.

A few reactions from these adolescents indicate their attitudes. Robert Utsumi, like Abu Keiokan, disregarded school, had a good-natured contempt for many of his minimally qualified teachers, particularly the Caucasian ones, and recalled with pleasure forty years later the pranks he and his friends played on them. Harry Kitano also remembered enjoying the freedom from parental restraints, as did his sister Chiz. John Hada recalled relocation as "just like going on a trip, perhaps to the Outback." Lee Suyemoto, who had been shy at home, remembered "hanging out" with a youth gang and taking the lead in some acts of defiance of authority. He began to smoke at age thirteen, despite his parents' disapproval. Hannah Hara, who was a preteen, also ran with a girls' gang, much to her mother and older sister's dismay. But gangs and social deviance did not lead these adolescents to crime, of which there was less than in ordinary American communities of the same size.[24]

Many Nisei, while in no way condoning the experience, found camp life itself quite tolerable. Tad Hayashi said, "I liked it. . . . We had dances once a week at least, . . . we played baseball . . . and I improved my bridge game. . . . Your needs are taken care of. You're fed three times a day." Scorpions he could live without, and the dust was annoying. However, he met and courted Fumi Manabe, his future wife. It was a carefree time. Kitty

[22]Daniels, *Concentration Camps USA,* p. 22; and Roger Daniels, "The Japanese," in John Higham, ed., *Ethnic Leadership in America* (Baltimore and London, 1978), p. 40; Bill Hosokawa, *Nisei: The Quiet Americans, The Story of a People* (New York: William Morrow, 1969), pp. 151–52. The federal census shows that in 1940 there were 79,642 Nisei and 47,305 Issei, totaling 126,947, in a total U.S. population of 131,669,275.

[23]James, *Exile Within,* p. 8.

[24]Interviews with Abu Keiokan and Robert Utsumi, San Francisco, May 11, 1988; Harry Kitano, Los Angeles, September 20, 1987; Chiz Kitano Iiyama, San Francisco, May 13, 1988; Dr. John Hada, San Francisco, November 2, 1987; Lee Suyemoto, Boston, June 21, 1988; Hannah Hara, New York City, October 5, 1987; Mari Eijima, New York City, October 5, 1987, and June 14, 1988; and Arrington, *Prejudice,* p. 27.

Nakagawa recalled camp as being fun in the beginning, but she noted, "I hadn't experienced enough of life to know that this was an outrage."[25]

Age alone did not necessarily turn teenaged Nisei into carefree camp dwellers. Adolescence is a turbulent time in American culture; these were second-generation youth caught between the expectations of their parents' Japanese generation and the changing mores of American culture. These teenagers had to cope not only with the stresses of growing up in a bicultural situation but also with the tensions and traumas of the uprooting they had experienced, which threw them into a very "Japanese" environment. At the same time, they attended schools that were determined to teach them about democracy and make them good American citizens.[26]

Those whose family background was insecure or who lost parents as the result of incarceration suffered proportionately more, and some bear lasting scars today. Maya Nagata's father had died prior to the evacuation from the West Coast, and she and her mother and two sisters entered camp without father or brothers to pave the way. She remembered bitterly how hard it was to acquire the makeshift furniture that the men and boys made of scrap lumber they found or stole. She and her sisters had to use the surfaces of exposed beams as shelves to store their meager possessions. She admitted that even today she distrusts Caucasians and still cannot stand in line to wait patiently for anything but shoulders her way to the front—a practice she knows embarrasses her children but one she cannot break, remembering the humiliation of queuing up in camp for everything.[27]

Michi Okamoto's father, like Maya's, was deceased. She and her mother had quarreled before camp over the question of whether to try to seek voluntary relocation and move to Denver with friends.[28] Michi pleaded to go there, but her mother hesitated just one day too long and they lost their chance for freedom when voluntary evacuation was abruptly terminated. Michi could not forgive her. The anger grew to the point that the two did not speak, and after camp they went their separate ways. Alienated and bitter, Michi found the camp high school inferior to hers in San Francisco and blamed this inadequate schooling for her difficulties in acquiring a higher education later. The scars still show.[29]

Don Nakahata's father was lost to him in another way; he was removed by the FBI after Pearl Harbor because he worked for the Japanese Association, an Issei organization that helped the first generation deal with life in America and maintain their connections in Japan. Don's father was sent to

[25]Interviews with Arthur Tadashi Hayashi, Berkeley, October 28, 1987, and Kitty Nakagawa, Leonia, N.J., June 15, 1988. AWC Collection.

[26]James, *Exile Within*, p. 8.

[27]Interview with Maya Nagata, Oakland, November 4, 1987, AWC Collection.

[28]Japanese Americans were allowed to relocate voluntarily for a brief few weeks in February 1942 before they were restricted in movement prior to being moved to assembly camps and then to the relocation centers.

[29]Interview with Michi Okamoto Kobi, New York City, October 5–6, 1987, and written memoir in possession of the author, AWC Collection.

a series of prison camps; interned without trial, separated from his family, his health deteriorated and he died. Don never saw his father alive again, and the family was never able to learn the circumstances of his death.[30]

For some a sense of discrimination in camp built upon feelings of inferiority that had developed throughout a childhood spent in a racist society that condemned them for their Japanese heritage and visage. Memories of discrimination haunted Tomoye Takahashi who had been a schoolgirl in San Francisco and Berkeley; she viewed her entire prewar life through the prism of racism. Mari Eijima believed that Topaz deepened a sense of inferiority she had long felt over being Japanese, and she overcame it only when she left camp early to pursue her secondary education with a Quaker family in Pennsylvania.[31]

Parents were not always ignored. Their attitudes affected the way these young people reacted to camp. The elder Suyemotos' anger over their incarceration was quickly communicated to their children, who shared it. Parental rage sustained Morgan Yamanaka and his brother when they decided to answer "no-no" to the two items on the loyalty questionnaire required in 1942 of all inmates to determine allegiance and willingness to serve in the military. Even though their answers meant that the family would be segregated in Tule Lake and could be sent to Japan, the Yamanakas agreed with their sons' actions. But a sense of the ultimate value of America and the belief that their children were, after all, American citizens, caused many parents, like Tom Kawaguchi's, to urge their sons to enlist. "Don't ever forget that it happened," he was counseled, and although he too was angry he chose to serve the country that disdained him. Tad Hayashi's father told him, "Well, you're an American citizen," so he said "yes-yes," and enlisted.[32]

Religious faith was also a determinant for both Buddhists and Christians. Fumi Manabe's parents were extremely devout Christians; her father did circuit preaching for the Christian Layman's church, and their faith and ability to accept camp as God's will sustained their children. Even today the elderly Chitose Manabe knows her faith sustained her, and because of that camp was not so bad; it was, in fact, a rest from a hard life. Tad Fujita had been active in his church before the war, and he continued to be involved with the Protestant church in camp. He too found camp life bearable. Buddhist families found a similar strength in their faith. Shig Sugiyama identified with his family's faith, and later in his life Buddhism became a great source of strength for him.[33] Above all, parents could reinforce a sense of

[30]Interview with Dr. Don Nakahata, Mill Valley, Calif., May 12, 1988, AWC Collection.

[31]Interviews with Tomoye Takahashi and Mari Eijima, AWC Collection.

[32]Interview with Kiyo Ito, Leonia, N.J., June 14, 1988; Morgan Yamanaka, San Francisco, May 11, 1988; interview with Tom Kawaguchi, San Francisco, November 5, 1987; interview with Tad Hayashi, AWC Collection.

[33]Interview with Fumi Hayashi, Berkeley, October 28, 1987; interview with Chitose Manabe, Berkeley, October 26, 1987; interview with Shigeki Sugiyama, Washington, June 9, 1988; interview with Tad Fujita, Berkeley, October 27, 1987; AWC Collection.

pride in ethnicity, of being able to survive because of their heritage, and this in some measure counterbalanced the sense of inferiority they felt because of their incarceration.

In addition to external circumstances, traits of character also affected the way individuals coped. Strength of character, resiliency, and the belief in being a "survivor" all determined responses to camp life. Kiyo Ito became the head of her family at age sixteen when her father was temporarily removed to a prison camp. Her parents feared a future life of discrimination in America and chose to return with their daughter to Japan after the war. There they had to cope with a devastated economy and a new kind of discrimination they felt as Americans in Japan.[34] But Kiyo's memories were not bitter: "People and governments make mistakes, but you have to be strong enough to rise above them." She returned to America as a survivor, and she sought to make sure her children were survivors, too, who appreciated both their Japanese heritage and the American way of life.[35]

Although most Japanese Americans were quick to spot the inequities and the ultimate injustice of the concentration camps and all they represented in the way of American racism, few could do anything about it. George Kondo and his young wife were not only angered by the internment but also were determined to get out as soon as possible. His parents reacted passively as did most: *Shakata ga nai,* "it can't be helped"; but George recalled that the camp made him feel like a criminal, and he reacted actively, seeking an exit.[36] As he put it, "It's the whole feeling that a person has that I shouldn't be here." As soon as the War Relocation Authority announced the new policy of relocation in October 1942—a resettlement program intended to spread Japanese Americans throughout the country—they applied for leave clearance and were successful. They left camp after only six weeks to take jobs as domestics, a position they quickly disliked, but it led to other work and enabled them to keep their freedom.[37] Others left for educational opportunities, as did Mari Eijima, Midori Shimanouchi, and Nobu Kumekawa Hibino.[38]

For some Nisei in their early twenties the camps provided an opportunity to develop professional experience, albeit in a specialized setting. It is a patronizing justification after the fact to suggest that Japanese American lives

[34]Some 1,447 Topaz internees moved to the camp at Tule Lake, of whom 859 had asked for repatriation or expatriation. Two hundred fifty-nine answered "no" on loyalty, and the rest accompanied relatives. Most were American citizens. Arrington, *Prejudice,* p. 22.

[35]Kiyo Ito, interview.

[36]See Harry H. L. Kitano, "Japanese American Mental Illness," in Sue and Wagner, *Asian-Americans,* p. 195, for a discussion of *shikata ga nai* as a way of coping.

[37]Interview with George Kondo, San Francisco, November 5, 1987, AWC Collection. Obtaining leave clearance involved an FBI check for loyalty, the very process that might have obviated the "need" for relocation to begin with. No Japanese American was ever found to be disloyal prior to internment, and those 5,000 who did reject the U.S. during the war did so as a result of internment.

[38]Interview with Midori Shimanouchi Lederer, New York City, June 17, 1988; interview with Nobu Hibino, Wakefield, R.I., June 20, 1988, AWC Collection.

were improved by the camp experience, but some did acquire skills or sharpen talents that they were able to use in the outside world. Mine Okubo, for example, wanting to record her experience, worked on illustrations of camp life that she later published as *Citizen 13660*. She also illustrated the three published issues of *Trek*, the camp literary magazine. Mine, who had graduated in fine arts from the University of California before the war and had won a scholarship to Europe, went to camp with a younger brother and was able to leave in 1943 when she was offered a position as an illustrator with *Fortune* magazine.[39] There were many other artists in camp, such as Hisako Hibi and her husband and Berkeley Professor Chiura Obata, and others who captured the experience later in words, as did Yoshiko Uchida in her memoir *Desert Exile*.[40] Most, however, just toiled in the fields, the mess halls, or the hospital in menial positions for which they received only $16, $19, or $21 a month, a wage deliberately set lower than an army private's pay.[41] Their records were kept in their minds.

The experiences of Dave Tatsuno and his associate Tad Fujita in managing the cooperative at Topaz helped both young men acquire useful skills in merchandising and business.[42] Dave's attitude toward camp was one of forbearance—*gaman*—as he put it, of making the best of it.[43] In his early twenties, he and his small family settled into camp and adapted quickly to his new surroundings. He showed little bitterness over the experience: the war had unsettled many lives, and he felt they were just part of the dislocation. Forty years later he remarked, "With the war going on, people killing each other, why any kind of protest would have been futile." Providing clothing and sundries for the camp inmates gave him a position that eventually brought travel outside the barbed wire, even outside the state, to stock the co-op's inventory. He even found the opportunity to record the camp with his home movie camera, smuggled into Topaz and loaded with film acquired on the outside. Dave later went into business for himself.[44]

Others, like Chiyoko Yano and Hiromoto Katayama, worked for the administration, made close friends with the Caucasians with whom they labored, and cherished the associations forty years later. Yano was proud of the statistics she kept for the camp and noted with pride that she had created the "tree of Topaz," a demographic profile of the camp that resembles the shape of a tree. Kazu Iijima remembered with fondness how she and her

[39]Mine Okubo, *Citizen 13660* (Seattle: University of Washington Press, 1946); interview with Mine Okubo, New York City, October 4, 1987, and written statement in possession of the author. See also Arrington, *Prejudice*, p. 16.

[40]Yoshiko Uchida, *Desert Exile: The Uprooting of a Japanese-American Family* (Seattle: University of Washington Press, 1982).

[41]See Weglyn, *Infamy*, p. 115.

[42]The co-op had a membership of more than 5,000 and employed over 500. Gross sales averaged over $40,000 a month. The co-op made enough to reimburse the WRA for all salaries and allowances paid employees and to pay rent for the WRA building space and equipment. Arrington, *Prejudice*, pp. 30–31.

[43]See Kitano, "Japanese American Mental Illness," pp. 191–92.

[44]Interview with Dave Tatsuno, San Jose, November 4, 1987, AWC Collection.

coworkers did not hesitate once to wake director Charles Ernst at 2 a.m. to tell him what was bothering them and how graciously he received them.[45] There were, all agreed, "good" and "bad" Caucasians, and among the former were those conscientious objectors who were assigned to the camp, like Emil Sekerak, and some truly gifted and dedicated teachers like Eleanor Gerard, Harry Kitano's favorite, who still attends reunions of the high school classes of the camp and was at the all-camp reunion held in the Bay Area in 1988. Many remembered Gerard, who married fellow administrator Eric Sekerak, with great affection.[46]

The lives of the Nisei of Topaz demonstrate how the human spirit survives in adversity. These lives also help us to understand the impact of incarceration upon a particular age group, young people in their teens and twenties, and especially the ways in which it could affect their growing up. Coming of age in a concentration camp was a painful thing. Young children could probably withstand the experience the best, but even they were traumatized by loss of parents, the breakdown of the family system, and the arbitrariness and routinization of life behind barbed wire. Teenagers were swept into gangs, a phenomenon unknown in prewar Japanese America, and some ran wild in school, while others only profited from their educations by dint of furious self-discipline, as did Shigeki Sugiyama.[47] The rest had, as Fumi Manabe put it, "an attitude problem."

There were also differences in the way males and females reacted. Young girls approaching maturity suffered keenly from the lack of privacy, especially in sanitary facilities. Disruption of the family appears to have had a more devastating effect on some of them. Although there were some notably strong women like Mine Okubo, the artist, who cared for herself and her brother, and Faith Terasawa, who as a single woman worked as a social worker in camp and aided others with her strong Christian faith, the breakdown in family life and the virtual disappearance of the individual home was devastating to women.[48] Some young women like Chiz Kitano found an outlet in political activism in a radical group known as the Young Democrats where she met her future husband Ernie Iiyama, but most did not stray far from school or job. Deviant behavior among women was virtually unknown; the Japanese American social ethic still prevailed, and the lack of private space curtailed actions as well.

Both sexes had to face the issue of renewed discrimination by the white community, something that the Nisei who were not interned (those living in the interior and East) already knew about. Salt Lake City's small Japanese American community, for example, was not interned and had long since developed strategies of survival in a Caucasian environment.

[45]Interviews with Chiyoko Yano, Berkeley, October 28, 1987; Hiromoto Katayama, Berkeley, October 27, 1987; and Kazu Iijima, AWC Collection.

[46]See Eleanor Gerard Sekerak, "A Teacher at Topaz," in Daniels, Taylor, and Kitano, *Japanese Americans*, pp. 38–43.

[47]See interview with Shig Sugiyama.

[48]Interview with Faith Terasawa, San Francisco, November 6, 1987, AWC Collection.

Some questions applied to both sexes: whether to return with the family to the Bay Area or to strike out on their own to find a new future in a different environment where being Japanese might not matter so much. Finding jobs also was a factor: whether to return to the fields and canneries of California or take a chance and do something radically different, as Michi Okamoto did when she went to New York to become an actress. Hardest of all was the choice of whether to follow parents who had rejected America back to Japan (a place many Nisei had never seen) or to cast one's lot with the U.S. despite the anger many felt over relocation. Gender did indeed play a role, posing different questions and choices, but making it easy for neither. For no Japanese American internee living through relocation and resettlement were the choices easy ones. The experience marked their lives.[49]

[49]See Harry H. L. Kitano, "The Effects of Evacuation on the Japanese Americans," in Daniels, Taylor, and Kitano, *Japanese Americans*, pp. 151–58.

*

"A Sad and Expensive Experience": Ernest L. Wilkinson's 1964 Bid for the U.S. Senate

GARY JAMES BERGERA

Utah's political history has long attracted the attention of Utah historians. In the following article Gary James Bergera examines Brigham Young University president Ernest L. Wilkinson's unsuccessful bid for a U.S. Senate seat in 1964. The election presented a clear choice between Wilkinson, an "exponent of hard-core conservative Republican politics," and the liberal Democratic incumbent, Frank E. Moss. Wilkinson launched aggressive attacks against his rival, moderate Republican Congressman Sherman Lloyd, in the primary and Moss in the general election. Moss won easily, however, much to Wilkinson's surprise and dismay. The loss was difficult for him and affected Brigham Young University as well. When he returned to the school, according to Bergera, he was "overly politicized by his foray into partisan politics, increasingly fearful of dissent, and preoccupied to the point of distraction with rumors of faculty disloyalty."

Gary James Bergera, "'A Sad and Expensive Experience': Ernest L. Wilkinson's 1964 Bid for the U.S. Senate," *Utah Historical Quarterly* 61 (Fall 1993): 304–24. Reprinted by permission of the publisher and the author.

Gary James Bergera is director of publishing at Signature Books in Salt Lake City and co-author of *Brigham Young University: A House of Faith*. He appreciates the advice and support of Alice Wilkinson Anderson, John T. Bernhard, Harvard S. Heath, Marian Wilkinson Jensen, Frank E. Moss, F. Ross Peterson, and John Sillito.

As ERNEST L. WILKINSON, scrappy sixty-four-year-old president of Brigham Young University, and other Utah politicos sensed, the 1964 U.S. Senate race promised the state's electorate a clear choice between an incumbent liberal Democrat and a conservative Republican challenger. Having flirted with the heady give-and-take of American politics as a patriotic circuit rider for free-market capitalism,[1] Wilkinson had emerged in the popu-

[1]For Wilkinson's political career before 1964, see Gary James Bergera, "A Strange Phenom-

lar Utah mind as an articulate, impassioned, if humorless and overbearing, exponent of hard-core conservative Republican politics.

In his twelve years since leaving a lucrative eastern law practice for BYU, Wilkinson had come to fear deeply for the future of the United States. With his country seemingly on a collision course with socialism, he was convinced he could be of greatest service in Washington, D.C. He had also concluded that his mission at BYU—particularly his expansive building program—had been accomplished and that continuing support for his educational agenda would not survive the death of David O. McKay, octogenarian president of the Church of Jesus Christ of Latter-day Saints and long-time Wilkinson booster. Finally, he knew his own age would soon be an obstacle to political ambition.[2]

Despite his well known behind-the-scenes involvement in statewide politics,[3] Wilkinson's decision to run for the Senate was not an easy one. For a brief time he toyed with entering the race for governor but could not shake the allure of national office.[4] When he finally resolved in November 1963

---

ena: Ernest L. Wilkinson, the LDS Church, and Utah Politics," *Dialogue: A Journal of Mormon Thought* 26 (Summer 1993): 89–115. During these years Wilkinson publicly addressed a variety of conservative subjects. Unquestionably his favorite was "The Founding, Fruition, and Future of Free Enterprise" (also known as "Free Enterprise for Everyone"), which he delivered to eager audiences at least twenty-one times from 1961 to 1963. Copies of this and other speeches can be found in Wilkinson's Biographical File, Brigham Young University Archives, Harold B. Lee Library, Brigham Young University, Provo (hereinafter BYU Archives).

[2]Wilkinson's bid was not the first such attempt by a BYU president. Both Karl G. Maeser and Franklin S. Harris had earlier campaigned unsuccessfully for public office: Maeser in 1895 for state superintendent of public instruction and Harris in 1938 for U.S. senator (see Maeser to George Reynolds, October 12, 1895, Maeser Presidential Papers, BYU Archives; Harris Journal, August 2, 9, 10, September 12–14, November 4–8, 1938, Harris Papers, BYU Archives). Other BYU administrators had also tested partisan waters, relying on their affiliation with the school and network of university contacts to improve their chances of winning. For example, the representative of one candidate reminded BYU's official fund raiser in the early 1960s: "You are going to contact the Dean's Council and the Administrative Council to obtain donations for the John Bernhard campaign fund" (Edwin Kimball to Noble Waite, September 12, 1962, Bernhard Biographical File, BYU Archives).

During the 1950s BYU's board of trustees, composed of high-ranking LDS officials, had ruled simply that faculty involvement in politics required administrative clearance (BYU Board of Trustees, Minutes, July 22, 1954, November 4, 1959, BYU Archives). By early 1962, and at Wilkinson's urging, the board had settled on allowing the university president "to judge each case on its merits and make such decisions as he thought proper with these guide lines": (1) "faculty members . . . [should] not be unduly partisan"; (2) "staff members running for political office or staff members occupying positions with political parties should not permit their duties to interfere with their regular work at the University"; and (3) "if the political campaign or office is of such a nature that they cannot give full attention to their regular work at the University, they should either be given a leave of absence without pay or resign" (Executive Committee, BYU Board of Trustees, Minutes, March 22, 1962).

[3]See Bergera, "A Strange Phenomena."

[4]Wilkinson, Memorandum for File, November 1, 1963, Wilkinson Papers, BYU Archives. Copies of virtually all documents from the Wilkinson Papers cited in this essay are also in private possession, which is my source for them. Additionally, many are referenced in Ernest L. Wilkinson, ed., *Brigham Young University: The First One Hundred Years,* vol. 2 (Provo: Brigham Young University Press, 1975), pp. 497–723; Wilkinson and Leonard J. Arrington, eds., *Brigham Young University: The First One Hundred Years,* vol. 3 (Provo: Brigham Young University Press, 1976), pp. 3–789; Wilkinson and W. Cleon Skousen, *Brigham Young University:*

that his chances would never be better, he put behind him months of agonizing indecision.[5] He and his supporters had sounded out a variety of sympathetic Mormon/non-Mormon business and political interests, securing verbal support and promises of assistance. They also knew that in 1962 Utah Republicans had retained their place in the Senate, captured both congressional seats, won control of both houses in the state legislature, and secured a majority of county offices.[6] Finally, Wilkinson had received reassurances from President McKay that if he "wanted to run for the Senate in 1964 [McKay] would give [him] a year's leave of absence" from his appointments as BYU president and chancellor of the entire education system of the LDS church.[7]

Although he would have preferred to see Wilkinson on the U.S. Supreme Court, McKay agreed in mid-October 1963 that the lawyer-turned-educator should run for the Senate. An astute partisan observer, McKay knew of Wilkinson's needs and appreciated as well as anyone the value of loyal associates in positions of national prominence and influence. According to Wilkinson, McKay voiced his concern that Wilkinson's likely Republican challenger in the primaries, incumbent congressman Sherman P. Lloyd, was becoming too soft on federal aid to education and Medicare and that the BYU president's brand of conservative Republicanism provided a better safeguard against socialist inroads.[8] The following month Wilkinson asked members of the church's budget committee, who jointly served on the executive committee of BYU's Board of Trustees, what they thought of his running for the Senate. They unanimously opposed the idea.[9] Undissuaded, he notified McKay by letter the next week that

> I might very shortly decide to run for [the] Senate, telling him that if he had any final objections to my doing so I would be happy not to run. In other words, I have placed myself squarely subject to his direction, although he may feel that he should not deprive me of my own free agency in this respect.[10]

A School of Destiny (Provo: Brigham Young University Press, 1976), pp. 429–759; and Woodruff J. Deem and Glenn V. Bird, *Ernest L. Wilkinson: Indian Advocate and University President* (Salt Lake City: Alice L. Wilkinson, 1978).

[5]For Wilkinson's vacillation, see Wilkinson Diary, March 1, 2, 13, October 11, November 27, 1963, photocopy in Wilkinson Collection, Special Collections, Marriott Library, University of Utah, Salt Lake City; original in Wilkinson Papers.

[6]See Stewart Grow, "The 1962 Election in Utah," *Western Political Quarterly* 16 (1963): 460.

[7]See Wilkinson, Memorandum of a Conference with McKay, March 7, 1962, Wilkinson Papers; see also Wilkinson Diary, March 2, 1963; Wilkinson, Memorandum of a Conference with McKay, October 17, 1963, Wilkinson Papers; compare Wilkinson Diary, April 9, 1958. In fact, McKay felt at first that "President Wilkinson should remain as president of the Brigham Young University while he is seeking the nomination, and if he gets the nomination then he can consider finding a successor. If he is not elected, then he should continue at the school" (McKay Diary, November 21, 1963, McKay Papers, LDS Church Archives, Salt Lake City).

[8]See Wilkinson, Memorandum of a Conference with McKay, October 17, 1963.

[9]McKay Diary, November 21, 1963.

[10]Wilkinson Diary, November 27, 1963.

That same day Wilkinson also began sounding out possible campaign managers.

Following a combined meeting of BYU's Board of Trustees and the church's General Board of Education one week later, Wilkinson announced that this would probably be his last meeting with them. "You mean the last meeting this year," Hugh B. Brown, McKay's counselor, said. "No," Wilkinson replied, "the last meeting, period." Overcome with emotion, Wilkinson "told them I took credit for only two things. One, that I had not loafed on the job and second, that I had not profited by it. . . . " Brown immediately praised Wilkinson's accomplishments and then asked him to meet with N. Eldon Tanner, Brown's nephew and co-counselor in the First Presidency, in his office. Alone with Wilkinson and Tanner, Brown asked moments later "what was all this about and if I had cleared it with President McKay." Wilkinson answered that he had. The usually stoical Wilkinson then broke down and wept.[11]

Wilkinson met the next week with McKay. He knew the church president supported his decision but nonetheless emphasized that

> I had no personal desire to go into politics; the so-called grandeur of public office never appealed to me at all nor to my wife who preferred for me not to go; that if I went it would be because I felt we all had a duty to respond to public office if there was a legitimate demand for us.

He knew he was safe in asking that if McKay wanted him to remain at BYU "all he needed to do was say so and I would stay—in fact," Wilkinson added, "I might be more happy." McKay answered less than a minute later, "I want you in the Senate." He also "reiterated our previous understanding that [a] temporary appointment should be made during the campaign and that if I should be defeated I should return to both of my previous positions" as BYU president and church chancellor of education.[12] By this time Wilkinson had concluded that a leave of absence could be a liability and was probably unnecessary given McKay's support.

News of Wilkinson's resignation was officially released to the press on January 9, 1964. "New challenges and responsibilities have developed which call for decisions in the near future," he explained.[13] Sensitive to Wilkinson's nuance, the *Salt Lake Tribune* speculated that "the move was . . . a prelude to his entry in the race for the U.S. Senate."[14] The same day the *Deseret News and Telegram* printed the results of its poll of twenty of Utah's twenty-nine Republican county chairmen, finding nine in favor of Wilkinson, nine supporting Sherman P. Lloyd, one for J. Bracken Lee, and one undecided. According to the paper, Wilkinson's supporters had contacted the same group and found fifteen favoring Wilkinson, six Lloyd, and

[11]Ibid., December 4, 1963.
[12]Ibid., December 10, 1963.
[13]*Daily Universe,* January 9, 1964.
[14]*Salt Lake Tribune,* January 9, 1964.

eight neutral.[15] The next day the *News* eulogized Wilkinson, praising the mark he left on BYU as one "such as few men have ever been privileged to leave in their lifetimes."[16] When Wilkinson finally announced his candidacy for the U.S. Senate on January 11,[17] the news came as no surprise to the state's political savants.

In his farewell address to BYU's student body, Wilkinson proved unusually self-revealing. "The intervening thirteen years [1951–64] have been the happiest years of our lives," he said, "not that there have not been problems. Sometimes I know that some members of my Board of Trustees have felt that I thought that too much of the income of the Church should be spent for the B.Y.U. And there may have been times when I pressed my viewpoints a little too hard," he confessed. "I told one of them one day that if what I was doing was treason he should make the most of it." He admitted that he may have been "unduly brusk, . . . and for this I apologize." But he had found students "the easiest of all to control, . . . because, based on my boyhood days, I understand you students better than I sometimes understood the Board and the faculty."[18]

Two days later, addressing faculty, he conceded: "Our decision to resign in order to run for political office was the most difficult decision we have had to make in our lives."[19] He had decided to run now because the government was spiritually bankrupt, men and women were too reliant on federal aid, government spending was steadily increasing, the national debt was burgeoning, the Monroe Doctrine had been abandoned, and the threat of communism was growing worldwide. "If the Constitution is to hang by a thread in this country," he vowed, alluding to popular Mormon tradition, "I want to be the one to save it."[20]

[15]*Deseret News and Telegram,* January 9, 1964.

[16]Ibid., January 10, 1964.

[17]*Daily Universe,* January 13, 1964.

[18]Wilkinson, "Valedictory Address," February 18, 1964, p. 6, Wilkinson Biographical File.

[19]Wilkinson, "Valedictory to Faculty," February 20, 1964, p. 7, Wilkinson Biographical File. In fact, Alice Ludlow Wilkinson, Wilkinson's wife of forty years, was even more apprehensive. "I was not very enthusiastic in the beginning," she later recalled. "I didn't want to see him get into politics because I had seen so many things happen in political life that I didn't like, but I knew that he loved politics. When President McKay asked him if he would run, of course he wanted to, and I said that I would support him" (Oral History, September 28, 1979, p. 11, BYU Archives).

[20]Wilkinson, "Valedictory to Faculty," February 20, 1964, pp. 8–9. The minutes of this meeting record Wilkinson's closing promise a little differently: "if the constitution [were] to hang by a thread he wanted to be one to help save it" (BYU Faculty Meeting, Minutes, February 20, 1964, BYU Archives).

"We have not yet determined when we will move from the campus," Wilkinson closed. "The Board of Trustees has said that in exchange for my 13 non-salaried years of service [to the university] we may remain in the [president's] home until we decide where to move permanently for the convenience of our son who is now enrolled in school. We may, however, open another home in Salt Lake also for I am there 6 out of every 7 days. But we hope to see all of you frequently. If I should become unemployed we may have the glorious privilege of seeing you more in social gatherings" ("Valedictory to Faculty," p. 11; on Wilkinson retaining occupancy of the president's home, see McKay Diary, February 4, 1964).

Early on Wilkinson found that staffing his campaign machine was more difficult than he had imagined. Salt Lake City businessman Joseph P. Rosenblatt had initially offered to help raise funds for the race. In mid-1963 he had publicly declared:

> I feel very strongly that this man has the voice of the conservative we need in this country, the mature, sound, reasonable, reliable voice of the conservative. He is not the conservative who plants his feet against all that represents progress, not one who is conservative because he may be the opposite of what you think of as a liberal, and indeed not one who is conservative because he is a reactionary, but he is a conservative in the true sense of what we in this country stand for.[21]

In fact, Wilkinson had concluded to run, in part, because of Rosenblatt's support. However, Rosenblatt subsequently changed his mind, preferring to remain on the sidelines. Angry over this turn of events, Wilkinson never forgave him. As a result, the former BYU president went for several months without a fund raiser[22]; and then, tragically, the next man who agreed to help died within the month, leaving a seriously handicapped Wilkinson to rely on part-time volunteers.

Securing a full-time campaign manager proved less difficult, though in some ways more problematic. Wilkinson's selection, John T. Bernhard, was a logical choice. He was trained as a political scientist, had loyally served Wilkinson for more than three years as administrative assistant, had cultivated strong ties to Utah's Republican party as a state legislator, and shared Wilkinson's conservative political views. With typical alacrity Wilkinson obtained David O. McKay's permission for Bernhard to take a "special [sabbatical] leave of absence" "at full compensation" to serve as his campaign director.[23] However, BYU's comptroller objected to the arrangement, arguing that he would only comply with it on the express order of the university's acting president or Board of Trustees.[24] The comptroller and others knew that Bernhard did not qualify under university policy for a paid sabbatical and probably feared as well the accusations of church support for Wilkinson that would erupt should the arrangement be made public.

Despite these concerns, the chair of BYU's Board of Trustees and president of the Quorum of Twelve Apostles notified BYU's acting president that in view of the "special circumstances"—that Wilkinson had served for thirteen years without compensation and that Bernhard's "services in his new assignment will redound to be benefit of B.Y.U."—"we believe it is proper

21"Introductory Remarks of Joseph Rosenblatt at Testimonial Dinner for Doctor Ernest L. Wilkinson, May 2, 1963," pp. 3–4, Wilkinson Biographical File.

22See Wilkinson, Memorandum of a Conference with McKay, November 13, 1966, Wilkinson Papers. BYU subsequently awarded Rosenblatt an honorary doctorate less than two weeks after Wilkinson died in April 1978.

23Bernhard to Joseph T. Bentley, January 8, 1964, BYU Archives. According to the terms of this special leave, Bernhard's pay totaled nearly $12,000.

24Joseph T. Bentley to Earl C. Crockett, acting BYU president, January 13, 1964, BYU Archives.

to grant him a special sabbatical leave with full pay from February 1, 1964, to November 15, 1964. This would be in accord with President McKay's desires, and this letter is your authority to grant the same, which we would appreciate your doing."[25] Still BYU administrators balked at the idea. Wilkinson then suggested that Bernhard be given an unpaid leave and that the church simply deduct his monthly salary from the school's operating budget and pay him from an account outside the university.[26] School officials found this alternative more acceptable,[27] and Bernhard, who had gone more than four months without pay, was able to concentrate entirely on the campaign.

With these and similar problems in mind, Wilkinson lamented less than six weeks after announcing his candidacy, "Frankly, were it possible to undo what has been done in the last two months and not resign at all, I would make that decision, but decisions once made and relied on by other people (hundreds are supporting me) cannot be undone and I must go forward."[28] "I, frankly, often regret that I am not still at the B.Y.U.," he later added.[29]

In his primary bid against Sherman P. Lloyd, the erstwhile educator found himself facing a man with considerable public service experience. A native of eastern Idaho and former general counsel for the Utah Retail Grocers Association, the forty-nine-year-old Lloyd had spent eighteen years in the Utah State Senate. Most recently he had served on the Utah Legislative Council, acted as Utah's representative on the board of managers of the Council of State Governments (CSG), and chaired the CSG Committee on State Taxation of Interstate Income. He had been a delegate to the State Republican Convention and the Republican National Convention. He had run unsuccessfully for Congress in 1960 and successfully in 1962. In fact, Wilkinson had earlier lauded Lloyd as one who "will help to restore sanity to the Congress of the United States,"[30] even crediting himself as "one responsible for getting Sherman Lloyd in the congressional Republican primary race and . . . [who] intended to continue to support him."[31] Times had changed, however, and Wilkinson clearly felt that Lloyd, a political moderate, had become ineffectual in corralling a runaway federal bureaucracy. Ironically, Lloyd had initially encouraged Wilkinson to run "because I mistakenly felt that I could defeat him and that it would be better if he ran for the Senate instead of governor because I thought if he ran for governor he would not help the ticket."[32]

[25]Joseph Fielding Smith to Crockett, May 20, 1964, BYU Archives.

[26]Bentley to Crockett, June 25, 1964, BYU Archives.

[27]Lyman J. Durfee to Bentley, December 11, 1964, BYU Archives; Bentley to Bernhard, January 4, 1964 [1965], BYU Archives.

[28]Wilkinson Diary, February 17, 1964.

[29]Wilkinson to Ben E. Lewis, May 21, 1964, BYU Archives.

[30]"Television Address of Ernest L. Wilkinson On Channel 5 KSL TV," October 29, 1962, p. 23, Wilkinson Biographical File.

[31]Wilkinson Diary, August 4, 1962.

[32]Sherman P. Lloyd, Oral History, November 21, 1974, pp. 2–3, Utah State Historical Society, Salt Lake City.

Wilkinson tried to portray himself as a hard-working, frugal, common man of the people, with strong ties to Utah and an even stronger commitment to its economy, who by sheer force of his will and managerial abilities would bring a recalcitrant federal government to its knees in service to the citizens of the United States. He was resolutely opposed to federal intervention in any but the narrowest aspect of daily life and liked to think of himself as conservative presidential candidate Barry Goldwater's ideological twin. "True dynamic progress," Wilkinson believed, "can only be achieved when individual citizens are left free to develop their own creative powers unfettered by government."[33] "I pledge a militant fight for the preservation of our inspired Constitution, and our Republican form of government," he promised at the Utah Republican Nominating Convention on June 13. "Each generation of free men has its rendezvous with destiny," he proclaimed, "and our rendezvous is to see that our Government remains our servant, and does not become our master."[34]

Initially, Wilkinson focused on differences between the Republican and Democratic parties, but his platform left little doubt as to those areas in which he felt Congressman Lloyd was weakest. Specifically, Wilkinson called for "curbing run-away government expenditures, and making a substantial payment on the federal debt"; selling to private enterprise all "government businesses, except those absolutely indispensable for national defense"; eliminating federal subsidy programs; encouraging "American private industries to invest in foreign countries"; defeating the federal Medicare bill; repealing the Civil Rights Act; fighting "for a strong and resolute foreign policy, based on formidable military strength"; adopting "a Constitutional Amendment permitting state legislatures to be based both on *geographical* as well as *popular* representation"; reopening investigations into government corruption; supporting legislation to benefit Utah such as "irrigation projects," "protect[ing] the cattle industry from threatened bankruptcy," and "full utilization of our missile industry"; and "us[ing] all my influence to persuade permanent peacetime industries to locate in Utah."[35]

Representative Lloyd adopted a more gentle approach, announcing ten "broad principles" at the nominating convention "on which you may judge whether I am the kind of man you would hire to send to Washington to secure results for you of lasting worth." He vowed not to "appeal to your prejudices," but to "your sense of justice"; not to "inflame you," but to "in-

[33]"Statement of Political Convictions of Dr. Ernest L. Wilkinson, former President of Brigham Young University, Republican Candidate for United States Senate from the State of Utah," July 10, 1964, p. 1, Wilkinson Biographical File.

[34]Quoted in *The Wilkinson Story* (Provo, Ut.: Volunteers for Wilkinson, 1964), p. 1, Wilkinson Biographical File.

[35]Excerpted from ibid., pp. 1–8; "Television Address of Ernest L. Wilkinson, Candidate for the Republican Nomination as United States Senator, over K.S.L.-T.V. on July 24, 1964," pp. 2–9, Wilkinson Biographical File; "Speech of Ernest L. Wilkinson, Wilkinson Family Program, August 10, 1964," pp. 2–3, Wilkinson Biographical File.

form you"; not to "close your minds," but to "open them"; not to be "influenced by distribution of scabrous literature or by the vices of bigotry"; not to "arouse your hates," but to "reason with you"; to "continue to give voice to the dignity of the individual by working to suppress excessive government"; to "work for unity" and to "oppose the forces which divide us"; to continue to "labor against waste and unwise public debt"; to be "positive and constructive"; to "respect the rights and opinions of others"; and not to be "one of your leaders," but "one of your servants."[36]

Lloyd enjoyed the advantages of incumbency—experience in elected office, public exposure, existing campaign staff, fund-raising resources—and Wilkinson knew that the congressman's supporters were confident their man would easily garner the nomination. After a lackluster start, the former BYU president campaigned with single-minded vigor and determination—or with acrimony and demagoguery, his opponents would charge.[37] In March he dramatically confronted head-on rumors that he was too old or in poor health by performing forty-eight push-ups before 10,000 enthusiastic fans during a BYU basketball game and then challenging Lloyd to a similar feat.[38] He subsequently charged the freshman congressman with missing nearly 40 percent of roll-call votes, including sessions when the House cut $2 million from an appropriation bill for Hill Air Force Base or voted on state reclamation projects. More damaging, he began picturing Lloyd as politically and economically liberal, alleging that he had voted conservatively "only 64% of the time" and condemning his support of the Civil Rights Act. "Is Lloyd Becoming a Liberal?" Wilkinson's ads asked. This aggressive strategy began to pay off when it became apparent that Lloyd's popularity was not as widespread as assumed. In fact, polls conducted after less than four months of campaigning showed Wilkinson capturing slightly more than 48 percent of delegates to the State Republican Convention.[39]

Lloyd was clearly not accustomed to such attacks, including innuendos that he drank to excess,[40] and angrily denied the charges, protesting that he was actually the most conservatively voting member of Utah's four-man congressional team. He also circulated photographs of himself with presidential contender Barry Goldwater. Wilkinson countered by securing Goldwater's endorsement (as well as that of Michigan governor George Romney, Illinois senator Everett M. Dirksen, Massachusetts senator

[36]Lloyd, "Speech Given before the Republican State Convention," June 13, 1964, in Lloyd, Oral History, November 21, 1974, p. 4.

[37]See Calvin L. Rampton, *As I Recall*, ed. Floyd A. O'Neil and Gregory C. Thompson (Salt Lake City: University of Utah Press, 1989), p. 124; Lloyd, Oral History, November 5, 1974, pp. 2–3.

[38]See "Wilkinson Keeps in Top Physical Condition," *The Wilkinson Story*, p. 3. Wilkinson's feat was later restaged for campaign photographs to document the candidate's "can-do spirit."

[39]See "Utah: How It Is Out There," *Time*, August 21, 1964, p. 18; "Wilkinson Beats Lloyd in Lloyd's Own District," in *The Wilkinson Story*, p. 3.

[40]See Rampton, *As I Recall*, p. 124.

Leverett Saltonstall, Kansas senator Frank Carlson, Maine senator Margaret Chase Smith, and former U.S. president Dwight D. Eisenhower), and proclaiming that he, not Lloyd, had Goldwater's real support.[41] From Lloyd's point of view the debate should have been between Democrat and Republican but Wilkinson turned against his own party. "Wilkinson campaigned against me," Lloyd complained. "I also say—and I think I could sustain it in court—that he distorted my votes, accused me of absenteeism, for which I was not guilty, and many other things."[42] Reportedly, the head of the firm handling Wilkinson's campaign advertising later apologized to Lloyd.[43]

Interest in the controversial campaign so intensified that by the time of the state Republican primary on August 11, a record number of 120,567 voters turned out. "Most attention, and most heat, centered in the Republican senatorial primary," the *Salt Lake Tribune* reported.[44] After spending more than $80,000 Wilkinson managed to carry nineteen counties—Lloyd ten—to barely edge past Lloyd 61,113 votes to 59,454.[45] "The students of BYU take pride in the accomplishment of their former leader," the school's student newspaper editorialized two days later, "and realize that if the same boundless energy and devotion to a cause for which he is famous, is incorporated in further campaigning Pres. Wilkinson will be a tough competitor in November."[46] With voters in the Republican primary exceeding those in the Democratic primary by more than 20,000, Wilkinson's "scant" 1.3 percent margin of victory heralded to some outsiders: "The way things stand now, Wilkinson can start packing to move back to Washington."[47]

Lloyd credited his support of civil rights legislation, and Wilkinson's calculated criticisms of it, as the major cause of his defeat. "I had a hard time trying to reason with people in 1964 on the Civil Rights issue," he noted, "which was the big issue and in Utah had a tremendous undercurrent of ugliness to it."[48] Following the bitter contest Lloyd resigned himself to endorsing Wilkinson's continuing bid, "even though I thought many Wilkinson views were extreme," and discouraged supporters from running a write-in campaign in his behalf. However, when Lloyd declined an offer to appear with Wilkinson in a large heart-shaped advertisement after the primary and later when his mother's funeral prevented him from attending a Wilkinson fund-raising dinner, Wilkinson condemned the former congressman's support as half-hearted at best. Years afterwards a resentful Wilkin-

[41]See "Utah: How It Is Out There."

[42]Lloyd, Oral History, November 21, 1974, p. 5.

[43]Ibid., p. 8.

[44]*Salt Lake Tribune,* August 13, 1964.

[45]Richard R. Wilkins to Wilkinson, February 3, 1965, Wilkinson Papers; *Deseret News,* August 12, 1964.

[46]*Daily Universe,* August 13, 1964.

[47]Ibid.; "Utah: How It Is Out There."

[48]Lloyd, Oral History, November 5, 1974, p. 11.

son would repeatedly insist that Lloyd was a poor loser and had refused to support his candidacy.[49]

Wilkinson's Democratic opponent, fifty-two-year-old incumbent senator Frank E. Moss, had earlier worked as an attorney for the Securities and Exchange Commission, been appointed judge advocate in Europe during World War II, and served for ten years as a Salt Lake City judge and another ten years as Salt Lake County attorney. In 1958 Moss had barely been elected to the U.S. Senate when a third candidate (J. Bracken Lee) split the Republican vote. Convinced a preemptive strike was now needed, the Salt Lake City native launched his first volley against Wilkinson almost immediately.[50]

> The victory of Ernest Wilkinson in the Republican Primary presages a bitter personal type of campaign directed to matters unrelated to the real issues before Utahns and Americans. . . . The capture of the Republican Party by the Goldwaterites has now been cemented in Utah with the nomination of Ernest Wilkinson. . . . Extremism now will be preached in Utah with fervor equalling or exceeding its national proclamation!

Moss promised to travel the moral and ethical high road and "keep on the real issues of the day": employment, education, industry, poverty, natural resources, tourism, recreation, civil rights, personal freedom, roads and highways, small business, Social Security, national defense, conservation, and world peace. "I invite Mr. Wilkinson," he announced "to rise above personal abuse, accusation, and innuendo to talk sense to the people of Utah."[51]

Wilkinson responded by attacking Moss's votes for increased federal spending and by repeatedly telling voters:

> At stake is YOUR decision whether we squander billions of dollars annually in foreign aid, buying more enemies, or whether we conserve our resources to balance our budgets; whether we continue borrowing money to subsidize government competition with private enterprise, or whether we commence reduction of our staggering national debt; whether we spend ourselves into oblivion, or whether we preserve this nation's financial stability and integrity and continue its blessings upon our children.[52]

[49]Ibid., pp. 3, 8, 9; November 21, 1974, pp. 7–8. Following his defeat Lloyd became vice-president of Prudential Federal Savings, in charge of public relations. He also lectured on politics at the University of Utah and was subsequently elected to the U.S. Congress in 1966, where he remained for six years. In 1973 he was appointed assistant director of the U.S. Information Agency and taught political science at Utah State University. He was then named trade specialist in charge of the Utah office of the Department of Commerce. He ran again for the Senate in 1976. After losing he retired to Salt Lake City, where he died in late 1979.

[50]Wilkinson's only sister, Elva Wilkinson Bell, was a Democrat and worked for Moss. When her older brother announced his candidacy, she "tearfully tendered her resignation." Moss quickly explained that "he had full confidence in her loyalty and integrity and that she need not resign." Bell "joyfully continued her services and," according to Moss, "was probably the most exultant Utah resident with the Moss re-election." In fact, Moss reported that he "can still hear her muttering, 'That damned Ernest' " (Moss to Gary J. Bergera, March 13, 1992).

[51]Untitled papers in Moss Papers, Special Collections, Marriott Library. See also "Senator Moss Position papers" in ibid.

[52]"Speech over KSL Television by Dr. Ernest L. Wilkinson, Fiscal Integrity vs Fiscal Insanity, October 7, 1964," p. 9, Moss Papers.

In a point-by-point rebuttal Moss charged that his opponent intentionally preyed "on the fears of our elder and retired citizens for political purposes"; that his position on foreign aid was "that of . . . the John Birch Society"; that he ignored important provisions of the Civil Rights bill that addressed his criticisms; that he deliberately manipulated federal budget figures; that he insincerely objected to federal aid to public education without offering a "constructive solution to our school financing problem"; and that his criticisms of foreign travel at federal expense were hypocritical: "Mr. Wilkinson . . . believes that travel broadens *Republicans,* but is a waste of money for *Democrats.*" Finally, Moss gave voice to rumors that Wilkinson had misrepresented his personal wealth and out-of-state financial interests:

> I have made a full public disclosure of all of my financial interests—and they are limited enough to embarrass some of my friends. May I ask Mr. Wilkinson if he favors full disclosure? Would he vote for it? . . . It would be interesting for the voters of Utah to know of Mr. Wilkinson's financial holdings, income, interests in property, etc., before they decide whether he should represent them.[53]

In subsequent advertisements Moss forces revealed that Wilkinson owned a multimillion-dollar luxury apartment building called Inwood Manor in a wealthy Houston neighborhood despite Wilkinson's public protests that "No—I don't have millions invested in Texas."[54] After quoting from the sales brochure, which extolled Wilkinson's development as "that mauve moment in history when the world had become gloriously rich but not yet grown unimaginatively equal," the ads asked: "Does this demonstrate any interest in the problems, dreams and hopes of the average Utah family . . . [A]ren't you more likely to protect your investment by working for the economy of Texas instead of Utah? . . . Is it your belief that to the strong belong the spoils . . . that the problems of the old, the poor and the ill can be disregarded?" "Lest we be misunderstood," the ads closed, "Mr. Wilkinson certainly has the right to invest his money in Texas instead of Utah—But the citizens of Utah also have a right, the right to know."[55]

In their own full-page response Wilkinson backers blasted the allegations as "low blows." They insisted that Wilkinson's investment in Texas totalled less than a million dollars; that some Inwood Manor apartments rented for $250 per month, not $1,000; that Wilkinson had not approved the sales brochure; that he was not as wealthy as opponents suggested; that he had investments in Utah as well; and that he intended to donate the major share of his wealth, including Inwood Manor, to BYU at his death. "Mr. Moss," Wilkinson's supporters retorted, "we ask you, does Mr. Wilkinson's years of unselfish service at the BYU and his generous dedication to the students of Utah justify insinuations, as contained in the ad—that he has

[53] "Senator Moss Position Papers."
[54] *Salt Lake Tribune,* October 11, 1964.
[55] Ibid.; see also *Daily Herald,* October 18, 1964.

sought or is seeking to do anything but devote himself to public service?"[56]

The candidate's critics countered:

> Mr. Wilkinson, why Texas—why not Utah? You have still not made a full fair disclosure of your Texas investment or anything else. Instead of replying yourself, you have imposed on your business associates to answer for you. It appears that an attempt is being made to distort the facts not only for the public, but also for your friends.

His opponents convincingly demonstrated that despite having publicly denied he had invested "millions in Texas," Wilkinson's Inwood Manor project was worth more than $6 million. With a Houston bank holding a $3.5 million mortgage on the upscale apartment building, the ad asked, "Could Mr. Wilkinson fairly represent the citizens of Utah with this huge personal liability owing to a Texas financial institution? . . . Why won't Mr. Wilkinson disclose? What is he hiding?"[57]

These and other accusations sallied back and forth, including charges that Wilkinson had a decade earlier backed a proposal to transfer Weber Junior College in Ogden to the LDS church and had tried to prevent Utah State University in Logan from entering the Western Athletic Conference.[58] Soon pro-Moss groups began emerging among disenchanted Republicans. In a barrage of newspaper, radio, and television assaults during the closing weeks of the campaign Wilkinson supporters charged that Moss was soft on communism, favored selling American wheat to Russians, called for officially recognizing mainland China, received an excessive amount of financing from out of state, had toured the world with his wife at government expense, and had blocked congressional ethics probes. Moss backers alleged that Wilkinson had used foreign steel in BYU construction projects, was more interested in promoting a right-wing political agenda than Utah interests, favored the "tactical" use of nuclear weapons, and was conducting a campaign of "distortion, fear-and-smear."[59]

[56]*Daily Herald,* October 19, 1964.

[57]Ibid., October 18, 1964. Shortly before his death in 1978 Wilkinson donated 42 percent of his interest in Inwood Manor as a tithing contribution earmarked for the LDS church's educational system. This contribution was estimated at the time to be worth $4 million. See Executive Committees, Church Board of Education and Boards of Trustees of Brigham Young University, Brigham Young University—Hawaii Campus, Ricks College, and LDS Business College, Minutes, May 4, 1977.

[58]Although he had not publicly endorsed the proposed transfer of Weber Junior College, as well as two other state colleges, to the LDS church, Wilkinson had carefully orchestrated the unsuccessful move from behind the scenes. See Gary J. Bergera and Ronald L. Priddis, *Brigham Young University: A House of Faith* (Salt Lake City: Signature Books, 1985), pp. 30–31, 385 n. 63.

[59]See advertisements in *Deseret News,* October 24, 1964; *Daily Herald,* October 16, 21, 26, 1964. In 1992 Moss recalled, with evident pleasure, a debate with Wilkinson on the BYU campus: "A speaker's stand and microphones were installed, reminding me of a ring for exhibition boxing." The two candidates spoke and fielded questions for nearly an hour. "Ernest was fair and advised the students that I was to be treated with respect," Moss said. "They heeded this request by bestowing on me applause in excess of that given to Ernest as we each made our points on most of all of the issues in that election campaign. My paralyzed staff members were breathing easy and smiling at the end. That debate was one highlight of that campaign" (Moss to Bergera).

As humiliating as the attacks on his character were, Wilkinson also scrambled to minimize the impact of President Lyndon Johnson's two providentially timed visits to David O. McKay prior to his November 3 face-off with Moss. Ostensibly seeking the Mormon leader's "strength and understanding,"[60] Johnson explained, "I always feel better after I have been in his presence."[61] For his part, McKay, a Republican, responded by wishing the Democratic president "continued success," which some saw as an implicit endorsement. Of course, cynics accused Johnson of manipulating the aged and frail McKay for political purposes, but newspaper photographs of their carefully managed meetings, which almost always included Moss, made it difficult for the majority of Mormons to believe their prophet had been so crassly used.[62]

Alarmed at McKay's apparent friendship with Johnson, Wilkinson subsequently attempted to secure McKay's endorsement of the Republican party and presumably his candidacy. McKay chose not to respond to Wilkinson's awkward public pleas directly. But when Barry Goldwater paid him a visit, McKay moved to even the score, commenting to reporters, "I wish him success and advise him to stand true to his principles."[63] McKay later offered, "I think you can put me down as favoring the success of the Republican party." Still, Wilkinson's determined, and occasionally inept, pressure for McKay's support may have backfired: while 50 percent of Utah voters disapproved of Moss's attempts to align himself with McKay, 74 percent took exception to Wilkinson's strong-arming of the church president.[64]

With only days left in an increasingly acrimonious campaign, an anonymous letter surfaced on college campuses throughout the state. The most vitriolic of any attack, the letter was evidently written by a disgruntled BYU employee and read in part:

> Here at the "Y" we were, at first, alarmed at having an attorney chosen to head the school. Later, when the needed buildings began to appear, we applauded his achievements, but for two years now, it has been clear that he has used the "Y" as a tool for his long-range ambitions. For over two years this campus has been a refuge for ex-politicians, Birchers, and relatives of influential men. Many of our assemblies have been nothing more than political rallies. For years the "Y" has been giving preferential treatment to builders, suppliers, contractors, advertising agencies who might serve as Wilkinson boosters. And they are serving as such during this campaign.
>
> Many of the faculty have been hired and fired to serve his personal ends, and the faculty has been helpless to curb such action. This cunning and ruthless man has even captured the President of the Church and has used his

[60]*Salt Lake Tribune,* September 17, 1964.

[61]*Deseret News,* September 18, 1964.

[62]See also Frank H. Jonas, "President Lyndon Johnson, the Mormon Church and the 1964 Political Campaign," *Proceedings, Utah Academy of Sciences, Arts, and Letters* 44 (1967), Part 1:67–90.

[63]*Salt Lake Tribune,* October 11, 1964.

[64]See Jonas, "President Lyndon Johnson," pp. 87–88.

> high and holy office to promote partisan politics. Wilkinson will do anything to gain his ends. As stated, what he now seeks is to wring another four million dollars from the federal government.[65]

Angered by the anonymous attack, McKay, at Wilkinson's urging, released a public statement one day before the November finals. He condemned in no uncertain terms the "vituperative attack" as "an error-filled anonymous letter now being examined by the Federal Bureau of Investigation." While remaining neutral, McKay praised Wilkinson's integrity, insisting that in administering the affairs of BYU he had merely "followed the instructions and directions of the Board of Trustees." McKay closed by affirming that Wilkinson had always been considered "a man of honor, integrity and sound principle."[66]

If Wilkinson knew that his $240,000[67] battle with Moss—the majority of which he financed personally—would be uphill, he rarely expressed it. Still he must have greeted with considerable disappointment the results of a last-minute poll. Labeling the Senate race "probably Utah's most heated contest," the *Salt Lake Tribune* reported 55 percent of the state's voters favored Moss, while 45 percent said they would vote for Wilkinson.[68] When the final results in "the most torrid state contest by long odds"[69] were tabulated two days later, not only was Wilkinson's margin of loss greater than that predicted (14.8 percent or 169,491 to 228,210),[70] he lost by more votes than Goldwater and even failed to carry his own home county.[71] In a stunning sweep, Democrats won the U.S. presidency, the governorship, the Senate, one of two congressional seats, and control of both houses in the Utah legislature.[72] "Senator Moss has an impressive mandate with a total that led the entire ticket," the *Deseret News* reported. The newspaper concluded that "Clearly, the people of Utah appreciate his leadership in . . . issues important to the state, and were not persuaded by the hard-hitting campaign waged against him."[73] While conceding Moss's victory, Wilkin-

[65]Photocopy of original letter, entitled "Dear Friend of Good Government," in my possession. This letter reportedly reached 115 BYU faculty members, 75 percent of Utah State University faculty members, 25 to 30 Weber College faculty members, and a similar but unspecified number of University of Utah faculty members. See Earl C. Crockett to Wilkinson, February 11, 1965; L. Mark Neuberger to Wilkinson, February 5, 1965; Wilkinson to L. Ralph Mecham, February 18, 1965; all in BYU Archives.

[66]See *Deseret News,* November 2, 1964; *Salt Lake Tribune,* November 3, 1964; *Daily Universe,* November 3, 1964. Much to Wilkinson's dismay the FBI failed to unmask the letter's author and closed its investigation after four months (see Herbert J. Miller to Wallace F. Bennett, undated but ca. March 3, 1965; Bennett to Wilkinson, March 5, 1965; all in BYU Archives). Wilkinson entertained the idea of having McKay intercede personally with Lyndon B. Johnson but changed his mind (see draft of letter to Johnson written by Wilkinson for McKay, February 13, 1965, BYU Archives).

[67]Wilkins to Wilkinson.

[68]*Salt Lake Tribune,* November 1, 1964.

[69]Ibid., November 3, 1964.

[70]*Deseret News,* November 4, 1964.

[71]Ibid.; *Daily Herald,* November 4, 1964.

[72]*Daily Universe,* November 5, 1964.

[73]*Deseret News,* November 4, 1964.

son announced: "I stand behind every statement I made during the campaign, and still believe in them."[74]

Wilkinson had hoped the grueling race would bring his family closer together,[75] but for several of his children the defeat was difficult. His wife Alice remembered:

> The family worked hard for him campaigning all the time, but it was an interesting experience for all of us. I think it's something that drew us together. There was a feeling of disappointment in the family, particularly with Douglas, he was very disappointed that his father didn't win.

As for herself, Alice Wilkinson was relieved:

> I was not sorry that he lost. I felt that he had a mission at BYU. As it turned out the democrats won by such a majority that it would have been like a voice crying in the wilderness for him in Washington, and that would be difficult for him.[76]

Wilkinson tried to be upbeat about the loss, but his disappointment was obvious. "I don't want you to think I am bitter about it," he shortly afterwards wrote to Ezra Taft Benson, a member of the Quorum of Twelve Apostles and a longtime friend, "because I am not. I sensed ahead of time that this might happen and I was much more prepared for defeat than most of my supporters. Nevertheless, it was a very sad and expensive experience."[77] He then enumerated five reasons for his defeat: (1) having been blamed for master-minding the failed 1954 referendum transferring three Utah junior colleges back to the LDS church; (2) having been charged with preventing Utah State University from entering the Western Athletic Conference; (3) having reportedly fired the director of the church's Institute of Religion adjacent to the University of Utah for differences over LDS doctrine; (4) University of Utah and Utah State University alumni being "natural[ly] jealous . . . over the growth of BYU"; and (5) Lyndon Johnson's having created "the impression that President McKay was an old time friend and [was] for him in the campaign."[78]

Later Wilkinson also cited the church's unwillingness to "do its duty in supporting the right candidates."[79] "If the Church and the forces of good

[74]Ibid., November 5, 1964. Moss ran again in 1970 and won, but lost six years later. While in the Senate he chaired the Committee on Aeronautical and Space Sciences, was secretary to the Democratic Conference, and served on the National Democratic Steering and Policy committees. After his loss in 1976 he resumed his law practice in Washington, D.C., and later in Salt Lake City, where he currently resides.

[75]See Wilkinson to Alice Ann Mangum, August 17, 1964, Wilkinson Papers.

[76]Wilkinson, Oral History, p. 12.

[77]Wilkinson to Benson, February 2, 1965, Wilkinson Papers.

[78]Ibid. In a second list Wilkinson added that because of its deficit spending policy, the Democratic party had succeeded in promoting a feeling of peace and prosperity nationally; Moss had run a better-financed, better-organized campaign; Lloyd had refused to endorse his candidacy; the state's school teachers had condemned him for opposing federal aid to education; and his own outspokenness and unwillingness to compromise had made him an easy target for "mud-slinging" tactics (Wilkinson, "Memorandum on Reasons for Election Defeat on November 3, 1964," undated, Wilkinson Papers).

are going to have political influence in this State," he complained to McKay the following year, "the leaders of the Church must use their individual influence in having proper men selected as leaders of our political parties."[80] Too, Wilkinson may have felt that his age, lack of a full-time fund raiser, and having to face an incumbent all contributed to the embarrassing defeat.[81] Finally, Wilkinson's politics may simply have been too conservative for the majority of Utah's electorate, many of whom voted straight-ticket Democrat.[82] In the end, a deeply disillusioned Wilkinson would chalk the tumultuous experience up as one of the greatest disappointments of his life.[83]

Wilkinson's ten months on the campaign trail crystallized his intense political views. Returning to BYU in early 1965, he regretted that in his absence "so-called 'liberal elements' [had taken] charge of the economic and political things of the university,"[84] and he determined to mold the school into a showcase of conservative politics. "We are facing a great crisis in this country," he would explain to McKay, "and many of our political science and economics teachers are teaching false doctrine."[85] In his diary he confided, "The problems that I will face are much larger than those I faced when I first came in as president of the B.Y.U. Whether I will have the energy and the fortitude and patience to solve some of them remains to be seen." But, he promised, "I am going to do what I can to reverse [this] trend."[86] As would become apparent in the ensuing years, one of the lega-

[79]See Wilkinson Diary, October 5, 1966.

[80]Wilkinson to McKay, April 26, 1965, Wilkinson Papers. His pleas fell on sympathetic but ultimately deaf ears, as more powerful voices in the LDS hierarchy determined not to mire the church in partisan intrigues. See Wilkinson Diary, October 14, 1970, when he was criticized for endorsing a congressional candidate. Wilkinson later noted: "I have been active [in giving political speeches] off-campus, which met with the enthusiastic approval of President McKay, but that's quite different than speaking on campus" which was "the policy I pursued when I was President, of not giving any political speeches on campus" (Wilkinson to Dallin H. Oaks, August 26, 1978, photocopy in private possession).

[81]See Wilkinson Diary, March 13, 1968.

[82]See Frank H. Jonas, "The 1964 Election in Utah," *Western Political Quarterly* 18 (June 1965), No. 2, Part 2:509–13. For Lloyd the reason was simple: "I say this firmly, honestly, and without any reservations in my own mind—that the principal reason for this very poor showing in the November election was the low quality, the low grade of the campaign which he ran against me" (Oral History, November 21, 1974, pp. 7–8).

Wilkinson's campaign manager, John T. Bernhard, identified his own reasons for the loss: Goldwater's candidacy proved more harmful than helpful; Moss's organization did an excellent job; Wilkinson's "campaign war chest was chronically inadequate"; Lloyd "and many of his followers sat on their hands instead of helping their party's chosen candidate"; and finally "I was still a greenhorn campaign manager! With more know-how, particularly in state-wide campaigning, an experienced manager might have made a difference." "My biggest challenge during the campaign," Bernhard reported, "was trying to 'soften' Wilkinson's negative impact on the electorate. He was so combative! Time and time again, he came across as irascible and dogmatic. I wasn't very successful in my efforts to moderate him" (Bernhard to Gary J. Bergera, March 24, 1992).

[83]Wilkinson, "Personal Disappointments in Life," in Deem and Bird, *Ernest L. Wilkinson,* p. 631.

[84]Wilkinson Diary, November 30, 1970.

[85]Wilkinson to McKay, July 1, 1965, Wilkinson Papers.

[86]Wilkinson Diary, January 2, April 7, 1965.

cies of Ernest Wilkinson's 1964 bid for the U.S. Senate would be a university president overly politicized for his foray into partisan politics, increasingly fearful of dissent, and preoccupied to the point of distraction with rumors of faculty disloyalty.[87]

[87]For Wilkinson's political agenda at BYU after 1965, see Bergera and Priddis, *Brigham Young University*, pp. 198–219.

*

The Successful Marketing of the Holy Grail

LINDA SILLITOE

In 1985 Mark Hofmann pleaded guilty to second-degree murder in the bombing deaths of two people in Salt Lake County whom he had killed in an effort to cover up his tens of thousands of dollars of sales over more than a decade of forged historical documents. This essay discusses that complex and tangled story. It focuses on Hofmann's activities as a dealer in, and forger of, historical documents and asks us to try to understand who he was, how he could fool so many people both in Utah's historical community and outside it, and what his actions tell us about ourselves.

Linda Sillitoe, "The Successful Marketing of the Holy Grail," *Dialogue, A Journal of Mormon Thought* 20 (Winter 1987): 97–104. Reprinted by permission of the publisher and the author.

Linda Sillitoe is an award-winning writer and historian. She has been poetry editor for *Exponent II* and *Dialogue: A Journal of Mormon Thought*. Her published works include a novel, *Sideways to the Sun*, a collection of poetry, *Crazy for Living*, and, with co-author Allen D. Roberts, *Salamander: The Story of the Mormon Forgery Murders*.

NOT LONG AGO AT A CONVENTION in Salt Lake City for police chiefs, a visiting law enforcer dubbed Utah a "white-collar crime capital." He was alluding to pyramid schemes and speculative investments initiated by unscrupulous LDS individuals preying upon the trust between people with cultural and religious bonds. Professional concern about involvement of LDS leaders in fraudulent businesses such as AFCO focused on these men's impact on rank and file member-investors, rather than upon the possibility of naiveté among the top Church elders. The participation of the victimized was at issue as well as the proclivities of the perpetrators.

Though no mention was made of old letters and early Mormon money, that market too involved speculative investments and high finance, as well as that most valuable currency—trust. For sale were many tangible bits of Mormon history. In Church offices, antique book departments, and conservative businesses, a fragmented community was involved in an increasingly inflated, highly competitive trade in Mormon documents. Information in media and scholarly publications soon reached an audience beyond that core of secretive document and book dealing. The salamander became a cultural folk creature that was soon relegated to myth following the Salt Lake bombings and the subsequent detection of forgery. These events raise questions not only for a court of law or a parole board, but for all of us who are part of a participating consciousness.

At a recent symposium at Brigham Young University, Robert Stott, lead prosecutor in the murder and forgery cases against Mark Hofmann, castigated Mormon historians and researchers for hindering the investigation by insisting upon the authenticity of Hofmann documents and by being generally reluctant to cooperate with the investigation. My own familiarity with the history community and its attitudes, my impressions from hundreds of interviews regarding the bombings and forgeries, and my own mixed feelings have left me acutely aware of the chasm of suspicion and hostility between the history and law enforcement camps.

In acknowledging that the many kinds and degrees of denial prominent among historians and researchers did complicate the prosecution of Mark Hofmann, it is only fair to emphasize that the history community unconsciously reacted to the investigation as fraud victims typically react—by denying they are victims and by accusing the investigators of creating the problems. Those close to murder typically react quite differently, by seeking protection, disclosing potentially damaging information, and expressing outrage. These murders erupted within the framework of a complex, secrecy-laced scam, which ultimately robbed many people in tangible and intangible ways. Nothing about the forgeries or bombings case has been simple, including the response of a well-educated and law-abiding community within which the unthinkable happened.

When Mark Hofmann was injured by a bomb of his own making 16 October 1985, the day after he killed Steven F. Christensen and Kathleen W. Sheets with similar bombs, people interested in Mormon history knew him as an extraordinary document dealer. His success depended not only upon the skill with which he researched and forged, but also upon his manipulation of public and private perceptions. To understand how this occurred, we need to take a step back—for perspective—and look at assumptions common at the time.

By the time Mark Hofmann returned from his mission in January 1976, professional LDS historians had been officially writing Mormon history for several years. However, Church leaders were giving mixed reviews to the efforts of Leonard Arrington's History Division. The sesquicentennial sixteen-volume history of the Church, scheduled to begin appearing in 1980, was abandoned as a project, Arrington was released, and research historians were moved to BYU. Despite criticism, the energy to write a new Mormon history did not disappear, nor did the Church's mandate to collect and study history. These conflicting forces may have created a vacuum that historical documents and research, speculation, and testimonial declarations about them soon filled.

History is crucial in Mormonism and among Mormons. Why? First of all, the Mormon church is authoritative, and official accounts of its origin link the current prophet and president to divine guidance through Joseph Smith's first vision and subsequent revelations. The Book of Mormon, introduced by Joseph as an ancient record, adds another layer of history. Since the Church is young, scholarly debate and research have only begun, and the Mormon past is near and personal to many members. Finally, history is political. History is everyone's means to every end. For some, it reinforces testimony and policy; for others, history "proves" that the Church is true and investigators should join; at times history provides the precedent for change and the rejection of change; and history even attacks the Church's claims, which are based on canonized history.

Mark Hofmann knew what history meant to the orthodox collector, the high Church leader, the liberal scholar, and the outside critic. His tactics between 1980 and 1985 convinced historians and collectors in Mormon studies that primary, handwritten documents were abundantly discoverable. The documents of lesser importance than the few that made news stories gave his major discoveries credibility, and vice versa. His customers knew that they could lose out on something big if they didn't carefully maintain a relationship with Hofmann. During 1985, Hofmann's success in the national antiquities market bolstered his local reputation.

A few who dealt with Hofmann frequently had some idea how many documents flowed through his hands. But they rationalized his prolific sales, for they, too, had in a fortunate moment found something interesting enough to carry a jolt of excitement. Hofmann, the story went, worked hard, had sufficient capital and time, developed original techniques, hired assistants, or had a spiritual gift to find Church documents. Repeatedly, scholars and collectors insisted that if they had Hofmann's time and money, they could find as much or more than Hofmann did.

Why did so many believe this illusion of plentiful, primary documents when very few handwritten documents penned by Church leaders before the railroad came to Utah have been found by anyone but Hofmann during the same years? For one thing, Hofmann's quiet demeanor, his reflection of the various Church-related values his associates held, and his suggestions of authentication procedures all inspired trust. In addition, the numbers of documents and Mormon currencies that were suddenly extant with no known link to Hofmann convinced many—including Church leaders, historians, and collectors—that the field of nineteenth-century documents was "white already to harvest." We apparently lived within a historical restoration of all things.

Hofmann says he began counterfeiting and forging literally as a child. In any case, he burst spectacularly into the Mormon history market in April 1980 at the age of twenty-five. The Church was celebrating its sesquicentennial despite the absence of the sixteen-volume history, and despite a ruckus in the national and Utah press regarding the Mormon effort in several states to defeat the Equal Rights Amendment and the excommunication of Sonia Johnson. So closely linked were these events, that President Gordon B. Hinckley, first counselor in the First Presidency, conducted an April 1980 conference session televised from the David Whitmer cabin on Sunday and appeared on a national morning talk show the next day to deny that the Church was busing Relief Society sisters to legislatures in Illinois and Missouri.

Approximately two weeks later, Mark Hofmann brought to the office of the First Presidency a transcript apparently copied by Joseph Smith from the gold plates. This young man claimed to have looked into a Bible, which evidently belonged once to the Smith family, and had found a treasure. Church leaders were very excited, particularly because this event occurred on the Church's anniversary. In-house authorities examined the document, and then the Church called a press conference. "Good press" abounded, and the rest is history.

By now the Sunstone Symposium and other gatherings were pumping energy through the independent sector of Mormon culture, which had an abiding interest in the Church's restrictions on historical research. Hofmann reinforced the growing suspicion that Church leaders would "grab-and-stash" controversial historical documents and then deny possession of them. Events surrounding the Church procurement of the 1825 Joseph Smith letter to Josiah Stowell particularly substantiated a mysterious variety of stories supporting that feeling. Many of those stories can be traced to Hofmann.

President Gordon B. Hinckley purchased the Stowell letter from Hofmann on 11 January 1983 for $15,000. Only after the sale of the salamander letter in 1984 did the 1825 Stowell letter, also involving Joseph Smith in money-digging, become an open secret in the historical community. (A number of typed transcripts were mailed from New York in August 1984 to various people in the history community.) A showdown between the Church and scholars at the Mormon History Association meetings in May 1985 led to the release of the Stowell letter, very soon after the Church released the text of the salamander letter. The impact of the two letters on the general public was great. Despite the Church's openness about the salamander letter, the "grab-and-stash" assumption was validated by the Stowell letter. That belief became increasingly exploitable as the Oliver Cowdery history and McLellin collection myths soon demonstrated.

In short, by the time of the Salt Lake bombings, readers of the *Los Angeles Times,* the *Deseret News,* the *Salt Lake Tribune,* and other publications, and the historical community in general, believed that nineteenth-century primary documents were abundantly discoverable and highly valuable and that the Church would publicize or suppress those documents, depending on their content. Both impressions had an aspect of truth. Both were exaggerated, reinforced, and exploited by Mark Hofmann.

Hofmann's distortions were supported by specific techniques used to market his forgeries. These four, used repeatedly, I call: (1) the shared discovery; (2) the self-identifying document; (3) cultural myths; and (4) preliminary discussion. Three of the four techniques were used with the Anthon transcript, the document that made a very minor forger of $60 letters into a major Mormon document dealer.

Hofmann shared the discovery of the Anthon transcript with several people. First, his bride of a few months, Doralee, noticed that two Bible pages were stuck together. The Anthon transcript, the young couple discovered, was inside. The following day, Hofmann took the Bible and transcript to a friend, A. J. Simmonds, director of special collections at Utah State University where Hofmann was a student in his junior year. Simmonds excitedly helped Hofmann open the document and compare it with various texts. Immediately Hofmann took the transcript to LDS Institute instructor Danel Bachman, who then called LDS historian Dean Jessee, who, within days, said the Joseph Smith holograph on the reverse side was apparently authentic. A few days later, Hofmann, Bachman, and Church Historian Leonard Arrington showed the transcript to Elders Gordon B. Hinckley and Boyd K. Packer, and then to the First Presidency. Throughout the fuss that followed his discovery, Mark Hofmann appeared pleased, becomingly shy with Church leaders, and rather cautious. He let others make the claims.

The Anthon transcript introduced itself. Even when the young couple found the page folded in quarters and glued into the book, hieroglyphs and Joseph Smith's name were visible. Like the Bible itself, which included a handwritten portion signed by Samuel Smith, the transcript announced itself with the first glance. The more experts studied it, the more the Anthon transcript appeared to be authentic. The arrangement of hieroglyphs matched Charles Anthon's description. Smith had apparently described the process of copying the characters in a brief note on the reverse side; and the Bible had Smith family signatures.

Hofmann's story of the Anthon transcript echoed cultural myth. His discovery parallels that of the young Joseph Smith seeking guidance in the Bible and later finding the gold plates and founding the Church. But the Anthon transcript story resonates further. Its discoverer is a worthy, poor young man, as shown by his status as a married pre-med student. He procures the Bible through good luck and friendship for only a few dollars, like a character in a Horatio Alger novel or a personal story in *The Ensign.* In some versions, Hofmann consecrates his find to the Church; in others, he receives a small compensation. (In fact, he received $20,000 in trade. He quit college the same quarter as his discovery and began his career as a document dealer.)

The technique of sharing the discovery varied with other documents, particularly as Hofmann's reputation grew. He began to attribute discovery or provenance or both to various colleagues, including antiquities author Charles Hamilton with the Josiah Stowell letter, and Hofmann's sometimes-partner, Lyn Jacobs, in the case of the salamander letter and several other documents.

According to court testimony, Hofmann gave Jacobs's name as the provenance for the salamander letter when he asked Kenneth Rendell to authenticate it in November 1983. As *discoverer,* Jacobs took the letter to President Hinckley in January 1984. Both Hofmann and Jacobs had a part in the sales contract with Steven Christensen, though Hofmann received the lion's share of the profit. Jacobs claimed ownership again in 1985 when the Church released the text. However, in court he testified that he had first heard of the salamander letter during a call from Hofmann in late 1983. He also testified that Hofmann paid Jacobs because he had played a role in supposedly leading him to the source of the letter.

Documents other than the Anthon transcript also identified themselves. The Joseph Smith III blessing, Hofmann's next major find, had a note, "Joseph Smith III," penned on the reverse side. The David Whitmer and Martin Harris testimonial notes (sold, respectively, to the Church and collector Brent Ashworth) were, reportedly, found in the same envelope. The Oath of a Freeman, reportedly the first printed document in colonial America, won over several national experts, who were charmed by sixteenth-century handwriting on the reverse side, identifying it.

One of the best-identified documents is the earliest forgery that investigators attribute to Hofmann—the supposed text of a second anointing sealing, first seen in 1978 and sold in 1979. This 5 inch by 7 inch letter identifies itself by a stamp in one corner reading SALT LAKE TEMPLE and a half-erased note in the other: "Destroy this copy." The stamp was not used in the temple. The note to destroy the blessing defies logic, since there is no contextual reason for writing the blessing and giving a copy to someone who should then destroy it. Nevertheless, these "clues" hint of a sinister authenticity. Hofmann sold this document to Simmonds, a non-Mormon, for $60 a few months before he brought in the Anthon transcript. (A young man allowed Sandra Tanner, in the Utah Lighthouse Ministry Bookstore, to photocopy the blessing in June 1978. Tanner now believes the man to have been Mark Hofmann.)

Many Hofmann documents entered the marketplace clothed in cultural myth. The Lucy Mack Smith letter, an obscure, unmailed cover letter (folded into a self-envelope) was hailed by the Church as "the most significant document outside the Book of Mormon"—a real-life Cinderella. The salamander letter and the Oath of a Freeman were reportedly plucked from heaps of documents by Mark Hofmann, soon to fool national experts like true Pygmalions. Also, rags-to-riches stories were common with Hofmann documents. Virtually every letter cost $25, then sold for $20,000, $40,000, or—

almost—more than $1 million. Even when the documents Hofmann sold were purchased—not made—he apparently needed the myth. For example, the newspapers reported that Mark Hofmann had sold an Al Capone signature for $5,000 that supposedly cost him $25. In fact, Hofmann had bought the signature from Brent Ashworth for $2,000 and added the story himself.

Many document deals were preceded by discussions during which Hofmann discovered an interest for a particular document he might create and ascertained specific information in order to assure its fit into a historical context.

One major investor told Hofmann he would like a first edition of the Book of Mormon. Within weeks, Hofmann brought him one, inscribed by the buyer's wife's third great-grandfather. Steven Christensen and his employee Brent Metcalf actually made up a list of areas of Mormon history in which Christensen would buy any documents Hofmann might find, according to Metcalfe. When Brent Ashworth saw letters Joseph Smith wrote from Carthage Jail, housed in the RLDS archives, he asked Mark to watch for such an item. They frequently discussed the possibility of Mark finding another Carthage letter. When one finally appeared, from Joseph Smith to General Jonathan Dunham, Hofmann sold it to another collector. Ashworth was incensed. A few months before the bombings, Hofmann took a substantial loss on the convoluted repurchase and resale of that letter to Ashworth for $90,000. Ashworth, probably Hofmann's hardest hit major financial victim, may take some comfort in knowing that it was the Dunham letter, and its dissimilarities to the RLDS Carthage letters written the same day, that raised forensic document analyst George Throckmorton's suspicions sufficiently to call the county attorney's office about six weeks after the bombings. The subsequent investigation then broke the stalemated circumstantial murder case.

Evidently, orders were placed more obliquely as well. When Hofmann asked a friend what he should look for if he was ever in the First Presidency's vault, the friend consulted with Jerald and Sandra Tanner of the Utah Lighthouse Ministry and then suggested the Oliver Cowdery history. Brent Metcalfe, also a friend of Hofmann's, asked him specifically if he had ever seen the history in the vault. Hofmann said no.

Sometime later, however, Hofmann told Metcalfe that the history did exist and the Church had it. In 1985, Hofmann described the history and a page or two of its contents in detail to Metcalfe and later to *Los Angeles Times* religion writer John Dart. Metcalfe, whose order had been surprisingly well filled, then was interviewed by Dawn Tracy at the *Salt Lake Tribune*.

History-oriented Church leaders also "placed orders," asking Hofmann and other document finders if they had leads on the lost 116 pages. Evidence taken from Hofmann's home suggests that he was out in front in that search as well.

Preliminary discussions in which Hofmann described a document he had a lead on and/or the client expressed an interest in a particular item preceded many a sale. Individually these do not seem unusual. At the time, they seemed ordinary. Now they fit a pattern that mocks our credulity. My first example is of the physical preparation for a document sale; the second example involves psychological preparation for a document's acceptance.

Hofmann extensively researched some documents, though others were hastily prepared and sold. He created a provenance for some, including the Oath of a Freeman, which he expected to sell for more than $1 million in the east. Using the pseudonym "Mike Harris" on 8 March 1985, Hofmann ordered a printing plate for a poem deliberately mistitled "The Oath of a Freeman" from Debouzek Engraving in Salt Lake City. On March 11, Mark Hofmann visited Argosy Bookstore in New York City. After browsing a bit, Hofmann bought a poem entitled "The Oath of a Freeman" and paid twenty-five dollars. His sales slip became a provenance.

On March 25, Mike Hansen—a name tied to Hofmann through telephone numbers, personal checks, items found in Hofmann's home, and a fingerprint—ordered a printing plate for the "Oath of a Freeman" with the text published by colonial printer Stephen Daye. That document and a second copy became crucial in Hofmann's escalating scams in 1985, which ultimately led to murder. Both Oath 1 and 2, demonstrably products of the printing negatives that investigators seized, were hotly defended by their investors.

Sometimes Hofmann paid attention to psychological preparation for a document. One example is the 1830 Martin Harris or salamander letter, which he read to friends in November 1983. One brainstorming session concerned not the literal sale of the letter, but the acceptance of the letter by the public, the Church, and the Mormon history community. The letter's controversial nature is due, in part, to the close relationship its author, Martin Harris, had with the prophet. Hofmann suggested that positive links be emphasized, such as the Anthon transcript, which Harris had carried to Anthon; the E. B. Grandin contract to print the Book of Mormon, which Harris had signed; and a testimonial note, evidently dictated and signed by Harris. All these documents are Hofmann originals. The conversation also identified one element as crucial to the salamander letter's success, which eventually proved prophetic—the support of Mormon historians.

Like the historians he hired to research the salamander letter, Steven Christensen had plenty of reason to believe it was authentic when he donated the letter to the Church. At the time of his death, Steve Christensen was intent on closing the McLellin transaction. He had locked up a papyrus fragment purported to be Facsimile 2 in order to keep Hofmann from selling it separately. He pressured Hofmann relentlessly to come through with the collection and repay an overdue bank loan arranged by a general authority. He rearranged a pressured business schedule in order to keep in touch with Hofmann, Church leaders, and the designated buyer. Christensen indicated both his desire to save the Church embarrassment and his interest to add to the known history of the Church, as he had with the study of the salamander letter. Close friends say "he was living and breathing that document deal."

Kathleen Sheets knew virtually nothing about Mormon documents. And yet, on one wall of her spacious home she had hung an ancestral mission call signed by Brigham Young, alongside a portrait of Young, a ram's head, and some dried flowers. History was simply part of her culture.

Kathy Sheets, a lively mother and grandmother, a bishop's wife distinguished by wit and compassion, died as a decoy, to disguise through her husband's troubled investment firm the motive for Steven Christensen's murder.

The Hofmann documents and the stories that surround them reach deep into our culture. Thus, even as the context of the Hofmann scam broadens to the national market and national investors, collectors and victims, the epicenter will remain in Utah. We may look less naive as we gain company, but we will be no less involved. These documents and their faith-promoting tales and horror stories fit our conscious and unconscious assumptions. Gradually, reality was distorted until many within the Church, the press, the market, and the historical community worked to further one man's scheme.

This murder mystery that has captured our attention for two years, a paper chase extraordinaire, therefore includes all of us in varying ways and degrees. As a community we need to gain a sense of proportion; the commandment "Thou Shalt Not Commit Murder" precedes those forbidding lying, stealing, and bearing false witness. The denial that complicated the investigation has also been hurtful to some who lost loved ones. Healing follows the acknowledgement of pain, and the trauma of lost lives exceeds other damages.

Also, as these stories unravel and the documents are understood in a different light, there is the temptation to belittle those who "should have been" smarter, better trained, more inspired. In that way we may continue the damage that has been done personally, professionally, spiritually, or financially. Or as we undo the stories, we can search for our own reflections in their shiny surfaces. We can reach for understanding with an accuracy that recognizes courage and integrity, sees clearly human deception, cowardice, and rage, and accepts the vulnerability that makes all of us human.

*

All Fall Down: Money Wins and History Loses at Canyon Road

LAURA FRIEL

Established in the late 1960s as the real estate arm of the Mormon church, Zion's Securities Corporation is one of the largest property owners in Salt Lake City and has consequently been a major force in shaping the downtown area. The corporation played a leading role in the dramatic facelifting of the central business district in the 1970s and 1980s. In the following article Laura Friel explores its controversial decision in the fall of 1980 to demolish three historic buildings in downtown Salt Lake. This occurred at a time when the demolition of historic buildings had emerged as an important issue in Utah and across the United States and a significant movement for historic preservation had developed. The author discusses the reasoning and motives behind the decision; the reaction of preservationists, architects, historians, and elected officials; and the issues the demolition raised. By the 1980s Salt Lake was clearly a modern urban center, and the article has much to say about how it got that way, who makes such decisions and why, and where the effective power lies. The article also offers considerable insight into the distance Salt Lake had moved from the original utopian vision of a cooperative, anticapitalistic society to one integrated and controlled by secular rather than religious motives.

Laura Friel, "All Fall Down: Money Wins and History Loses at Canyon Road," *Utah Holiday*, December 1980, 42–58. Reprinted by permission of the author.

Laura Friel is a writer and also teaches English at Skyline High School in Salt Lake City.

ON THE MORNING OF SEPTEMBER 24, Lavon Cannon, 84, widow of the late General John K. Cannon, rested while waiting for her grandchildren to visit. She thought how fortunate she was to live protectively for 23 years in her large Canyon Road Apartment. "A person could pay $1,000 a month for a place like this in New York," she had often told friends, pointing out the beauty of the marble entry and the handcrafted, solid oak stairs, She felt secure, knowing that friends, shopping and entertainment were nearby.

When the knock came at the door, it was not her grandchildren, but a young man who handed her a letter. "I'm sorry," he said, "if we can be of any help, please let us know." Marcia Hurst, a neighbor, was reading a similar letter across the hall. Lavon Cannon took the paper inside and read the eviction notice three times before the shock registered.

MEMORANDUM

TO: ALL TENANTS, CANYON ROAD and
WASATCH APARTMENTS
DATE: September 23, 1980

Salt Lake City has enacted a new ordinance requiring certain changes to be made in the buildings listed above effective January 1, 1981. This ordinance effects changes to be made regarding fireproofing and safety. It has been determined that it is not economically feasible to comply with the city's requirements. For this reason and because the sites are under consideration for further development, we regret to inform you that the buildings must be closed.

Notice is hereby given that all tenants in the Canyon Road and Wasatch Apartments must vacate the same on or before December 31, 1980. We trust this advance notice will be helpful in your relocation.

Your understanding and cooperation will be sincerely appreciated.

ZIONS SECURITIES CORPORATION
O. Claron Alldredge
Vice President

The eviction notice may have signaled more than a disruption in the lives of senior citizens and other low income tenants, for whom appropriate housing is becoming increasingly scarce. It appeared to be the latest and most ominous round in a potential downtown demolition derby that could gradually chip away several buildings of Salt Lake City's historic and architectural legacy.

The proposal to demolish the Medical Arts Building and the Wasatch and Canyon Road Apartments should not have come as a complete shock. The buildings are located on expensive ground—a five-minute walk from the LDS Temple, the ZCMI Center, Crossroads Plaza and the LDS Church Office Building.

Other buildings in the downtown and midtown area have been threatened or have gone down in recent years. Five homes in the 500 block of First South and the 100 block of Sixth East, including the important Story Mansion, were lost in August of 1979.

"I heard one day that they were going to take down the homes," says Stephanie Churchill, director of the Utah Heritage Foundation, "and by the next day they were starting demolition."

The Hermes Corporation, which had indicated it would build its headquarters on the corner of First South and Sixth East, has now erected a sign on the site which reads, "Available," and lists a telephone number. The

Moormeister Home on South Temple also went down a year ago. This historic street, the backbone of the historic district that includes the Avenues, lost the Hogle Mansion and the Bamberger Home three years ago.

While all of the above were individual decisions by private developers, Zions Securities also had its hand in the demolition of historic homes in the past year. To make way for expansion of Zions Securities' Garden Apartments complex, seven houses and an apartment house went down on West Temple between North Temple and Second North. Many of the homes were owned by early LDS apostles, including Mathias Cowley and Anton Lund. The especially attractive Doctor Whitney home was under the wrecker's ball in early November.

Left standing forlornly alone was the Senator Elbert E. Thomas home, which is privately owned and is on the National Register of Historic Sites.

"The streetscape that was destroyed was one of the most intact block faces remaining from the early residential settlement that became the downtown area," Churchill notes.

The preservation fight seems to have gained ground on some fronts in recent years and lost ground on others.

"The designation of historic districts has allowed us to save whole patches of important buildings," Churchill observes. "And there have been a number of investors in the downtown area who have seen the financial and historic wisdom in rehabilitating old buildings." Others, however, haven't got the message, citing the need to bring older buildings up to code as prohibitive. "As wise investors and developers have shown, there are many ways to deal with bringing buildings up to code. This is often more economically feasible than replacing old buildings with new structures," Churchill says.

The Zions Securities Corporation, the financial arm of The Church of Jesus Christ of Latter-day Saints, has for years hinted at the eventual destruction of Canyon Road, Wasatch and Medical Arts. Why, then, the uproar? Part of the objection appears to lie in the way the announcement was made. Some of it may be reflected in the attitude that such decisions are strictly business considerations. And some of the concern may center on the fact that if the LDS Church has a master plan in relation to its properties, city planners and church planners should know each other's intentions rather than stumbling over constant surprises.

"Not knowing the church's plans poses potential difficulties for the city, since a city isn't static but dynamic," Churchill observes.

Some of the people who have spoken out on both sides of the issue have been less than familiar with the buildings in question. A tour of the structures and a review of their history and of the involvement of Zions Securities lends insight.

The ten-story Medical Arts Building on South Temple is dwarfed by the vastness of the ZCMI Center. It appears to be in good shape internally and externally.

"It's a good building," opines Verene Olsen, who has worked in it for Dr. Max Sharp for nearly 20 years, "and would have been better had they put money into it over the years."

O. Claron Alldredge, vice president of Zions Securities, says the mechanical systems in the building have failed.

"That building," says Alldredge, "is only 60 percent full now because doctors want their offices located near hospitals. Why do you think they (a group of doctors) sold it to us? Had an individual rather than Zions Securities bought it eight years ago, he would be bankrupt now. Anyone with an understanding of business operation couldn't defend that for five minutes."

Dr. Lyndon D. Snow, a salty optometrist who has served patients in the Medical Arts Building for 45 years, values old buildings. He owns the Heber J. Grant home on South Temple and will relocate his office in its basement after remodeling. His home, located in the Avenues, is on the Utah and National Registers for Historic Sites. Proudly, he points out that he bought the first vacancy in the medical building.

Snow doesn't want the Medical Arts Building torn down because it "fills a definite need for the people in downtown Salt Lake. It has been a great convenience for people who don't drive, the elderly, and those who work nearby," he says. "Patients have been deeply disturbed about doctors moving since it is the only medical building in the area." He feels the move will be costly to doctors who do not expect to re-establish in offices as convenient nor as spacious. He thinks the Medical Arts Building still has many years of good use in it, but is reconciled to the fact that "the owner is the boss."

When Zions Securities built the ZCMI Center, it land-locked the Medical Arts Building, then owned by a corporation of resident doctors. Because the mall left the MA Building without parking, Zions Securities was able to pick up the property with a guarantee that parking would be provided and tenant rights protected for seven years.

"Most of those practicing in the building have been there 20 to 30 years," says a patient. "Some have only a couple of years before retirement. Without advance notice, Zions tells them they have to be out by Dec. 31. That gives them less than six months to re-establish a practice. For many it is impossible because they are too close to retirement."

Dr. Max Sharp, a former tenant now relocated, confirms the agreement to protect tenant rights for seven years. Since Zions has fulfilled that requirement and is no longer legally bound, it recognizes no further obligation.

"To be honest, the planned demolition of Medical Arts hasn't stirred me as much as to see the low income housing destroyed," says Mayor Ted Wilson. "Commercial buildings are commercial buildings." Preservationists, meeting to map strategy in the wake of Zions Securities decision, have virtually ignored the Medical Arts Building.

Previously known as the Louise Grace Emery Apartments, the Canyon Road at 101 First Avenue contains eighteen units, six in each of the three sections. The wood on the sun porches is in poor condition, and the sandstone foundation is showing wear. Atop the building is a parapet and a cornice with brackets and a molding of white sandstone. Leafy carvings frame oval windows. Indentations and curves in the buff-colored brickwork give the building a charm that is unaffordable at today's labor and material costs.

Martha Hurst stands in the doorway of her home, glad for a chance to show her "lovely apartment." She apologizes for packing and happily points out conveniences she has enjoyed for 28 years. She especially likes the ample closet space, her large bedroom and her nicely tiled bathroom. "I am glad," she says, "that I had the privilege of living here, and I hate to leave, but one must face reality." She praises Alldredge and has good feelings toward her landlord.

The elegant atmosphere of long ago survives in Mrs. Hurst's large living quarters. (She figures she has about 1,400 square feet in her unit.) Ten-foot ceilings, large living rooms, quality copper fixtures, butler closets, eighteen-inch-thick walls and sun porches are typical of the early 1900s elegance. The staircases, made from the finest cuts of oak, are irreplaceable.

Directly south of the Canyon Road stands the red-bricked, four-story Wasatch Apartments. It is quickly apparent that the Wasatch does not have the intricate exterior design of the Canyon Road.

Inside, the halls are so narrow that people must step aside to pass one another. The staircases are curved and steep. An apartment in the Wasatch includes a bath and two small rooms, connected by a hallway that has been converted into a kitchen area. Vistas here are often grim. Bathtubs are stained, and faucets drip. There are no individual thermostats, and rooms are very hot.

It appears, just as Alldredge claims, "unfit to live in."

Cesar Adams occupies one of the small apartments with his young wife and a new baby girl. He says he has enjoyed the low rents and likes his place. In a charming Spanish accent, he empathizes with those in the building who are elderly.

"I know we are the younger generation; we can work and we can find a place, but these old people, you know, they can't find a place. Some, you know, cannot talk real good, cannot walk real good. They have lived for years in that very same place, and I don't know why they are doing this to them. They need consideration."

There are a variety of opinions about the historical significance of the three buildings and about whether their history should preclude their destruction. Even those who know the buildings will point out that the structures cannot easily be lumped in the same category.

The Medical Arts Building was completed in 1927. Just inside the front door in the marble foyer is a plaque dedicated to the doctors who promoted its construction. It was the first strictly medical structure built and owned by Salt Lake doctors and dentists and was designed to provide badly needed medical office space downtown. The building has always maintained its own dental laboratory and pharmacy. Zions Securities has owned it for eight years.

The Wasatch Apartments were constructed in 1916 by Wallace Bransford, son of Salt Lake Mayor John S. Bransford, as a dormitory for nurses who trained at LDS Hospital. The property was acquired by Zions Securities several years ago and has remained one of the sources of low income housing in the downtown area.

The Canyon Road Apartments have the most colorful history of the three structures. They were built in 1902 by the Park City "Silver Queen," Susanah Bransford Emery Holmes Delitch Galicheff. (She didn't stay married to anyone for long.) Susanah was a partner with Thomas Kearns and owned a share in the Silver King mine in Park City, Utah. She bought the property, originally part of Brigham Young's estate, from the estate of Luna Young Thatcher for $30,000.

John C. Craig, an architect from Chicago, included many of the latest inventions of the day, including mail boxes, speaking tubes to the entrance, a button to open the front door, electric lights and plumbing. The building had a steam furnace, a laundry and rooms for a janitor in the basement. Newspaper articles on its construction described it as one of the finest in the west and similar to apartment complexes in New York and Chicago.

The building was originally set back from First Avenue, with a front lawn and green areas around it. A Salt Lake *Herald* article on August 3, 1902, listed the prospective residents—a Who's Who of Salt Lake society: George Blood, a leading mining figure and later governor of the state; William S. Walker, assistant postmaster; Jay T. Harris, president and treasurer of the Daily Reporter Company; and William B. Lanius, manager of William A. Stickney Cigar Company.

Susanah built the apartments as an investment for her foster daughter, Louise Grace Emery, after whom the three famous entrances were named. The final cost of $60,000 was thought exorbitant for the time.

John McCormick, a specialist in Utah history at the Utah Historical Society, says buildings are considered important if associated with a distinctive person or event. Under that strict criterion, he says, the Canyon Road and Wasatch Apartments might not qualify.

"However," he notes, "in a larger sense, they are important because they reflect the history, values and tastes of Salt Lake's turn-of-the-century community. They were constructed when Salt Lake was growing rapidly (between 1900 and 1920), when the population more than doubled. Salt Lake changed from a basically agricultural, isolated, Mormon population to one that was economically diversified with a lot of wealthy people and secular diversification."

McCormick notes that the Utah Historical Society has successfully nominated the Avenues area as a historic district on both the Utah and National Registers. That historic district is bordered by First and Seventh Avenue on the south and north and by Canyon Road on the west and Virginia Street on the east. In that area are 2,100 buildings that are more than 50 years old—a basic requirement for registration. Of those, only 125 (including the

Canyon Road and the Wasatch) are considered historically significant.

McCormick's major concern, however, is that the proposed demolition would not stop with the Canyon Road, the Wasatch and the Medical Arts Building. He worries that Zions Securities will eventually destroy more buildings of increasingly greater significance.

"I dislike seeing the Medical Arts Building torn down because it logically follows that they (Zions Securities) would want the Bank of Utah destroyed." Next to go, he fears, would be the Eagle Gate Apartments and the Gateway Apartments. "We're not just talking about three buildings coming down; we're talking about six, and that would drastically alter the character of the area."

McCormick's uneasiness is apparently not just idle anxiety. O. Claron Alldredge, vice president of Zions Securities, who has stayed away from the press during most of the controversy that erupted after the announcement of the company's demolition plans, took this reporter on a tour of all three buildings. Between stops, he gestured straightforwardly to the Bank of Utah. "I guess," he said, "that that will have to come down someday too."

Peter Goss, architectural historian at the University of Utah, is also concerned that the destruction of the Canyon Road and Wasatch will be a foot-in-the-door in public consciousness that will then allow Zions Securities to replace other buildings.

"I'm convinced that the Canyon Road, the Gateway, the Wasatch and the Eagle Gate are going to go, no matter what. I don't believe Zions Securities will put apartments there because there are other things that would make more money. If they could make $2 million on a Big Mac stand, they'd build one on that site. Zions Securities is a business; any company that is a business corporation would do the same thing. It's investment money. If they act as they have in the past, they won't give a damn what it looks like, and they won't give a damn what they put there as long as it makes money—because the aesthetic value is not important to them."

While Zions Securities doesn't deny the value of history in shaping the character of a city, company officials by no means see it as a determining factor.

"We considered the historical aspect," says Alldredge, "but there has to be a better reason than that. Who would finance it? We had to temper it with economic reality. The board members were apprised of all the information on which we based the decision. They know about this thing inside and out, and it was not a precipitous decision."

Among those who would save the buildings are aestheticians who argue that they should not be torn down since they serve as architectural examples of the past.

Gayl Baddeley, a member of the American Society of Interior Design and prominent Salt Lake interior designer, contributed to the restoration of the Mayflower, the Maryland and the Belvedere Apartments. He argues against destruction of the Canyon Road and Wasatch Apartments and is especially fond of Canyon Road.

"I can tell you that the Canyon Road is as fine a building as any of the other three structures I've restored. To say that it is too expensive or beyond means to repair these buildings is really laughable."

He suspects the Zions Securities is using the fire codes as an "excuse," and expresses his own fears that the Eagle Gate Apartments will be next to go.

"Only fools tear down things that are good and can not be built again. I have just been in London and in Paris. Tourists from all over the world go to see buildings that they've been restoring. They come to Salt Lake City to see the same styles of architecture," he says.

Baddeley believes it is Zions Securities' debt to the public to make clear what it plans to erect on the sites of the buildings marked for destruction.

Debbie Temme, assistant state architectural historian for the Utah State Historical Society, refers to the Eagle Gate, the Wasatch and the Canyon Road apartments as "a group that makes a nice streetscape. The scale of the buildings is very much in keeping with the scale of the Beehive House," she says, "and the feeling of the area could be destroyed with any building that overshadowed the rest."

Because they "represent buildings of their time," and reflect the ornamentation of Louis Sullivan, father of the skyscraper, Temme feels they are of architectural value.

Goss agrees. "The buildings from the Eagle Gate Apartments to the Canyon Road Apartments are architecturally significant to the area north of the city's commercial district. They tie in with the scale of other buildings and the religious theme of the Beehive House, the Hotel Utah and the Church Offices," he says.

He has mixed feelings about their architectural importance, however. Taken separately and out of their environment, they are not necessarily "architecturally distinctive," he believes.

"I personally like the Gateway more than any of the others because it is in the Prairie School style, is low in scale and fits nicely in that space," Goss says. "There is a level of craftsmanship that can't be denied in the Canyon Road, and they all symbolize a part of the architectural variety of downtown Salt Lake in what could be a bland or boring combination of designs."

Goss also has mixed feelings about the fight for preservation in Salt Lake City. He is worried about preservationists "who try to save every blasted thing. Perhaps we should put our efforts into saving more important things. The other approach could put a bad taste in a lot of peoples' mouths. When something more important comes up for demolition, the fight might be lost."

While the fight might be "a lot of wasted effort, it may be worth it, because maybe, after 50 fights—150 or 2,000 fights, someone might get the picture."

Goss says the LDS Church, not Zions Securities Corporation, must ultimately decide what it will preserve in the area that represents the church to the rest of the world.

"If the church really wants to save the buildings, all its leaders have to do is say, 'Don't tear them down.' If the church doesn't say that, it seems to mean it doesn't care about preserving the quality of environment around its own international headquarters. And it seems to mean its leaders don't care about the impact it would have on the very city they have created for themselves."

"The church does not seem to have a policy on preservation of its historical buildings. On the one hand, they went to great pains to tastefully duplicate the new addition on the Hotel Utah; on the other, they destroyed the Coalville Tabernacle."

In the wake of the furor over the destruction of the Coalville Tabernacle, the Division of Arts and Sites of the LDS Church Historical Department was organized several years ago. (While the Coalville incident was not the only factor in the creation of the division, it was a catalyst.) One of the functions of Arts and Sites has been to compile a list of buildings owned by the church that are deemed worthy of preservation. While the list does not guarantee preservation, it serves as an internal guideline for church departments.

The list, however, according to a division staff member, generally includes only those buildings used for ecclesiastical purposes and has never charted any building owned by Zions Securities. "It has never been clear if we have any role as a consultant in the case of Zions Securities–owned structures," the staffer said.

Nonetheless, approximately five years ago the Church Arts and Sites Division sent an architect to a meeting with Howard Dunn and Claron Alldredge, president and vice president of Zions Securities. Stephanie Churchill, director of the Utah Heritage Foundation, also attended, as did Vee Carlisle, who at the time represented the Avenues district in the Utah Legislature. The group toured the Eagle Gate Apartments, and Churchill, Carlisle and the Arts and Sites architect all expressed concern that it be preserved. Also expressed at the time by all three was the opinion that the Canyon Road and Wasatch Apartments were worthy of preservation.

Churchill proposed to Dunn that a feasibility study, at least partially funded by the Heritage Foundation, be undertaken to determine the condition and preservation-worthy status of the Eagle Gate Apartments. Dunn asked her to get something down on paper. Churchill later sent a formal proposal for such a study to Dunn, asking for his response. He never replied. (In the recent case of the historic homes destroyed on West Temple between North Temple and Second North, Churchill sent Dunn information on how such blocks in the middle of downtown areas had been preserved elsewhere in the country, and proposed a feasability study. Again Dunn did not reply.)

It seems hopeful to some observers that the LDS Church seems committed to exact and painstaking restoration of historic ecclesiastical sites in other states (the Grandin Building in Palmyra, N.Y., where the Book of

Mormon was published; the Newell K. Whitney store in Kirtland, Ohio, among others). Yet the church is much more tentative in involving itself where business and financial decisions may seem to clash with historical and aesthetic concerns in the shadow of church headquarters.

While Salt Lake Mayor Ted Wilson recognizes that Zions Securities is legally entitled to do with its property as it wishes and that while neighborhoods may not have "rights" that stand up to property rights, they have a certain character and cohesion that any corporation considering itself part of a community may not wisely choose to ignore.

"My feeling is that if they say, 'Yes, we're going to take this building out, but we're going to add these delightful buildings to provide architecturally significant housing for people,' that could carry a lot of weight. The more modern approach might be the best way to go. But I want Zions to tell me what their plans are. If they have a positive plan, that would make the argument more in their favor."

Not only historians and architects are dismayed at the changing face of State Street, but area residents are also clamoring in opposition to the proposed move they say will drastically alter the charm of an architecturally unique area.

According to Councilwoman Sidney Fonnesbeck, who attends the Greater Avenues Association meetings, many people in the area are "deeply frustrated at having a historic district that is gradually being destroyed.

"This is just another encroachment on something that is beautiful by something that may not be." She maintains that Salt Lake City needs to improve and strictly enforce zoning for the area with restrictions that require preservation. "This area is a vital key to the tourist industry, and people in the Greater Avenues Association are disappointed that this historic district is gradually being destroyed."

Laura Young Wells, a tenant of the Canyon Road Apartments, is an active volunteer for the Utah Heritage Foundation. She is a Salt Lake tour guide who knows as much about the history of the apartments as anyone. A petite woman, she seems larger because of her strong, eloquent voice.

"I would very much like to see not only the old Canyon Road Building saved because it's a lovely old building, I'd like to see the Eagle Gate Building saved," Wells says.

"You know, I take a great many people on tours around the city, and one of the things that strikes everyone who comes to the city (and me everytime I do it) is the fact that from West Temple to State Street you have the most incredible display of architecture, the majesty of history, the elegance of a bygone day and the shining modern. You've got the Symphony Hall; you've got the temple grounds, the Hotel Utah and executive offices, the Lion House, the Beehive House, the Eagle Gate and the old Canyon Road. That, plus the trees and the flowers in such profusion, make this a city center like no other that I have ever seen in this country. I think it would be tragic beyond belief if we changed it."

The last and most explosive case against Zions Securities' plan to destroy the buildings is people oriented. Unusually moderate rents have been a godsend to those on fixed incomes. The convenient downtown location has enabled them to handle daily living with ease. Some of them view a move from a "home" they expected to enjoy for the rest of their lives as unthinkable, bringing financial, emotional and physical upset. Most of them now hope only to be recognized as individuals with dreams, memories and special problems that conflict with the proposed demolition.

There is real poignancy in their pleas. Yet some, not accustomed to speaking up for themselves, now find themselves in the midst of a battle they never imagined they'd fight.

"I'm not much of a speaker," Canyon Road occupant Bernie Lutz said at a meeting of tenants. "I know many tenants have moved into places that are not adequate for them. They've got rid of a lot of their things they've kept for years. Of course, maybe *we* should get rid of all those things. It's hard to get rid of them." (Listening quietly, Frances Farley, State Senator for District 1, ducked her head to hide her tears.)

"I know that some are really scared. You know, you get up in your older years and you are told you've got to get out. You thought you could stay there until the end of your time. It's hard on you. It's emotional and physical. 'What am I going to do, where can I go, I can't get my things in this little place,' you say.

"They say, of course, that they've got to make more money on them (the apartments). Well, it's whether you want the money or the people. There's got to be someplace for people to live."

"Younger people can't comprehend what it is like to be old," says one retired renter. "The slightest change, like the moving of a rug or a visit from the grandchildren, can be upsetting to us." She worries over her husband who is extremely upset about relocation. She feels a bit betrayed by the church she has loved and served most of her life.

Seventy-six-year-old Lucy Baugh opened one tenants' meeting with a prayer in her antique-filled apartment. "When we came here, we came with an understanding that this would be our home as long as we lived," Baugh said. "But," she slyly glanced at others, "maybe they didn't think I was going to live this long."

She is proud of her collection of antique furniture, including two pianos and an organ, which she has gathered since she was first married. Lucy teaches music lessons and hopes to "teach until the last breath I draw." She says she cannot afford to sell her furniture because "it is my savings, which I will convert into cash, if and when I do not teach." She speaks softly, "I don't know how I would adjust; it's so much a part of me."

Where will evicted tenants find comparable housing? Some sources claim that if the buildings come down, the downtown housing shortage will become even more acute.

"I think one of the big concerns of the Council is that we are losing low income housing," says Ted Wilson. "There are 222 apartment houses, from our last report, that will come under this fire code restriction. Some of those may be economically impossible to bring up to code. But we need to save as many as possible because we're losing them so fast that the elderly people just can't find housing that they can afford."

City Councilman Grant Mabey echoes the mayor's concern that low income housing is disappearing in Salt Lake City. He is concerned that "we are losing housing so fast that the elderly people can't find a place to live."

Betty Wilkins, a Canyon Road occupant, has unsuccessfully looked for housing throughout the valley since the eviction notice. She indicates she has found virtually nothing in her price range, that is located close in and is adequate. Vacancies far out in the county obviously do not have the conveniences she has enjoyed downtown. If tenants must move, Wilkins asks for more time so the tenants can adjust to the idea of the move and aren't forced to make hasty decision they may later regret. (Extending the fire code deadline is a responsibility no one wants.)

Alldredge says that Zions Securities has been aware of the need for low income housing in the downtown area for some time. That is why it has built the Garden Apartments, which contain 200 units. An additional 100 units are planned in the expansion.

"Mayor Wilson has lately made a speech about getting more living units downtown," Alldredge recalls. "But you see, we have eighteen units where the Canyon Road now sits, and I am sure we'll probably build more than 100 on that same site." He feels the Zions Securities has been responsive to the need for low income housing and adds that Zions Securities has been sensitive to the needs of tenants in Zions' buildings.

"We've been careful to help anyone who is displaced; we have vacancies in the Garden Apartments right now. Some of the tenants have come over and said, 'I will not live on the west side,' so what can I say? We've made offers to them; we've actually moved some in."

Some of the residents have accepted the situation with better feelings than others. They credit Zions with being a good landlord.

"The Zions Securities has been bad-mouthed like they're not helping—as if they were so mean, and it's just not true," says Vicki Stevenson, a young woman who works in the church offices and is a resident of the Wasatch. "When I first came into the Wasatch, Brother Alldredge had the walls all painted and a new carpet put in. When my fridge needed fixing, they repaired it right away.

"I think we've taken for granted what we've had here. My apartment is only $90 a month, utilities paid. So we've been spoiled a lot."

One of the basic conflicts lies in peoples' perceptions of Zions Securities. The people at Zions see the firm purely and simply as a corporation with a goal of investing wisely and making money. From this perspective, Alldredge says, "For the tenants to demand that we find them a place to live and move them at our expense is a demand they wouldn't make on any other landlord in the city without being told to get out. But this is a business proposition. We have a program in the LDS Church if people need welfare assistance. That's handled through their bishop, not through Zions Securities Corporation."

But because Zions Securities is an arm of the LDS Church, some people cannot regard it as they would "any other landlord in the city." That is especially so, considering the fact that the firm's board of directors is made up of General Authorities of the church. They somehow expect more from it than other corporations. They expect it to contribute to preservation of the community—even when such a solution is not as cost effective as other alternatives. Justifiable or not, they want more than a business response.

Most tenants of Canyon Road and Wasatch attest that communication from Zions Securities has in the past been unquestionably responsive and helpful. But the door to effective communication seems to have closed since the eviction notice.

Alldredge says there is no percentage in "hashing it over" with those people who want to save the buildings because he is quite aware of their views.

"Mr. Blaze Wharton from the Senior Citizens Coalition made an appointment to talk with us personally, but he arrived with a big delegation of everybody and their friends," Alldredge reports. "So, the president of the company, Mr. Howard Dunn, said, 'If you'd like to bring a couple of your representatives in, we'll be glad to talk with you; otherwise, there's no useful purpose served in having another hearing.' They responded that if all of them couldn't attend the meeting, none of them wanted to, and they left.

"They all had their say before the City Council," Alldredge says. "It's the same group who were there. I know because I was at the City Council meeting, but there was no point in my refuting all those emotional statements made by people who didn't know the facts, so I just sat there and listened to the whole thing and went home."

Why hasn't Zions Securities attempted to inform people why it has decided to replace the buildings? In an issue as important as this, if there are cracks in the foundation of the Canyon Road, people should be told. They may want to know that the water heater for that building is located across the street, and that people aren't always getting hot water. They may also be interested in knowing that the corporation is losing $6,000 a month on the apartments and that the stairs are in need of bracing.

"If they're going to try our case in the City Council, in the Historical Society and with the Community Action Program, on T.V. and in the papers, there isn't anything we can say or do to change their minds," Alldredge maintains.

"I'd rather save my breath, and maybe they'll get the idea that our decision was arrived at as equitably and fairly as we could arrive at it. We would never have issued those instructions unless we intended to carry them out. So is there any useful purpose served in my hashing over these questions and going into details about how much it costs to do this and that when the answer is already determined? That's *our* business."

Many people have devised elaborate (and not-so-elaborate) schemes to try to save the buildings. Some have offered to "chip money into a kitty to help bring the buildings up to fire code standards." Others have offered to pay more rent. There are estimates that it would cost $32 a square foot to restore the buildings.

"I can't quite buy that the fire code is the only reason the buildings are being torn down," Wilson said at a Council meeting. "They cited this on the eviction notice, but when we talked to them, they spoke of other things like the electrical and plumbing systems. Yet, publicly they only talk about the fire code. I feel, frankly, that the city is being scape-goated, and to some degree, I resent it. The fire code is very important to preserve lives. When a prestigious firm like Zions Securities uses that as the number one excuse, it creates the mood for other apartment owners to use a similar excuse."

Claron Alldredge responds that the basic reason for Zions' decision to demolish the buildings is that they are in "such poor shape" and that the Canyon Road should be used for "a much larger development." Zions Securities has planned demolition for years, and has not kept that from the tenants, Alldredge says.

"What triggered it now (earlier than planned) is the requirement of the city and the fact that the Canyon Road sits on the most underused piece of property in the city," he continues.

"We were told about the fire code several months ago," he says frankly. "We needed some time to make an investigation as to whether or not it was in our interest to bring that up to standard. Our conclusion was that it was not.

"It's not our decision to put a bandaid on anything. If we're going to fix something, we want to do it right. If you think there's a furor now, this is nothing compared to what there would be if we had an electrical fire with fatalities. We'd be condemned for having an old fire trap.

"Their wanting to pay a little more rent to bring it up to code wouldn't make any difference." If Zions decided to restore, occupants would have to move anyway while the buildings were gutted. "We're in a no-win position," he says. "That's why we have to do what we have to do and weather this."

People who have been most angered and who oppose demolition of the buildings have generally been the most verbal. A majority of the residents seem to have accepted the situation and credit Zions for being a "model landlord."

A woman in the Wasatch Apartments, who really doesn't "want to talk about it," says, "this building is old. It's condemned. Nobody can tell me they're going to save it. Most everyone has moved out, and I'm moving too."

Another older woman who has just moved looks back at the situation this way: "I cried when I left Canyon Road. We've heard about it for years, but we just hoped it wouldn't be in our lifetimes. Can you imagine a building this large housing only twenty people when a hundred could enjoy living on this site?"

Any court would ultimately uphold Zions Securities' right to dispose of its property in the manner it sees fit. Yet that will not prevent members of a community from feeling they have a stake in community landmarks.

"Some buildings, in a sense, belong to the community as well as to the owner," says Stephanie Churchill, director of the Utah Heritage Foundation. "Too often people are willing to settle for easy solutions rather than realizing that the sensitive and conjunctive mixture of the old and new makes a community special and gives it interest.

"The city has designated the Eagle Gate Apartments as a landmark," she states, "and they are recognized as a benefit to the whole community. Because the Wasatch and Canyon Road apartments are in the Avenues Historical District designated by the city, the city has power to delay demolition up to five months. The city can also regulate the design, which includes height, mass, scale and compatibility with other buildings." What it cannot do, finally, is prevent demolition.

"There is a basic issue at stake here," says Alldredge. "It concerns private property rights. I don't want to go out of my way to duck any honest criticism, but I think in this case we have had our real rights usurped, our motives have been impinged, and emotionalism and special interests have propounded their proposals above and beyond the real rights of the owner. Everyone has so much to say when they have no financial interest in it. How much would they pay to keep those buildings? All they want to do is abuse us, and they think by public pressure and demand they can get us to change our minds. But in the end, I think it's still America, and you can do with your property as you see fit."

"We can't legally do anything," admits Mayor Wilson. "It is clear that the law allows them to demolish the buildings. However, I do sense that Mr. Alldredge and Mr. Dunn have a real sense of social commitment toward the residents. Toward the buildings, of course, not so much."

When the Utah Heritage Foundation's board of trustees met at the Alta Club in October, in the wake of the announcement of Zions Securities' demolition plans, Architect Steve Smith was remembering some words he heard two months earlier. They were the words of Spencer W. Kimball, president of The Church of Jesus Christ of Latter-day Saints:

"People who care nothing for the past," President Kimball said on August 13 at the World Conference on Records in Salt Lake City, "usually have no thought for the future and are selfish in the way they use the present. When there is proper regard for the past and its people, we enrich the present, as well as the future."

Those leaving the meeting at the Alta Club who glanced across the street at the Eagle Gate Apartments may have seen the past, the present and the future fused in a single building—likely the next landmark to be considered for demolition.

In the basement of the Gateway Apartments, hissing and popping noises emanate from the pipes which carry heated water to the Wasatch and Canyon Road Apartments. A bucket is placed in the middle of the hall to catch dripping water. But some of the drops fall directly onto the floor. Plaster has broken away from the walls in several places and the temperature is uncomfortable.

While tempers flared, and there was a mild public furor over the impending demolition of Canyon Road, the Wasatch and the Medical Arts Building, it doesn't appear to have stopped the inevitable. But there are those observers who predict that if the Gateway and the Eagle Gate Apartments are threatened, the heat that Zions Securities has taken this time won't compare with the coming confrontation. That hissing and popping you hear is the muffled sound of a future showdown.

*

Culture Shock

PHYLLIS BARBER

Through the nineteenth century perhaps Utah's most compelling aspect was the division of the population into two hostile groups, Mormons and non-Mormons, those who considered themselves inside the Kingdom of God and those they considered outside. The question Phyllis Barber raises in the following essay is the extent to which that situation remains true today, and why. She asks a number of questions: How do newcomers respond to Utah? What cultural adaptation is required of those who come here? How well does Utah assimilate novelty and differences? How well does it accept and provide for newcomers? How much does it value diversity? For Ms. Barber Utah is a complex place, easy to oversimplify and challenging to describe fairly. It is more diverse and multidimensional than it might first appear to be. Yet the omnipresence of Mormon culture remains unavoidable. "All non-Mormons in Utah share one thing in common, that supersedes race, creed, or religion," she asserts, "the fact that they are not Mormon." Newcomers typically experience what can fairly be called "culture shock."

Phyllis Barber, "Culture Shock," *Utah Holiday,* November 1981:31–40. Reprinted by permission of the author.

Phyllis Barber earned an MFA degree from Vermont College and was a cofounder of Park City's Writers at Work Conference. Her published works include *And the Desert Shall Blossom; How I Got Cultured: A Nevada Memoir;* and *The School of Love: Short Stories.*

AUTHOR CLIFTON FADIMAN tells of his move from a restful Connecticut town to Los Angeles: "I was felled by a shotgun burst of odd physical and mental ailments . . . In the course of six months my illness got straightened out. The neurologist diagnosed my trouble as 'culture shock.' "

A newcomer to the Arctic snow can be "shocked" by a grey, undefined world without proportion, dimension or color while the native views the snow as a gift from the gods—a fortification against the winds, a highway for travel, the material for the blocks of his home. The snow is a reality which must be understood for survival.

Newcomers to Utah come to a land once called Deseret (Honey bee) where beehives are cast in the center of UTA bus tokens, poised at the apex of Eagle Gate and stamped onto squad car doors of the Utah Highway Patrol. The people, descendants of industrious pioneers, are inheritors of a hive consciousness—the collective good is more important than one individual. The beehive is a shared religious and political symbol of Utah, of a sacred and professional ethic. Newcomers need to perceive the nature of this hive, its call to join up and make honey, before drawing conclusions about themselves relative to the culture.

Culture shock, not unique to Los Angeles, the Arctic or Utah, could also describe a move from Ephraim to Tooele. Even long-time residents can be on the receiving end of the shock waves as their habitat changes before their eyes—as immigrants devour their land, restructure their social scene, and clog their streets, their skies and their sense of security. Newcomers have a more immediate problem with assimilation. Old relationships have been ruptured—dentists, car mechanics, hairdressers and friends—and a new society has to be encountered. It can be a time of temporary loneliness and seeming invisibility accentuated by the stark realization that a new bee in a hive doesn't add much buzz or honey.

Some people thrive on change and wandering, on dipping in and out of places and lives. Others do not. Successful relocation for most comes with a sense of acceptance by the community.

"I feel so at home here," some say; "No matter how long I live here, I will never feel at home," others say.

What does it mean to feel at home? Is it the sight of an open irrigation ditch, blossoms of an apricot tree, the smell of water on grass in summer, of mentholatum or a pot of minestrone? Is feeling at home a real possibility or is it an idyll, an imaginary yesterday, a chimera? To most, being at home means a place to rest, a niche with shelter, food and comfort, and a forum where one's opinions, ideas and life's experiences receive respect. It does not mean being a wisp of hay left over after the bales are stacked.

Home is spoken of frequently in Utah. Generations have lived and died here, and many return after living away. Obviously, many feel at home; but how well does Utah assimilate newness and differences, accept and provide for newcomers? What culture adaptation is required: what social purchase does a newcomer feel obliged to make? Are people expected to follow the when-in-Rome admonition?

New people are arriving every day, and the statistics are staggering. The state experienced a 38 percent growth rate in the last ten years; the Wasatch Front region, 32.7 percent. According to Chamber of Commerce figures, Sandy City grew from a population of 6,438 in 1970 to 51,022 in 1980. Though this increase includes some annexation, the percentage change represents a 692½ percent growth in population.

Today, a million and a half people call Utah home. Many of them love the state and maintain that the sun not only rises and sets, but resides here. People continue to move to the state and sing praises to "ye mountains high, where the clear blue sky arches over the vale of the free."

"This is one of the most beautiful places that we have ever lived," says Judy Hagerman from Cortez, Colorado.

"I love the seasons, the skiing, the family closeness, the parks and places for children," says a single parent from southern California who maintains that her children "were subjected to peer pressure and drugs in Hollywood."

"People are in extremely good physical condition because of the recreation and low incidence of smoking and drinking," a physician comments.

"Salt Lake City has a rich cultural community and excellent spectator sports."

"People are warm, communal and friendly—there are no class distinctions."

The accolades go on. Yet, mingled with the praise is a buzz at the periphery:

"I feel like I have been taken out of the real world and put in a place where everybody responds mostly to family orientation," says Marilyn Casey, mother of five. "We have a big family, but there's still a shock."

Paradoxically, many feel crowded by, as well as grateful for, the community emphasis on family. When family is everything, those without one are not part of that everything. One newcomer called three people she had met briefly and invited them to lunch. "I'd love to, but I'm busy with my family," she was told in essence each time.

Psychiatrist Benjamin Lee, returning to Utah roots after twelve years away, has his own idea of heaven—Manhattan—but didn't feel that he could transmit the values he most cared about to his children in that culture. "With our reentry, we found what we expected. Utah has a relatively simple culture characterized by self-denial for the greater good. It offers a children oriented life and if heaven is a nursery, this has got to be paradise. The hard part is being here for myself."

Tiffany Pyle likes Utah for her children, but worries that "Women have no place here in the work world. They are subservient and can't find a job for decent money." (The average 1980 earnings of full-time, year-round workers, according to Utah Job Service, is approximately $21,000 for men, but only $12,000 for women.)

Many people will take a cut in salary to stay in Utah, opting for perceived safety for their families, for right-to-work laws, for sagebrush independence—and people usually work hard for that lesser salary. The work ethic is a bonus for employers and productivity—"no three-hour lunch breaks, people generally don't rip you off, folks take pride in their work," says one resident. At the same time, it has side effects: "Utahns are industrious," says a midwestern arrival, "to the point that they rarely have unregimented fun. Spontaneity doesn't seem a legitimate way to approach one's free time."

"I don't have a sense of adventure here," says Carol Lee, a former resident of northern California who appreciates Utah for her family's benefit. "There's a certain lethargy, even mediocrity when everyone has their nose to the grindstone and is so involved."

Precipice psychology, the call to risk and adventure, is not the prevalent mode of thought.

Utah surroundings can be jarring and literally shocking to the alien sensibility: adjustment to westernness (watching pick-up trucks with gun racks mounted on the rear window roll down dusty rural roads or Salt Lake City's State Street), adjustments to Great Basin aridity (nursing bloody cracks in fingernail crevices or purchasing mounds of moisture cream), adjustments to Great Basin urban problems (moving to increasing pollution and an apparent lack of outrage rather than cleaner, fresher air and wide open spaces), and adjustments to western landscape.

"The most devastating difference," says Ann Hart from Michigan and Washington, D.C., "is that there aren't enough trees here. The extraordinarily different landscape is desolate and frightening. Though the openness of the west is beautiful, it's very jolting to be without trees." Conversely, when Hal Cannon, a native Utahn, moved to Rhode Island, the countryside was too lush for him. "I had a sense of being closed in by all of the trees, by too many things growing all over the place."

Geographically, Utah is an insular, isolated state; it isn't a seaport, wide open to winds of change, or a bustling emporium with many diverse ideas and behaviors. Utah is a desert, a severe land. Its people have paid a price for their "blossom as a rose" ideal, perceived by some as a lack of diversity, a stasis, an inbreeding of ideas as well as people ("Nothing new can get past those high mountains").

"It bothers me," says Meg Brady, assistant professor of English at the University of Utah, "to walk down the street and rarely see a black person. I don't like a completely homogenous group of people."

Georganne Sugden "misses diversity . . . a real cultural mix. People do not grow up with the same value systems and I want my children to know that."

"The people here are close-minded," says Jim Galletta from New York City, Berlin and Tokyo. "They have good book knowledge, but have not taken the opportunity to expand their thoughts and see things from a different point of view."

"So many people have lived here for generations," says Linda Boekelheide, a native of Boston. "They think this is the place to be and the way to live, and that makes any other way of living somewhat questionable."

The buzz goes on.

* * *

Because one "doesn't live with the mountains or the desert, but with the people," according to University of Utah sociologist Ricardo Garcia, a specialist in majority/minority group relationships, the peoples of Utah are the essential consideration when analyzing culture shock.

Most agree that every culture has its quirks and that Utah has a lot to offer. A glance at this magazine's events calendar makes it clear that the state is considerably more diverse and multidimensional than may appear to the uneducated eye. Yet, unavoidable for most newcomers is the omnipresence of Mormon culture—from the towering world headquarters building of the Church of Jesus Christ of Latter-day Saints to its prescription for the everyday life of the body and mind. Yesterday's settling of the state by Mormons, their comprehensive lifestyle and their numbers (71 percent of the state, 66 percent of Salt Lake County according to LDS Church statistics) are inextricably woven into strands of Utah life.

Utah Mormonism—a unique blend of theology, history, insularity and colonialism influenced by western middle class and agrarian values—is a culture as much as it is a religion. To outsiders, the culture can have a tribal feel about it, complete with a language (brothers, sisters, stake, ward, branch, Relief Society), a behavioral norm (a health code called the Word of Wisdom, special standards of sexual ethics, strict rites of passage), a dress (private vestments) and a temple (a holy place like an Indian kiva, where outsiders are barred unless they adopt tribal ways).

Non-Mormon newcomers are suddenly a minority, most of them for the first time in their lives, even if they had never recognized their majority status elsewhere.

"It's painful for a WASP to be a minority anywhere in the United States," says Dean May, a professor of history at the University of Utah and a former LDS bishop, "to not be a part of all the important things taking place."

"All non-Mormons in Utah share one thing in common," says Mike Weathers, "that supersedes race, creed or religion: the fact that they are not Mormon."

Even Mormon newcomers may experience some pain on becoming a high-profile majority person, identified and numbered with a mass for the first time in their lives, and in the process, struck by the feeling that they are losing individuality.

"It's like I'm not a person with unique characteristics anymore," says Suzanne Beck from Santa Barbara, California, "only a Mormon."

Incomers of all faiths and creeds experience much the same perplexity in their search for "feeling at home" in Utah—scratching out a place among strongly-bonded lifetime friendships, a subtle pioneer/spiritual aristocracy, and generations-old social patterns and attitudes. But bonds often get sifted out, forgotten, lost in a locked polarity which neither side intends to create, all because of one of the most commonly asked questions in the state—"Are you a Mormon?" The question is an effective device for establishing lines of demarcation, analyzing social expectations and cutting to the bone.

Playwrights Nancy Borgenicht and Michael Buttars conceived of a custom Utah license plate—I M 1 R U—to parody the inimical question.

"Only in this community," say most of those interviewed, "has anybody asked me where I go to church." Some people, tired of the question, tired of the "Yes" or "No" categorical answer, respond with a non sequitur:

"Does it make a difference?"

"I'm a Twin Peaks Methodist," says an avid mountain climber.

"And what religion are you?"

If one tunes in to the flow of conversation on buses, in corners, at parties and over the fences of this community, one is likely to hear a discussion of churchly topics. "I've never been in a place," says Linda Boekelheide, "where people discuss religion so much."

Some people talk about it because they are curious, some because they feel a need to establish their identity, often in self-defense, and others because the topic fuels the great armchair sport of testing who can outdo whom with horror stories. But regardless of reasons, the bottom line reality is that many people feel isolated. The following quotes are variations on the single most repeated theme from thirty-five interviews and multiple informal conversations with Utah incomers, old and new:

"People are often involved only with their families and the same friends through elementary, high school and college," observes a retired businessman from California.

"We couldn't ask for nicer neighbors," says Jan Gillilan. "They are friendly, generous and offer us vegetables from their gardens. But there is no social mixing, just a respectful tolerance of each other."

"That I am a guest on Mormon turf is a pervasive feeling," says Hugh Gillilan, a former Unitarian minister in Salt Lake City, now a practising psychologist. "The ward structure is an intense community, and with all of the various ward activities, there is a natural feeling of exclusion."

"It hit me after six to eight months," says Judy Hagerman. "Suddenly you realize that you're happy in your work, but you don't have a social core unless you are LDS. People are friendly and say 'We've got to have you over,' but they never do."

When people feel isolated they start to wonder why. "They could solve all their problems if they'd join the group," is not a satisfactory answer for everyone. The paradox is that no one likes to be left out, even if they don't want to belong. It's like hearing a party down the block and knowing that you haven't been invited. It's like watching a steady stream back and forth to a meeting and knowing you aren't privy to the topic of discussion nor part of the bonding process. In this mix of fears and sensitivities, a gulf grows.

The polarity is most formidable in the abstract, but specific factors do crate distance:

The bees. Stereotypes would have Mormon mothers baking bread, canning and singing to their children, "During all the long hours till daylight is through, there is plenty indeed for my two hands to do," and Mormon fathers listening to Book of Mormon cassette tapes while they shave. Often this emphasis on working one's way to perfection leaves little extra time.

"You will probably not be able to have close personal friends among Mormons," advises Noel de Nevers (professor of Chemical Engineering at the University of Utah and self-styled expert on local culture) in his "Suggestions for Outsiders Moving to Utah—A Purely Personal View." "They are not unfriendly, simply busy."

"You get the feeling it's immoral to sit and relax," observes Gloria Skurzynski, a children's book writer. "Some people never light long enough to sit and enjoy. They always have one foot pointed to the door."

Sharing the honey. The desire to share religious faith is not unique to Mormons, to this century, to Utah or the United States. "Sharing the gospel," at its ideal best, is an act of love—"the supreme compliment," says President Jonathan Snow of the Salt Lake South LDS Mission.

The missionary thrust is met with simultaneous acceptance and rejection. On one hand, the Salt Lake North and Salt Lake South Missions combined (encompassing the state) baptize approximately 325 people per month, the largest rate of LDS baptisms in the United States and Canada.

"The converts are mainly transfers into Salt Lake City," says a full-time missionary from Australia, "impressed to listen because of the friendliness, the good family example, and the feeling of being welcomed."

On the other hand, the intended fellowship may cause resentment:

"When I had a hysterectomy recently," says one woman, "I was upset. My doctor came in to console me and in the process took an hour and a half to tell me what I really needed—the Mormon Church. I had been receiving Holy Communion for the duration of my hospital stay and he knew this. It was like he was saying, 'What you do and believe doesn't count.' I would feel better if Mormons were happy with me where I am."

"It is an 'all give and no take' proposition," says Tiffany Pyle. "I can accept people on their own terms, but I am not entitled to my own viewpoint unless it agrees with theirs."

Health in the hive. Intertwined with a utilitarian lifestyle is the Word of Wisdom, a health law originally discouraging (now prohibiting) the use of coffee, tea, tobacco, alcohol and other drug-related substances and encouraging wise eating habits. Much of the polarity in the community can be attributed to this Word.

A new-to-town, professionally trained actress wins a part in a play at Promised Valley Playhouse, not knowing that it is an LDS Church-affiliated theater. When she brings a thermos of tea to rehearsal she is told by a young cast member, "Do you realize that we are rehearsing in a sacred building? Please leave the tea at home."

When the Word of Wisdom is presented on moral grounds, defensiveness raises its eighty-nine-toothed head. Some non-Mormons start to criticize the cookies and red punch refreshments at PTA, school or neighborhood parties ("excess sugar destroys health as much as caffeine or nicotine") and cite scientific studies showing that wine is beneficial to health.

"One of the problems," says Allen Swan, a former mission president and regional representative for the LDS Church, "is that many social relationships are built around liquor and coffee—the neighborhood women getting together over a cup of coffee, families getting together for cocktails—so common in other areas. The LDS family often doesn't know what to do instead, possibly afraid of rejection on any other basis. We are too prone to figure out what the answer is going to be ahead of time, and therefore, don't make the approach at all. We are timid."

Many people paint themselves into opposing corners: "I can't be comfortable with people who won't accept *my* standards."

Also potentially distancing are strict customs (no dating until age sixteen, no dating outside of the religion, modest dress) and religious laws (no fornication, adultery, homosexuality or masturbation) related to sexual morality. Worthiness to receive a *recommend* to LDS temples and to be called as a missionary depends on adherence to these laws. But sometimes, somewhere between worthiness and uprightness, pharisaical attitudes seep through:

The same actress who took the thermos of tea to the Promised Valley Playhouse buys a modest, full-length slip, goes to a costume fitting and soon after receives a phone call from the theater's secretary who says, "I really don't know how to tell you this . . . " ("do I need Scope?" the actress panics), "but there is a policy here in the theater that you must wear a brassiere."

"I wouldn't have minded so much if I had any bosom to speak of or if the costumes hadn't been period pieces, huge things up to my neck," the actress says.

"Here, whether you are a Mormon or a non-Mormon," says Scott Gillilan, a college student who grew up in Salt Lake City, "determines if you're thought of as good or bad. Some Mormon kids act as if there are no standards in non-LDS homes: 'It wouldn't matter if you came in drunk, your parents won't care how late you are out.' "

Order of the hive. Because of the erosion of respect for authority in the twentieth century, aided by Adolf Hitler, Idi Amin and Jim Jones, obedience to authority is often viewed with suspicion. Authority vibrates with connotations of power, coercion and dominion. People—especially minorities—are suspicious of absolute dicta, and uneasy with relationships where one group or individual always has the last say.

"When I saw crowds of middle-aged women in pink jogging suits suddenly appear in the streets," says Boekelheide, "I thought that the Mormon Church must have said something about running. I found out that it had. It is frightening to think that a group can have such a rapid effect on its members. Obedience has great potential for good and change, but blind obedience led to Jonestown. That's frightening."

"This [fright] stems from a failure to appreciate that a communal culture," says historian Dean May, "is a less individualistic one, collectively more important than the individual. Most people don't see it that way. However, the obedience is voluntary, not a psychologically coerced obligation."

The Sting. "Three days after you die," explains a five-year-old metaphysician, "you get a big rock, and if you can move it, you get to go to heaven." Serious issues are pondered in the realm of Big Wheels, Mother Goose and used tire swings, and serious accusations are made:

"You're bad if you ride your bike on Sunday."

"Your baptism doesn't count. You're not a Mormon."

Twenty-three percent of Utah's population is below the age of nine as compared to 14.6 percent nationwide. For all of the blesseds showered on the heads of children (which they occasionally deserve), little minds can be insensitive and even cruel, especially when speaking from the my-dad-is-bigger-than-your-dad position.

"The adults can cope," says one mother, "but what about the children?"

Surveys conducted by the Brigham Young University *Daily Universe* in the early and late seventies asked non-LDS people how they had been treated in public schools. The response was unanimous: They were stereotyped, left out, and had problems with dating. (More than one LDS girl has cried her heart out over a barred-from-the-door "gentile" suitor.) A 1981 survey in Box Elder High School in Brigham City showed that more than 50 percent of its 1,500 students felt they had witnessed religious discrimination at some time.

Of nine non-Mormon families interviewed for this article, all volunteered the information that their children had been made to feel inferior because of their choice of religion or no religion.

Marilyn Casey, a Catholic mother who once worked as a nanny in an LDS family's home in California, came to Salt Lake City with enthusiastic anticipation:

"The first year here we didn't notice any differences. We loved the mountains and were thrilled to be alone with our family. But the second year, it hit us. My eight-year-old daughter came home one day and said, 'You and Daddy will never see how aggravating it is where if you wear a cross and have a black friend, the kids think you are ridiculous.' Too many people here don't make their children realize how to respect all feelings. They teach their children to love only Mormonism."

"Children seem to go through a rigid period where anything that isn't Mormon is no good," observes Gloria Skurzynski whose two oldest daughters moved into Salt Lake at junior high age, have since moved away and have sworn never to move back. "In junior high especially, kids start to feel that they have to uphold their religion against anyone who is not of the same faith."

Some people who hear these stories pooh-pooh them, saying that these newcomers must have a chip on their shoulders, must not be well adjusted or have the right attitude. Growing up is not an uncomplicated proposition, but no one likes to feel left out. Even if children in a majority group are not bosom buddies, one isolated child's viewpoint when he sees a group of kids trailing together is: "I don't belong and everybody else does."

The LDS ward/stake network, the fact that Mormon children interact socially and religiously on weekends, that they speak the same language and disapprove certain behaviors is no flimsy web. The message perceived by many non-Mormons, especially children, is "This is the way to be; you're not this way; what's wrong with you?" Isolating begins when a majority forms.

"You expect the phenomenon in a small community," says college student David Gillilan, "but for a metropolitan area to be like that is unusual."

"No one has malice," says sociologist Ricardo Garcia, "just a lack of understanding that differences are not necessarily good or bad."

"The intent of the church is good," say most of those interviewed, "but it doesn't always come across that way."

Any emphasis on resisting the evils of the world, on being an example to others by good works, and loving neighbors by sharing a knowledge of "the truth," unintentionally categorizes. These are admonitions that provide the backbone and strength of a sincere people, but are paradoxical when the implications are examined: If the world is evil, does "the world" mean anything different from me? Does being an example imply the capability of being better or above others, a model worthy of imitation? Does it promote an unnecessary self-consciousness or a loss of compassion? If one says the "truth" is in one place, does it imply that it is not in another? The problem was analogized by Esther Landa in a speech at a forum on extremism at the University of Utah: "When I first heard the name 'Moral Majority' I thought that since I was not of the 'Moral Majority' I was consigned to the immoral minority."

Some people find themselves reacting defensively: Mormons are sure they are right→there's no room for me→they isolate me because I might warp their beeline to perfection→I feel alone→I'll find my own group→I'll exclude those who exclude me→I'll prove they're wrong→I'm sure I'm right.

Bees who get stung. "What happens when you first come to Utah," says Meg Brady, "is that almost immediately people who have been here for a short period of time descend on you. Even if you have no preconceptions, all of a sudden you are part of this group that sets itself in contrast to the majority culture. Most of the time, people who have been here for a while and have found their place, don't bother."

The Nouveau Minorité, having been consigned automatically to limbo as the other (the *non*-righteous, the *non*-supporter of family life, the *non*-everything), have to scramble for position. Some choose to ignore the fray and find a quiet place for themselves and like-minded friends. Others rail at their displacement and demand justice, justice that often includes the same condescension of which newcomers complain:

"I'm not inviting any Mormons to my party," says a Holladay man. "I don't want them criticising me."

"I," says an Ogden woman, "don't want my son to move to Brigham or to Logan . . . too many Mormons. I don't want to even eat lunch with a Mormon."

" . . . Seek friendship in other groups," advises de Nevers. "You will find numerous congenial people who will strike you as being just ordinary Americans."

Some relate to Mormonism as the Ultra Bright Clean Machine moving solemnly onward like an armored tank, adorned with beehive decals and a Hear No Evil, See No Evil, Speak No Evil bumper sticker. Just as the *Church News* editorials in the *Deseret News* warn against outside evils, disgruntled snipers take potshots in the *Tribune* or the *Daily Utah Chronicle*. Mormons are cast as sheep and non-Mormons as sheep gone astray. The Shepherdsons and the Grangerfords.

"The *Chronicle* gives vent to anti-Mormon feelings," says Dean May, "with stereotyped images of members as clones, a mindless group of people wearing dark suits with nameplates who don't do anything unless told to." There is a tendency to attribute ignorance, narrowness and blind obedience across the board to a wide spectrum of Utahns.

"This 'uneasy-with-the-majority' sentiment is promoted by realtors who steer clients clear of Bountiful and other heavily LDS-populated areas, by solemn *griots* bearing tales of horror, and by assorted others who wish to sound the knell and save others from the pain of a minority experience. "Remember—this is *Utah*."

"When people are warned about Mormons," says sociologist Garcia, "they start applying selective perception and looking for certain behaviors. They make generalizations from their observations and say 'that's how Mormons are.'"

How does this affect Mormons? Some never recognize the hostility, totally engaged in their sphere; some hear the hostility and chalk it up to persecution of "God's work"; but many who have made considerable effort to handle differences with discretion and to dredge open channels of communication feel cheated when they are labeled and categorized in sweeping generalizations.

"Members of my department go to a private club once a week," says an LDS visiting professor at the University of Utah. "As a Mormon, the invitation is not extended to me. People are very concerned as to whether my wife and I are Mormons or not. Once they find that we are, if they are non-Mormons, most pretty quickly and definitively write us out of their social calendar. They assume that we don't want to be invited to a cocktail party or that we don't enjoy visiting."

An often unrecognized group who undergo Utah shock are Mormon newcomers. Used to dealing and being dealt with as individuals, they are confused when they become a category, "bad guys" in some eyes. One woman learned very abruptly that "Hi, I met you at Relief Society" was not only a gauche move at her tennis club, but also grounds for ostracism by non-Mormons whereas the same statement would fall on deaf ears elsewhere.

Many assume that the ward community will open like a pop-up book and that any LDS newcomer can walk in, sit down, and become a popping part too. Not so simple. Utah Mormonism is like a southern accent, the same language with differences. If a newcomer doesn't instantly accept local ways or wonders why LDS prayers are offered at PTA meetings, other Mormons may pat their hand and say, "Oh, you must be a convert."

"Unless you grew up as a Mormon in Utah," says Jim Galleta, a Swiss-Italian convert, "you are considered different."

Today's incoming Mormons are often used to being considered unique in a wider society, a minority, even an interesting oddity. Expecting to be embraced by Utah Mormons ("real saints") and drawn to the bosom of the faith, they are often shocked as their uniqueness turns commonplace, as they fall into line as foot soldiers in the battalion of the righteous. Their whole way of viewing themselves turns upside down as they become a majority, and a personality shift is often required.

"It has been difficult to find our place," says a retired couple from California, returned missionaries for the LDS Church. "The real question for my husband and me is, can we contribute here?"

A newcomer may choose a combination of responses to a culture: *Accept everything* (embrace it, kiss it, wave flags about it and say it's the best place in the world). *Ignore it* (it doesn't exist). *Be horrified* ("those natives!"). *Stereotype* ("Yes, they are like that, this place is full of them, what else can you expect?"). *React defensively* ("these folks don't accept me because I'm different; their tunnel vision prevents them from seeing this fine specimen, me, and appreciating my delicate sensibilities . . . the creeps."). *Do the chameleon* (adopt an accent within five days, cut or grow hair, add four-letter words to—or drop them from—your vocabulary, buy-burn-or-stuff a bra). *Become an anthropologist/ornithologist* (observe the behaviors of local birds—how they fly or why they don't).

Moving and separation are traumatic at best. Many new Utahns are able to make inroads after they accept the culture as it is, stop waiting for others to accept them on their terms, and take responsibility for their own experience.

One individual concluded that "this place does not do the adjusting for you. I have really had to clarify my values and generate my own milieu in a way that has been valuable, and one that I am in no position to resent."

"Everybody makes their own community," says Georganne Sugden. "Why continue to complain about this one? Newcomers should jump in and create their own alternative."

"Once we got over having a chip on our shoulder and realized that

Utahns were just people," admits Judy Hagerman who found her friends through jogging and old-time fiddle music, "we started to enjoy it. You've got to be smart enough and strong enough to go out and find your own thing. Otherwise, you'll get bummed out about it."

Misunderstanding in any of the world's neighborhoods is often filtered through second-hand sources. "She said that he said . . . I think that's what they're thinking . . . " Rather than subscribing to rumor, storm warnings and hearsay, check to see if offenses are intended before deciding to be offended. Ask: "Is it true that you want to convert me? "Is it true that you're not going to let my children play with yours?" "Do I look like a sheep to you?"

"Blaming Salt Lake City is not realistic, not productive," says Ann Hart, "and there's nothing much wrong with this place. There's a variety of people, landscape, a beautiful manner of human exchange—forthright and respectful."

The fact is that the world is full of sensitive people, none of whom think they are stereotypes, yet most of whom find it easy to sit with compatriots and analyze, categorize and stigmatize.

"We maintain our self-delusive ideas," says Everett "Doc" Murdock, "by stereotyping others."

"It is simpler to deal in categories," says de Nevers. "Habit means conservation of thought. Why should I have to think about brushing my teeth every morning?"

Categorization, a guillotine, separates head from body, body from body.

"You can be threatened or shocked by this culture," says Hal Cannon, Folk Arts Coordinator for the Utah Arts Council, "or you can take joy in finding it. It is hidden. It has an internal language. People in the culture may not see it as readily as the newcomer. For instance, most people hadn't noticed all of the beehive symbols until we had our exhibit" (the Grand Beehive Exhibit at the Salt Lake Art Center and at the Renwick Gallery of the National Collection of Fine Arts, Smithsonian Institution).

Call it an adventure and go beehive symbol hunting, or hiking, backpacking, skiing, climbing or gold mining; read Don Marshall's *Frost in the Orchard* or *Rummage Sale* for an affectionate view of rural Utah; see *Saturday's Voyeur* (July–August) for an unaffectionate view of Mormon Utah. Attend the U.S. Film Festival in Park City (January), buy binoculars and go Redford/Redford-clone watching at Sundance. Visit the Southern Utah Folklife Festival in September. Read Al Church's piece in the September 1981 issue of *Network,* "Stalking the Wild Gentile," complete with a survival kit.

None of this is guaranteed to make you feel at home. But home may be a state of mind. People cling to some rather amazing places—in a crab-like clutch to ocean cliffs, to dusty roadside towns, to freezing Alaskan outposts—because that place, for some reason, speaks of home to them. Some element holds them—roots, tradition, inertia, friends. Even those who leave eventually turn their thoughts to the green grass, the sunbaked sands or the crashing waves of home. Those sights, those sounds, those smells have been delicately carved—or are eventually carved—in all of us. It happens everywhere. Even in Utah.

*

Next Time

MICHAEL N. MARTINEZ

In this brief personal reminiscence, Michael N. Martinez touches on a number of subjects, including growing up Hispanic in Lark, Utah, a small mining town at the base of the Oquirrh Mountains where most people worked for Kennecott Copper Corporation or Hercules, an aerospace company. He also tells of returning from a two-year tour of duty in Vietnam; his experiences there; and the impact Vietnam had on him as well as on his friends and relatives.

Michael N. Martinez, "Next Time," *Utah Holiday,* June 1991:26–27. Reprinted by permission of the author.

Michael N. Martinez is an attorney in Salt Lake City and a member of Salt Lake Community College's Board of Trustees..

ST. THERESA'S CHURCH HALL was filled for this noisy celebration of proud parents, relatives, and friends all anxious to participate in the victory over Iraq. Harold, a marine, an eldest son, had just returned from Saudi Arabia. A hero! Alive! He represented our pride. He gave us the opportunity to share the celebrations we had seen on television for returning troops. Even a local news station was interviewing our marine.

The parish priest greeted everyone paternally. After all, what is a Hispanic celebration if not a secular and religious choreography of prayer, giving thanks for what is and what will be (although we accept it is beyond our control) but never for what might be. We accepted, but this night we also celebrated, we American Hispanics.

As I entered the hall I saw familiar faces and, as happens more often, new faces. Faces of children, of friends, the spouses of acquaintances, distant cousins who'd traveled in for the festivity. Standing in line for my feast of green chili, beans, turkey, and cake, I noticed Paul. He stood out in his camouflage army fatigues. The same kind of fatigues I had worn. I heard someone whisper that Paul wasn't all there and watched him move through the crowd, shaking hands and smiling between sips of beer.

I filled my plate and looked for an empty seat along the two tables that filled the hall. I felt comfortable sitting with my parents' contemporaries. After all, I came to such events mostly to see old friends, meet their kids, and reminisce with others who once lived in Lark and Bingham Canyon. I had grown up in the two mining towns, neither of which survived the growth of the bordering copper mine. Some of the people then had lived in log cabins on the lower tiers of the mine, others in row housing built on company land. Both towns exist now only in the memories of what I am rapidly becoming—old-timers.

Our pastor sat with us. He spoke of the difficulty in getting parishioners from the "east side" to attend mass in Midvale. The parish is largely Hispanic. We spoke of how well everyone looked and, again, I noticed Paul.

After dinner was savored, the party was ready for music and dancing to Mexican "rancheras" and rock'n' roll tunes, played as if they were country and western ballads. Sons and daughters made "don't embarrass me" faces as their parents danced. After a few numbers, relatives danced with relatives, mothers with sons, and fathers with daughters. Entire families danced and traded partners as the music continued nonstop.

I stepped outside to find an audible conversation and ran into an old friend, the proud uncle of the marine. Of course we talked about how long it had been since we had been in the army, both drafted to Vietnam at the same time. Paul joined us. I asked, tongue in cheek, if the uniform he wore was his original issue. He raised his beer and asked if I knew what it was like to fight in a war that no one cared about. He wasn't mad, just matter-of-fact. He asked if it mattered to anyone that he had put his life on the line. He was less than sober, yet not drunk. Now he asked his beer, more than me, if I knew what it was like to come home from a war and not grow up.

I did know. Paul stirred memories that floated back like artifacts from a former life someone else lived. I remembered days I'll never forget, yet won't think about. Not bad memories, mostly distant. I realized I still carried them like someone else's baggage. I hadn't ingested Vietnam, I only remembered it. Life had changed for me but not for Paul. Paul, as he said, hadn't grown up. He had come home, moved home, stayed home. He had ventured nowhere, stayed safe. I had ventured far.

THE EXPERIENCE OF VIETNAM

I was nineteen when I went to Vietnam. I was twenty-one when I returned. I experienced life, death, pain, anger, frustration, denial, and—most of all—loneliness or maybe it was despair. I also learned to make tough decisions quickly. I learned to trust my judgment because it was as good as anyone else's. I learned friendship based on mutual goals and caring about one another's successes and letdowns.

I had been a good soldier and was awarded several medals. My father said they were more than anyone else in our family received before me, and all the fathers I knew had been in the army. Years later when others threw their medals during peace marches, I kept mine. Although I came to understand that the war wasn't worth a generation of cripples and drug addicts, I was still proud I had served. Proud I fought. Proud I had gone. My father served. My brother served. My uncles served. My Lark buddies served. To Hispanic males, Catholicism and military service are the reality of youth. The rite of passage to manhood was military service, more so during a conflict. This celebration for Harold was not because he had come home alive but because he had served, he was a man. Like his father and his father's father.

The draft is gone but my nephew joined the reserves. I asked him why. He said he wanted to go to college and he wanted to do the right thing. His father had been a marine. I told him that when he becomes a lawyer, which he plans, he will meet very few who have served. Professionals have other rites of manhood like hiking through Europe. He didn't understand. He will. His service will later be a reflection of where he grew up.

Now Paul looked at me as if I couldn't understand. He wanted everyone to acknowledge that he, Paul, had served. He had done so longer and under worse conditions than those in Saudi Arabia. He had gone into the jungle and one year later come out alive. If you think about it, it is truly a miracle that he could do such a thing. Yet the toll was paid in the afterlife. Paul had never grown up. He said that.

HOMECOMING

One day I had been in the jungle, the next on a plane home, the next at the San Francisco Airport. Seventeen months in the Nam and one day to adjust. I couldn't go home, not yet. I went to San Francisco, uniform and all. On the way to a hotel, any hotel, a lady called me a killer. The hotel clerk asked where I was headed. I said I was out and going home. He said I shouldn't be in uniform if I was out. I hadn't adjusted to the time change. I fell asleep at 2 p.m. and awoke at 11 p.m. I slipped into a pair of Levis I had bought at the PX and a khaki shirt. As much as people hated the war, they loved khaki, especially with military epaulets.

I wandered for several hours. I finally heard music and entered a bar. The music was loud. The bartender yelled at me to order. I ordered a warm beer. A women came over to me and asked if I would buy her a drink. I did, for $10. I imagined that she must be like the Saigon bar girls I had heard about, but maybe the drinks were cheaper in Saigon.

She asked me if I wanted to go to her place, only, she said, because I looked like a nice guy. She said she was afraid to go out alone. I asked if she knew where the bathroom was. She did. I got up and walked out the front door and kept on going. At 21, I could shoot at someone but girls scared me a little, especially after two years. My last encounter with a woman had been a date with the nicest Catholic girl you could meet. I'd barely kissed her good night.

I returned to the hotel. I packed my duffle bag and headed for the bus station. By 6 a.m. I was at the airport. By noon I was home, Salt Lake City. My parents had gotten a telephone while I was away, so I called them. They came and picked me up. Some high school friends came over once I was back in Lark. We had called ourselves the Spanish Armada because we thought we were invincible on the basketball court. Part of the Armada was still away. Within two months we were all home again.

And the following month, my father died on the first day I was to attend university classes. It snowed that September 18, 1971—my brother's birthday. He was given leave from Nam to come to the funeral. While some never grew up, I did. I was in a hurry. I finished college and graduated from law school and by age 26 was practicing law. In between I would visit the bar in Lark where the Armada played pool. I saw Paul there. We talked about Nam and more Nam. We were our own support. We knew we had done something to be proud of, but others took it so matter-of-factly that it was almost as if we'd just gone to work.

All my friends went to work at Kennecott or Hercules. They married or played. They bought cars and houses. They recalled heroic missions, boot camp, and lost loves over our infrequent Armada poker games. I bought a house for my family on the "east side." I met people who thought serving was a joke. People who thought I was different than other Mexicans because I'm a lawyer. And Lark people who knew me but treated me differently because I'm a lawyer.

Now I'm sorry Paul wasn't given a party when he came home. He might have grown up. And even then, what would he have done differently? Most likely nothing. But, to him, it would have been different. He never grew up. I was never young. I was in a hurry, fearful of death and believing I had been spared for a reason. Luck, it had been, and I gave it a meaning. Paul can still grow up, whatever that means to him. I can't be young.

I'm proud of Harold. He represents victory and all who served. I hope Harold doesn't think he is different than Paul. I hope he doesn't think the next time it will be like Saudi Arabia. I hope, for his son, that the next time is not like Vietnam, or Korea, or World War II.

*

Expanding Our Moral Vision Beyond the Human Community

DONALD WORSTER

In this interview conducted by Elbert Peck of Sunstone Magazine *in 1988, award-winning historian Donald Worster discusses the nature and causes of the environmental crisis faced by Utah and the world. The two men converse about such topics as the contradictory attitudes that Americans have toward the natural environment; Utahns' lack of concern in general for environmental issues; and the biblical injunction to take dominion over the earth. We are invited to take a hard look at the issues facing us through pointed, sometimes rhetorical, questions: How big should Salt Lake City be? How can we possibly continue indefinitely on our present course? How can you endlessly sustain the American lifestyle in a desert? In Worster's view, meeting the crisis requires expanding our old moral vision beyond the human community to accept moral responsibility for the whole community of life on this planet, and he asserts that it cannot be solved within the framework of a capitalistic economic system. Capitalism, he says, is not a system well designed for living within ecological limits because it is premised on endless economic growth and endless envy. Nature is viewed as the capital on which the increase is to be based. "I don't see how you can sustain forever a system that is based on calling vice a virtue," he says. "I don't know of any other system that has tried to make greed a virtue."*

"Interview: Expanding Our Moral Vision Beyond the Human Community; A Conversation with Donald Worster," *Sunstone* 12 (September 1988): 30–34. Reprinted by permission of the publisher and author.

Donald Worster teaches at the University of Kansas. He is the author of *The Dust Bowl: The Southern Plains in the 1930s,* which was awarded the 1980 Bancroft Prize in American History, and *Rivers of Empire: Water, Aridity, and the Growth of the American West,* as well as several other books dealing with environmental history.

In *Rivers of Empire* your chapter on the Mormons is entitled "The Lord's Beavers."

That's because the role that water has played in Mormon history has not been given enough attention. Generally, people who study their own religion tend to take an idealist approach—they see those ideas as having an independent life and an ideal set of origins. But material conditions do affect the way people think, even the way they think religiously. I think it is hard to understand Mormonism as we know it today apart from its Utah setting, its setting in the arid west, its relation to water.

The reference to beavers was not meant to be degrading. I've always been amazed at how much identification there has been with the bee and the beehive in Utah; but it seems to me to be a mischosen or inappropriate metaphor, given the role of water in Utah history and in the formation of its communal culture and religion.

Like bees, beavers are communal; they are very family centered. There's probably no more appropriate totem for this state and its people. It strikes me as interesting how in many societies we identify with animals—sometimes insects, but mainly the larger animals. Even today within the Judeo-Christian tradition we do what native peoples in North America did: we often identify ourselves with an animal. A number of American Indian tribes identified with the bear. Mormons have done that with the bee. The point is we continue to do this, and yet it strikes me that in modern society we don't take seriously the implications of doing it. For us it's simply a kind of symbolic relationship; it's not a genuine ethical relationship, it's not a spiritual relationship with what we've chosen. That makes us different from, say, the Australian aborigines who choose the wallaby, with which they have a fraternal as well as a symbolic relationship. They're allied together in a spiritual harmony and unity, and I doubt if that really ever developed here in Utah, not just with the bee but with all of what was here before, with the natural world.

Did the scriptural command to have dominion prevent that unity?

Anyone who came West in the middle of the nineteenth century, Mormons included, came with a lot of cultural attitudes about water and land. It was hard to grow up in America at that point and avoid developing an ethos of domination over the natural world. Curiously, at the same time Americans were generally celebrating the natural world. That was all we had to give us a sense of identity in term of the world of nations. We didn't have cathedrals, we didn't have an old civilization, old cultural institutions, and so on, but what we had was nature in abundance. So in the nineteenth century America became "nature's nation." A nation that was peculiarly blessed by nature, a nation that had a peculiarly close relationship with the natural world. However, at the same time we were saying all that endlessly to ourselves, we were also bent on domination and conquest over the natural world; people saw no real contradiction in their set of attitudes.

I think the Mormons who came to Utah had precisely that same sort of contradiction, a deep contradiction that they were not aware of. It looks like a contradiction to us today because it is hard to see how you can celebrate something you are in the process of dominating, but that was a common American characteristic. We've done this with American Indians, too. We celebrated them at the same time we were setting out to dominate and even in some cases exterminate them. That is an old pattern in American society—ruining, spoiling, and killing what we most cherish. Even today, from the president on down, we somehow consider ourselves a more natural people than others. When Reagan gets on his horse and rides around the ranch that he cherishes, I'm sure he feels in some sense that he is an environmentalist. But his political policies don't follow that; in fact they're almost diametrically opposed to it. It's not just his peculiar contradiction, it's a national and cultural contradiction. It's so in Utah, and it's so in Massachusetts.

At some point we must become more self-aware of the contradiction between our values and policies, and that's where we seem to be arriving in the country as a whole. When you become more aware of the contradiction, you try to resolve it. That greater self-awareness is what environmentalism is about, and I must say that Utah is still not on the cutting edge of the environmental movement. There is still not much awareness of contradiction in this state.

IDEALLY, WHAT IS THE CORRECT RELATIONSHIP TO THE LAND, ESPECIALLY FOR THE DESERT?

The primary thing that is necessary today, for anyone living anywhere in the country, but especially for people living in areas such as Utah where vital natural resources are scarce, is to get control of one's needs. That is, to determine which are our real needs and which are the needs that we've just invented, created, or thought up. This is a challenge which we have to face all through the American West.

I often quote William Mulholland, the water and power director for Los Angeles in the early part of the twentieth century, who said, "If we don't get the water we won't need it." That is, go and get everything you can get out of the environment and then discover how you can use it later. That same philosophy has been applied up and down the whole Colorado River Basin—"Let's get the water before someone else gets it and then we'll discover how to put it to use." So, the primary challenge in every state is to put some limits on our sense of need. Until we do that we are vulnerable to manipulative, powerful forces that move us this way and that, and then our lives are out of our control. Unless you can control your needs, which partly means to define them, then you have no control over yourself, over your community, over your destiny.

That is a very abstract answer, but it speaks on the deepest metaphysical, spiritual and psychological levels about what is needed in the West. What is the amount of water we really need in this state to serve vital human functions, to provide a sense of community, to preserve our traditions, and to provide a home for our children? We have to identify our values and personal values and then ask, what do we need in the way of natural resources to get them? That's not been done so far in any advanced consumer society.

In Utah any extension of large-scale intensive agriculture is clearly out of the question; it cannot even be sustained at present levels. I think small-scale agricultural uses of water in various valleys can probably be sustained for a long time to come. But large-scale intensive uses, involving inter-basin transfers of water that tie in up and down the Colorado River and so forth, are responsible for a whole series of environmental problems. We have assumed for the last 100 to 150 years that we could turn the West into a major agricultural producer. That was unrealistic. It can't be sustained, and over the next fifty years everybody in the West is going to have to accept a much smaller agricultural base than what we now have or what we wanted to have. Agriculture is going to migrate back East where there is more natural rainfall and where the environmental and ecological problems are less overwhelming. Water in the West is going to be increasingly used for other purposes, urban and industrial. We also have to arrive at some idea of how many people we can optimally support. Again, we have had extravagant ideas: the nineteenth century had a vision of hundreds of millions of people living here. I think Westerners are beginning to recognize that extravagance, but we must ask very specifically, "How big should Salt Lake City be?" "How can it possibly go on and on?" "How can we sustain Los Angeles as the second biggest city in this country—a city in a desert?" At some point those questions must bring us to consider population control—the size of families, etc. I realize that this is a particularly sensitive issue in pro-family Utah. But we have almost a quarter of a billion of people in this country, and if you consider not just our numbers but the demands those numbers make on the environment, we are one of the most over-populated countries on earth. In a great many ways the American West is one of the most over-populated regions of this continent. We don't want to think of ourselves in that way—overpopulation is supposed to be a problem in Calcutta, not Salt Lake City. How can you endlessly sustain that American lifestyle in a desert? Especially a lifestyle which is bent on endless economic growth, endless want, endless proliferation of demand.

Seems like you're anti-capitalistic.

There isn't going to be a solution to the challenge of environmental limits anywhere on the planet within a purely capitalistic framework. I'm not anti-capitalistic in some absolute sense. Capitalism is a great system in many respect, certainly for its achievements in production and technology. The whole world recognizes those achievements. But it's not a system that is well designed for living within ecological limits because it's premised not only on endless economic growth but on endless envy.

There are other disadvantages: I don't see how you can sustain forever a system that is based on calling vice a virtue. I don't know of any other system that has tried to make greed a virtue. We all know that it's a trick, a trick we've tried to learn to play on ourselves, but I don't see how we can continue to fool ourselves that greed is a virtue or believe that we can find a virtuous society emerging from the pursuit of personal greed. In environmental terms it leads to endless emulation and endless envy, so that no matter how much you have you've got to have more to be worthy in the eyes of society. How can you sustain that in the desert? How can you sustain that in a shrinking biosphere?

THE MORMON COMMUNITARIAN EXPERIMENT TRIED TO MASTER NATURE THROUGH TECHNOLOGY, BUT IT WAS ALSO ANTI-CAPITALISTIC. WAS IT A FAILED ATTEMPT?

It represented an important exception to what was going on in the culture at that time. Mormons felt that the idea of turning vice into virtue was phony; I don't think they felt that way for environmental reasons, but their stance had important environmental implications. Maybe we will come back to such religious responses as the best way to deal with capitalism. I'm not personally convinced, however, that any traditional religion has been very successful in returning us to a sense of values. It may be that Christianity and all the religious traditions of the world still have the possibility of an important function here, and I would include Mormonism in that. But they will have to go a step further than they did in the nineteenth century. That is, Mormonism will have to correct its indifference to our ecological situation—the predicament we're in as far as resources—and will have to expand its old moral vision beyond the human community, to accept moral responsibility for the whole community of life on this planet, which includes a great deal more than the people sitting in church.

We cannot get an effective solution to any of our environmental problems—water scarcity and so forth—until we develop what Aldo Leopold called the "land ethic." That is not, as far as I can see, on the agenda of any of the traditional religions in this country. It's about time that they began to take the idea of a land ethic seriously and to expand their moral horizons—to grow ethically. That's one kind of growth I'm in favor of—ethical growth. The next step in such growth in the country must be to move beyond a narrow anthropocentricism in our attitude toward the land. I mean "land" in the collective sense—plants, animals, the soils, the river systems, the whole biosphere. We need to understand that now that we have power over the biosphere, we also must have moral responsibility. We must develop a community sense, a sense of mutual interaction and mutual benefit. This is what was missing in the nineteenth century generally, and what was missing in the Mormon experiment here in Utah. I don't mean to say having it would have changed things, but only that it just wasn't there. It wasn't a possibility for the culture at that point. It may be a possibility for the culture today, for Utah today and for Mormonism.

Since it was founded, Mormonism has been through some significant changes in its moral vision, and it seems to me that it is possible for people like Ezra Taft Benson and others to lead the Church to a land ethic; to lead others to become more ecocentric instead of anthropocentric. I see that not just as a Utopian ideal but as a practical necessity if we're to develop new ways of making a safe and sustainable living here in the West. I'm quite skeptical that our religions' leaders are willing to do that. Some of them are taking seriously our moral responsibility to the poor and suffering of the Third World, and that's a step forward. But I don't see many churchmen, many key religious leaders anywhere in this country, who really address the environmental and ecological issues. In Japan there are thousands of local environmental organizations, and many of them are led by Buddhist monks. It may be that the only way we can come up with a strong counterforce to our economic institutions is to use some sort of religious counterforce. If so, our religions do not yet appear ready or willing to do that.

Is this "religious counterforce" rooted in spiritual motivation?

Call it pantheism, call it bio-regional consciousness, there are lots of labels being thrown around. Call it an ecological consciousness. Some kind of *holism* is what I'm getting at. That is, a sense that there is a whole out there that includes more than the human species, and that it is in our own self-interest to develop a sense of that whole and a responsibility for it. Otherwise we will continue to have power without responsibility. That is what I see in our water projects all over the West: we've got enormous technological power without any kind of moral responsibility to everything that lives, that is a part of those river systems. We've abstracted water out of all those complex living systems, and we've denied moral responsibility for the consequences. So we have power without responsibility. That cannot go on very long in any culture or society. If you do not expand your ethics along with your power—your capacity to do harm—you self destruct. That's what the history of ethics on this planet teaches.

Does addressing water issues address all ecological issues?

Of course not everything. It wouldn't help us solve our problems with the grizzly bear population in Yellowstone, or a lot of other issues. But if we began to put water back into rivers, instead of extracting it as a commodity and ignoring the whole complex of ecological relations of which water is a part; if we began to think about rivers and watersheds and their limits and all that lives in them and the cycles in them, we would cover most of the issues affecting the American West today. I think it would be the single biggest step forward we could take. To see the West not simply as a struggle of Utah versus Arizona versus California over water, but to understand that the Colorado River was once a living entity, and to see that we've killed it, it's dead. There are bits and pieces of it that are struggling to stay alive, but it's "a river no more," as one author calls it. It never reaches the ocean in most years. We've dismantled a lot of living systems in the West, dismantled whole watersheds because we somehow couldn't conceive of them as whole entities. The same thing is true of the Missouri river, it's been totally taken apart. We thought we knew what we were doing, but there is an enormous illusion in all of this.

If we began to think about all of our major rivers in the West as living entities based around water but including all kinds of organisms, vegetation patterns, climate cycles, the whole complex of nature—in other words, if we began to think about them holistically—that would have a profound effect on the politics and economics of this region. Undoubtedly we'd begin to ask questions about the extent which the West has been committed to military and atomic development. All of that gets into the water in some way or another—radiation, for example—everything finally gets into the water. You can't think holistically about rivers without thinking about everything else that goes on in the West.. This is true in the East, too, but it is especially true out here where life is on the biological edge, where there are very strict limits to the key natural resource that life needs to sustain itself.

WHAT ABOUT THE PROMISE OF NEW TECHNOLOGICAL ADVANCES?

Every recent technological panacea we've come up with has encountered more and more problems as we began to deploy it. I do believe in new technologies; I'm just leery of big technological panaceas.

The latest one that is clearly a disaster is the nuclear power industry. It is the biggest failure in the history of industrial civilization. We now know that it is not going to be the great way to the future. Some people still won't accept that outcome, but, by and large, people all over the world are beginning to do so. It is an enormous failure in which we've invested hundreds of billions of dollars as a way out of our problems.

I can't believe that any administration in Washington is going to revive the project to turn around Arctic rivers to make them flow to Arizona. They would be in the U.S. and Canadian courts for decades trying to push that scheme through. It would involve so many complex issues, and there would be so many people angry about it, that it is just not going to be the way out.

We thought we could desalinize the ocean water; that sounded like a great scheme if we could build the nuclear power plants to provide endless energy to do it. Now, not only do we not have an energy source for the scheme, but we don't even know where we are going to dump all the brine we're going to have left over. Who's going to get it? Where is it going to go?

Yes, I think there is a need for new technologies, for some technological solutions. But like more and more Americans I am skeptical of these big solutions. Finally, I don't think we've got the capital surplus we once had. We're in an economic struggle with very powerful competitors in Western Europe, Japan, and East Asia; how are we going to find the capital to address that kind of competition and at the same time push forward these enormous water and energy projects? The projects we have now were begun at a time when we could ignore cost-effectiveness or any kind of rational economic analysis.

Suppose we don't adopt a holistic approach, how will we then deal with this approaching crisis?

If we fail to adapt and find new ways of producing a living, and if we don't get control of our numbers and demands, we'll simply disappear as a nation. Large numbers of people may actually die. The risks will get more and more scary.

Are we going to see violent mobs searching for food?

Not in the United States, because for a while we've got a comfortable surplus of food. But certainly in other parts of the world that will be the case. Especially if we simply seek short-term solutions to food supplies for the rest of the world, which would probably undermine our capacity to provide long-range food supplies. We've got to do both.

I'm not really a prophet of doom. I'm a little more optimistic than I may sound. I am a believer in the possibility of change. We're not the first society to face problems of depletion of resources and undermining our resource base. I teach environmental history, and if you look at the world from that perspective it seems clear to me that most societies have been driven by environmental and ecological constraints—demands to adapt and change their ways of thinking—to reinvent what they do. There are societies that have disappeared in the past, and we could face that fate in this country. If we believe that we have to go down with all of our economic solutions intact, all our water projects intact, then we'll probably disappear as a people. But I suspect that this country is a little more adaptive and flexible than that. We are already beginning to rethink most of these questions. I don't think there is much popular sentiment nationally, and less and less in the West, for building new water projects, although there's a sense that we've got to finish the projects we've started like the Central Utah Project. California is a bellwether state when it comes to water. Nobody knows what Los Angeles is going to do over the next fifty years, but the defeat of the Peripheral Canal, stopping the diversion of more water from Northern California, is clear evidence that Californians are not going to follow old patterns. The states are not going to come up with the money on their own for big projects, and the Federal government certainly is not going to do it.

So we're adopting the holistic view only because we have to?

It may be that when we look back fifty or a hundred years from now we will see that we lived through a cultural revolution. We wouldn't have wanted to call it that at the time, of course.

As far as urban centers are concerned, there's enough water in the West to sustain urban development for some time to come. The people who are not going to get more water in the future, who are going to be forced to sell their existing water, are the farmers. What we'll do then with that water, until we learn differently, will be to build more swimming pools and do less irrigating of cotton. But already researchers are working on new varieties of grass that require half as much water. We won't give up our lawns, but we won't be growing Kentucky Blue Grass in L.A. We will search every way we can to find solutions. We've done rather well in energy conservation, and we can do even better in water conservation in the West, and that will stave off any absolute growth ceiling for a while.

Most people won't do much adapting strictly out of total altruism for the whole ecosphere. I don't have any faith in pure altruism to find our way to the future, but I do think altruism will be part of the solution. There is a growing sense of responsibility to the land and other forms of life in this country. It may not be the only reason we do things, it may not even be the most important reason. Sometimes, it is true, we give reasons that are really not the real reason—we give economic reasons when we want to give moral reasons. But I have no quarrel with the idea that we are likely to find our way to the future through economic pressures changing our economic thinking, that there will be a lot of fundamental self-interest at work. I see nothing wrong with self-interest being a factor. If it is self-interest to develop a broader holistic vision, then I don't find any real contradiction.

How would self-interest move us toward greater responsibility toward other animals?

Probably the biggest environmental issue on this planet right now is the loss of biological diversity. And most of that is happening in the Third World through the destruction of the rain forest. Preserving biological diversity on this planet is a moral and altruistic ideal, but it is also in our self-interest. I don't mean to say that every plant we save is going to contain a cure for cancer, but arguments like that are part of the self-interest aspect. We can't separate our health and well being on this planet from the survival and health of so many other organisms and whole communities of organisms. In the past we have thought that our self-interest was totally insulated from the well being and survival of other species, that if we eliminated the passenger pigeon in North America it didn't affect us, that we could do these things with impunity. Maybe we're more aware than we were in the nineteenth century. When we lose a species, it has become a moral issue and we see that it can affect us; it can affect our future and our survival on this planet.

Some Christians take the biblical commands to tend the garden and to have dominion over the earth as an active stewardship of responsibility for nature.

There are people who criticize the idea of stewardship because it is nothing more than enlightened anthropocentricism. That is, it still tends to assume that the earth was created for humans and their welfare. Also, with that sort of thinking the creation becomes a piece of property. The concept of stewardship comes out of a lord and master social world, where the steward was commanded to look after the lord's property to ensure that when he came back it would be in good shape, humming along and producing. Of course, one doesn't have to approach stewardship in so property-conscious a way. Stewardship, for all its faults, would certainly be an advance over what we have now; it would be a form of moral responsibility.

I don't go as far as some critics who believe that our environmental problems today are due to the Book of Genesis. That's much too simplistic. The Judeo-Christian tradition got bent pretty far out of shape by the rise of modern technology, industrialism, and capitalism, and themes of domination were given a lot more emphasis than they had received in the traditional religion. The Christian concept of the natural world is essentially the concept of the Creation—and that's a holistic concept. The Creation is a whole. You can take the view that the whole has got to be understood and appreciated, valued and saved. If that's what one means by stewardship then it seems about as effective as anything else we could invent or create.

I'm a little more nervous about the idea of stewardship as a chain of hierarchy, because that way of thinking seems to be full of possibilities for exploitation. What we need is a much more democratic sense of our relationship to that whole, one that does not place us near the top of a chain of being, somewhere between the angels and the apes, enjoying a special privilege to use and appropriate. I think the direction that we must move is toward a more egalitarian relationship with the natural world. If stewardship can be expanded to include that, then I think it's a useful teaching.

What about other religious traditions?

The other religions have not seen much thinking about our environmental predicament. I mentioned the Japanese Buddhist monks leading environmental causes, but Japan has also been driving the whales to extinction. They've been polluting the world. Recently, I read about a group of Japanese businessmen who want to set up a penguin hide factory in Patagonia and make penguin gloves to sell to American teenagers. Apparently, this is going to be a hot new consumer item. A lot of Buddhist businessmen, like their Christian counterparts, have not yet begun to see the contradictions in what they're doing. We've got to get some new awareness of our responsibility awakened in many religious traditions.

Islam has great potential for taking moral responsibility toward the earth, but I don't find the Moslems who are eager to sell oil to the rest of the world and to bring Kentucky Fried Chicken into their countries have discovered that potential. There has been little self-analysis about how to enter a capitalistic economy, little asking how they can build an industrial society and still maintain their traditional moral insights, let alone strengthen them and allow them to grow.

I don't see most of the world's religious leaders doing all that they could to promote this holistic point of view and vision. In the future, the even larger challenge is going to be: How can we move from our multiplicity of religious traditions to a common environmental ethic? That is clearly what we will need. It is too small a planet these days for people to simply go off in completely different, conflicting moral directions. We've got to come together on some sort of planetary consciousness and planetary environmental ethic. Traditionally our ethics have grown out of our religious traditions. But if our religious traditions continue to be as disparate as they have been, then we have to wonder what language we are going to use to talk about these things. We have lots of such communication trouble in this country. Try inviting a Protestant clergyman, a Jewish rabbi, a Catholic priest and a Mormon bishop to discuss these issues: "Give us an answer as to what we are going to do with water in Utah or with endangered species in Alaska." "Tell us what the earth was made for." "What is the proper role of humans on earth?" You know what chaos that is likely to produce. I don't know how we get beyond such chaos except by sitting around and talking at great length and by finding common ground within these moral traditions. The environmental issues of this country require that sort of discussion. We simply can't withdraw into our different religious sects and expect each of them to come up with its own environmental ethic based on its own tradition. You can look at the abortion issue and see what kind of difficulties there are in trying to reach a consensus among these religious traditions. It's a serious dilemma we're facing, and when you stretch that to the world it's going to be even more serious. How does an American environmentalist raised in a Protestant tradition, for example, talk to a Japanese businessman about whaling?

We Americans have had an extraordinarily confused answer to give to the question of our role in the natural world. We have not yet come up with a single clear, satisfactory answer. Still, the discussion has moved a long way from what it was when the Puritans arrived in Massachusetts. At least we're much more aware of the many dimensions of the question than we ever were before.

Whatever will emerge, it will have to be pluralistic. It will have to involve a pulling together from various places. This is not the first time we've tackled difficult issues or confronted our differences. We're a diverse nation, racially, ethnically, regionally, and yet we somehow function. We've learned ways to talk to each other. That's what democratic societies are about—that's what democratic pluralism is. An environmental ethic is something we have to find collectively.

*

Zion in Eden: Phases of the Environmental History of Utah

DAN L. FLORES

Utah has faced increasingly serious environmental problems for a long time; however, according to Dan Flores in the following article, present-day Utah is "less open to environmental sympathies than almost any other part of the Mountain West." He asks the question, "What does it take to develop and act on an environmental ethic?" His answer, based on his interpretation of the history of environmental attitudes and practices in Utah, is this: "Either we must find a religious tradition capable of imparting spiritual force to empirical ecological realities, or else make our environmentalism a religion."

Dan L. Flores, "Zion in Eden: Phases of the Environmental History of Utah," *Environmental Review* 7 (Winter 1983), pp. 325–44. Reprinted by permission of the publisher and the author.

Dan L. Flores teaches history at the University of Montana. He is the author of *Canyon Visions: Photographs and Pastels of the Texas Plains* and *Caprock Canyonlands: Journeys into the Heart of the Southern Plains,* and he is editor of *Journal of an Indian Trader: Anthony Glass and the Texas Trading Frontier, 1790–1810.*

> SALT LAKE CITY—Gov. Scott Matheson and Senate President Cap Ferry, R-Corinne, squared off for their much-heralded debate . . . over disagreements between the Democratic governor and the Republican-dominated Legislature as to the best way to deal with the state's flooding problems.
>
> *The Herald Journal,* August 18, 1983

> That man is, in fact, only a member of a biotic team is shown by an ecological interpretation of history. Many historical events, hitherto explained solely in terms of human enterprise, were actually biotic interactions between people and land.
>
> Aldo Leopold, *A Sand County Almanac*

IN SEEKING TO DISCOVER the causes of modern ecological dilemmas, the environmental movement of the past two decades has developed a penetrating critique of a number of mainstream American institutions. Historians Lynn White, Jr., and Roderick Nash, for example, have identified the Judeo-Christian religious ethic, which places man at the center of a subservient biosphere, as central to the development of environmental callousness and mismanagement.[1] Philosopher Eugene Hargrove has argued that western, Lockean property concepts are too exclusive to permit the emergence of an ecologically sound society.[2] Yet another historian, Donald Worster, in a recent study, lays the responsibility for a major environmental disaster, the Dust Bowl of the 1930's, on capitalism's relentless drive for profits.[3] While disposed to trace many current problems to technology and scientific specialization, ecologist and political figure Barry Commoner, in a number of widely-read books, also portrays capitalism as disharmonious with ecological values.[4] Thus mainstream environmental philosophy in the United States finds itself largely in sympathy with government ownership and strong legal restraints on private development of national resources, while the environmental left openly urges communal, "ecotopian" institutions.[5]

Environmental historians can point for documentation of these views to the example of the American West. Initially settled between 1865 and 1900, the heyday of laissez-faire economic doctrines, the West appears to offer in its history a portentous example of unplanned, wasteful, disruptive, and undemocratic natural resources exploitation.[6]

Many questions yet remain unanswered, however, with respect to the environmental history of western America. For example, given the institu-

---

[1]Lynn White, Jr., "The Historical Roots of Our Ecologic Crisis," *Science* 155 (March 1967): 1203–7; Roderick Nash, *Wilderness and the American Mind* (New Haven, 1973, revised edition), pp. 13–20. See also James Barr, "Man and Nature: The Ecological Controversy and the Old Testament," Rene Dubos, "Franciscan Conservation versus Benedictine Stewardship," and Arnold Toynbee, "The Religious Background of the Present Environmental Crisis," in David and Eileen Spring, eds., *Ecology and Religion in History* (New York, 1974).

[2]Eugene Hargrove, "Anglo-American Land-use Attitudes," *Environmental Ethics* 2 (Summer 1980): 121–148.

[3]Donald Worster, *Dust Bowl: The Southern Plains in the 1930's* (New York, 1979). Worster's book won the Bancroft Prize in 1979.

[4]Barry Commoner, *The Closing Circle: Nature, Man & Technology* (New York, 1971), pp. 253–259.

[5]See Joseph Petulla, *American Environmentalism: Issues, Tactics, and Priorities* (College Station, Texas, 1980). Mark Satin's *New Age Politics* (New York, 1978) includes a "new age" political platform (chapter 24), based largely on Friends of the Earth philosophy for its environmental sections. Influenced by E. F. Schumacher's *Small Is Beautiful* (New York, 1973), many radical environmentalists advocate decentralization and community control, to which Barry Commoner's environmentalist Citizen's Party paid lip-service in the presidential election of 1980. Mainstream environmental groups still place their faith in a strong, centralized approach to dealing with environmental problems.

[6]Stuart Chase, *Rich Land, Poor Land: A Study of Waste in the Natural Resources of America* (New York, 1936); Roy Robbins, *Our Landed Heritage: The Public Domain, 1776–1970* (Lincoln, Nebraska, 1976, revised edition).

tional complex and cultural trends, was it actually possible to have had a planned, egalitarian society, let alone a non-exploitive one, on the American frontier of the 19th century? Necessarily lacking today's environmental grasp, how successful would such a society have been in modern ecological terms? And finally, has the modern federal policy of attempting to educate Westerners to the ecological realities of the region, with its arid plains and deserts surrounding high mountain oases, been the most successful approach to creating a stable western civilization?

While contemporary trends in the West enable us to address the last of these questions only tentatively, it is possible to explore the two former questions more fully. For a colonizing group with some of these ideals did exist in the 19th century American West and for nearly half a century it brought to bear upon one of the most ecologically sensitive regions of North America a set of values much in line with modern environmental philosophy. This society was created by members of a religious sect known as the Mormons, who in 1847 initiated a series of settlements along the western edge of the Rocky Mountains, centering in present Utah. Their experiences provide us with a model from which to speak to the hypotheses of present environmental philosophy.

Founded by Joseph Smith of upstate New York in the 1820's, the Mormon Church (or Church of Jesus Christ of the Latter-day Saints, as the preferred) emerged in America at a time when utopian, communal, and socialistic experimentation was widespread. These influences on Smith's pronouncements have been well-documented: one of his close collaborators in the early years of the church, Sidney Rigdon, was an intellectual reformer who had been involved in several communal experiments in the Midwest.[7] The societal plan which emerged from Smith's one hundred or more "revelations" (some of which were canonized in *The Doctrine and Covenants*) featured the essence of the liberal thought of the time. The Law of Consecration and Stewardship (later a basis for the Mormon communal societies of the United Order) attempted to establish a socialism for the Saints by conveying all individual wealth to the church, which would then redistribute it according to need.[8] After an initial experiment with this doctrine in the Midwestern Mormon communities it was abandoned, although some of its principles were tried sparingly in the West. But its existence in the early doctrines did pave the way for a number of radical doctrines which were widely promulgated in Utah. The two most important of these from an environmental perspective were church stewardship over natural resources and the communalism practiced by Mormon pioneers, who endeavored to

[7]Leonard J. Arrington, "Mormon Economic Policies and Their Implementation on the Western Frontier, 1847–1900" (Ph.D. diss., University of North Carolina, 1952), pp. 96–97. The best survey study of Mormon cooperation is Leonard J. Arrington, Feramorz Y. Fox, and Dean May, *Building The City of God* (Salt Lake City: Deseret Book Co., 1976).

[8]". . . if ye are not equal in earthly things ye cannot be equal in obtaining heavenly things." *The Doctrine and Covenants of the Church of Jesus Christ of Latter-day Saints* (Salt Lake City, 1921 edition), 76: 6.

prepare for the Millennium by creating a society ("Zion") which, working collectively under divine guidance, would cleanse and beautify a "cursed earth" through a "pragmatic mastery of the forces of nature."[9]

The opportunity to try these ideas in a virgin setting did not come before Smith's death. But he was ably succeeded by Brigham Young, a pragmatist who nonetheless shared Smith's utopian concerns. Hounded and persecuted in the Midwest, by 1846 the Mormons were considering an emigration to Texas, Oregon, California, even Vancouver Island. But in May of 1844, explorer John C. Fremont had returned from an expedition to California by way of the Great Basin, and at the foot of the Wasatch Front had found "a region of great pastoral promise abounding with fine streams . . . [and] soil that would produce wheat," although "this fertility of soil and vegetation does not extend far into the Great Basin."[10] Before his death, Smith had written in his diary that he had dreamed that "the Saints . . . would be driven to . . . [and] become a mighty people in the midst of the Rocky Mountains."[11] Given that prophecy and the desired isolation of the Wasatch Front, when Fremont's report was read to the assembled Mormon Quorum, the issue was settled. The American "Great Trek" was about to begin.

In order to understand the environmental history which follows, it is necessary to establish, with as much scientific precision as possible, the ecological outlines of the setting which the Mormon pioneers entered when they emerged from Emigration Canyon in the late summer of 1847. Fortunately, a number of accurate first-hand accounts, as well as subsequent studies by ecologists, exist to make this possible.

The environment of the region pioneered by the Mormons was the result of both natural and man-made forces which had been at work for tens

[9]It is not clear whether the Mormons saw themselves, and Utah, in Old Testament terms before the migration, but in the later Mormon mythology which Young and other church leaders consciously sought to promote, they came to. In time the Mormons saw themselves as emulating the ancient Hebrews, who had viewed the arid plains of the Middle East as cursed wilderness (Genesis, 3:17, 18) the antithesis of the green, lush "Garden" from which man had been expelled (Genesis, 2:9). Both the name "Zion" and Young's promise that the Lord would help the Saints transform the environment of the Wasatch Front came from the Book of Isaiah (51:3): "For the Lord shall comfort Zion; he will comfort all her waste places; and he will make her wilderness like Eden, and her desert like the garden of the Lord." Time evidently dimmed the very favorable first impression the Wasatch Front made on the Mormon Pioneers, setting the stage for the Mormon mythology of environmental transformation, with Young invoking these images: "We had to leave our homes and possessions on the fertile plains of Illinois to make our dwelling places in these desert wilds, on barren, sterile plains amid lofty, rugged mountains." And later: "We were the first to plant our orchards and to improve this desert country, making it like the Garden of Eden." *Journal of Discourses* 26 vols. (Liverpool, 1852–1886), XX, p. 233; XIX, p. 60.

[10]Donald Jackson and Mary Spence, eds., *The Expeditions of John Charles Fremont,* 3 vols. (Urbana, 1970–1973), I, p. 695.

[11]As Richard H. Jackson has shown in his fine dissertation, "Myth and Reality: Environmental Perceptions of The Mormons, 1840–1865, An Historical Geosophy" (Ph.D. diss., Clark University, Worcester, Mass., 1970), contrary to Mormon mythology, both Young and Joseph Smith had carefully studied the records of early trappers and explorers in the Rockies. Brigham Young knew the Wasatch Front was "the place" long before the migration of 1847. See Jackson, pp. 56–86.

of thousands of years. The setting was dominated by the massive Wasatch Range, the product of nearly 300 million years of uplift, erosion, faulting, and sedimentation.[12] Stretching like a wall more than 200 miles north and south, and rising to elevations exceeding 12,000 feet, the Wasatch was rent by a series of structural troughs which had been carved into steep canyons by water and glaciers. To the westward through these tumbled sparkling rivers which the Anglo-Americans would name Bear, Ogden, Weber, Provo, Jordan, and Sevier, as well as dozens of smaller streams.

Rivaling the mountains in importance were the contours of the basin floor which abutted them. Nearly perfectly flat out away from the mountains, the basin was the legacy of ancient Lake Bonneville, a gigantic freshwater lake produced from the melt of the Wisconsin Age glaciers. Over thousands of years Lake Bonneville had alternately risen and fallen to create a series of lakeshore terraces on the Wasatch and on the smaller Oquirrh Range twenty-five miles to the west, as well as numerous deltas and benches where the rivers had spilled their sediments into the lake. As the climate became warmer and drier, Lake Bonneville had shrunk to a salty remnant without drainage—the Great Salt Lake. But it had left deposited along the Transition Zone of the Wasatch a narrow, rich, alluvial piedmont of fans, deltas, and terraces, through which meandered the sweet, clear water of the mountains.[13]

A rain shadow cast by the Sierra Nevada to the west produced desert conditions in the basin itself, with fewer than five inches of precipitation annually. But the Wasatch, thrusting up at right angles to prevailing winds, formed an orographic barrier to induce precipitation, so that the narrow Transition Zone at its base received 13 to 18 inches, and the high mountains up to 50 in most years. The great bulk of the precipitation on the highlands fell as snow, and its melting annually sent from 8 to 10 million acre-feet of water surging through the drainage in late spring and early summer.[14] Local convectional cells formed over the mountains in summer to produce often violent rainstorms (at intensities up to eight inches per hour for short periods). Yet the thickly-vegetated watersheds handled these without problems in the natural setting.[15]

The altitude and precipitation zones effected a corresponding zonation of soils, and hence biological life. In the high mountains were chernozem

[12]For the geologic history of the Central Rockies, see Philip King, *Evolution of North America* (Princeton, 1959), pp. 90–128.

[13]W. E. Coffman, "The Geography of the Utah Valley Crescent" (Ph.D. diss., Ohio State University, 1944), pp. 10, 24; Wasatch Front Regional Council, *Historical Settlement and Population Patterns Along the Wasatch Front* (Bountiful, Utah, 1976), pp. 1–2; Wallace Stegner, "Dead Heart of the West: Reflections on the Great Salt Lake," *Rocky Mountain Magazine* 3 (November 1981): 56–59

[14]Elmo Coffman, "Our Resources," Ralph Woolley, "Our Resources—Water," Reed Bailey, "Utah's Watersheds," in *Proceedings, Utah Academy of Sciences, Arts and Letters* 25 (1947–48): 24–25, 36.

[15]*Historical Settlement and Population Patterns Along the Wasatch Front,* p. 4; Coffman, "Geography of the Utah Valley Crescent," pp. 34–35, 40.

soils that were dark and humus-rich but often rocky, while on the flats below, where the drainage had brought the salts down, alkaline sierozem soils prevailed. Between these, the deltas and fans at the bases of the mountains featured sandy, porous chestnut soils, fertile and rich in lime.[16]

Combined with the diversity of altitudes and precipitation, these soils grew a remarkable array of vegetation which, from the reports of early observers, ecologists are now able to reconstruct. On the tops of the mountains the elevation and short growing season produced an alpine tundra featuring short sedges, dwarf bluegrass and wheatgrass. Below the tundra lay the narrow Hudsonian Zone, occupied by elfinwood timber where Engelmann spruce was the chief dominant. Lower down there existed the montane forest of the Canadian Zone, where ponderosa pine, lodgepole pine, and Douglas firs predominated, with interspersed meadows of tall grasses such as Letterman needlegrass and beardless wheatgrass. In the canyons and on the lower slopes there existed a diversified understory, of which the Utah juniper was most important. The Transition Zone benches and valley were largely carpeted with tall, waving wheatgrasses and bluegrasses and a variety of forbs. Less than 20% of this original Transition Zone flora were shrubs (such as big sagebrush and rabbitbrush). Salt-tolerant shrubs such as greasewood were the principal flora of the desert basin.[17] Most of the principal native fauna of the region, including bighorn sheep, wapiti, mule deer, pronghorn antelope, and white-tailed jackrabbit, ranged over the entire region, the larger ungulates often migrating from one biome zone to another with the changing seasons. In contrast, the black-tailed jackrabbit was confined to the desert floor, while Utah grizzly, black bear, moose, and mountain bison ranged only in the mountains and high valley meadows.[18]

A question of increasing ecological interest is the role American Indians played in modifying the environment of North America. The evidence is

[16]Ibid., pp. 76–77; James Carley, et al., "A Soil Survey and Soil Interpretations of Ogden Valley, *Utah Agricultural Experiment Station Research Reports, No. 14* (1973); "Report of the Secretary of the Interior," *House Exec. Doc. No. 1*, 34th Cong., 3d sess., pp. 546–47.

[17]Although the primary documents exist to do it here and elsewhere in the Mountain West, excellent work by Utah scientists on historical ecology has made it unnecessary for the author to re-create the pre-settlement ecology from the original sources. See, for example: Early M. Christensen and Myrtis A. Hutchinson, "Historical Observations on the Ecology of Rush and Tooele Valleys, Utah," *Utah Academy Proceedings* 42 (1965): 90–105; A.C. Hull, Jr., and Mary Kay Hull, "Presettlement Vegetation on Cache Valley, Utah and Idaho," *Journal of Range Management* 27 (January 1974): 27–29; Walter P. Cottam, "An Ecological Study of the Flora of Utah Lake, Utah" (Ph.D. diss., University of Chicago, 1926); Richard D. Guyom, "Ecological History and Biological Resources of San Juan County, Utah" (M.A. thesis, University of Utah, 1964); Heber H. Hall, "The Impact of Man on the Vegetation and Soil of the Upper Valley Allotment, Garfield County, Utah" (M.A. thesis, University of Utah, 1954); and John H. Wakefield, "A Study of the Plant Ecology of Salt Lake and Utah Valleys Before the Mormon Immigration" (M.A. thesis, Brigham Young University, 1933).

[18]See Christensen and Hutchinson, "Historical Observations on the Ecology of Rush and Tooele Valleys, Utah," 99–103; and, for original range of the faunal subspecies herein indicated, E. Raymond Hall and Keith R. Kelson, *The Mammals of North America*, 2 vols. (New York, 1959). For both floral and faunal climax dominants, see Victor E. Shelford, *The Ecology of North America* (Urbana, 1963), pp. 152–68.

clear that men and women had lived on the flanks of the Wasatch for at least 10,000 years prior to the coming of the Mormons. At first, they were hunters who stalked and killed the megafauna of the Pleistocene age; these were replaced by the Basket Makers, who practiced an archaic way of life; and by A.D. 1,000 by the agriculturalists known as the Anasazi. These peoples were themselves replaced by Shoshonean peoples—ancestors of the Utes and Paiutes encountered by the Mormons. Indian religious enspiritualization of nature played a role in their treatment of the Utah environment, but a biodegradable technology and population constraints imposed by hunter-gatherer subsistence were also important. Instructively, the one population of farmers was unable to maintain colonies in Utah. The natural swings of a climate already marginal for agriculture, along with localized overpopulation and soil exhaustion, most likely were the causes of the Anasazi evacuation of the Utah area.[19]

All these peoples utilized fire as a hunting practice and to produce succulent pasturage for game, leading, it is believed, to far-reaching ecological results along the Wasatch Front. The highly-respected Utah ecologist Walter Cottam has argued that through the use of fire, Indians were able to maintain, against the true bench and foothill climax of shrubs and junipers, a relict population of grasses from an earlier, wetter age.[20]

Into this centuries-old environment, with its delicate balance of water, slope, vegetation, and fire, stepped more than 1,600 Anglo-American farmers, with 30,000 cattle and "an immense number of sheep," and armed with the unusual cultural baggage of Mormonism.[21] Interestingly for environmental history, as Richard Jackson has shown, the impression of the early Mormon pioneers was not of a "desert," but of "the most fertile valley . . . clothed with a heavy garment of vegetation."[22] To people used to the prairies and woods of Illinois and Missouri, this mountain country must have seemed strange and incomprehensible. But under Young's leadership the Mormons threw themselves zealously into the task of colonizing Utah, thus proving that in communal action there existed an alternative to the capital-

[19]Jesse D. Jennings, *Prehistory of North America* (New York, 1968), pp. 183, 264, 274–76; Jesse D. Jennings and Edward Norbeck, eds., *Prehistoric Man, in the New World* (Chicago, 1964), p. 162; James H. Gunnerson, "Plateau Shoshonean Prehistory: A Suggested Reconstruction," *American Antiquity* 28 (July 1962): 44; David Madsen, et al., "Man, Mammoth, and Lake Fluctuations in Utah," *University of Utah Antiquities Section Selected Papers*, No. 5 (1977); Ross T. Christensen, "On the Prehistory of Utah Valley," *Proceedings, Utah Academy of Science, Arts and Letters* 25 (1947–48): 101–9; Ralph V. Chamberlain, "Man and Nature in Early Utah," *Proceedings, Utah Academy of Science, Arts and Letters* 24 (1946–47): 3–22.

[20]Walter P. Cottam, "The Impact of Man on the Flora of the Bonneville Basin" (Salt Lake City, 1961), pamphlet housed in Special Collections, Milton R. Merrill Library, Utah State University, Logan. Cottam cites primary documents on Indian fire ecology, pointing out the fact that both big sagebrush and Utah juniper are fire intolerant.

[21]Leonard J. Arrington, *Great Basin Kingdom: An Economic History of the Latter-Day Saints, 1830–1900* (Cambridge, 1958), p. 18.

[22]Wilford Woodruff, "Journal," entry for July 24, 1847, quoted in Jackson, "Myth and Reality: Environmental Perceptions of the Mormons," p. 168. See, for a discussion, pp. 151–73.

istic order which worked, as Young put it, "to make a few rich, and to sink the masses of the people in poverty and degradation."[23]

With their centralized leadership and their belief that the earth and all its products were the property of a divine entity,[24] the Mormon brand of stewardship was at once less theoretical than Christian stewardship as it is generally understood: individual Mormons, for example, held ceremonies dedicating land and projects to the divinity. Additionally, the doctrine of continuing revelation was not only a boon for coping with a new environment, but endowed church decrees on natural resources with the power of supernatural sanction. The Mormons thus provide the closest American example of the Judeo-Christian stewardship ethic, or the "Abrahamic Land Concept," in action on a pristine frontier.

Mormon stewardship modified the Lockean view of private property use. The earth could not be "owned," but it could be occupied temporarily provided the occupant "improved" it, or used it "beneficially." To Mormon thinking this meant changing the natural order to make it more productive of the things most useful to themselves. Land, it was decreed, must be distributed democratically, and members were even expected to give over part of theirs if a project or a new arrival needed it. Between 1847 and 1869 the church assigned parcels of usually no more than twenty acres by drawing and petition.[25] These small plots were a clear recognition that arable lands were limited in Zion, although such Jeffersonianism was also encouraged by the irrigation which made their mountain benchland farming possible.

The mountain topography of the country they now inhabited had left the areas receiving the most adequate rainfall too high and rocky to farm. To combine the water of the highlands with the fertile land below, the Mormons followed the lead of both Indians and Spaniards in North America. In this way the Wasatch environment reinforced their yen for communal action, for irrigation was an intimidating undertaking for even the most of rugged of individualists. The church leaders also borrowed certain features of Hispanic water law, specifically public ownership combined with a priority right of diversion for users. It planned and controlled the collective construction of canals and laterals, and the allotment of water. An early historian of

[23]*Journal of Discourses,* II, p. 348. Mere subsistence obviously was not the goal of this co-operation: "If we will work unitedly, we can work ourselves into wealth, health, prosperity and power . . . " Ibid., XII, p. 376.

[24]See *Doctrine and Covenants,* sec. 104: 13–18, 55–56. Young's pronouncements were consistent with those of Smith on stewardship and cooperation: "There is any amount of property, and gold and silver in the earth . . . and the Lord gives to this one and that one . . . but it all belongs to Him. . . . No person on earth can truly call anything his own . . . " And on cooperation: "This co-operative movement is only a stepping stone to what is called the Order of Enoch, but which is in reality the Order of Heaven." *Journal of Discourses,* XVI, p. 10; IX, p. 106; XIII, p. 2.

[25]Leonard J. Arrington, "Property Among the Mormons," *Rural Sociology* 18 (December 1951): 345; and Feramorz Y. Fox, "The Mormon Land System: A Study of the Settlement and Utilization of Land Under the Direction of the Mormon Church" (Ph.D. diss., Northwestern University, 1937).

institutions called these projects "one of the greatest and most successful community or cooperative undertakings in the history of America."[26]

Centralized control over land and water also extended to other major resources, notably timber and grass, and even minerals. As Young told a band of new arrivals in 1847:

> There shall be no private ownership of the streams that come out of the canyons, nor the timber that grows on the hills. These belong to the people: all the people.[27]

Timber was obviously sparse compared to the Eastern conditions the Mormons had known, and it was much more difficult of access. Using it sensibly necessitated restraint. After a brief experiment with unfettered use, the church decided to grant monopolies, or concessions, to responsible persons who would open roads onto the slopes. The extent of this regulation went beyond the charge of a toll for road use, for in 1851 a territorial ordinance established the rather stupendous fine of $1,000 for anyone convicted of wasting or burning timber. Yet full use was implied, and since there were no attempts at reseeding, the stands of lodgepole and ponderosa pine and douglas fir were drawn down quickly by the steady increase in population.[28]

With grass the approach was similar, and oriented more towards democratic distribution than conservation.[29] The herding of stock communally did eliminate competitive use of the range so long as the Mormons had only themselves to compete against. Yet Mormon stockmen, possibly somewhat bewildered by the strangeness of the Mountain West, with its complicated arrangement of life and water zones, appear to have overgrazed much of their country rather quickly. The Indians first voiced concern over the decline of grass for game herds in the 1850's. By the 1860's, the Mormons themselves were uneasy over its scarcity.[30]

Mormon communities, unlike those which sprang up elsewhere in the Mountain West, were not organized around exploitation of only one resource, but made use of a variety of natural products. Parley P. Pratt's scout-

[26]George Thomas, *Development of Institutions Under Irrigation with Special Reference to Early Utah Conditions* (New York, 1920), p. 27.

[27]B. H. Roberts, *A Comprehensive History of the Church of Jesus Christ of Latter-Day Saints,* 6 vols. (Salt Lake City, 1930), III, p. 269.

[28]Arrington, "Property Among the Mormons," 348. The Territorial Ordinance of 1850, signed by Governor Brigham Young, is reprinted in George Stewart, "Utah's Biological Heritage and the Need for its Conservation," *Proceedings, Utah Academy of Science, Arts and Letters* 25 (1947–48), 7–8. See also, Ezra C. Knowlton, *History of Highway Development in Utah* (Salt Lake City, 1967), p. 24. At first Young also determined that his constituency should use "Dead Wood" for fuel so as "to foster the growth of timber." Roberts, *A Comprehensive History of the Saints,* III, p. 269. This must have become impractical rather early on.

[29]Arrington, "Mormon Economic Policies and Their Implementation on the Western Frontier," p. 178.

[30]Works Progress Administration History of Grazing Collection, 1690–1941. Special Collections, Milton R. Merrill Library, Utah State University, Logan. Box 15, Folder 2. See also note 35.

ing parties ranged up and down the Wasatch Front in search of suitable Transition Zone sites where later farm villages (or "stakes") could be begun. This farm village community pattern was particularly suited to the mountain frontier, although the idea predated the move west, coming from Joseph Smith's "Plat of the City of Zion," itself evolving as a utopianist adaptation of the New England village. Church policies respecting natural resources were handled regionally by Stake Presidents and Councils, and locally by the ward bishop, a necessary delegation of powers given the distances and transportation facilities. Far from being independent and self-sufficient city-states, however, the farm villages were actually cogs in a societal economic network. By 1900 nearly 500 of them had been established along the western slope of the Rockies, extending even into Arizona and Idaho.[31]

Out of step with the spirit of laissez-faire which came to characterize American society during the post–Civil War years, the Mormons struggled against outsiders, and themselves, to remain uncontaminated. Brigham Young remained unyielding. During the 1870's he resurrected the communism of Smith's early theories by starting several United Order colonies—small, self-sufficient, entirely communal villages—and as late as 1868 held before the Saints this vision of collectivism:

> I have looked upon the community of Saints in vision and beheld them organized as one great family of heaven . . . working for the good of the whole more than one individual aggrandizement; and in this I have beheld the most beautiful order that the mind of man can contemplate . . .[32]

For a variety of reasons, however, the communal, egalitarian society advocated by the early church leaders began to crumble during the 1870's. "Gentiles" who found Mormon ways authoritarian and un-American began passing through Utah regularly as early as 1849, and with the completion of the transcontinental railroad in 1869 arrived in numbers which soon rivaled the Mormon presence. Forced increasingly to compete for resources with them, many Mormons (such as the Godbeite organization of Mormon Businessmen) lost their affection for egalitarianism. When Young's death in 1877 removed the major advocate of the old order, Mormons in Utah began a process of "Americanization" (which one author has compared to Southern Reconstruction) that ended in 1896 with Utah's statehood and an almost complete incorporation into the laissez-faire American mainstream.

[31]Lowery Nelson, *The Mormon Village: A Pattern and Technique of Land Settlement* (Salt Lake City, 1962), pp. xv, 11, 26–27, 38–40, 53; Joel E. Ricks, *Forms and Methods of Early Mormon Settlement in Utah and the Surrounding Region, 1847 to 1877* (Logan, 1964); Lynn A. Rosenvall, "Defunct Mormon Settlements: 1830–1930," in Richard Jackson, ed., *The Mormon Role in the Settlement of the West* (Provo, 1978), p. 60.

[32]*Journal of Discourses,* XII, p. 153. On United Order settlements, see Leonard J. Arrington, *Orderville, Utah: A Pioneer Mormon Experiment in Economic Organization* (Logan, 1954), and Feramorz Y. Fox, *Experiments in Cooperation and Social Security Among the Mormons: A Study of Joseph Smith's Order of Stewardship and Consecration, and Brigham Young's United Order* (Salt Lake City, 1937).

Although separation of church and state and abandonment of plural marriage were the most symbolic reforms required to "bring the territory into conformity with national standards," Americanization also meant a tacit recognition that resource use was a matter of competition rather than planning.[33]

Although Leonard J. Arrington, the dean of Utah historians, has asserted that Mormon resource policy "seems to have protected Utah from the abuses and wastes which characterized many frontier communities in the West," from the perspective of environmental health, Utah's very landscape, read as an historical document, indicates otherwise. Even before the rush of individualistic Gentiles into the territory, the sensitive setting of the Western Rockies was showing signs of deterioration. In its efforts to provide for the growing numbers of converts by making "the desert bloom as the rose," the Mormons quite clearly overstrained the Wasatch environment.[34] Accustomed to Eastern conditions, lacking scientific knowledge of plant succession, or of the relationship between water, vegetation, and slope; forced increasingly to both provide for larger numbers and compete for resources with non-Mormons, the church did not develop an adequate land ethic. Its doctrine provided for egalitarian resource distribution, but by its own definition, it was no longer using Zion beneficially, for Zion land was becoming yearly less productive and more unstable. Rather than taking a desert and making it bloom like the rose, the Mormons had settled lush mountain valleys which now were in danger of being overgrown with pigweed and juniper, and inundated in flood debris.

The consequences of disrupting the natural stability seem not to have occurred to many Mormons, but one who did worry was Orson Hyde. Addressing the General Conference of Saints in 1865, Hyde invoked both profit and stewardship as reasons why the Mormons should promote the conservation of their grass:

> I find the longer we live in these valleys that the range is becoming more and more destitute of grass; the grass is . . . eaten up by the great amount of stock . . . and where once grew luxuriantly there is now nothing but the desert weed . . . There is not profit in this, neither is it pleasing in the sight of God . . . that we should continue a course of life like unto this.[35]

Although Hyde did not mention it, timber was likewise beginning to come under heavy assault by the 1860's. At the beginning of that decade

[33]Gustave O. Larson, *The "Americanization" of Utah for Statehood* (San Marino, Calif., 1971), introduction, p. 35.

[34]Arrington, "Mormon Economic Policies and Their Implementation on the Western Frontier," p. 178. Wayne L. Wahlquist, "Population Growth in the Mormon Core Area: 1847–90," in Jackson, *The Mormon Role in the Settlement of the West,* has worked out a population schedule for Utah which he believes to be more accurate than the Census Reports. According to his figures (Table 2), the population in Utah increased from 1,637 in 1847 to 97,229 by 1870, with 55% of these residing along the Wasatch Front. Between 1848 and 1883, he estimates (his Table 5) that the Mormons had to provide homes for some 72,551 who emigrated to Zion from abroad.

[35]*Deseret News,* November 16, 1865.

there were 28 sawmills operating in the Wasatch. Twenty years later they had increased to 100, and by 1900 the entire west slope of the mountains had been denuded to such an extent that, according to Forest Reserve employee Albert Potter, "it would be difficult to find a seedling big enough to make a club to kill a snake."[36]

Because of traffic over the Mormon Cutoff, Gentiles were obviously in Utah with their herds during much of the 1850's and 1860's. According to Works Progress Administration grazing researchers, the "chief injustice" done to Utah grasslands was done by these transient operators rather than Mormon herders. Utah's cattle population peaked before 1880, and soon cattle were giving way to sheep, many of them herded around the West wherever forage could be found. By 1889 a million sheep and 350,000 cattle were in Utah; by 1899 the cattle population had stabilized, but the sheep count had increased four-fold. Like the wild grazers which they considerably replaced, these stock animals grazed the valleys in winter and followed the melting snows into the high mountains during spring and summer. Supplemental winter feeding of stock broke the old natural balance by keeping alive thousands of animals which, had they been wild grazers, would have died. The enormous stock herds tramped and gouged the waterlogged spring soils, and ate the meadows down until individual sheep bands could be spotted from the valleys below by the dust clouds they raised.[37]

Another barometer of change set into motion by the Mormons and accelerating with the coming of non-Mormons was an almost complete change in the vegetation patterns of the Western front. By comparing the records kept by early observers such as Peter Skene Ogden with those of later scientific and survey expeditions, it is obvious that as early as the 1870's an unexpected transformation was taking place. For almost two decades the grasslands of the valleys and lower slopes managed to recover from grazing of Mormon stock. But overgrazing combined with the suppression of Indian and natural fires led by the 1870's to the unfolding of a new succession pattern in Utah which erased forever the flora of the natural setting. Gradually the grasses gave way to sagebrush, rabbitbrush, and shadscale, fol-

[36]The quote is Albert Potter's, in Charles S. Peterson, "Albert F. Potter's Wasatch Survey, 1902: A Beginning for Public Management of Natural Resources in Utah," *Utah Historical Quarterly* 39 (Summer 1971): 249; See also, "Forest Reserves," *19th Annual Report of the U.S. Geological Survey* (Washington, 1898), p. 22; "Report on the Forests," *House Misc. Doc. 1*, 47th Cong., 2nd Sess., Vol. 13, pt. 9, pp.567–69.

[37]Will C. Barnes, "The Story of the Range," in the WPA Grazing Collection, Box 6, Folder 11; see also, Box 15, Folder 2; Box 7, Folder 3. In addition, Don Walker, "The Cattle Industry of Utah, 1850–1900: An Historical Profile," *Utah Historical Quarterly* 32 (Summer 1964): 34; Leonard J. Arrington and Thomas G. Alexander, *A Dependent Commonwealth: Utah's Economy From Statehood to the Great Depression,* Dean May, ed. (Provo, 1974), p. 16; N. Keith Roberts and B. Delworth Gardner, "Livestock and the Public Lands," *Utah Historical Quarterly* 32 (Summer 1964): 286; *U.S. Census Report,* 1880, Volume on Agriculture, pp. 144–76. For a fuller discussion of altitudinal grazing migrations and the mountain environment, see Dan Flores, "Island in the Desert: An Environmental Interpretation of the Rocky Mountain Frontier" (Ph.D. diss., Texas A&M University, 1978), pp. 404–10.

lowed by a rapid invasion of juniper, which in a century would expand its range six-fold. After 1900, exotic invading annual weeds such as cheatgrass and the tumbleweed, Russian thistle, began overspreading the range to take the place of the native grasses.[38]

In 1878, emerging from the scientific study of the Mountain West which had begun with Ferdinand Hayden's Geological and Geographical Survey of the Territories, John Wesley Powell's landmark "Report on the Lands of the Arid Region of the United States, with Special Reference to Utah," was published, arguing that the cooperative nature of early Mormon society ought to be adopted as a general plan of settlement in the West.[39] Although not adopted (perhaps fortunately due to some serious flaws) the Powell monograph pointed up the growing belief among American scientists that a land-use plan for the West had become a critical necessity. Many within American scientific circles—among them Chief Forester B. E. Fernow, and Franklin B. Hough of the American Association for the Advancement of Science—were beginning to agree with George Perkins Marsh, author of *Man and Nature* (1864), that the high mountains of the West must be retained in public ownership and their use regulated in order to protect the watersheds upon which the entire region was dependent.[40]

Public retention of the mountains, perhaps the most critical legislation ever passed for the perpetuation of civilization in the American West, came about with astonishingly little fanfare. In 1891 there was attached to the end of a twenty-four-part land revision bill a section which empowered the

[38]Christensen and Hutchinson, "Historical Observations on the Ecology of Rush and Tooele Valleys, Utah," 98; Cottam, "The Impact of Man on the Flora of the Bonneville Basin," 9. Respecting the area of what is now the Manti/La Sal National Forest in southeastern Utah, Cottam says: "Local history and ecological data regarding Mountain Meadows establish a record of almost complete change in vegetation since settlement in 1862." Walter Cottam and George Stewart, "Plant Succession as a result of Grazing and of Meadow Dessication by Erosion Since Settlement in 1862," *Journal of Forestry* 38 (August, 1940): 31. For a species and habits breakdown of the *Chenopodiaceae,* or "pigweeds," which have replaced the native grasses in many areas of Utah and the West, see Harold W. Rickett, *The Central Plains and Mountains,* vol. VI of *Wild Flowers of the United States,* 6 vols. (New York, 1966), p. 110.

[39]John Wesley Powell, *Report on the Lands of the Arid Region of the United States, With a More Detailed Account of the Lands of Utah* (Washington, 1878). For a laudatory assessment of Powell's plan, based on local and collectivist "grazing and water districts" and (later) legal right and institutional lines conforming with natural drainage, consult Wallace Stegner, *Beyond the Hundredth Meridian: John Wesley Powell and the Second Opening of the West* (Boston, 1954). In light of subsequent scientific finds, the major flaw of Powell's plan was his failure to recognize the link between the mountain forests and streamflow. His plan would have turned the mountain watersheds over to the lumber companies for clearcutting. See Flores, "Island in the Desert," pp. 283–89, for a more critical analysis of Powell's land-use plan.

[40]"Every civilized government," Fernow wrote, "must in time own or control the forest cover of the mountains in order to secure desirable water conditions." B.E. Fernow, "Report Upon the Forestry Investigations of the U.S. Department of Agriculture, 1877–1898," *House Doc. 181,* 55th Cong., 3rd sess., p. 316. Marsh had opened this debate in America with his *Man and Nature,* now recognized as a work of major significance to American environmental history. Marsh spoke of the disasters which had befallen China and areas of the French Alps when mountainous areas were stripped of their trees. By 1891 eight European nations already had moved to public ownership of their mountains, among them Germany, Fernow's homeland.

president to set aside forest reserves in the West. It passed both Senate and House virtually without comment.[41] Within fifteen years, aided by the ideas and support of Forester Gifford Pinchot and President Theodore Roosevelt, the principles of federal ownership and regulated multiple use (with fees and permits for some uses) had been established for the National Forest system. With the passage of the Taylor Grazing Act in 1934, these principles were extended to desert and valley lands, first regulated by the Grazing Service and then the Bureau of Land Management.

The year following statehood Utah got its first Forest Reserve (Uinta); by 1910 there were ten more, now called National Forests, and covering nearly all of the mountainous areas, or about 14% of Utah land. Perhaps because early church regulation of resources had established a precedent of control, the people of Utah were more solidly in favor of the National Forest plan than was generally the case in the West. The concept was supported by the Mormon Church, and Senator Reed Smoot of Utah was one of the only western legislators who championed its cause.[42] Yet for users, immediate economics still outweighed "theories" such as conservation. Their constant pressure on the Forest Service for more freedom was indirectly aided by a number of scientists and scientific bureaus (notably the Army Corps of Engineers and the U.S. Weather Service) which openly began to doubt the postulated relationship between vegetation and runoff that had provided the rationale for the creation of the system.[43]

[41]Lands Committee Chairman Payson of Illinois implied in the House that the reserves might be "temporary," but were necessary for "conserving the general good by preserving the watersheds . . . " Mcrae of Arkansas noted prophetically that "we shall hear from it [the reservation clause] in the future." *Congressional Record,* 51st Cong., 2nd sess., vol. 22, pp. 3613–16. Bills to establish such a mountain reserve system in the West had been introduced in every session of Congress beginning in 1882. In 1890 both the American Association for the Advancement of Science and the National Academy of Science lobbied for the idea, the National Academy opining that "no other problem confronting the government of the United States is equal in importance to that offered by the present condition and future fate of the forests of western North America." Quoted in Robbins, *Our Landed Heritage,* p. 312.

[42]Thomas G. Alexander, "Senator Reed Smoot and Western Land Policy, 1905–1920," *Arizona & The West* 13 (Autumn, 1971): 245–64; Peterson, "Albert F. Potter's Wasatch Survey, 1902," 249–53. Smoot was one of the few Western legislators who also supported the Pettigrew Amendment which opened the Reserves to multiple use, and the fee and permit system later implemented by Pinchot. The question of support for the National Forest system was not, we now know, the clear-cut "people vs. special interests" confrontation of Progressive rhetoric, but subsequent research has not erased the suspicions that the opponents were motivated by greed. Generally speaking, farmers and urban dwellers in the West were supportive of the system, as was the National Forestry Association and some of the individual timbermen and cattlemen. The most vehement opponents were (and still are) the sheepmen, the mining industry, and the majority of cattlemen. See Lawrence Rakestraw, "Uncle Sam's Forest Reserves," *Pacific Northwest Quarterly* 44 (October 1953): 145–46; and by the same author, "The West, States' Rights and Conservation: A Study of Six Public land Conferences," *Pacific Northwest Quarterly* 47 (July 1957): 89–99.

[43]Again contrary to popular impression, not all Eastern government scientists supported the rationale of the Forest system. In addition to the two entities mentioned, Hiram M. Chittenden of the reservoir survey also expressed doubts regarding the beneficial effects of vegetation upon streamflow. The science of "oekologie" was then in its infancy. For a discussion of their arguments, see Gordon B. Dodds, "The Streamflow Controversy: A Conservation Turning Point," *Journal of American History* 56 (June, 1969): 56–69.

Ironically, the very land of the Mormon experiment provided the ultimate proof for the hypothesis. Beginning in 1881, and continuing thereafter with mounting fury and frequency, the now deteriorated mountain watersheds, which geological evidence proved had not flooded since Lake Bonneville had receded 25,000 years before, began periodically to send tons of water, soil, and boulders roiling into the streets and irrigation works of the town below them. The Manti area of southeastern Utah, settled by Mormons in 1862, began flooding in 1888, and although local petitions closed the Manti National Forest to grazing in 1904, nine devastating floods struck the area between 1888 and 1909. By 1930 thirteen Mormon communities in southern Utah had been abandoned because of flooding.[44]

Even with Forest Service regulation and the Manti lesson, grazing and logging pressure continued to be too intense on the Wasatch. By the 1920's a widespread land collapse had begun. Between 1923 and 1930, sixteen Utah counties suffered devastating floods, finally leading Governor George Dern to appoint a Flood Commission to study the causes of the phenomenon, unknown to the early settlers. After two years of study, the Commission concluded that the mountain topography of Utah was incapable of absorbing heavy rains with the watersheds so critically depleted by overgrazing, fires, and over-cutting of timber, and warned of continuing catastrophe if large-scale mitigation was not undertaken.[45] Although a few watersheds were cross-terraced, at considerable expense, to break up the

[44]Robert V. R. Reynolds, "Grazing and Floods: A Study of Conditions in the Manti National Forest, Utah," *U.S. Department of Agriculture Forest Service Bulletin 91* (Washington, 1911). Of a total of forty-three Mormon settlements which were abandoned because of environmental factors, the highest number of failures (16) was due to flooding. All but three of these were located in southern Utah, in the Colorado Plateau country. Rosenvall, "Defunct Mormon Settlements: 1830–1930," 60–61, Table 2. At this time, it cannot be said whether environmental disruption caused by overgrazing or cutting was responsible, but since all but two were abandoned after more than a decade of occupation, it appears likely that this was the cause. Rosenvall, who is unfamiliar with the techniques of historical ecology, assumes the rivers were simply unpredictable.

[45]The point of the Weather Service that bared slopes yield more runoff than vegetated ones was ably documented in Utah, where some studies indicated that as much as sixty-two times the amount of water came from bare slopes. But the Utah experiences made the further point that without vegetation, mountains shed their soil, boulders, and other debris along with the water, in destructive and erosive floods. Whereas vegetation slopes normally lose *no* soil from rainfall, bare slopes average 100 cubic feet per acre soil loss during heavy storms. Further, the rapid runoff of degraded mountain slopes interfered with water percolation, causing streams to dry up prematurely. In one of the 1920's floods, gullies were cut 75 feet deep to bedrock, rock and debris covered the ground to a depth of eight feet at the mouths of canyons, and boulders of 300 tons weight rolled through towns and irrigation systems. Sixty years later, those gullies are still etched into the slopes. Utah ecologists proved that they could revegetate a slope and stop floods in no more than a decade, but when flood-fears subsided found the public apathetic to their arguments that use ought to be severely curtailed. For several score high quality black-and-white photographs which graphically illustrate the seriousness of this mountain lands collapse, see: Utah Land Board, Intermountain Forest and Range Experiment Station, U.S. Forest Service, and the Utah Agricultural Experiment Station, *Report of Utah Flood Survey, 1931, 1932*, Special Collections, Milton R. Merrill Library, Utah State University, Logan. Other major studies documenting the relationship between watershed abuse and ecological collapse in Utah include: C.L. Forsling, "A Study of Herbaceous Plant Cover and Soil Erosion in Relation to Grazing on the Wasatch Plateau in Utah," *U.S. Department of Agriculture*

gullying, and then replanted and closed to grazing, no widespread reforms ensued. In 1945 Salt Lake City suffered a flood which caused nearly a half million dollars in damage, its first flood in 98 years of occupation, when a single square-mile of the highly flammable alien, cheatgrass, burned and left the ground exposed. By 1950, after only one century of White occupation, twenty watersheds, from one end of the Wasatch Mountains to the other, were open to flooding.[46]

In the mid-1930's it had become apparent in Utah that floods and altered plant succession were only two manifestations of the widespread environmental deterioration. During that decade, the area at the north end of the Oquirrh Range, specifically Tooele, Skull, Cedar, and Rush valleys—only sixty years before praised as an excellent grassland of waving native species—became the only Dust Bowl in Rocky Mountain history. Eventually 46,000 acres lay bare to the winds, and in 1935 the Department of Agriculture anticipated that the town of Grantsville would have to be abandoned. The Soil Conservation Service closed the area to use and made it a demonstration plot on revegetation, but Utah's battle with surface wind erosion and dust bowls did not abate. After particularly severe problems struck again in 1955 and 1960–61, Utah ecologist Walter Cottam predicted that Utah was, as he put it, "Sahara-Bound."[47]

Contributing to the general ecological degradation was the 20th century transformation of Utah's agriculture. Encouraged by government reservoir development and indicated by an increase in average farm size from 30 acres in 1870 to 212 in 1900 (and 1,032 in 1977), commercial agriculture and its techniques now held sway. When the Office of Foreign Seed and Plant Introduction imported strains of strong red winter wheat from Siberia, a flurry of dry farming began, pushing the fields up mountain slopes as steep as 20%. Yet even the booms in wheat, sugar beets, and horticulture could not submerge the serious problems in soil erosion, malaccumulations of water and salt from irrigation, and canal seepage losses which in some irrigation systems exceeded 50%. By mid-century half the arable lands in Utah had been exhausted to the point of requiring artificial fertilizing. And while one of the legendary events of early Mormon history, the devouring of a grasshopper plague by gulls, had established a precedent for biological pest control, commercial monoculture built up harmful insect populations to the point that

---

Experiment Station Circular 92 (Logan, 1931); Reed Bailey, C.L. Forsling, R. J. Becraft, "Floods and Accelerated Erosion in Northern Utah," *U.S. Department of Agriculture Misc. Publication 196* (Washington, 1934); Richard Marston, "Effect of Vegetation on Rainstorm Runoff," *Proceedings, Utah Academy of Science, Arts and Letters* 26 (1948–49); Ernest O.Buhler, "Forest and Watershed Fires in Utah," *Utah Agriculture Experiment Station Circular 115* (Logan, 1940); Raphel Zon, "Forests and Water in Light of Scientific Evidence," *Sen. Doc.* 469, 62nd Cong., 2nd sess.

[46]Stewart, "Utah's Biological Heritage," 14; George W. Craddock, "Salt Lake City Flood, 1945," *Proceedings, Utah Academy of Science, Arts and Letters* 23 (1945–1946): 51–61.

[47]Cottam, "The Influence of Man on the Flora of the Bonneville Basin," p. 10; Christensen and Hutchinson, "Historical Observations on the Ecology of Rush and Tooele Valleys, Utah."

first DDT, and later 2,4-D, malathion, endrin, and other pesticides were sprayed on crops with malevolent effects upon the food chain.[48]

Strangely, in view of its environmental history, contemporary Utah seems less open to environmental sympathies than almost any other part of the Mountain West. Utah ecologists such as J. H. Paul, Ray Becraft, C. L. Forsling, Reed Bailey, and Walter Cottam, ably assisted by native literary sons Barnard DeVoto and Wallace Stegner, appear to have been far less convincing with their empirical data than the early Mormon leadership was with its religious pronouncements. Their conclusive documentation of detrimental vegetation changes since settlement, as well as of the critical relationship between abused watersheds and floods, have been unsuccessful in convincing a clear majority in Utah. Although a Utah Conservation Association was formed in the 1930's, and the Utah Academy of Science, Arts and Letters promoted an omnibus State Department of Conservation to consolidate and centralize resource use planning in 1948 (in the process invoking images of a collapse like that of China's mountain lands if nothing were done), sportsmen's groups defeated the movement, [49] delaying creation of a Natural Resources department to the 1960s.

During the "environmental decade" (1965–1975), Utah did pass a Land and Water Conservation Fund Act (1965) to stimulate conservation, but did not make participation mandatory. Three years later a Conference on the Future of Utah's Environment, held in Salt Lake City, resurrected the ecologist's

[48]*U.S. Census Report,* 1900. Volume on Agriculture; Stewart, "Utah's Biological Heritage," 7; George F. Knowlton, "Our Resources—Beneficial Insects," *Proceedings, Utah Academy of Science, Arts and Letters* 25 (1947–48): 39; Charles S. Peterson, "The 'Americanization' of Utah's Agriculture," *Utah Historical Quarterly* 42 (Spring 1974), 109–125; John E. Lamborn, "A History of the Development of Dry Farming in Utah and Southern Idaho," (M.A. thesis, Utah State University, 1978). For early reservoir development, see Thomas C. Alexander, "An Investment in Progress: Utah's First Federal Reclamation Project, The Strawberry Valley Project," *Utah Historical Quarterly* 39 (Summer, 1971): 286–304. Although not considered in this paper, mining also had an adverse impact on the Utah agricultural environment. Silting and pollution of streams used for irrigation, and sulphur poisoning of stock and crops emerged as a major problem around 1900. See John A. Widtsoe, "The Relation of Smelter Smoke to Utah Agriculture," *Utah State Agriculture College Experiment Station Bulletin No. 88* (Logan, 1903). The author also wishes to thank John Lamborn of the Special Collections Library at Utah State University for allowing him to peruse his unpublished paper, "The Smelter Cases of 1904 and 1906."

[49]Walter Cottam, "General Plan for Conservation," and Ross Hardy, "Our Program for Action," *Proceedings, Utah Academy of Science, Arts and Letters* 25 (1947–48): 69–70, 77. Paul was professor of Natural Science at the University of Utah, as was Cottam. Becraft was Professor of Range Management at Utah State, Bailey for years the Director of the Intermountain Forest and Range Experiment Station at Ogden, and Forsling, Research Ecologist in the U.S. Forest Service. Bernard DeVoto, a well-known historian and literary figure who died in 1955, spent years trying "to save the West from itself" through his *Harper's* columns. See Peter Wild, *Pioneer Conservationists of Western North America* (Missoula, 1979), chapter 9, for a good sketch of Devoto. Wallace Stegner is a widely acclaimed writer and environmentalist.

[50]Michael Treshow and C.M. Gilmour, eds., *Proceedings, Conference on the Future of Utah's Environment* (Salt Lake City, 1968); "An Analysis of Counties and Municipalities which did not Participate in the Land and Water Conservation Fund Act of 1965, Utah: 1965–1970," (M.A. thesis, Utah State University, 1974).

fears for the state once again, but to little avail.[50] Modern Mormons have not only embraced capitalism and state's rights, but most are rather hostile to environmental concerns of any kind. Utah Senator Orrin Hatch, who in 1980 introduced Bill S. 1680 calling for the "return" to Utah of all National Forest and BLM lands within the state (a beginning for what he has termed "the second American Revolution") is a major spokesman for the Sagebrush Rebellion who regards ecologists as "toadstool and dandelion worshippers." A poll taken in late 1979 indicated that nearly half of Utahns agree with his sentiments. And the classic Mormon concept of divine environmental transformation continues: "In the [modern] Mormon mind," environmental researcher Don Snow has written, "the earth as we know it is a temporary state of affairs, soon to be cleansed 'in the twinkling of an eye' by the redeemer. If industry makes a mess of air and watersheds, that's of little consequence."[51] Only those who know Utah's early history would understand the appropriate irony of representing a Mormon bishop as the antienvironmental antagonist in Edward Abbey's novel, *The Monkey Wrench Gang* (1975).

Although it continues to send mixed signals to Utahns, alternately threatening the state with such environmental disasters as the MX Missile and holding forth promises of development with the current $325 million Central Utah Water Project, the Federal government still remains the major force of environmental sensitivity in Utah. Since 1925 the Department of Agriculture has attempted to reverse watershed deterioration by cutting back on both permits and grazing seasons. In the 1970's Environmental Impact Statements on grazing in BLM lands and the Wasatch National Forest concluded that "the declining condition of millions of acres of rangelands caused by overgrazing" was still so widespread that a massive reduction would be necessary to show a reversal by the year 2000.[52] Helped by the passage of the BLM Organic Act in 1976, this reduction is now under way in Utah. Unfortunately, it was not implemented soon or rigorously enough to mitigate against a disastrous Utah land collapse in the form of floods and mudslides when the climate swung to a wet cycle in the spring and summer of 1983.

For environmental historians, the lessons of the Utah experience are intriguing although not simple. The Mormon experiment is useful in testing

[51]Don Snow, "Squeezing the Daylights out of Zion," *High Country News* (July 25, 1980), pp. 5–6; Wallace Stegner, "If the Sagebrush Rebels Win, Everybody Loses," *The Living Wilderness* 45 (Summer, 1981): 30–35. Stegner points out that the permit owners are the most vocal members of the "rebellion." Some 70% of land within the boundaries of the state is federally owned, with 45% in BLM lands and 14% in National Forest. Only 13% is privately-owned, while 5% is in state hands.

[52]Arthur H. Roth, Jr., "A Graphic Summary of Grazing on the Public Lands of the Intermountain Region," *U.S. Department of Agriculture, U.S. Forest Service, and Intermountain Forest and Range Experiment Station Project 3298* 3 parts; (Washington, 1940), Pt. 1, pp. 1–6; U.S. Forest Service, Intermountain Region, *Draft Environmental Impact Statement and Proposed Land Management Plan: Wasatch National Forest, Utah* (Ogden, 1977); U.S. Bureau of Land Management, *Final Environmental Impact Statement: Livestock Grazing Management on National Resource Lands* (Washington, 1974), I-1 through I-10; Deevon Bailey, "Economic Impacts of Public Grazing Reductions in the Livestock Industry with Emphasis on Utah" (M.A. thesis, Utah State University, 1980).

some of the hypotheses of the environmental movement's critique of American institutions, although it is complicated by the relict nature of Utah grasslands, and the relatively early presence of "Gentiles" whose free abuse of resources was beyond the pale of the church. Early Mormonism, it is clear, did possess the democratic and communal impulses valued by environmentalists, and the centralization and support necessary to carrying out a land ethic program. And yet, it seems that without an empirical understanding of how mountain land worked—and despite Mormon mythology to the contrary—even practical stewardship of the Mormon variety was unable to do so.[53]

The cultural transformation wrought on Mormondom by "Americanization" offers a unique opportunity to examine the effects of two belief systems—supernaturalism and scientism—on behavior towards the environment. The evidence here indicates that the former is probably the more effective in compelling people to act in a certain way towards the land. Yet, while it is conversely true that scientism offers the most pragmatic means of understanding why an ecoregion (or the biosphere) demands ethical treatment, and how to go about providing it, as a belief system it has not proved itself so universally compelling as religion. From this it may be conjectured that, ecologically, only the society which combines the two can be expected to create an effective and workable land ethic. Either we must find a religious tradition capable of imparting spiritual force to empirical ecological realities, or else make our environmentalism a religion.

[53]Jackson, in "Myth and Reality: Environmental Perceptions of the Mormons" argues that the mythology, accepted widely by both Mormons and non-Mormons, that the Wasatch Front was a stark, barren desert converted into a garden by the Mormon pioneers, was a theme deliberately played up by Brigham Young. Thus was he able to induce reluctant saints to found settlements in Zion's "Dixie," the increasingly arid country south of Utah Lake, by holding forth this mythic example of environmental transformation.

*

Building Zions: A Conceptual Framework

ROBERT ALAN GOLDBERG

The success of Mormons in settling the semi-arid Great Basin has long fascinated historians. In this article Robert Goldberg offers an explanation for that success. He proposes a model by which the Mormon experience can be examined and applies it as well to the failed colonizing effort of Jewish settlers at Clarion in Utah's Sanpete County in the early twentieth century and the Jewish experience in Israel. He concludes: "The defeat of the Clarion colonists and the victories of the Mormons in the Great Basin and the Jews in Israel differ in degree rather than in kind and thus represent different ends of the same continuum. Rather than a regional, ethnic, or cultural interpretation, the histories of these colonization efforts were written in the interplay of five factors—experience, environment, capital, morale, and alternatives."

Robert Alan Goldberg, "Building Zions: A Conceptual Framework," *Utah Historical Quarterly* 57 (Spring 1989): 165–79. Reprinted by permission of the publisher and the author.

Robert A. Goldberg teaches history at the University of Utah. He is the author of *Back to the Soil: The Jewish Farmers of Clarion, Utah, and Their World; Hooded Empires: The Ku Klux Klan in Colorado;* and *Grassroots Resistance: Social Movements in Twentieth Century America.*

LEONARD J. ARRINGTON, IN HIS SEMINAL WORK *Great Basin Kingdom: An Economic History of the Latter-day Saints, 1830–1900,* detailed the course of Mormon colonization in the nineteenth-century West. Through Mormon efforts a wilderness became a functioning society and economy. Arrington determinedly resisted extensive speculation upon the reasons for the success of Mormon colonization. Only briefly did he succumb, discussing the underlying patterns of discipline, careful organization and planning, and the homogeneity of the settlers to explain the spread of Mormon outposts throughout the Great Basin.

This paper seeks to cast Arrington's observations into a wider conceptual scheme to understand the factors that influenced not only Mormon settlement but the process of colonization in a larger context. These factors will be uncovered and probed in a case study of a Jewish colony of the Great Basin. The Jewish settlement of Clarion, Utah, founded in 1911 and dissolved in 1916, was the last of the approximately forty attempts to colonize Jews on the land in the United States. It was the largest in population and land area and had the longest temporal existence of any Jewish colony west of the Appalachian Mountains. What light does its defeat shed upon Mormon victories? Why did Clarion fail when all around it was evidence of Mormon success? Finally, parallels will be drawn between Mormon colonization in the Great Basin and Jewish settlement in the land of Israel, using the insights gleaned from the Clarion experiment. In this way the variables underlying the success and failure of colonization efforts may be ascertained and subject to research in other times and places in world history.[1]

Between 1881 and 1915 Jewish agricultural colonies were planted in New Jersey, North and South Dakota, Kansas, Louisiana, Oregon, Colorado, and Utah. This American effort was ideologically, ethnically, and temporally part of an international Back to the Soil Movement that saw Jewish farming settlements established in Argentina, Canada, and Israel. In America advocates seeking to end urban congestion and to restructure Jewish economic life encouraged immigrants to take up the plow. They listed a number of intriguing benefits. Farming would decrease the oversupply of labor in the cities, create a proper environment for child rearing, and accelerate Americanization. Further, the farm would inhibit anti-Semitism by smothering the stereotype of the Jew as a commercial parasite. A return to agriculture would, moreover, bring Jewish spiritual and physical revival, restore a sense of dignity, free Jews from the economic uncertainties of the sweatshop, and demonstrate to Christians the Jews' stake in their new homeland.[2]

The seeds sown by the advocates of a Jewish return to the soil grew in the mind of Benjamin Brown, a Russian immigrant to America. In 1909 he began agitating in New York and Philadelphia for the creation of a farming colony whose success would generate a wave of Jewish agricultural settlements throughout the United States. His message was always multifaceted, extolling the good life on the farm while reminding his listeners of the impelling need to ameliorate the Jewish condition in the eastern cities. Brown's words touched a wide range of people. Socialists, anarchists, Zionists, the religious Orthodox, and those seeking a more comfortable life for them-

[1]For a detailed discussion of the Clarion colony see Robert Alan Goldberg, *Back to the Soil: The Jewish Farmers of Clarion, Utah, and their World* (Salt Lake City, 1986).

[2]*Jewish Exponent*, July 5, 1889; Gabriel Davidson, "The Jew in Agriculture in the United States," *American Jewish Year Book* 37 (Philadelphia, 1935–36), p. 134; Rabbi Joseph Krauskopf, "What to Do with the Russian Refugee," *Sunday Discourses Before the Congregation Keneseth Israel, 1905–6*, 19 (Philadelphia, 1906), p. 52; Uri D. Herscher, *Jewish Agricultural Utopias in America, 1880–1910* (Detroit, 1981), pp. 23–24, 37–48.

selves and their families joined. Each would conceive the colony in his own image. In such diversity the weed of dissension was well fertilized.[3]

By 1911 Brown had attracted 200 men, most with families, and had accumulated $60,000 in investment capital for land, equipment, livestock and building supplies. (While a substantial outlay for the time and the people involved, it would prove insufficient to support the colony during reverses.) Brown suggested a western site for the colony, for land was cheaper there than in the East; the temptation to return to the cities less; and the likelihood of the settlement becoming a boarder-resort, as had occurred to Jewish farms in upstate New York, remote.[4]

On a trip to the West to view land for the proposed colony, Brown visited Utah. State officials greeted him eagerly, offering to sell a prime tract of land that would be irrigated with water from a canal under construction. The more than 8,000 acres offered for sale were located in south-central Utah, three miles from the small town of Gunnison. The canal, state officials boasted, would provide abundant water and eliminate the caprice of weather. Impressed by the state's claims and assurances, Brown purchased 6,000 acres of land for his colony.[5]

The canal was crucial to the colony's future. Yet, at the time of purchase, canal construction had reached only the southern one-third of the eight-mile-long tract of Jewish colony land. The canal would not serve all of the land until two years after the colony's demise. The newly built canal had sides and bottom of dirt and lacked the necessary gates and weirs designed to regulate the water received by each farmer. Moreover, because there were no past data concerning canal capacity, state engineers could only estimate water seepage and quantity available for delivery.[6]

The first twelve colonists, chosen for their mechanical skills, experience with horses, and "seriousness," arrived at the settlement site in September 1911. Only two of the men had any agricultural background, and their knowledge was geared to eastern conditions. None had any practical experience with irrigation or drainage. Although urban dwellers, the men became concerned as they surveyed the tract. The land sloped steeply and was

[3]Interview with Lillian Brown Vogel, Los Angeles, June 17, 1983; Interview with Sarah Brown, Phoenix, by Michael and Patricia Walton, November 6, 1982; Benjamin Brown, "Memoirs," trans. Sarah Brown, typewritten, n.d., pp. 1–2, in the author's possession; Esther Radding, "Journal," handwritten, 1962, p. 157, in the author's possession.

[4]Brown, "Memoirs," pp. 1–2; Barney Silverman, "A Short History of Clarion," typewritten, 1967, pp. 3–5, 7, in the author's possession.

[5]Brown, "Memoirs," p. 6; Silverman, "Short History," pp. 21, 34–36; *Jewish Exponent,* September 15, 1911; "In re Clarion Colony, Utah," p. 2, Ben Roe Papers, Special Collections, Marriott Library, University of Utah, Salt Lake City; *First Successful Jewish Colony in the United States* (Salt Lake City, 1912), pp. 3, 5.

[6]Everett L. Cooley, "Clarion, Utah—Jewish Colony in Zion," *Gunnison Valley News,* March 12, 19, 1970; Conrad Frischknecht to Everett Cooley, October 3, 1960, Everett L. Cooley Papers, Special Collections, Marriott Library, University of Utah; C. J. Ullrich, "Report on the Water Supply—Piute Project," (typewritten, Salt Lake City, 1917?) in the author's possession. *Gunnison Gazette,* October 14, 1910; Interview with Carl Carpenter, Clarion, May 15, 1982; Interview with Lamont Nielsen, Clarion, June 26, 1982.

covered by sagebrush, tall grasses, and weeds. Large patches of ground were bare of any vegetation. Closer inspection of the soil revealed a sandy, gravelly consistency underlain by a hardpan subsoil. Although they were unaware at the time, the area had a short growing season with frosts coming late in the spring and early in the fall. Rainfall was minimal.[7]

Despite these difficulties the Jews immediately began to clear the land for cultivation. During the next five years they prepared 2,600 acres for planting. They laid out and dug irrigation channels from the canal to the fields, built homes to house fifty-two families, constructed a school, and experimented with chicken and hog raising. More than 200 people would attempt to realize their dream of going back to the soil. The colonists believed that they had received a call. They perceived themselves as the harbingers of the Jewish economic and social future in America. It was appropriate, then, that they named their colony Clarion.[8]

Between 1911 and 1916 setback after setback, both external and internal, eroded the human and financial resources that the Clarion colonists had mustered. Drought and an unreliable canal combined with marginal soil and farming inexperience to doom the first year's harvest. Already behind in payments to the state for land and water rights, the colonists could not pull themselves out of their financial hole. The support of Salt Lake City's Jewish community and Jews nationally was never sufficient to stem the hemorrhaging of funds. The 1913 harvest brought no respite. Heavy mountain rains in August had sent torrents of water into the dry washes and toward the colony. The water breached the canal and flooded the hay, wheat, and alfalfa fields. In 1914 drought and a water shortage resulting from their neighbors' greed again doomed the harvest. In the colony's last year a late frost was sufficient to break the colonists' spirit, already numbed by the misery of a hard and resisting land.[9]

Adding to this distress was the only crop that grew in abundance in Clarion's soil, dissension. When the colony's future dimmed, Benjamin Brown's judgment and qualifications came under attack, and he was accused of mismanagement and dictatorial practices. Exacerbating tensions was the factionalism inherent in the heterogeneous membership. Anarchists, international socialists, Jewish socialists, and Zionists found no unity as they now had evidence to substantiate their pre-Clarion suspicions. Even the religious Orthodox minority found itself embroiled in the mayhem.[10]

Further, the Mormon community did not present a unifying enemy around which to rally. Mormon welcomed Jew as neighbor and Biblical

[7]Silverman, "Short History," pp. 42–44; Interview with Harry Kimura, Clarion, September 20, 1983; Interview with Samuel Chatsky by Ronald Goldberg, Miami, May 18, 1982; U.S. Department of Agriculture, *Soil Survey of Sanpete Valley Area, Utah* (Washington, D.C., 1981), pp. 76–77, 80–81; Isaac Friedlander, *Virgin Soil,* trans. Louis Zucker (Los Angeles, 1949), p. 14; Interview with Allen Frandsen, Clarion, September 20, 1983

[8]Goldberg, *Back to the Soil,* chaps. 3, 4, 5 passim.

[9]Ibid.

[10]Ibid.

brother, tendering advice, food, friendship, tools, labor, and moral support. While the colony was an organizational entity, Mormons respected Jewish beliefs and attempted no proselytizing. A sense of common identity, past and present, religious and pioneering, united the two peoples.[11]

In January 1916, with the colony unable to pay the state the monies owed for land and water rights, Utah officials auctioned off the Clarion tract, selling just over one-tenth of the land. Most of the colonists returned to Philadelphia and New York City or went on to Los Angeles. Others took up land in New York, Michigan, Pennsylvania, and California. Some continued to farm in the Clarion area, with the last Jews leaving in the mid-1920s. The latter left because they feared the loss of their children's religious identities through assimilation rather than as a result of financial hardship.[12]

Five interrelated variables, their influence changing with time, were crucial in determining Clarion's fate: farming experience, environmental conditions, capital availability, colonists' morale, and the existence of alternatives. Clarion's people were urbanites familiar with the sweatshop, store, and the pushcart. Even the few with farming experience were unprepared for the semiarid conditions of Utah. Added to the ordinary toil attendant upon colony ground-breaking, inexperience was a difficult burden to bear. A poor site choice compounded inexperience-generated problems. Water scarcity, an undependable irrigation canal, marginal soil, and capricious weather drained the colony of enthusiasm and its meager supply of funds.

Yet, neither the lack of experience nor the environment is sufficient explanation for Clarion's fall. Each day on the land increased the colonists' store of agricultural knowledge. Hard work, trial and error, and Mormon farmers' aid and advice strengthened the Jews in their physical, emotional, and mental ability to stay on the land. The success of those Jews who remained in the Clarion area for a decade after the colony's demise or who took to the land elsewhere is evidence of their will to adapt to farming. Moreover, those who persisted saw a change in environmental conditions. While life was never easy, the environment had begun to shed its harshness and become more predictable. The most difficult tasks had been accomplished. The land had been cleared and fields created. Fences and outbuildings had been erected. The canal had become increasingly dependable.

Clarion's life could have been extended if it had had the means to sustain it through the difficult years—available capital and high morale. Without either of these vital assets the impact of alternatives became pronounced. Adequate financial resources would have bought the settlers time to survive the early colonization period, gain experience, and control their environment. Still, if the patronage of an outside benefactor with abundant funds would have softened the hard times, it would not alone have ensured the colony's future. To hold the colonists to a resisting land also required a

[11]Ibid.

[12]Ibid., pp. 124–28.

morale that was intense and cohesive. The hardship, denial, and self-doubt that accompany any colonization project can be held at bay, if not dispelled, when men and women are bound mentally and emotionally to a common goal. The colony's avowed purpose was to rebuild the Jewish people through agriculture. The colonists lost sight of this mission as personal animosities, ideological conflicts, and cultural disagreements caused diverse factions to focus their energies against one another, thus dissipating trust, goodwill, and strength. Further eroding morale was the silence of the outside world. When Clarion's call was ignored and financial contributions failed to materialize, the colonists' greatest fears were reified; their mission had no meaning.

Directly related, yet separate, was the existence of alternatives. New York City, Philadelphia, and Los Angeles beckoned Jews as they did Christians, offering rescue and release from farm life. The familiar urban world, even with its drawbacks, promised solutions to economic uncertainty, deteriorating relations with fellow colonists, and idealism gone sour. Without the bulwarks of high morale, financial security, and agricultural achievements, the siren of alternatives could not be silenced. Clarion's obstacles to economic self-reliance and ethnic viability proved too formidable to conquer.

With Clarion as background and the five variables as a framework, let us briefly review the Mormon colonization experience in the Great Basin. In the second half of the nineteenth century Mormon colonists established nearly five hundred settlements in seven states. Professor Arrington conceptualized this colonization movement in a series of stages. In the first stage Mormons initially populated the Salt Lake Valley. Radiating from this nucleus, they built communities in the Utah, Tooele, Sanpete, Box Elder, Pahvant, Juab, Parowan, and Cache valleys. Expansion in the second stage was accomplished beyond Utah's "inner cordon of settlement."[13] Choosing sites for geopolitical and missionary reasons, Mormons colonized San Bernardino, California; Las Vegas and Carson Valley, Nevada; Moab, Utah; Forts Supply and Bridger, Wyoming; and Lemhi, Idaho. By 1857 they had founded ninety-six colonies. During the next forty years, and in a continuing series of stages, Mormons reached central, southern, and northeastern Utah; the Salt and Gila River valleys in Arizona; the Upper Snake River Valley in Idaho; the Big Horn Basin and the Star Valley in Wyoming; the San Luis Valley in southern Colorado; White Pine County in Nevada; and the Grand Ronde Valley in eastern Oregon. Even lands in Canada and Mexico came under the Mormon plow. The success rate of the Mormon colonies is very impressive. Geographer Lynn Rosenvall calculated that only sixty-nine, or less than 14 percent, of the settlements had failed.[14]

[13]Quoted in Leonard J. Arrington, *Great Basin Kingdom: An Economic History of the Latter-day Saints, 1830–1900* (Cambridge, Mass., 1958), p. 84.

[14]Arrington, *Great Basin Kingdom,* pp. 84–88, 215–17, 354, 383–84; Dean May, "Problems of Mormon Settlement," p. 60, typewritten, 1977; Lynn A. Rosenvall, "Defunct Mormon Settlements: 1830–1930," in Richard H. Jackson, ed., *The Mormon Role in the Settlement of the West* (Provo, 1978), pp. 51–52.

We can account for this remarkable achievement with the same variables that determined Clarion's fate. Unlike Clarion's Jews, the Mormon pioneers were steeped in an agrarian tradition. Nineteenth-century America was a nation of farmers, and there were few who were not raised on the land or did not earn their bread from the soil. Rather than stepping into an alien world, Mormon colonists could farm from habit, having learned the skills inculcated through experience, generation to generation. They knew how to fence, cultivate, and care for livestock. Harnesses, hitches, and tools were not mysterious or foreboding. Still, the Great Basin was not New England or the Midwest. Wilford Woodruff reminds us, "of course, we had no experience with irrigation."[15] Yet, using their abundant store of agricultural resources, the Mormons adapted with trial and error techniques to the new environment. This can be illustrated in Woodruff's account of the first attempt to plant in the Salt Lake Valley. Finding the ground resistant to their plows, the pioneers turned water on the land only to watch their teams sink to their bellies in the mud. When the soil had dried, wrote Woodruff, "We then plowed our land."[16] Such incidents would be repeated many times over until the settlers had mastered farming in the Great Basin. Similarly, in this testing period the Mormons were confronted with environmental disasters. Marginal soil, inadequate water supply, insects, drought, bitter winters, and floods plagued the colonists. Man-made dangers appeared in the form of Indians, federal officials, and soldiers. Setbacks in diversifying the economy compounded harvest failures and at times brought famine and food rationing. Yet the Mormons persevered, stubbornly holding on to the land and gradually subduing it.[17]

The surmounting of these obstacles describes Mormon success. It does not, however, yield a sufficient explanation for their achievements in colonization. In the faces of adversity Mormon morale was sustained by the belief that God had invested them with a mission to prepare the earth for the second coming of Christ. In light of this, all Mormon activities, social, economic, and cultural, were infused with an intensity that could only come from active participation in the building up of the kingdom of God. "High on the mountain top a banner is unfurled," they sang in the ward houses, "Ye nations, now look up; It waves to all the world. . . . "[18] What had occurred, wrote Leonard Arrington, was a "spiritualization of temporal activity."[19]

Mormon history and the geography of the Great Basin bolstered theological doctrine to assure the pioneers of their destiny as the chosen of God. In the 1830s and 1840s the Mormons had suffered violence as they fled before mobs in Ohio, Missouri, and Illinois. After the murder of Joseph

[15]Quoted in May, "Problems of Mormon Settlement," p. 29.

[16]Ibid.

[17]Ibid., pp. 29–30; Rosenvall, "Defunct Mormon Settlements," pp. 52–53, 62–67; Arrington, *Great Basin Kingdom*, pp. 170–94.

[18]"High on the Mountain Top," in *Hymns* (Salt Lake City, 1968), p. 62.

[19] Arrington, *Great Basin Kingdom*, pp. 4–5, 27, 33–34.

Smith, Brigham Young led the Saints in an exodus across the Mississippi River and into the wilderness. The self-proclaimed "Camp of Israel" found its promised land in Utah. It was hardly coincidental, they believed, that the climate and topography of the region resembled the land of Israel.

Colonization, then, became the means to fulfilling a divine will that seemed partially revealed. This interpretation was made even more convincing when church leaders in conference called pioneers to missions to manufacture iron, raise silk, or till land. Under the direction of the church, colony sites were chosen, settlers selected, and tools and equipment assigned. The church also allocated property rights according to the principles of stewardship. The colonists were, as Charles Peterson suggested, like "children of God thrust from Eden into the hard, cruel world and charged to rebuild the garden in each desert outpost by the sweat of their brow."[20] Practical tasks of community building, maintenance, and defense when added to the concept of mission intensified this solidarity.[21]

The result was a nation of highly communal, homogeneous, and close-knit villages composed of individuals prepared to sacrifice their self-interest for the common good. They had taken Joseph Smith's admonition seriously: "I say unto you, be one; if ye are not one ye are not mine."[22] With hardships seen as tests of faith, the future of history on their shoulders, and identities as God's missionaries secure, the Mormons found that colonization efforts gave meaning to life, strength to the community, and success to the communal endeavor.

In addition to farming experience, overcoming the environment, and high morale, capital was necessary to sustain the Mormon experiment. Church leaders were able to pool their followers' savings and invest it for the collective good through the tithing office. Resources gathered through tithing, or as Arrington phrased it, the "socialization of surplus incomes,"[23] were partially spent furnishing settlers with food, livestock, equipment, tools, and seed. With the land financially free, settlement costs would not drain Mormon coffers. The church's financial sponsorship of colonization would last into the early twentieth century. The church also created the Perpetual Emigration Fund to bring needy Saints from Europe to Utah for religious reasons. This fund served economic functions as well. It efficiently worked to increase the region's labor supply and to create an effective means whereby payments in cash and kind were transferred and distributed according to need. Gold rushers and western travelers contributed as well to the building of the Great Basin kingdom. Bringing scarce currency, they opened an internal market for Mormon goods. With these resources the

[20]Charles S. Peterson, "Imprint of Agricultural Systems on the Utah Landscape," in Jackson, ed., *The Mormon Role in the Settlement of the West*, 92.

[21]Ibid., pp. 94–95, 102; Lowry Nelson, *The Mormon Village: A Pattern and Technique of Land Settlement* (Salt Lake City, 1952), p. 261; Thomas F. O'Dea, *The Mormons* (Chicago, 1957), p. 186; Wallace Stegner, *Mormon Country* (New York, 1942), pp. 30–32, 62–64.

[22]Doctrine and Covenants, 38:27.

[23]Arrington, *Great Basin Kingdom*, p. 7.

Mormons had the means to pass through the ground-breaking period of colonization and achieve economic stability and growth.[24]

Finally, the Mormons had few alternatives to the Great Basin. Recently chased by mobs, few cared to return to the American "Babylon." Church leaders actively pursued a policy of economic, cultural, and political self-sufficiency. Yet, distance did not eliminate harassment. Throughout the second half of the nineteenth century Congress rejected rapprochement and vigorously acted to abolish polygamy and the church's influence in economic and political affairs. Mormon hymns such as "Zion Stands with Hills Surrounded," "For the Strength of the Hills," and "Come, Come, Ye Saints" reflect a sense of siege and necessary isolation from the "proud boasting nation." In "Up, Awake, Ye Defenders of Zion" congregations pledged to "Remember the wrongs of Missouri; Forget not the fate of Nauvoo. When the God-hating foe is before you, Stand firm and be faithful and true. . . . "[25] Not until the beginning of the twentieth century, after Utah had achieved statehood, would a ceasefire exist and alternatives to the Great Basin become more visible. By then departure could not destroy the experiment because the long period of community building had created a foundation difficult to unearth.[26]

The men and women who colonized Israel were as prepared for the fields as their Clarion coreligionists. The environment they encountered was equally hostile with poor soil, a shortage of water, swamps, and insufficient rainfall. Over the centuries, since the Jews had farmed the land of Israel, soils had eroded, the forests had been cut down, and the streams filled with silt. Despite these restraints, a quarter of a million Jews inhabit the land today, and hundreds of *moshavot* ("settlements"), *kibbutzim* ("collectives"), and *moshavimovdim* ("workers' cooperatives") dot the Israeli landscape.[27]

The Jewish return to the soil began in the 1830s when 20,000 to 30,000 Jews left pogrom-ravaged eastern Europe for Palestine. By 1898 these men and women had launched twenty-five *moshavot.* The settlements had not rooted easily. Inexperience, a lack of funds, malaria, and Arab harassment had combined in the first years to choke growth. Only the timely financial intervention of philanthropist Baron Edmund de Rothschild averted the colonies' collapse. The settlements would require a quarter-century of financial weaning before they had stabilized and could stand by themselves.[28]

[24]Ibid., pp. 7–9, 18, 25–27, 34, 51, 77–79, 89–93, 97–108, 133; May, "Problems of Mormon Settlement," p. 46.

[25]*Hymns,* pp. 37–38. The LDS hymnal currently in use presents an amended wording for this song by Charles Penrose.

[26]Arrington, *Great Basin Kingdom,* pp. 24, 353–79; *Hymns,* pp. 13–14, 62, 212, 241.

[27]Henrik Infield, *Cooperative Living in Palestine* (New York, 1944), pp. 38–39.

[28]Mark Wischnitzer, *To Dwell in Safety: The Story of the Jewish Migration Since 1800* (Philadelphia, 1948), pp. 52, 57–60; Nora Levin, *While Messiah Tarried: Jewish Socialist Movements, 1871–1917* (New York, 1977), pp. 47–50; Arthur Ruppin, "Agricultural Achievements in Palestine," *Contemporary Jewish Record* 5 (June 1942): 268–70; D. Weintraub, M. Lissak, and Y. Azmon, *Moshava, Kibbutz, and Moshav: Patterns of Jewish Rural Settlement and Development in Palestine* (Ithaca, New York, 1969), pp. 3–4; Alex Bein, *The Return to the Soil: A History of Jewish Settlement in Israel* (Jerusalem, 1952), pp. 5–10.

The *moshavot* had initiated modern Jewish agriculture in Palestine. They would not, however, serve as ideological or practical precursors for the major thrust of Jewish agrarianism. Zionist leaders disparaged these villages because they did not offer a sufficient foundation to erect a national homeland for Jews. The twenty-five *moshavot* had lost their idealistic drive, becoming divorced from national goals. To carry forth efforts to accelerate immigration, expand territorial possessions, and reform Jewish society, the Zionist searched for a different solution.[29]

The pragmatic needs of Zionist organizers fused with the ideological dreams of the members of an immigration wave that touched Palestine's shores between 1904 and 1914. Many of these immigrants came to Palestine to build a new Jewish nation upon socialist principles. They hoped to establish settlements that would draw strength from their ideals: from each according to ability and sharing according to need. In such communities property would be owned collectively while decisions were made democratically. Firing hopes and actions was a perception that they stood at a crossroad of history and by their efforts would decide the Jewish future. Bolstering this self-conception was the enormous interest that world Jewry paid to this handful of men and women. This hothouse atmosphere of intense attention and idealism helped push these Jewish pioneers to conquer themselves and their environment.[30]

In 1909 Degania, the first *kibbutz* or collective farm, was organized. It proved successful and became the model for hundreds of Jewish colonies. The *kibbutz* fulfilled settlers' needs for independence and self-management, a decent standard of living, and the pursuit of national aims. Often built in a circular pattern for defense, it cultivated a sense of mutuality and self-reliance. Yet it did not stifle colonists' idealism or shield them from larger goals. The *kibbutz* became a crucial Zionist channel for dispersing immigrants, providing farm experience, building an agricultural sector for a Jewish state, and gathering lands to the end of nation-building. In the 1920s those who sought a cooperative agricultural life but were unable to accommodate to the *kibbutz* regimen formed *moshavim-ovdim* or workers' cooperatives. In these communities the central role of the family was recognized, land was privately owned, and members engaged in cooperative buying and selling.[31]

[29]Arthur Ruppin, *The Agricultural Colonisation of the Zionist Organization in Palestine* (London, 1926), p. 5; Arthur Ruppin, *Three Decades of Palestine: Speeches and Papers on the Upbuilding of the Jewish National Home* (Jerusalem, 1936), pp. 49–50; Eliyahu Kanovsky, *The Economy of the Israeli Kibbutz* (Cambridge, Mass. 1966), p. 12.

[30]Weintraub, et al., *Moshava,* p. 8; Levin, *While Messiah Tarried,* pp. 377–406; Melford E. Spiro, *Kibbutz; Venture in Utopia* (New York, 1970), pp. 32–36; Kanovsky, *Economy,* pp. 3–4, 25, 31–32; Paula Rayman, *The Kibbutz Community and Nation Building* (Princeton, 1981), pp. 11–16.

[31]Bein, *Return,* pp. 61–62; Kanovsky, *Economy,* pp. 7–9, 16, 126; Ruppin, *Agricultural Colonisation,* 132–33; Weintraub, et al., *Moshava,* pp. 10–11, 128; Harry Viteles, *A History of the Cooperative Movement in Israel* (London, 1966), vol 4: *Co-Operative Smallholders' Settlements (The Moshav Movement),* pp. 4, 23; vol 1: *The Evolution of the Co-Operative Movement,* p. 33.

The *kibbutz* and *moshav* concepts were conducive to Zionism's limited budget. The pioneers arrived with no resources to begin an agricultural life. Their inexperience amid severe conditions, plus the strategic and geopolitical nature of site selection, meant that the settlements would suffer heavy financial losses in a prolonged period of dependency. Settlement of families on dispersed farms was not only defensively unwise but beyond Zionist capabilities. A variety of organizations existed to provide the subsidization the colonies could not survive without. The Jewish National Fund acquired land which the settlers cultivated. The JNF also extended credits to aid the work of settlement and the purchase of livestock, equipment, and building materials. The *Keren Hayesod* ("Palestine Foundation Fund") granted loans to facilitate the colonization effort. Additional assistance was provided by the Jewish Agency, the Anglo-Palestine Bank, the *Histadrut* or General Federation of Jewish Labor, *kibbutzim* and *moshavim* federations, and the Israeli government.[32]

The Jewish colonies in Palestine and later Israel had found the means to ethnic and economic viability. The capital resources of the Zionist organizations gave settlers the opportunity gradually to loosen the shackles of inexperience and poor site selection. Their sense of purpose, and even destiny, sustained them when life was difficult and primitive. Self-selection in the migration process, which led to a Palestine destination rather than to the United States, guaranteed a core of men and women hardened in their idealism. Persecution and Arab attack at home combined with aid and attention from abroad to increase their determination. In addition, the *kibbutz* and *moshav* support group, its ideology and aims consistent, stiffened resolve and heightened the level of pain and despair that could be endured. At the same time, few alternatives were sufficiently attractive to tempt colonists from what had become their raison d'etre.

The defeat of the Clarion colonists and the victories of the Mormons in the Great Basin and the Jews in Israel differ in degree rather than in kind and thus represent different ends of the same continuum. Rather than a regional, ethnic, or cultural interpretation, the histories of these colonization efforts were written in the interplay of five factors—experience, environment, capital, morale, and alternatives. In the negative or positive interaction of the variables may be discerned the course of colonization. Hopefully, continuing research on the colonial mosaic will be as favorable to these concepts as it has been in substantiating the work of Professor Arrington.

[32]Kanovsky, *Economy,* p. 47; Ruppin, *Agricultural Colonisation,* p. 69; 98–99; Weintraub, et al., *Moshava,* pp. 6–7, 12, 185–227; Ruppin, *Three Decades,* pp. 131–32.

*

Salt Lake City: Zion at the Crossroads

PETER WILEY AND ROBERT GOTTLIEB

In many ways the history of Salt Lake City, indeed, all of Utah, in the last generation is the story of its complex interaction and confrontation with economic, political, social, and cultural forces of the outside world pressing in upon it and the extent to which they have increasingly shaped it. This is the subject of the following selection. After providing an insightful overview of the city's history from its founding in 1847 to the early 1980s the authors discuss the issues residents have had to deal with in the post–World War II era, including rapid urbanization, scarce water resources, the exploitation of vast energy resources on public land and Indian reservations, the activities of multinational corporations, and the influx of an increasingly heterogeneous population. One result is that Salt Lake City has increasingly become something of a battleground between contrasting cultures and lifestyles.

"Salt Lake City: Zion at the Crossroads," in Peter Wiley and Robert Gottlieb, *Empires in the Sun; The Rise of the New American West* (New York: G.P. Putnam's Sons, 1982), pp. 140–64. Reprinted by permission of the authors and the publisher.

Peter Wiley and Robert Gottlieb are co-authors of *Empires in the Sun: The Rise of the New American West* and *America's Saints: The Rise of Mormon Power.*

IT WAS 1969 AND THIS WAS to be the last meeting of this self-appointed group of three, a most unusual and perhaps fitting finale to nearly two decades of information-swapping, problem-solving, and decision-making in an effort to keep their city in hand. A meeting in an oxygen tent! What a sad but apt way to describe the end of an era.

First and foremost there was David O. McKay. The silver-haired president of the Church of Jesus Christ of Latter-day Saints was the "prophet, seer, and revelator," the spiritual and temporal leader of the church for which Salt Lake City was the capital, the centerpiece of the Mormon economic, political, and religious empire of Zion. McKay was a key figure in the growth and development of Salt Lake City from World War II through the 1960s. Intensely interested in political and economic affairs, he had set up regular breakfast meetings at the Mormon-owned Hotel Utah, where McKay lived, to keep abreast of city affairs and to direct them in appropriate ways. McKay was also something of a folk legend in his declining years, a man who liked big, fast cars, although he could not always control them, a man about whom everybody in the city had some kind of story to tell.

Now the ninety-six-year-old David O. McKay was in an oxygen tent, plagued with the illnesses that would define his remaining days. A new church leadership had emerged to take over the practical affairs of the church. This new leadership was best represented by Nathan Eldon Tanner, the dour and efficient Canadian oilman who reorganized the church's vast economic holdings along more modern corporate lines, and Spencer W. Kimball, who assumed the office of "first president" in 1973.

Next to McKay in the oxygen tent stood Gus Backman, the head of the Salt Lake City Chamber of Commerce, the non-Mormon businessman who linked the gentile and Mormon business worlds. Backman was a business fixer who derived his power from his connections and the pivotal role he occupied between Salt Lake City's two elites. He had led the fight for Utah's share of the Colorado River and had been instrumental in making non-Mormon businessmen feel more comfortable with these "peculiar people," as the Mormons called themselves. But Gus Backman was also getting on in years. He could see the passing of an era and the arrival of new businessmen from the outside, many of them from California, eyeing the rich coal deposits on the Colorado Plateau. These businessmen had already begun to bypass Backman and go directly to the new fixers in the state—politicians like Governor Calvin Rampton and his successor Scott Matheson.

The third man in the oxygen tent was John Gallivan, the publisher of the gentile *Salt Lake Tribune,* a comparative youngster although already in his late fifties. The *Tribune* was the establishment paper and spoke for the business community as a whole. In 1950 the *Tribune* made peace with its Mormon-owned rival, the *Deseret News,* through a joint operating agreement that pooled the advertising, distribution, and production of the papers into a single corporate entity. Now, nearly twenty years later, with both papers running in the black, the *Salt Lake Tribune* helped direct the business affairs of the city with its Mormon counterpart. It was a far cry from the origins of the *Tribune* in 1870, when it led the attack on Mormon control of the territory.

Gallivan had replaced his father-in-law, John F. Fitzpatrick, the *Tribune*'s longtime publisher, at the breakfast meetings when Fitzpatrick died in 1960. Gallivan came into his own by successfully establishing and promoting, like the Chandlers in Los Angeles and Donald Seawell at the *Denver Post,* a downtown cultural center. The idea for the Salt Palace had originally been advanced at the Hotel Utah breakfast meetings. The group of three quickly realized the benefits of such a project for the downtown district and the business community as a whole. "It was our finest moment," Gallivan recalled. Indeed, the idea capped a long history of Mormon-gentile cooperation that began tentatively when both Mormons and gentiles signed the articles of incorporation for the new Salt Lake City Chamber of Commerce in 1887.

Every Wednesday the three men met at the Hotel Utah. The gentiles drank their coffee and McKay his Postum while they exchanged bits of information and gossip, discussed who was buying and who was selling, and decided, when a big issue came along, what needed to be done. Although their time was now passing, Salt Lake was still their kind of city. The planned capital of Brigham Young's State of Deseret, Salt Lake was more of a village than the other sprawling, amorphous metropolises of the West, a city where close personal ties were still important—what Mayor Ted Wilson would later call a city of brothers-in-law. On the horizon loomed new, powerful forces eager to turn Utah inside out to satisfy their thirst for energy.

THE DEPENDENT COMMONWEALTH

Born of the martyred prophet Joseph Smith's socialistic frontier evangelism, reared and given identity during their dramatic exodus to the Promised Land on the shores of the Great Salt Lake, and consolidated and expanded into the communitarian and centralized State of Deseret by the organizational genius Brigham Young, the Mormons created their own commonwealth in the West in the days of the first Anglo migrations. "The Mormons had, in effect," wrote Leonard J. Arrington and Davis Bitton, "leaped beyond the line of American frontier settlement, moving to a region that others would not approach in significant numbers for three decades."

Utah's history derives from the efforts of the Saints to build an autonomous society in a largely hostile world of gentiles. From their arrival in 1847 through the coming of the transcontinental railroad in 1869, the Saints, with Brigham Young's leadership, attempted to establish a self-sufficient theocratic society based primarily on irrigated agriculture and village industry. Defying the federal invasion of 1857 and a series of natural disasters, the Saints created their state as a grand experiment in centralized planning and cooperative organization. At first, Deseret was bypassed by the chaotic and antagonistic mining frontier and the schemes of Manifest Destiny emanating from Washington.

With the driving of the golden spike at Promontory north of Ogden, signaling the completion of the transcontinental railroad, the Saints could no longer avoid a confrontation with the gentile world. The coming of the railroad coincided with the opening of the Utah mining frontier and the arrival of eastern capital to finance the new mines. When the railroads marched across northern Utah and the local silver kings and eastern mining companies opened Utah's ore veins, boomtowns sprang up with values diametrically opposed to the Mormons' tightly controlled theocracy.

With his community threatened to its roots by the corruption and departure of its young people, Young preached against mining. After the arrival of the railroads, Young reemphasized the need for the church to build and direct its own economy according to its own principles. At the same time, he tried to accommodate some of the new outside forces. Beginning with the Union Pacific, Young organized work crews to subcontract grade work for the new railroads, gave church land for stations and warehouses, and later sold the church-developed intrastate roads to the Union Pacific. In the process, the church developed a close relationship with the Union Pacific that has continued to the present. As *Fortune* magazine once commented, "You can't do business with the [Union Pacific] unless you work through Utah." Young's relationship with the emerging world of corporate capital was facilitated by Mormon businessmen, like David Eccles, who were strong links between the church community and eastern-based power.

Despite eastern fears of theocracy, which were aroused to a new pitch by the early feminists' campaign against polygamy, the church continued to maintain its control over the territory's politics and economy. Local gentile merchants feared that church economic schemes, such as Zion's Cooperative Mercantile Institute, were an attempt to monopolize all economic activity. Led by the *Tribune,* the local merchants argued for the development of mining and the freeing of politics from "ecclesiastical directive and control." The fight raged until the church, weakened by the attacks of the federal government, began the inevitable process of accommodation by officially opposing polygamy in exchange for statehood.

By the turn of the century the conflict between the Mormon and gentile elites within Utah had diminished. Mining had become the dominant economic activity. The early mining which attracted thousands of speculators and individual mining entrepreneurs soon gave way to forms of mining dependent on large capital expenditures. The shift to this kind of mining paralleled the rise of such eastern-based companies as Kennecott, which became, along with the Union Pacific, the major corporate power in the state.

By 1914, Utah had become the most industrialized state in the interior West through the processing of ore. Since a high percentage of the profits and products of the mines were taken out of the state, mining did not provide a sufficient foundation for broader economic development. The mining profits that remained went to build the great mansions east of the Temple or were siphoned off into political contributions to keep the state legislature in tow. When Thomas Kearns, whose family operated one of the Park City mines, bought the *Tribune* in 1901, he also became a major political power in the state.

With the rise of mining and a new business class, a local financier named Heber Grant led the church to rebuild its own economic base, much of which had been confiscated by the federal government or quietly sold to high-ranking church members. In the 1890s Grant, a member of the church's Council of Twelve (the highest ranking body in the hierarchy below the president), went hat in hand to Wall Street to attract outside capital to Utah. He was told to come back when economic conditions were more propitious. Grant then turned to a number of wealthy Mormons, including David Eccles, and persuaded them to purchase $1 million worth of church bonds. Looking for profitable business ventures, the church decided to make a second attempt at sugar-beet production—its first effort having failed in Young's day. The Saints first guaranteed a $400,000 bond issue, which was sold to an eastern financier. Then Grant consolidated several processing plants into a $13 million agribusiness giant called Utah and Idaho Sugar Company (U and I). With the help of Utah Senator Reed Smoot, a member of the Twelve and a prominent Republican, U and I successfully sought the imposition of high tariffs to protect its output from the cheap imports from American-owned plantations in Cuba and Hawaii.

Grant was also instrumental in the formation, with church funds, of Utah Power and Light, Utah's principal utility. The church later sold Utah Power to E. H. Harriman, whose ownership of both the Union Pacific and Southern Pacific made him the foremost eastern capitalist seeking to control western resources. Utah Power was eventually reacquired by Mormons, and the church became the largest single stockholder.

After Heber Grant became church president in 1918, the Utah economy began a long slide that hit bottom in the Great Depression. Output had been artificially expanded during World War I, but soon after, the mining economy collapsed, and farmers faced a severe downturn from which they would not recover until World War II. Discriminatory freight rates further hurt local industry, which also suffered from growing competition with California. The decline in basic industries through the 1920s and 1930s became so severe that the state's industrial capacity, despite the recovery during World War II, was smaller in 1950 than it had been in 1920.

With the economy in a state of collapse, people began to leave the state in large numbers. Nearly thirty thousand people emigrated from Utah in the 1920s. Radical insurgencies erupted after World War I, culminating in a Workers, Soldiers, and Sailors Council in Salt Lake City in 1918 and a bitter miners' strike in 1922. Under the influence of radicals, the Utah Federation of Labor endorsed the Russian Revolution. Soon a concerted counterattack led by the church and local bankers, Marriner Eccles among them, virtually destroyed the labor movement.

During the Great Depression, United Orders—local communal organizations that had been promoted by Brigham Young—were revived, and many poor Mormons established cooperatives throughout the state. The growing popularity of the United Orders and the defeat of Reed Smoot by Elbert Thomas, a pro–New Deal professor of political science at the University of Utah, frightened the church hierarchy. J. Reuben Clark, Grant's top adviser, attacked the revival, saying that "Communism and the United Order are the same thing, Communism being merely a forerunner, so to speak, of a reestablishment of the United Order. . . . I am informed that ex-bishops, and indeed bishops, who belong to Communistic organizations are preaching this doctrine."

In reaction to the revival of the United Orders, the church established the Church Security Program under Clark's leadership. This self-help program, the hierarchy's version of the correct connection with its socialistic past, was presented as an alternative to New Deal relief programs. Encouraged by articles in such conservative publications as the *Saturday Evening Post, Cosmopolitan,* and *American Banker,* the Republican-oriented church leadership touted the church program as the answer to Roosevelt's "big government." It claimed to have taken more than eighty-five thousand Mormons off the dole, but in fact, Utah's proportion of indigents on relief remained high throughout the decade. At the height of the depression, more federal funds poured into Utah than most other states. The Mormon welfare program ultimately failed to stem the "revolt of the Mormon congregations" as Carey McWilliams characterized it. Utah residents through the 1930s and 1940s remained attracted to New Deal programs and candidates. Church members frequently preferred government relief checks to bishops' storehouse supplies.

The Great Depression also hit the church hard economically despite Heber Grant's attempts to rebuild its economic base. Church investments in the late 1920s and early 1930s were largely unproductive. One of its major banks was sold for a song to the Eccles interests in order to forestall a collapse of the entire Salt Lake banking system. Utah and Idaho Sugar was also forced to sell its Canadian factory to meet long-overdue payments for the sugar beets and to gain capital to keep the company going.

While the church floundered, the Eccles interests prospered. Led by George Eccles after Marriner went to Washington, the family was more in tune with the shifts in the regional economy and the new forces emerging from the New Deal. The Eccles brothers in the late 1920s had created the first bank holding company in the interior West, which allowed their First Security Corporation not only to weather the depression but to swallow up at bargain prices weaker banks in Utah and Idaho. The central organizing force in the region, First Security maintained influence throughout Utah, southern Idaho, and Wyoming and established a presence in Nevada and northern Arizona. First Security became heavily involved in the home-mortgage market by tapping loans from the new Federal Housing Administration, in the design of which Marriner had played a central role.

The Eccles brothers were not the only Utah businessmen to establish a Washington link. By the late 1930s, a number of key people, some of them Mormons who had gotten their start as Reed Smoot's bright young men, became a force in the Washington bureaucracy. These Washington connections paid off for Utah with the advent of World War II. George Eccles promoted Ogden as a desirable site for military installations because of its role as a railroad nexus. In the late 1930s, Hill Air Force Base was established on land donated by Eccles and other members of the Ogden Chamber of

Commerce. During the war, ten major military bases were opened in Utah. New capital investment from 1941 to 1945, almost all of it from federal sources, equaled the total capital investment in the state in 1939.

Wartime expenditures soon led to the diversification of Utah's mining-dominated economy. Hill Air Force Base became a magnet for further defense installations and for defense-related industries. By 1960, Hill was the major missile center in the West, and Utah was the third most defense-oriented state in the nation. At the same time, Utah's military installations attracted such corporation as Thiokol Chemical Corporation, Sperry Rand, and Hewlett-Packard.

Utah farming was also undergoing major changes. The size of farms grew as they came to resemble large outdoor factories. First Security worked closely with the Idaho-based Jack Simplot agribusiness interests and U and I Sugar to foster the integration of farming with processing and packing. Simplot is best known for its development of mass marketing of potatoes for the McDonald's fast-food chain.

The war was also responsible for the interior West's first steel plant at Geneva, Utah, south of Salt Lake City. Built with federal funds by Utah Construction, the plant was leased during the war to United States Steel. When United States Steel proposed purchasing the plant outright in 1948, the church opposed the move because it feared the plant would disorganize nearby communities and undermine the church's influence in an area not far from Brigham Young University at Provo. Negotiations between J. Reuben Clark and United States Steel's Dr. Walter Mathesius eventually led to an agreement over hiring policies and the role of the corporation in the community. With United States Steel firmly established in Utah, the Geneva plant played a major role in generating related economic activity in the area. Utah resources, in the spirit of the self-industrializing West, were being fully processed within the state and used to build its own economy.

The momentum from the war-inspired boom had carried Utah forward, eventually establishing it as an important growth center of the interior. The strong presence of corporations from outside the state was complemented by the rise of such regional powers as First Security, U and I, Simplot Industries, Idaho-based Morrison-Knudsen, the Browning armament interests, and regional marketing operations such as Albertson's and Food King. "If one word had to be chosen to summarize the economic history of Utah for the past thirty years," wrote James Clayton in *Utah's History,* "a good choice would be *dependency.*" According to J. L. Shoemaker, a Utah Power and Light executive who had worked for Dun and Bradstreet, the New York brokerage houses were still identifying Utah as federally dominated in the 1960s.

By the late 1960s the boom began to shift toward resource development. The issues underlying this boom traced back to the very roots of Deseret, when control over resources, particularly control of water, the most precious western resource, was considered the key not just to growth but to survival. Despite its dependency, Salt Lake City grew apace, fueled by Mormon population policies. As the city spread along the Wasatch Front, the city's leaders mounted a campaign to get Utah's share of the Colorado.

GRABBING UTAH'S SHARE: THE CENTRAL UTAH PROJECT

Immediately upon arriving in the Salt Lake Valley in 1847, the Mormon settlers realized that the proper development of water was the key to food production and economic self-sufficiency. By the following spring, over 5,000 acres had been brought under cultivation by diverting the streams that flowed from the Wasatch Mountains. Settlements were established near the mouth of every canyon with at least one irrigation system for each settlement. The effort was entirely on a cooperative basis defined by a system of "beneficial use." Brigham Young told the settlers, "No man has the right to waste one drop of water that another man can turn into bread." Consistent with the practice of "prior appropriations," which would later develop in Colorado and other western states to serve mining, the Mormons linked water use to their overall concept of the cooperative community, in which no individual rights for use of the water were recognized. Prior appropriation, with its principle of "first in time, first in right," was a mechanical application of a western-invented system for an arid environment, which required control with some degree of cooperation. The Mormon model of cooperative action impressed the first great appraiser of western water, John Wesley Powell, who believed further land development in the West could only be achieved through cooperative action rather than individual, government, or corporate action.

Throughout the late nineteenth century, the Mormon settlements experimented with dam and reservoir construction, encountering the usual difficulties with financing. By the turn of the century, irrigation efforts began to dwindle in number because of the growing costs of projects. One of the key projects explored but postponed was a diversion of the Strawberry River into the area of Spanish Fork in the Utah Valley southeast of Salt Lake City, one of the major agricultural valleys in central Utah. The local farmers realized that they would need to find outside financing and resources to pay the high costs of diverting the water through the mountains north and east of the valley. With the creation of the Reclamation Service, the farmers quickly turned to the federal government for irrigation subsidies. The Strawberry Creek Project, one of the Reclamation Service's first, was initiated in 1906 and completed in 1922.

When Utah agriculture was in collapse during the 1920s and 1930s, the Reclamation Service became the central planning body for future Utah water development. The bureau conducted nearly all the field investigations and planning for a series of projects for the storage and diversion of water.

By the mid-1940s local Utah business and agricultural interests formed the Utah Water Users Association and later the Water and Power Board to build the state's own water lobby rather than relying solely on the Bureau of

Reclamation. The plans of Arizona and California to take more water from the Colorado generated the first systematic push for water development among the upper-basin states. Utah water interests began to talk of massive development of the upper Colorado basin, including a series of long-term projects known collectively as the Central Utah Project.

The Colorado had been a major concern of the Mormons ever since they had built early settlements adjacent to the river. Brigham Young had explored the possibility of using the Colorado as the main transportation route from Salt Lake City to the sea. In the late 1920s Senator Reed Smoot, in response to California's plans for the Colorado, raised the possibility of a dam at Flaming Gorge on the Utah-Wyoming border.

By the late 1940s Utah's growing water lobby was committed to large-scale utilization of the Colorado for agricultural and urban needs as well as a source of cheap hydroelectric power. The upper-basin agreement of 1948 made water allotments by state, with Utah entitled to 23 percent of the upper-basin total. The upper-basin states, working with the Bureau of Reclamation, planned a series of major multipurpose dams called the Colorado River Storage Project, which was introduced in Congress in the early 1950s. The major Utah components of the plan, the Central Utah Project, were budgeted at more than a billion dollars.

In a curious episode in 1950, the head of southern California's Metropolitan Water District, Joseph Jensen, used his Utah Mormon background to try to persuade church officials to back California instead of Arizona in the fight over the Central Arizona Project. In a letter to J. Reuben Clark, Jensen argued that the Mormon church in southern California was growing rapidly. The increase in Mormons meant in turn a greater church investment in the area, thanks to tithing and other income-generating activities. Such growth and economic investment, Jensen argued, was "dependent upon the security of the water supply in southern California." Jensen then set up a meeting with Clark in Salt Lake City through Gus Backman while simultaneously attempting to influence his cousin, senatorial candidate Wallace Bennett, and Governor J. Bracken Lee. Jensen argued with the conservative Lee that the Arizona project ought to be opposed because it was "federally dominated."

Jensen's efforts were to no avail. The church stood by its support for Arizona and its substantial Mormon population, located in the area where development by the project might occur. Church counselor Clark also felt that California represented the major obstacle to the plans of Utah and the upper-basin states. "We have large areas in Utah that might be irrigated from the Colorado River," Clark wrote back to Jensen, arguing that "Arizona has elaborate ambitions along the same direction of providing water for their lands and they have great quantities of land." Clark concluded, "In all of these, we have and must have a direct interest."

Jensen discovered that the growing consensus in the state around the Central Utah and Colorado River Storage projects was overwhelming. Even

Lee, although strongly opposed to federal government intervention, backed them. The breakfast trio of McKay, Backman, and Fitzpatrick, along with other Salt Lake business leaders, had a hand in mobilizing support through the Aqualantes, the promotional organization of the upper-basin states. The *Deseret News,* treating the Colorado River Storage Project as a crusade, called on upper-basin groups to subscribe to a publicity fund to fight the conservationists who opposed the project.

Republican Senator Arthur Watkins became the state's chief spokesman on water issues through the 1950s. Watkins, with senators from Wyoming, Colorado, and New Mexico, became a field general for the storage-project legislation and maintained an almost evangelical fervor in promoting the reclamation project. When the bitter fight between Senator Joseph McCarthy and the Eisenhower administration broke out in 1954–1955, Watkins played a pivotal role. He eventually introduced the successful censure motion against the Wisconsin senator. Watkins' emergence as a key figure in the McCarthy situation was a trade-off for Eisenhower's reluctant support for the storage project. Watkins denied any explicit deal but explained in his autobiography that when Eisenhower called him in to congratulate him after the censure motion, the Utah senator "quite coincidentally—because a State of the Union message was in preparation—asked him [Eisenhower] to include a statement in support of the Colorado River project, and he did."

After Congress passed the storage-project act in 1956, the Central Utah Water Conservancy District was established to act as local government sponsor for the Central Utah Project. The Water Conservancy Board, appointed by state judges, became a self-perpetuating pro-water-development lobbying group that functioned as tax collector, administrator, and lobbyist.

As it was originally designed in the 1950s, the Central Utah Project was structured to divert water from the south slopes of the Uinta Mountains and the Colorado River to the Great Basin in Central Utah. The water from the Bonneville unit of the project would be diverted via extensive reservoirs, tunnels, and canals over the Wasatch Mountains, a substantial distance to marginal farmland in central Utah as well as the more densely populated and industrialized Wasatch Front. The project's six separate units, Bonneville, Vernal, Jensen, Uintah, Upalco, and the Ute Indian unit, were designed for different urban and agricultural purposes.

From the outset, the Central Utah Project was never a clearly defined project. When it was authorized, it was presented primarily as a plan to bring irrigation water to previously unirrigated lands. After 1956 the overall project, particularly the key Bonneville unit, was modified several times to offset criticisms of excessive costs and unwarranted subsidies. Ultimately, a substantial amount of the water was redefined as supplemental municipal water so that the quantity of water for urban and industrial use could be increased. "In analyzing the CUP, the economist does not know exactly what to analyze," wrote University of Montana economist Tom Powers. "The CUP is a shifting project," he concluded.

The shifting rationale for the project paralleled similar shifts involving other Colorado basin projects. The underlying motivation for completing the revised projects revolved around the fears associated with the "use it or lose it" mentality. "The goal to 'fully utilize the whole supply' has had all the force of revealed truth from pioneer days to the present," wrote Utah water analyst Jay Bagley. "Every generation sees some unrealized water development opportunities and is driven toward development from an implicit faith in the economic and social transformation that could be triggered by it. This faith has been reinforced by a constant fear that if water-development potentials are not soon realized, someone else will find a way to put the water to use so that identified opportunities are lost forever." In Utah's case, that "someone else" was primarily California, with its apparently insatiable thirst for the Colorado.

"For those of us who live in the arid West," Utah Water Conservancy District attorney Ed Clyde declared in defense of the project, "it is unthinkable that we should permit our water resources to waste, either by nondevelopment or wasteful use." Such thinking became the rationale underlying support for the project as well as the basis for environmental opposition to the Central Utah Project and other massive western water projects. Through the 1970s, public criticism mounted over project costs and subsidies. As the attacks increased, advocates of the Utah project restructured the project to allow for greater urban use. Under the new plan up to 99,000 acre-feet were to be delivered to the urban corridor stretching from Salt Lake in the north to Provo and Orem in the south. The new urban-oriented system meant additional costs from plans to deliver the water to satisfy summer peak loads, particularly during a drought.

One Salt Lake County water study estimated that upward of 40 percent of residential and municipal water use during the year was earmarked for such nonconsumptive purposes as watering lawns, trees, and flower gardens. "Thus the Bureau of Reclamation is using federal subsidies intended for support of family farms," Powers wrote, "to construct mammoth facilities so that suburban lawns in prosperous communities can be watered whenever their owners desire."

The Central Utah Project also generated criticism concerning the project's diversion and storage components, which would, according to one critic, "hack up the mountains and screw up the stream flows." Another key area of concern was the problems related to the Ute tribe, which was entitled to a substantial portion of the project. Many of these criticisms were incorporated into the arguments justifying Jimmy Carter's hit list, which jeopardized the project's future when the list was first announced. Unlike the situation in Colorado, Utah water lobbyists were already united and prepared to act to save their project. Farming and urban interests, along with the Mormon church, had long maintained a common front for the project. Time and again Utah's governor, congressional delegation, and legislature would invoke their support of the lake project. One exception to this powerful support was Paul Van Dam, Salt Lake County Attorney from 1975 to 1979. Van Dam and his assistant Gerald Kinghorn risked career and political backing by issuing two reports questioning CUP economics and its ostensible advantages for the Salt Lake area.

The strong support for the Central Utah Project proved crucial in the months following the hit-list announcement. The Utah water lobby continued to pressure Congress for new authorizations on the Bonneville unit. The lobby used considerable muscle to fend off the Carter administration's attempts to scale down the project. In 1979 the EPA, working closely with local critics, proposed an independent review process for the project that would have substantially delayed the project and quite possibly killed it. But the Utah water lobby immediately moved to keep the project on line using its biggest weapon, Congressman Gunn McKay, the nephew of David O. McKay. Gunn McKay was a strong project advocate and a power in the House as chairman of the House Military Appropriations Subcommittee. When the EPA began to move on its independent-review proposal, the Carter administration sought support for the MX missile system to be built in Utah and Nevada. McKay would clearly play a central role in the MX debates.

By late 1979, an obvious quid pro quo had been arranged. If Carter would agree to support McKay and the project, McKay would support basing the MX missile in Utah and Nevada. As the EPA started to make its move for an independent review, the agency was called off. "EPA got a call from [the president's] Domestic Council saying do not defer this project," the Environmental Policy Center's Peter Carlson told *High Country News*. "For various political reasons, Interior Secretary Cecil Andrus has committed his agency to constructing the CUP, and EPA's involvement was just not acceptable," said Carlson. As a consequence, CUP not only remained on line, but in January 1980 an additional $20 million was added to the appropriation request for the project. "Utah has found itself marvelously favored by Mr. Carter," the *Deseret News* noted in March 1980, in light of the situation. "The number of federal policy reversals in the past three months has been amazing," the *Deseret News* concluded. MX support eventually helped deny McKay his reelection in 1980.

Despite lobbying successes, the project continued to face a range of criticisms, particularly as the project shifted to a more urban orientation. EPA administrator Alan Merson pointed out in 1979 that construction of the Utah project would "defer the need for water conservation measures for several decades, and this in a metropolitan area with one of the highest per capita water use rates in the nation."

Using conservation and cost comparisons as their yardstick, critics were able to develop full-blown alternatives. Gerald Kinghorn, director of Salt Lake County's Division of Water Quality and Water Pollution Control, proposed an urban-oriented "dual water system." Such a system would provide low-quality water for such uses as watering lawns, while high-quality water would be earmarked for personal consumption. In this way enough high-quality water would be conserved to eliminate the need for Bonneville-unit supplies to urban areas. This alternative plan would cost only about one-fourth as much as the Central Utah Project.

The idea of an alternative to the project, particularly one of limited size and purpose, was anathema to the development-oriented business and political leadership in Utah. By the late 1970s, a small but significant opposition to that development ethic had emerged. The opposition called attention to the "physical limitations of the region," as Powers put it. Utah's water lobby, committed for so long to the completion of the project, still dominated the politics of water in the state. But Utah, which never had as powerful an agribusiness lobby as California or Arizona, found it increasingly difficult to justify the project. With the question of resource development in flux, the problems with the CUP refocused that other central resource issue of the Interior: energy, by whom and for whom.

ENERGY BROKER

While the focus of efforts to divert the Colorado River shifted toward the urban corridor, the attention of the major energy players was fixed on the rich deposits of coal, uranium, oil shale, and a variety of other mineral ores in eastern, central, and southern Utah. Increasingly Salt Lake City's future was tied to its new role as an energy broker.

Utah coal deposits had been coveted by energy producers since the development of deep mines in the Emery County coal fields in central Utah in the late nineteenth and early twentieth century. By the 1960s, with the emergence of the Grand Plan and WEST Associates' regional energy strategy, attention shifted from central Utah to strip mines on the Colorado Plateau. The region's rich deposits of low-sulfur coal offered a major opportunity for energy producers, particularly the California utilities attracted by its proximity to California.

The first big play for these coal deposits on the Utah side of the Utah-Arizona border was the epic Kaiparowits fight in the early 1970s. The Kaiparowits project fit the state's development ethos. Local residents accepted the argument that construction of the plant would aid the local community. Unlike the urban corridor to the north, southeastern Utah, according to sociologist Ronald Little, had been "undergoing dedevelopment since 1940, and its residents faced a reality of high unemployment, low wages, and the expected outmigration of its youth." The utilities argued that the Kaiparowits plant would revitalize the area economically, providing more than six thousand new jobs as well as indirect economic benefits. Most important, the utilities appeared to offer the solution for halting outmigration. Widespread concern over the exodus of the young was particularly intense in Mormon communities, in which people desperately wanted to keep their families and communities intact.

As the Kaiparowits fight heated up, local residents felt torn between the different parties to the dispute. The major participants—the utilities, the environmentalists, the federal government (which owned the land on which the coal was located), and the railroads (which debated whether to build a new transportation route for the coal)—were all outsiders. No one seemed to have much concern for the impact on the residents, whatever the outcome. Even the church, which strongly backed the Kaiparowits project, appeared more interested in the overall dynamic of energy development in the state than the actual impact on the local Mormon communities.

The effects, many argued, would be severe. In an area that was basically agricultural, the Kaiparowits project would consume 41,400 acre-feet of Utah's annual allotment from the Colorado River. The project would also create boomtown conditions then prevalent in other energy development areas such as Page, Arizona, across the border. A number of boomtown studies pointed out that jobs for local residents generated by projects like Kaiparowits were few and far between, primarily because of the skill requirements of the jobs. A transient work force would be brought in that would likely undermine local institutions and sharply conflict with community values. Ultimately, the studies concluded, the economic impact—including increased property-tax, welfare, sewer, police, and education assessments and skyrocketing inflation in such areas as housing—would be extremely negative.

One Mormon academic who had studied the potential impact of Kaiparowits concluded that the plant would indeed hurt the area, contrary to what the utilities were saying. The academic met with a member of the church hierarchy who followed the Kaiparowits situation, to communicate his views. "We are now an international church," the church leader told the professor. "Do you realize how many members we now have in Latin America, in Europe? How many new stakes, how many new temples we're building? We can't be oriented just toward a few small communities in southern Utah."

When the Kaiparowits project was suspended after Southern California Edison dropped out, the decision highlighted the crucial role of the California utilities and the California market in the Utah energy situation. While the Kaiparowits fight was being waged, another proposed coal-fired plant in southern Utah, the Intermountain Power Project (known as Son of Kaiparowits), began to wend its way through the federal bureaucracy. The Interior Department approved the project after its relocation to Lynndyl, north of Interstate 70. After Kaiparowits, the Intermountain project became the focus of efforts to develop Utah's energy resources. Once again California utilities, led by the Los Angeles Department of Water and Power, provided a major share of the project's front end financing and planned to take 58 percent of the power supply Their presence on the project was, like Edison at Kaiparowits, essential to its survival. Further, the proposed coal-fired Warner Valley plant, also in southern Utah and advocated by southern Utah development interests, was equally dependent on California participation.

The dependence on California, particularly after the Kaiparowits fight, became more and more unpopular in the state. The opposition was joined by some southern Utah residents formerly wedded to energy development. The state's major electrical utility, Utah Power and Light, took note of the increased antagonism toward California and used the opportunity to shift away from an integrated regional energy strategy with California in the driver's seat toward a new role for Utah as an energy broker.

The Mormon church had for a number of years owned and controlled Utah Power and Light, but in the dispersal of church investments at the turn of the century, it divested itself of most of its interest in the company. Through the 1970s, there was a strong Mormon presence within the company's management and on its board, although many of the utility's stockholders were eastern investors. During the 1960s and early 1970s, Utah Power and Light had been a participant in WEST Associates, sharing the assumptions of the Grand Plan. But shortly after Kaiparowits collapsed, the company's leadership decided to pull out of the WEST group and reorient its approach. It decided to extricate itself from the southern Utah situation by seeking to trade long-term leases held on the Kaiparowits Plateau for coal leases in Emery County that were held by the Bureau of Reclamation. The company continued to consider coal development central to its continuing strategy as a self-sufficient energy broker. But even the wily utility realized it could never maintain a fully independent role, given the great energy play developing within the state and throughout the interior West. Utah Power's primary source of capital now came from California rather than the East, as in the past. Utah, like Colorado and Arizona, was a capital-deficit state and showed no signs in the foreseeable future of generating its own funds. Despite significant church investment, Utah Power and Light had to look outside the state for funding for new projects.

Utah Power and Light pursued a regional energy strategy even after pulling out of WEST. As part of an overall campaign to promote the Utah boom, the utility ran a series of ads in the *Wall Street Journal.* "We sit atop some of the world's great coal deposits," the utility proclaimed to these national business readers, encouraging them to tap into Utah's boom. Utah Power and Light, despite its fling as an independent energy broker, still expressed the same "Come and Get 'Em" attitude that dominated the mood of the state.

The emergence of the energy issue in the 1960s and 1970s witnessed the rise of a new type of power broker in the state—the energy-connected lawyer and politician. Two of the most influential figures were Calvin Rampton and Scott Matheson, who occupied the governor's post through most of the period. Rampton, elected in 1964 as a moderate Democrat over weak Republican opposition, was a consummate politician. The son of a Mormon salesman from Bountiful, Utah, Rampton became a powerful local lawyer with a wide range of political and corporate ties. As governor, he worked closely with Pro-Utah, a Republican-oriented business group, to establish the Utah Industrial Promotion Council and the Utah Travel Council.

As governor when the boom took off in Utah, Rampton established himself as a champion of corporate relocation and a probusiness environment. His prodevelopment stance made him equally attractive to Republicans and Democrats, allowing him to become the consensus candidate of the business and political establishment. Rampton also became the champion of energy development in Utah, declaring that he was "perfectly willing to produce energy for sale outside the state." The foremost champion of the Kaiparowits project, he scoffed at the anti-California perspective and worked closely with corporate lobbyists to promote the big energy developments.

Although Rampton won reelection easily in 1968 and again in 1972, he decided to leave office in 1976 to devote his time to his law practice, in which he functioned as a high-powered broker on the statewide, western, and national levels. Rampton's handpicked successor, Scott Matheson, narrowly defeated Vernon Romney in the 1976 election. Matheson, the son of a Mormon judge, had worked for eighteen years in the legal department of the Union Pacific and as legal counsel for the Anaconda Copper Company.

Although Matheson was a less crafty politician than Rampton, he was nevertheless a crucial link between the big energy companies and the new Democratic politicians of the 1970s: Lamm of Colorado, Judge of Montana, Herschler of Wyoming, and Babbitt of Arizona. When Matheson became chairman of the Western Governors' Policy Office (WESTPO) in 1979, his election was welcomed by the Western Regional Council. The council's chairman during that period was James Wilson, the head of the Union Pacific's energy subsidiary, Rocky Mountain Energy Company. Wilson characterized Matheson's ascendancy in WESTPO as providing "a basis of trust already established."

Matheson in turn looked to the council as a key component of what the Utah governor characterized as "the new coalition of the 1980s." Speaking at the council's annual meeting in Phoenix in December 1979, Matheson described "the fast-blooming romance" between WESTPO and the council, comparing their relationship to the "romance period" that precedes the marriage. Looking to the big energy play in the West and in his own state, Matheson also spoke of "a new western consciousness" underlying his proposed coalition of governors, the congressional delegation, the various federal bureaucrats overseeing development in the western states, and the corporate community. WESTPO and the council would provide the leadership for this coalition, Matheson declared. The Utah governor projected a new kind of regionalism—not the conservative and potentially unproductive concept of the Sagebrush Rebellion, which neither he nor his corporate hosts backed, but a regionalism based on a developing energy economy.

Matheson knew that Utah was well situated to cash in on the development of its resources. He actively backed the mammoth Intermountain Power and Warner Valley plants, hoping they might launch a new coal boom in southern Utah. Anticipating such tentative projects as a proposed coal-gasification plant in the California desert or the Harry Allen coal-fired plant in Nevada might use Utah coal, Matheson and his allies explored the possibility of constructing a coal-slurry pipeline, using Utah water to transport coal to the California coast, where it could be shipped to Japan.

Shale was another resource being touted. Every participant in the proposed Matheson coalition saw rich possibilities for Utah shale, particularly after the "money supermarket" became available in 1980. The possibility of shale development turned cautious Utah bankers and businessmen into wild-eyed optimists. "We're incredibly optimistic about future growth in the area and energy is the key to it all," Kelly Matthews, chief economist of the First Security Corporation, said of the Utah economy. "Right now, however, we're the weak sister to Denver in the battle for the big money coming in around that development, especially oil and gas exploration. But most of the synthetics are on our side of the mountain," Matthews happily went on, "and all that money for development should rub off on us here in Salt Lake."

Matthews and other Utah businessmen realized that shale could be a tremendous boon, but even the massive subsidies from the Energy Security Corporation would be dwarfed by what could be the largest and most expensive public-works project and boom stimulator in history—the MX missile project. "The MX," Matthews declared in 1980, "is an absolutely imponderable situation. They're talking about $60 billion or more, much of which will undoubtedly be oriented toward Salt Lake City. Even if the people here in Utah don't like it, I'm not sure they can block it in any case. The MX could be our blockbuster."

The MX idea was initially proposed by the Carter administration in June 1979, shortly after the president signed the SALT II treaty. The system consisted of a looped track winding twenty-five square miles through the desert along the Nevada-Utah border. Two hundred missile transporters or launchers would move up and down the track through twenty-three horizontal shelters on each loop, creating all together forty-six hundred different shelters. This MX was a monstrosity, a multibillion-dollar project that some estimates projected would cost as much as $100 billion or more. It would have employed more than twenty-three hundred construction workers, creating boomtown conditions far greater than any previous project. The Carter administration and the Air Force dismissed the boomtown problems by emphasizing, as with the Kaiparowits project, the economic advantages for the area.

Unlike Kaiparowits, local residents, particularly in the south-central part of the state and Nevada, where the MX was to be built, quickly opposed the project. Opposition building through 1979 and 1980 focused not only on boomtown fears but also the availability of water. Politicians such as Matheson soon began to retreat on the issue, shifting from their earlier advocacy to a more studied neutrality or opposition. The MX opposition signaled a shift in attitude that raised the question of large-scale development throughout the state.

Mistrust of the federal government, always present, grew in the late

1970s because of the effects of the 1950s atom bomb tests that were conducted in Nevada upwind from southern Utah. With neighbors and family members dying of cancer and the federal government's Nuclear Regulatory Commission continuing to downplay the consequences of the tests, the Utah media quickly moved in on the story, transforming the tests into a major issue in the state. Even the Mormon church maintained a neutral position on the MX in part because of the anger of a number of church members over the nuclear-test issue. By 1981, opposition to the MX had spread to a substantial number of the state's residents. The Mormon church, after major internal debate, issued a strong statement attacking not only the MX, but the proliferation of nuclear weapons as well.

For the first time, Utahns began to question the impact of the massive projects—whether the MX, the Intermountain Power Project, or the huge nuclear park proposed for the Green River area—on local communities. Residents were more amenable to the arguments of environmentalists, although a great deal of mistrust still remained. The actor Robert Redford, who had been involved in the fight against Kaiparowits, had symbolized unwelcome outsider meddling in Utah's affairs. At the height of the controversy, Redford had been burned in effigy in Kanab. But in the period after Kaiparowits, the actor tried to mend fences in the state while continuing his opposition to big energy projects. Now established as a Utah resident, he criticized, in retrospect, the way he and fellow environmentalists had disregarded the fears and needs of the local residents. Redford now supported the idea of economic development but proposed instead "nonpolluting" industry, such as film production, as an alternative to the energy game plans.

The film *The Electric Horseman,* shot both in Las Vegas and southern Utah in 1978 and released in 1979, was conceived in part as an element of Redford's "southern Utah strategy." It provided some employment for local residents. Redford also attempted to establish an interesting counterpoint through the story line of the film. The cowboy played by Redford is linked to the good people of southern Utah and its celebrated landscape but is pitted against a rapacious development-minded corporation that operates out of the iniquitous Las Vegas.

Despite the success of the film, the local residents ultimately remained interested in Redford the celebrity—the quintessential outsider—more than Redford the advocate. But by 1980 the hostility toward environmentalists had begun to dissipate. The idea of resource development no longer produced an easy consensus. Utah, indeed, was a changing state, susceptible to all the characteristics of the western boom. The speed and direction of that change could no longer just be a simple matter of what someone in New York, Los Angeles, Denver, or even downtown Salt Lake City, decided to do.

CHURCH POWER

When Heber Grant made his pilgrimage to Wall Street in the 1890s, he embraced Brigham Young's realpolitik of seeking accommodation with the larger economic and political forces shaping Utah. Before he reached the top of the church hierarchy, the uneasy relationship between leaders of the Mormon and gentile communities had developed into a more permanent detente. The Grant presidency (1918–1945) became a pivotal era for the church.

The church had begun as one of the great nineteenth-century millenarian movements emphasizing that the creation of Deseret through cooperative action meant the realization of the commonwealth of heaven on earth. With the growing ties between church and gentile leaders, church attitudes shifted profoundly. The attack on the church led by feminists and a number of exposés written during the early muckraking period had identified the church in the popular mind with socialistic practices and polygamy. In response to this popular view of the church and the changes in the Utah economy that weakened church-controlled enterprise, church leaders began to preach the virtues of Americanism, hard work, and free enterprise. Politically, the church became identified with the most orthodox wing of the Republican party. According to Robert Mullen, Heber Grant's time "was taken up in forwarding the economic interests of the church."

The first two decades of the Grant presidency embraced a period of difficulties and decline for the church. Restrictive immigration laws cut off the church from its main source of new recruits—its missionary efforts in northern and western Europe. The collapse of the Utah economy forced more and more saints to emigrate, many to California. The Saints had weathered infinitely more difficult periods, and they survived the Great Depression, divided politically but still intact.

With the rapid spread of American influence overseas after World War II, the church renewed its missionary effort in countries from which it had previously been excluded. Consistent with the Mormon definition of success as success in the business world, the church developed a missionary approach modeled after sales techniques used in the commercial world. In the postwar era the church identified itself not only as the one Christian church native to America but also as the fastest-growing church in the country. By the 1960s the top levels of the church hierarchy—the First Presidency, the Quorum of Twelve, the presiding bishopric, and the Quorum of Seventy—were overwhelmingly composed of small businessmen or corporate executives.

In addition to being the principal center of influence in what Arrington called the Great Basin Kingdom, the church was heard in Washington. The role of Marriner Eccles and other Mormons in the Roosevelt administration highlighted Roosevelt's alliance of regional power centers. The New Deal Mormons represented a liberal tendency within the church, but they did not speak for the hierarchy, which was decidedly anti-Roosevelt. During the Eisenhower years, Ezra Taft Benson served as secretary of agriculture, symbolizing the emergence of Great Basin agribusiness and representing an important tie to western conservatives. Eisenhower characterized Benson's church connections as "a distinct asset." In every election year, presidential candidates regarded an appearance at the Tabernacle as a must. Despite its power, the church remained passive in many crucial areas, following rather than initiating key economic and political decisions. From the Great Depression through the 1950s, the federal government played the major role in reviving a moribund Utah economy. In this period New York investment houses defined Utah as "a sphere of influence" of the federal government and tended to discount the nature and importance of the influence of the Mormon church and its extensive holdings.

Throughout David O. McKay's presidency, the church's holdings grew steadily in value, beginning with the assets left intact or reacquired after the divestitures forced by the Edmunds-Tucker Act of 1887. These assets included several insurance companies, a local bank, a woolen mill, the ZCMI department store chain, Utah and Idaho Sugar, and large amounts of land around the Temple in downtown Salt Lake City, plus the growing holdings of local stakes (parishes). Other major economic powers such as Kennecott Copper, the Union Pacific, and the Eccles interests continued to be linked to the church. During the McKay presidency, George Eccles was a regular visitor to McKay's suite at the Hotel Utah, while Marriner maintained a suite upstairs. Although George in particular became an informal adviser to the church and church leaders sat on the First Security Board, both George and Marriner remained distinct from the church.

After Marriner returned to Salt Lake City, he decided to run for the United States Senate as a Republican against Arthur Watkins. Out of tune with the state's conservative politics, he was accused of aiding and abetting Communists because he advocated recognition of China and was soundly defeated. Soon after the defeat, Marriner began dividing his time between Salt Lake City and San Francisco. As Utah Mining and Construction expanded in the Pacific basin, Marriner decided that San Francisco was a much more appropriate city for the headquarters of a major multinational corporation.

The church, having weathered a liberal challenge from within its own ranks during the New Deal, felt much more at home with the conservative politics of the cold-war era. In 1948 and 1950 the church played a role in the defeat of pro–New Deal candidates for governor and United States senator. Then with the advent of the Eisenhower years, McKay became the new prophet, seer, and revelator. He and church leader Henry D. Moyle began to orient the church away from its earlier passive and reactive role to a more aggressive policy of growth and recruitment. McKay and Moyle put particular emphasis on the international missionary effort. To send thousands of missionaries around the world and build new stakes and temples required a great deal of money.

Under Moyle, the church upgraded its portfolio, even selling its own Zion's First Security Bank to Mormon businessmen, who kept the bank within the church's sphere of influence. By 1962, Moyle would boast to Salt Lake City's Mayor J. Bracken Lee that church investments and internal sources of income such as tithing were generating an annual income of $1 million a day. But the church was also spending its money as fast as it was coming in. The drive for new members overwhelmed all other aspects of church policy. As a regional economic power, the church continued to remain relatively passive, removed from, although supportive of, the gradual growth that preceded the takeoff of the economy in the 1960s.

When Moyle died in 1963, his place as counselor and chief economic policy maker was assumed by Nathan Eldon Tanner, who became the pivotal figure in church economic affairs for most of the next two decades. Tanner, who comes from an old Mormon family, settled in western Canada in the early part of the twentieth century and became active in politics. Elected to the Alberta legislature, he eventually became speaker of its house. With a background in mining, oil, and gas, Tanner later became minister of lands and mines in the provincial government. He developed extensive interests in the energy area, becoming the head of the Trans-Canada Pipeline Company and the Canadian Gas Association. Called to Zion in 1960, he was soon appointed to the Council of Twelve and then became second counselor in the First Presidency on Moyle's death.

As counselor, Tanner reorganized the economic side of the church, attempting to create a more professional, corporate-oriented approach that treated church investments more as a business opportunity than simply as a source of expansion funds. He was able to consolidate his power and overcome remaining resistance in the wake of a scandal in the late 1960s. Two church accountants had been able to embezzle at least $600,000 before getting caught because of the antiquated nature of the church bookkeeping system. The embezzlement so shocked church authorities that Tanner was able to computerize the accounts and to bring in a number of "money managers." These professional aides were in charge of day-to-day decisions under Tanner, as well as the preparation of annual budgets and long-term investment strategies.

In 1968, Tanner created the Deseret Management Corporation as an overall holding company for church-owned businesses. Zion's Securities Corporation was established as the holding company for the church's real estate interests, stock portfolio, and other investments. Further reorganization took place in 1972 as the corporatist approach became entrenched within the church organization and Tannerism became synonymous with church economics.

In economic affairs the church also turned to several national corporate figures, who were given no formal leadership position but served as informal financial advisers and decision-makers. Such behind-the-scenes figures included David Kennedy, Richard Nixon's Secretary of Treasury, and J. Willard Marriott, founder of the Marriott hotel and entertainment empire. Kennedy, prior to his Treasury appointment, had been Nixon's roving ambassador, a kind of international economic troubleshooter, a natural outgrowth of his work as head of the internationally minded Chicago-based Continental Illinois Bank. In his memoirs, Nixon said of Kennedy, "He also met my requirement that my Secretary of the Treasury not be part of the New York-Boston banking establishment that had dominated the department for too long." During the 1970s Kennedy, relying on earlier contacts, also functioned as the church's international ambassador.

The expansion of the church's media holdings showed best how the church used its economic power to further its spiritual quest. Prior to Tanner's emergence, the church's media holdings were limited to Salt Lake's afternoon newspaper, the *Deseret News;* a couple of radio stations in southern Idaho; and KSL, the CBS television and radio outlet in Salt Lake City. Under Tanner, the church reorganized its media holdings into what would ultimately become a major international media conglomerate. In 1964 the church leadership called on Arch Madsen, the sharp-tongued conservative head of the church's Salt Lake broadcast operations, to head up this new church-media operation. Madsen had lived in New York, operated an advertising agency, and had some contact with the world of media financing. With Madsen in charge, the church created the Bonneville International Corporation and immediately acquired radio and television properties in Seattle and New York City to expand its holdings. Through the late 1960s and 1970s Bonneville systematically picked up broadcast properties in Los Angeles, Kansas City, San Francisco, Chicago, and Washington, D.C., and created a broadcast consulting arm to advise Bonneville's stations and other like-minded media groups. Bonneville also created a film-production arm, a computer operation, and a number of audio production facilities.

Under Madsen's leadership, Bonneville functioned as a professional, "profit-oriented" operation within which church policies and goals would still be implemented. Madsen and other church leaders became wedded to the idea that mass communications were, as Madsen put it, "the ultimate power on the face of the earth today. . . . The proper use of the mass media is going to mean the difference between chaos and the solid values of civilization." Madsen referred in part to Bonneville's decision to buy a couple of Dallas radio stations in 1978 in order to "clean them up."

As Bonneville attempted to project itself as a modern media conglomerate subject to Federal Communications Commission (FCC) programming standards, the appearance of overt church influence on programming, news, and public affairs, particularly in its Salt Lake outlets, had to be diminished. Nevertheless, when conflict developed because church interests were at stake, invariably the church hierarchy would step in, stories would be killed, and programming would be affected.

By 1980 the church had greatly expanded its area of economic influence. Since Eldon Tanner's appointment to the first-presidency seventeen years earlier, the church had moved from a passive supporter of downtown redevelopment to an active participant in reshaping the area. New high-rises were built, notably the church's own twenty-six-story office building adjacent to the Temple. The church also leased land to Salt Lake County for the Salt Palace Convention Center. It ultimately attempted to influence the direction of development in both the downtown and outlying areas of Salt Lake City through its own real estate activities as well as links with individual real estate developers. In the process, redevelopment obliterated some of the most spectacular examples of Utah's architectural heritage, including a number of beautiful church and commercial buildings and stately downtown mansions associated with the heyday of the mining frontier. The church was obsessed with recording its own history, but history could not stand in the way of making Salt Lake City a modern, more characterless metropolis.

Tanner's effort to reorganize the church economic holdings was part of a larger effort to consolidate church functions and programs to bring them under centralized control from Salt Lake City. Through its missionary effort, the church had become a worldwide organization with more and more of its membership located overseas in Asia, Europe, Latin America (particularly Mexico), the Pacific basin and Africa. This new situation required a more streamlined administrative structure and greater control over the content of church programs.

The general consolidation of church authority paralleled changes in the use and disposition of its political power in its historical area of influence. The church was especially concerned about its influence in the Utah state legislature, where direct church interests were at stake. "Clear it with the church" was an unwritten rule for politicians in areas in which church policy was directly involved. The church, for example, was active in the right-to-work issue, a long-standing church concern, and it played a prominent role in passage of the provision in Utah as well as in Nevada, Idaho, and Arizona. By 1980 the Utah legislature was overwhelmingly Mormon and conservative, by some estimates as high as 80 percent Mormon.

The increasing political turmoil of the 1960s had a profound effect on the church. The most publicized issue was the church's policy on black members. Although the church was actively recruiting in Third World countries, black members were banned from the priesthood, a position attained by white Mormon men at the age of thirteen. In Joseph Smith's day, ironically, the church was considered abolitionist. Civil rights activists began to attack the church, and Brigham Young University sports teams were often picketed when they appeared out of the state.

Divisions within the church over the civil rights issue were exacerbated by a growing right wing within the church. Divisions became increasingly pronounced between an Ezra Taft Benson wing and a more moderate faction led by First Counselor Hugh B. Brown. By the early 1960s Benson had become a confirmed "conspiracy" advocate who praised the John Birch Society and called its founder, Robert Welsh, "a great American patriot." When Benson's son Reed became Utah chairman of the John Birch Society, father and son were constantly inveighing against liberal-cum-socialist perfidy. "Today the devil as a wolf in a supposedly new suit of sheep's clothing is enticing some men to parrot his line by advocating planned government-guaranteed security programs at the expense of liberty," the elder Benson wrote in 1962 about John Kennedy's New Frontier.

By the mid-1960s the Benson followers found themselves increasingly isolated within the church. Brown was able to stave off the Benson thrust within the church by sending Reed Benson to London on a church mission and by attempting to tone down some of the more virulent anti-Communism and liberal-baiting that had characterized the church over the previous decade. With the collapse of the civil rights movement and the end of the war in Vietnam in the early seventies, the moral issues that most concerned the church leadership became increasingly important political issues throughout the country.

In 1973 Spencer W. Kimball became the new prophet. Kimball came from an old and worthy Mormon family. His grandfather was Heber Kimball, Brigham Young's closest adviser. Spencer was related through complex and extensive family ties to many past and present church leaders. He grew up in Thatcher, Arizona, in the Gila Valley east of Phoenix, where he counted Stewart and Morris Udall's father among his high school classmates. Before becoming president of the church, Kimball was best known for his missionary work among the Indians, whom the Saints identified as their brothers, the Lamanites. In 1978 he announced that he had a revelation that called for the admission of blacks into the priesthood. Kimball's revelation ended a bitter fight within the church and appeared to represent a new move toward the mainstream.

In Utah this was the period of the consensus candidacy of Calvin Rampton. The common understanding among Utah politicians by the mid-1970s was that the church, although not necessarily endorsing particular candidates, would still actively oppose those who attacked or threatened church interests or opposed a prodevelopment approach. Thus a politician like Salt Lake Mayor Ted Wilson, with his youthful liberal image, could get elected mayor of Salt Lake City twice in the 1970s precisely because of the absence of any active church opposition. Wilson brought a new image to the city, the publicity-conscious church hierarchy decided. Such prestige was considered crucial in changing the image of Salt Lake from its "once provincial, religiously oriented" aura to a "cosmopolitan city," as a Hotel Utah promotional brochure put it. Wilson was inevitably influenced by the church, however. He consulted with church leaders on a number of issues and his reelection campaign was run by J. Allen Blodgett, the church's comptroller.

The turmoil of the civil rights and Vietnam eras led the church to create a new institutional mechanism to look after its interests in the political sphere. The new Special Affairs Committee included Gordon Hinckley from the Council of Twelve; James Faust, also a member of the Twelve and a former member of the Utah legislature; David Haight, former mayor of Palo Alto, California; and Neal Maxwell, the former director of the church's educational institutions. The committee was staffed by a number of individuals who played an active role in Utah and western politics. Special Affairs member Maxwell, for one, symbolized the new breed of church leadership involved in political affairs. Formerly a member of the CIA and vice-president of public affairs at the University of Utah during the turbulent 1960s, the smooth-talking Maxwell blended in well with the more modern-sounding corporate-oriented leadership emerging within the church.

The Special Affairs Committee became the leading edge of the church's new role in politics. Its members looked into issues the church considered crucial, such as the MX, how changes in the 160-acre law would affect the church agricultural holdings, how the Indian Child Welfare Act of 1976 related to the church's Indian programs, and the fate of the Central Utah Project. Mormons in Congress—and the entire Utah delegation was Mormon—also looked after the church's interests, getting the church's Indian programs exempted from the Indian Child Welfare Act and promoting the version of the reclamation reform bill that exempted church holdings from the 160-acre limit.

The relatively bland probusiness political outlook of the Special Affairs Committee did not lay to rest the long-simmering right-wing traditions within the church. In 1974 the church took a dramatic stand against the Equal Rights Amendment (ERA) and subsequently helped defeat passage of the measure in at least five states, including Virginia, Florida, and Nevada. This new line on the ERA grew out of the response to the liberal and permissive trends of the 1960s and put a renewed emphasis on what the church considered the moral issues confronting and threatening the family—issues such as the role of women, abortion, and homosexuality. This increasing concern over family issues led to a conservative revival in the church. While some members attacked this conservative revival and questioned the patriarchal and authoritarian outlook associated with it, a new and more powerful right wing began to gather momentum within the church.

Meanwhile, the church, more than ever, actively encouraged its members to get involved in politics. Such activities were extraordinarily effective, since the church remained a highly disciplined, centralized structure with a strong authoritarian cast in all its internal procedures. When the church decided to get involved, it was capable of mobilizing large numbers of people at short notice, as it proved during the International Women's Year meetings in 1977.

In many minds, the question boiled down to whether the eighty-two-year-old Ezra Taft Benson would outlast the ailing eighty-six-year-old Kimball and assume the role of prophet. Once that question is settled, then the conflict within the church between the more modernist element and the Benson conservatives will be resumed within the newly arranged hierarchy.

A NEW SALT LAKE CITY

In the early 1970s, the Eastman Kodak Company decided to open a regional headquarters in the interior West. Company officials narrowed the choice of location to Denver or Salt Lake City. An internal study was commissioned to weigh the pros and cons of each city. When the firm issued a report, Kodak's choice was Denver. Calvin Rampton, recalling the report, commented that what made it so unusual was that it openly referred to Mormon influence in Salt Lake as a crucial factor. "Those fears about the church are seldom articulated and thus seldom addressed," Rampton commented. "When you're trying to persuade a company to bring their headquarters here, you have to raise the problem, since they're undoubtedly thinking about it." Rampton concluded a little wistfully, "But the problem is hopefully diminishing."

Discussing the problem, one non-Mormon Utah Power and Light executive compared his feelings about working in a state surrounded by the pervasive Mormon cultural, political, and economic influence to the feelings of a young man he read about in *National Geographic.* The magazine profiled a man who was walking across the country. When he crossed the Utah state line, the walker commented that entering Utah felt like entering a foreign country.

Northwest Energy, a major pipeline company and the largest single corporation headquartered in Salt Lake City, decided that church influence had its advantages. "The church people are businessmen and that's what's important," Vice-President William Owens said of the situation. "They will support growth and development," he declared, referring to the state's business and tax climate.

Despite this favorable assessment, Owens, like other non-Mormon executives, complained of feeling that he and his wife were "strangers in a strange land." The company was also concerned for its younger, non-Mormon employees with children who had to deal with the thoroughly Mormon-influenced school system. It was fearful that its employees' social life was inevitably constricted by the community's prohibitions on drinking and the general stern moral tone projected by the church and its active believers. "You know, you can't just invite people over for drinks or maybe some bridge, or a cup of coffee," an executive's wife complained.

Despite its rapid growth, Utah remains a relatively small state, with a population under 2 million. While the recent rise in population was in part related to the development of new plants and new jobs, Utah also maintained the highest birthrate in the country, a phenomenon directly related to the church's emphasis on large families. "If we can't beat 'em, we can outpopulate 'em" is a common quip among the Mormons. Utah's growth has not fully weakened Mormon influence, with the exception, perhaps, of Salt Lake City. The Mormon population in the state hovered around 72 percent, while it dipped to slightly over 50 percent in the Salt Lake metropolitan area and under 50 percent in Salt Lake City proper.

As the Mormon factor prevents a greater shift of regional headquarters to Salt Lake, the city will fall short of achieving the status of a new energy capital like Denver. The large corporations, which have moved so easily into Denver and assumed power, remain wary of Salt Lake and the church, although they are tempted by such favorable variables as the probusiness environment, the large energy deposits, the high level of education, and the focus on maintaining a nonunion labor force.

New industries recently attracted to Utah include energy-related companies and a range of labor-intensive operations such as electronics, light industry, and the garment industry. New companies opening plants in the state include multinationals such as Litton, General Telephone and Electric, and Union Carbide and big energy combines such as Standard of Indiana, Exxon, Texaco, and Union Oil.

Energy-related growth was clearly the key to Utah's economic development. Mining operations were a big source of employment, and copper was to a great extent still king, with the value of its output still surpassing the value of coal output, although not for long. Kennecott, with its regional headquarters in Salt Lake City, was still a major influence in the state. In fact, the company was crucial in the initial organization of the Western Regional Council. In the mid-1970s, Kennecott faced increasing difficulties over the extensive pollution generated from its massive smelter west of Salt Lake City, pollution that was contributing heavily to the rapid decline of Salt Lake's air quality. The EPA attempted to force Kennecott to put in new antipollution equipment or face a possible plant closure. Kennecott, at that point, turned to several of its business and political allies, including the head of the Mountain Fuel Supply Company, the local gas company, and Calvin Rampton, who had recently stepped down as governor. The newly formed Western Regional Council took on the Kennecott air-quality issue as its first major project, and Kennecott regional vice-president Robert Pratt was the council's first chairman.

After the council began operations in 1977, staff work was contracted to a newly formed consulting firm called Bonneville Associates, based in Salt Lake. Bonneville was part of a new breed of ambitious, young Salt Lake professionals and entrepreneurs attracted to the potential power and profits of the intermountain region. The Bonneville staff was more attracted to the sleek corporate world of Denver than the stuffy "Neanderthal" world of Salt Lake. Although Bonneville helped smooth the council's transition from a Salt Lake–oriented to a multinational-oriented and Denver-influenced organization, Bonneville remained in Salt Lake City because many of the staff liked what they perceived as a new Salt Lake emerging from the confines of an earlier Mormon-shaped city.

Around the time that Bonneville began operations in the late 1970s, Salt Lake City began to witness a growing influx of like-minded young professionals and middle-management figures. The arrival of new corporate types who liked to drink in turn led to the proliferation of private clubs, the only places in which the state's liquor laws permit the sale by the drink of alcohol. These private clubs, resembling a cross between a singles' bar and a businessman's club, were the main center of afterwork socializing. A rapidly growing ski culture, similar to the fast-growing areas that had so influenced the political climate of Colorado, began to take off in the late 1970s with Park City, about thirty miles from Salt Lake City, providing the proper old mining-town setting. The notion of a new outdoor life-style, complete with booze, drugs, and wife-swapping, became the new Salt Lake's answer to that pervasive "other" culture.

A counterpoint of change and reaction set in. Salt Lake, unlike any other western city, resembled something of a battleground between contrasting cultures and life-styles. As the new corporate life-style invaded Salt Lake, Mormon fundamentalism, linked in part to the revived Mormon right wing, also began to grow. Inspired by the church's own strong emphasis on the social issues surrounding the family, a number of Mormons reacted strongly to what they perceived as new antifamily values. This reaction was intensified by the contemporary corporate ideology, which emphasized loyalty to the company above loyalty to the family. As several business publications pointed out, the preferred 1980s executive, as opposed to the 1950s executive, was someone engaged in the more open-ended, less attached life-style of a single or divorced person.

With growing mistrust of the modern life-style, Mormon fundamentalists became more aggressive in seeking out new political solutions to combat these contemporary trends. There were even widespread signs that polygamy has never fully disappeared. Some estimates put the number of polygamists as high as 35,000. Polygamous households, including one behind a high wall in Salt Lake City, existed throughout the state. Polygamists could be spotted on the street because of their distinctive old-fashioned dress and were treated by some with a measure of respect due to society's committed traditionalists.

Groups like the Salt Lake–based Freemen Institute, headed by former Salt Lake police chief and FBI man W. Cleon Skousen, combined a profamily position with a new conspiracy theory focused on such corporate pillars as the Trilateral Commission. Skousen's group, which claimed that more than twenty members in the state legislature had gone through the group's intensive seminar program, represented one possible direction for a Salt Lake caught between countervailing cultural and political currents.

Ezra Taft Benson's sons, Reed and Mark, who continue to work with right-wing groups, contrast sharply with the more moderate go-getters such as J. Allen Blodgett and Mayor Ted Wilson. Blodgett, one of the rising men in the church financial bureaucracy, is a technocrat whose moderate conservatism was shaped more by business issues than an ideological anti-Communism. Blodgett, in turn, contrasts with the young Bonneville Associates staff. The Bonneville people are more representative of the new corporate-influenced generation on the rise in Salt Lake. Deeply attracted to the values of money and corporate power, wedded to the outdoor life-style of the new Utah, these corporate go-fers simply ignore that "other" culture, which intersects and severely contrasts with their own.

Behind this unique cultural confrontation lie the region's two contending, but essentially linked, powers. On the inside sits the church, looking once again to become a power in the West and beyond. And on the outside, looking in, are the big energy companies and their corporate counterparts. They are ready to make their move, potentially capable of overwhelming the region in their search for new sources of energy and other investments.

*

Suggestions for Further Reading

As noted in the introduction, the literature on Utah history is abundant. Over the years a number of book-length studies, as well as scholarly and popular articles, have (with some notable exceptions) examined major areas of Utah's growth and development. As might be expected, many of these writings have directly or indirectly focused on Mormonism. Consequently, a gap in our understanding of Utah's non-Mormon experience represents an important challenge for future historians to address. Moreover, there is a need for studies that expand our knowledge of Utah's racial and ethnic minorities, the lives and experiences of average citizens, and the state's contemporary economic, political, and social development. Still, there is a vast body of works available for the scholar and general reader alike.

An essential beginning place is *Utah's History* edited by Richard D. Poll, Thomas G. Alexander, Eugene E. Campbell, and David E. Miller. First published in 1977 by Brigham Young University Press, and reissued a dozen years later by Utah State University Press, this excellent volume surveys the social, political, economic, ethnic, and religious development of the state. Reflecting the work of many of the ablest students of Utah history, the volume also contains a valuable bibliography. Similarly, Robert Gottlieb and Peter Wiley extensively surveyed sources on Utah for their books *Empires in the Sun* and *America's Saints*. Using those bibliographies as a starting place, this essay points the reader to some of the most significant books and articles which have appeared since the late 1970s.

In terms of general overviews of the state, several important titles stand out. Charles S. Peterson's *Utah: A Bicentennial History* (Norton, 1977), and Dean L. May's *Utah: A People's History* (University of Utah [U of U] Press, 1980) provide concise summaries of Utah's growth and development. Helen Papanikolas's *The Peoples of Utah* (Utah State Historical Society, 1976) is the standard work on Utah's diverse peoples and cultures. Her collection of folk tales, *Small Bird, Tell Me* (Swallow, 1993), is also valuable. Papanikolas has fostered a growing interest in Utah ethnicity and encouraged a whole generation of scholars in their efforts to understand the impact of diversity in the state's development. Leslie G. Kelen and Sandra T. Fuller explore Utah ethnicity in *The Other Utahns* (U of U Press, 1990). This book also contains a number of excellent photographs by some of the finest contemporary Utah photographers. Another important volume is Jessie L. Embry's *Black Saints in a White Church* (Signature, 1993) which focuses on the particular challenges facing black Mormons in Utah and elsewhere. *Hecho en Utah* edited by Carol A. Edison, Anne F. Hatch, and Craig R. Miller for the Utah Arts Council contains several essays dealing with Hispanics in Utah. With a particular emphasis on folk arts, the text is written in both English and Spanish.

As a part of observances of the centennial of statehood in 1995–96, several respected historians have been commissioned to chronologically survey the state's development. These forthcoming volumes will include a one-volume survey written by Thomas G. Alexander, and four other volumes, by James B. Allen, Charles E. Peterson, S. Lyman Tyler and John R. Alley, Jr., and Ronald W. Walker.

The centennial has also sparked interest in county history. A number of Utah historians and writers—Martha Bradley, Linda K. Newell, Ross Peterson, Allen Roberts, Linda Sillitoe, Richard Roberts, and Richard Sadler, among many others—are working on studies of each of the state's twenty-nine counties. The recently published *Utah History Encyclopedia* (U of U Press, 1994), edited by Allan Kent Powell with articles by more than 270 individual writers, provides pertinent information on the events and individuals who have contributed to Utah's growth.

In addition to these general surveys, a significant number of books that examine various aspects of Utah history have been published in the last fifteen years. Several have dealt with nineteenth-century Utah history. Among them are E. B. Long, *The Saints and the Union: Utah Territory During the Civil War* (University of Illinois Press, 1981); Clifford L. Stott, *Search For Sanctuary: Brigham Young and the White Mountain Expedition* (U of U Press, 1984); and Donald R. Moorman and Gene A. Sessions, *Camp Floyd and the Mormons: The Utah War* (U of U Press, 1992).

Brigham D. Madsen is one of Utah's most prolific and respected historians. Among his most important works examining nineteenth-century topics are *Corinne: The Gentile Capital of Utah* (Utah State Historical Society, 1980); *Gold Rush Sojourners* (U of U Press, 1983); *The Shoshoni Frontier and the Bear River Massacre* (U of U Press, 1985); and *Glory Hunter: A Biography of Patrick Edward Connor* (U of U Press, 1990).

Any understanding of Utah history prior to statehood must take into account Mormon church president Brigham Young. Leonard J. Arrington's *Brigham Young: American Moses* (Knopf, 1985) is the standard biography; Newell Bringhurst's *Brigham Young and the Expanding Mormon Frontier* (Little, Brown, 1986) is also valuable. Thomas G. Alexander's *Things In Heaven and Earth: The Life and Times of Wilford Woodruff, A Mormon Prophet* (Signature, 1991) is the definitive study of the Mormon leader whose actions facilitated the entrance of the Saints into the American mainstream. It is not an exaggeration to assert that Arrington and Alexander have had a major impact on our understanding of Utah's past both in terms of their scholarly works and in the mentoring role they have played with other historians. Alexander's *Mormonism in Transition: A History of the Latter-day Saints, 1890–1930* and E. Leo Lyman's *Political Deliverance: The Mormon Quest for Utah Statehood,* both published by the University of Illinois Press in 1986, provide important background on the coming of statehood and the first quarter-century of Utah political developments. Another important examination of events of this period can be found in Peggy Pascoe's *Relations of Rescue: The Search for Female Moral Authority in the American West, 1874–1939* (Oxford University Press, 1990), which deals in part with efforts of non-Mormons in Utah to oppose plural marriage. Edwin Brown Firmage and Richard Collin Mangrum examine nineteenth-century Mormon attitudes and the development of the church court system in *Zion in the Courts: A Legal History of the Church of Jesus Christ of Latter-day Saints, 1830–1900* (University of Illinois Press, 1988). In his book *Presbyterian Missions and Cultural Interaction in the Far Southwest, 1850–1950* (University of Illinois Press, 1993) Mark T. Banker discusses the attitudes of Presbyterian missionaries toward three "exceptional populations" of the American West—Mormons, Native Americans, and New Mexicans. Ronald L. Holt, *Beneath These Red Cliffs: An Ethnohistory of the Utah Paiutes* (University of New Mexico Press, 1992) is a significant account of a much-ignored Utah tribe.

The period between statehood and the Great Depression awaits additional scholarly attention. Important developments in Utah's political, social, and business history occurred during these years, and, though examined somewhat, they deserve greater attention. One Utahn who played an important role in both the state and the national scenes during this period was J. Reuben Clark. His life and contributions are chronicled in D. Michael Quinn, *J. Reuben Clark: The Church Years* (Brigham Young University Press, 1980), and in Gene A. Sessions, *Prophesying Upon the Bones: J. Reuben Clark and the Foreign Debt Crisis 1933–39* (University of Illinois Press, 1992).

World War II is a subject of growing interest to students of recent Utah history. Allan Kent Powell has examined this topic in two books: *Utah Remembers World War II* (Utah State University Press, 1991) and *Splinters of a Nation* (U of U Press, 1989). One of the most interesting chapters in Utah history during the war surrounds the Japanese-American internment camp at Topaz. This has been examined in a personal memoir by Yoshiko Uchida, *Desert Exile* (University of Washington Press, 1982) and has also been studied by Sandra Taylor in *Topaz: Jewel of the Desert* (University of California Press, 1993).

Robert Gottlieb and Peter Wiley have provided significant assessments of contemporary Utah life and economic developments in their aforementioned books *Empires in the Sun* (Putnam's, 1982) and *America's Saints* (Putnam's, 1984). Three valuable books for understanding contemporary Utah political developments are Dennis L. Lythgoe, *Let 'Em Holler: A Political Biography of J. Bracken Lee* (Utah State Historical Society, 1982); Scott Matheson and James E. Kee, *Out of Balance* (Peregrine Smith, 1986); and Calvin L. Rampton, Floyd A. O'Neil, and Gregory C. Thompson, *As I Recall* (U of U Press, 1989), the reminiscences of Utah's only three-term governor.

The activities of Mark Hofmann as murderer and forger in the mid-1980s received considerable attention. The best account is Linda Sillitoe and Allen D. Roberts, *Salamander: The Story of the Mormon Forgery Murders* (Signature, 1989). The perspective of the LDS church is represented by Richard Turley, *Victims: The LDS Church and the Mark Hofmann Case* (University of Illinois Press, 1992).

Other books have examined specific topics in Utah history. The nature and practice of plural marriage has been extensively chronicled in Richard Van Wagoner's *Mormon Polygamy* (Signature, 1986) and in Jessie L. Embry's *Mormon Polygamous Families* (U of U Press, 1987). Also valuable is the work of Lawrence Foster, *Religion and Sexuality: Three American Communal Experiments of the Nineteenth Century* (Oxford University Press, 1981), which compares Mormon experiences with those of the Shakers and the Oneida Community. Levi S. Peterson's *Juanita Brooks, Mormon Woman Historian* (U of U Press, 1988) tells the story of one of the most important historians of the state. Roger D. Launius's and Linda Thatcher's edited collection *Differing Visions: Dissenters in Mormon History* (University of Illinois Press, 1994) considers the fate of dissenters within Mormonism from David Whitmer of the 1840s to Sonia Johnson of the 1980s. Little-known aspects of the "underside" of Utah life have been explored by Larry Gerlach in *Blazing Crosses in Zion* (Utah State University Press, 1982) and by L. Kay Gillespie in *The Unforgiven: Utah's Executed Men* (Signature, 1991). Two recent books on atomic testing and the MX missile controversy in contemporary Utah stand out as significant: Carole Gallagher, *America Ground Zero: The Secret Nuclear War* (MIT Press, 1993) and Matthew Glass, *Citizens Against the MX: Public Languages in the Nuclear Age* (University of Illinois Press, 1993).

Utah's capital city is chronicled in John S. McCormick's *Salt Lake City: The Gathering Place* (Windsor, 1980) and in Thomas G. Alexander's and James B. Allen's *Mormons and Gentiles: A History of Salt Lake City* (Pruett, 1984). Important area landmarks are discussed in Nancy D. McCormick and John S. McCormick, *Saltair* (U of U Press, 1985); Leonard J. Arrington and Heidi K. Swinton, *The Hotel: Salt Lake's Classy Lady, the Hotel Utah, 1911–1986* (Publishers Press, 1986); and Mark Angus, *Salt Lake Underfoot* (Signature, 1993). Also valuable are John S. McCormick, *The Historic Buildings of Downtown Salt Lake City* (Utah State Historical Society, 1982), and Karl T. Haglund and Philip F. Notarianni, *The Avenues of Salt*

Lake City (Utah State Historical Society, 1980), both of which explore the architecture and history of important parts of the built environment of the capital city.

Richard Roberts and Richard Sadler have written *Ogden: Junction City* (Windsor, 1983) and *The Weber River Basin: Grass Roots Democracy and Water Development* (Utah State University Press, 1994); these books and Kenneth L. Cannon II's *Provo and Orem: A Very Eligible Place* (Windsor, 1987) deal with the growth of two major metropolitan areas to the north and south of Salt Lake City. One of Utah's fastest-growing and most important communities is chronicled in Martha S. Bradley's *Sandy City: The First 100 Years* (Sandy City Corporation, 1993). Other important areas of Salt Lake County are examined in G. Wesley Johnson and David L. Schirer, *Between The Cottonwoods: Murray City in Transition* (Timpanogos Research Associates, 1992); Michael Gorrell, *The History of West Valley City, 1848–1990* (West Valley City, 1994); and Melvin L. Bashore and Scott Crump, *Riverton: The Story of a Utah Country Town* (Riverton Historical Society, 1994).

A preliminary assessment of three of Utah's southeastern counties is found in Philip F. Notarianni, *Carbon County: Eastern Utah's Industrialized Island* (Utah State Historical Society, 1980); Allen Kent Powell, ed., *Emery County: Reflections on its Past and Future* (Utah State Historical Society, 1979), and Powell, ed., *San Juan County: People, Resources and History* (Utah State Historical Society, 1983). Another important study of "place" in Utah is Terry Tempest Williams's highly regarded *Refuge: An Unnatural History of Family and Place* (Pantheon, 1991).

Utah's religious diversity has been explored in Stan Larson and Lorille Miller, *Unitarianism in Utah: A Gentile Religion in Salt Lake City, 1891–1991,* (Free Thinker Press, 1991); Bernice Maher Mooney, *Salt of the Earth: The Catholic Church in Utah* (Catholic Diocese of Utah, 1992); and Robert A. Goldberg, *Back to The Soil: The Jewish Farmers of Clarion and Their World* (U of U Press, 1986). The Episcopal Diocese is currently working on a volume that will explore the contributions made by that denomination to Utah's development.

In recent years a number of writers and historians have turned their attention to Utah's artistic heritage. Two of the most important books are Dan E. Burke, *Utah Art of the Depression* (Utah Arts Council, 1986) and Vern G. Swanson, Robert S. Olpin, and William C. Seifrit, *Utah Art* (Peregrine Smith, 1991). On Utah architecture generally see Thomas Carter and Peter L. Goss, *Utah's Historic Architecture, 1847–1940* (U of U Press, 1988). Also valuable is Hal Cannon, ed., *Utah Folk Art: A Catalog of Material Culture* (BYU Press, 1980).

Utah labor history is an area that still awaits more attention. Important preliminary appraisals, however, include J. Kenneth Davies, *Deseret's Sons of Toil: A History of Worker Movements in Territorial Utah, 1850–1896,* (Olympus, 1977) and Allan Kent Powell, *The Next Time We Strike* (Utah

State University Press, 1985). Also valuable is Gibbs M. Smith, *Joe Hill* (Peregrine Smith, 1984), which remains the best source on the case of the legendary IWW organizer and songwriter who was executed in Utah in 1915.

Journal articles continue to be a major resource on the Utah experience. Prominent among these journals is the *Utah Historical Quarterly (UHQ);* significant articles are also found in the *Journal of Mormon History, Dialogue, Sunstone,* and the *Western Historical Quarterly (WHQ)*. For articles of a popular interest one should also consult *Beehive History,* which is published by the Utah State Historical Society. For more than twenty years *Utah Holiday* magazine provided unique insights into various aspects of Utah life. The magazine's demise in 1993 created a significant, and so far unfilled, void in investigative reporting on contemporary Utah life. Part of the niche carved out by *Utah Holiday* has been filled by two Salt Lake publications, *The Private Eye* and *Catalyst,* each of which has featured investigative stories on contemporary Utah life. Also valuable for an overview of trends in Utah business, as well as an occasional examination of historical developments, are *Utah Economic and Business Review* and *Utah Business.*

Important journal examinations of Utah in the period prior to Mormon settlement are found in Alan R. Schroedel, "The Archaic Inhabitants of the Northern Colorado Plateau," and C. Gregory Crampton's "Utah's Spanish Trail," both published in the Fall 1979 issue of *Utah Historical Quarterly (UHQ)*. Also valuable is Joel C. Janetski's "Utah Lake: Its Role in the Prehistory of Utah Valley," *UHQ* (Winter 1990).

Several important articles relating to the nineteenth century are worth reading. A seminal article is David Brion Davis, "Some Themes of Countersubversion: An Analysis of Anti-Masonic, Anti-Catholic and Anti-Mormon Literature," *Mississippi Valley Historical Review* (September 1960), which compares common themes of hostility toward these groups in the 1820s and 1830s. Another important essay is Christopher Lasch, "The Mormon Utopia," first published in the *New York Review of Books,* 26 January 1967, and then included in his collection *The World of Nations: Reflections on American History, Politics and Culture* (Knopf, 1973). Lasch believes that as long as the Mormons "were different from their neighbors, their neighbors hounded them mercilessly. Only when they gave up their chief distinguishing features of their faith" did they become another tolerated minority. This development, according to Lasch, "may well be the most important fact of Mormon history." On the immigration of Mormons to Utah see John K. Hulmston, "Mormon Immigration in the 1860s: The Story of the Church Trains," *UHQ* (Winter 1990). Thomas G. Alexander examines Mormon "beliefs and understandings of the relationship of human beings to the environment" in "Stewardship and Enterprise: The LDS Church and the Wasatch Oasis Environment, 1847–1930," *WHQ* (Autumn 1994). Other articles examining specific aspects of Utah during this period include Charles S. Peterson, "The Americanization of Utah's Agriculture," *UHQ*

(Spring 1974); Jean M. Westwood, "Richard Dallin Westwood: Sheriff and Ferryman of Early Grand County," *UHQ* (Winter 1987); and Davis Bitton, "Zion's Rowdies: Growing Up on the Mormon Frontier," *UHQ* (Spring 1982).

Aspects of nineteenth-century society and culture in Utah are examined in Charles S. Peterson, "The Limits of Learning in Pioneer Utah," *Journal of Mormon History* (1983) and Peterson, "A New Community: Mormon Teachers and the Separation of Church and State in Utah Territorial Schools, *UHQ* (Summer 1980); Richard Sadler, "The Impact of Mining in Salt Lake City," *UHQ* (Summer 1979); Donald R. Murphy, "One Hundred Years of Utah Climate," *UHQ* (Fall 1978); Janice P. Dawson, "Chautauqua and the Utah Performing Arts," *UHQ* (Spring 1990); and Martha S. Bradley, "Hide and Seek: Children on the Underground," *UHQ* (Spring 1983), and Bradley, "Reclamation of Young Citizens: Reform of Utah's Juvenile Legal System," *UHQ* (Fall 1983).

The history of nineteenth-century Utah women has attracted considerable scholarly attention. The *Utah Historical Quarterly* devoted the Spring 1978 and Summer 1982 issues to Utah women's history. These issues contain discussions of suffrage, women editors, women miners, and socialist and political activists. Also valuable is David Whittaker and Carol Cornwall Madsen, "History's Sequel: A Source Essay on Women in Mormon History," *Journal of Mormon History* (1979). Among the most interesting studies are Maureen Ursenbach Beecher, "Women's Work on the Utah Frontier," *UHQ* (Summer 1981); Martha S. Bradley and Jessie L. Embry, "Mothers and Daughters in Polygamy," *Dialogue* (Fall 1985); and Lawrence Foster, "From Frontier Activism to Neo-Victorian Domesticity: Mormon Women in the 19th and 20th Centuries," *Journal of Mormon History*, (1979). Gary Topping touches on the role of non-Mormon women in nineteenth-century Utah in his article "The Ogden Academy: A Gentile Assault on Mormon Country," *Journal of the West* (January 1984). Other aspects of Utah women's history are examined in Lawrence Foster, "Polygamy and the Frontier: Mormon Women in Early Utah," *UHQ* (Summer 1982); Audrey M. Godfrey, "Housewives, Hussies and Heroines, The Women of Johnston's Army," *UHQ* (Spring 1986); Beverly Beeton, "Woman Suffrage in Territorial Utah," *UHQ* (Spring 1978); Linda Thatcher and John Sillito, "Sisterhood and Sociability: The Utah Women's Press Club," *UHQ* (Spring 1985); and Constance L. Lieber, "The Goose Hangs High: Excerpts from the Letters of Martha Hughes Cannon," *UHQ* (Winter 1980). Finally, an on-going question of interest to scholars and general readers alike is considered in Jeffery Ogden Johnson, "Determining and Defining 'Wife': The Brigham Young Households," *Dialogue* (Fall 1987).

Tensions within Mormonism and between Mormons and Gentiles are dealt with in David Whittaker, "The Bone in the Throat: Orson Pratt and the Public Announcement of Plural Marriage," *WHQ* (April 1987); Ronald W. Walker, "The Liberal Institute: A Case Study of National Assimilation,"

Dialogue (Autumn 1977); and Thomas G. Alexander, "Wilford Woodruff and the Mormon Reformation of 1855–1857," *Dialogue* (Summer 1992). The attitudes of one critic of Mormonism are discussed in John Sillito and Martha S. Bradley, "Franklin Spencer Spalding: An Episcopal Critic of Mormonism," *Journal of the Protestant Episcopal Church* (Winter 1985). The relationship between Mormonism and Masonry has been an interesting aspect of Utah history. Among the best accounts are Michael W. Homer, "Masonry and Mormonism in Utah, 1847–1984," *Journal of Mormon History* (Fall 1992) and Fred S. Buchanan, "Masons and Mormons: Released Time in Salt Lake City, 1930–1956," *Journal of Mormon History* (Spring 1993). For a discussion of one aspect of Jewish activities in Utah see Hynda L. Rudd, "Congregation Kol Ami: Religious Merger in Salt Lake City," *Western States Jewish Historical Quarterly* (July 1978).

Examinations of life in early twentieth-century Utah are numerous. A good starting point is Thomas G. Alexander and Jessie L. Embry, "Toward a Twentieth Century Synthesis: The History of Utah and Idaho," *Pacific Historical Review* (Fall 1981). Other important studies covering a variety of topics include Charles S. Peterson, "Life in A Village Society, 1877–1920," *UHQ* (Winter 1981); Walter E. Pittman, Jr., "The Smoke Abatement Campaign in Salt Lake City, 1890–1925," *Locus* (1989); John L. Lamborn and Charles S. Peterson, "The Substance of the Land: Agriculture vs. Industry in the Smelter Cases of 1904 and 1906," *UHQ* (Fall 1985); Douglas E. Kupel, "Beyond the Wasatch: The History of Irrigation in the Uintah Basin and Upper Provo River Area of Utah," *Public Historian* (Winter 1991); Brent G. Thompson, "Standing Between Two Fires: Mormons and Prohibition, 1908–1917," *Journal of Mormon History* (1983); David L. Buhler, "The Peculiar Case of James Lynch and Robert King," *UHQ* (Spring 1992); and Roger D. Launius, "Crossroads of the West: Aviation Comes to Utah," *UHQ* (Spring 1990). The role of working women in the Beehive State is examined by Michael Vinson in "From Housewife to Office Clerk: Utah Working Women, 1870–1901," *UHQ* (Fall 1985).

Early twentieth-century Utah politics are examined in E. Leo Lyman, "The Political Background of the Woodruff Manifesto," *Dialogue* (Fall 1991) and Kenneth L. Cannon II, "After the Manifesto: Mormon Polygamy, 1890–1906," *Sunstone* (January–April 1983). One of Utah's most controversial politicians is examined by Linda Thatcher in "The 'Gentile Polygamist': Arthur Brown, Ex-Senator From Utah," *UHQ* (Summer 1984). While dealing with the West generally, David Sarasohn's "The Election of 1916: Realigning the Rockies," *WHQ* (July 1980) argues that Utah voters "succumbed to Woodrow Wilson's charms" and supported him in his bid for re-election. A glimpse of social and political interactions is found in Jean B. White, "The Right To Be Different: Ogden and Weber County Politics, 1890–1924," *UHQ* (Summer 1979) and in Brian Q. Cannon, "Change Engulfs a Frontier Settlement: Ogden and its Residents Respond to the Railroads," *Journal of Mormon History* (1985). For a discussion of socialism in Utah see John R. Sillito, "Women and the Socialist Party in Utah," *UHQ* (Summer 1981); John S. McCormick, "Hornets in the Hive: Socialists in Early Twentieth Century Utah," *UHQ* (Summer 1982); and Sillito and McCormick, "Socialist Saints: Mormons and the Socialist Party, 1900–1920," *Dialogue* (Spring 1985).

Aspects of Utah life at the time of World War I are examined in Robert S. McPherson, "The Influenza Epidemic of 1918: A Cultural Response," *UHQ* (Spring 1990); Leonard J. Arrington, "The Influenza Epidemic of 1918–1919 in Utah," *UHQ* (Spring 1990); Richard C. Roberts, "The Utah National Guard in the Great War, 1917–1918," *UHQ* (Fall 1990); David L. Wood, "Gosiute-Shoshoni Draft Resistance, 1917–1918," *UHQ* (Spring 1981); and Miriam B. Murphy, "'If Only I Shall Have the Right Stuff': Utah Women in World War I," *UHQ* (Fall 1990). War-time pressures brought about the removal of Utah Episcopal Bishop Paul Jones because of his opposition to the war; see John R. Sillito and Timothy S. Hearn, "A Question of Conscience: The Resignation of Bishop Paul Jones," *UHQ* (Summer 1982).

An interesting chapter of Utah history in the 1920s is chronicled in Ann Weaver Hart, "Religion and Education: The Scopes Controversy in Utah," *UHQ* (Spring 1983). The central fact of the 1930s was the Great Depression. For insights on Utah during this period see Wayne K. Hinton, "Some Historical Perspectives on the Mormon Response to the Great Depression," *Journal of the West* (Fall 1985) and his later article, "The Economics of Ambivalence: Utah's Depression Experience," *UHQ* (Summer 1986). Also worthwhile is Leonard J. Arrington, "Utah's Great Drought of 1934," *UHQ* (Summer 1986) and his "Utah, The New Deal, and The Great Depression of the 1930s," the 1982 Dello G. Dayton lecture, published by Weber State College.

Valuable studies of Utah during and after World War II include Thomas G. Alexander, "The Utah War Industry During World War II: A Human Impact Analysis," *UHQ* (Winter 1983); Yoshiko Uchida, "Topaz: City of Dust," *UHQ* (Summer 1980); Antonette Chambers Noble, "Utah's Defense Industries and Workers in World War II," *UHQ* (Fall 1991); and Roger D. Launius, "Home on the Range: The U.S. Air Force Range in Utah, A Unique Military Resource," *UHQ* (Fall 1991).

Post-war educational developments are the subject of Elinore H. Partridge, "A. Ray Olpin and Postwar Emergency at the University of Utah," *UHQ* (Spring 1980). The significance of Mormon leader and conservative activist Ezra Taft Benson is the subject of D. Michael Quinn's article "Ezra Taft Benson and Mormon Political Conflict," *Dialogue* (Summer 1993). Two other important conservatives are the subjects of Dennis L. Lythgoe's "Political Feud in Salt Lake City: J. Bracken Lee and the Firing of W. Cleon Skousen," *UHQ* (Fall 1974).

Important discussions of sports in Utah include Melvin R. Bashore, "The Salt Lake Seagulls Professional Football Team," *UHQ* (Winter 1993); Afton

Bradshaw, "Tennis in Utah: The First Fifty years, 1885–1935," *UHQ* (Spring 1984); Larry Gerlach, "Best in the West? Corinne Utah's First Baseball Champions," *UHQ* (Spring 1984); and Kenneth L. Cannon, "Deserets, Red Stockings and Out-of-Towners: Baseball Comes of Age in Salt Lake City, 1877–1979," *UHQ* (Spring 1985). For a view of Salt Lake baseball of a later vintage see John Sillito, "The Bees of Summer," *Utah Holiday* (May 1984).

Helen Papanikolas is the preeminent historian of the Greek experience in Utah. Among her important articles are "Growing Up Greek in Helper, Utah," *UHQ* (Summer 1980), "Wresting with Death: Greek Immigrant Funeral Customs in Utah," *UHQ* (Winter 1984); and "Immigrants, Minorities and the Great War," *UHQ* (Fall 1990). Immigrants to Utah from the Pacific Islands are discussed in Tracey E. Panek, "Life at Josepa, Utah's Polynesian Colony," *UHQ* (Winter 1992). The Fall 1984 issue of the *Utah Historical Quarterly* is devoted to the "German Speaking Immigrants of Utah." An early examination of Utah's black history can be found in Newell Bringhurst, "The Mormons and Slavery—A Closer Look," *Pacific Historical Review* (August 1981), and in Larry R. Gerlach, "The Lynching of George Segal," *UHQ* (Spring 1981).

The history of Native Americans is becoming increasingly recognized as important. Among the most interesting articles are Ronald W. Walker, "Native Women on the Utah Frontier," *BYU Studies* (Fall 1992) and Walker's earlier "Toward a Reconciliation of Mormon and Indian Relations, 1847–77," *BYU Studies* (Fall 1989). Another interesting article is Beverly P. Smaby, "The Mormons and the Indians: Conflicting Ecological Systems in the Great Basin," *American Studies* (Spring 1975). Other valuable studies include Gregory C. Thompson, "The Unwanted Indians: The Southern Utes in Southeastern Utah," *UHQ* (Spring 1982); Steven Crum, "The White Pine War of 1875: A Case of White Hysteria," *UHQ* (Summer 1991); Crum, "The Skull Valley Band of Goshute Tribe: Deeply Attached to their Homeland," *UHQ* (Summer 1987); and Albert Winkler, "The Circleville Massacre: A Brutal Incident in Utah's Black Hawk War," *UHQ* (Winter 1987).

A good starting point for Utah architecture studies is the Winter 1986 issue of the *Utah Historical Quarterly,* edited by Peter L. Goss, which explores various aspects of Utah architecture at the turn of the century. Thomas Carter's "North European Horizontal Log Construction in the Sanpete-Sevier Valleys," *UHQ* (Winter 1984) is a valuable addition to the literature, as is the Fall 1988 issue of *Utah Historical Quarterly* dealing with material culture which Carter edited. Other important articles include Richard C. Poulsen, "Folk Material Culture of the Sanpete-Sevier Area: Today's Reflections of a Region's Past," *UHQ* (Spring 1979), and Larry Jones, "Utah's Vanishing Log Cabins, *Utah Preservation/Restoration* (1979). John S. McCormick's "Utah's Constitution Was Framed in the Salt Lake City and County Building," *Beehive History* (December 1994) is a brief overview of that important building.

Tourism is an increasingly important fact of Utah life. The significance to tourism of the Salt Lake Temple is traced in M. Guy Bishop and Richard Neitzel Holzapfel, "The St. Peter's of the New World: The Salt Lake Temple, Tourism and a New Image for Utah," *UHQ* (Spring 1993). Utah's red rock country is discussed in Roy Webb "'Until Dissolved by Consent . . . ': The Western River Guides Association," *UHQ* (Spring 1992); Gary Topping, "Charles Kelly's Glen Canyon Ventures and Adventures," *UHQ* (Spring 1987), and Topping, "Harry Aleson and The Place No One Knew," *UHQ* (Spring 1984); Thomas G. Smith, "The Canyonlands National Park Controversy, 1961–1964," *UHQ* (Summer 1991); Richard E. Westwood, "Howard W. Balsley: Dean of Uranium Miners and Civic Leader of Moab," *UHQ* (Fall 1991); Michael B. Husband, "History's Greatest Metal Hunt: The Uranium Boom on the Colorado Plateau," *Journal of the West* (October 1982); and the Spring 1987 special issue of the *Utah Historical Quarterly* devoted to the Colorado River Country. Particularly valuable in that issue is Melvin T. Smith, "Before Powell: Explorations of the Colorado River." The northeastern corner of the state is the subject of Mark W. T. Harvey, "Utah, The National Park Service, and Dinosaur National Monument 1909–1956," *UHQ* (Summer 1991).

Examinations of legal history include Carol Cornwall Madsen, "Sister's at the Bar: Utah Women in Law," and John R. Alley, Jr., "Utah Supreme Court Justice Samuel R. Thurman," both found in *UHQ* (Summer 1993). Ken Driggs, "Lorenzo Snow's Appellate Court Victory," *UHQ* (Winter 1990) chronicles the case that "brought a shift of Mormon defense strategy from one of flight on the underground to . . . a policy of civil disobedience." Another important perspective is found in Edwin B. Firmage, "Religion and the Law: The Mormon Experience in the 19th Century," in the *Cardozo Law Review* (February–March 1991).

Another area that has only recently attracted historical attention concerns gender and sexuality issues. An early effort in this area is Vern Bullough and Bonnie Bullough, "Lesbianism in the 1920s and 1930s: A Newfound Study," *Signs* (Summer 1977), which draws upon an unpublished account of two dozen lesbian women in Salt Lake City. A more recent examination is Rocky O'Donovan, "'The Abominable and Detestable Crime Against Nature': A Brief History of Homosexuality and Mormonism, 1840–1980," in Brent Corcoran, *Multiply and Replenish: Mormon Essays on Sex and Family* (Signature, 1994).

The above barely scratches the surface of the important studies of Utah life and history produced in the last few years. As the state enters its second century, writers and historians face the challenge of chronicling and interpreting the events and peoples who contribute to Utah's development. If past scholarship is any indicator, the years ahead will likely see important new perspectives on the Utah experience. Such a body of literature represents one of the state's most important resources.

*

ABOUT THE EDITORS

John S. McCormick is Associate Professor of History at Salt Lake Community College. John R. Sillito is Archivist and Associate Professor at Weber State University, Ogden, Utah. They each have published widely in Utah history. They have also collaborated on a number of projects, and their joint articles have appeared in *Utah Historical Quarterly*, *Dialogue*, *Weber Studies*, and *Southwest Economy and Society.* Their essay "Henry Lawrence: A Life in Dissent" appeared in the recently published collection *Differing Visions: Dissenters in Mormon History*. They are currently completing a study of the Socialist party and other political movements in Utah.